with MyFinanceLab

D0140363

- **Worked Solutions**—Provide step-by-step explanations on how to solve select problems using the exact numbers and data that were presented in the problem. Instructors will have access to the Worked Solutions in preview and review mode.

- **Algorithmic Test Bank**—Instructors have the ability to create multiple versions of a test or extra practice for students.

- **Financial Calculator**—The Financial Calculator is available as a smartphone application, as well as on a computer, and includes important functions such as cash flow, net present value, and internal rate of return. Fifteen helpful tutorial videos show the many ways to use the Financial Calculator in MyFinanceLab.

- **Reporting Dashboard**—View, analyze, and report learning outcomes clearly and easily. Available via the Gradebook and fully mobile-ready, the Reporting Dashboard presents student performance data at the class, section, and program levels in an accessible, visual manner.

- **LMS Integration**—Link from any LMS platform to access assignments, rosters, and resources, and synchronize MyLab grades with your LMS gradebook. For students, new direct, single sign-on provides access to all the personalized learning MyLab resources that make studying more efficient and effective.

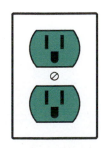

- **Mobile Ready**—Students and instructors can access multimedia resources and complete assessments right at their fingertips, on any mobile device.

PEARSON

The Pearson Series in Finance

Berk/DeMarzo
Corporate Finance*
Corporate Finance: The Core*

Berk/DeMarzo/Harford
Fundamentals of Corporate Finance*

Brooks
Financial Management: Core Concepts*

Copeland/Weston/Shastri
Financial Theory and Corporate Policy

Dorfman/Cather
*Introduction to Risk Management
and Insurance*

Eakins/McNally
Corporate Finance Online*

Eiteman/Stonehill/Moffett
Multinational Business Finance*

Fabozzi
Bond Markets: Analysis and Strategies

Foerster
*Financial Management: Concepts
and Applications**

Frasca
Personal Finance

Gitman/Zutter
Principles of Managerial Finance*
*Principles of Managerial Finance—
Brief Edition**

Haugen
*The Inefficient Stock Market: What Pays
Off and Why*
Modern Investment Theory

Holden
Excel Modeling in Corporate Finance
Excel Modeling in Investments

Hughes/MacDonald
International Banking: Text and Cases

Hull
*Fundamentals of Futures and Options
Markets*
Options, Futures, and Other Derivatives

Keown
*Personal Finance: Turning Money
into Wealth**

Keown/Martin/Petty
*Foundations of Finance: The Logic and
Practice of Financial Management**

Madura
Personal Finance*

Marthinsen
*Risk Takers: Uses and Abuses of Financial
Derivatives*

McDonald
Derivatives Markets
Fundamentals of Derivatives Markets

Mishkin/Eakins
Financial Markets and Institutions

Moffett/Stonehill/Eiteman
Fundamentals of Multinational Finance

Nofsinger
Psychology of Investing

Pennacchi
Theory of Asset Pricing

Rejda/McNamara
*Principles of Risk Management
and Insurance*

Smart/Gitman/Joehnk
Fundamentals of Investing*

Solnik/McLeavey
Global Investments

Titman/Keown/Martin
*Financial Management: Principles
and Applications**

Titman/Martin
*Valuation: The Art and Science of
Corporate Investment Decisions*

Weston/Mitchell/Mulherin
*Takeovers, Restructuring, and
Corporate Governance*

---

* Denotes titles with MyFinanceLab. Log onto http://www.myfinancelab.com to learn more.

PERSONAL FINANCE

Sixth Edition

JEFF MADURA
Florida Atlantic University

Boston   Columbus   Indianapolis   New York   San Francisco
Amsterdam   Cape Town   Dubai   London   Madrid   Milan   Munich   Paris   Montréal   Toronto
Delhi   Mexico City   São Paulo   Sydney   Hong Kong   Seoul   Singapore   Taipei   Tokyo

Vice President, Business Publishing: Donna Battista
Editor-in-Chief: Adrienne D'Ambrosio
Acquisitions Editor: Kate Fernandes
Editorial Assistant: Kathryn Brightney
Vice President, Product Marketing: Maggie Moylan
Director of Marketing, Digital Services and Products: Jeanette Koskinas
Senior Product Marketing Manager: Alison Haskins
Executive Field Marketing Manager: Adam Goldstein
Product Marketing Assistant: Jessica Quazza
Team Lead, Program Management: Ashley Santora
Program Manager: Kathryn Dinovo
Team Lead, Project Management: Jeff Holcomb
Project Manager: Heather Pagano
Operations Specialist: Carol Melville
Creative Director: Blair Brown
Art Director: Jonathan Boylan
Vice President, Director of Digital Strategy and Assessment: Paul Gentile
Manager of Learning Applications: Paul DeLuca
Digital Editor: Brian Hyland
Director, Digital Studio: Sacha Laustsen
Digital Studio Manager: Diane Lombardo
Digital Studio Project Managers: Andra Skaalrud, Alana Coles, Robin Lazarus
Digital Content Team Lead: Noel Lotz
Digital Content Project Lead: Miguel Leonarte
Full-Service Project Management and Composition: SPi Global
Interior Designer: SPi Global
Cover Designer: Lumina Datamatics
Cover Art: Oleksiy Mark/Shutterstock
Printer/Binder: LSC Communications / Kendallville
Cover Printer: LSC Communications / Kendallville

Library of Congress Cataloging-in-Publication Data
Names: Madura, Jeff, author.
Title: Personal finance / Jeff Madura, Florida Atlantic University.
Description: Sixth Edition. | New York: Pearson, 2016. | Revised edition of
   the author's Personal finance, 2014. | Includes index.
Identifiers: LCCN 2015044458 | ISBN 0134082567
Subjects: LCSH: Finance, Personal.
Classification: LCC HG179 .M252 2016 | DDC 332.024—dc23
LC record available at http://lccn.loc.gov/2015044458

KV 04.08.2019 1551

PEARSON

ISBN 10: 0-13-408256-7
ISBN 13: 978-0-13-408256-1

For Mary

BRIEF CONTENTS

DETAILED CONTENTS

PART 1 TOOLS FOR FINANCIAL PLANNING

Chapter 2 Planning with Personal Financial Statements 34

PART 2 MANAGING YOUR LIQUIDITY

Chapter 5   Banking and Interest Rates 128

Chapter 8   Managing Your Credit 209

PART 3 PERSONAL FINANCING

PART 4 PROTECTING YOUR WEALTH

Chapter 13 Life Insurance

PART 5 PERSONAL INVESTING

Chapter 14 Investing Fundamentals 404

PART 6 RETIREMENT AND ESTATE PLANNING

PART 7 SYNTHESIS OF FINANCIAL PLANNING

Chapter 21 Integrating the Components of a Financial Plan 578

The Most Interactive Book on the Market

The Sixth Edition of Personal Finance *integrates the Building Your Own Financial Plan and case study worksheets into each chapter, helping students to create their own personalized plan for financial success.*

BUILDING YOUR OWN FINANCIAL PLAN

Personal Finance's structure mirrors a comprehensive financial plan, teaching students the skills they need to build their own financial plan. The **Building Your Own Financial Plan** chapter-ending case studies are presented as an integrated series of exercises and worksheets that represent a portion of a financial plan. At the end of the course, students will have completed a financial plan that they can continue implementing beyond the school term. All of the Financial Planning Software worksheets are available in MyFinanceLab™ and also at http://www.pearsonhighered.com/madura.

BUILDING YOUR OWN FINANCIAL PLAN

Based on the goals that you established in Chapter 1 and the personal cash flow statement that you created in Chapter 2, you are now ready to begin determining how to go about achieving many of your goals. Most financial goals are achieved by some sort of savings/investment plan.

Go to the worksheets at the end of this chapter to continue building your financial plan.

NAME   DATE

CHAPTER 3: BUILDING YOUR OWN FINANCIAL PLAN

YOUR GOALS FOR CHAPTER 3

1. Determine how much savings you plan to accumulate by various future points in time.

ANALYSIS

1. Assume that you have $1,000 to invest, so insert 1000 as your Present Value in the following table. Assume that you want to invest your money for 5 years (insert 5 for Number of Periods). Assume an annual interest rate of 3.00% (insert 3 for Interest Rate per Period). The table will determine the Future Value of your investment. If you input the numbers correctly, your Future Value is computed to be $1,159, which is what your investment will be worth in 5 years. Now revise the input to reflect your actual savings and the prevailing interest rate so that you can see how your savings will grow in 5 years. Even if you have no savings now, you can at least see how the interest rate affects the future value of savings by revising your input in the Interest Rate per Period, and then observing the change in the Future Value.

Future Value of a Present Amount

Present Value	
Number of Periods	
Interest Rate per Period	
Future Value	

2. Assume that you have $1,000 to invest at the end of each of the next 5 years, so insert 1000 as your Payment per Period in the following table. Assume that you want to invest your money for 5 years (insert 5 for Number of Periods). Assume an annual interest rate of 3.00% (insert 3 for Interest Rate per Period). The following table will determine the Future Value of your investment. If you input the numbers correctly, your Future Value is computed to be $5,309, which is what your investments will be worth in 5 years. Now revise the input to reflect your actual expected savings per year over the next 5 years, and existing interest rate quotations so that you can estimate how your savings will grow in 5 years. You can now revise the table to fit your own desired level of saving.

Future Value of an Annuity

Payment per Period	
Number of Periods	
Interest Rate per Period	
Future Value	

3. Assume that you want to deposit savings that will be worth $10,000 in 5 years, so insert 10000 as the Future Amount and 5 as the Number of Periods in the following table. Assume an annual interest rate of 3.00% (insert 3 for Interest Rate per Period). The following table will determine the Present Value, which represents the amount of savings you need today that would accumulate to be worth $10,000 in 5 years. If you input the numbers correctly, the Present Value is estimated

---

NAME   DATE

the table to be $8,606. Now revise the input to reflect your own desired savings amount in 5 years so that you can estimate how much you need now to achieve your savings goal in 5 years.

Present Value of a Future Amount

Future Amount	
Number of Periods	
Interest Rate per Period	
Present Value	

4. Assume that you want to deposit savings at the end of each of the next 5 years so that you will have $10,000 in 5 years. So insert 10000 as the Future Amount, and 5 for Number of Periods. Assume an annual interest rate of 3.00% (insert 3 for Interest Rate per Period). The following table will determine the Annual Payment, which represents the annual payments that will accumulate to your future desired investment. If you input the numbers correctly, your Annual Payment is computed to be $1,884. Now revise the input to reflect your own desired savings amount in 5 years so that you can estimate how much you need to save per year to achieve your savings goal in 5 years.

Present Value of an Annuity

Payment per Period	
Number of Periods	
Interest Rate per Period	
Present Value	

DECISIONS

1. Report on how much you must save per year and the return you must earn to meet your savings goal in 5 years.

An Interactive Approach

Personal Finance's interactive approach incorporates Internet-based resources along with many examples, problems, and ongoing case studies, all of which focus on providing students with hands-on practice applying financial concepts.

FREE APPS
for Personal
Finance

Estimating Growth in Savings

Application:

The Future Value app (by Garinet Media Company, LLC) illustrates how your money will grow based on input that you provide about your savings plans.

To Find It:

Search for the "Future Value" app on your mobile device.

Free Apps for Personal Finance highlights useful apps students can download to their smartphones for free that apply to some of the key concepts covered in the chapter.

Financial Planning
ONLINE

Go to:
The banking section of
About.com

To get:
Information on how to
pay bills online.

Financial Planning Online in every chapter highlights Internet resources for more information on a chapter topic. Each includes an Internet address and a description of what the Web site provides.

FINANCIAL PLANNING PROBLEMS

All Financial Planning Problems are available in MyFinanceLab at http://www.myfinancelab.com. A financial calculator is recommended for Problems 4, 8, 11, 12, 14, and 15. The financial tables are recommended to answer Problems 1, 2, 3, 5, 6, 7, 9, 10, and 13.

1. **Future Value.** Kyle has $1,000 in cash received for high school graduation gifts from various relatives. He wants to invest it in a certificate of deposit (CD) so that he will have a down payment on a car when he graduates from college in five years. His bank will pay 6% per year, compounded that she will have a "nest egg" to start her off. Michelle works out her budget and decides she can afford to set aside $50 per month for savings. Her bank will pay her 3% per year, compounded monthly, on her savings account. What will Michelle's balance be in five years?

Financial Planning Problems require students to demonstrate knowledge of mathematically based concepts by performing computations to make well-informed personal finance decisions. All Financial Planning Problems are available in MyFinanceLab.

FINANCIAL PLANNING ONLINE EXERCISES

1. Go to the banking section of About.com, read about the bill paying process, and answer the following questions:

   a. Is setting up online bill pay a difficult process? Explain fully.

   b. What are the two basic types of online bill pay, and what information is needed to use each?

Financial Planning Online Exercises show students how to obtain, critically evaluate, and use Internet-based resources in making personal finance decisions.

Real-Life Scenarios

EXAMPLE

Stephanie Spratt believes that she may be able to save about $5,000 per year. She wants to know how much she will have in 30 years if she earns 6% annual interest on her investment. The annuity in this example is $5,000. As you can see in Table C.3 in Appendix C, the future value annuity factor based on a 30-year period and a 6% interest rate is 79.057. Thus, the future value is

$$\$5,000 \times 79.057 = \$395,285$$

If she could earn 7% instead of 6% on her savings, the future value annuity factor would be 94.459 and the future value would be:

$$\$5,000 \times 94.459 = \$472,295$$

A running example of Stephanie Spratt, a recent college graduate and new entrant into the workforce, helps students apply concepts to real-life situations. Students are commonly faced with dilemmas similar to those Stephanie faces, such as how to control recreational spending or whether to buy or lease a car.

THE SAMPSONS—A Continuing Case

Recall that Dave and Sharon Sampson established a plan to save $300 per month (or $3,600 per year) for their children's education. Their oldest child is six years old and will begin college in 12 years. They will invest the $300 in a savings account that they expect will earn interest of about 2% a year over the next 12 years. The Sampsons wonder how much additional money they would accumulate if they could earn 5% a year on the savings account instead of 2%. They also wonder how their savings would accumulate if they could save $400 per month (or $4,800 per year) instead of $300 per month.

Go to the worksheets at the end of this chapter to continue this case.

Build a financial plan for the Sampson family! The parents of two children, Dave and Sharon Sampson have made few plans regarding their financial future and are eager to start saving toward a new car, their children's college education, and their retirement. Students apply chapter concepts to counsel the Sampsons on the accompanying worksheets.

PART 1: BRAD BROOKS—A Continuing Case

Your childhood friend, Brad Brooks, has asked you to help him gain control of his personal finances. Single and 30 years old, Brad is employed as a salesperson for a technology company. His annual salary is $48,000. He claims no exemptions (he enjoys the big refund check in May), and after Social Security, Medicare, and federal, state, and local income taxes, his monthly disposable income is $2,743. Brad has recently moved from his comfortable two-bedroom apartment with rent of $600 per month to a condo that rents for $1,000 per month. The condo is in a plush property owner's association with two golf courses, a lake, and an activity center.

At the end of each part, students are prompted to **build a financial plan for Brad Brooks** using the accompanying worksheets. Brad has expensive tastes—as evidenced by his soaring credit card balance—and he needs assistance in gaining control over his finances.

Learning Tools

chapter 3

Applying Time Value Concepts

Scott Pilar has been smoking two packs of cigarettes a day. Today, on his 18th birthday, he decided to give up smoking for health reasons. He does not realize that this is an important financial decision as well. If Scott invests the money that he would have spent on smoking over the next 50 years, he could become a millionaire.

Karen Roach/Fotolia

Let's assume that a pack of cigarettes is priced at $8. Scott will save $16 per day (2 packs × $8 per pack), or $5,840 per year ($16 × 365 days). If Scott could invest that money in a bank deposit account and earn 5% per year, his investment would accumulate to be worth $1,222,592 in 50 years. The specific method to estimate this amount of accumulated funds can be done in less than one minute, as explained in this chapter.

Cash accumulates when it is invested and earns interest because of the time value of money. Over a long period of time, money can grow substantially because interest is earned both on the deposited funds and on the interest that has already accumulated. The lesson is that saving even a small amount per month or year at an early age can enhan

The concepts in this chapter can help you determine how much yo on a particular savings level per month or year. You can also deter need to save per month or year to achieve a specific savings goal able to calculate how much monthly or annual savings you will nee on a new car or home, or to make other types of purchases at a fu

MyFinanceLab helps you master the topics in this chapter and study efficiently. Visit http://www.myfinancelab.com for more details.

Chapter Introductions
The opening of each chapter provides an interest-grabbing scenario that previews the chapter's content.

Learning Objectives
Corresponding to the main headings in each chapter, the list of learning objectives guides students through the material.

The objectives of this chapter are to:
- Describe the importance of time value of money
- Calculate the future value of a dollar amount that you save today
- Calculate the present value of a dollar amount that will be received in the future
- Calculate the future value of an annuity
- Calculate the present value of an annuity
- Explain how time value can be used to estimate savings
- Explain how time value fits within your financial plan

EXAMPLE

Suppose you want to know how much money you will have in five years if you invest $5,000 now and earn an annual return of 4%. The present value of money (*PV*) is the amount invested, or $5,000. The *FVIF* for an interest rate of 4% and a time period of five years is 1.217 (look down the 4% column and across the row for year 5). Thus, the future value (*FV*) of the $5,000 in five years will be:

$$FV = PV \times FVIF_{i,n}$$
$$FV = PV \times FVIF_{4\%,5}$$
$$= \$5,000 \times 1.217$$
$$= \$6,085$$

Affordable Care Act of 2010
Legislation that introduced the Individual Mandate to acquire health care coverage or face a penalty for not having coverage.

earned income
Earned income represents salary or wages.

FICA (Federal Insurance Contributions Act)
Taxes paid to fund the Social Security System and Medicare.

Marginal Glossary
Throughout the text, key terms and their definitions appear in the text margin where they are first introduced.

Explanation by Example
Practical examples applying concepts in realistic scenarios throughout chapters help cement student understanding.

PSYCHOLOGY of Personal Finance   **Paying Bills on Time** Your checking account provides a quick and convenient means of paying bills. There are psychological forces that influence how people pay bills. Although no one enjoys paying bills, people deal with the process in different ways. Some people try to avoid the stress of bill paying by ignoring their bills. They defer payment, perhaps with the hope that their creditors will forget about the bills. But creditors tend to remember what they are owed, and, if you fail to pay by the deadline, you will receive a late notice and will be charged a late fee.

Psychology of Personal Finance

Personal finance behavior is influenced by psychology. For example, some spending decisions are made on impulse due to the desire for immediate satisfaction.

ECONOMIC IMPACT   Economic conditions also affect the value of your assets. Favorable economic conditions result in a high demand to purchase homes, which increases the values of homes. In addition, the values of stocks rise when economic conditions are favorable because corporations experience higher sales of the products or services they produce. Conversely, weak economic conditions result in lower values of assets. Home prices decline as demand for homes declines.

Economic Impact

The Economic Impact logo identifies text that emphasizes how economic conditions can affect personal finance.

SUMMARY

Importance of Time Value of Money. A dollar today has more value than a dollar received one year from now. Consequently, many decisions about saving for the future are influenced by the time value of money. Proper decisions based on the time value of money can allow you to accumulate more wealth.

Summary

In paragraph form, the chapter summary presents the key points of the chapter to aid in student study.

REVIEW QUESTIONS

All Review Questions are available in MyFinanceLab at http://www.myfinancelab.com.

1. **Time Value of Money.** What is the time value of money? How is it related to opportunity costs?
2. **Importance of the Time Value of Money.** List one reason why the time value of money is an

c. You received $500 as a gift for graduation, and you want to know how much it will be worth in three years if you deposit it in a savings account.

Review Questions

Test knowledge of material by comparing and contrasting concepts, interpreting financial quotations, and understanding how financial data can be used to make personal finance decisions. All Review Questions are available in MyFinanceLab.

Ethical Dilemmas

Real-life ethical situations are presented along with questions to encourage students' critical thinking about ethics.

19. **Ethical Dilemma.** Cindy and Jack have always practiced good financial habits, in particular, developing and living by a budget. They are currently in the market to purchase a new car and have budgeted $300 per month for car payments.

WEB SEARCH EXERCISE

You can develop your personal finance skills by conducting an Internet search for related articles. Find a recent online article about personal finance that reinforces one or more concepts covered in this chapter. If your class has an online component, your professor may ask you to post your summary of the article there and provide a link to the article so that other students can access it. If your class is live, your professor may ask you to summarize your application of the article in class. Your professor may assign specific students to complete this assignment or may allow any student to do the assignment on a volunteer basis.

Web Search Exercises

This exercise allows students to conduct an online search for real-world events related to the key content of each chapter.

VIDEO EXERCISE: Banking Tips

Go to one of the Web sites that contain video clips (such as http://www.youtube.com) and view some video clips about banking tips. You can use search phrases such as "banking tips." Select one video clip on this topic that you would recommend for the other students in your class.

Video Exercises

This activity has students find a video on an important finance topic discussed in the chapter.

Psychology of Personal Finance Questions

At the end of every chapter is a section on the Psychology of Personal Finance that tests students' understanding of how psychological forces such as desire for immediate satisfaction can influence personal finance decisions.

PSYCHOLOGY OF PERSONAL FINANCE: Future Value of Your Cash

1. This chapter explains how your cash deposited in a bank can grow over time. Some people are only willing to save if they are rewarded with a high interest rate. However, the interest rate on deposits has been relatively low lately. Does this influence your willingness to save? Would you save more money if interest rates were higher?

2. This chapter illustrates how the amount of debt you owed would not grow as quickly when interest rates are low. Because interest rates have been low lately, are you more willing to borrow money?

Financial Literacy Tests

A Financial Literacy Pre-Test is included just before Chapter 1. Answers are provided so that students can grade their performance. This test allows students to discover how much they do not know about personal finance and motivates them to develop their skills. A Financial Literacy Post-Test is provided immediately following Chapter 21. This test lets students discover how much they have learned after finishing the course. Answers are supplied so that students can easily assess their performance.

Financial Literacy POST-TEST

The following test will help you determine how much you learned about personal finance. It contains basic questions on material you learned from the text that can determine your ability to make proper financial planning decisions.

After taking the test, grade your performance based on the answers provided at the end of the test.

1. The _____ specifies the financial decisions that result from your personal financial planning.
   a. personal financial plan
   b. personal budget
   c. personal finance objective
   d. none of the above

2. When constructing a budget, it is helpful to use a personal cash flow statement, which measures a person's _____ and _____.
   a. cash inflows; cash outflows
   b. assets; expenses
   c. assets; liabilities
   d. none of the above

3. The time value of money implies that a dollar received today is worth _____ a dollar received tomorrow.
   a. more than
   b. the same as
   c. less than
   d. none of the above

4. Which of the following will not affect the amount of taxes you pay?
   a. Purchasing a home that will be financed with a mortgage
   b. Contributing a portion of your salary to your retirement account
   c. Taking a third job to enhance your wealth
   d. All of the above will affect the amount of taxes you pay.

5. _____ are not a type of depository institution.
   a. Credit unions
   b. Savings institutions
   c. Commercial banks
   d. Securities firms

6. Individuals with short-term funds would probably not invest them in _____.
   a. CDs
   b. NOW accounts
   c. corporate bonds
   d. checking accounts

7. Credit cards that allow consumers to borrow up to a specified maximum amount are examples of _____.
   a. installment credit
   b. collateral-based credit
   c. noninstallment credit
   d. revolving open-end credit

8. When applying for a credit card, you will probably not be asked for information regarding _____.
   a. your cash inflows and outflows
   b. your capital
   c. your credit history
   d. your criminal record

9. When applying for a loan, borrowers will probably need to provide information regarding their _____.
   a. personal balance sheet
   b. assets
   c. personal cash flow statement
   d. Borrowers probably need to provide information regarding all of the above.

10. The _____ the cost of a home, the _____ the insurance.
    a. higher; higher
    b. higher; lower
    c. lower; higher
    d. none of the above

601

Appendix B PROJECTS

The following pages include projects for you to complete relating to specific aspects of personal finance. They are also available on this book's companion Web site http://www.pearsonhighered.com/madura.

- Assessing Your Credit
- Career Planning Project
- Leasing an Apartment
- Stock Market Project
- Comparison Shopping: Online versus Local Purchases

Assessing Your Credit

If you do not own a credit card, answer the following questions based on how you think you would use a credit card:

1. **Credit Spending.** How much do you spend per month on your credit card?
2. **Number of Credit Cards.** Do you have many credit cards? Are all of them necessary? Do you spend more money than you would normally as a result of having extra credit cards?
3. **Credit versus Cash.** Would you make the most of your purchases if you used cash instead of a credit card? Do you feel like purchases have no cost when you use a credit card instead of cash?
4. **Pay Off Part or All of Balance.** What is your normal strategy when you receive a credit card bill? Do you only pay the minimum amount required? Do you typically pay off your entire balance on a monthly basis? If you do not pay off the entire balance, is it because you cannot afford to pay it off, or because you would prefer to have extra cash on hand? If you have a positive balance, how do you plan to pay off that balance? Pay all of it off next month? Or pay only the minimum amount required next month?
5. **Credit Limit.** Consider the limit on the amount you can spend using your credit cards. Does the limit restrict your spending? Would you benefit if the limit were increased? Or reduced?
6. **Obtaining Your Credit Report.** Go to the Federal Trade Commission Web site, http://www.ftc.gov to obtain your free credit report. If you recently obtained your report, just review that report rather than obtaining a new one. Notice the types of companies that requested information on your credit. Is your credit report accurate? If not, you can write to the credit bureau to have the wrong information corrected, as explained in the text.
7. **Assessing Your Credit Report.** Are you satisfied with your existing credit rating? If not, what steps do you plan to take to improve your credit rating? For example, could you reduce some debt in the future? See Chapter 7 for more ideas on improving your credit rating.

Career Planning Project

Personal financial planning involves how you budget your money, manage your liquidity, finance purchases, protect your assets, invest your money, and plan your retirement and estate. All these activities are focused on your money. A related task is career planning, which determines the amount of money that you can earn over time. Furthermore, your career determines your quality of life. Most people think about their ideal career (such as rock star, professional athlete, movie star), but do not spend enough time planning a realistic career. This project allows you learn about possible career opportunities in which you might have an interest. Your instructor may offer you additional details regarding the deadline date and length of the project.

619

Projects

Several projects are available in Appendix B.

- *Assessing Your Credit* prompts students to evaluate their credit card balance and credit limit. It also guides students to obtain their credit score and to consider whether they should implement a strategy to pay down their existing credit balance.

- *Career Planning Project* allows students to research a particular career that they plan to pursue and report on their research.

- *Leasing an Apartment* allows students to assess the cost and potential benefits of leasing a particular apartment that they have identified.

- *Stock Market Project* allows students to simulate the investing process, monitor a particular stock, and analyze how stock values respond to economic conditions.

- *Comparison Shopping: Online versus Local Purchases* allows students to compare the prices of products in stores versus online and to assess the pros and cons of purchasing products online.

PREFACE

Ask yourself these financial questions:

- Should you buy a new car or pay off your credit card balance first?
- How much can you borrow?
- Which bank offers the best services to satisfy your needs?
- How can you obtain easy access to funds in an emergency situation?
- Do you have enough insurance?
- Will you be able to retire at an early age?

This textbook allows you to address these and other related financial dilemmas. It equips you with the knowledge and tools to help you make sound decisions. It also guides you to create a financial plan for yourself. This textbook gives you the opportunity to develop the skills that can improve your financial position over time.

New to the Sixth Edition

All chapters have been updated to present complete and current coverage at time of publication. The key changes in the Sixth Edition of *Personal Finance* include the following:

- A new feature, **Web Search Exercise**, allows students to develop personal finance skills by conducting a search on the Internet for articles related to the chapter content. This exercise can facilitate classroom or online participation.
- The feature called **Psychology of Personal Finance** is retained in the Sixth Edition, but is applied to additional situations, such as how the behavior toward spending can either ruin a budget or create wealth.
- The feature called **Free Apps for Personal Finance** is retained in the Sixth Edition, and is updated to reflect new free opportunities available so that students can make informed personal finance decisions.
- **The Sampsons** case has been revised to ensure consistency throughout the text, and also now uses lower interest rates in examples to reflect realistic conditions because interest rates have declined since the previous edition.
- The case of **Brad Brooks** has been revised to ensure consistency throughout the text, and now uses lower interest rates in examples to reflect realistic conditions because interest rates have declined since the previous edition.
- The **Building Your Own Financial Plan** feature has been revised to ensure consistency throughout chapters and to allow for lower interest rates in computations because interest rates have declined since the previous edition.
- Updates have been included on information such as the salaries for various levels of education and growing occupations, and new rules for issuers of credit cards that can protect students from excessive fees.
- **Chapter 1** contains more information about how to select a college (or graduate school), a major, and an occupation. It also provides updated salary information about occupations and explains how to implement a financial plan to accomplish financial goals.
- **Chapter 5**, "Banking and Interest Rates," contains more discussion on checking services, debit cards, mobile banking, checking account fees, and savings accounts.
- **Chapter 6**, "Managing Your Money," uses lower interest rates in examples to reflect realistic conditions because interest rates have declined since the previous edition.
- **Chapter 7**, "Assessing and Selecting Your Credit," contains more discussion of student credit cards, credit bureaus, improving your credit score, and prevention of identity theft.

- Chapter 8, "Managing Your Credit," contains more discussion of secured and prepaid credit cards and rules for credit card issuers that protect card users.
- Chapter 9, "Personal Loans," contains more discussion of peer-to-peer lending, warranty rules for car dealers, student loans, and home equity loans.
- Chapter 10, "Purchasing and Financing a Home," now uses lower interest rates in examples to reflect realistic conditions because interest rates have declined since the previous edition. There is now more discussion on the impact of credit ratings on one's ability to obtain a mortgage, new rules that ensure mortgage contracts are understandable, and private mortgage insurance.
- Chapter 16, "Investing in Bonds," now uses lower interest rates in examples to reflect realistic conditions because interest rates have declined since the previous edition.
- Chapter 19, "Retirement Planning," contains updated information on all the different retirement plans that are available because many of the rules, such as the maximum allowable contribution per year, have changed since the previous edition.

Hallmarks of Personal Finance

The first chapter establishes the text's organization by introducing the key components of a financial plan. The balance of the text is organized into the following seven parts, which are keyed to the financial plan components introduced in Chapter 1, concluding with the synthesis of those components into a comprehensive financial plan in Chapter 21:

1. *Tools for Financial Planning* covers budgeting and tax planning.
2. *Managing Your Liquidity* covers banking, credit, and money management.
3. *Personal Financing* covers financing large purchases.
4. *Protecting Your Wealth* covers insurance planning.
5. *Personal Investing* covers a variety of investments and investing strategy.
6. *Retirement and Estate Planning* covers plans, strategies, and tax considerations related to retirement and estate planning.
7. *Synthesis of Financial Planning* covers the integration of the components into a comprehensive personal financial plan.

Decision Making

All the information presented in this book is geared toward equipping students with the expertise they need to make informed financial decisions. Each chapter establishes a foundation for the decisions that form the basis of a financial plan. When students complete each chapter, they are therefore prepared to complete the related financial plan subsection. The key to understanding personal finance is applying concepts to real-life planning scenarios.

Personal Finance calls attention to the trade-offs involved in financial decisions. The decision to buy a new car affects the amount of funds available for recreation, rent, insurance, and investments. The text uses ongoing scenarios woven throughout all the chapters to illustrate the interdependence of personal finance decisions, including the following:

- *Examples* feature Stephanie Spratt, a recent college graduate and new entrant into the workforce.
- *Building Your Own Financial Plan* exercises prompt students to revise their goals, personal cash flow statement, and personal balance sheet to reflect their shifting priorities.
- *The Sampsons* case at the end of each chapter highlights a family with two young children that face common financial dilemmas.
- The part-ending *Brad Brooks* case challenges students to offer advice that will improve Brad's financial condition.

- The capstone Chapter 21 synthesizes all parts of the text to highlight the interrelationships among the components of a financial plan and presents a completed plan for Stephanie Spratt. It also contains a *Certified Financial Planner Exercise* that challenges students to offer advice on how financial planning should be adjusted in response to a change in economic conditions.

Math-Friendly Presentation

The quantitative side of financial planning intimidates many students. This book simplifies the mathematics of personal finance by explaining the underlying logic. Formulas and calculations are explained in the text and then illustrated in examples. Examples that can be solved using a financial calculator are depicted with a calculator illustration. Students are referred to Web sites with online calculators whenever pertinent. The Financial Planning Problems provide students with ample opportunity to practice applying math-based concepts.

Instructor and Student Support Package

The following array of supplementary materials is available to help busy instructors teach more effectively and to allow busy students to learn more efficiently.

MyFinanceLab

This fully integrated online homework tool gives students the hands-on practice and tutorial assistance they need to learn finance skills efficiently. Ample opportunities for online practice and assessment in MyFinanceLab are seamlessly integrated into the content of each chapter and organized by section within the chapter summaries. All end-of-chapter Review Questions and Financial Planning Problems are available in MyFinanceLab. Please visit http://www.myfinancelab.com for more information and to register.

Instructor's Resource Center

This password-protected site, accessible at http://www.pearsonhighered.com/irc, hosts all the instructor resources that follow. Instructors should click on the "IRC Help Center" link for easy-to-follow instructions on getting access or may contact their sales representative for further information.

Instructor's Manual

Prepared by Mike Casey, University of Central Arkansas, this comprehensive online manual pulls together a wide variety of teaching tools. Each chapter contains an overview of key topics, teaching tips, and detailed answers and step-by-step solutions to the Review Questions, Financial Planning Problems, and Sampson family case questions. Each part concludes with answers to the Brad Brooks case questions. The Instructor's Manual has been updated to reflect the revised content of each chapter.

Test Bank

Prepared by Alan Wolk, University of Georgia, the online Test Bank contains over two thousand questions in true-false, multiple-choice, and short-essay format that can be used for quick test preparation. The Test Bank has been updated to reflect the revised content of each chapter.

PowerPoint Lecture Presentation

Authored by Mike Casey, University of Central Arkansas, this useful tool provides slides illustrating key points and exhibits as well as Web site information from the text in lecture note format. The PowerPoint Presentation has been updated to reflect the revised content of each chapter.

Financial Planning Workbook

The workbook is fully integrated into the text. At the end of each chapter, the student is prompted to complete the Building Your Own Financial Plan exercises and the Sampson family continuing case. At the end of each part, the student is prompted to complete the Brad Brooks continuing case. Students can easily rip out the perforated worksheets to build their financial plan. These same workbook sheets are available in Excel software, via MyFinanceLab and at http://www.pearsonhighered.com/madura.

The software templates prompt students through the key steps in the financial decision-making process as they complete the Building Your Own Financial Plan exercises. The software's true power lies in the linking of all the worksheets; students are prompted to revise their goals, cash flow statement, and personal balance sheet to demonstrate their understanding of the interrelationships among their financial decisions. Creating a complete and integrated plan has never been this easy!

Additional software features include the following:

- Calculation-based templates on topics such as determining one's federal income tax liability, reconciling a checking account, estimating the time it will take to pay off credit card debt, and determining disability insurance needs.
- For decisions that require time value of money analysis, the software directs students for input and then performs the calculations.
- Enhanced graphics such as pie charts and bar graphs that are generated based on user input aid students in visualizing their cash outflows and asset allocation.

Companion Web site

Available at http://www.pearsonhighered.com/madura, the Web site provides online access to innovative teaching and learning tools, including

- Financial Planning Workbook Software
- Links to Updated Tax Information

List of Reviewers

Pearson sought the advice of many excellent reviewers, all of whom strongly influenced the organization, substance, and approach of this book. The following individuals provided extremely useful evaluations:

Shannon Donovan,
Bridgewater State University

Michael S. Gutter,
University of Florida

David Marlett,
Appalachian State University

Thomas Matula,
Great Basin College

Jake Posey,
Florida State College at Jacksonville, Nassau Campus

Greg M. Richey,
California State University, San Bernardino

Tom Severance,
Mira Costa College

Pearson would also like to thank the following individuals who provided feedback in previous editions:

Tim Alzheimer,
Montana State University, Bozeman

Pat Andrus,
University of Louisiana, Lafayette

Eddie Ary,
Ouachita Baptist University

Albert L. Auxier,
University of Tennessee, Knoxville

H. David Barr,
Blinn College

Omar Benkato,
Ball State University

Charles Blaylock,
Lamar University

John Blaylock,
Northeast Community College

Lyle Bowlin,
University of Northern Iowa

Kathleen Bromley,
Monroe Community College

Ted Caldwell,
California State University, Fullerton

Margaret A. Camp,
University of Nebraska, Kearney

Joyce Cantrell,
Kansas State University

Steven L. Christian,
Jackson Community College

Conrad Ciccotello,
Georgia State University

Bruce A. Costa,
University of Montana

Richard L. Craig,
Western State College

John Cross,
California State University, Fullerton

Charles E. Downing,
Massasoit Community College

Dorsey Dyer,
Davidson County Community College

Sidney W. Eckert,
Appalachian State University

Brenda Eichelberger,
Portland State University

Sharon Farley,
Saddleback Community College

James Farris,
Golden West College

Michael Fenick,
Broward College

Cheryl J. Fetterman,
Cape Fear Community College

Michael Finke,
University of Missouri

Thomas M. Finnicum,
Oklahoma State University, Oklahoma City

Joseph F. Fowler,
Florida Community College

Glenn Gelderloos,
Grand Rapids Community College

Garry Grau,
Northeast State Technical Community College

Joseph D. Greene,
Augusta State University

Joyce Griffin,
Kansas City Kansas Community College

Ramon Griffin,
Metropolitan Community College, Denver

Reynolds Griffith,
Stephen F. Austin State University

Clark Grinde,
Iowa State University

Michael Gutter,
University of Wisconsin–Madison

Donald G. Hardwick,
Lexington Community College

Eric Hayden,
University of Massachusetts, Boston

Celia Ray Hayhoe,
University of Kentucky

Richard Healy,
Canyon College

Ruth Henderson,
Union County College

Jeanne Hilton,
University of Nevada, Reno

David R. Hoffman,
Arizona State University

M. Janice Hogan,
University of Minnesota

Marilynn E. Hood,
Texas A&M University

Samira Hussein,
Johnson County Community College

Roger Ignatius,
Husson College

Jan R. Jasper,
Prairie View A&M University

Debora C. Johnson,
Southeastern Louisiana University

Ronald R. Jordan,
New Mexico State University

Raymond Kerlagon,
Webster University

Judith Mae King,
Western Carolina University

Lee Kitchen,
Tallahassee Community College

Daniel Klein,
Bowling Green State University

Kenneth Knauf,
University of Wisconsin–Green Bay

Tina Knickerbocker,
Sam Houston State University

Dave Kraemer,
Maysville Community College

Edward Krohn,
Miami-Dade Community College, Kendall Campus

Andrew H. Lawrence,
Delgado Community College

Lauren Leach,
Northwest Missouri State University

John R. Ledgerwood,
Bethune-Cookman College

Catherine H. LoCascio,
Niagara County Community College

Robert A. Lupton,
Central Washington University

Robert A. Lutz,
University of Utah

Willard Machen,
Amarillo College

Kjartan T. Magnusson,
Salt Lake City Community College

James Mallett,
Stetson University

Ken Mark,
Kansas City Kansas Community College

Maggie L. McDermott,
Winona State University

Cindy Miglietti,
Bowling Green State University

Geofrey Mills,
University of Northern Iowa

Diann Moorman,
University of Georgia

Dianne R. Morrison,
University of Wisconsin–La Crosse

David W. Murphy,
Madisonville Community College

John V. O'Connor,
California State University, Fullerton

David Oliver,
Edison Community College

Susan L. Pallas,
Southeast Community College

Armand Picou,
University of Central Arkansas

Aimee D. Prawitz,
Northern Illinois University

Barbara Rice,
Florida College

Julia Sampson,
Malone College

Nick Sarantakes,
Austin Community College

Larry Schrenk,
American University

Elizabeth Scull,
University of South Carolina

A.S. Sethi,
University of Montana, Western

Gerald Silver,
Purdue University

Marilynn K. Skinner,
Central Georgia Technical College

Carolyn Strauch,
Crowder College

Timothy Strudell,
University of Texas at San Antonio

Melinda Taintor,
City University

Nancy Titus-Piersma,
Oklahoma State University

Robert S. Walsh,
SUNY Oswego

Marsha Weber,
Minnesota State University, Moorhead

Sally Wells,
Columbia College

Wayne Williams,
University of North Florida

Tony Wingler,
University of North Carolina at Greensboro

Michael J. Woodworth,
Purdue University

Myrna Wulfson,
SUNY Rockland Community College

Carol Wysocki,
Columbia Basin College

Robert S. Young,
Salt Lake Community College

Austin Zekeri,
Lane College

Acknowledgments

I benefited from the insight of John Bernardin, Kevin Brady, Dave Brooks, Ping Cheng, Inga Chira, Sean Davis, Ed Everhart, Marianne Hudson, Victor Kalafa, Ken Johnson, Pat Lewis, Mary Madura, Arjan Premti, Oliver Schnusenberg, Garret Smith, Ariel Viale, and Nik Volkov regarding various personal finance issues. I also benefited from many individuals whom I surveyed to identify the personal finance concepts that were most important to them, and to determine how I could most effectively communicate common personal finance dilemmas and solutions.

I am especially indebted to Michael J. Woodworth for his contributions to the tax and retirement chapters in the Sixth Edition. I am also grateful to Mike Casey for his work on the end-of-chapter content.

I wish to acknowledge the help and support of many people associated with Pearson who made this textbook possible. First and foremost, I wish to thank Kate Fernandes, my editor, for her continual support. The efforts of Program Manager Kathryn Dinovo and Editorial Assistant Kathryn Brightney are also noteworthy.

I greatly appreciated the copy editing by Karen Slaght. Other contributors in the production process whose commitment to quality benefited the project are Heather Pagano, project manager; Kristina Mose-Libon, cover designer at Lumina Datamatics, Inc.; and Karen Berry, project manager at SPi Global.

Financial Literacy
PRE-TEST

The following test will help you determine how much you already know about personal finance. It contains basic questions that can determine your ability to make proper financial planning decisions. This text explains the concepts identified in the test that are essential to make financial planning decisions. It also covers more analytical concepts that can allow you to develop an effective financial plan.

After taking the test, grade your performance based on the answers provided at the end of the test.

1. If you give something up as a result of making a decision, you are incurring a(n) _____.
   a. liquidity problem
   b. net cost
   c. opportunity cost
   d. none of the above

2. _____ sell shares to individuals and invest the proceeds in investment instruments such as bonds or stocks.
   a. Financial plans
   b. Budget plans
   c. Mutual funds
   d. none of the above

3. When finding the present value of a future value or the present value of an annuity, the _____ the interest rate, the _____ the present value.
   a. higher; higher
   b. lower; lower
   c. higher; lower
   d. none of the above

4. _____ reduce taxable income even if the taxpayer does not itemize.
   a. Exemptions
   b. Tax credits
   c. Capital gains
   d. none of the above

5. When the Federal Reserve wishes to _____ interest rates, it _____ the amount of funds at commercial banks.
   a. reduce; reduces
   b. increase; increases
   c. reduce; increases
   d. Answers (a) and (b) are correct.

6. A _____ offered by a depository institution specifies a minimum amount that must be invested, a maturity date on which the deposit matures, and an annualized interest rate.
   a. NOW account
   b. money market deposit account
   c. certificate of deposit
   d. savings account

7. In all cases of identity theft, you should notify the _____.
   a. FTC
   b. U.S. Postal Service
   c. FBI
   d. Secret Service

8. The _____ quoted on credit represents the simple interest rate charged after including any fees imposed by the creditor.
   a. annual percentage rate (APR)
   b. money market rate (MMR)
   c. effective annual rate (EAR)
   d. debit card rate (DCR)

9. Which of the following is not a disadvantage of leasing?

   a. You may have to purchase more car insurance than you already have.

   b. You must worry about finding a buyer for the car at the end of the lease period.

   c. You have no equity investment in the car.

   d. You may be charged if you drive more than a maximum number of miles specified in the original lease agreement.

10. When purchasing a home, which of the following costs will you not incur?

    a. Closing costs

    b. Loan application fee

    c. Real estate broker's commission

    d. Down payment

11. A deductible of $500 requires _____.

    a. you to pay the first $500 in damages

    b. the party at fault to pay the first $500 in damages

    c. the insurance company to pay the first $500 in damages

    d. none of the above

12. _____ is not a source of disability income insurance.

    a. Insurance from Social Security

    b. Employer disability insurance

    c. Insurance from worker's compensation

    d. All of the above are sources of disability income insurance.

13. For a given life insurance policy with specific benefits, the insurance premium is _____ related to one's age.

    a. rarely

    b. never

    c. positively

    d. inversely

14. _____ is not a common investment mistake made by individuals.

    a. Making decisions based on unrealistic goals

    b. Borrowing to invest

    c. Taking risks to recover losses from previous investments

    d. All of the above are common investment mistakes made by individuals.

15. When investors purchase stock on margin, they

    a. are buying stock in the over-the-counter market.

    b. are using a buy-stop order.

    c. are borrowing money from the brokerage firm to fund part of the purchase.

    d. are lending money to the brokerage firm.

16. The _____ a bond provides credit.

    a. shareholder of

    b. investor in

    c. issuer of

    d. none of the above

17. Which of the following is not a motive for investing in mutual funds?

    a. The expertise of the portfolio managers who decide how to invest the money you provide

    b. Mutual funds designed to meet specific investment goals

    c. Investing in a broadly diversified portfolio with a small initial investment

    d. All of the above are motives for investing in mutual funds.

18. The price at which an option can be exercised is the _____.

    a. premium

    b. put add-on

    c. call price

    d. exercise price

19. Individuals subject to a _____ income tax rate enjoy the greatest tax benefits as a result of using a retirement plan.

    a. middle

    b. high

    c. zero

    d. low

20. The executor of a will is also referred to as the _____.

    a. grantor

    b. guardian

    c. personal representative

    d. trustee

Answers

1. C	11. A
2. C	12. D
3. C	13. C
4. A	14. D
5. C	15. C
6. C	16. B
7. A	17. D
8. A	18. D
9. B	19. B
10. C	20. C

Overview of a Financial Plan

Imagine that you are taking a vacation next year. You have many financial choices to make. How big is your vacation budget, and how do you want to allocate it? The more money that you save now, the more you will have to spend on your vacation.

rh2010/Fotolia

Now, imagine that you are planning your financial future. You have many choices to make. How much of your budget should be allocated to food and utilities? How much can you afford to spend on clothes? Should you spend all of your money as you earn it, or should you use some money for investment opportunities? Should you buy a new car? Should you buy a house? If so, what type of house should you buy? When do you want to retire? Do you want to leave an estate for your heirs? All these decisions require detailed planning.

In a world where there are few guarantees, thorough financial planning, prudent financial management, and careful spending can help you achieve your financial goals.

The personal financial planning process enables you to understand a financial plan and to develop a personal financial plan. The simple objective of financial planning is to make the best use of your resources to achieve your financial goals. The sooner you develop your goals and a financial plan to achieve those goals, the easier it will be to achieve your objectives.

MyFinanceLab helps you master the topics in this chapter and study more efficiently. Visit http://www.myfinancelab.com for more details.

3

The objectives of this chapter are to:

- Explain how you benefit from personal finance
- Identify the key components of a financial plan
- Explain how financial planning affects your cash flows
- Outline the steps involved in developing your financial plan

How You Benefit from Personal Finance

personal finance (personal financial planning)
The process of planning your spending, financing, and investing to optimize your financial situation.

personal financial plan
A plan that specifies your financial goals and describes the spending, financing, and investing plans that are intended to achieve those goals.

Personal finance (also referred to as **personal financial planning**) is the process of planning your spending, financing, and investing to optimize your financial situation. A **personal financial plan** specifies your financial goals and describes the spending, financing, and investing plans that are intended to achieve those goals. Although the United States is one of the wealthiest countries in the world, many Americans do not manage their financial situations well. Consequently, they tend to rely too much on credit and have excessive debt. Consider these statistics:

- More than 1 million people filed for personal bankruptcy in 2013.
- The level of savings in the United States is less than 5% of income earned. (Some investments, including retirement accounts, are not included as savings.)
- About half of all surveyed people in the United States who are working full-time state that they live from one paycheck to the next, without a plan for saving money.
- About 40% of people who work full-time do not save for retirement. Those who do typically save a relatively small amount of money.

ECONOMIC IMPACT

Personal finance has become even more critical since the 2008–2009 financial crisis, as this caused the wealth of many people to be reduced substantially. The values of many homes and other types of investments were cut in half or more, and some still have not fully recovered. Economic conditions are still not as strong as in the period before the crisis, which have limited the available jobs. Overall, people have less wealth and fewer opportunities to earn income. Thus, they need an effective financial plan to achieve their financial goals.

You will have numerous options regarding the choice of bank deposits, credit cards, loans, insurance policies, investments, and retirement plans. With an understanding of personal finance, you will be able to make decisions that can enhance your financial situation.

How much do you know about personal finance? Various government agencies in different countries have attempted to assess financial literacy in recent years. Surveys have documented that people tend to have very limited personal finance skills. In addition, surveys have found that many people who believe they have strong personal finance skills do not understand some basic personal finance concepts. If you haven't already taken the Financial Literacy Pre-Test that precedes this chapter, be sure to take it. You can substantially increase your understanding and improve your financial planning skills by reading this text. An understanding of personal finance is beneficial to you in many ways, including the following.

Make Your Own Financial Decisions

opportunity cost
What you give up as a result of a decision.

An understanding of personal finance enables you to make informed decisions about your financial situation. Each of your spending decisions has an **opportunity cost**, which represents what you give up as a result of that decision. By spending money for a specific purpose, you forgo alternative ways that you could have spent the money and also forgo saving the money for a future purpose. For example, if your decision to use your cell phone costs $100 per month, you have forgone the possibility of using that money to buy concert tickets or to save for a new car. Informed financial decisions increase the amount of money that you accumulate over time and give you more flexibility to purchase the products and services you want in the future.

Judge the Advice of Financial Advisers

The personal financial planning process will enable you to make informed decisions about your spending, saving, financing, and investing. Nevertheless, you may prefer to rely on advice from various types of financial advisers. An understanding of personal finance allows you to judge the guidance of financial advisers and to determine whether their advice is in your best interest (or in their best interest).

EXAMPLE You want to invest $10,000 of your savings. A financial adviser guarantees that your investment will increase in value by 20% (or by $2,000) this year, but he will charge you 4% of the investment ($400) for his advice. If you have a background in personal finance, you would know that no investment can be guaranteed to increase in value by 20% in one year. Therefore, you would realize that you should not trust this financial adviser. You could either hire a more reputable financial adviser or review investment recommendations made by financial advisers on the Internet (often for free).

Become a Financial Adviser

An understanding of personal finance may interest you in pursuing a career as a financial adviser. Financial advisers are in demand because many people lack an understanding of personal finance or are not interested in making their own financial decisions. A single course in personal finance is insufficient to start a career as a financial adviser, but it may interest you in taking additional courses to obtain the necessary qualifications.

Components of a Financial Plan

A complete financial plan contains your personal finance decisions related to six key components:

1. Budgeting and tax planning
2. Managing your liquidity
3. Financing your large purchases
4. Protecting your assets and income (insurance)
5. Investing your money
6. Planning your retirement and estate

Each of the first six parts of this text is devoted to one component of the financial plan, and the seventh part synthesizes these components. To begin your introduction to the financial planning process, let's briefly explore each component.

A Plan for Your Budgeting and Tax Planning

budget planning (budgeting)
The process of forecasting future expenses and savings.

Budget planning (also referred to as **budgeting**) is the process of forecasting future expenses and savings. That is, it requires you to determine how you spend money, the amount of money to spend, and how much to save. Your spending decisions are critical because they determine how much of your income can be used for other purposes.

FREE APPS
for Personal
Finance

Your Spending Decisions

Application:

The Spending Tracker app (by MH Riley Ltd) allows you to easily monitor how you spend your money.

To Find It:

Search for the "Spending Tracker" app on your mobile device.

assets
What you own.

liabilities
What you owe; your debt.

net worth
The value of what you own minus the value of what you owe.

If you receive $750 in income during one month, your amount saved is the amount of money (say, $100) that you do not spend. The relationship between income received, spending, and saving is illustrated in Exhibit 1.1. Some individuals are "big spenders": They focus their budget decisions on how to spend most or all of their income and therefore have little or no money left for saving. Others are "big savers": They set a savings goal and consider spending their income received only after allocating a portion of it toward saving. Budgeting can help you estimate how much of your income will be required to cover monthly expenses so that you can set a goal for saving each month.

The first step in budget planning is to evaluate your current financial position by assessing your income, your expenses, your **assets** (what you own), and your **liabilities** (debt, or what you owe). Your **net worth** is the value of what you own minus the value of what you owe. You can measure your wealth by your net worth. As you save money, you increase your assets and therefore increase your net worth. Budget planning enables you to build your net worth by setting aside part of your income to either invest in additional assets or reduce your liabilities.

Your budget is influenced by your income, which in turn is influenced by your education and career decisions. Individuals who pursue higher levels of education tend to have smaller budgets during their education years. After obtaining their degrees, however, they typically are able to obtain jobs that pay higher salaries and therefore have larger budgets.

A key part of budgeting is estimating the typical expenses that you will incur each month. If you underestimate expenses, you will need more cash inflows (money that you receive) than you expected to cover your cash outflows (money that you spend). Achieving a higher level of future wealth requires you to maintain your spending at a lower level today.

EXHIBIT 1.1   How a Budget Plan Affects Savings

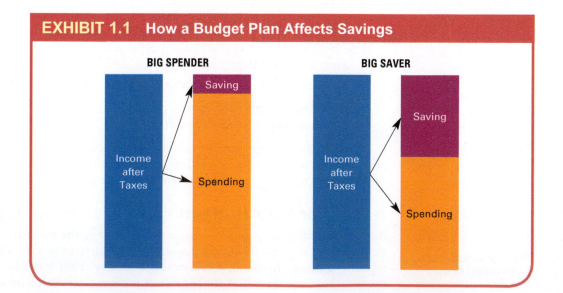

Many financial decisions are affected by tax laws, as some forms of income are taxed at a higher rate than others. By understanding how your alternative financial choices would be affected by taxes, you can make financial decisions that have the most favorable effect on your cash flows. Budgeting and tax planning are discussed in Part 1 because they are the basis for decisions about all other parts of your financial plan.

A Plan to Manage Your Liquidity

liquidity
Access to funds to cover any short-term cash needs.

You should have a plan for how you will cover your daily purchases. Your expenses can range from your morning cup of coffee to major car repairs. You need to have **liquidity**, or access to funds to cover any short-term cash needs. You can enhance your liquidity by utilizing money management and credit management.

money management
Decisions regarding how much money to retain in a liquid form and how to allocate the funds among short-term investment instruments.

Money management involves decisions regarding how much money to retain in a liquid form and how to allocate the funds among short-term investments. If you do not have access to money to cover your cash needs, you may have insufficient liquidity. That is, you have the assets to cover your expenses, but the money is not easily accessible. Finding an effective liquidity level involves deciding how to invest your money so that you can earn a return, but also have easy access to cash if needed. At times, you may be unable to avoid cash shortages because of unanticipated expenses.

credit management
Decisions regarding how much credit to obtain to support your spending and which sources of credit to use.

Credit management involves decisions about how much credit you need to support your spending and which sources of credit to use. Credit is commonly used to cover both large and small expenses when you are short on cash, so it enhances your liquidity. Credit should be used only when necessary, however, as you will need to pay back borrowed funds with interest (and the interest expenses may be very high). The use of money management and credit management to manage your liquidity is illustrated in Exhibit 1.2.

A Plan for Your Financing

Loans are typically needed to finance large expenditures, such as the payment of college tuition or the purchase of a car or a home. The amount of financing needed is the difference between the amount of the purchase and the amount of money you have available, as illustrated in Exhibit 1.3. Managing loans includes determining how much you can afford to borrow, deciding on the maturity (length of time) of the loan, and selecting a loan that charges a competitive interest rate.

A Plan for Protecting Your Assets and Income

insurance planning
Determining the types and amount of insurance needed to protect your assets.

To protect your assets, you can conduct **insurance planning**, which determines the types and amount of insurance that you need. In particular, automobile insurance and homeowner's insurance protect your assets, and health insurance limits your potential medical expenses. Disability insurance and life insurance protect your income.

EXHIBIT 1.2   Managing Your Liquidity

Money Management → Keep some money available in case it is needed → Access to money and/or credit → Cover expenses that cannot be covered by current income

Credit Management → Ensure access to credit in case it is needed → Access to money and/or credit

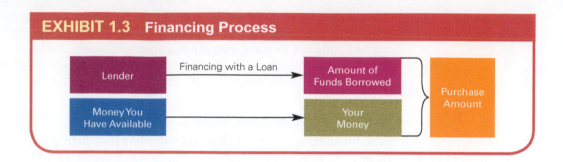

EXHIBIT 1.3 Financing Process

A Plan for Your Investing

Any funds that you have beyond what you need to maintain liquidity should be invested. Because these funds normally are not used to satisfy your liquidity needs, they can be invested with the primary objective of earning a high return. Potential investments include stocks, bonds, mutual funds, and real estate. You must determine how much of your funds you wish to allocate toward investments and what types of investments you wish to consider. Most investments are subject to **risk** (uncertainty surrounding their potential return), however, so you need to manage them so that your risk is limited to a tolerable level.

risk
Uncertainty surrounding the potential return on an investment.

A Plan for Your Retirement and Estate

Retirement planning involves determining how much money you should set aside each year for retirement and how you should invest those funds. Retirement planning must begin well before you retire so that you can accumulate sufficient money to invest and support yourself after you retire. Money contributed to various kinds of retirement plans is protected from taxes until it is withdrawn from the retirement account.

retirement planning
Determining how much money you should set aside each year for retirement and how you should invest those funds.

Estate planning is the act of planning how your wealth will be distributed before or upon your death. Effective estate planning protects your wealth against unnecessary taxes and ensures that your wealth is distributed in the manner that you desire.

estate planning
Determining how your wealth will be distributed before or upon your death.

Building Your Own Financial Plan

An effective financial plan enhances your net worth and therefore builds your wealth. In each part of this text, you will have the opportunity to develop a component of your financial plan. At the end of each chapter, the Building Your Own Financial Plan exercise offers you guidance on the key decisions that you can make after reading that chapter. Evaluate your options, and make decisions using the Excel-based software available with your text. By completing the Building Your Own Financial Plan exercises, you will build a financial plan for yourself by the end of the school term.

How Financial Planning Affects Your Cash Flows

All components of your financial plan affect your cash inflows and cash outflows and therefore affect the amount of cash you have available. This section explains how each component of your financial plan affects your cash flows.

Part 1: Tools for Financial Planning

Part 1 of this text focuses on the tools required for budgeting, which is the first component of your financial plan. Budgeting allows you to plan how you will use the cash you receive in a given period (such as a month). Your salary is probably your most important source of cash inflows each month, and it might be your only source of income. You may rely on cash inflows from your income so that you can purchase products or services each month. Your budget decisions determine how much you spend and the amount of your cash outflows each month. If your spending exceeds your income, your cash inflows cannot cover your cash outflows in a particular month, and therefore you will not have any cash to allocate for savings.

Your budget decisions include

- How much should you work this month (if your employer allows flexibility)? This decision determines your cash inflows for the month.
- What products or services should you purchase this month? This decision determines your cash outflows for the month.

CASH FLOWS DUE TO YOUR BUDGETING DECISIONS

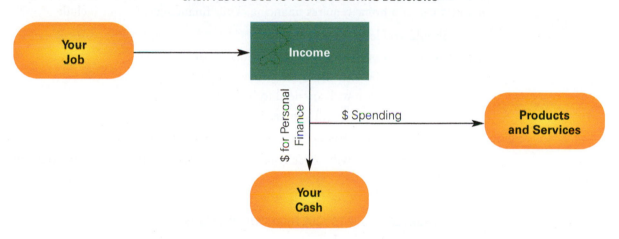

Part 2: Managing Your Liquidity

Part 2 of this text focuses on liquidity management, which is the second component of your financial plan. When your cash inflows exceed your cash outflows (covered in Part 1) in a particular month, you use liquidity management to decide how much of this cash should be allocated to savings at your financial institution. Conversely, if your cash inflows are less than your cash outflows, you use liquidity management to withdraw savings or obtain funds from another source to cover your spending for the month. Your liquidity management decisions include

- If you have excess cash this month, how much cash should you add to your checking or savings account?
- If you have a cash deficiency this month, how much cash should you withdraw from your checking or savings account?
- If you have a cash deficiency this month, how much credit should you use from credit cards or other sources?

CASH FLOWS DUE TO YOUR LIQUIDITY MANAGEMENT DECISIONS

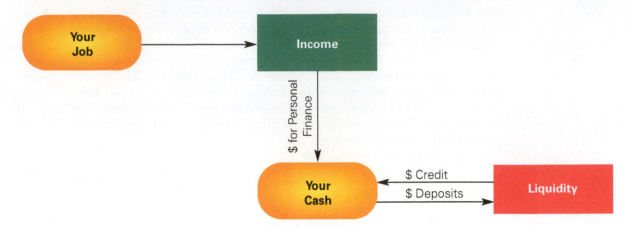

Part 3: Personal Financing

Part 3 of this text summarizes your financing, which represents the third component of your financial plan. Financing is needed to support your large purchases. The purchase of a new car or a home requires financing. Your financing decisions include

- Should you lease a car?
- Should you borrow money to purchase a car?
- Should you borrow money to purchase a home?
- How much cash will you need to borrow?
- How long a period will you need to borrow funds?
- What is the ideal source from which you will borrow funds?

All these decisions will affect your monthly interest payment (a cash outflow) on your loan.

CASH FLOWS DUE TO YOUR FINANCING DECISIONS

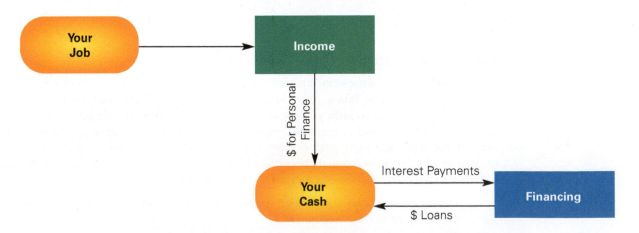

Part 4: Protecting Your Wealth

Part 4 of this text explains how to use insurance to protect your assets and your income, which represents the fourth component of your financial plan. Your insurance decisions include

- What types of insurance do you need?
- How much insurance should you purchase to protect your assets?
- How much insurance should you purchase to protect your income?

These decisions will affect your monthly insurance premiums (a cash outflow) that you must pay.

CASH FLOWS FROM PROTECTING YOUR ASSETS AND INCOME

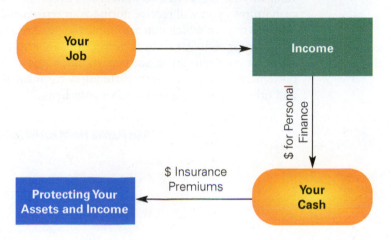

Part 5: Personal Investing

Part 5 of this text focuses on investing, which represents the fifth component of your financial plan. Common investing decisions include

- How much cash should be used to make investments?
- What types of investments should you make?
- How much risk should you tolerate when making investments?

These decisions will determine how much money you allocate for investments, and how much cash these investments generate for you over time.

CASH FLOWS FROM INVESTING

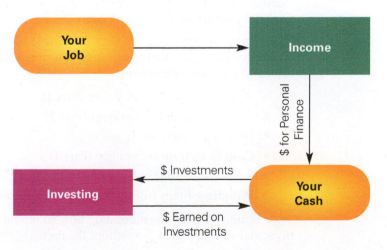

Part 6: Retirement and Estate Planning

Part 6 of this text focuses on retirement and estate planning, which represents the sixth component of your financial plan. Common retirement and estate planning decisions include

- How much cash should you invest toward your retirement each month?
- What types of investments should you make for your retirement accounts?

These decisions will determine your cash outflows that you will contribute to your retirement account while working. These decisions also will affect the degree to which the value of your retirement account grows over time and therefore will determine how much cash inflows you will receive during your retirement. Normally, the more you contribute over the time in which you are employed, the larger are the cash inflows you will receive during your retirement. In addition, the higher the performance of the investments you select for your retirement account, the larger the cash inflows you will receive during your retirement. Also, your estate planning decisions will determine how your remaining cash and other assets are distributed to your heirs.

CASH FLOWS FROM RETIREMENT AND ESTATE PLANNING

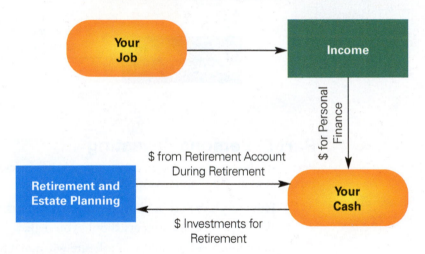

Summary of Financial Plan Components

Notice in the previous six diagrams (one for each financial plan component) how the decisions made within each component can either cause you to make cash payments (outflows) or generate cash (inflows). A summary of financial plan components is provided in Exhibit 1.4. This summary is a consolidation of the diagrams for each of the six financial plan components.

Summary of Sources of Cash As you review the six components in Exhibit 1.4, notice that each component can help you obtain cash. When you need more cash, you can consider these alternatives:

- Attempt to work more hours (Part 1)
- Withdraw cash from savings (Part 2)
- Obtain a loan (Part 3)
- Cash in an insurance policy (Part 4)
- Sell some of your investments (Part 5)
- Withdraw funds from your retirement account (Part 6)

Your optimal choice when deciding how to obtain cash is dependent on various conditions that are explained throughout the text.

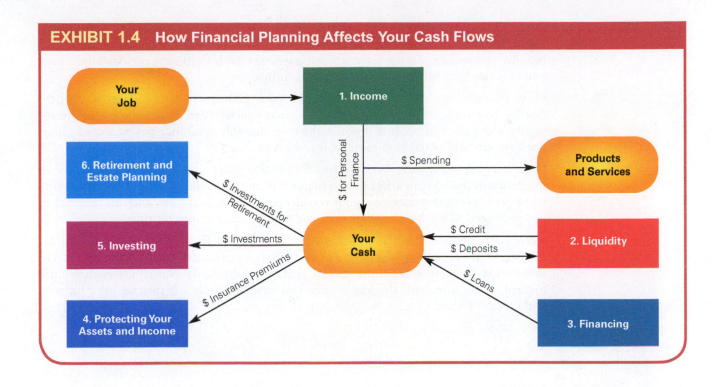

EXHIBIT 1.4   How Financial Planning Affects Your Cash Flows

Summary of Uses of Cash As you review the six components in Exhibit 1.4, notice that each component can help you decide how to use cash. When you have cash, you can consider these alternatives:

- Purchase products and services (Part 1)
- Deposit cash in your checking or savings account (Part 2)
- Pay interest payments on a loan or pay off a loan (Part 3)
- Make insurance payments (Part 4)
- Make new investments (Part 5)
- Contribute toward your retirement account (Part 6)

Your optimal choice when using cash is dependent on various conditions that are explained throughout the text.

Integration of the Financial Plan Components

As you learn about each of the six components of your financial plan, keep in mind that your decisions about one component of the plan can affect all the other components. The integration of financial plan components is covered in Chapter 21. It is important to understand how components are integrated, so that you recognize trade-offs before you finalize your conclusions about any component of your financial plan.

How Budgeting Decisions Affect Other Financial Plan Components Your budgeting decisions (Part 1) affect your liquidity management decisions (Part 2) because if you decide to spend all of your income, you will not be able to accumulate savings in your bank accounts.

How Managing Liquidity Affects Your Other Financial Plan Components Your liquidity management (Part 2) can affect your financing decisions (Part 3) because if you do not accumulate savings in your bank accounts, you may not have funds to make a down payment on a home in the future.

How Financing Affects Your Other Financial Plan Components Your financing decisions (Part 3) can affect your insurance decisions (Part 4) because if you borrow heavily, you will be making large interest payments (cash outflows) periodically. Thus, you may not have sufficient funds to pay for insurance.

How Protecting Your Assets Affects Your Other Financial Plan Components Your decisions to buy insurance to protect yourself (Part 4) can affect your investing decisions (Part 5) because if you make large monthly insurance payments, you may not have any additional cash to make investments.

How Investing Affects Your Other Financial Plan Components Your investing decisions (Part 5) can affect your retirement planning decisions (Part 6) because if you make poor investment decisions, your wealth could decline over time, and this means that you may need to work more years than you had expected before retiring.

How Retirement Planning Affects Your Other Financial Plan Components Your retirement planning decisions (Part 6) can influence your budget decisions (Part 1) because the more money that you voluntarily contribute each month toward your retirement, the less money you have available for purchasing products and services today.

FREE APPS
for Personal
Finance

Help on Personal Finance

Application:

The Dollarbird—Smart Personal Finance app (by Halcyon MD SRL) allows you to set financial plans, forecasts how much money you will have in the future, and provides reminders about paying bills.

To Find It:

Search for the "Dollarbird" app on your mobile device.

How Psychology Affects Your Financial Plan

PSYCHOLOGY
of Personal
Finance

Psychology has a major impact on human behavior and decision making. Therefore, it has a major impact on your spending behavior and your ability to implement an effective financial plan. For this reason, the impact of psychology on financial planning is given attention in various sections, like this one, throughout the text. Consider the two completely different types of spending behavior described here, so that you can determine which type reflects your own behavior.

Focus on Immediate Satisfaction and Peer Pressure Some people allow their desire for immediate satisfaction and their focus on peer pressure to make most of their financial planning decisions. This causes them to spend excessively, meaning that they make purchases that are not necessary. They tend to spend every dollar they earn, without serious consideration to use any money for other purposes. Consumers often tend to make many impulse purchases, which are purchases made on the spur of the moment, even though they don't need the products or were not even shopping specifically for those products. They get a strong dose of pleasure from the purchase, perhaps more so than the ultimate use of some of the products that they buy. This type of behavior may be referred to as "shopping therapy" or "retail therapy" because the act of shopping (and buying) boosts the morale of some people. However, the boost provided by the therapy may quickly vanish, so that additional therapy (shopping) is needed. The spending can become addictive.

People who spend based on peer pressure may purchase a new car that they cannot afford, even when they already own a reliable car, just because their friends or neighbors have a new car. Although they receive immediate satisfaction from having a new car, they may now have the obligation of a $500 monthly car payment for the next four years. This decision will use up much of their monthly income and could prevent them from allocating any funds toward all the other financial planning functions such as managing liquidity, insurance, investments, and retirement planning. Notice that all these other financial planning functions are intended to offer future benefits. Thus, the behavior of people to spend based on immediate satisfaction and peer pressure causes them to spend excessively now, which leaves nothing for the future. They may say that all of their spending was on necessities and they did not have any extra funds to use for financial planning purposes. Their perception of necessities, however, is whatever allows them to achieve immediate satisfaction.

People with this type of mind-set may make promises to themselves that they will reduce their spending in the future to focus on financial planning functions. But with this mind-set, they may always find reasons to justify spending their entire paycheck—or more.

Another psychological force is a hopeless feeling that is used to justify spending. Some people think that if they can allocate only a small amount such as $50 for saving or other forms of financial planning, they will never be able to achieve any long-term goals. Thus, they use this reasoning to justify spending all their income. Their logic is that they might as well enjoy the use of the money now.

Focus on the Future Other people have more discipline when deciding whether to spend all their income, and their decision making is influenced by other psychological forces. They may have a strong desire to avoid debt at this point in their lives because they would feel stress from the obligation of making large debt payments. For this reason, they may avoid purchasing a new car or any types of purchases that would cause large credit card payments, and this allows them to use their income for other purposes. They recognize that by spending conservatively today, they will have additional money available that they can use for financial planning functions to improve their financial future.

Assess Your Own Spending Behavior How would you describe your spending behavior? Do you focus only on achieving immediate satisfaction, or are you disciplined so that you can improve your financial future? If you spend conservatively now so that you can improve your financial future, you'll benefit from this text because it explains how you can conduct your financial planning. Conversely, if you spend excessively now to achieve immediate satisfaction, you have no money left to direct toward financial planning functions discussed in this text, such as managing liquidity, insurance, investing, or retirement planning. Take this brief quiz to determine which behavior category you are in.

- Do you pay rent for a single apartment rather than share an apartment?
- Do you have large monthly car payments?
- Do you have credit card bills that you only make the minimum monthly payment toward each month?
- Do you spend all your income that is not needed for rent or car loan payments within the first day or two of receiving your paycheck on clothes or electronic games or other items?
- Do you always find a reason each month to spend all your income?

If you answered "yes" to any of these questions, you might be able to reduce your spending behavior so that you could allocate more money toward financial planning functions. This will allow you to accumulate more wealth in the future, and with that wealth, you will be able to afford more spending in the future. This text will help guide you to achieve these goals.

Developing Your Financial Plan

Six steps are involved in developing your financial plan.

Step 1. Establish Your Financial Goals

You must determine your financial goals.

First, identify your general goals in life. These goals do not have to be put in financial terms. For example, you may have goals such as a family, additional education, or a vacation to a foreign country for one week every year. You may envision owning a five-bedroom house, or having a new car every four years, or retiring when you reach age 55.

Types of Financial Goals Your general goals in life influence your financial goals. It takes money to support many of your goals. If you want to have a family, one of your financial goals may be that you and your spouse earn enough income and save enough money over time to financially support a family. If you want a vacation to a foreign country every year, one of your financial goals may be that you earn enough income and save enough money to financially support your travel. If you want a large home, one of your financial goals should be that you earn enough income and save enough money over time to make a substantial real estate purchase. If you want to retire by age 55, this will require you to save enough money by then so that you could afford to stop working. You may also establish financial goals such as helping a family member or donating to charities.

Set Realistic Goals You need to be realistic about your goals so that you can have a strong likelihood of achieving them. A financial plan that requires you to save almost all your income is useless if you are unable or unwilling to follow that plan. When this overly ambitious plan fails, you may become discouraged and lose interest in planning. By reducing the level of wealth you wish to attain to a realistic level, you will be able to develop a more useful plan.

Timing of Goals Financial goals can be characterized as short term (within the next year), intermediate term (typically between one and five years), or long term (beyond five years). For instance, a short-term financial goal may be to accumulate enough money to purchase a car within six months. An intermediate-term goal would be to pay off a school loan in the next three years. A long-term goal would be to save enough money so that you can maintain your lifestyle and retire in 20 years. The more aggressive your goals, the more ambitious your financial plan will need to be.

Step 2. Consider Your Current Financial Position

Your decisions about how much money to spend next month, how much money to place in your savings account, how often to use your credit card, and how to invest your money depend on your financial position. A person with little debt and many assets will clearly make different decisions than a person with mounting debt and few assets. And a single individual without dependents will have different financial means than a couple with children, even if the individual and the couple have the same income. The appropriate plan also varies with your age and wealth. If you are 20 years old with zero funds in your bank account, your financial plan will be different than if you are 65 years old and have saved much of your income over the last 40 years.

ECONOMIC IMPACT

How Your Future Financial Position Is Tied to the Economy Economic conditions affect the types of jobs that are available to you and the salary offered by each type of job. They also affect the price you pay for services such as rent, the value of assets (such as a home) that you own, and the return that you can earn on your investments.

The financial crisis of 2008–2009 affected the financial position of individuals in many ways. First, it caused a reduction in new job opportunities. Second, it resulted in the elimination of some jobs. Third, it resulted in lower pay for the existing job positions, as employers could not afford to give generous raises to their employees. These first three effects resulted in a general decline in income for many individuals.

The financial crisis also resulted in a decline in the value of housing. The reason for the decline in price was due to shifts in the demand for homes versus the supply of available homes. As incomes of individuals declined, the demand for homes declined because individuals could not afford to buy a home. Meanwhile, many individuals who owned a home could no longer afford it. They had borrowed money to finance the purchase of their homes and now were unable to make their loan payments because their income had declined. With many homeowners trying to sell a home and very few people seeking to purchase homes, it was difficult for homeowners to sell homes. They had to lower the price of their home to attract possible buyers. Consequently, the values of many homes declined by 50% or more during the financial crisis. As a result of the financial crisis, some individuals had to revise their financial goals to make them attainable or allow for a longer period in which to reach their goals.

Step 3. Identify and Evaluate Alternative Plans That Could Achieve Your Goals

Given your financial goals (which you defined in Step 1), you need a financial plan that could help move you from your existing financial position (which you assessed in Step 2) toward achieving your financial goals. Your financial plan will require various types of decisions that will influence your career, income level, and savings over the next several years.

Pursuing Additional Education Your pursuit of additional education might enable you to achieve the credentials to obtain the career and income level that you desire to fulfill your long-term financial goals. The more education that you have, the higher your earnings will likely be. As Exhibit 1.5 shows, the average annual income for people with a bachelor's degree is much higher than the average income for people without a bachelor's degree. In addition, the average annual income is even higher for people who have earned a master's degree.

A degree might also allow you to pursue a wider range of job opportunities. Exhibit 1.6 shows the proportion of unemployed people in specific education categories. Notice from this exhibit that the more education you have, the less likely it is that you will be unemployed.

Selecting Your Major One of your most important education decisions is selecting your major (journalism, nursing, etc.). Your skills and general interests will naturally influence your selection. Your choice of a major will determine your career, and your career determines your lifestyle and income over time. Therefore, your chosen major can help you achieve your financial plans.

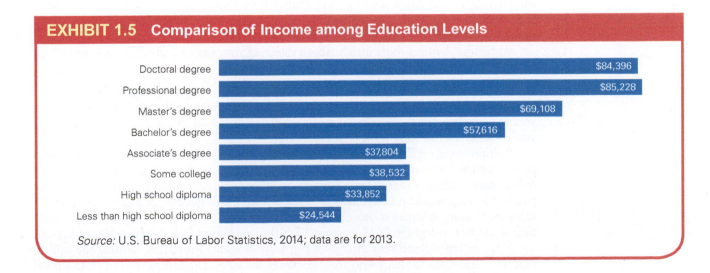

EXHIBIT 1.5   Comparison of Income among Education Levels

Education Level	Income
Doctoral degree	$84,396
Professional degree	$85,228
Master's degree	$69,108
Bachelor's degree	$57,616
Associate's degree	$37,804
Some college	$38,532
High school diploma	$33,852
Less than high school diploma	$24,544

Source: U.S. Bureau of Labor Statistics, 2014; data are for 2013.

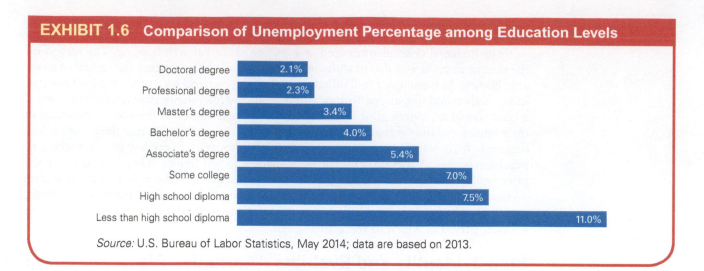

EXHIBIT 1.6 Comparison of Unemployment Percentage among Education Levels

Education Level	Unemployment %
Doctoral degree	2.1%
Professional degree	2.3%
Master's degree	3.4%
Bachelor's degree	4.0%
Associate's degree	5.4%
Some college	7.0%
High school diploma	7.5%
Less than high school diploma	11.0%

Source: U.S. Bureau of Labor Statistics, May 2014; data are based on 2013.

The fastest-growing occupations are identified in the first column of Exhibit 1.7. The expected growth rate in the employment level for each of these occupations is shown in the second column, and the median pay is shown in the third column.

If you become a social worker, you will be in a different financial position than if you choose to work as an electrical engineer. As a social worker, you will need to save a much higher proportion of your income to achieve the same level of savings that you could achieve as an electrical engineer. If you choose a career that pays a low salary, you will need to set attainable financial goals. Or you may reconsider your choice of a career in pursuit of a higher level of income. However, be realistic. You should not decide to be a doctor just because doctors' salaries are high if you dislike health-related work. You should choose a career that will be enjoyable and will suit your skills. If you like your job, you are more likely to perform well. Because you may be working for 40 years or longer, you should seriously think about the career that will satisfy both your financial and personal needs.

Various Web sites can help you estimate the income level for a specific career. Additional information about salary levels for various types of careers, types of colleges, and various college majors is provided at http://www.payscale.com. Even if the income level for a particular career you desire is less than what you expected, you may be able to maintain the same financial goals by extending the period in which you hope to achieve those goals.

Many people change their career over time. As the demand for occupations changes, some jobs are eliminated, and others are created. In addition, some people grow tired of their occupation and seek a new career. Thus, career choices are not restricted to students who are just completing their education. As with your initial career decision, a shift to a new career should be influenced by your views of what will satisfy you.

Appendix A offers more insight about selecting your major and other decisions about your education.

Selecting Your College Your selection of a college is crucial because the cost of an education can vary substantially among colleges. Therefore, a wise selection may enable you to complete your education at a relatively low cost and therefore make it easier for you to achieve your long-term financial plans.

Tuition at state colleges is typically less than tuition at private colleges. However, tuition at state colleges also varies substantially among states, and even within states. Conduct an online search using a search term such as "college tuition," and specify the state where you live to review the annual tuition levels. Some state colleges charge $6,000 per year for full-time tuition, whereas others charge more than $16,000 per year. The average annual tuition at state colleges in 2015 is about $9,000 according to *U.S. News & World Report*.

State colleges commonly charge out-of-state students more than double the tuition that they charge for students who are residents of the state. The average out-of-state annual

EXHIBIT 1.7   Fastest-Growing Occupations

Occupation	Growth Rate Over the 2012–2022 Period	Annual Median Pay
Industrial organizational psychologist	53%	$83,580
Personal care aides	49%	$19,190
Home health aides	48%	$20,820
Insulation workers	47%	$39,170
Interpreters and translators	46%	$45,430
Diagnostic medical sonographers	46%	$65,860
Masons	43%	$28,220
Occupational therapy assistants	43%	$53,240
Genetic counselors	41%	$56,800
Physical therapy assistants	41%	$52,160
Physical therapy aides	40%	$23,880
Skincare specialists	40%	$28,640
Physician assistants	38%	$90,930
Segmental pavers	38%	$33,720
Helpers for electricians	38%	$27,670
Information security analysts	37%	$86,170
Occupational therapy aides	36%	$26,850
Health specialties	36%	$81,140
Medical secretaries	36%	$31,350
Physical therapists	36%	$79,860

Source: U.S. Bureau of Labor Statistics, 2014.

tuition charged at state colleges in 2015 is about $20,000 according to *U.S. News & World Report*, but it is more than $30,000 at some state colleges.

Many private colleges charge more than $40,000 for full-time annual tuition, but there are some private colleges that charge less than $10,000 a year. The average annual cost of tuition at private schools as of 2015 is more than $30,000 according to *U.S. News & World Report*.

All the estimated tuition levels above are for one year, so assuming that four years of full-time coursework is needed to complete a degree, the estimated cost of a college education might range from about $24,000 to about $200,000. Given the large difference in tuition among colleges, it is well worth your time to compare tuition levels before deciding where to further your education.

Ideally, you should decide on your major before you select your college to ensure that the college offers the major that you desire. However, if you are unsure of your specific major, you may want to focus on colleges that offer majors within your general area of interest, such as health, science, liberal arts, or business.

The benefits from a given degree and major might vary with the college you attend. For example, you might prefer to earn a degree in nursing at one particular college because of the specific nursing courses offered there or because of the course delivery (online versus in classroom). In addition, a degree earned at one particular college might lead to better job opportunities and higher income if that college has a very strong reputation. For this reason, assess not only the cost of tuition but also the job marketability when comparing colleges that offer a particular major.

Establishing a Strategy to Accumulate Wealth   Along with planning for additional education, you also need a plan for saving money to achieve your long-term financial goals. For example, you might establish a goal of saving a large portion of your income over the next several years. However, this plan requires much discipline.

Alternatively, you could plan to save only a small portion of your income, but to invest your savings in a manner that earns a very high return so that you can accumulate a substantial amount of money in 10 years. This alternative plan does not require you to save as much money. However, it places more pressure on you to earn a high return on your investments. To earn such a high return, you will likely have to make risky investments to achieve your goals. You might not achieve your goals with this alternative plan because your investments might not perform as well as you expected.

Step 4. Select and Implement the Best Plan for Achieving Your Goals

You need to analyze and select the plan that will be most effective in achieving your goals. Many alternative plans that could possibly achieve your goals involve trade-offs. For example, you may have a long-term financial goal of accumulating a large amount of money by the time you are 50 years old so that you can retire at that time. One plan to achieve this goal may be to pursue a career that generates a higher income level, but this type of career might first require you to pursue additional education to have the credentials you need. Consequently, you may have to spend money and time in education over the next few years to achieve this long-term goal. Alternatively, you may decide not to pursue additional education, but plan to save a very high proportion of your income from your existing career to achieve your goal. However, this strategy may require that you forgo some spending over the next several years to achieve your long-term financial goal of early retirement.

Many individuals do not meet their financial goals because they establish unrealistic financial plans. For example, they may set a plan of saving at least half of their income every month to satisfy their financial goal of retiring by age 50. Yet, they spend all their income every month and therefore are unable to satisfy their goal. In this case, they should consider revising their financial plan and financial goal so that it is achievable.

Using the Internet   The Internet provides you with valuable information for making financial decisions. Your decision to spend money on a new camera versus saving the money may be dependent on how much you can earn from saving the money. Your decision of whether to purchase a new car depends on the prices of new cars and financing rates on car loans. Your decision of whether to purchase a home depends on the prices of homes and financing rates on home loans. Your decision of whether to invest in stocks is influenced by the prices of stocks. Your decision of where to purchase insurance may be influenced by the insurance premiums quoted by different insurance agencies. All these financial decisions require knowledge of prevailing prices or interest rates, which are literally at your fingertips on the Internet.

The Internet also provides updated information on all parts of the financial plan, such as:

- Current tax rates and rules that can be used for tax planning
- Recent performance of various types of investments
- New retirement plan rules that can be used for long-term planning

Many Web sites offer online calculators that you can use for a variety of financial planning decisions, such as:

- Estimating your taxes
- Determining how your savings will grow over time
- Determining whether buying or leasing a car is more appropriate

Financial Planning ONLINE

Go to:
The finance section of Yahoo.com

To get:
A lot of information and many tools for all aspects of financial planning, including tax rates, bank deposit rates, loan rates, credit card information, mortgage rates, insurance policies, and investment information.

Financial Planning Online exercises are provided at the end of each chapter so that you can practice using the Internet for financial planning purposes. URLs in this text are available and updated on the text's Web site for easy navigation.

When you use online information for personal finance decisions, keep in mind that some information may not be accurate. Use reliable sources, such as Web sites of government agencies or financial media companies that have a proven track record for reporting financial information. Also, recognize that free personal finance advice provided online does not necessarily apply to every person's situation. Get a second opinion before you follow online advice, especially when it recommends that you spend or invest money.

Step 5. Evaluate Your Financial Plan

After you develop and implement each component of your financial plan, you must monitor your progress to ensure that the plan is working as you intended. Keep your financial plan easily accessible so that you can evaluate it over time.

Step 6. Revise Your Financial Plan

If you find that you are unable or unwilling to follow the financial plan that you developed, you need to revise the plan to make it more realistic. Of course, your financial goals may have to be modified as well if you are unable to maintain the plan for achieving a particular level of wealth.

As time passes, your financial position will change, especially with specific events such as graduating from college, marriage, a career change, or the birth of a child. As your financial position changes, your financial goals may change as well. You need to revise your financial plan to reflect such changes in your means and priorities.

The steps in developing a financial plan are summarized in Exhibit 1.8. To see how the steps can be applied, consider the following example.

EXHIBIT 1.8   Summary of Steps Used to Develop a Financial Plan

1. Establish your financial goals.

   - What are your short-term financial goals?
   - What are your intermediate-term financial goals?
   - What are your long-term financial goals?

2. Consider your current financial position.

   - How much money do you have in savings?
   - What is the value of your investments?
   - What is your net worth?

3. Identify and evaluate alternative plans that could achieve your goals.

   - How can you obtain the necessary funds to achieve your financial goals?
   - Will you need to reduce your spending to save more money each month?
   - Will you need to make investments that generate a higher rate of return?

4. Select and implement the best plan for achieving your goals.

   - What are the advantages and disadvantages of each alternative plan that could be used to achieve your goals?

5. Evaluate your financial plan.

   - Is your financial plan working properly? That is, will it enable you to achieve your financial goals?

6. Revise your financial plan.

   - Have your financial goals changed?
   - Should parts of your financial plan be revised to achieve your financial goals? If so, how?

EXAMPLE

Stephanie Spratt graduated from college last year with a degree in marketing. After job searching for several months, she was just hired by the sales department of an advertising firm at an annual salary of $38,000. She is eager to have money from her salary to spend and to give up her interim part-time job waiting tables.

Stephanie plans to save a portion of every paycheck so that she can invest money to build her wealth over time. She realizes that by establishing a financial plan to limit her spending today, she can increase her wealth and therefore her potential spending in the future. At this point, Stephanie decides to develop an overview of her current financial position, establish her goals, and map out a plan for how she might achieve those goals, as shown in Exhibit 1.9.

EXHIBIT 1.9   Overview of Stephanie Spratt's Financial Plan

Step 1. Financial Goals:

I would like to:

- *buy a new car within a year,*
- *buy a home within two years,*
- *make investments that will allow my wealth to grow over time, and*
- *build a large amount of savings for retirement in 20 to 40 years.*

Step 2. Current Financial Position:

I have very little savings at this time and own an old car. My income, which is about $30,000 a year after taxes, should increase over time.

Step 3. Plans to Achieve the Goals:

Since my current financial position does not provide me with sufficient funds to achieve these financial goals, I need to develop a financial plan for achieving these goals. I want to save enough money to make a down payment on the car and home and to obtain financing to cover the rest of the cost. This plan allows me to allocate some of my income toward investments.

My financing decisions will determine the type of car and home that I will purchase and the amount of funds I will have left to make other investments so that I can build my wealth over time.

Step 4. Selecting and Implementing the Best Plan:

Financing the purchase of a car and a home is a more appropriate plan for me. I will prepare a budget so that over time I can accumulate savings that will be used to make a down payment on a new car. Then, I will attempt to accumulate savings to make a down payment on a new home. I need to make sure that I can afford financing payments on any money that I borrow.

Step 5. Evaluating the Plan:

Once I establish a budget, I will monitor it over time to determine whether I am achieving the desired amount of savings each month.

Step 6. Revising the Plan:

If I cannot save as much money as I desire, I may have to delay my plans for purchasing a car and a home until I can accumulate enough funds to make the down payments. If I am able to exceed my savings goal, I may be able to purchase the car and the home sooner than I had originally expected.

Key decisions that relate to Stephanie's financial plan will be summarized at the end of each chapter. Your financial planning decisions will differ from Stephanie's or anyone else's. Nevertheless, the process of building the financial plan is the same. You need to establish your goals, assess alternative methods for reaching your goals, and decide on a financial plan that can achieve your goals.

SUMMARY

Benefits of Personal Finance. Personal financial planning is the process of planning your spending, financing, and investing to optimize your financial situation. Your financial planning decisions allow you to develop a financial plan, which involves a set of decisions about how to manage your spending, financing, and investments.

Components of a Financial Plan. A financial plan has six components: (1) budgeting, (2) managing your liquidity, (3) financing large purchases, (4) protecting your assets and income, (5) investing, and (6) planning for retirement and the future.

Financial Planning Process. The financial planning process involves six steps: (1) establishing your financial goals, (2) considering your current

financial position, (3) identifying and evaluating alternative plans that could achieve your goals, (4) selecting and implementing the best plan for achieving your financial goals, (5) evaluating your financial plan over time to ensure that you are meeting your goals, and (6) revising your financial plan when necessary.

How Financial Planning Affects Your Cash Flows. Notice that each component of your financial plan affects your cash flows. If you make a decision about one component that increases your future cash outflows, you may need to complement that with a decision about another financial planning component that either reduces your cash outflows or increases your cash inflows. Thus, the decisions about all your financial planning components are integrated.

REVIEW QUESTIONS

All Review Questions are available in MyFinanceLab *at http://www.myfinancelab.com.*

1. **Personal Finance Decisions.** Define personal financial planning. What types of decisions are involved in a personal financial plan?

2. **Opportunity Cost.** What is an opportunity cost? What might be some of the opportunity costs of spending $10 each week on the lottery?

3. **Personal Finance Benefits.** How can an understanding of personal finance benefit you?

4. **Financial Plan Components.** What are the six key components of a financial plan?

5. **Budget Planning.** Why is it important to track your spending before creating a budget?

6. **Net Worth.** How is your net worth calculated? Why is it important?

7. **Income and Budgeting.** What factors influence income? Why is an accurate estimate of expenses important in budget planning? How do tax laws affect the budgeting process?

8. **Liquidity.** What is liquidity? What two factors are considered in managing liquidity? How are they used?

9. **Financing.** Why do most people need access to financing at some point in their life?

10. **Investing.** What is the primary objective of investing? What else must be considered? What potential investment vehicles are available?

11. **Protecting Your Assets.** What are the three elements of planning to protect your assets? Define each element.

12. **Your Cash Flows.** How does each element of financial planning affect your cash flows?

13. **Steps in Financial Planning.** What are the six steps in developing a financial plan?

14. **Financial Goals.** How do your financial goals fit into your financial plan? Why should goals be realistic? What are three time frames for goals? Give an example of a goal for each time frame.

15. **Your Financial Position.** Name some factors that might affect your current financial position.

16. **Financial Goals and Planning.** Jill has decided to save 50% of her income for retirement. Her father told her she needed to set a different goal. Why do you think he gave her this advice?

17. **Implementing Your Plan.** Once your financial plan has been implemented, what is the next step? Why is it important?

18. **Revising Your Plan.** Why might you need to revise your financial plan?

19. **Online Information.** List some information available on the Internet that might be useful for financial planning. Describe one way you might use some of this information for financial planning purposes.

20. **Economic Impact on Net Worth.** Assume that you have established a plan to achieve a particular level of wealth in three years, but the economic conditions suddenly cause both your existing income and the value of your existing assets to decline. Should you leave your financial plan as it is or adjust it?

21. **Economic Impact on Job Strategy.** During a weak economy jobs are scarce, so some individuals may consider starting their own businesses. What is the disadvantage of this idea during a weak economy?

22. **Peer Pressure and Your Finances.** How can peer pressure impact your spending habits?

23. **Selecting the Right College.** Explain why it is important to select the right university or college.

24. **Selecting Your Major.** How does your choice of career impact your financial plan?

25. **Your Career and Lifetime Goals.** Ricardo wants a career where he can help people. He also wants to travel and see the world. He is thinking about becoming a personal care aide. What advice would you give him?

FINANCIAL PLANNING PROBLEMS

All Financial Planning Problems are available in MyFinanceLab *at* http://www.myfinancelab.com.

1. **Estimating Savings.** Julia brings home $1,600 per month after taxes. Julia's rent is $350 per month, her utilities are $100 per month, and her car payment is $250 per month. Julia is currently paying $200 per month to her orthodontist for her braces. If Julia's groceries cost $50 per week and she estimates her other expenses to be $150 per month, how much will she have left each month to put toward savings to reach her financial goals?

2. **Estimating the Opportunity Cost.** Julia (from problem 1) is considering trading in her car for a new one. Her new car payment will be $325 per month, and her insurance cost will increase by $60 per month. Julia determines that her other car-related expenses (gas, oil) will stay about the same. What is the opportunity cost if Julia purchases the new car?

3. **Estimating Net Worth.** Mia has $3,000 in assets, a finance company loan for $500, and an outstanding credit card balance of $135. Mia's monthly cash inflows are $2,000, and she has monthly expenses of $1,650. What is Mia's net worth?

4. **Estimating Net Worth.** At the beginning of the year, Arianne had a net worth of $5,000. During the year she set aside $100 per month from her paycheck for savings and borrowed $500 from her cousin that she must pay back in January of next year. What was her net worth at the end of the year?

5. **Estimating Net Worth.** Anna has just received a gift of $500 for her graduation, which increased her net worth by $500. If she uses the money to purchase a tablet computer, how will her net worth be affected? If she invests the $500 at 4% interest per year, what will it be worth in one year?

6. **Estimating Cash Flows.** Jason's car was just stolen, and the police informed him that they will probably be unable to recover it. His insurance will not cover the theft. Jason has a net worth of $3,000, all of which is easily convertible to cash. Jason requires a car for his job and his daily life. Based on Jason's cash flow, he can't currently afford more than $200 in car payments. What options does he have? How will these options affect his net worth and cash flow?

7. **Ethical Dilemma.** Sandy and Phil have recently married and are both in their early 20s. In establishing their financial goals, they determine that their three long-term goals are to purchase a home, to provide their children with a college education, and to plan for their retirement.

They decide to seek professional assistance in reaching their goals. After considering several financial advisers who charge an annual fee based on the size of their portfolio, they decide to go to Sandy's cousin Larry, who is a stockbroker. Larry tells them that he is happy to help them, and the only fee he will charge is for transactions. In their initial meeting, Larry recommends stocks of several well-known companies that pay high dividends, which they purchase. Three months later, Larry tells them that due to changing market conditions, they need to sell the stocks and buy several others. Three months later, the same thing happens. At the end of the year Phil and Sandy, who had sold each of the stocks for more than they had paid for them, were surprised to see that the total dollar value of their portfolio had declined. After careful analysis, they found the transaction fees exceeded their capital gains.

a. Do you think Larry behaved ethically? Explain.

b. Would Larry have a personal reason for handling Sandy and Phil's portfolio as he did? Explain.

FINANCIAL PLANNING ONLINE EXERCISES

1. The purpose of this exercise is to introduce you to one of the online tools that are available to help with budgeting and financial planning. Go to http://www.mint.com, and review the information available on this Web site. Don't sign up yet, although you may want to before the course is completed.

   a. How does Mint help you with your personal finances?

   b. List some examples of the information Mint can access.

   c. How can Mint help you save money?

PSYCHOLOGY OF PERSONAL FINANCE: Your Spending Behavior

1. This chapter explains how consumers may make purchases that they cannot afford to keep up with their friends. This could prevent them from allocating any funds toward all the other financial planning functions such as liquidity, insurance, investments, and retirement planning. Are your spending decisions influenced by the need for immediate satisfaction or by peer pressure? Or are your spending decisions influenced more by the desire to avoid debt? What factors have the most influence on your spending behavior?

2. Read one practical article of how psychology affects spending behavior. You can easily retrieve possible articles by doing an online search using the terms "psychology" and "spending." Summarize the main points of the article.

WEB SEARCH EXERCISE

You can develop your personal finance skills by conducting an Internet search for related articles. Find a recent online article about personal finance that reinforces one or more concepts covered in this chapter. If your class has an online component, your professor may ask you to post your summary of the article there and provide a link to the article so that other students can access it. If your class is live, your professor may ask you to summarize your application of the article in class. Your professor may assign specific students to complete this assignment or may allow any student to do the assignment on a volunteer basis.

For recent online articles related to this chapter, consider using the following search terms (be sure to include the current year as a search term to ensure that the online articles are recent):

- Financial goals
- Identifying your financial goals
- Setting your financial goals
- Realistic financial goals
- Achieving financial goals
- Saving money
- Spending decisions

VIDEO EXERCISE: Benefits of Financial Planning

Go to one of the Web sites that contain video clips (such as http://www.youtube.com), and view some video clips about financial planning. Conduct a search of the site using phrases such as "value of financial planning" or "benefits of financial planning." Select one video clip on this topic that you would recommend for the other students in your class.

1. Provide the Web link for the video clip.

2. What do you think is the main point of this video clip?

3. How might you change your financial planning as a result of watching this video clip?

BUILDING YOUR OWN FINANCIAL PLAN

These end-of-chapter exercises are designed to enable you to create a working life-long financial plan. Like all plans, your personal plan will require periodic review and revision. In this first exercise, you should review your current financial situation. If you are a full-time student, base your review on what you anticipate your financial situation will be upon your graduation. After carefully reviewing your current or antici-pated financial situation, create three short-term goals and three intermediate-term and long-term goals.

Your short-term goals should be goals that you can realistically accomplish in one year. They may include, but are not limited to, paying off credit card balances, begin-ning a 401(k) or other retirement-type savings program, or getting your cash inflows and outflows in balance.

Your intermediate-term goals are goals that you should realistically be able to accom-plish in one to five years. They may include, but are not limited to, purchasing a new vehicle or paying off school loans.

Long-term goals will take longer than five years to accomplish realistically. They may include, but are not limited to, purchasing a home, taking a major trip (such as a sum-mer in Europe), or saving sufficient funds to retire at a predetermined age.

The goals that you develop are a first draft and may be added to or modified as you proceed through this course. This course is designed to provide you with information and insight that will help you make informed decisions about your financial future. As you gain experience in financial planning, new goals may emerge, and existing goals may change. Once you have completed your financial plan, you should review your goals annually or whenever a significant change occurs in your life (e.g., mar-riage, divorce, birth of a child, or a significant change in employment circumstances).

Go to the worksheets at the end of this chapter to begin building your financial plan.

THE SAMPSONS—A Continuing Case

Dave and Sharon Sampson are 30 years old and have two children, who are five and six years old. Since marrying seven years ago, the Sampsons have relied on Dave's salary, which is currently $48,000 per year. They have not been able to save any money, as Dave's income is just enough to cover their mortgage loan payment and their other expenses.

Dave and Sharon feel they need to take control of their finances. Now that both chil-dren are in school, they have decided that Sharon will look into getting a part-time job.

She was just hired for a part-time position at a local department store at a salary of $12,000 per year. Dave and Sharon are excited by the prospect of having additional cash inflows—they now feel they can start working toward their financial goals.

The Sampsons own a home valued at about $100,000, and their mortgage is $90,000. They have a credit card balance of $2,000. They own two cars and do not have any car loans, but Sharon's car is old and will need to be replaced soon. Sharon would really like to purchase a new car within the next year; she hopes to save $500 each month until she has accumulated savings of $5,000 to use for a down payment.

The Sampsons are also concerned about how they will pay for their children's college education. Sharon plans to save an additional $300 each month that will be set aside for this purpose.

The Sampsons have decided to develop a financial plan. They realize that by formally identifying their main goals, they will be able to implement and monitor their plan over time. At the end of every chapter, you will help the Sampsons develop their financial plan using the key concepts presented in the chapter.

Go to the worksheets at the end of this chapter to begin this case.

CHAPTER 1: BUILDING YOUR OWN FINANCIAL PLAN

YOUR GOALS FOR CHAPTER 1

1. Set financial goals such as the purchase of a car or paying your education expenses.

2. Identify one or two possible career goals.

ANALYSIS

1. Complete the following worksheet regarding specific purchases (such as a car or education) that you wish to make in the future. You can focus on just one or two goals for now if you wish.

Your Personal Financial Goals

1. _____

2. _____

3. _____

2. Go to the Web site http://www.bls.gov, and insert the search term "occupation." Review one or two careers in the Occupational Outlook Handbook that interest you. Summarize what you learn about the career by completing the following table.

Personal Career Goals

	Career One	Career Two
Job Title		
Educational Requirements		
Advancement Potential		
Job Outlook		
Salary Range		
Continuing Education Requirements		
Related Occupations		
Brief Description of Working Conditions		
Brief Job Description		

DECISIONS

1. Explain whether your planned career will allow you to afford the future purchases (such as a home) that you plan to make. You may revise your plan later after you learn more about personal finance during this school term.

_____

_____

_____

_____

_____

_____

_____

_____

_____

_____

_____

_____

CHAPTER 1: THE SAMPSONS—A Continuing Case

CASE QUESTIONS

1. Help the Sampsons with their financial plans by filling out the worksheet below:

Goal 1: Purchase a new car for Sharon this year.

Plan to achieve Goal 1:	Sharon will set aside savings of $500 per month until she has a down payment of $5,000 to buy a car.
How can the Sampsons periodically evaluate whether their plan to achieve Goal 1 is successful?	

Goal 2: Pay for the children's college

Plan to achieve Goal 2.	The Sampsons will set aside savings of $300 per month to save for their children's college educations.
How can the Sampsons periodically evaluate whether their plan to achieve Goal 2 is successful?	

2. Should the Sampsons make one of these goals a priority over the other goal?

Tools for Financial Planning

The chapters in this part introduce the key tools used to make financial planning decisions. Chapter 2 describes the personal financial statements that help you to monitor your spending and guide your budgeting decisions. Chapter 3 illustrates how you can use time value of money concepts to make decisions about saving. Chapter 4 explains how to use tax concepts to assess and minimize your tax liability. Your budget, saving, and tax plans all influence your cash flows and wealth.

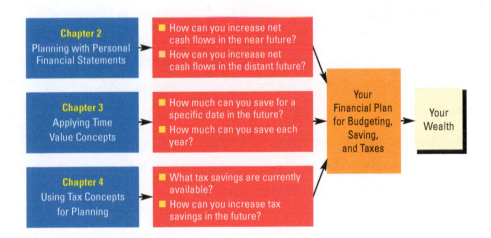

Planning with Personal Financial Statements

WavebreakMediaMicro/Fotolia

Where does it all go? It seems like the last paycheck is gone before the next one comes in. Money seems to burn a hole in your pocket, yet you don't believe that you are living extravagantly. Last month you made a pledge to yourself to spend less than the month before. Some-

how, though, you are in the same position as you were last month. Your money is gone. Is there any way to plug the hole in your pocket?

What are your expenses? For many people, the first obstacle is to correctly assess their true expenses. Each expense may seem harmless and worthwhile, but combined they can be like a pack of piranhas that quickly gobble up your modest income. What can you do to gain control of your personal finances?

Just read on in this chapter, and you will see how to take control of your finances. However, your task is not easy because it takes self-discipline, and there may be no immediate reward. The result is often like a diet: easy to get started, but hard to carry through.

Your tools are the personal balance statement, the personal cash flow statement, and a budget. These three personal financial statements show you where you are, predict where you will be after three months or a year, and help you control expenses. The potential benefits are reduced spending, increased savings and investments, and peace of mind from knowing that you are in control.

MyFinanceLab helps you master the topics in this chapter and study more efficiently. Visit http://www.myfinancelab.com for more details.

The objectives of this chapter are to:

- Explain how to create your personal cash flow statement
- Identify the factors that affect your cash flows
- Forecast your cash flows
- Explain how to create your personal balance sheet
- Explain how your personal financial statements fit within your financial plan

Personal Cash Flow Statement

You may commonly ask whether you can afford a new television, a new car, another year of education, or a vacation. You can answer these questions by determining your financial position. Specifically, you use what you know about your income and spending habits to estimate how much cash you will have at the end of this week, or quarter, or year. Once you obtain an estimate, you can decide if there are ways in which you can either increase your income or reduce your spending to achieve a higher level of available cash.

PSYCHOLOGY of Personal Finance

Psychology can discourage many individuals from assessing their financial position because they are afraid the assessment will lead to a conclusion that they should not make specific purchases at this time. They may decide to defer their assessment of their financial position, which allows them to make some purchases without feeling guilty. Naturally, individuals want support for financial decisions (including purchases) that they make. Making purchases might be enjoyable when done with friends who encourage the spending, especially when those friends are also making purchases that they cannot afford.

However, assessing your financial position does not have to be so painful. It allows you to estimate how much you need to save each period to make specific purchases in the future with cash instead of borrowing money. This type of analysis can make you realize how your efforts to save will ultimately be rewarded and therefore might encourage you to establish a plan for saving money.

personal cash flow statement
A financial statement that measures a person's cash inflows and cash outflows.

As mentioned in Chapter 1, budgeting is the process of forecasting future expenses and savings. When budgeting, the first step is to create a **personal cash flow statement,** which measures your cash inflows and cash outflows. Comparing your cash inflows and outflows allows you to monitor your spending and determine the amount of cash that you can allocate toward savings or other purposes.

Cash Inflows

The main source of cash inflows for working people is their salary, but there can be other important sources of income. Deposits in various types of savings accounts can generate cash inflows in the form of interest income. Some stocks also generate quarterly dividend income.

Cash Outflows

Cash outflows represent all your expenses, which are the result of your spending decisions. Expenses are both large (for example, monthly rent) and small (for example, dry cleaning costs). It is not necessary to document every expenditure, but you should track how most of your money is spent. Recording transactions in your checkbook when you write checks helps you to identify how you spent your money. Using a credit card or debit card for your purchases also provides a written record of your transactions. Many people use software programs such as Quicken and Microsoft Money Plus Sunset to record and monitor cash outflows.

Creating a Personal Cash Flow Statement

You can create a personal cash flow statement by recording how you received cash over a given period and how you used cash for expenses.

EXAMPLE

Stephanie Spratt tried to limit her spending in college but never created a personal cash flow statement. Now that she has begun her career and is earning a salary, she wants to monitor her spending on a monthly basis. She decides to create a personal cash flow statement for the last month.

Stephanie's Monthly Cash Inflows. Stephanie's present salary is about $3,170 per month ($38,000 annually) before taxes. For budgeting purposes, she is interested in the cash inflow she receives from her employer after taxes.

About $670 per month of her salary goes to taxes, so her disposable (after-tax) income is:

Monthly Salary	$3,170
− Monthly Taxes	− $670
Monthly Cash Inflow	$2,500

Then Stephanie considers other potential sources of cash inflows. She does not receive any dividend income from stocks, and she does not have any money deposited in an account that pays interest. Thus, her entire monthly cash inflows come from her paycheck. She inserts the monthly cash inflow of $2,500 at the top of her personal cash flow statement.

Stephanie's Monthly Cash Outflows. Stephanie looks in her checkbook register to see how she spent her money last month. Her household payments for the month were as follows:

- $600 for rent
- $50 for Internet
- $60 for electricity and water
- $60 for cellular expenses
- $300 for groceries
- $130 for a health care plan provided by her employer

Next, Stephanie reviews several credit card bills to estimate her other typical expenses on a monthly basis:

- About $100 for clothing
- About $200 for car expenses (insurance, maintenance, and gas)
- About $600 for recreation (including restaurants and a health club membership)

Stephanie uses this cash outflow information to complete her personal cash flow statement, as shown in Exhibit 2.1. Her total cash outflows were $2,100 last month.

Stephanie's Net Cash Flows. Monthly cash inflows and outflows can be compared by estimating **net cash flows**, which are equal to the cash inflows minus the cash outflows. Stephanie estimates her net cash flows to determine how easily she covers her expenses and how much excess cash she has to allocate to savings or other purposes. Her net cash flows during the last month were:

Net Cash Flows = Cash Inflows − Cash Outflows

= $2,500   − $2,100

= $400

Stephanie enters this information at the bottom of her personal cash flow statement.

net cash flows
Cash inflows minus cash outflows.

EXHIBIT 2.1   Personal Cash Flow Statement for Stephanie Spratt

Cash Inflows	Last Month
Disposable (after-tax) income	$2,500
Interest on deposits	0
Dividend payments	0
Total Cash Inflows	**$2,500**

Cash Outflows	Last Month
Rent	$600
Internet	50
Electricity and water	60
Cellular	60
Groceries	300
Health care insurance and expenses	130
Clothing	100
Car expenses (insurance, maintenance, and gas)	200
Recreation	600
Total Cash Outflows	**$2,100**
Net Cash Flows	**+$400**

Factors That Affect Cash Flows

To enhance your wealth, you want to maximize your (or your household's) cash inflows and minimize cash outflows. Your cash inflows and outflows depend on various factors, as will be described next.

Factors Affecting Cash Inflows

Cash inflows are highly influenced by factors that affect your income level. The key factors to consider are the stage in your career path and your job skills.

Stage in Your Career Path The stage you have reached in your career path influences cash inflows because it affects your income level. Cash inflows are relatively low for people who are in college or just starting a career (like Stephanie Spratt). They tend to increase as you gain job experience and progress within your chosen career.

Your career stage is closely related to your place in the life cycle. Younger people tend to be at early stages in their respective careers, whereas older people tend to have more work experience and are thus further along the career path. It follows that cash inflows tend to be lower for younger individuals and much higher for individuals in their 50s.

There are many exceptions to this trend, however. Some older people switch careers and therefore may be set back on their career path. Other individuals who switch careers from a low-demand industry to a high-demand industry may actually earn higher incomes. Many women put their careers on hold for several years to raise children and then resume their professional lives.

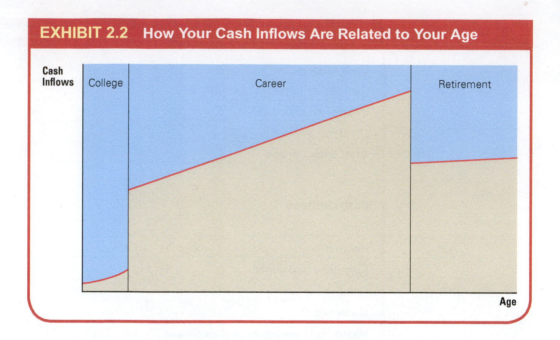

EXHIBIT 2.2   How Your Cash Inflows Are Related to Your Age

The final stage in the life cycle that we will consider is retirement. The cash flows that come from a salary are discontinued at the time of retirement. After retirement, individuals rely on Social Security payments and interest or dividends earned on investments as sources of income. Consequently, retired individuals' cash inflows tend to be smaller than when they were working. Your retirement cash inflows will come from income from your investments and from your retirement plan. The manner in which age commonly affects cash inflows is summarized in Exhibit 2.2. Notice that there are three distinct phases.

Type of Job Income also varies by job type. Jobs that require specialized skills tend to pay much higher salaries than those that require skills that can be obtained very quickly and easily. The income level associated with specific skills is also affected by the demand for those skills. The demand for people with a nursing license has been very high in recent years, so hospitals have been forced to pay high salaries to outbid other hospitals for nurses. Conversely, the demand for people with a history or an English literature degree is low because the number of students who major in these areas outnumbers available jobs.

Number of Income Earners in Your Household If you are the sole income earner, your household's cash inflows will typically be less than if there is a second income earner. Many households now have two income earners, a trend that has substantially increased the cash flows to these households.

Factors Affecting Cash Outflows

The key factors that affect cash outflows are a person's family status, age, and personal consumption behavior.

Size of Family A person who is supporting a family will normally incur more expenses than a single person without dependents. The more family members, the greater the amount of spending, and the greater the cash outflows. Expenses for food, clothing, day care, and school tuition are higher for families with many dependents.

Age As people get older, they tend to spend more money on expensive houses, cars, and vacations. This adjustment in spending may result from the increase in their income (cash inflows) over time as they progress along their career path.

PSYCHOLOGY
of Personal
Finance

Personal Consumption Behavior Most people's consumption behavior is affected by their income. For example, a two-income household tends to spend more money when both income earners are working full-time. Yet, people's consumption behavior varies substantially. At one extreme are people who spend their entire paycheck within a few days of receiving it, regardless of the size of the paycheck. Although this behavior is understandable for people who have low incomes, it is also a common practice for some people who have very large incomes. At the other extreme are "big savers" who minimize their spending and focus on saving for the future.

Some consumers spend excessively to achieve immediate satisfaction, without any attempt to plan for their financial future. Their consumption may be intended to match what they consider to be their peer group. They attempt to have a car or a home that is at least the same value as those of their peers. This behavior can lead to financial problems for consumers whose cash inflows are less than those of their peers because they may not be able to afford their lifestyle. Alternatively, they may be attempting to match peers who are also living beyond their means. They (and perhaps even their peers) may need to constantly borrow to support their excessive consumption, which could ultimately result in credit problems.

You can assess your spending behavior by measuring the proportion of your cash outflows over a recent period (such as the last month) for each purpose. First, classify all your spending into categories such as car, rent, school expenses, clothing, and entertainment. Then determine the proportion of your cash outflows that are allocated toward each of these categories. If a very high percentage of your cash outflows are allocated toward your car, it might suggest that your car dictates your lifestyle because it leaves very little money for you to spend on anything else. You can also determine the proportion of your income that is spent on each category, so that you can assess where most of your money is spent.

Forecasting Your Cash Flows

budget
A cash flow statement that is based on forecasted cash flows for a future time period.

The next step in the budgeting process is an extension of the personal cash flow statement. You can forecast net cash flows by forecasting the cash inflows and outflows for each item on the personal cash flow statement. We refer to a cash flow statement that is based on forecasted cash flows for a future time period as a **budget**. For example, you may develop a budget to determine whether your cash inflows will be sufficient to cover your cash outflows. If you expect your cash inflows to exceed your cash outflows, you can also use the budget to determine the amount of excess cash that you will have available to invest in additional assets or to make extra payments to reduce your personal debt.

EXAMPLE

Stephanie Spratt wants to determine whether she will have sufficient cash inflows this month. She uses the personal cash flow statement she developed last month to forecast this month's cash flows. However, she adjusts that statement for the following additional anticipated expenses:

1. Total health care expenses will be $430 this month, due to a minor health care procedure she had done recently that is not covered by her insurance.

2. Car maintenance expenses will be $500 this month, mainly due to the need to purchase new tires for her car.

Stephanie revises her personal cash flow statement from last month to reflect the expected changes this month, as shown in Exhibit 2.3. The numbers in brackets show the revised cash flows as a result of the unusual circumstances for this month.

The main effects of the unusual circumstances on Stephanie's expected cash flows for this month are summarized in Exhibit 2.4. Notice that the expected cash outflows for this month are

$2,700, or $600 higher than the cash outflows in a typical month. In this month, the expected net cash flows are

$$\text{Expected Net Cash Flows} = \text{Expected Cash Inflows} - \text{Expected Cash Outflows}$$

$$= \$2,500 \qquad - \$2,700$$

$$= -\$200$$

The budgeting process has alerted Stephanie to this $200 cash shortage.

EXHIBIT 2.3 Stephanie Spratt's Revised Personal Cash Flow Statement

Cash Inflows	Actual Amounts Last Month	Expected Amounts This Month
Disposable (after-tax) income	$2,500	$2,500
Interest on deposits	0	0
Dividend payments	0	0
Total Cash Inflows	**$2,500**	**$2,500**

Cash Outflows	Actual Amounts Last Month	Expected Amounts This Month
Rent	$600	$600
Internet	50	50
Electricity and water	60	60
Cellular	60	60
Groceries	300	300
Health care insurance and expenses	130	[430]
Clothing	100	100
Car expenses (insurance, maintenance, and gas)	200	[500]
Recreation	600	600
Total Cash Outflows	**$2,100**	**$2,700**
Net Cash Flows	**+$400**	**−$200**

EXHIBIT 2.4 Summary of Stephanie Spratt's Revised Cash Flows

	Last Month's Cash Flow Situation	Unusual Cash Flows Expected This Month	This Month's Cash Flow Situation
Cash inflows	$2,500	$ 0	$2,500
Cash outflows	$2,100	$600	$2,700
Net cash flows	$400	−$600	−$200

FREE APPS
for Personal
Finance

Managing Your Budget in Real Time

Application:

The Mint Money Manager, Budget, and Personal Finance app (by Mint.com) sends you reminders about future bills that are due and helps you schedule the payment of your future bills. This allows you to ensure that you manage your cash outflows more effectively.

To Find It:

Search for the "Mint" app on your mobile device.

Financial Planning
ONLINE

Go to:
http://www.moneycrashers.com and search "five steps to effective budgeting."

To get:
Tips on effective budgeting based on your goals.

PSYCHOLOGY
of Personal
Finance

Anticipating Cash Shortages

In a month with a large amount of unexpected expenses, you may not have sufficient cash inflows to cover your expected cash outflows. If the cash shortage is small, you would likely withdraw funds from your checking account to make up the difference. If you expect a major deficiency for a future month, however, you might not have sufficient funds available to cover it. The budget can warn you of such a problem well in advance so that you can determine how to cover the deficiency. You should set aside funds in a savings account that can serve as an emergency fund in the event that you experience a cash shortage.

In reality, unanticipated expenses can occur very often because of various unexpected events such as a car repair. Although you may not always be able to predict the specific event that will cause your expenses to be higher than normal, you might consider budgeting for unanticipated expenses. You could include an amount such as $30 per month for unanticipated expenses, even though you do not know what the expense will be. This may allow you to establish a more realistic budget, with more accurate estimates of how much money you will spend per month, and therefore more accurate estimates of how much you can save per month. Such a budgeting strategy might seem painful because it will result in a smaller amount of expected savings. But to the extent that it allows you to more accurately estimate your savings, it can help you achieve the savings goals that are set by your budget.

Assessing the Accuracy of the Budget

Periodically compare your actual cash flows over a recent period (such as last month) to the forecasted cash flows in your budget to determine whether your forecasts are on target. Many individuals tend to be overly optimistic about their cash flow forecasts. They overestimate their cash inflows and underestimate their cash outflows; as a result, their net cash flows are lower than expected. By detecting such forecasting errors, you can take steps to improve your budgeting. You may decide to limit your spending to stay within your budgeted cash outflows. Or you may choose not to adjust your spending habits, but to increase your forecast of cash outflows to reflect reality. By budgeting accurately, you are more likely to detect any future cash flow shortages and therefore can prepare in advance for any deficiencies.

EXAMPLE

Recall that Stephanie Spratt forecasted cash flows to create a budget for this coming month. Now it is the end of the month, so she can assess whether her forecasts were accurate. Her forecasted cash flows are shown in the second column of Exhibit 2.5. She compares the actual cash flows (third column) to her forecast and calculates the difference between them (shown in the fourth column). This difference between columns two and three is referred to as the *forecasting error*. A positive difference means that the actual cash flow level was less than forecasted, whereas a negative difference means that the actual cash flow level exceeded the forecast.

Reviewing the fourth column of Exhibit 2.5, Stephanie notices that total cash outflows were $100 more than expected. Her net cash flows were −$300 (a deficiency of $300), which is worse than the expected level of −$200 Stephanie assesses the individual cash outflows to determine where she underestimated. Although grocery expenses were slightly lower than expected, her clothing and recreation expenses were higher than she anticipated. She decides that the expenses were abnormally high in this month only, so she believes that her budgeted cash flows should be reasonably accurate in most months.

Forecasting Net Cash Flows over Several Months

To forecast your cash flows for several months ahead, you can follow the same process as for forecasting one month ahead. Whenever particular types of cash flows are expected to be normal, they can be forecasted from previous months when the levels were normal. You can make adjustments to account for any cash flows that you expect to be unusual in a specific month in the future. (For example, around the winter holidays you can expect to spend more on gifts and recreation.)

Expenses such as health care, car repairs, and household repairs often occur unexpectedly. Although such expenses are not always predictable, you should budget for them periodically. You should assume that you will likely incur some unexpected expenses for

EXHIBIT 2.5   Comparison of Stephanie Spratt's Budgeted and Actual Cash Flows for This Month

Cash Inflows	Expected Amounts (forecasted at the beginning of the month)	Actual Amounts (determined at the end of the month)	Forecasting Error
Disposable (after-tax) income	$2,500	$2,500	$0
Interest on deposits	0	0	0
Dividend payments	0	0	0
Total Cash Inflows	**$2,500**	**$2,500**	**$0**

Cash Outflows	Expected Amounts	Actual Amounts	Forecasting Error
Rent	$600	$600	$0
Internet	50	50	0
Electricity and water	60	60	0
Cellular	60	60	0
Groceries	300	280	+20
Health care insurance and expenses	430	430	0
Clothing	100	170	−70
Car expenses (insurance, maintenance, and gas)	500	500	0
Recreation	600	650	−50
Total Cash Outflows	**$2,700**	**$2,800**	**−$100**
Net Cash Flows	**−$200**	**−$300**	**−$100**

health care as well as for repairs on a car or on household items over the course of several months. Thus, your budget may not be perfectly accurate in any specific month, but it will be reasonably accurate over time. If you do not account for such possible expenses over time, you will likely experience lower net cash flows than expected over time.

Creating an Annual Budget

If you are curious about how much money you may be able to save in the next year, you can extend your budget out for longer periods. You should first create an annual budget and then adjust it to reflect anticipated large changes in your cash flows.

EXAMPLE

Stephanie Spratt believes her budget for last month (except for the unusual health care and car expenses) is typical for her. She wants to extend it to forecast the amount of money that she might be able to save over the next year. Her cash inflows are predictable because she already knows her salary for the year. Some of the monthly cash outflows (such as rent and the Internet bill) in her monthly budget are also constant from one month to another. To forecast these types of cash outflows, she simply multiplies the monthly amount by 12 (for each month of the year) to derive an estimate of the annual expenses, as shown in the third column of Exhibit 2.6.

Some other items vary from month to month, but last month's budgeted amount seems a reasonable estimate for the next 12 months. Over the next 12 months Stephanie expects net cash flows of $4,800. Therefore, she sets a goal of saving $4,800, which she can place in a bank account or invest in stocks.

EXHIBIT 2.6   Annual Budget for Stephanie Spratt

Cash Inflows	Typical Month	This Year's Cash Flows (equal to the typical monthly cash flows × 12)
Disposable (after-tax) income	$2,500	$30,000
Interest on deposits	0	0
Dividend payments	0	0
Total Cash Inflows	**$2,500**	**$30,000**

Cash Outflows	Typical Month	This Year's Cash Flows
Rent	$600	$7,200
Internet	50	600
Electricity and water	60	720
Cellular	60	720
Groceries	300	3,600
Health care insurance and expenses	130	1,560
Clothing	100	1,200
Car expenses (insurance, maintenance, and gas)	200	2,400
Recreation	600	7,200
Total Cash Outflows	**$2,100**	**$25,200**
Net Cash Flows	**+$400**	**$4,800 (difference between cash inflows and outflows)**

FREE APPs
for Personal
Finance

Establishing a 12-Month Budget Plan

Application:

The moneyStrands app (by Strands, Inc.) establishes a 12-month budget so that you can determine whether you can afford your planned spending over this period. You can also have your upcoming bills displayed on a calendar.

To Find It:

Search for the "Money Strands" app on your mobile device.

Improving the Budget

As time passes, you should review your budget to determine whether you are progressing toward the financial goals that you established. To increase your savings or pay down more debt so that you can more easily achieve your financial goals, you should identify the components within the budget that you can change to improve your budget over time.

EXAMPLE

Recall that Stephanie Spratt expects to spend about $2,100 and invest the remaining $400 in assets (such as bank accounts or stocks) each month. She would like to save a substantial amount of money so that she can purchase a new car and a home someday, so she considers how she might increase her net cash flows.

Stephanie assesses her personal income statement to determine whether she can increase her cash inflows or reduce her cash outflows. She would like to generate more cash inflows than $2,500, but she is already paid well, given her skills and experience. She considers pursuing a part-time job on weekends, but does not want to use her limited free time to work. Therefore, she realizes that given her present situation and preferences, she will not be able to increase her monthly cash inflows. She decides to reduce her monthly cash outflows so that she can save more than $400 per month.

Stephanie reviews her budget's summary of cash outflows to determine how she can reduce spending. Of the $2,100 that she spends per month, about $1,500 is spent on what she considers necessities (such as her rent and utilities). The remainder of the cash outflows (about $600) is spent on recreation; Stephanie realizes that any major reduction in spending will have to be in this category of cash outflows.

Most of her recreation spending is on her health club membership and eating at restaurants. She recognizes that she can scale back her spending while still enjoying these activities. Specifically, she observes that her health club is upscale and overpriced. She can save about $60 per month by going to a different health club that offers essentially the same services. She also decides to reduce her spending at restaurants by about $40 per month. By revising her spending behavior in these ways, she can reduce her cash outflows by $100 per month, as summarized here:

	Previous Cash Flow Situation	Planned Cash Flow Situation
Monthly cash inflows	$2,500	$2,500
Monthly cash outflows	$2,100	$2,000
Monthly net cash flows	$400	$500
Yearly net cash flows	$4,800	$6,000

This reduction in spending will increase net cash flows from the present level of about $400 per month to a new level of $500 per month. Over the course of a year, her net cash flows will now be $6,000. Although Stephanie had hoped to find a solution that would improve her personal cash flow statement more substantially, she believes this is a good start. Most important, her budget is realistic.

Updating Your Visual Budget

Application:

The Visual Budget app (by Kiwi Objects) allows you to easily classify your transactions into cash inflows and outflows so that you can have a continually updated balance. It also monitors how you spend your money over time.

To Find It:

Search for the "Visual Budget" app on your mobile device.

Personal Balance Sheet

The next step in the budgeting process is to create a personal balance sheet. A budget tracks your cash flows over a given period of time, whereas a personal balance sheet provides an overall snapshot of your wealth at a specific point in time. The **personal balance sheet** summarizes your *assets* (what you own), your *liabilities* (what you owe), and your *net worth* (assets minus liabilities).

Financial Planning ONLINE

Go to:
The "save" section of http://www.dailyfinance.com and search the site for Calculators

To get:
An estimate of the savings that you can accumulate over time if you can reduce your spending on one or more of your monthly expenses.

personal balance sheet
A summary of your assets (what you own), your liabilities (what you owe), and your net worth (assets minus liabilities).

liquid assets
Financial assets that can be easily sold without a loss in value.

household assets
Items normally owned by a household, such as a home, car, and furniture.

bonds
Certificates issued by borrowers to raise funds.

stocks
Certificates representing partial ownership of a firm.

Assets

The assets on a balance sheet can be classified as liquid assets, household assets, and investments.

Liquid Assets Liquid assets are financial assets that can be easily sold without a loss in value. They are especially useful for covering upcoming expenses. Some of the more common liquid assets are cash, checking accounts, and savings accounts. Cash is handy to cover small purchases, and a checking account is convenient for larger purchases. Savings accounts are desirable because they pay interest on the money that is deposited. For example, if your savings account offers an interest rate of 4%, you earn annual interest of $4 for every $100 deposited in your account. The management of liquid assets for covering day-to-day transactions is discussed in Part 2.

Household Assets Household assets include items normally owned by a household, such as a home, car, and furniture. The financial planning involved in purchasing large household assets is discussed in Part 3. These items tend to make up a larger proportion of your total assets than the liquid assets.

When creating a personal balance sheet, you need to assess the value of your household assets. The market value of an asset is the amount you would receive if you sold the asset today. For example, if you purchased a car last year for $20,000, the car may have a market value of $14,000 today, meaning that you could sell it to someone else for $14,000. The market values of cars can easily be obtained from various sources on the Internet, such as kbb.com. Although establishing the precise market value of some assets such as a house may be difficult, you can use recent selling prices of other similar houses nearby to obtain a reasonable estimate.

Investments Some of the more common investments are in bonds, stocks, and rental property.

Bonds are certificates issued by borrowers (typically firms and government agencies) to raise funds. When you purchase a $1,000 bond that was just issued, you provide a $1,000 loan to the issuer of the bond. You earn interest while you hold the bond for a specified period. (Bonds are discussed further in Chapter 16.)

Stocks are certificates representing partial ownership of a firm. Firms issue stock to obtain funding for various purposes, such as purchasing new machinery or building new facilities. Many firms have millions of shareholders who own shares of the firm's stock.

The investors who purchase stock are referred to as *shareholders* or *stockholders*. You may consider purchasing stocks if you have excess funds. You can sell some of your stock holdings when you need funds.

The market value of stocks changes daily. You can find the current market value of a stock at many Web sites, including the finance section of Yahoo.com. Stock investors can earn a return on their investment if the stock's value increases over time. They can also earn a return if the firm pays dividends to its shareholders.

Investments such as stocks normally are not considered liquid assets because they can result in a loss in value if they have to be sold suddenly. Stocks are commonly viewed as a long-term investment and therefore are not used to cover day-to-day expenses. (Stocks will be discussed in detail in Chapter 15.)

Mutual funds sell shares to individuals and invest the proceeds in an overall portfolio of investment instruments such as bonds or stocks. They are managed by portfolio managers who decide what securities to purchase so that the individual investors do not have to make the investment decisions themselves. The minimum investment varies depending on the particular fund, but it is usually between $500 and $3,000. The value of the shares of any mutual fund can be found in periodicals such as *The Wall Street Journal* or on various Web sites. We'll examine mutual funds in detail in Chapter 17.

Real estate includes holdings in rental property and land. **Rental property** is housing or commercial property that is rented out to others. Some individuals purchase a second home and rent it out to generate additional income every year. Others purchase apartment complexes for the same reason. Some individuals purchase land as an investment.

Liabilities

Liabilities represent debt (what you owe) and can be segmented into current liabilities and long-term liabilities.

Current Liabilities

Current liabilities are debt that you will pay off in the near future (within a year). The most common example of a current liability is a credit card balance that will be paid off in the near future. Credit card companies send the cardholder a monthly bill that itemizes all the purchases made in the previous month. If you pay your balance in full on receipt of the bill, no interest is charged on the balance. The liability is then eliminated until you receive the next monthly bill.

Credit cards deserve special attention when discussing the personal budget. Although they offer a convenient source of funds, they also create serious credit problems for many people. Some people use credit cards to purchase products or services that they do not need and cannot afford. There are two psychological forces that cause this behavior. First, some people make unnecessary purchases with credit cards that they cannot afford to achieve immediate satisfaction and to keep up with their peers. Second, some people are especially willing to spend excessively when using a credit card to make purchases because a credit card avoids the use of cash. That is, they would rather create a current liability (debt) than use an asset (cash) to make their purchases. They would feel more pain from using their cash and are more disciplined about how to spend the cash they have. They know that taking $50 out of their wallet to make a purchase will leave $50 less for other cash purchases. Yet when they use a credit card and keep their cash, they feel like they are able to obtain products or services for free. Because the focus of their purchases is on achieving immediate satisfaction by making purchases they cannot afford, they ignore the fact that they will have to pay off the credit card in the future. This type of behavior tends to result in a large accumulation of current liabilities, which can result in credit problems.

Long-Term Liabilities

Long-term liabilities are debt that will be paid over a period beyond one year. A common long-term liability is a student loan, which reflects debt that a student must pay back to a lender over time after graduation. This liability requires you to pay an interest expense periodically. Once you pay off this loan, you eliminate this liability and do not have to pay any more interest expenses. In general, you should limit your liabilities so that you can limit the amount of interest owed.

---

mutual funds
Investment companies that sell shares to individuals and invest the proceeds in investment instruments such as bonds or stocks.

real estate
Rental property and land.

rental property
Housing or commercial property that is rented out to others.

Financial Planning
ONLINE

Go to:
http://calculatorweb.com

To get:
A means for comparing your actual budget versus your desired budget (based on your income and spending habits) and shows how you could improve your budget.

PSYCHOLOGY
of Personal Finance

current liabilities
Debt that will be paid within a year.

long-term liabilities
Debt that will be paid over a period longer than one year.

Other common examples of long-term liabilities are a car loan and a mortgage (housing) loan. Car loans typically have a maturity of between 3 and 5 years, whereas mortgages typically have a maturity of 15 or 30 years. Both types of loans can be paid off before their maturity date.

Net Worth

Your net worth is the difference between what you own and what you owe.

$$\text{Net Worth} = \text{Value of Total Assets} - \text{Value of Total Liabilities}$$

In other words, if you sold enough of your assets to pay off all of your liabilities, your net worth would be the amount of assets you would have remaining. Your net worth is a measure of your wealth because it represents what you own after deducting any money that you owe.

Some people tend to assess their financial wealth by reviewing their assets without consideration of their liabilities. Psychologically, they can see the new car or their home or other assets. Yet, they cannot see their liabilities. This might even encourage them to make purchases that they cannot afford as long as they can obtain the credit. To illustrate the point, consider a student who purchased a $20,000 car last month with all borrowed funds. The market value of the car if he had to sell the car is about $16,000 today because the market value of a car commonly declines by 20% as soon as the car is purchased (as explained in Chapter 9). The student's liabilities equal $20,000. If the student has no other assets or liabilities, his net worth is estimated as:

Assets of	$16,000
Liabilities of	$20,000
Net worth of	−$ 4,000

Whenever assets are less than liabilities, net worth is negative. Many people who rely heavily on credit cards and do not pay off the balance each month tend to have negative net worth. This means that they could not repay their debt even if they sold all of their assets. This type of condition can lead to bankruptcy.

Creating a Personal Balance Sheet

You should create a personal balance sheet to determine your net worth. Update it periodically to monitor how your wealth changes over time.

EXAMPLE

Stephanie Spratt wants to determine her net worth by creating a personal balance sheet that identifies her assets and her liabilities.

Stephanie's Assets. Stephanie owns:

- $500 in cash
- $3,500 in her checking account
- Furniture in her apartment that is worth about $1,000
- A car that is worth about $1,000
- 100 shares of stock that she just purchased for $3,000 ($30 per share), which does not pay dividends

Stephanie uses this information to complete the top of her personal balance sheet, shown in Exhibit 2.7. She classifies each item that she owns as a liquid asset, a household asset, or an investment asset.

Stephanie's Liabilities. Stephanie owes $2,000 on her credit card. She does not have any other liabilities at this time, so she lists the one liability on her personal balance sheet under "Current Liabilities" because she will pay off the debt soon. Because she has no long-term liabilities at this time, her total liabilities are $2,000.

Stephanie's Net Worth. Stephanie determines her net worth as the difference between her total assets and total liabilities. Notice from her personal balance sheet that her total assets are valued at $9,000, whereas her total liabilities are valued at $2,000. Thus, her net worth is:

Net Worth = Total Assets − Total Liabilities

$$= \$9,000 \quad - \$2,000$$

$$= \$7,000$$

Changes in the Personal Balance Sheet

If you earn new income this month but spend all of it on products or services such as rent, food, and concert tickets that are not personal assets, you will not increase your net worth. As you invest in assets, your personal balance sheet will change. In some cases, such as when you purchase a home, your assets increase while at the same time your liabilities may increase from taking on a mortgage. In any case, your net worth will not grow unless the increase in the value of your assets exceeds the increase in your liabilities.

EXHIBIT 2.7 Stephanie Spratt's Personal Balance Sheet	
Assets	
Liquid Assets	
Cash	$500
Checking account	3,500
Savings account	0
Total liquid assets	$4,000
Household Assets	
Home	$0
Car	1,000
Furniture	1,000
Total household assets	$2,000
Investment Assets	
Stocks	$3,000
Total investment assets	$3,000
Total Assets	**$9,000**
Liabilities and Net Worth	
Current Liabilities	
Credit card balance	$2,000
Total current liabilities	$2,000
Long-Term Liabilities	
Mortgage	$0
Car loan	0
Total long-term liabilities	$0
Total Liabilities	**$2,000**
Net Worth	$7,000

EXAMPLE

Stephanie Spratt is considering purchasing a new car for $20,000. To make the purchase, Stephanie would do the following:

- She would trade in her existing car, which has a market value of about $1,000.
- She would write a check for $3,000 as a down payment on the car.
- She would obtain a five-year loan for $16,000 to cover the remaining amount owed to the car dealer.

Her personal balance sheet would be affected as shown in Exhibit 2.8 and explained next.

Change in Stephanie's Assets. Stephanie's assets would change as follows:

- Her car would now have a market value of $20,000 (at the time of purchase, assuming depreciation would occur later) instead of $1,000.
- Her checking account balance would be reduced from $3,500 to $500.

Thus, her total assets would increase by $16,000 (her new car would be valued at $19,000 more than her old one, but her checking account would be reduced by $3,000).

EXHIBIT 2.8   Stephanie Spratt's Personal Balance Sheet if She Purchases a New Car

Assets

	Present Situation	If She Purchases a New Car
Liquid Assets		
Cash	$500	$500
Checking account	3,500	500
Savings account	0	0
Total liquid assets	$4,000	$1,000
Household Assets		
Home	$0	$0
Car	1,000	20,000
Furniture	1,000	1,000
Total household assets	$2,000	$21,000
Investment Assets		
Stocks	$3,000	$3,000
Total investment assets	$3,000	$3,000
Total Assets	**$9,000**	**$25,000**

Liabilities and Net Worth

	Present Situation	If She Purchases a New Car
Current Liabilities		
Credit card balance	$2,000	$2,000
Total current liabilities	$2,000	$2,000
Long-Term Liabilities		
Mortgage	$0	$0
Car loan	0	16,000
Total long-term liabilities	$0	$16,000
Total Liabilities	**$2,000**	**$18,000**
Net Worth	**$7,000**	**$7,000**

Change in Stephanie's Liabilities. Stephanie's liabilities would also change:

- She would now have a long-term liability of $16,000 as a result of the car loan.

Therefore, her total liabilities would increase by $16,000 if she purchases the car.

Change in Stephanie's Net Worth. If Stephanie purchases the car, her net worth would be:

Net Worth = Total Assets − Total Liabilities

$$= \$25,000 \quad - \$18,000$$

$$= \$7,000$$

Stephanie's net worth would remain unchanged. Yet it may actually decline if she considers that the market value of the car she purchases is probably less than the $20,000 price she would pay for the car.

Stephanie's Decision. Because the purchase of a new car will not increase her net worth, she decides not to purchase the car at this time. Still, she is concerned that her old car will require expensive maintenance in the future, so she will likely buy a car in a few months after she improves her financial position.

How Cash Flows Affect the Personal Balance Sheet

The relationship between the personal cash flow statement and the personal balance sheet is shown in Exhibit 2.9. This relationship explains how you build wealth (net worth) over time. If you use net cash flows to invest in more assets, you increase the value of your assets without increasing your liabilities. Therefore, you increase your net worth. You can also increase your net worth by using net cash flows to reduce your liabilities. So, the more of your income that you allocate to investing in assets or to reducing your debt, the more wealth you will build.

Your net worth can change even if your net cash flows are zero. For example, if the market value of your car declines over time, the value of this asset is reduced, and your net worth will decline. Conversely, if the value of a stock that you own increases, the value of your assets will rise, and your net worth will increase.

Impact of the Economy on the Personal Balance Sheet

Economic conditions can affect your cash flows and therefore affect your personal balance sheet, as illustrated in Exhibit 2.10. Favorable economic conditions can increase job opportunities and therefore your income. Conversely, unfavorable economic conditions can result in the elimination of jobs and reduced income for some individuals.

ECONOMIC IMPACT

Economic conditions also affect the value of your assets. Favorable economic conditions result in a high demand to purchase homes, which increases the values of homes. In addition, the values of stocks rise when economic conditions are favorable because corporations experience higher sales of the products or services they produce. Conversely, weak economic conditions result in lower values of assets. Home prices decline as demand for homes declines. Stock prices decline when corporations experience a reduction in sales. Many individuals experience a large decline in their asset value during weak economic conditions. For some individuals, the value of their assets declines to a level that is lower than the value of their liabilities. That is, their net worth becomes negative.

EXHIBIT 2.9   How Net Cash Flows Can Be Used to Increase Net Worth

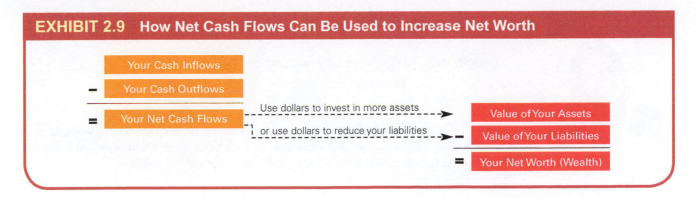

Analysis of the Personal Balance Sheet

The budgeting process helps you monitor your cash flows and evaluate your net worth. In addition, by analyzing some financial characteristics within your personal balance sheet or cash flow statement, you can monitor your level of liquidity, your amount of debt, and your ability to save.

Liquidity Recall that liquidity represents your access to funds to cover any short-term cash needs. You need to monitor your liquidity over time to ensure that you have sufficient funds when they are needed. Your liquidity can be measured by the liquidity ratio, which is calculated as:

$$\text{Liquidity Ratio} = \text{Liquid Assets/Current Liabilities}$$

A high liquidity ratio indicates a higher degree of liquidity. For example, a liquidity ratio of 3.0 implies that for every dollar of liabilities that you will need to pay off in the near future, you have $3 in liquid assets. Thus, you could easily cover your short-term liabilities.

A liquidity ratio of less than 1.0 means that you do not have sufficient liquid assets to cover your upcoming payments. In this case, you might need to borrow funds.

EXHIBIT 2.10   Impact of the Economy on the Personal Balance Sheet

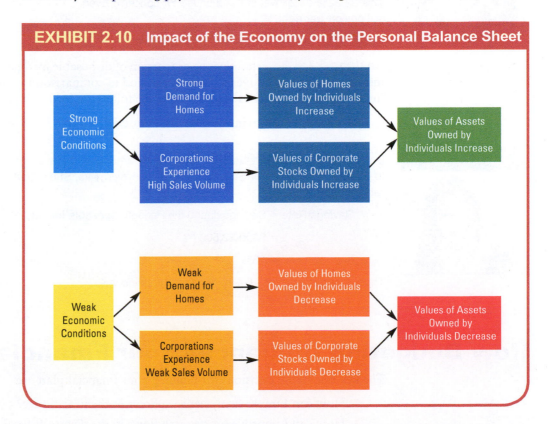

EXAMPLE

Based on the information in her personal balance sheet shown in Exhibit 2.7, Stephanie measures her liquidity:

Liquidity Ratio = Liquid Assets/Current Liabilities

= $4,000/$2,000

= 2.0

Stephanie's liquidity ratio of 2.0 means that for every dollar of current liabilities, she has $2 of liquid assets. This means that she has more than enough funds available to cover her current liabilities, so she is maintaining sufficient liquidity to cover her current liabilities.

Debt Level You also need to monitor your debt level to ensure that it does not become so high that you are unable to cover your debt payments. A debt level of $20,000 would not be a serious problem for a person with assets of $100,000, but it could be quite serious for someone with hardly any assets. Thus, your debt level should be measured relative to your assets, as shown here:

$$\text{Debt-to-Asset Ratio} = \text{Total Liabilities/Total Assets}$$

A high debt ratio indicates an excessive amount of debt and should be reduced over time to avoid any debt repayment problems. Individuals in this position should review their cash flows to maximize inflows and minimize outflows.

EXAMPLE

Based on her personal balance sheet, Stephanie calculates her debt-to-asset ratio as:

Debt-to-Asset Ratio = Total Liabilities/Total Assets

= $2,000/$9,000

= 22.22%

This 22.22% debt level is not a cause for concern. Even if Stephanie lost her job, she could still pay off her debt.

Savings Rate To determine the proportion of disposable income that you save, you can measure your savings over a particular period in comparison to your disposable income (income after taxes are taken out) using the following formula:

Savings Rate = Savings during the Period/Disposable Income during the Period

EXAMPLE

Based on her cash flow statement, Stephanie earns $2,500 in a particular month and expects to have net cash flows of $400 for savings or investments. She calculates her typical savings rate per month as:

Savings Rate = Savings during the Period/Disposable Income during the Period

= $400/$2,500

= 16%

Thus, Stephanie saves 16% of her disposable income.

How Budgeting Influences Your Financial Plan

The key budgeting decisions for building your financial plan are

- How can I improve my net cash flows in the near future?
- How can I improve my net cash flows in the distant future?

These decisions influence all aspects of your financial plan, including your liquidity, personal financing, protection of wealth, personal investing, and retirement and estate planning. By limiting your spending, you may be able to increase your net cash flows, your liquidity, and your net worth. Exhibit 2.11 provides an example of how the budgeting decisions apply to Stephanie Spratt's financial plan.

EXHIBIT 2.11   Application of Budgeting Concepts to Stephanie Spratt's Financial Plan

GOALS FOR A BUDGETING PLAN

1. *Determine how I can increase my net cash flows in the near future.*
2. *Determine how I can increase my net cash flows in the distant future.*

ANALYSIS

Present Situation:

Cash Inflows = *$2,500 per month*

Cash Outflows = *$2,100 per month*

Net Cash Flows = *$400 per month*

Estimated Savings per Year = *$4,800 ($400 per month × 12 months)*

Increase Net Cash Flows by:

Increasing my salary? (New job?)	*No. I like my job and have no plans to search for another job right now, even if it would pay a higher salary.*
Increasing my income provided by my investments?	*No. My investments are small at this point. I cannot rely on them to provide much income.*
Other? (If yes, explain.)	*No.*

Reduce Cash Outflows by:

Reducing my household expenses?	*No.*
Reducing my recreation expenses?	*Yes (by $100 per month).*
Reducing my other expenses?	*No.*

Overall, I identified only one adjustment to my budget, which will increase monthly net cash flows by $100.

DECISIONS

Decision to Increase Net Cash Flows in the Near Future:

I initially established a budget to save $4,800 per year. During the next year, I can attempt to save an additional $100 per month by reducing the amount I spend on recreation. I can increase my savings if I reduce cash outflows. By reducing cash outflows by $100 per month, my savings will increase from $400 to $500 per month. The only way that I can reduce cash outflows at this point is to reduce the amount I spend for recreation purposes.

Decision to Increase Net Cash Flows in the Distant Future:

My cash inflows will rise over time if my salary increases. If I can keep my cash outflows stable, my net cash flows (and therefore my savings) will increase. When I buy a new car or a home, my monthly cash outflows will increase as a result of the monthly loan payments. If I buy a new car or a home, I need to make sure that I limit my spending (and therefore limit the loan amount) so that I have sufficient cash inflows to cover the monthly loan payments along with my other typical monthly expenses.

If I get married someday, my husband would contribute to the cash inflows, which would increase net cash flows. We would be able to save more money and may consider buying a home. If I marry, my goal will be to save even more money per month than I save now, to prepare for the possibility of raising a family in the future.

DISCUSSION QUESTIONS

1. How would Stephanie's budgeting decisions be different if she were a single mother of two children?

2. How would Stephanie's budgeting decisions be affected if she were 35 years old? If she were 50 years old?

SUMMARY

Personal Cash Flow Statement. The personal cash flow statement measures your cash inflows, your cash outflows, and their difference (net cash flows) over a specific period. Cash inflows result from your salary or from income generated by your investments. Cash outflows result from your spending.

Factors Affecting Cash Flows. Your cash inflows are primarily affected by your stage in your career path and your type of job. Your cash outflows are influenced by your family status, age, and personal consumption behavior. If you develop specialized skills, you may be able to obtain a job position that increases your cash inflows. If you limit your consumption, you can limit your spending and therefore reduce your cash outflows. Either of these actions will increase net cash flows and thus allow you to increase your wealth.

Forecasting Your Cash Flows. You can forecast your net cash flows (and therefore anticipate cash deficiencies) by creating a budget, which is based on forecasted cash inflows and outflows for an upcoming period.

Comparing your forecasted and actual income and expenses will show whether or not you were able to stay within the budget. By examining the difference between your forecast and the actual cash flow, you can determine areas of your budget

that may need further control or areas of your budget that required less in expenditures than you predicted. This analysis will help you modify your spending in the future or perhaps adjust your future budgets.

Personal Balance Sheet. The personal balance sheet measures the value of your assets, your liabilities, and your net worth. The assets can be categorized into liquid assets, household assets, and investments. Liabilities can be categorized as current or long-term liabilities. The difference between total assets and total liabilities is net worth, which is a measure of your wealth.

The net cash flows on the personal cash flow statement are related to the net worth on the personal balance sheet. When you have positive net cash flows over a period, you can invest that amount in additional assets, which results in an increase in your net worth (or your wealth). Alternatively, you may use the net cash flows to pay off liabilities, which also increases your wealth.

How Your Personal Financial Statements Fit Within Your Financial Plan. Your personal financial statements help you make your decisions about spending, and therefore they influence your financial plan, including your liquidity, personal financing, protection of wealth, personal investing, and retirement and estate planning.

REVIEW QUESTIONS

All Review Questions are available in MyFinanceLab *at* http://www.myfinancelab.com.

1. **Personal Financial Statements.** What two personal financial statements are most important to personal financial planning?

2. **Cash Flows.** Define cash inflows and cash outflows and identify some sources of each. How are net cash flows determined?

3. **Changing Your Cash Flows.** Jeremey wants to increase his net worth. What advice would you give him?

4. **Factors Affecting Cash Inflows.** Identify some factors that affect cash inflows.

5. **Factors Affecting Cash Outflows.** List your monthly cash outflows. Will everyone have similar cash outflows?

6. **Purpose of a Budget.** What is a budget? What is the purpose of a budget? How can a budget help when you are anticipating cash shortages or a cash surplus?

7. **Budget Accuracy.** How do you assess the accuracy of your budget? How can finding forecasting errors improve your budget?

8. **Unexpected Expenses.** How are unexpected expenses and liquidity related?

9. **Creating an Annual Budget.** Describe the process of creating an annual budget.

10. **Changing Your Budget.** Suppose you want to change your budget to increase your savings. What could you do?

11. **Cash Deficiencies.** How do you think people who do not create a budget may deal with cash deficiencies? How can this affect their personal relationships?

12. **Personal Balance Sheet.** What is a personal balance sheet?

13. **Asset Classifications.** Name three classifications of assets. Briefly define and give examples of each.

14. **Types of Investments.** What are bonds? What are stocks? What are mutual funds? Describe how each of these provides a return on your investment.

15. **Real Estate Investment.** Describe two ways real estate might provide a return on an investment.

16. **Types of Liabilities.** What are liabilities? Define current liabilities and long-term liabilities.

17. **Measuring Net Worth.** How does a personal balance sheet help you track your net worth?

18. **Change in Net Worth.** When does your net worth increase? Will the purchase of additional assets always increase your net worth? Why or why not?

19. **Financial Characteristics.** What three financial characteristics can be monitored by analyzing your personal balance sheet?

20. **Liquidity Ratio.** What is the liquidity ratio? What does it indicate? How is the debt-to-asset ratio calculated? What does a high debt ratio indicate? How is your savings rate determined? What does it indicate?

21. **Personal Financial Statements.** Justin's stock portfolio increased in value during the year, and the balance on his mortgage declined. What happened to his net worth over the course of the year?

22. **Economic Impact on Asset Values.** Explain in logical terms why values of assets such as homes and stocks may decline during a weak economy.

23. **Economic Impact on Net Worth.** Explain in logical terms why a weak economy can cause the net worth of individuals to decline.

24. **Credit Cards and Spending Psychology.** Explain how credit card usage can impact your spending habits.

25. **Market Values of Assets and Net Worth.** Heather purchased a new car for $18,000 three years ago and listed the new car as an asset with a value of $18,000 on her personal balance sheet. She was able to borrow the entire $18,000 to purchase the car and listed the car loan as a liability with a value of $18,000. She just made the last payment on the car loan, so the liability is no longer on her personal balance sheet. However, the asset value of the car is still listed as $18,000. What adjustments should Heather make to the value of her assets in order to make her personal balance sheet more accurate?

26. **Factors Affecting Cash Flows.** What are two factors that impact your cash inflows?

FINANCIAL PLANNING PROBLEMS

All Financial Planning Problems are available in MyFinanceLab *at http://www.myfinancelab.com.*

1. **Estimating Disposable Income.** Angela earns $2,170 per month before taxes in her full-time job and $900 before taxes in her part-time job. About $650 per month is needed to pay taxes. What is Angela's disposable income? Why is it important to track disposable income?

2. **Estimating Net Cash Flow.** Angela (from problem 1) inspects her checkbook and her credit card bills and determines that she has the following monthly expenses:

Rent	$500
Internet	30
Electricity	100
Water	25
Cellular	40
Groceries	400
Car expenses	350
Health insurance	200
Clothing and personal items	175
Recreation	300

What is Angela's net cash flow?

3. **Impact on Net Cash Flow.** Angela makes a budget based on her personal cash flow statement. In two months, she must pay $375 for tags and taxes on her car. How will this payment affect her net cash flow for that month? Suggest ways that Angela might handle this situation.

4. **Estimating Savings.** From the information in Problems 1 through 3, how much can Angela expect to save in the next 12 months?

5. **Change in Savings.** Angela analyzes her personal budget and decides that she can reduce her recreational spending by $50 per month. How much will that increase her annual savings? What will her annual savings be now?

6. **Savings Rate.** If Angela is saving $350 per month, what is her savings rate (i.e., savings as a percentage of disposable income)?

7. **Estimating Liquidity.** Jarrod is a college student. All of Jarrod's disposable income is used to pay his college-related expenses. Although he has no liabilities (Jarrod is on a scholarship), he does have a credit card that he typically uses for emergencies. He and his friend went on a vacation in New York City costing $2,000, which Jarrod charged to his credit card. Jarrod has $20 in his wallet, but his bank accounts are empty. What is Jarrod's liquidity ratio? What does this ratio indicate about Jarrod's financial position?

8. **Estimating Debt.** Jarrod (from Problem 7) has an old TV worth about $100. Jarrod's other assets total about $150. What is Jarrod's debt-to-asset ratio? What does this indicate about Jarrod's financial position?

9. **Asset Levels.** Ryan and Nicole have the following assets:

	Fair Market Value
Home	$85,000
Cars	22,000
Furniture	14,000
Stocks	10,000
Savings account	5,000
Checking account	1,200
Bonds	15,000
Cash	150
Mutual funds	7,000
Land	19,000

What is the value of their liquid assets? What is the value of their household assets? What is the value of their investments?

10. **Liability Levels.** Ryan and Nicole (from Problem 9) have the following liabilities:

Mortgage	$43,500
Car loan	2,750
Credit card balance	165
Student loans	15,000
Furniture loan (6 months)	1,200

What are their current liabilities? What are their long-term liabilities? What is their net worth?

11. **Impact on Net Worth.** Jasmine has been saving for the past five years for a European vacation. Her vacation account currently has $5,000, and she is ready to book her trip. If she takes the vacation, what impact will it have on her net worth? Should she take the trip?

12. **Liquidity and Debt.** Based on the information in Problems 9 and 10, what is Ryan and Nicole's liquidity ratio? What is their debt-to-asset ratio? Comment on each ratio.

13. **Ethical Dilemma.** Jason and Mia are in their early 20s and have been married for three years. They are eager to purchase their first house, but they do not have sufficient money for a down payment. Mia's Uncle Chris has agreed to loan them the money to purchase a small house. Uncle Chris requests a personal balance sheet and cash flow statement as well as tax returns for the last two years to verify their income and their ability to make monthly payments.

The cash flow statements for the last two years show that Mia and Jason will have no difficulty making the payments Uncle Chris requires. However, Mia just lost her job. Without her income, they will not be able to afford the house payments. Because Mia is confident she will find work soon, they decide to keep the job loss a secret from Uncle Chris.

a. Comment on Mia and Jason's decision not to provide the information about Mia's job loss. What potential problems could result from their decision?

b. Discuss in general the disadvantages of borrowing money from relatives.

FINANCIAL PLANNING ONLINE EXERCISES

1. Go to the Web site http://www.moneycrashers.com. In the search box, search for "five steps to effective budgeting" and answer the following questions:

   a. What are three good sources of information that can be accessed to begin the budgeting process?

   b. How important is it to write out your budget? What is a good software program you can use that provides a template should you wish to write out your budget?

   c. Explain what is meant by "looking ahead budgeting."

   d. Explain one effective method discussed on the Web site for organizing your budget.

2. Go to the finance section of Yahoo.com. This Web site has various calculators that demonstrate the value of reducing your expenses. You can input various expenses that can be reduced and determine the savings that will accrue over time.

   a. If you waited to buy a car, you could, perhaps, save $220 monthly. Use the appropriate calculator to determine how much extra savings you could accumulate by the time you retire if you avoid a $220 payment on a monthly basis.

   b. If you had your meals at home instead of at restaurants, you could save, say, $150 monthly. Enter this information to determine how much this could add to your retirement savings.

   c. If you went to fewer movies and reduced expenses by $50 monthly, enter this information to determine how much extra you could save by retirement.

PSYCHOLOGY OF PERSONAL FINANCE: Your Cash Outflows

1. Review your largest cash outflows over the last year, and identify your largest expenses (for example, rent, a car loan, and tuition). Were any of your major purchases influenced by psychological forces such as peer pressure? If you could redo last year, would you change any of your major purchases to improve your personal financial situation?

2. Classify all your spending into categories such as car, rent, school expenses, clothing, and entertainment. Determine the proportion of your cash outflows that is allocated toward each of these categories. Describe the results, and explain whether you have any plans to change your consumption pattern.

WEB SEARCH EXERCISE

You can develop your personal finance skills by conducting an Internet search for related articles. Find a recent online article about personal finance that reinforces one or more concepts covered in this chapter. If your class has an online component, your professor may ask you to post your summary of the article there and provide a link to the article so that other students can access it. If your class is live, your professor may ask you to summarize your application of the article in class. Your professor may assign specific students to complete this assignment or may allow any student to do the assignment on a volunteer basis.

For recent online articles related to this chapter, consider using the following search terms (be sure to include the current year as a search term to ensure that the online articles are recent):

- Budgeting
- Budgeting tips

- Your assets and liabilities
- Your net worth
- Improving your net worth
- Your debt
- Reducing your debt

VIDEO EXERCISE: Budgeting

Go to one of the Web sites that contains video clips (such as http://www.youtube.com) and view some video clips about budgeting. You can use search phrases such as "budgeting tips." Select one video clip on this topic that you would recommend for the other students in your class.

1. Provide the Web link for the video clip.

2. What do you think is the main point of this video clip?

3. How might you change your budgeting as a result of watching this video clip?

BUILDING YOUR OWN FINANCIAL PLAN

Two major components of any good personal financial plan are a personal cash flow statement and a balance sheet. If you are a full-time student, prepare your cash flow statement based on your anticipated cash flow after graduation.

To prepare your personal balance sheet and cash flow statement, turn to the worksheets at the end of this chapter. When listing your liabilities, be sure to include any educational loans, even if they are not payable until after graduation.

When preparing your personal cash flow statement, break down all expenses into the frequency in which you are/will be paid. For example, if your car insurance is $700 per year and you are paid monthly, divide the $700 by 12. If you are paid biweekly, divide the $700 by 26. Personal cash flow statements should be set up based on the frequency of your pay. This way, each time you are paid, you can distribute your paycheck to the appropriate cash outflow categories.

If, after preparing your personal cash flow statement, you have an excess of cash outflows over cash inflows, you should review in detail each cash outflow to determine its necessity and whether it can realistically be reduced to balance your cash inflows and outflows. Using Web sites with budget calculators, you can also estimate the savings that you can accumulate over time by reducing your cash outflows.

Personal financial statements should be reviewed annually or whenever you experience a change that affects your cash inflows such as getting a raise, obtaining a new job, marrying, or getting divorced.

THE SAMPSONS—A Continuing Case

The Sampsons realize that the first step toward achieving their financial goals is to create a budget capturing their monthly cash inflows and outflows. Dave and Sharon's combined income is now about $4,000 per month after taxes. With the new cash inflows from Sharon's paycheck, the Sampsons have started spending more on various after-school programs for their children, such as soccer leagues and tennis lessons. In Chapter 1, they resolved to save a total of $800 per month for a new car and for their children's education.

Reviewing their checking account statement from last month, Dave and Sharon identify the following monthly household payments:

- $900 for the mortgage payment ($700 loan payment plus home insurance and property taxes) (Note that this loan payment is high because the Sampsons obtained the mortgage when interest rates were high. They are in the process of refinancing their mortgage with a lower interest rate; this will be discussed in Chapter 10.)
- $60 for Internet
- $80 for electricity and water
- $70 for cellular expenses
- $500 for groceries
- $160 for a health care plan provided by Dave's employer (this expense is deducted directly from Dave's salary)

The Sampsons also review several credit card bills to estimate their other typical monthly expenses:

- About $180 for clothing
- About $300 for car expenses (insurance, maintenance, and gas)
- About $100 for school expenses
- About $1,000 for recreation and programs for the children
- About $20 as a minimum payment on their existing credit card balance

To determine their net worth, the Sampsons also assess their assets and liabilities, which include the following:

- $300 in cash
- $1,700 in their checking account
- Home valued at $100,000
- Furniture worth about $3,000
- Sharon's car, which needs to be replaced soon, is worth about $1,000; Dave's car is worth approximately $8,000
- They owe $90,000 on their home mortgage and about $2,000 on their credit cards

Go to the worksheets at the end of this chapter to continue this case.

CHAPTER 2: BUILDING YOUR OWN FINANCIAL PLAN

YOUR GOALS FOR CHAPTER 2

1. Complete your Personal Cash Flow Statement.
2. Complete your Personal Balance Sheet.
3. Determine possible ways in which you could improve your Personal Cash Flow Statement.

ANALYSIS

1. Prepare your personal cash flow statement.

Personal Cash Flow Statement

Cash Inflows	This Month
Disposable (after-tax) income	
Interest on deposits	
Dividend payments	
Other	
Total Cash Inflows	
Cash Outflows	
Rent/Mortgage	
Internet	
Electricity and water	
Cellular	
Groceries	
Health care insurance and expenses	
Clothing	
Car expenses (insurance, maintenance, and gas)	
Recreation	
Other	
Total Cash Outflows	
Net Cash Flows	

If you enter your cash flow information in the Excel worksheet, the software will create a pie chart of your cash outflows.

2. Prepare your personal balance sheet.

Personal Balance Sheet

Assets

Liquid Assets

Cash	
Checking account	
Savings account	
Other liquid assets	
Total liquid assets	

Household Assets

Home	
Car	
Furniture	
Other household assets	
Total household assets	

Investment Assets

Stocks	
Bonds	
Mutual funds	
Other investments	
Total investment assets	

Real Estate

Residence	
Vacation home	
Other	
Total real estate	
Total Assets	

Liabilities and Net Worth

Current Liabilities

Loans

Credit card balance

Other current liabilities

   Total current liabilities

Long-Term Liabilities

Mortgage

Car loan

Other long-term liabilities

   Total long-term liabilities

Total Liabilities

Net Worth

3. Reevaluate the goals you set in Chapter 1. Based on your personal cash flow statement, indicate how much you can save each year to reach your goals.

DECISIONS

1. Explain how you may be able to improve your personal cash flow situation by increasing your cash inflows or reducing your cash outflows (if possible) in the near future. Be realistic.

CHAPTER 2: THE SAMPSONS—A Continuing Case

CASE QUESTIONS

1. Using the information in the case, prepare a personal cash flow statement for the Sampsons.

Personal Cash Flow Statement

Cash Inflows	This Month
Total Cash Inflows	

Cash Outflows

Include categories for cash outflows as follows:

Rent/Mortgage	
Internet	
Electricity and water	
Cellular	
Groceries	
Health care insurance and expenses	
Clothing	
Car expenses (insurance, maintenance, and gas)	
School expenses	
Recreation	
Credit card minimum payments	
Other	
Total Cash Outflows	
Net Cash Flows	

2. Based on their personal cash flow statement, will the Sampsons be able to meet their savings goals? If not, how do you recommend that they revise their personal cash flow statement to achieve their savings goals? (One solution is to refinance their mortgage, but ignore that solution for now. It will be covered in Chapter 10.)

3. Prepare a personal balance sheet for the Sampsons.

Personal Balance Sheet

Assets

Liquid Assets

Cash	
Checking account	
Savings account	
Total liquid assets	

Household Assets

Home	
Car	
Furniture	
Total household assets	

Investment Assets

Stocks	
Bonds	
Mutual funds	
Total investment assets	
Total Assets	

Liabilities and Net Worth

Current Liabilities

Loans

Credit card balance

   Total current liabilities

Long-Term Liabilities

Mortgage

Car loan

   Total long-term liabilities

Total Liabilities

Net Worth

4. What is the Sampsons' net worth? Based on the personal cash flow statement that you prepared in question 1, do you expect that their net worth will increase or decrease in the future? Why?

Applying Time Value Concepts

Scott Pilar has been smoking two packs of cigarettes a day. Today, on his 18th birthday, he decided to give up smoking for health reasons. He does not realize that this is an important financial decision as well. If Scott invests the money that he would have spent on smoking over the next 50 years, he could become a millionaire.

Karen Roach/Fotolia

Let's assume that a pack of cigarettes is priced at $8. Scott will save $16 per day (2 packs × $8 per pack), or $5,840 per year ($16 × 365 days). If Scott could invest that money in a bank deposit account and earn 5% per year, his investment would accumulate to be worth $1,222,592 in 50 years. The specific method to estimate this amount of accumulated funds can be done in less than one minute, as explained in this chapter.

Cash accumulates when it is invested and earns interest because of the time value of money. Over a long period of time, money can grow substantially because interest is earned both on the deposited funds and on the interest that has already accumulated. The lesson is that saving even a small amount per month or year at an early age can enhance your wealth over time.

The concepts in this chapter can help you determine how much you may save over time based on a particular savings level per month or year. You can also determine how much money you need to save per month or year to achieve a specific savings goal in the future. Thus, you'll be able to calculate how much monthly or annual savings you will need to make a down payment on a new car or home, or to make other types of purchases at a future point in time.

MyFinanceLab helps you master the topics in this chapter and study more efficiently. Visit http://www.myfinancelab.com for more details.

The objectives of this chapter are to:

- Describe the importance of time value of money
- Calculate the future value of a dollar amount that you save today
- Calculate the present value of a dollar amount that will be received in the future
- Calculate the future value of an annuity
- Calculate the present value of an annuity
- Explain how time value can be used to estimate savings
- Explain how time value fits within your financial plan

Importance of Time Value of Money

The value of money is affected by the point in time it is received. Would you rather receive $1,000 five years from now or one year from now? It is better to receive the money one year from now because its value is higher if received in one year than in five years. If you wanted to spend the money, you could buy more with the money today than if you waited for five years. In general, prices of the products you might purchase rise over time due to inflation. Therefore, you can buy more products with $1,000 in one year than in five years.

If you wanted to save the money that you receive, you could earn interest on it if you deposited the money in an account with a financial institution. If you receive the money in one year, you would be able to earn interest on that money over the following four years. Its value would accumulate and would be worth more than the money received four years later. Thus, the value of money received in one year would be greater than the value of money received in five years.

Would you rather receive $1,000 now or $1,000 at the end of one year from now? As with the preceding example, it's better to receive the money now because its value is higher now than it will be in one year. If you wanted to spend the money, you could buy more with the money today than if you waited for a year. If you wanted to save the money, you could earn interest on money received today over the next year. Thus, the value of money received today would be greater than the value of money received in one year.

In general, the value of a given amount of money is greater the earlier it is received. A dollar today has more value than a dollar received in one year. A dollar received in one year has more value than a dollar received in five years. A dollar received in five years has more value than a dollar received in ten years.

The time value of money is especially important when considering how much money you may have at a specific point in the future. The earlier you start saving, the more quickly your money can earn interest and grow, and the greater the amount of money you can accumulate by a given future point in time.

annuity (or ordinary annuity)
A series of equal cash flow payments that are received or paid at equal intervals in time.

The time value of money is most commonly applied to two types of cash flows: a single dollar amount (also referred to as a lump sum) and an annuity. An **annuity** is a stream of equal payments that are received or paid at equal intervals in time. For example, a monthly deposit of $50 as new savings in a bank account at the end of every month is an annuity. Your telephone bill is not an annuity, as the payments are not the same each month. This chapter will discuss time value of money computations related to the future and present value of both lump-sum and annuity cash flows. Calculations are illustrated using both time value tables and a financial calculator.

Future Value of a Dollar Amount

When you deposit money in a bank savings account, your money grows because the bank pays interest on your deposit. The interest is a reward to you for depositing your money in the account, is normally expressed as a percentage of the deposit amount, and is paid either monthly, quarterly, or annually.

You may want to know how your money will grow to determine whether you can afford specific purchases in the future. For example, you may want to estimate how much your existing bank balance will have accumulated in six months, when you will need to make a tuition payment. Alternatively, you may want to estimate how much that money will have accumulated in one year, when you hope to make a down payment on a new car. To do this, you can apply the interest rate that you expect to earn on your deposit to the deposit amount.

To determine the future value of an amount of money you deposit today, you need to know:

- The amount of your deposit (or other investment) today
- The interest rate to be earned on your deposit
- The number of years the money will be invested

EXAMPLE	If you make a bank deposit of $1,000 that earns 4% annually, the deposit will earn an annual interest of:

Interest rate times deposit
4% × $1,000 = $40

Thus, your deposit will accumulate to be worth $1,040 by the end of one year.

In the next year, the interest rate of 4% will be applied not only to your original $1,000 deposit, but also to the interest that you earned in the previous year. The process of earning interest on interest is called **compounding**.

Assuming that the interest rate is 4% in the second year, it will be applied to your deposit balance of $1,040, which results in interest of $41.60 (4% × $1,040). Thus, your balance by the end of the second year will be $1,081.60.

Notice that the interest of $41.60 paid in the second year is more than the interest paid in the first year, even though the interest rate is the same. This is because the interest rate was applied to a larger deposit balance.

In the third year, a 4% interest rate would result in interest of $43.26 (4% of $1,081.60). Your deposit balance will be $1,124.86 by the end of the third year.

compounding
The process of earning interest on interest.

In some cases, you may want to know how your deposit will accumulate over a long period of time, such as 20 or 30 years. You can quickly determine the future value for any period of time by using the **future value interest factor** (*FVIF*), which is a factor multiplied by today's savings to determine how the savings will accumulate over time. It is dependent on the interest rate and the number of years the money is invested. Your deposit today is multiplied by the *FVIF* to determine the future value of the deposit.

future value interest factor (*FVIF*)
A factor multiplied by today's savings to determine how the savings will accumulate over time.

Using the Future Value Table

Table C.1 in Appendix C shows the *FVIF* for various interest rates (*i*) and time periods (*n*). Each column lists an interest rate and each row lists a possible time period.

EXAMPLE

Suppose you want to know how much money you will have in five years if you invest $5,000 now and earn an annual return of 4%. The present value of money (*PV*) is the amount invested, or $5,000. The *FVIF* for an interest rate of 4% and a time period of five years is 1.217 (look down the 4% column and across the row for year 5). Thus, the future value (*FV*) of the $5,000 in five years will be:

$$FV = PV \times FVIF_{i,n}$$

$$FV = PV \times FVIF_{4\%,5}$$

$$= \$5,000 \times 1.217$$

$$= \$6,085$$

Impact of a Longer Period

By reviewing any column of the *FVIF* table in Appendix C, you will notice that as the number of years increases, the *FVIF* increases. This means that the longer the time period in which your money is invested at a particular interest rate, the more your money will grow. This relationship is illustrated in the following example.

EXAMPLE

What if you invested your $5,000 for 20 years instead of 5 years? Assuming that the interest rate is still 4%, the future value (*FV*) will be:

$$FV = PV \times FVIF_{i,n}$$

$$FV = PV \times FVIF_{4\%,20}$$

$$= \$5,000 \times 2.191$$

$$= \$10,955$$

This result shows how your $5,000 grows if you invest it for a longer period of time.

Impact of a Higher Interest Rate

By reviewing any row of the *FVIF* table in Appendix C, you will notice that as the interest rate increases, the *FVIF* increases. This means that the higher the interest rate at which your money is invested for a particular number of years, the more your money will grow. This relationship is illustrated in the following example.

EXAMPLE

What if you could invest your $5,000 at an interest rate of 9% instead of 4%? Assuming a period of 20 years (like in the previous example), the future value (*FV*) will be:

$$FV = PV \times FVIF_{i,n}$$

$$FV = PV \times FVIF_{9\%,20}$$

$$= \$5,000 \times 5.604$$

$$= \$28,020$$

Thus, your $5,000 will be worth $28,020 in 20 years if you can earn 9% interest, versus only $10,955 in 20 years if you only earn 4% interest. This comparison illustrates the benefit of investing your money at a higher interest rate.

Using a Financial Calculator to Compute Future Value

You can buy financial calculators, which greatly simplify time value calculations. The typical financial calculator lets you easily estimate the future value that you would accumulate at a specific point in time as a result of an initial deposit today. The main function keys on the calculator for this purpose are

N = number of periods in which your deposit will be invested

I = interest rate per period

PV = present value (the initial amount deposited)

FV = future value of your initial deposit

CPT = the compute function, which you press just before the function you want the calculator to compute

EXAMPLE

Input	Function
20	N
9	I
−5000	PV
0	PMT
CPT	FV
Solution	
$28,022.00	

Repeat the previous problem in which you could earn an annual rate of 9% over 20 years using the financial calculator instead of the future value table, and follow these steps:

- Press 20 and then press *N* (number of periods).
- Press 9 and then press *I* (interest rate).
- Press −5000 and then press *PV* (present value of the money you invest); the negative sign is used to represent your deposit.
- Press 0 and then press *PMT* (which means that there are no periodic payments in this problem).
- Press *CPT* (the compute function) and then press *FV* (future value).

Your calculator should display the computed future value, $28,022.

EXAMPLE

Input	Function
12	N
10	I
−5687	PV
0	PMT
CPT	FV
Solution	
$17,848.24	

Suppose you have $5,687 to invest in the stock market today. You like to invest for the long term and plan to choose your stocks carefully. You will invest your money for 12 years in certain stocks on which you expect a return of 10% annually. Although financial calculators can vary slightly in their setup, most would require inputs as shown at left.

Using the calculator, follow these steps:

- Press 12 and then press *N* (number of periods).
- Press 10 and then press *I* (interest rate).
- Press −5687 and then press *PV* (present value, which represents the value of today's investment).
- Press 0 and then press *PMT* (which means that there are no periodic payments in this problem).
- Press the *CPT* function and then *FV* (future value), so that the calculator will compute and display the future value answer.

The *PV* is a negative number here, reflecting the outflow of cash to make the investment. The calculator computes the future value to be $17,848.24, which indicates that you will have $17,848.24 in your brokerage account in 12 years if you achieve a return of 10% annually on your $5,687 investment.

Use a financial calculator to determine the future value of $5,000 invested at 9% for 20 years. (This is the same problem as an earlier example used for the *FVIF* table.) Your answer should be $28,022.05. The small difference in answers using the *FVIF* table versus using a financial calculator is due to rounding.

FREE APPS
for Personal
Finance

Estimating Growth in Savings

Application:

The Future Value of Your Money app (by Garinet Media Network, LLC) illustrates how your money will grow based on input that you provide about your savings plans.

To Find It:

Search for the "Future Value" app on your mobile device.

The Power of Compounding

As a result of compounding, an amount of savings can grow substantially. Exhibit 3.1 illustrates how a deposit of $1,000 grows over time. Notice that your initial $1,000 deposit almost doubles in seven years when considering the compounding effect (you earn interest on your initial deposit and on any interest that has already accumulated). With the assumed interest rate of 10%, it would take 10 years for your deposit to double if you only earned interest on the initial deposit and not on the accumulated interest as well.

The Future Value of Debt

Just as compounding can expand your savings, it can also expand your debt. For example, if you had debt today of $1,000 and were charged 10% on the debt per year, and you did not pay off any of your debt, Exhibit 3.1 could be applied to illustrate how your debt would grow over time. Notice how the debt would grow because you would pay interest not only on your initial debt amount but also on the interest that accumulates over time.

Deferring Student Loan Debt Students who obtain student loans to fund their education sometimes have difficulty paying off their loans after they graduate, especially when they are allowed to defer (postpone) making any payments on their student

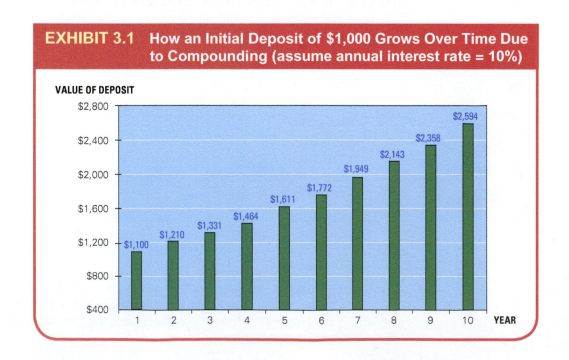

EXHIBIT 3.1   How an Initial Deposit of $1,000 Grows Over Time Due to Compounding (assume annual interest rate = 10%)

loan debt for a specific period. For some types of student loans, no interest is charged during this period, but, for many student loans, interest will be charged and will be added to your debt. For example, if you defer $50,000 in student loans for three years, and the interest rate is 5%, you will owe $57,881.25 at the end of that period because $7,881.25 in interest will be added to your debt. Chapter 9 discusses student loans in more detail.

Twisted Logic About Long-Term Debt

PSYCHOLOGY
of Personal
Finance

Unfortunately, some consumers use twisted logic when assessing their long-term debt. They believe that avoiding the payment of debt for as long as possible is advantageous because it allows them to spend money on other purchases instead of paying off the debt. They receive immediate satisfaction from this logic because they put off the pain associated with using their income to pay off debt. Their use of credit to make purchases is much more enjoyable than their use of existing income to pay off debt. Thus, they can easily justify their decision to spend excessively today without considering how difficult it may be to pay off the debt in the future. They might not recognize how debt can accumulate over a long period. Instead, they are more comfortable with long-term debt because there is much time before they must face the reality of paying off the debt.

Present Value of a Dollar Amount

discounting
The process of obtaining present values.

In many situations, you will want to know how much money you must deposit or invest today to accumulate a specified amount of money at a future point in time. The process of obtaining present values is referred to as **discounting**. Suppose that you want to have $20,000 for a down payment on a house in three years. You want to know how much money you need to invest today to reach a total of $20,000 in three years. That is, you want to know the present value of $20,000 that will be needed in three years, based on an interest rate that you could earn over that period.

To determine the present value of an amount of money expected in the future, you need to know:

- The future amount of money
- The interest rate to be earned on your deposit
- The number of years the money will be invested

present value interest factor (*PVIF*)
A factor multiplied by a future value to determine the present value of that amount.

The present value can be calculated by using a **present value interest factor (*PVIF*)**, which is a factor multiplied by the future value to determine the present value of that amount. It is dependent on the interest rate and the number of years the money is invested.

Using the Present Value Table

Table C.2 in Appendix C shows the *PVIF* for various interest rates (i) and time periods (n). Each column lists an interest rate, and each row lists a time period.

You will notice that in any column of the table the *PVIF* is lower as the number of years increases. This means that less money is needed to achieve a specific future value when the money is invested for a greater number of years.

Similarly, an inspection of any row reveals that less money is needed to achieve a specific future value when the money is invested at a higher rate of return.

EXAMPLE

You would like to accumulate $50,000 in five years by making a single investment today. You believe you can achieve a return from your investment of 7% annually. What is the dollar amount that you need to invest today to achieve your goal?

The *PVIF* in this example is 0.713 (look down the 7% column and across the row for year 5). Using the present value table, the present value (*PV*) is:

$$PV = FV \times PVIF_{i,n}$$

$$PV = FV \times PVIF_{7\%,5}$$

$$= \$50,000 \times 0.713$$

$$= \$35,650$$

Thus, you need to invest $35,650 today to have $50,000 in five years if you expect an annual return of 7%.

Using a Financial Calculator to Compute Present Value

Using a financial calculator, present values can be obtained quickly by inputting all known variables and solving for the one unknown variable.

EXAMPLE

Input	Function
20	N
8.61	I
500000	FV
CPT	PV

Solution

$95,845.94

Loretta Callahan would like to accumulate $500,000 by the time she retires in 20 years. If she can earn an 8.61% return annually, how much must she invest today to have $500,000 in 20 years? Because the unknown variable is the present value (*PV*), the calculator input will be as shown at left.

Where:

N = 20 years

I = 8.61%

PV = present value, or the amount that would have to be deposited today

FV = amount of money desired at a future point in time

Thus, Loretta would have to invest $95,845.94 today to accumulate $500,000 in 20 years if she really earns 8.61% annually.

Use a financial calculator to determine the present value of a single sum by calculating the present value of $50,000 in five years if the money is invested at an interest rate of 7%. This is the example used earlier to illustrate the present value tables. Your answer should be $35,650. Your answer may vary slightly due to rounding.

Future Value of an Annuity

Earlier in the chapter, you saw how your money can grow from a single deposit. An alternative way to accumulate funds over time is through an ordinary annuity, which represents a stream of equal payments (or investments) that occur at the end of each period. For example, if you make a $30 deposit at the end of each month for 100 months, this is an ordinary annuity. As another example, you may invest $1,000 at the end of each year for 10 years. There is a simple and quick method to determine the future value of an annuity. If the payment changes over time, the payment stream does not reflect an annuity. You can still determine the future value of a payment stream that does not reflect an annuity, but the computation process is more complicated.

An alternative to an ordinary annuity is an **annuity due**, which is a series of equal cash flow payments that occur at the beginning of each period. Thus, an annuity due

annuity due
A series of equal cash flow payments that occur at the beginning of each period.

timelines
Diagrams that show payments received or paid over time.

differs from an ordinary annuity in that the payments occur at the beginning instead of the end of the period.

The best way to illustrate the future value of an ordinary annuity is through the use of **timelines**, which show the payments received or paid over time.

EXAMPLE

You plan to invest $100 at the end of every year for the next three years. You expect to earn an annual interest rate of 10% on the funds that you invest. Using a timeline, the cash flows from this annuity can be represented as follows:

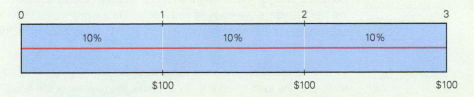

You would like to know how much money will be in your investment account at the end of the third year. This amount is the future value of the annuity. The first step in calculating the future value of the annuity is to treat each payment as a single sum and determine the future value of each payment individually. Next, add up the individual future values to obtain the future value of the annuity.

Because the first payment will be invested from the end of year 1 to the end of year 3, it will be invested for two years. Because the second payment will be invested from the end of year 2 to the end of year 3, it will be invested for one year. The third payment is made at the end of year 3, the point in time at which we want to determine the future value of the annuity. Hence, the third-year payment will not accumulate any interest. Using the future value in Table C.1 in Appendix C to obtain the future value interest factor for two years at 10% ($FVIF_{10\%,2} = 1.21$) and the future value interest factor for one year at 10% ($FVIF_{10\%,1} = 1.10$), the future value of your annuity can be determined as follows:

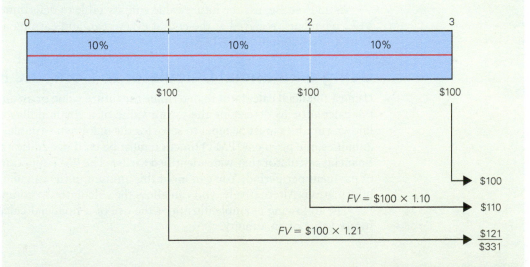

Adding up the individual future values shows that the future value of this annuity is $331 (i.e., you will have $331 in your account at the end of the third year). Notice that $300 of the $331 represents the three $100 payments. Thus, the remaining $31 of the $331 is the combined interest you earned on the three payments.

Using the Future Value Annuity Table

future value interest factor for an annuity (*FVIFA*)
A factor multiplied by the periodic savings level (annuity) to determine how the savings will accumulate over time.

Computing the future value of an annuity by looking up each individual single-sum future value interest factor (*FVIF*) is rather tedious. Consequently, Table C.3 in Appendix C lists the factors for various interest rates and periods (years). These factors are referred to as **future value interest factors for an annuity** ($FVIFA_{i,n}$), where i is the periodic interest rate and n is the number of payments in the annuity. The annuity payment (*PMT*) can be multiplied by the *FVIFA* to determine the future value of the annuity ($FVA = PMT \times FVIFA$). Each column in the table lists an interest rate, and each row lists the period of concern.

EXAMPLE

Suppose that you have won the lottery and will receive $150,000 at the end of every year for the next 20 years. As soon as you receive the payments, you will invest them at your bank at an interest rate of 7% annually. How much will be in your account at the end of 20 years (assuming you do not make any withdrawals)?

To find the answer, you must determine the future value of an annuity. (The stream of cash flows is in the form of an annuity because the payments are equal and equally spaced in time.) Using the future value annuity table to determine the factor, look in the $i = 7\%$ column and the $n = 20$ periods row. The table shows that this factor is 40.995.

The next step is to determine the future value of your lottery annuity:

$$FVA = PMT \times FVIFA_{i,n}$$
$$= PMT \times FVIFA_{7,20}$$
$$= \$150,000 \times 40.995$$
$$= \$6,149,250$$

Thus, after 20 years, you will have $6,149,250 if you invest all your lottery payments in an account earning an interest rate of 7%.

As an exercise, use the future value annuity table to determine the future value of five $172 payments, received at the end of every year, and earning an interest rate of 14%. Your answer should be $1,137.

Using a Financial Calculator to Compute FVA

Using a financial calculator to determine the future value of an annuity is similar to using the calculator to determine the future value of a single dollar amount. As before, the known variables must be input to solve for the unknown variable. For problems involving annuities, the payment (PMT) function must be used in addition to the other keys on the financial calculator that were identified earlier. The PMT function represents the amount of payment per period. You can input this amount in the calculator along with the other information. Alternatively, you can allow the calculator to compute this amount.

The following example illustrates the use of a financial calculator to determine the future value of an annuity.

EXAMPLE

You have $80 of each monthly paycheck invested in a retirement account. You expect to earn 5% annually on this account. How much will be in the account in 30 years?

This problem differs from the problems we have seen so far, in that the payments are received on a monthly (not annual) basis. You would like to obtain the future value of the annuity and

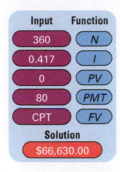

Input	Function
360	N
0.417	I
0	PV
80	PMT
CPT	FV

Solution

$66,630.00

consequently need the number of periods, the periodic interest rate, the present value, and the payment. Because there are 12 months in a year, there are $30 \times 12 = 360$ periods. Furthermore, because the annual interest rate is 5%, the monthly interest rate is $5/12 = 0.417\%$. Also, note that to determine the future value of an annuity, most financial calculators require an input of 0 for the present value. The payment in this problem is 80.

The input for the financial calculator would be as shown at left.

Thus, you will have $66,630 when you retire in 30 years as a result of your monthly investment.

FREE APPS
for Personal
Finance

Calculating Your Savings

Application:

The Quick Compound Interest Calculator app (by Goran Rauker) allows you to calculate the savings that you will accumulate in the future, based on how much you plan to save each month and the interest rate to be earned on your savings.

To Find It:

Search for the "Quick Compound Calculator" app on your mobile device.

Present Value of an Annuity

Just as the future value of an annuity can be obtained by compounding the individual cash flows of the annuity and then adding them up, the present value of an annuity can be obtained by discounting the individual cash flows of the annuity and adding them up.

Referring to our earlier example of an ordinary annuity with three $100 payments and an interest rate of 10%, we can graphically illustrate the process as follows:

Financial Planning
ONLINE

Go to:
The calculators in the personal finance section of Yahoo.com

To get:
An estimate of the future value of your savings, based on your initial balance, the amount saved per period, the interest rate, and the number of periods.

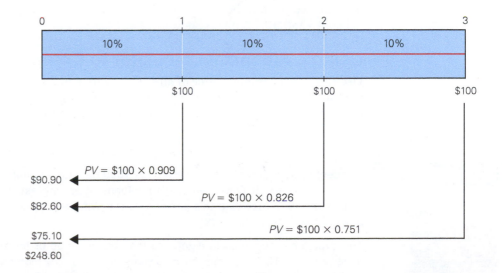

Adding up the individual present values leads to the conclusion that the present value of this annuity is $248.60. Therefore, three $100 payments received at the end of each of the next three years are worth $248.60 to you today if you can invest your money at an interest rate of 10%.

present value interest factor for an annuity (*PVIFA*)
A factor multiplied by a periodic savings level (annuity) to determine the present value of the annuity.

Using the Present Value Annuity Table

Table C.4 in Appendix C shows the **present value interest factors for an annuity** ($PVIFA_{i,n}$) for various interest rates (i) and time periods (n) in the annuity. Each column in the table lists an interest rate, and each row lists a time period.

EXAMPLE

You have just won the lottery. As a result of your luck, you will receive $82,000 at the end of every year for the next 25 years. Now, a financial firm offers you a lump sum of $700,000 in return for these payments. If you can invest your money at an annual interest rate of 9%, should you accept the offer?

This problem requires you to determine the present value of the lottery annuity. If the present value of the annuity is higher than the amount offered by the financial firm, you should reject the offer. Using the present value annuity table to determine the factor, we look in the $i = 9\%$ row and the $n = 25$ periods column. The table shows that this factor is 9.823.

The next step is to determine the present value of the annuity:

$$PVA = PMT \times PVIFA_{i,n}$$
$$= PMT \times PVIFA_{9,25}$$
$$= \$82,000 \times 9.823$$
$$= \$805,486$$

Thus, the 25 payments of $82,000 each are worth $805,486 to you today if you can invest your money at an interest rate of 9%. Consequently, you should reject the financial firm's offer to purchase your future lottery payments for $700,000.

As an exercise, use the present value annuity table to determine the present value of eight $54 payments, received at the end of every year and earning an interest rate of 14%. Your answer should be $250.50, which means that the eight payments have a present value of $250.50.

Using a Financial Calculator to Compute PVA

Determining the present value of an annuity with a financial calculator is similar to using the calculator to determine the present value of a single-sum payment. Again, the values of known variables are inserted to solve for the unknown variable.

EXAMPLE

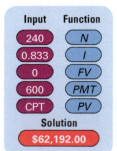

Input	Function
240	N
0.833	I
0	FV
600	PMT
CPT	PV

Solution
$62,192.00

A recent retiree, Dave Buzz, receives his $600 pension monthly. He will receive this pension for 20 years. If Dave can invest his funds at an interest rate of 10%, he should be just as satisfied receiving this pension as receiving a lump-sum payment today of what amount?

This problem requires us to determine the present value of the pension annuity. Because there are $20 \times 12 = 240$ months in 20 years, $n = 240$. The monthly (periodic) interest rate is $10/12 = 0.833\%$. Thus, $i = 0.833$. Using these inputs with a financial calculator, we obtain the inputs shown to the left.

The present value is $62,192. If Dave is offered a lump sum of $62,192 today, he should accept it if he can invest his funds at an interest rate of 10%.

Using Time Value to Estimate Savings

Now that you understand the various time value calculations, you can apply them to financial planning. The key time value tools for building your financial plan are estimating the future value of annual savings and determining the amount of annual savings necessary to achieve a specific amount of savings in the future.

Estimating the Future Value from Savings

The future value of an annuity is especially useful when determining how much money you will have saved by a future point in time if you periodically save a specific amount of money every year. You can apply this process when you are saving for a large purchase (such as a down payment on a home) in the near future or even for your retirement in the distant future.

EXAMPLE

Stephanie Spratt believes that she may be able to save about $5,000 per year. She wants to know how much she will have in 30 years if she earns 6% annual interest on her investment. The annuity in this example is $5,000. As you can see in Table C.3 in Appendix C, the future value annuity factor based on a 30-year period and a 6% interest rate is 79.057. Thus, the future value is

$$\$5,000 \times 79.057 = \$395,285$$

If she could earn 7% instead of 6% on her savings, the future value annuity factor would be 94.459 and the future value would be:

$$\$5,000 \times 94.459 = \$472,295$$

Estimating the Annual Savings That Will Achieve a Future Amount

The future value of annuity tables are also useful for determining how much money you need to save each year to achieve a specific amount of savings at a designated future point in time. Thus, you can estimate the size of the annuity that is necessary to achieve a specific future value of savings that you desire. Because $FVA = PMT \times FVIFA$, the terms can be rearranged to solve for the annuity:

$$FVA/FVIFA = PMT$$

Exhibit 3.2 shows how Stephanie Spratt uses the time value tools to develop a financial plan. Stephanie developed a tentative plan to save $5,000 per year. After applying the time value tools, however, she recognizes that she could accumulate $600,000 in 30 years by saving $6,352 per year. She decides to strive for this higher level of annual savings. Because she realizes that this goal is ambitious, she sets a minimum goal of saving $5,000 per year.

EXAMPLE

Stephanie Spratt now wants to know how much money she must save every year to achieve $600,000 in 30 years, based on a 7% interest rate. In this example, the future value is $600,000, and the future value interest factor is 94.459. The unknown variable is the annuity.

$$PMT = FVA/FVIFA$$

$$= \$600,000/94.459$$

$$= \$6,352$$

Thus, Stephanie would need to invest $6,352 each year to accumulate $600,000 in 30 years.

EXHIBIT 3.2 **How Time Value of Money Decisions Fit Within Stephanie Spratt's Financial Plan**

GOALS FOR A SAVINGS PLAN

1. Calculate how much savings I will accumulate by various future points in time.
2. Determine how much I need to save each year to ensure a comfortable living upon retirement.

ANALYSIS

Present Situation:

Expected Savings per Year = $5,000

Expected Annual Rate of Return = 6% or 7%

Estimated Amount of Savings to Be Accumulated:

Savings Accumulated over:	Assume Annual Return = 6%	Assume Annual Return = 7%
5 years	$28,185	$28,753
10 years	65,905	69,080
15 years	116,380	125,645
20 years	183,930	204,975
25 years	274,325	316,245
30 years	395,290	472,305

Annual Savings Needed to Achieve a Specific Savings Goal:

Savings Goal = $80,000 in 10 years, $200,000 in 20 years, $600,000 in 30 years

Expected Annual Rate of Return = 6% or 7%

Savings Goal	Assume Annual Return = 6%	Assume Annual Return = 7%
$80,000 in 10 years	$6,069	$5,790
$200,000 in 20 years	5,437	4,879
$600,000 in 30 years	7,589	6,352

To achieve a savings goal of $80,000 in 10 years, I would need to save $6,069 per year (assuming an annual return of 6% on my money). To achieve a goal of $200,000 in 20 years, I would need to save $5,437 per year (assuming a 6% annual return).

DECISIONS

Decision on My Savings Goal in the Future:

If I can save $5,000 a year, I should accumulate $28,185 in 5 years and $65,905 in 10 years. These estimates are based on an assumed annual return of 6%. If my annual return is higher, I should accumulate even more than that. The estimated savings for longer time periods are much higher.

A comparison of the third column with the second column in the table shows how much more savings I could accumulate if I can earn an annual return of 7% instead of 6%.

Decision on My Savings Goal per Year:

Although my initial plan was to develop a budget for saving about $5,000 a year, I will try to save more so that I can achieve my savings goals. I will use a minimum savings goal of $5,000, but will try to save about $6,000 per year.

How Time Value Can Motivate Saving

PSYCHOLOGY
of Personal
Finance

The results from estimating the future value of an annuity may surprise you. Your money can grow substantially over time when you invest periodically and when interest is earned on your savings over time. The exercise of estimating the future value of an annuity might encourage you to develop a savings plan because you see the reward as a result of your willingness to save. Consider how much you may be able to save over each of the next five years, and estimate the future value of an annuity over this period based on the prevailing interest rate. Then, apply it to a 10-year period and also to a 20-year period. Notice how the amount saved over 10 years is more than twice the amount saved over 5 years, and the amount saved over 20 years is more than twice the amount saved over 10 years. Your estimates might convince you to save more money each year, so that you can build your savings and wealth over time and therefore have more money to spend in the future.

How Time Value Fits Within Your Financial Plan

The key time value decisions for building your financial plan are

- How much should I attempt to accumulate in savings for a future point in time?
- How much should I attempt to save every month or every year?

These decisions require an understanding of the time value of money. Exhibit 3.2 shows how these savings decisions apply to Stephanie Spratt's financial plan.

DISCUSSION QUESTIONS

1. How would Stephanie's savings decisions be different if she were a single mother of two children?

2. How would Stephanie's savings decisions be affected if she were 35 years old? If she were 50 years old?

SUMMARY

Importance of Time Value of Money. A dollar today has more value than a dollar received one year from now. Consequently, many decisions about saving for the future are influenced by the time value of money. Proper decisions based on the time value of money can allow you to accumulate more wealth.

Future Value of a Dollar Amount. You can estimate the future value of a single dollar amount to determine the future value of a bank deposit or a fund established for retirement. It is determined by estimating the compounded interest that is generated by the initial amount. The future value can be determined by using a future value table or a financial calculator.

Present Value of a Dollar Amount. You can estimate the present value of a single dollar amount so that you know what a future payment

would be worth if you had it today. The present value of a single dollar amount to be received in the future is determined by discounting the future value. The present value of a future amount to be received can be determined by using a present value table or a financial calculator.

Future Value of an Annuity. You can estimate the future value of an annuity so that you can determine how much a stream of payments will be worth at a specific time in the future. This involves determining the future value of every single dollar amount contained within the annuity, which is easily estimated by using a future value annuity table or a financial calculator.

Present Value of an Annuity. You can estimate the present value of an annuity so that you can determine how much a stream of future payments is worth today. This involves determining the present value of every single dollar amount contained within the annuity, which is easily estimated by using a present value annuity table or a financial calculator.

Using Time Value to Estimate Savings. Time value can be applied to estimate your future savings, which enables you to make decisions about how much to save to achieve a specific savings goal in the future.

How Time Value Fits Within Your Financial Plan. You will likely need to save money to achieve some of your financial goals. Because time value can be applied to estimate savings, it is an important tool for you to establish your financial plan.

REVIEW QUESTIONS

All Review Questions are available in MyFinanceLab *at* http://www.myfinancelab.com.

1. **Time Value of Money.** What is the time value of money? How is it related to opportunity costs?

2. **Importance of the Time Value of Money.** List one reason why the time value of money is an important concept.

3. **Time Value of Cash Flows.** To what types of cash flows is the time value of money concept most commonly applied?

4. **Annuity.** What is an annuity?

5. **Compounding.** Define compounding. How is it used in financial planning?

6. **Calculating Future Values.** What two methods can be used to calculate future values?

7. **Future Value Formula.** What is the formula for determining the future value of a single sum when using the future value interest factor table? What information must be known to find the correct future value interest factor?

8. **Discounting.** What is discounting?

9. **Present Value.** Describe some instances when determining the present value of an amount is useful.

10. **Using Proper Tables.** In questions a through d, indicate whether you would use the table for determining the future value of a single sum (*FVIF*), the present value of a single sum (*PVIF*), the future value of an annuity (*FVIFA*), or the present value of an annuity (*PVIFA*).

    a. You want to know how much you must deposit today to have $5,000 in five years.

    b. You plan to contribute $300 per month to your company's retirement plan and want to know how much you will have at retirement.

    c. You received $500 as a gift for graduation, and you want to know how much it will be worth in three years if you deposit it in a savings account.

    d. You must decide between accepting a lump-sum settlement and annual payments.

11. **Present Value of Annuity.** What formula is used to determine the present value of an annuity? What does the present value of an annuity indicate?

12. **Future Value of Annuity.** How would you modify the FVA equation to determine how much you would need to save each month to have a specific amount at a specific time in the future?

13. **Number of Periods.** In determining the future value of an annuity to be invested monthly over a five-year period, what number of periods should you use?

14. **Time Value of Money and Debt.** Lakesha recently found out that her credit card balance was compounded daily rather than monthly. How will this compounding frequency impact the outstanding debt she owes on her credit card?

15. **Time Value of Money and Your Financial Plan.** Jerry would like to save the same amount every month until he turns 40. Which time value concept should he use to compute the value of his savings at that time?

16. **Time Value of Money Tools.** Winston will receive $100,000 on his 25th birthday. Which time value of money concept would you use to compute the value of his future inheritance?

FINANCIAL PLANNING PROBLEMS

All Financial Planning Problems are available in MyFinanceLab *at http://www.myfinancelab.com. A financial calculator is recommended for Problems 4, 9, 11, 12, 13, 15 and 16. The financial tables are recommended to answer Problems 1, 2, 3, 5, 6, 7, 9, 10, and 13.*

1. **Future Value.** Kyle has $1,000 in cash received for high school graduation gifts from various relatives. He wants to invest it in a certificate of deposit (CD) so that he will have a down payment on a car when he graduates from college in five years. His bank will pay 6% per year, compounded annually, for the five-year CD. How much will Kyle have in five years to put down on his car?

2. **Future Value.** Sandra wants to deposit $100 each year for her son. If she places it in a savings account that pays 5% per year, what amount will be in the account in 20 years?

3. **Future Value.** Luis wants to know how much he will have available to spend on his trip to Belize in three years if he deposits $3,000 today at an annual interest rate of 9%.

4. **Future Value.** How much will you have in 36 months if you invest $75 a month at 10% annual interest?

5. **Using Time Value to Estimate Savings.** DeMarcus wants to retire with $1 million in savings by the time he turns 60. He is currently 18 years old. How much will he need to save each year, assuming he can get a 12% annual return on his investments?

6. **Present Value.** Cheryl wants to have $2,000 in spending money to take on a trip to Disney World in three years. How much must she deposit now in a savings account that pays 5% per year to have the money she needs in three years?

7. **Present Value.** Juan would like to give his newly born grandson a gift of $10,000 on his 18th birthday. Juan can earn 7% annual interest on a certificate of deposit. How much must he deposit now to achieve his goal?

8. **Present Value.** Winners of the Georgia Lotto drawing are given the choice of receiving the winning amount divided equally over 20 years or as a lump-sum cash option amount. The cash option amount is determined by discounting the winning amount at 7% over 20 years. This week the lottery is worth $6 million to a single winner. What would the cash option payout be?

9. **Future Value of Annuity.** Michelle is attending college and has a part-time job. Once she finishes college, Michelle would like to relocate to a metropolitan area. She wants to build her savings so

that she will have a "nest egg" to start her off. Michelle works out her budget and decides she can afford to set aside $50 per month for savings. Her bank will pay her 3% per year, compounded monthly, on her savings account. What will Michelle's balance be in five years?

10. **Future Value of Annuity.** Twins Jessica and Joshua, both 25, graduated from college and began working in the family restaurant business. The first year, Jessica began putting $2,000 per year in an individual retirement account and contributed to it for a total of 10 years. After 10 years, she made no further contributions until she retired at age 65. Joshua did not start making contributions to his individual retirement account until he was 35, but he continued making contributions of $2,000 each year until he retired at age 65. Assuming that both Jessica and Joshua receive 10% interest per year, how much will Jessica have at retirement? How much did she contribute in total? How much will Joshua have at retirement? How much did he contribute in total?

11. **Estimating the Annuity Amount.** Amy and Vince want to save $7,000 so that they can take a trip to Europe in four years. How much must they save each month to have the money they need if they can get 8% per year, compounded monthly, on their savings?

12. **Future Value of Annuity.** Lena has just become eligible to participate in her company's retirement plan. Her company does not match contributions, but the plan does average an annual return of 12%. Lena is 40 and plans to work to age 65. If she contributes $200 per month, how much will she have in her plan at retirement?

13. **Future Value of Annuity.** Stacey would like to have $1 million available to her at retirement. Her investments have an average annual return of 11%. If she makes contributions of $300 per month, will she reach her goal when she retires in 30 years?

14. **Future Value of Annuity.** Jesse has just learned that she won $1 million in her state lottery. She has the choice of receiving a lump-sum payment of $312,950 or $50,000 per year for the next 20 years. Jesse can invest the lump sum at 8%, or she can invest the annual payments at 6% per

year. Which should she choose for the greatest return after 20 years?

15. **Future Value of Annuity.** Jen spends $10 per week on lottery tickets. If she takes the same amount that she spends on lottery tickets and invests it each week for the next five years at 10%, compounded weekly, how much will she have in five years?

16. **Future Value of Annuity.** Kirk can take his $1,000 income tax refund and invest it in a 36-month certificate of deposit at 7%, compounded monthly, or he can use the money to purchase a home entertainment system and put $30 a month in a bank savings account that will pay him 7% annual interest, compounded monthly. Which choice will give him more money at the end of three years?

17. **Future Value of Debt.** Jim accepted a $3,000 loan from his Uncle Kurt. Uncle Kurt agreed to defer payments for two years until after Jim graduates from college. How much will Jim owe in two years if his uncle charges him 6% interest compounded annually?

18. **Future Value of Debt.** Elizabeth borrowed $1,000 from her credit union. She has to make only one payment at the end of the loan. How much will she owe at the end of the year if the credit union charges her 5% interest?

19. **Ethical Dilemma.** Cindy and Jack have always practiced good financial habits, in particular, developing and living by a budget. They are currently in the market to purchase a new car and have budgeted $300 per month for car payments.

While visiting a local dealership, a salesman, Scott, shows them a car that meets their financial requirements. Then he insists that they look at a much more expensive car that he knows they would prefer. The more expensive car would result in payments of $500 per month.

In discussing the two cars, Cindy and Jack tell Scott that the only way they can afford a more expensive car would be to discontinue making a $200 monthly contribution to their retirement plan, which they have just begun. They plan to retire in 30 years. Scott explains that they would only need to discontinue the $200 monthly payments for five years, that is, the length of the car loan. Scott calculates that the $12,000 in lost contributions over the next five years could be made up over the remaining 25 years by increasing their monthly contribution by only $40 per month, and they would still be able to achieve their goal.

a. Comment on the ethics of a salesperson who attempts to talk customers into spending more than they had originally planned and budgeted.

b. Is Scott correct in his calculation that Cindy and Jack can make up the difference in their retirement by increasing their monthly contributions by only $40 per month for the remaining 25 years? (*Note*: Assume an annual rate of return of 6% on Cindy and Jack's investment and assume that they make the investments annually.)

FINANCIAL PLANNING ONLINE EXERCISES

1. Go to the banking section of About.com, read about the bill paying process, and answer the following questions:

   a. Is setting up online bill pay a difficult process? Explain fully.

   b. What are the two basic types of online bill pay, and what information is needed to use each?

PSYCHOLOGY OF PERSONAL FINANCE: Future Value of Your Cash

1. This chapter explains how your cash deposited in a bank can grow over time. Some people are only willing to save if they are rewarded with a high interest rate. However, the interest rate on deposits has been relatively low lately. Does this influence your willingness to save? Would you save more money if interest rates were higher?

2. This chapter illustrates how the amount of debt you owed would not grow as quickly when interest rates are low. Because interest rates have been low lately, are you more willing to borrow money?

WEB SEARCH EXERCISE

You can develop your personal finance skills by conducting an Internet search for related articles. Find a recent online article about personal finance that reinforces one or more concepts covered in this chapter. If your class has an online component, your professor may ask you to post your summary of the article there and provide a link to the article so that other students can access it. If your class is live, your professor may ask you to summarize your application of the article in class. Your professor may assign specific students to complete this assignment or may allow any student to do the assignment on a volunteer basis.

For recent online articles related to this chapter, consider using the following search terms (be sure to include the current year as a search term to ensure that the online articles are recent):

- How savings grows
- The magic of compounding
- How debt accumulates
- How interest rate affects your saving
- How interest rate affects your debt payment
- Impact of debt repayment period
- How much to save to achieve your goal

VIDEO EXERCISE: How Your Savings Grows

Go to one of the Web sites that contain video clips (such as http://www.youtube.com), and view some video clips about how savings grows. You can use search phrases such as "future value of savings." Select one video clip on this topic that you would recommend for the other students in your class.

1. Provide the Web link for the video clip.
2. What do you think is the main point of this video clip?
3. How might you change your savings plans as a result of watching this video clip?

BUILDING YOUR OWN FINANCIAL PLAN

Based on the goals that you established in Chapter 1 and the personal cash flow statement that you created in Chapter 2, you are now ready to begin determining how to go about achieving many of your goals. Most financial goals are achieved by some sort of savings/investment plan.

Go to the worksheets at the end of this chapter to continue building your financial plan.

THE SAMPSONS—A Continuing Case

Recall that Dave and Sharon Sampson established a plan to save $300 per month (or $3,600 per year) for their children's education. Their oldest child is six years old and will begin college in 12 years. They will invest the $300 in a savings account that they expect will earn interest of about 2% a year over the next 12 years. The Sampsons wonder how much additional money they would accumulate if they could earn 5% a year on the savings account instead of 2%. They also wonder how their savings would accumulate if they could save $400 per month (or $4,800 per year) instead of $300 per month.

Go to the worksheets at the end of this chapter to continue this case.

CHAPTER 3: BUILDING YOUR OWN FINANCIAL PLAN

YOUR GOALS FOR CHAPTER 3

1. Determine how much savings you plan to accumulate by various future points in time.

ANALYSIS

1. Assume that you have $1,000 to invest, so insert 1000 as your Present Value in the following table. Assume that you want to invest your money for 5 years (insert 5 for Number of Periods). Assume an annual interest rate of 3.00% (insert 3 for Interest Rate per Period). The table will determine the Future Value of your investment. If you input the numbers correctly, your Future Value is computed to be $1.159, which is what your investment will be worth in 5 years. Now revise the input to reflect your actual savings and the prevailing interest rate so that you can see how your savings will grow in 5 years. Even if you have no savings now, you can at least see how the interest rate affects the future value of savings by revising your input in the Interest Rate per Period, and then observing the change in the Future Value.

Future Value of a Present Amount

Present Value	
Number of Periods	
Interest Rate per Period	
Future Value	

2. Assume that you have $1,000 to invest at the end of each of the next 5 years, so insert 1000 as your Payment per Period in the following table. Assume that you want to invest your money for 5 years (insert 5 for Number of Periods). Assume an annual interest rate of 3.00% (insert 3 for Interest Rate per Period). The following table will determine the Future Value of your investment. If you input the numbers correctly, your Future Value is computed to be $5,309, which is what your investments will be worth in 5 years. Now revise the input to reflect your actual expected savings per year over the next 5 years, and existing interest rate quotations so that you can estimate how your savings will grow in 5 years. You can now revise the table to fit your own desired level of saving.

Future Value of an Annuity

Payment per Period	
Number of Periods	
Interest Rate per Period	
Future Value	

3. Assume that you want to deposit savings that will be worth $10,000 in 5 years, so insert 10000 as the Future Amount and 5 as the Number of Periods in the following table. Assume an annual interest rate of 3.00% (insert 3 for Interest Rate per Period). The following table will determine the Present Value, which represents the amount of savings you need today that would accumulate to be worth $10,000 in 5 years. If you input the numbers correctly, the Present Value is estimated in

the table to be $8,626. Now revise the input to reflect your own desired savings amount in 5 years so that you can estimate how much you need now to achieve your savings goal in 5 years.

Present Value of a Future Amount

Future Amount	
Number of Periods	
Interest Rate per Period	
Present Value	

4. Assume that you want to deposit savings at the end of each of the next 5 years so that you will have $10,000 in 5 years. So insert 10000 as the Future Amount, and 5 for Number of Periods. Assume an annual interest rate of 3.00% (insert 3 for Interest Rate per Period). The following table will determine the Annual Payment, which represents the annual payments that will accumulate to your future desired investment. If you input the numbers correctly, your Annual Payment is computed to be $1,884. Now revise the input to reflect your own desired savings amount in 5 years so that you can estimate how much you need to save per year to achieve your savings goal in 5 years.

Compute Payment Needed to Achieve Future Amount

Future Amount	
Number of Periods	
Interest Rate per Period	
Present Value	

DECISIONS

1. Report on how much you must save per year and the return you must earn to meet your savings goal in 5 years.

_____

_____

_____

_____

_____

_____

_____

CHAPTER 3: THE SAMPSONS—A Continuing Case

CASE QUESTIONS

1. Help the Sampsons determine how much they will have for the children's education by calculating how much $3,600 in annual savings will accumulate to if they earn interest of (a) 2% and (b) 5%. Next, determine how much $4,800 in annual savings will accumulate to if they earn interest of (a) 2% and (b) 5%.

Savings Accumulated Over the Next 12 Years
(Based on Plan to Save $3,600 per Year at 2% or 5%)

Amount Saved Per Year	$3,600	$3,600
Interest Rate	2%	5%
Years	12	12
Future Value of Savings		

Savings Accumulated Over the Next 12 Years
(Based on Plan to Save $4,800 per Year at 2% or 5%)

Amount Saved Per Year	$4,800	$4,800
Interest Rate	2%	5%
Years	12	12
Future Value of Savings		

2. What is the impact of the higher interest rate of 5% (instead of 2%) on the Sampsons' accumulated savings?

3. What is the impact of the higher savings of $4,800 (instead of $3,600) on their accumulated savings?

4. If the Sampsons set a goal to save $70,000 for their children's college education in 12 years, how would you determine the yearly savings necessary to achieve this goal? How much would they have to save by the end of each year to achieve this goal, assuming a 5% annual interest rate?

Calculator: Savings Needed Each Year

Future Value	$70,000
Interest Rate	5%
Years	12
Savings Needed Each Year	

Using Tax Concepts for Planning†

When is an itemized deduction really a deduction?

Often when asked for a charitable contribution, you may be reminded that the donation is deductible on your taxes because the organization is a not-for-profit agency. You may also hear, at some point in your life, that you should purchase a home because the mortgage interest is tax deductible. Giving clothes to Goodwill? Another gift that can be deducted on your tax return. Donating money to your favorite university? Deduct it from your taxes.

Karen Roach/Shutterstock

What you might not realize is that all the deductions just mentioned are itemized deductions. Their benefit does not really begin until the sum total of all of your itemized deductions exceeds the standard deduction. As you will learn in this chapter, for single taxpayers that threshold is $6,300 in 2015 and double that for married taxpayers. So, if you purchase a home and pay $4,500 in mortgage interest, you will not have any real tax benefit unless you can add other deductions to total more than the standard deduction amount. Then your true benefit is the amount that exceeds the standard deduction multiplied by your marginal tax rate.

So go ahead and be generous; the charitable organizations will appreciate it. But remember that such donations are only financially beneficial if you can itemize your deductions. Give for the right reasons, and any potential tax benefit is just extra.

In this chapter, you will learn the basics of income taxes. Knowledge of the tax laws can help you conserve your income, enhance your investments, and protect the transfer of wealth when you die. Understanding the taxation of income and wealth is crucial to sound financial planning.

MyFinanceLab helps you master the topics in this chapter and study more efficiently. Visit http://www.myfinancelab.com for more details.

†2014 IRS forms are displayed in this chapter because 2015 forms were not available at the time of publication. 2015 IRS forms can be obtained online from irs.gov as they become available, and they will also be accessible via http://www.pearsonhighered.com/madura.

The objectives of this chapter are to:

- Provide a background on taxes
- Explain how to determine your tax filing status
- Demonstrate how to calculate your gross income
- Show how deductions and exemptions can be used
- Explain how to determine your taxable income, tax liability, and refund or additional taxes owed
- Explain how tax planning fits within your financial plan

Background on Taxes

Taxes are an integral part of our economy. They are paid on earned income, consumer purchases, wealth transfers, and capital assets. Special taxes are levied on certain consumer products such as cigarettes, alcohol, and gasoline. Corporations pay corporate income taxes on corporate profits. Homeowners pay property taxes on the value of their homes and land. In 2013, $2.775 trillion was paid in taxes in the United States. These taxes are a significant source of funding for governments and governmental agencies. Taxes are used to pay for a wide variety of governmental services and programs, including national defense, Social Security, fire and police protection, government employees, road construction and maintenance, and our education systems.

Individuals pay taxes at the federal, state, and local levels. The federal tax system is administered by a branch of the U.S. Treasury Department called the Internal Revenue Service (IRS). Although Congress passes federal tax laws, it is the IRS that enforces those laws and prepares the forms and publications that taxpayers use to calculate their income taxes.

Many taxes, such as sales taxes, are paid at the time of a transaction. Income taxes are generally paid as income is earned in a process called withholding. Taxes are withheld as income is earned throughout the year. Self-employed individuals have to estimate the amount of taxes to withhold and therefore pay estimated tax withholdings. Employees file a form with their employer, which helps the employer calculate the amount of taxes to withhold. Individuals are allowed to withhold more than the minimum from each pay cycle, but are not allowed to reduce the amount of withholding below the amount specified by the IRS.

The tax year for federal income taxes ends on December 31 of each calendar year. Individual income taxes must be filed and paid by April 15 of the following year. Occasionally, the tax filing deadline is extended a day or two because the actual deadline falls on a weekend date or holiday. The IRS allows taxpayers to file an extension to send in their tax return up to six months after April 15, but all taxes due for the tax year must be paid by the tax filing deadline.

Tax Law Changes

Before you prepare your own tax return, you should familiarize yourself with the latest changes in the tax laws and IRS instructions. Due to inflation, some three dozen individual and business tax provisions increase each year, including tax brackets, standard deductions, and personal exemptions. Major changes to the tax code occur less frequently and are usually the result of philosophical and political changes in our country. In addition, due to economic conditions, some minor and temporary modifications are provided by congressional legislation, including tax relief for natural disasters and tax-related economic stimulus provisions. In the past, special tax relief has been directed toward hurricane victims and first-time homebuyers, and, in 2011–2012, a one-time reduction in Social Security tax withholding was approved as a means of stimulating the economy.

The last two major revisions to the tax code occurred in 2001 and 2003. In the summer of 2001, Congress passed the **Economic Growth and Tax Relief Reconciliation Act of 2001** (more commonly referred to as the Tax Relief Act of 2001). Provisions of the new law began taking effect in 2001 and were scheduled to be phased in gradually until the law expired in 2011. The Act reduced inequities in the tax code, simplified several sections of tax law, and provided educational incentives to a broad range of taxpayers. Tax relief for parents included an increase in the child tax credit and an expansion of the dependent care credit. The 2001 law also expanded contribution limits to retirement plans. In 2003, Congress passed the **Jobs and Growth Tax Relief Reconciliation Act of 2003**. The Act accelerated much of the tax relief scheduled to occur as a result of the 2001 Tax Relief Act. Specifically, individual tax rates were lowered by 2%–3%, the child tax credit was increased to $1,000 per child, the standard deduction for married taxpayers was increased to twice the standard deduction for single taxpayers, the 15% tax bracket for married taxpayers was increased to twice that of single taxpayers, and investors were rewarded with lower long-term capital gains and dividend tax rates.

All the measures of the 2001 law, as modified in 2003, were scheduled to end in 2011. In December 2010, Congress passed the Tax Relief, Unemployment Insurance Reauthorization, and Job Creation Act of 2010, which extended these rates through 2012. Finally in early 2012, President Obama signed the **American Taxpayers Relief Act of 2012**, which permanently set in place many existing features of the tax law. Specifically, the Child Tax Credit was made permanent and no longer will be refundable (paid to the claimant when their tax liability is less than the credit) after 2017. Student loan interest deductions, employer-provided education assistance benefits, and the dependent care credit were finally made permanent. Two other tax law changes came about as a result of court action. In 2013, the Supreme Court handed down a decision invalidating a key provision of the 1996 Defense of Marriage Act. As a result, the U.S. Department of the Treasury and the Internal Revenue Service issued a ruling regarding the tax treatment of same-sex couples. Under the ruling, same-sex couples will be treated as married for all federal tax purposes, including income and gift and estate taxes. The ruling applies to all federal tax law provisions where marriage is a factor, including filing status, claiming personal and dependency exemptions, taking the standard deduction, employee benefits, contributing to an IRA, and claiming the earned income tax credit or child tax credit. In 2015, the court made an additional ruling that requires same-sex marriage to be recognized in all states. The application of the treatment of same-sex couples for federal tax purposes now applies in all jurisdictions. As a result of these two rulings, married same-sex couples will receive equal treatment when it comes to federal tax and benefits.

The **Affordable Care Act of 2010**, or Obamacare, later upheld by a narrow margin in the Supreme Court, requires that everyone must report their medical coverage status and the coverage status of all their dependents on their Tax Form 1040. If everyone had health coverage for the entire year, there are no complications. However, if a taxpayer or dependent was not covered and does not meet one of the exemptions, a penalty will apply. In 2016, the penalty is the greater of $695 per adult and $347.50 per child (up to $2,085 per family) or a penalty of 2.5% of family income. The 2016 penalty will be adjusted in subsequent years for the cost of living. Although there has been some resistance to the Affordable Care Act, it is here to stay for now. In June 2015, the Supreme Court ruled that the intent of the law was to improve the health care market and defended against some challenges to the act. However, there might be other legal challenges to the act in the future.

Social Security and Medicare Taxes

Your **earned income** (wages or salary) is subject to **FICA (Federal Insurance Contributions Act)** taxes that fund Social Security and Medicare. Your employer withholds FICA taxes from each of your paychecks. The Social Security Administration uses the funds to make payments to you on your retirement (subject to age and other requirements). The Social

---

Economic Growth and Tax Relief Reconciliation Act of 2001
Tax cut package designed to provide short-term economic stimulus through tax relief for taxpayers.

Jobs and Growth Tax Relief Act of 2003
An act that accelerated much of the tax relief resulting from the 2001 Tax Relief Act.

American Taxpayers Relief Act of 2012
This law permanently set in place many existing features of the tax law that previously had been extended from time to time and faced a return to pre-2001 tax codes unless permanently fixed into law.

Affordable Care Act of 2010
Legislation that introduced the Individual Mandate to acquire health care coverage or face a penalty for not having coverage.

earned income
Earned income represents salary or wages.

FICA (Federal Insurance Contributions Act)
Taxes paid to fund the Social Security System and Medicare.

Financial Planning ONLINE

Go to:
http://www.irs.gov/

To get:
Information about tax rates, tax forms, guidelines, and deadlines.

Security tax is equal to 6.20% of your salary up to a maximum level (the level is $118,500 in 2015 and changes over time). The only Social Security tax on income beyond this maximum level is an additional 0.90% of Medicare tax on wages and self-employment income in excess of $200,000 for individuals ($250,000 for couples).

Medicare
A government health insurance program that covers people mostly over age 65 and provides payments to health care providers in the case of illness.

Medicare is a government health insurance program that covers people 65 years of age and older and some people with disabilities under age 65. Medicare provides payments to health care providers in the case of illness. Medicare taxes are 1.45% of your earned income, regardless of the amount. Your employer pays the same amount of FICA and Medicare taxes on your behalf.

The FICA taxes just described also apply if you are self-employed. Self-employed persons serve not only as the employee but also as the employer. Their FICA taxes are equal to 15.3% of 92.35% of net business income, which represents the 7.65% FICA tax paid by the employee plus the 7.65% FICA tax paid by the employer. The Social Security tax rate is again capped at the maximum limit, while the Medicare tax rate applies to the entire earnings. One-half of the FICA taxes paid by the self-employed is tax-deductible (i.e., half can be deducted from income when determining adjusted gross income).

EXAMPLE

Stephanie Spratt earned $38,000 in 2015. She is subject to total FICA taxes of 7.65%, which is based on 6.20% for Social Security and 1.45% for Medicare. Thus, her Social Security taxes and Medicare taxes are as follows:

	Social Security Tax	Medicare Tax
Tax rate	6.2% (up to a maximum of $118,500)	1.45%
Tax amount	$0.062 \times \$38,000 = \$2,356.00$	$0.0145 \times \$38,000 = \$551$

Her total FICA taxes are $2,907 (computed as $2,356 + $551).

Personal Income Taxes

personal income taxes
Taxes imposed on income earned.

Your income is also subject to **personal income taxes,** which are taxes imposed on income you earn as a salary or wage. For any year that you earn income, you must file a tax return that consists of a completed Form 1040, Form 1040A, or 1040EZ, plus supporting documents. Your tax return will show whether a sufficient amount of taxes was already withheld from your paycheck, whether you still owe some taxes, or whether the government owes you a refund. If you still owe taxes, you should include a check for the taxes owed along with your completed tax return.

Form 1040EZ, the simplest tax form to use, is an appropriate alternative to Form 1040 in some cases. Generally, this form is used by individuals whose filing status is either single or married filing jointly, who have no dependents, and whose taxable income is less than $100,000. Tax forms can be downloaded from several Web sites. Several software programs, including TurboTax, e-file TaxCut, and TaxACT, are also available to help you prepare your return. An example of Form 1040 is shown in Exhibit 4.1. Refer to this form as you read through the chapter. The most current year's Form 1040 can be downloaded from http://www.irs.gov. Click on Forms and Pubs, and then locate the appropriate form.

Notice from Exhibit 4.1 that determining taxes requires you to address filing status, gross income, adjusted gross income, exemptions, itemized deductions, standard deduction, taxable income (adjusted gross income), tax credits, and capital gains and losses. Each of these topics is covered in this chapter so that you will be prepared to file your taxes.

Form **1040** Department of the Treasury—Internal Revenue Service (99)

U.S. Individual Income Tax Return **2014** OMB No. 1545-0074 | IRS Use Only—Do not write or staple in this space.

For the year Jan. 1–Dec. 31, 2014, or other tax year beginning , 2014, ending , 20 | **See separate instructions.**

Your first name and initial | Last name | **Your social security number**

If a joint return, spouse's first name and initial | Last name | **Spouse's social security number**

Home address (number and street). If you have a P.O. box, see instructions. | Apt. no. | ▲ **Make sure the SSN(s) above and on line 6c are correct.**

City, town or post office, state, and ZIP code. If you have a foreign address, also complete spaces below (see instructions).

Foreign country name | Foreign province/state/county | Foreign postal code

Presidential Election Campaign
Check here if you, or your spouse if filing jointly, want $3 to go to this fund. Checking a box below will not change your tax or refund. ☐ You ☐ Spouse

Filing Status

Check only one box.

1 ☐ Single
2 ☐ Married filing jointly (even if only one had income)
3 ☐ Married filing separately. Enter spouse's SSN above and full name here. ▶
4 ☐ Head of household (with qualifying person). (See instructions.) If the qualifying person is a child but not your dependent, enter this child's name here. ▶
5 ☐ Qualifying widow(er) with dependent child

Exemptions

6a ☐ **Yourself.** If someone can claim you as a dependent, **do not** check box 6a . . . . . .
b ☐ **Spouse** . . . .

c **Dependents:**		(2) Dependent's social security number	(3) Dependent's relationship to you	(4) ✓ if child under age 17 qualifying for child tax credit (see instructions)
(1) First name	Last name			
				☐
				☐
				☐
				☐

If more than four dependents, see instructions and check here ▶ ☐

Boxes checked on 6a and 6b

No. of children on 6c who:
• lived with you
• did not live with you due to divorce or separation (see instructions)

Dependents on 6c not entered above

Add numbers on lines above ▶

d Total number of exemptions claimed

Income

Attach Form(s) W-2 here. Also attach Forms W-2G and 1099-R if tax was withheld.

If you did not get a W-2, see instructions.

7 Wages, salaries, tips, etc. Attach Form(s) W-2 . . . . | 7
8a **Taxable** interest. Attach Schedule B if required . . . . | 8a
b **Tax-exempt** interest. **Do not** include on line 8a . . . | 8b
9a Ordinary dividends. Attach Schedule B if required . . . . | 9a
b Qualified dividends . . . . | 9b
10 Taxable refunds, credits, or offsets of state and local income taxes . . . . . | 10
11 Alimony received . . . . | 11
12 Business income or (loss). Attach Schedule C or C-EZ . . . . | 12
13 Capital gain or (loss). Attach Schedule D if required. If not required, check here ▶ ☐ | 13
14 Other gains or (losses). Attach Form 4797 . . . . | 14
15a IRA distributions . | 15a | b Taxable amount . . . | 15b
16a Pensions and annuities | 16a | b Taxable amount . . . | 16b
17 Rental real estate, royalties, partnerships, S corporations, trusts, etc. Attach Schedule E | 17
18 Farm income or (loss). Attach Schedule F . . . . | 18
19 Unemployment compensation . . . . | 19
20a Social security benefits | 20a | b Taxable amount . . . | 20b
21 Other income. List type and amount | 21
22 Combine the amounts in the far right column for lines 7 through 21. This is your **total income** ▶ | 22

Adjusted Gross Income

23 Educator expenses . . . . | 23
24 Certain business expenses of reservists, performing artists, and fee-basis government officials. Attach Form 2106 or 2106-EZ | 24
25 Health savings account deduction. Attach Form 8889 . | 25
26 Moving expenses. Attach Form 3903 . . . . | 26
27 Deductible part of self-employment tax. Attach Schedule SE . | 27
28 Self-employed SEP, SIMPLE, and qualified plans . | 28
29 Self-employed health insurance deduction . . | 29
30 Penalty on early withdrawal of savings . . . . | 30
31a Alimony paid b Recipient's SSN ▶ | 31a
32 IRA deduction . . . . | 32
33 Student loan interest deduction . . . . . | 33
34 Tuition and fees. Attach Form 8917 . . . . | 34
35 Domestic production activities deduction. Attach Form 8903 | 35
36 Add lines 23 through 35 . . . . ▶ | 36
37 Subtract line 36 from line 22. This is your **adjusted gross income** . . . ▶ | 37

For Disclosure, Privacy Act, and Paperwork Reduction Act Notice, see separate instructions. | Cat. No. 11320B | Form **1040** (2014)

EXHIBIT 4.1 Form 1040 (Page 2)

Form 1040 (2014)   Page **2**

	38	Amount from line 37 (adjusted gross income)	**38**

Tax and Credits

39a	Check if: □ **You** were born before January 2, 1950, □ Blind. / □ **Spouse** was born before January 2, 1950, □ Blind. } **Total boxes checked ▶ 39a**		
b	If your spouse itemizes on a separate return or you were a dual-status alien, check here ▶ **39b** □		

Standard Deduction for—
- People who check any box on line 39a or 39b **or** who can be claimed as a dependent, see instructions.
- All others:
Single or Married filing separately, $6,200
Married filing jointly or Qualifying widow(er), $12,400
Head of household, $9,100

40	**Itemized deductions** (from Schedule A) **or** your **standard deduction** (see left margin) . .	**40**
41	Subtract line 40 from line 38	**41**
42	**Exemptions.** If line 38 is $152,525 or less, multiply $3,950 by the number on line 6d. Otherwise, see instructions	**42**
43	**Taxable income.** Subtract line 42 from line 41. If line 42 is more than line 41, enter -0- . . .	**43**
44	**Tax** (see instructions). Check if any from: **a** □ Form(s) 8814 **b** □ Form 4972 **c** □	**44**
45	**Alternative minimum tax** (see instructions). Attach Form 6251	**45**
46	Excess advance premium tax credit repayment. Attach Form 8962	**46**
47	Add lines 44, 45, and 46 . . . . ▶	**47**
48	Foreign tax credit. Attach Form 1116 if required	**48**	
49	Credit for child and dependent care expenses. Attach Form 2441	**49**	
50	Education credits from Form 8863, line 19 . . .	**50**	
51	Retirement savings contributions credit. Attach Form 8880	**51**	
52	Child tax credit. Attach Schedule 8812, if required . . .	**52**	
53	Residential energy credits. Attach Form 5695 . . .	**53**	
54	Other credits from Form: **a** □ 3800 **b** □ 8801 **c** □	**54**	
55	Add lines 48 through 54. These are your **total credits**	**55**
56	Subtract line 55 from line 47. If line 55 is more than line 47, enter -0- . . ▶	**56**

Other Taxes

57	Self-employment tax. Attach Schedule SE	**57**
58	Unreported social security and Medicare tax from Form: **a** □ 4137 **b** □ 8919	**58**
59	Additional tax on IRAs, other qualified retirement plans, etc. Attach Form 5329 if required	**59**
60a	Household employment taxes from Schedule H	**60a**
b	First-time homebuyer credit repayment. Attach Form 5405 if required . . .	**60b**
61	Health care: individual responsibility (see instructions) Full-year coverage □ .	**61**
62	Taxes from: **a** □ Form 8959 **b** □ Form 8960 **c** □ Instructions; enter code(s)	**62**
63	Add lines 56 through 62. This is your **total tax** . . . . . . ▶	**63**

Payments

If you have a qualifying child, attach Schedule EIC.

64	Federal income tax withheld from Forms W-2 and 1099 . .	**64**	
65	2014 estimated tax payments and amount applied from 2013 return	**65**	
66a	**Earned income credit (EIC)**	**66a**	
b	Nontaxable combat pay election	**66b**	
67	Additional child tax credit. Attach Schedule 8812	**67**	
68	American opportunity credit from Form 8863, line 8 . . .	**68**	
69	Net premium tax credit. Attach Form 8962	**69**	
70	Amount paid with request for extension to file	**70**	
71	Excess social security and tier 1 RRTA tax withheld	**71**	
72	Credit for federal tax on fuels. Attach Form 4136 . . .	**72**	
73	Credits from Form: **a** □ 2439 **b** □ Reserved **c** □ Reserved **d** □	**73**	
74	Add lines 64, 65, 66a, and 67 through 73. These are your **total payments** . . . ▶	**74**

Refund

Direct deposit? See instructions.

75	If line 74 is more than line 63, subtract line 63 from line 74. This is the amount you **overpaid**	**75**
76a	Amount of line 75 you want **refunded to you.** If Form 8888 is attached, check here ▶ □	**76a**
▶ **b**	Routing number [_____] ▶ **c** Type: □ Checking □ Savings	
▶ **d**	Account number [_____]	
77	Amount of line 75 you want **applied to your 2015 estimated tax** ▶	**77**

Amount You Owe

78	**Amount you owe.** Subtract line 74 from line 63. For details on how to pay, see instructions ▶	**78**
79	Estimated tax penalty (see instructions)	**79**

Third Party Designee

Do you want to allow another person to discuss this return with the IRS (see instructions)? □ **Yes.** Complete below. □ **No**

Designee's name ▶   Phone no. ▶   Personal identification number (PIN) ▶ [_____]

Sign Here

Joint return? See instructions. Keep a copy for your records.

Under penalties of perjury, I declare that I have examined this return and accompanying schedules and statements, and to the best of my knowledge and belief, they are true, correct, and complete. Declaration of preparer (other than taxpayer) is based on all information of which preparer has any knowledge.

Your signature	Date	Your occupation	Daytime phone number
Spouse's signature. If a joint return, **both** must sign.	Date	Spouse's occupation	If the IRS sent you an Identity Protection PIN, enter it here (see inst.) [_____]

Paid Preparer Use Only

Print/Type preparer's name	Preparer's signature	Date	Check □ if self-employed	PTIN
Firm's name ▶			Firm's EIN ▶	
Firm's address ▶			Phone no.	

www.irs.gov/form1040   Form **1040** (2014)

Source: U.S. Department of the Treasury and the Internal Revenue Service, Form 1040 (2014).

Filing Status

Each year, taxpayers must specify a filing status when submitting their income tax return. The alternatives are

- Single
- Married filing jointly
- Married filing separately
- Head of household
- Qualifying widow(er) with dependent child

Married people usually combine their incomes and file a joint return. However, each may file a separate tax return in some circumstances. In that case, they each must file as "married filing separately" rather than as a "single" taxpayer. The "head of household" status can be selected by single people who have at least one dependent in their household. The tax rates applied when using this status may be more favorable than when filing under the "single" status. If you are a qualifying widow(er) with a dependent child, you are entitled to use the joint tax rates for two years following the death of your spouse, assuming that you do not remarry, do have a child for whom you can claim an exemption, and pay more than half the cost of maintaining your residence.

Gross Income

gross income
All reportable income from any source, including salary, net business income, interest income, dividend income, and capital gains received during the tax year.

To calculate your federal income tax, first determine your gross income. **Gross income** consists of all reportable income from any source. It includes your salary or wages, interest income, dividend income, and capital gains received during the tax year. It also includes income from your own business, as well as from tips, prizes and awards, rental property, and scholarships that exceed tuition fees and book costs. Some types of income are not taxed, including health and casualty insurance reimbursements, child support payments received, reimbursements of moving expenses and other expenses by an employer, veteran's benefits, and welfare benefits.

Wages and Salaries

If you work full-time, your main source of gross income is probably your salary. Wages and salaries, along with any bonuses, are subject to federal income taxes. Contributions to your employer-sponsored retirement account, whether made by you or your employer, are not subject to income taxes until those funds are withdrawn from the account. Consequently, they are not subject to immediate taxation. Many employees take advantage of their employer-sponsored retirement plans to reduce their current income taxes and obtain tax-deferred growth of their retirement fund.

Interest Income

interest income
Interest earned from investments in various types of savings accounts at financial institutions, from investments in debt securities such as Treasury bonds, or from providing loans to other individuals.

Individuals can earn **interest income** from investments in various types of savings accounts or certificates of deposit at financial institutions. They can also earn interest income from investing in debt securities such as Treasury bonds or from providing loans to other individuals. Note that interest income earned from investments in municipal bonds issued by state and local government agencies is normally excluded from federal taxation. Any tax-exempt interest income is not included when determining taxes.

Dividend Income

dividend income
Income received in the form of dividends paid on shares of stock or mutual funds.

Individual taxpayers can earn **dividend income** by investing in stocks or mutual funds. Some firms pay dividends to their shareholders quarterly. Other firms elect not to pay dividends to their shareholders and instead reinvest all their earnings to finance their existing operations. This can benefit shareholders because a firm's share price is more likely to appreciate over time if the firm effectively reinvests all its earnings.

Dividend income is taxed at a rate of 15% for individuals in the tax brackets of 25%, 28%, 33%, and 35%. Taxpayers in the 39.6% bracket must pay a 20% rate on their dividends. Taxpayers in the 10% and 15% tax brackets are not taxed on their dividend income as of 2015.

The worksheet for figuring your interest income and dividend income—Schedule B of Form 1040—is shown in Exhibit 4.2.

Capital Gains

capital gain
Income earned when an asset is sold at a higher price than was paid for the asset.

You can purchase securities (also called financial assets) such as stocks or debt instruments (such as bonds) that are issued by firms to raise capital. You can also invest in other income-producing assets such as rental properties. When you sell these types of assets at a higher price than you paid, you earn a **capital gain**. If you sell the assets for a lower price than you paid, you sustain a capital loss.

short-term capital gain
A gain on assets that were held less than 12 months.

long-term capital gain
A gain on assets that were held for 12 months or longer.

A **short-term capital gain** is a gain on assets that were held 12 months or less. A **long-term capital gain** is a gain on assets that were held for longer than 12 months. The short-term **capital gains tax,** the tax that is paid on short-term capital gains, is based on your marginal tax rate, as if it were additional income. The capital gains tax on a long-term capital gain mirrors the rates for taxable dividends at 0%, 15%, or 20%, depending on the taxpayer's tax bracket, and is usually lower than the tax on short-term gains. Net short-term gains and long-term gains are reported on Form 1040 in the section on gross income.

capital gains tax
The tax that is paid on a gain earned as a result of selling an asset for more than the purchase price.

Holding an investment for more than one year can yield significant tax benefits, assuming that you have a gain. As of 2015, the long-term capital gains tax is 15% for taxpayers in the 25% and higher tax brackets, but has been eliminated for taxpayers in the 10% and 15% tax brackets. Although both long-term and short-term gains from investments you have sold can be offset by realized capital losses (if you have any), the best strategy now is not to use them against each other in the same year. Consider taking short-term losses against ordinary income in one year, and allowing your long-term gain to be taxed at a preferential rate in the next year. But remember, taxation of your investments is just one consideration when deciding when to buy or sell your stocks, bonds, or mutual funds.

EXAMPLE

Suppose your income places you in the 28% tax bracket. You must pay a tax of 28% on any additional income that you earn. Stock that you purchased nearly 12 months ago has increased in value by $20,000. If you sell the stock today, your capital gain will be classified as "short-term," and you will pay a tax of 28% ($5,600) on that gain. If you hold the stock for 12 months and a day, your capital gain will be classified as "long-term," subjecting it to a 15% tax rate. Assuming the value of the stock remains unchanged, your tax on the long-term gain will be $3,000. Thus, holding the stock for at least one year would cut your taxes by $2,600.

Use the Schedule D worksheet of Form 1040, shown in Exhibit 4.3, to determine your capital gains taxes.

Determining Gross Income

Gross income is determined by adding your salary, net business income, interest income, dividend income, and capital gains.

EXAMPLE

Stephanie Spratt earned a salary of $38,000 in 2015. She earned no income from interest, dividends, or short-term capital gains. Her gross income over the year is

Salary	$38,000
+ Interest Income	0
+ Dividend Income	0
+ Capital Gain	0
= Gross Income	$38,000

EXHIBIT 4.2   Schedule B of Form 1040

SCHEDULE B			
(Form 1040A or 1040)			OMB No. 1545-0074

Interest and Ordinary Dividends
► **Attach to Form 1040A or 1040.**
► **Information about Schedule B and its instructions is at** *www.irs.gov/scheduleb.*

Department of the Treasury
Internal Revenue Service (99)

20**14**
Attachment
Sequence No. **08**

Name(s) shown on return

Your social security number

Part I

Interest

(See instructions on back and the instructions for Form 1040A, or Form 1040, line 8a.)

Note. If you received a Form 1099-INT, Form 1099-OID, or substitute statement from a brokerage firm, list the firm's name as the payer and enter the total interest shown on that form.

		Amount
1	List name of payer. If any interest is from a seller-financed mortgage and the buyer used the property as a personal residence, see instructions on back and list this interest first. Also, show that buyer's social security number and address ►	
	---	1

2	Add the amounts on line 1	2
3	Excludable interest on series EE and I U.S. savings bonds issued after 1989. Attach Form 8815	3
4	Subtract line 3 from line 2. Enter the result here and on Form 1040A, or Form 1040, line 8a . . . . ►	4

Note. If line 4 is over $1,500, you must complete Part III.

Part II

Ordinary Dividends

(See instructions on back and the instructions for Form 1040A, or Form 1040, line 9a.)

Note. If you received a Form 1099-DIV or substitute statement from a brokerage firm, list the firm's name as the payer and enter the ordinary dividends shown on that form.

		Amount
5	List name of payer ► ------------------------------	
	---	5

6	Add the amounts on line 5. Enter the total here and on Form 1040A, or Form 1040, line 9a . . . . ►	6

Note. If line 6 is over $1,500, you must complete Part III.

Part III

Foreign Accounts and Trusts

(See instructions on back.)

You must complete this part if you **(a)** had over $1,500 of taxable interest or ordinary dividends; **(b)** had a foreign account; or **(c)** received a distribution from, or were a grantor of, or a transferor to, a foreign trust.

		Yes	No
7a	At any time during 2014, did you have a financial interest in or signature authority over a financial account (such as a bank account, securities account, or brokerage account) located in a foreign country? See instructions		
	If "Yes," are you required to file FinCEN Form 114, Report of Foreign Bank and Financial Accounts (FBAR), to report that financial interest or signature authority? See FinCEN Form 114 and its instructions for filing requirements and exceptions to those requirements		
b	If you are required to file FinCEN Form 114, enter the name of the foreign country where the financial account is located ►		
8	During 2014, did you receive a distribution from, or were you the grantor of, or transferor to, a foreign trust? If "Yes," you may have to file Form 3520. See instructions on back		

For Paperwork Reduction Act Notice, see your tax return instructions.   Cat. No. 17146N   **Schedule B (Form 1040A or 1040) 2014**

Source: U.S. Department of the Treasury and the Internal Revenue Service, Form 1040 (2014).

EXHIBIT 4.3   Schedule D of Form 1040 (Page 1)

SCHEDULE D (Form 1040) Department of the Treasury Internal Revenue Service (99)	**Capital Gains and Losses** ▶ Attach to Form 1040 or Form 1040NR. ▶ Information about Schedule D and its separate instructions is at *www.irs.gov/scheduled*. ▶ Use Form 8949 to list your transactions for lines 1b, 2, 3, 8b, 9, and 10.	OMB No. 1545-0074 20**14** Attachment Sequence No. **12**

Name(s) shown on return	Your social security number

Part I   Short-Term Capital Gains and Losses—Assets Held One Year or Less

See instructions for how to figure the amounts to enter on the lines below. This form may be easier to complete if you round off cents to whole dollars.	**(d)** Proceeds (sales price)	**(e)** Cost (or other basis)	**(g)** Adjustments to gain or loss from Form(s) 8949, Part I, line 2, column (g)	**(h) Gain or (loss)** Subtract column (e) from column (d) and combine the result with column (g)
1a Totals for all short-term transactions reported on Form 1099-B for which basis was reported to the IRS and for which you have no adjustments (see instructions). However, if you choose to report all these transactions on Form 8949, leave this line blank and go to line 1b .				
1b Totals for all transactions reported on Form(s) 8949 with **Box A** checked				
2 Totals for all transactions reported on Form(s) 8949 with **Box B** checked				
3 Totals for all transactions reported on Form(s) 8949 with **Box C** checked				

4 Short-term gain from Form 6252 and short-term gain or (loss) from Forms 4684, 6781, and 8824 .	**4**	
5 Net short-term gain or (loss) from partnerships, S corporations, estates, and trusts from Schedule(s) K-1	**5**	
6 Short-term capital loss carryover. Enter the amount, if any, from line 8 of your **Capital Loss Carryover Worksheet** in the instructions	**6**	( )
7 **Net short-term capital gain or (loss).** Combine lines 1a through 6 in column (h). If you have any long-term capital gains or losses, go to Part II below. Otherwise, go to Part III on the back	**7**	

Part II   Long-Term Capital Gains and Losses—Assets Held More Than One Year

See instructions for how to figure the amounts to enter on the lines below. This form may be easier to complete if you round off cents to whole dollars.	**(d)** Proceeds (sales price)	**(e)** Cost (or other basis)	**(g)** Adjustments to gain or loss from Form(s) 8949, Part II, line 2, column (g)	**(h) Gain or (loss)** Subtract column (e) from column (d) and combine the result with column (g)
8a Totals for all long-term transactions reported on Form 1099-B for which basis was reported to the IRS and for which you have no adjustments (see instructions). However, if you choose to report all these transactions on Form 8949, leave this line blank and go to line 8b .				
8b Totals for all transactions reported on Form(s) 8949 with **Box D** checked				
9 Totals for all transactions reported on Form(s) 8949 with **Box E** checked				
10 Totals for all transactions reported on Form(s) 8949 with **Box F** checked				

11 Gain from Form 4797, Part I; long-term gain from Forms 2439 and 6252; and long-term gain or (loss) from Forms 4684, 6781, and 8824	**11**	
12 Net long-term gain or (loss) from partnerships, S corporations, estates, and trusts from Schedule(s) K-1	**12**	
13 Capital gain distributions. See the instructions	**13**	
14 Long-term capital loss carryover. Enter the amount, if any, from line 13 of your **Capital Loss Carryover Worksheet** in the instructions	**14**	( )
15 **Net long-term capital gain or (loss).** Combine lines 8a through 14 in column (h). Then go to Part III on the back	**15**	

For Paperwork Reduction Act Notice, see your tax return instructions.   Cat. No. 11338H   **Schedule D (Form 1040) 2014**

EXHIBIT 4.3   Schedule D of Form 1040 (Page 2)

Schedule D (Form 1040) 2014   Page **2**

Part III   **Summary**

16	Combine lines 7 and 15 and enter the result	**16**

- If line 16 is a **gain,** enter the amount from line 16 on Form 1040, line 13, or Form 1040NR, line 14. Then go to line 17 below.
- If line 16 is a **loss,** skip lines 17 through 20 below. Then go to line 21. Also be sure to complete line 22.
- If line 16 is **zero,** skip lines 17 through 21 below and enter -0- on Form 1040, line 13, or Form 1040NR, line 14. Then go to line 22.

17   Are lines 15 and 16 **both** gains?
☐ **Yes.** Go to line 18.
☐ **No.** Skip lines 18 through 21, and go to line 22.

18   Enter the amount, if any, from line 7 of the **28% Rate Gain Worksheet** in the instructions . . ▶   **18**

19   Enter the amount, if any, from line 18 of the **Unrecaptured Section 1250 Gain Worksheet** in the instructions . . . . ▶   **19**

20   Are lines 18 and 19 **both** zero or blank?
☐ **Yes.** Complete the **Qualified Dividends and Capital Gain Tax Worksheet** in the instructions for Form 1040, line 44 (or in the instructions for Form 1040NR, line 42). **Do not** complete lines 21 and 22 below.

☐ **No.** Complete the **Schedule D Tax Worksheet** in the instructions. **Do not** complete lines 21 and 22 below.

21   If line 16 is a loss, enter here and on Form 1040, line 13, or Form 1040NR, line 14, the **smaller** of:

- The loss on line 16 or
- ($3,000), or if married filing separately, ($1,500)   } . . . .   **21** ( )

Note. When figuring which amount is smaller, treat both amounts as positive numbers.

22   Do you have qualified dividends on Form 1040, line 9b, or Form 1040NR, line 10b?

☐ **Yes.** Complete the **Qualified Dividends and Capital Gain Tax Worksheet** in the instructions for Form 1040, line 44 (or in the instructions for Form 1040NR, line 42).

☐ **No.** Complete the rest of Form 1040 or Form 1040NR.

Schedule D (Form 1040) 2014

Source: U.S. Department of the Treasury and the Internal Revenue Service, Form 1040 (2014).

Adjusted Gross Income

adjusted gross income (AGI)
Adjusts gross income for contributions to IRAs, alimony payments, interest paid on student loans, and other special circumstances.

Your **adjusted gross income** (AGI) is calculated by adjusting your gross income for contributions to individual retirement accounts (IRAs), alimony payments, interest paid on student loans, and other special circumstances. Note that student loan interest up to $2,500 is deductible whether or not you elect to itemize and is not included as one of your itemized deductions. If you do not have any special adjustments, your adjusted gross income is the same as your gross income.

EXAMPLE

Stephanie Spratt did not contribute any of her salary to an IRA in 2015. She also does not qualify for any other special adjustments to her gross income. Therefore, her adjusted gross income is $38,000, the same as her gross income.

Deductions and Exemptions

You may be able to claim deductions and exemptions, which reduce the amount of your gross income subject to taxation. Taxpayers can choose between the higher of the standard deduction or their total itemized deductions, as described later.

Standard Deduction

standard deduction
A fixed amount that can be deducted from adjusted gross income to determine taxable income.

The **standard deduction** is a fixed amount deducted from adjusted gross income to determine taxable income. The amount of the standard deduction is not affected by the amount of income you earned during the year; instead, it varies according to your filing status and whether you are over age 65. Each year the IRS adjusts the amount of the standard deduction to keep pace with inflation. Exhibit 4.4 lists the standard deduction amounts for the 2015 tax year.

EXAMPLE

Stephanie Spratt's tax filing status is single. Therefore, she can take a standard deduction of $6,300 from her adjusted gross income. Alternatively, she can itemize her deductions (as explained next). She will take the standard deduction unless her itemized deductions exceed the standard deduction.

Itemized Deductions

itemized deductions
Specific expenses that can be deducted to reduce taxable income.

Itemized deductions are specific expenses that can be deducted to reduce taxable income. Congress has approved these itemized deductions as tax preference items to encourage certain behavior such as home ownership and support of not-for-profit organizations. We now examine several of the more common itemized deductions.

EXHIBIT 4.4	Standard Deduction Amounts for the 2015 Tax Year
Filing Status	**Standard Deduction**
Married filing jointly and surviving spouses	$12,600
Head of household	9,250
Single individuals	6,300
Married, filing separately	6,300

Interest Expense When people borrow funds to purchase a home, they pay interest expense, or interest on the money that they borrow. The annual interest payments made on such a loan are an itemized deduction. Interest payments made on car loans or personal loans, annual credit card fees, and loan fees are not tax deductible. Itemized deductions are subject to a phaseout based on the taxpayer's income. The phaseout for single taxpayers begins at $258,250, and for married, filing jointly, the phaseout begins at $309,900.

state income tax
An income tax imposed by some states on people who receive income from employers in that state.

State and Local Taxes Many states impose a **state income tax** (between 3% and 10%) on people who receive income from employers in that state. Local municipalities such as large cities or counties may also impose an income tax. These state and local taxes are deductible as itemized deductions. Deductible state and local taxes for a tax year include any amounts withheld by the taxpayer's employer and amounts paid within the calendar year for a previous tax year. Some taxpayers may elect to use the amount of their sales tax instead of state and local income taxes as an itemized deduction.

real estate tax
A tax imposed on a home or other real estate in the county where the property is located.

Real Estate Taxes Owners of homes or other real estate are subject to a **real estate tax** imposed by the county where the property is located. Real estate tax can be deducted as an itemized deduction.

Medical Expenses Taxpayers with medical expenses that exceed 10% of adjusted gross income may deduct that excess amount as an itemized deduction. Notice that the amount of medical expenses that is equal to or less than 10% of the taxpayer's AGI is not deductible. This deduction is specifically for people who incur an unusually high level of medical expenses in relation to their income in a particular year. A special 7.5% rate applies to seniors age 65 or older until 2017 when they, too, will have to meet the 10% standard.

Eligible medical expenses include diagnosing, treating, easing, or preventing disease; health insurance premiums paid for policies that cover medical care or long-term care insurance; and the cost of prescription drugs and insulin. For more examples of costs you can deduct, see IRS Publication 502, Medical and Dental Expenses. Only unreimbursed medical expenses are deductible.

Financial Planning
ONLINE

Go to:
http://www.taxadmin.org

To get:
Income tax rates and information on personal exemptions for each state.

Charitable Gifts People who make charitable gifts to qualified organizations (such as the Humane Society) can deduct their contribution as an itemized deduction. You should keep track of all your charitable contributions throughout the year, whether you paid by cash, check, or credit card. For large contributions you will need a receipt from the charitable organization, and many organizations, such as churches, will send a confirmation of all donations as a matter of policy. You may deduct the value of property donated to charitable organizations, but be careful not to overstate the value of the donated property. If it is a large amount, you should probably get a professional appraisal.

Other Expenses It may be possible to deduct a portion of losses due to casualties or theft and major job-related expenses that are not reimbursed by employers. However, these expenses are deductible only if they are substantial, as they must be in excess of specified minimum levels (based on a percentage of adjusted gross income). Note that qualified higher education expenses (other than room and board) may also be deducted.

Summary of Deductible Expenses Taxpayers add up their deductions to determine whether to itemize or use the standard deduction. If a taxpayer's itemized deductions exceed his or her standard deduction, the taxpayer should take the itemized deduction in lieu of the standard deduction.

EXAMPLE

Stephanie Spratt does not own a home; therefore, she pays no interest expense on a mortgage and pays no real estate taxes. She does not pay state income taxes in her state of Texas. She made charitable contributions amounting to $200. Her total eligible itemized deductions are

Deductions

Interest Expense	$0
State Income Taxes	0
Real Estate Taxes	0
Unreimbursed Medical	0
Charity	200
Total	$200

If Stephanie decides to take the standard deduction, she can deduct $6,300 from her gross income instead of the itemized deductions described. Because the standard deduction far exceeds her itemized deductions of $200, she elects to take the standard deduction.

The worksheet for itemized deductions is Schedule A of Form 1040 for individuals. An example of Schedule A is shown in Exhibit 4.5.

Exemptions

personal exemption
An allowable amount by which taxable income is reduced for each person supported by income reported on a tax return.

A **personal exemption** is permitted for each person who is supported by the income reported on a tax return. For example, children in a household are claimed as exemptions by their parents. Exemptions reduce taxable income even if the taxpayer decides to take the standard deduction rather than itemizing. A personal exemption can be claimed for the person filing a tax return, for a spouse, and for each dependent. Each year the amount of the exemption is adjusted for inflation. For the 2015 tax year, each personal exemption is $4,000. The total amount for exemptions is deducted from gross income to determine taxable income. Personal exemptions are subject to phaseout based on income. In 2015, the phaseout begins at $258,250 for single taxpayers and $309,900 for married taxpayers.

EXAMPLE

Stephanie Spratt is single and has no children living in her household. She can claim one exemption for herself, which allows her to deduct $4,000 from her adjusted gross income.

Taxable Income and Taxes

Before calculating the taxes that you owe, you need to determine your taxable income, as explained next.

Taxable Income

Taxable income is equal to adjusted gross income (AGI) minus deductions and exemptions.

EXHIBIT 4.5   Schedule A of Form 1040

SCHEDULE A
(Form 1040)

Department of the Treasury
Internal Revenue Service (99)

Itemized Deductions

▶ Information about Schedule A and its separate instructions is at *www.irs.gov/schedulea*.
▶ Attach to Form 1040.

OMB No. 1545-0074

20**14**

Attachment
Sequence No. **07**

Name(s) shown on Form 1040

Your social security number

Medical and Dental Expenses		**Caution.** Do not include expenses reimbursed or paid by others.	
	1	Medical and dental expenses (see instructions)	1
	2	Enter amount from Form 1040, line 38 **2**	
	3	Multiply line 2 by 10% (.10). But if either you or your spouse was born before January 2, 1950, multiply line 2 by 7.5% (.075) instead	3
	4	Subtract line 3 from line 1. If line 3 is more than line 1, enter -0-	4
Taxes You Paid	5	State and local **(check only one box):**	
		a ☐ Income taxes, **or**	5
		b ☐ General sales taxes	
	6	Real estate taxes (see instructions)	6
	7	Personal property taxes	7
	8	Other taxes. List type and amount ▶ _____	
			8
	9	Add lines 5 through 8	9
Interest You Paid	10	Home mortgage interest and points reported to you on Form 1098	10
	11	Home mortgage interest not reported to you on Form 1098. If paid to the person from whom you bought the home, see instructions and show that person's name, identifying no., and address ▶ _____	
Note. Your mortgage interest deduction may be limited (see instructions).			11
	12	Points not reported to you on Form 1098. See instructions for special rules .	12
	13	Mortgage insurance premiums (see instructions)	13
	14	Investment interest. Attach Form 4952 if required. (See instructions.)	14
	15	Add lines 10 through 14	15
Gifts to Charity	16	Gifts by cash or check. If you made any gift of $250 or more, see instructions	16
If you made a gift and got a benefit for it, see instructions.	17	Other than by cash or check. If any gift of $250 or more, see instructions. You **must** attach Form 8283 if over $500 . . .	17
	18	Carryover from prior year	18
	19	Add lines 16 through 18	19
Casualty and Theft Losses	20	Casualty or theft loss(es). Attach Form 4684. (See instructions.)	20
Job Expenses and Certain Miscellaneous Deductions	21	Unreimbursed employee expenses—job travel, union dues, job education, etc. Attach Form 2106 or 2106-EZ if required. (See instructions.) ▶ _____	21
	22	Tax preparation fees	22
	23	Other expenses—investment, safe deposit box, etc. List type and amount ▶ _____	
			23
	24	Add lines 21 through 23	24
	25	Enter amount from Form 1040, line 38 **25**	
	26	Multiply line 25 by 2% (.02)	26
	27	Subtract line 26 from line 24. If line 26 is more than line 24, enter -0-	27
Other Miscellaneous Deductions	28	Other—from list in instructions. List type and amount ▶ _____	
			28
Total Itemized Deductions	29	Is Form 1040, line 38, over $152,525?	
		☐ **No.** Your deduction is not limited. Add the amounts in the far right column for lines 4 through 28. Also, enter this amount on Form 1040, line 40.	29
		☐ **Yes.** Your deduction may be limited. See the Itemized Deductions Worksheet in the instructions to figure the amount to enter.	
	30	If you elect to itemize deductions even though they are less than your standard deduction, check here . . . . ▶ ☐	

For Paperwork Reduction Act Notice, see Form 1040 instructions.   Cat. No. 17145C   Schedule A (Form 1040) 2014

Source: U.S. Department of the Treasury and the Internal Revenue Service, Form 1040 (2014).

EXAMPLE

Recall that Stephanie Spratt's adjusted gross income is $38,000, her standard deduction is $6,300, and her personal exemption is $4,000. Therefore, her taxable income for the year is

Adjusted Gross Income	$38,000
− Deductions	6,300
− Exemptions	4,000
= Taxable Income	$27,700

Calculating Taxes

Once you know what your taxable income is, you can use a table such as Exhibit 4.6 to determine the taxes that you owe. Taxes are dependent not only on your taxable income, but also on your filing status. Exhibit 4.6 shows the tax schedules for different filing statuses for the 2015 tax year. Notice that the income tax system in the United States is progressive. That is, the higher an individual's income, the higher the percentage of income paid in taxes.

There are seven different tax rates or brackets. For 2015, those income tax rates are 10%, 15%, 25%, 28%, 33%, 35%, and 39.6%. Each taxpayer begins paying taxes at the lowest level until their income exceeds that level. Then, their next dollars are taxed at the next higher level until that bracket is exceeded and so on. In general, for the two lowest levels, the married filing jointly brackets are twice as broad as similar brackets for single taxpayers. Eventually, however, at the highest level, the 39.6% level, all taxpayers begin to pay the same rate once their income reaches $464,850, no matter what filing status the taxpayer claims.

Determining Your Tax Liability To determine your tax liability, simply refer to your filing status and follow the instructions at the top of the columns of the tax schedule. Converting the instructions into a formula gives the following equation for the tax liability:

$$\text{Tax Liability} = \text{Tax on Base} + [\text{Percentage on Excess over the Base} \times (\text{Taxable Income} - \text{Base})]$$

Financial Planning
ONLINE

Go to:
http://www.turbotax.com

To get:
An estimate of your tax liability for the year and the tax refund that you will receive (if you already paid in more taxes than your tax liability), based on your income, filing status, exemptions, and deductions.

EXAMPLE

marginal tax bracket
The tax rate imposed on any additional (marginal) income earned.

Stephanie Spratt's taxable income is $27,700. Her filing status is single.

Stephanie uses the following steps to determine her taxes:

- Her 2015 taxable income falls within the second bracket in Panel A, from $9,225 to $37,450.

- The base of that bracket is $9,225. The tax on the base is $922.50, as shown in the second column of Panel A.

- The tax rate applied to the excess income over the base is 15%, as shown in the third column of Panel A. This means that Stephanie's **marginal tax bracket** is 15%, so any additional (marginal) income that she earns is subject to a 15% tax. Note that if she had earned an additional $9,750, her marginal income tax rate would have increased to 25% making any subsequent income taxable at the 25% rate.

- Stephanie's excess income over the base is $18,475 (computed as $27,700 − $9,225). Thus, the tax on the excess over the base is $2,771.25 (computed as $18,475 × 15%).

EXHIBIT 4.6   Tax Rate Schedules for 2015

Tax Rate – Single Taxpayers – 2015

Taxable income:

Over—	But not over—	Tax	+%	On amount over—
$ 0	$ 9,225	$ 0.00	10	$ 0
9,225	37,450	922.50	15	9,225
37,450	90,750	5,156.25	25	37,450
90,750	189,300	18,481.25	28	90,750
189,300	411,500	46,075.25	33	189,300
411,500	413,200	119,401.25	35	411,500
413,200	--------	119,996.25	39.6	413,200

Tax Rates – Married Individuals Filing Jointly and Surviving Spouses – 2015

Taxable income:

Over—	But not over—	Tax	+%	On amount over—
$ 0	$ 18,450	$ 0.00	10	$ 0
18,450	74,900	1,845.00	15	18,450
74,900	151,200	10,312.50	25	74,900
151,200	230,450	29,387.50	28	151,200
230,450	411,500	51,577.50	33	230,450
411,500	464,850	111,324.00	35	411,500
464,850	--------	129,996.50	39.6	464,850

Tax Rates – Married Individuals Filing Separately – 2015

Taxable income:

Over—	But not over—	Tax	+%	On amount over—
$ 0	$ 9,225	$ 0.00	10	$ 0
9,225	37,450	922.50	15	9,225
37,450	75,600	5,156.25	25	37,450
75,600	115,225	14,693.75	28	75,600
115,225	205,750	25,788.75	33	115,225
205,750	232,425	55,662.00	35	205,750
232,425	--------	64,989.25	39.6	232,425

Tax Rates – Head of household – 2015

Taxable income:

Over—	But not over—	Tax	+%	On amount over—
$ 0	$ 13,150	$ 0.00	10	$ 0
13,150	50,200	1,315.00	15	13,150
50,200	129,600	6,872.50	25	50,200
129,600	209,850	26,722.50	28	129,600
209,850	411,500	49,192.50	33	209,850
411,500	439,000	115,737.00	35	411,500
439,000	--------	125,362.00	39.6	439,000

In summary, her tax liability is:

Tax = Tax on Base

Liability + [Percentage on Excess over the Base × (Taxable Income − Base)]

$= \$922.50 + [15\% \times (\$27,700 - \$9,225)]$

$= \$922.50 + [15\% \times \$18,475]$

$= \$922.50 + \$2,771.25$

$= \$3,693.75$

This tax liability represents about 10% of her income. However, recall that she also paid $2,907 in FICA taxes. Thus, Stephanie's total taxes are $6,600.75 (calculated as $3,693.75 + $2,907), or about 17% of her income.

Tax Credits

tax credits
Specific amounts used to directly reduce tax liability.

You may be able to reduce your tax liability if you are eligible for tax credits. **Tax credits** offset taxes, as the full amount of the tax credit is subtracted from taxes owed: A tax credit of $1,000 will reduce your taxes by $1,000. Compare this result with the effect of a $1,000 deduction. The deduction reduces your taxable income by $1,000, but reduces your taxes by only a proportion of that amount. For this reason, a dollar's worth of tax credits is more valuable than a dollar's worth of deductions.

child tax credit
A tax credit allowed for each child in a household.

Child Credits   A **child tax credit** is a tax credit allowed for each child in a household who is less than 17 years old at the end of the tax year. The child must be either a U.S. citizen or a resident alien. The current level of the child tax credit is $1,000 per child. The child tax credit is not available to households above certain income levels. A key provision of the child tax credit is that it is available as a refund to low-income workers who owe no income tax. Beginning in 2017, the part of the Child Tax Credit that is refundable will no longer be available. The credit will not be allowed to exceed the taxpayer's liability.

college expense credits
A tax credit allowed to those who contribute toward their own or their dependents' college expenses.

College Expense Credits   There are two available **college expense credits**, which can help you or your parents to pay for your college expenses. The American Opportunity Tax Credit (formerly the Hope tax credit) allows parents or students to receive a tax credit equal to $2,000 for the first $2,000 that they spend on college expenses in each of the first four years of college. They also receive a 25% tax credit on the next $2,000 spent on college (or up to $500) for each child or by the student in each of the first four years of college. The maximum credit per student is $2,500 per year, and, if the credit is claimed by the parent, the child must be claimed as a dependent on his or her parents' tax return. Self-supporting students can use the tax credits to reduce their own taxes. If the credit pays your tax down to zero, you can have 40% of the remaining amount of the credit (up to $1,000) refunded to you.

The Lifetime Learning tax credit allows students or their parents to claim 20% of the first $10,000 of college expenses per year as a tax credit. Educational institutions issue Form 1098-T, Tuition Statement, to students by January 31. This form will help you determine your eligibility for education credits. The Lifetime Learning Credit is not refundable. So, you can use the credit to pay any tax you owe, but you won't receive any of the credit back as a refund. Both the American Opportunity Tax Credit and the Lifetime Learning tax credit are phased out for higher-income taxpayers. The American Opportunity Tax Credit and the Lifetime Learning tax credit cannot both be claimed for the same student in the same year.

Coverdell Savings Accounts
Tax-free accounts that can be used for a variety of school expenses.

Coverdell Savings Accounts As a result of the Tax Relief Act of 2001, **Coverdell Savings Accounts** (previously called Education IRAs) allow contributions of up to $2,000 per year (the previous limit was $500 per year). Once used solely to save for college expenses, these accounts can now be used for a wide variety of elementary and high school expenses including tuition, fees, academic tutoring, books, supplies, equipment, and "special needs services" for special needs students. Contributions are in after-tax dollars, but become tax-free if withdrawals are used for appropriate education expenses. The 2001 Tax Relief Act also extended the contribution deadline from December 31 to April 15 to resemble other IRA accounts. In 2013, the $2,000 contribution limit was made permanent, and the Coverdell Savings Accounts continues to be available for K–12 educational expenses as well as college expenses.

Section 529 College Savings Plan State and private universities can also offer prepaid tuition programs with tax benefits. In 2001, the tax laws were changed to allow substantial tax benefits for parents who wish to set aside money for their children's future college expenses. When parents invest funds in the Section 529 college savings plan, any income or gains from the investment will not be taxed at the federal level as long as the funds are ultimately used to pay for college expenses. Some states impose a state tax when funds are withdrawn and used to pay college expenses.

All parents are eligible for the 529 plan, regardless of their income. They can contribute up to $300,000 in the account, depending on the state's requirements. If the parents decide not to use the funds to pay for the designated child's college expenses, they can withdraw the funds but are subject to significant penalties.

There are expenses associated with college savings plans. Advisers who help parents establish the accounts and investment firms that manage the accounts charge fees. Each state has its own specific investment manager and investment options. Parents can request that the money be invested in a specific portfolio by the designated investment firm for that state. The performance of the money contributed by the parents will match the growth or decline of the portfolio value.

earned income credit
A credit used to reduce tax liability for low-income taxpayers.

Earned Income Credit The **earned income credit** is a special credit for low-income taxpayers that reduces the amount of taxes owed, if any. To qualify, you must work, have earned income, and have investment income of less than $3,400 in 2015. Adjusted gross income in 2015 for single taxpayers must be less than $14,820 for taxpayers without a qualifying child, less than $39,131 for those with one qualifying child, less than $44,454 for those with two qualifying children, and less than $47,747 for those with three or more qualifying children. The income limits for married taxpayers are slightly higher.

FREE APPS
for Personal Finance

Qualifying for the Earned Income Tax Credit

Application:
The TurboTax Tax Preparation app (by Intuit) allows you to determine if you qualify for the earned income tax credit.

To Find It:
Search for the "TurboTax" app on your mobile device.

Other Tax Credits Other tax credits are available for those who qualify. For example, there are tax credits for child care and adoptions. The child and dependent care tax credit amount is based on the expenses incurred if you paid someone to care for a child under age 13 or a disabled person who could not care for herself or himself. This tax credit may be reduced due to income limits.

How Tax Planning Fits Within Your Financial Plan

Tax planning involves taking actions throughout the year to be able to pay the least amount of taxes allowed by law. The key tax planning decisions for building your financial plan are

- What tax savings are currently available to you?
- How can you increase your tax savings in the future?
- Should you increase or decrease the amount of your withholding?
- What records should you keep?

If you are about to file your taxes, it is generally too late to take steps to lower your taxes other than to make sure that you include all the exemptions and deductions for which you are eligible. One exception is a contribution to a traditional IRA for those without a qualified plan at work.

Tax planning is more effective when done in advance of the tax year and throughout the tax year. When you are considering whether or not to make a donation to a charitable organization, you should recognize that contributing a larger amount may increase your itemized deductions, but will be totally ineffective as a tax reduction strategy if the total of your itemized deductions fails to exceed the standard deduction amount. If you own stocks, bonds, or mutual funds that are valued at less than their purchase price, you may want to sell the losers this year to apply the capital loss (up to $3,000) against ordinary income. Likewise, you can delay selling winners until after December 31 to push the taxable income into the next tax year.

Because individuals who earn a high level of income can be exposed to very high tax rates, they should consider ways to reduce their tax liability. Some of the most useful strategies to reduce taxes are having a mortgage (because mortgage interest payments can be claimed as an itemized deduction), investing in retirement accounts that offer tax advantages, investing in stocks that pay no dividends, and investing in municipal bonds whose interest is exempt from federal taxes. These strategies are discussed in more detail later in the text.

You may be one of those taxpayers who enjoys getting a large tax refund each year, but in reality that is not an efficient use of your capital. If you have too much withheld in taxes, you are in effect making an interest-free loan to the government while foregoing the use of that cash to pay off credit cards or make investments. However, if withholding too much helps to ensure that you do not have to scramble to make your tax payment on April 15, then consider doing so. Some taxpayers use their tax refund to pay for upcoming summer vacations or large consumer purchases for which they may not have the self-discipline to save.

Some actions that you take now will make tax filing easier in the future. For example, if you buy stock within the year but expect to retain the stock for several years, you should always maintain a record of the purchase transaction so that you will be able to calculate the gain or loss when you eventually sell the stock. You need to retain a copy of each of your tax returns for at least seven years and retain your supporting documents as well.

An example of how the tax concepts apply to Stephanie Spratt's financial plan is provided in Exhibit 4.7.

Free Apps
for Personal
Finance

Estimating Your Tax

Application:

Use the TaxCaster app (by Intuit) to estimate your taxes, and estimate the tax refund that you are due based on the input (your income, etc.) you provide.

To Find It:

Search for the "TaxCaster" app on your mobile device.

EXHIBIT 4.7   Application of Tax Concepts to Stephanie Spratt's Financial Plan

GOALS FOR TAX PLANNING

1. *Reduce taxable income (thereby reducing taxes paid) to the extent allowable by the IRS.*
2. *Reduce taxes paid by deferring income.*

ANALYSIS

Present Situation:

Gross Income = *$38,000*

Federal Income Taxes = *$3,693.75*

Taxes (excluding FICA) as a Percentage of Income = *10%*

Reduce Taxes by:	Comment
Increasing deductions?	*The only qualified deduction I had was a charitable contribution of $200, so this is not an option for me this year.*
Reducing gross income?	*I did not contribute any portion of my income to an individual retirement account or a qualified retirement plan.*
Total tax savings?	*$0 per year*

Long-Term Tax Plan:

Reduce Taxes by:	Comment
Increasing deductions?	*If I purchase a home, the interest expense on my mortgage loan, as well as the real estate taxes, will help boost my itemized deductions. These deductions will likely be higher than the standard deduction to which I would be entitled. In addition, my sales taxes can be counted toward my itemized deductions.*
Reducing gross income?	*I can also contribute to an IRA or to my employer's qualified retirement plan. If I can afford to contribute $5,000 of my salary to either the IRA or the qualified plan, I will reduce my gross income and defer taxes on that portion of my income.*

Tax savings (computed below) *$877.50*

To compute my estimated tax savings, I will compare the taxes paid under my current situation to what I would pay if I bought a home and paid $6,000 in mortgage interest and real estate taxes and contribute $5,000 to my IRA. My estimated tax deduction will be $600 and my charitable contributions will remain at $200.

Category	Current Situation	Long-Term Plan
Gross Income	$38,000	$38,000
– IRA contribution	$0	$5,000
= Adjusted gross income	$38,000	$33,000
– Deductions	$6,300	$6,800
– Exemptions	$4,000	$4,000
= Taxable income	$27,700	$22,200
Tax liability (based on applying tax rates to the taxable income)	$3,693.75	$2,868.75

Approximate Total Tax Savings = *$825.00 per year**

*Actual tax savings will change each year as the mortgage interest declines, as changes occur in other itemized deductions, and as the standard deduction increases.

(continues)

EXHIBIT 4.7   Application of Tax Concepts to Stephanie Spratt's Financial Plan

DECISIONS

Decisions Regarding Tax Savings for This Year:

So far I have only taken advantage of one tax reduction strategy.

Decisions Regarding Tax Savings in the Future:

I can improve my cash flows over time by taking advantage of tax deductions. If I buy a home, the interest that I would pay on the mortgage loan, as well as the real estate taxes I would be assessed, is tax-deductible. The purchase of a home would likely increase my monthly cash outflows, but I would benefit from deducting the interest payments and real estate taxes as itemized deductions, thereby reducing my taxable income.

As my income increases, my tax bracket may increase. I need to maximize my potential tax savings to limit the taxes I will pay. I should contribute the maximum allowable amount to my retirement plan (without compromising my cash budget) so that I can take full advantage of the related tax savings. Also, I hope to buy a home in the future. The interest I will pay on a mortgage loan for this home will be high, but I will enjoy tax savings, while also building equity in my home.

DISCUSSION QUESTIONS

1. How would Stephanie's tax planning decisions be different if she were a single mother of two children?

2. How would Stephanie's tax planning decisions be affected if she were 35 years old? If she were 50 years old?

SUMMARY

Tax Filing Status. The first step in filing a federal income tax return is to determine your filing status. It is important to select the correct filing status so that you pay the correct amount of taxes. In a few cases, you may have a choice, and the status chosen can affect the taxes that you owe. Gross income consists primarily of your salary or wages, interest income, dividend income from investments in stocks, and capital gains. A short-term capital gain is realized on an asset held for a period one year or less and is counted as ordinary income. A long-term capital gain is subject to a capital gain tax, which is generally lower than a person's ordinary income tax rate.

Gross Income. Your adjusted gross income (AGI) is calculated by adjusting gross income for any contributions to an individual retirement account (IRA) and for some other special circumstances. The adjusted gross income must be determined because it is used to determine eligibility for personal exemptions, itemized deductions, and IRA contributions.

Deductions and Exemptions. Deductions and exemptions are relevant because they are subtracted from your adjusted gross income before determining your taxes. Thus, they reduce the amount of taxes owed. Deductions include interest expenses incurred from holding a mortgage, state income taxes, property taxes, unreimbursed medical expenses, charitable contributions, and some other expenses. Exemptions are allowed for persons supported by the income reported on a tax return. You can elect to use itemized deductions instead of the standard deduction, if doing so provides you with greater tax benefits.

Taxable Income. Your taxable income is determined by subtracting the total value of your deductions and exemptions from your adjusted gross income. Your tax liability is dependent on your taxable income, and the tax rate applied is dependent on your filing status and income level.

REVIEW QUESTIONS

All Review Questions are available in MyFinanceLab at http://www.myfinancelab.com.

1. **Tax Consequences.** Why is it important to understand the tax consequences of your financial decisions?

2. **FICA Taxes.** What are FICA taxes? Describe the two portions of FICA and explain what they pay for. Who pays FICA?

3. **Self-Employment Taxes.** How are FICA taxes for self-employed individuals handled?

4. **Tax Forms.** Who typically files Form 1040EZ? Which tax form do most other individual taxpayers file?

5. **Filing Status.** What are the five filing statuses? Briefly describe how your filing status is determined. What parts of the tax form are affected by your filing status?

6. **Gross Income.** What is gross income? List some types of income that are included in gross income. What are some types of payments that you might receive that would not be included in gross income?

7. **Capital Gains.** What are capital gains? When is a capital gain considered short term? When is it considered long term? Why is this distinction important?

8. **Adjusted Gross Income.** How is adjusted gross income determined?

9. **Standard Deduction.** What is a standard deduction? What is the standard deduction based on?

10. **Itemized Deductions.** What are itemized deductions? How do itemized deductions relate to standard deductions? Provide some examples of itemized deductions.

11. **Exemptions.** What is an exemption? How many exemptions may a taxpayer claim?

12. **Taxable Income.** How is taxable income calculated?

13. **Marginal Tax Bracket.** What is a marginal tax bracket? Why is it important?

14. **Tax Deduction versus Credit.** What is the difference between a tax deduction and a tax credit? Which is more valuable?

15. **Tax Credits.** List some common types of tax credits.

16. **Gross Income.** Which of the following would be included in gross income?

Salary	Prizes
Business income	Tips
Veteran's benefits	Welfare benefits
Alimony	Dividend income
Child support	Interest income

17. **Interest versus Dividend Income.** Distinguish between interest income and dividend income. Does their treatment differ for tax purposes?

18. **Medical Expenses.** Are your total medical expenses deductible? Explain.

19. **Capital Gains Taxes.** Do investors in a low tax bracket or a high tax bracket benefit to a greater degree from the long-term capital gains tax? Explain.

20. **Tax Form.** Which form must be filed with the IRS for itemized deductions?

21. **Federal Tax System.** What is the purpose of income tax? Who administers the federal tax system?

22. **Affordable Care Act of 2010.** How did the Affordable Care Act of 2010 affect tax filing?

23. **Special Tax Relief.** In the past, the federal government has implemented tax relief initiatives for various reasons. List some recent examples of targeted tax relief.

24. **American Taxpayers Relief Act of 2012.** List some of the primary features of the American Taxpayers Relief Act of 2012.

25. **Marital Status.** How are same-sex couples treated for tax purposes?

26. **Coverdell Savings Account.** What is a Coverdell Savings Account? List some expenses that can be paid with Coverdell funds.

27. **Earned Income Credit.** What is an earned income credit? Explain why this credit is sometimes called a negative income tax.

28. **Section 529 College Savings Plan.** What is a Section 529 College Savings Plan? What are the income limits for parents who desire to take advantage of this plan?

FINANCIAL PLANNING PROBLEMS

All Financial Planning Problems are available in MyFinanceLab *at http://www.myfinancelab.com.*

1. **Tax Calculations.** Alys makes $450 per week. How much will be withheld from her weekly check for Social Security tax? Medicare tax? Total FICA taxes?

2. **FICA Contributions.** Brian makes $27,000 per year. How much can he expect to contribute to FICA taxes in 2015? How much will his employer contribute?

3. **FICA Taxes.** Matt is self-employed as a carpenter. He made $42,000 after expenses in 2015. How much did he contribute to FICA taxes?

4. **Capital Gains Tax.** Stephen is in a 15% marginal tax bracket. In 2015, he sold stock that he had held for nine months for a gain of $1,900. How much tax must he pay on this capital gain? How much would the tax be if he had held the stock for 13 months?

5. **Capital Gains Tax.** Stuart is in the 25% tax bracket. Recently, he sold stock that he had held longer than a year for a gain of $20,000. How much tax will Stuart pay on this gain?

6. **Capital Gains Tax.** Jordan sold a stock that he held for 11 months at a capital gain of $10,000. He is in the 25% marginal tax bracket. What taxes will he pay on this gain?

7. **Deductions.** Emily and Paul are married and filed a joint return for 2015. The standard deduction for their filing status is $12,600. They have the following itemized deductions:

Medical bills above the 10% limit	$400
Mortgage interest	3,500
State income taxes	1,500
Charitable contributions	250

Should Emily and Paul itemize their deductions or use the standard deduction?

8. **Itemized Deduction.** Emma's adjusted gross income is $24,200. She has $1,800 in unreimbursed medical expenses. How much in medical expenses can Emma claim as an itemized deduction?

9. **Itemized Deduction.** Dawn's adjusted gross income is $16,700. Dawn has $1,800 in unreimbursed medical expenses. How much can Dawn claim as an itemized deduction?

10. **Taxable Income.** Nick and Nora are married and have three children in college. They have an adjusted gross income of $47,400. If their standard deduction is $12,600, itemized deductions are $14,200, and they get an exemption of $4,000 for each adult and each dependent, what is their taxable income?

11. **Change in Taxable Income.** Using the information in problem 10, if Nick and Nora's itemized deductions increase by $2,000, how will their taxable income be affected?

12. **Impact on Taxes.** Daniel has a marginal tax rate of 25%. He suddenly realizes that he neglected to include a $1,000 tax deduction. How will this oversight affect his taxes?

13. **Impact on Taxes.** If Daniel (from problem 12) had forgotten a $1,000 tax credit (instead of a $1,000 tax deduction), how would his taxes be affected?

14. **Itemized Deductions.** Tracy is single and had an adjusted gross income of $37,000 in 2015. Tracy also has the following items:

Unreimbursed medical expenses	$3,000
State income tax	1,850
Interest expense (first mortgage)	3,040
Interest expense (second mortgage)	1,200
Real estate tax	700
Interest expense—car loan	550
Interest expense—credit card	125
Gifts to charity	300

How much may Tracy claim as itemized deductions?

15. **Taxable Income.** Using the information in problem 14, if Tracy's standard deduction is $6,300 and her exemption is $4,000, what is her taxable income?

16. **Dividend Income.** Margo is in the 39.6% marginal tax bracket. What is her tax liability on dividend income of $6,000?

17. **FICA Taxes and High Incomes.** Jauna made $178,400 in salary during 2015. How much were her FICA withholdings for that year?

18. **Ethical Dilemma.** The IRS tax code allows for the deduction of expenses incurred in traveling to a job interview. Sean, Erica, and their two children have used this deduction to fund their vacations for the last eight years. Each year, several months prior to their vacation, Sean and Erica begin reviewing the online job ads in the cities they plan to visit. They each apply for several jobs for which they are qualified. Any applications that result in interviews are scheduled during their vacation. They are careful to deduct only those expenses allowed under the IRS tax code, such as mileage, meals (not the children's), and hotel and motel expenses (not their children's). This plan

has resulted in between $300 and $500 in allowable tax deductions each year. Sean and Erica have determined that in most cases they would not accept the jobs if offered; however, if the perfect offer presents, they would give it serious consideration.

a. Discuss whether you think Sean and Erica are being ethical in using the IRS tax code to fund part of the expenses of their family vacation.

b. Do you see other areas of the tax code discussed in this chapter that could be subject to abuses?

FINANCIAL PLANNING ONLINE EXERCISES

1. Go to http://www.smbiz.com and, in the Reference Section, click on Corporate and Individual Tax Rates to find the latest individual tax rates, deductions, exemptions, and other tax data.

   a. What is the 2015 income limit that may entitle a single taxpayer with no dependents to the earned income tax credit?

   b. What is the maximum amount of the adoption credit?

   c. What is the modified adjusted gross income at which the American Opportunity Tax Credit begins to phase out for joint returns? For all others?

2. Go to Federation of Tax Administrators' Web site at http://www.taxadmin.org, click on "Tax Rates/Surveys," then "State Tax Summary Tables Updated through January 1, 2015." Finally, click on "State Individual Income Taxes," and answer the following questions based on the state in which you live (if there are no taxes in your state, select another state where taxes are imposed):

   a. What are the lowest and highest tax rates in your state?

   b. How many tax brackets are there?

   c. What is the exemption for a single taxpayer, for a married couple, and per child?

   d. Are your federal taxes deductible?

3. Go to http://www.turbotax.com, go to "Tax calculators" under "Tools & Tips," and click "TaxCaster calculator" to answer the following questions:

   a. Assume that your filing status is single, you are not head of household, and you are 35 years old. Compute your refund based on the following data: Your wages were $65,000, and you had $15,000 withheld for federal taxes and $3,000 for state taxes.

   b. Compute your refund using the same data as in 3a except that you are married and filing jointly, and your spouse is also 35 years old.

   c. Assume the same facts as in 3b except that you own a home on which you paid $15,000 in interest and $5,000 in real estate taxes during the tax year. Compute your refund.

   d. Using the same facts as in 3c, assume that you and your spouse both contributed $2,000 to a traditional IRA. Compute your refund.

PSYCHOLOGY OF PERSONAL FINANCE: Your Taxes

1. This chapter explains how a portion of your income is withheld throughout the year by your employer, as required by the Internal Revenue Service (IRS). You may have some flexibility on how much income can be withheld. A psychological advantage of this so-called withholding tax is that the funds are pulled from your income before you receive your paycheck. It is as if that portion of your income was never yours anyway. It may be even more painful to receive all the income and then have to pay a portion of the income in taxes later. If you have a choice, would you prefer to have a higher or lower amount of income withheld? Explain your opinion.

2. Read one practical article of how psychology affects behavior when paying taxes. You can easily retrieve possible articles by doing an online search using the terms "psychology" and "paying taxes." Summarize the main points of the article.

WEB SEARCH EXERCISE

You can develop your personal finance skills by conducting an Internet search for related articles. Find a recent online article about personal finance that reinforces one or more concepts covered in this chapter. If your class has an online component, your professor may ask you to post your summary of the article there and provide a link to the article so that other students can access it. If your class is live, your professor may ask you to summarize your application of the article in class. Your professor may assign specific students to complete this assignment or may allow any student to do the assignment on a volunteer basis.

For recent online articles related to this chapter, consider using the following search terms (be sure to include the current year as a search term to ensure that the online articles are recent):

- How taxes affect your lifestyle
- How to reduce your taxes
- Tax tips
- Organizing your tax receipts
- How education can reduce your taxes
- Your tax planning

VIDEO EXERCISE: Tax Saving Tips

Go to one of the Web sites that contains video clips (such as http://www.youtube.com) and review some video clips that are available about reducing your taxes. You can use search phrases in the Web site such as "tax savings tips." Select one video clip on this topic that you would recommend for the other students in your class.

1. Provide the Web link for the video clip.
2. What do you think is the main point of this video clip?
3. How might you reduce your taxes as a result of watching this video clip?

BUILDING YOUR OWN FINANCIAL PLAN

By properly managing your tax situation, you can significantly improve your annual cash flow situation and enhance your ability to achieve your goals in a timely fashion.

This case will give you some insights into what employee benefits you should look for from a prospective employer. Talk to friends and relatives, and find out how they reduce their taxes and achieve their financial goals.

Another crucial element of proper tax management is the selection of an appropriate tax preparer. Your options vary from doing your own tax return to engaging the services of a certified public accountant. As your personal financial situation becomes more complex (e.g., you have a home, you itemize, your portfolio grows to include international stocks), you may need a tax preparer with more advanced skills. Be sure that the skills of your tax preparer are a match for the sophistication level of your personal financial situation.

Go to the worksheets at the end of this chapter to continue building your own financial plan.

THE SAMPSONS—A Continuing Case

Dave and Sharon Sampson want to determine their taxes for the current year. Dave will earn $48,000 this year, while Sharon's earnings from her part-time job will be $12,000. Neither Dave nor Sharon contributes to a retirement plan at this time. Recall that they have two children. Assume child tax credits are currently $1,000 per child. The Sampsons will pay $6,300 in home mortgage interest and $1,200 in real estate taxes this year, and they will make charitable contributions of $600 for the year. The Sampsons are filing jointly.

Go to the worksheets at the end of this chapter to continue this case.

PART 1: BRAD BROOKS—A Continuing Case

Your childhood friend, Brad Brooks, has asked you to help him gain control of his personal finances. Single and 30 years old, Brad is employed as a salesperson for a technology company. His annual salary is $48,000. He claims no exemptions (he enjoys the big refund check in May), and after Social Security, Medicare, and federal, state, and local income taxes, his monthly disposable income is $2,743. Brad has recently moved from his comfortable two-bedroom apartment with rent of $600 per month to a condo that rents for $1,000 per month. The condo is in a plush property owner's association with two golf courses, a lake, and an activity center. You review his other monthly expenses and find the following:

Renter's insurance	$20
Car payment (balance on car loan $10,000; market value of car $11,000)	500
Utilities (gas, electric, Internet)	200
Smartphone	250
Miscellaneous expenses	50
Groceries	200
Clothes	100
Car expenses (gas, insurance, maintenance)	250
Entertainment (dining out, golf, weekend trips)	400

Brad is surprised at how much money he spends on clothes and entertainment. He uses his credit cards for these purchases (the balance is $8,000 and climbing) and has little trouble making the required monthly payments. He would, however, like to see the balance go down and eventually pay it off completely.

Brad's other goal is to save $4,000 a year so that he can retire 25 years from now. Brad currently has about $4,000 in his checking account and $200 in his savings account (the balance necessary to receive no-fee checking). He has furniture valued at $1,500 and owns $1,300 of tech stocks, which he believes have the potential to make him rich.

Turn to the worksheets at the end of this chapter to continue this case.

CHAPTER 4: BUILDING YOUR OWN FINANCIAL PLAN

YOUR GOALS FOR CHAPTER 4

1. Reduce taxable income (thereby reducing taxes paid) to the extent allowable by the IRS.
2. Reduce taxes paid by deferring income.

ANALYSIS

1. Use the following worksheet to estimate your federal income tax liability based on the 2012 guide-lines presented in the text or current tax regulations and rates. (The Excel worksheet will calculate your tax liability based on your input.)

Select one of the following as your Filing Status:

- Single   _____
- Married, Filing Joint Return   _____
- Married, Filing Separate Return   _____
- Head of Household   _____
- Qualifying Widow(er) with Dependent Child _____

Your status will determine how you compute your taxes.

Gross Income Computation:

Salary (After Retirement Contribution)	$	
Interest Income	$	
Dividend Income	$	
Long-Term Capital Gains	$	
Short-Term Capital Gains	$	
Gross Income		$
Standard Deduction	**$**	
Itemized Deductions		
Medical Expenses	$	
Minus 10% Adjusted Gross Income	$	
Deductible Medical Expenses	$	
State Income Taxes		$
Real Estate Taxes		$
Interest Expense		$
Charitable Contributions		$
Total Itemized Deductions		$

Enter the Larger of the Total Itemized Deductions or Standard Deduction			$
Exemptions	$4,000 × _____ (Number of exemptions)		$
Taxable Income (Gross Income − Deductions and Exemptions)			$
Tax Liability			
Capital Gains Tax			
Long-Term Capital Gains	$		
Long-Term Capital Gains Tax Rate	%		
Capital Gains Tax			$
Your Total Tax Liability (Capital gains tax plus tax liability)			$

DECISIONS

1. Describe the actions you will take (i.e., increasing deductions or reducing gross income) to achieve tax savings in the present year.

_____

_____

_____

_____

_____

_____

_____

_____

2. Describe the means by which you will reduce your tax liability (i.e., increasing deductions or reducing gross income) in the future.

_____

_____

_____

_____

_____

_____

_____

CHAPTER 4: THE SAMPSONS—A Continuing Case

CASE QUESTIONS

1. Help the Sampsons estimate their federal income taxes for this year by filling in the following worksheet.

Gross Income	_____
Retirement Plan Contribution	_____
Adjusted Gross Income	_____
Deductions	
Interest Expense	_____
Real Estate Taxes	_____
Contributions	_____
Exemptions ($4,000 each)	_____
Taxable Income	_____
Tax Liability before Tax Credits	_____
Child Tax Credit(s)	_____
Tax Liability	_____

2. The Sampsons think that it will be very difficult for them to pay the full amount of their taxes at this time. Consequently, they are thinking about underreporting their actual income on their tax return. What would you tell the Sampsons in response to this idea?

_____

_____

_____

_____

_____

_____

_____

_____

_____

_____

_____

_____

_____

PART 1: BRAD BROOKS—A Continuing Case

CASE QUESTIONS

1 a. Prepare personal financial statements for Brad, including a personal cash flow statement and personal balance sheet.

Personal Cash Flow Statement

Cash Inflows	This Month
Total Cash Inflows	

Cash Outflows	
Total Cash Outflows	
Net Cash Flows	

Personal Balance Sheet

Assets

Liquid Assets

Cash	
Checking account	
Savings account	
Other liquid assets	
Total liquid assets	

Household Assets

Home

Car

Furniture

Other household assets

   Total household assets

Investment Assets

Stocks

Bonds

Mutual funds

Other investments

   Total investment assets

Total Assets

Liabilities and Net Worth

Current Liabilities

Loans

Credit card balance

Other current liabilities

   Total current liabilities

Long-Term Liabilities

Mortgage

Car loan

Other long-term liabilities

   Total long-term liabilities

Total Liabilities

Net Worth

b. Based on these statements, make specific recommendations to Brad about what he needs to do to achieve his goals of paying off his credit card balance and saving for retirement.

_____

_____

_____

c. What additional goals could you recommend to Brad for the short and long term?

_____

_____

_____

2. Consider Brad's goal to retire in 25 years by saving $4,000 per year.

a. Based on your analysis of Brad's cash flow and your recommendations, is saving $4,000 per year a realistic goal? If not, what other goal would you advise?

_____

_____

_____

b. For Brad to know what his $4,000 per year will accumulate to in 25 years, what additional assumption (or piece of information) must he make (or have)?

_____

_____

_____

c. Assuming that Brad invests the $4,000 per year for 25 years, and achieves a return of 5% per year, how much will he accumulate in 25 years? (In reality, Brad should not build his savings until he pays off the credit card balance, but the exercise here will help him understand how annual savings can help him achieve his goal.)

Future Value of an Annuity

Payment per Period	$4,000
Number of Periods	20
Interest Rate per Period	5%
Future Value	

d. Compare the alternative of investing $4,000 every year for 25 years if he earns 8% instead of 5%.

Future Value of an Annuity

Payment per Period	$4,000
Number of Periods	25
Interest Rate per Period	8%
Future Value	

3. Develop three or four suggestions that could help Brad reduce his income tax exposure.

Suggestions to Reduce Taxes	**Pros**	**Cons**

4. If Brad was presently 40 (instead of 30) years old and had the same financial situation, explain how his goal to retire by age 55 might need to be revised.

_____

_____

_____

5. After you informed Brad of his negative monthly net cash flow, Brad indicated that he may delay paying his credit card bills for a couple of months to reduce his cash outflows. What is your response to his idea?

_____

_____

_____

Managing Your Liquidity

The chapters in this part explain the key decisions you can make to ensure adequate liquidity. Chapter 5 describes how to select a financial institution for your banking needs. Chapter 6 details how you can manage your money to prepare for future expenses. Chapter 7 explains how you can assess your credit situation, and Chapter 8 explains how to manage your credit. Your selection of a financial institution, money management, and credit management will influence your liquidity and therefore affect your cash flows and wealth.

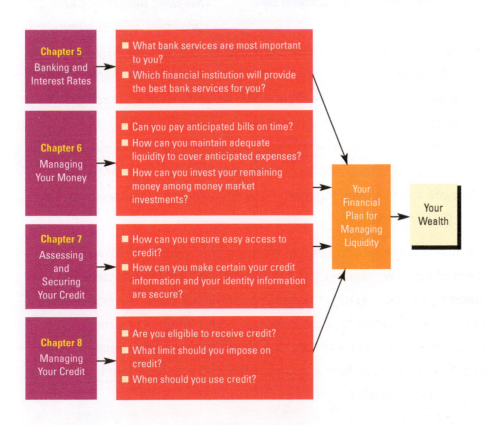

Chapter 5
Banking and Interest Rates

- What bank services are most important to you?
- Which financial institution will provide the best bank services for you?

Chapter 6
Managing Your Money

- Can you pay anticipated bills on time?
- How can you maintain adequate liquidity to cover anticipated expenses?
- How can you invest your remaining money among money market investments?

Chapter 7
Assessing and Securing Your Credit

- How can you ensure easy access to credit?
- How can you make certain your credit information and your identity information are secure?

Chapter 8
Managing Your Credit

- Are you eligible to receive credit?
- What limit should you impose on credit?
- When should you use credit?

Your Financial Plan for Managing Liquidity

Your Wealth

Banking and Interest Rates

WavebreakmediaMicro/Fotolia

When Shawna arrived on campus for her first year of college, she relied on an automated teller machine (ATM) to obtain cash for the many little necessities of college life (food, movies, and more food).

It was only on a weekend trip back home, where she reviewed her latest bank statement, that Shawna became aware of a problem. Her bank statement showed 39 separate charges for ATM fees. She had been charged $1.00 for each trip to an "out-of-network" ATM not owned by her bank. There was another $1.50 fee charged by the bank that owned the ATM, so each ATM visit created two charges. In addition, Shawna discovered that she had made five balance inquiries on "out-of-network" ATMs, and her bank charged $0.50 for each of them. Altogether, for her 17 visits to the ATM, Shawna had accrued $42.50 in ATM fees and $2.50 in inquiry fees for a total of $45.00. Shocked at this discovery, Shawna found a bank that had a branch on campus and several ATM locations that were convenient for her to use.

This chapter explains how to use a financial institution to manage your daily cash flow. A good bank is an essential ingredient of liquidity, whether you are depositing funds in an interest-earning account or are in need of a loan. You may choose a commercial bank, a credit union, or an online bank. In each case it is important to know how well your money is secured. You should also be interested in knowing how the bank sets its interest rates on your deposits and on any loan you might take out. Interest rates fluctuate frequently and are dependent on several factors, as you will find out later in this chapter.

MyFinanceLab helps you master the topics in this chapter and study more efficiently. Visit http://www.myfinancelab.com for more details.

The objectives of this chapter are to:

- Describe the types and functions of financial institutions
- Describe the banking services offered by financial institutions
- Explain how to select a financial institution for personal use
- Identify the components of interest rates
- Explain why interest rates change over time
- Explain how banking services fit within your financial plan

Types of Financial Institutions

Individuals rely on financial institutions when they wish to invest or borrow funds. In this chapter we'll examine the two major types of financial institutions: depository institutions and nondepository institutions.

Depository Institutions

depository institutions
Financial institutions that accept deposits (which are insured up to a maximum level) from individuals and provide loans.

Depository institutions are financial institutions that offer traditional checking and savings accounts for individuals or firms and also provide loans. They pay interest on savings deposits and charge interest on loans. The interest rate charged on loans exceeds the interest rate paid on deposits. The institutions use the difference to cover expenses and to generate earnings for their stockholders.

Depository institutions are skilled in assessing the ability of prospective borrowers to repay loans. This is a critical part of their business because the interest from loans is a key source of their revenue.

There are three types of depository institutions: commercial banks, savings institutions, and credit unions.

commercial banks
Financial institutions that accept deposits and use the funds to provide commercial (business) and personal loans.

Commercial Banks   **Commercial banks** are financial institutions that accept deposits in checking and savings accounts and use the funds to provide commercial (business) and personal loans. The checking accounts normally do not pay interest. The savings accounts pay interest, and certain other accounts pay interest and can be used to write checks. These accounts are described in more detail in the next chapter. Deposits at commercial banks are insured up to $250,000 per depositor by the Federal Deposit Insurance Corporation (FDIC), a government-owned insurance agency that ensures the safety of bank deposits. During the financial crisis in 2008–2009, several banks experienced problems because many of their mortgage loans defaulted. Depositors were protected as long as the deposits were insured by the FDIC. Without deposit insurance, the impact of the crisis on individuals would have been even worse.

Commercial banks provide personal loans for the purchase of a car or other big-ticket items. They also offer mortgage loans for purchasing a home. Some commercial banks own other types of financial institutions (such as those described next) that provide additional services to individuals.

savings institutions (or thrift institutions)
Financial institutions that accept deposits and provide mortgage and personal loans to individuals.

Savings Institutions   **Savings institutions** (also referred to as thrift institutions) accept deposits and provide mortgage and personal loans to individuals. They differ from commercial banks in that they tend to focus less on providing commercial loans. They typically offer the same types of checking and savings deposits as banks, and these deposits are also insured up to $250,000 per depositor by the FDIC. Like commercial banks, savings institutions also experienced problems during the financial crisis because many of their mortgage loans defaulted. However, depositors at savings institutions were protected as long as their deposits were insured.

credit unions
Nonprofit depository institutions that serve members who have a common affiliation (such as the same employer or the same community).

Credit Unions
Credit unions are nonprofit depository institutions that serve members who have a common affiliation (such as the same employer or community). Credit unions have been created to serve the employees of specific hospitals, universities, and even some corporations. They offer their members deposit accounts that are similar to the accounts offered by commercial banks and savings institutions; the accounts are insured by the National Credit Union Share Insurance Fund (NCUSIF) for up to $250,000 per member. Credit unions also provide mortgage and personal loans to their members. They may even issue credit cards, and the financing rates on these cards are sometimes lower than those issued by other types of financial institutions.

Nondepository Institutions

nondepository institutions
Financial institutions that do not offer federally insured deposit accounts, but provide various other financial services.

Nondepository institutions provide various financial services but do not receive federal insurance for their deposits. The main types of nondepository institutions that serve individuals are finance companies, securities firms, insurance companies, and investment companies.

finance companies
Nondepository institutions that specialize in providing personal loans to individuals.

Finance Companies
Finance companies specialize in providing personal loans to individuals. These loans may be used for various purposes, such as purchasing a car or other products, or adding a room to a home. Finance companies tend to charge relatively high rates on loans because they lend to individuals who they perceive to have a higher risk of defaulting on the loans. When the economy weakens, borrowers may have more difficulty repaying loans, causing finance companies to be subject to even higher levels of loan defaults. For example, during the financial crisis of 2008–2009, many individuals lost their jobs and were unable to repay their personal loans. Thus, finance companies experienced more defaults on the personal loans that they provided.

securities firms
Nondepository institutions that facilitate the purchase or sale of securities by firms or individuals by providing investment banking services and brokerage services.

Securities Firms
Securities firms facilitate the purchase or sale of securities (such as stocks or bonds) by firms or individuals by offering investment banking services and brokerage services. Investment banking services include (1) placing securities that are issued by firms, meaning that the securities firm finds investors who wish to purchase those securities; (2) advising firms regarding the sale of securities, which involves determining the price at which the securities may be sold and the quantity of securities that should be sold; and (3) advising firms that are considering mergers about the valuation of a firm, the potential benefits of being acquired or of acquiring another firm, and the financing necessary for the merger to occur.

In addition to offering investment banking services, securities firms also provide brokerage services, which facilitate the trading of existing securities. That is, the firms execute trades of securities for their customers. One customer may desire to sell a specific stock while another may want to buy that stock. Brokerage firms create a market for stocks and bonds by matching willing buyers and sellers.

insurance companies
Nondepository institutions that provide insurance to protect individuals or firms from the financial consequences of possible adverse events.

Insurance Companies
Insurance companies are nondepository institutions that provide insurance to protect individuals or firms from the financial consequences of possible adverse events. Specifically, life insurance companies provide insurance in the event of a person's death. Property and casualty companies provide insurance against damage to property, including automobiles and homes. Health insurance companies insure against specific types of health care costs. Insurance serves a crucial function for individuals because it compensates them (or their beneficiaries) in the event of adverse conditions that could otherwise ruin their financial situation. Chapters 11–13 discuss insurance options in detail.

investment companies
Nondepository institutions that sell shares to individuals and use the proceeds to invest in securities to create mutual funds.

Investment Companies
Investment companies use money provided by individuals to invest in securities to create mutual funds. The minimum amount an individual can invest in a mutual fund is typically between $500 and $3,000. Because the investment company pools the money it receives from individuals and invests in a portfolio of securities, an individual who invests in a mutual fund is part owner of that portfolio. Thus, mutual funds provide a means by which investors with a small amount of money can invest in a

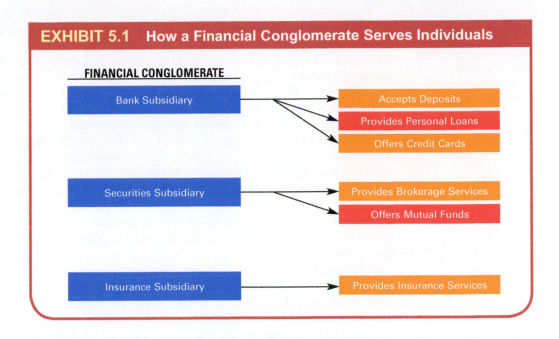

EXHIBIT 5.1   How a Financial Conglomerate Serves Individuals

portfolio of securities. More than 8,000 mutual funds are available to individual investors. More details on mutual funds are provided in Chapter 17.

Financial Conglomerates

financial conglomerates
Financial institutions that offer a diverse set of financial services to individuals or firms.

Financial conglomerates offer a diverse set of financial services to individuals or firms. Examples of financial conglomerates include Citigroup and Bank of America. In addition to accepting deposits and providing personal loans, a financial conglomerate may also offer credit cards. It may have a brokerage subsidiary that can execute stock transactions for individuals. It may also have an insurance subsidiary that offers insurance services. It may even have an investment company subsidiary that offers mutual funds containing stocks or bonds. Exhibit 5.1 shows the types of services offered by a typical financial conglomerate. By offering all types of financial services, the conglomerate aims to serve as a one-stop shop where individuals can conduct all their financial activities.

Banking Services Offered

A depository institution may offer you a wide variety of banking services. Although a nondepository institution does not offer banking services, it may own a subsidiary that can provide banking services. Some of the more important banking services offered to individuals are described here.

Checking Services

You use a checking account to draw on funds by using a debit card, making online payments, or writing checks against your account. Most individuals maintain a checking account for paying bills and to avoid having to carry large amounts of cash to make purchases. Although people today increasingly use debit cards, online payment systems, or mobile apps for making payments, checks are still used, especially for large transactions. To illustrate how your checking account works, assume that you write a check for $1,500 to your college to pay your fall tuition. The college deposits your check at the bank where it has an account. The bank electronically increases the college's account balance by $1,500. At the same time, it reduces your checking account balance by $1,500 if your account is at that bank. If your checking account is at another bank, the bank receiving the check sends an electronic signal to that bank to reduce your balance by $1,500.

Debit Cards

A **debit card** is a payment card that can be used to make purchases that are charged against the cardholder's checking account. If you use a debit card to pay $100 to a car repair shop, your checking account balance is reduced by $100, while the account balance at the car repair shop is increased by $100. Thus, using a debit card has the same result as writing a check from your checking account. Most individuals prefer to use a debit card because it is easier to carry than their checkbook. Many merchants accept payments by debit card. In fact, some merchants may accept payments by debit card but not a check because they fear that a check may bounce. Although a debit card looks similar to a credit card, a debit card is intended to be used for convenience and does not provide credit. That is, the holder can only use a debit card to make purchases up to the checking account balance. The use of a debit card does not create debt and can be especially valuable for individuals who prefer that their purchases be constrained by the balance in their checking account. In contrast, a credit card allows individuals to spend beyond their checking account balance but creates a debt to the credit card holder that must be repaid.

Although debit cards are convenient, they have some disadvantages. If your debit card is stolen, the thief can empty your entire checking account within a very short time, perhaps by using the debit card to make online purchases. Although you are not liable for the loss if you report the stolen card immediately to your bank, the bank may not restore the funds to your account for a period of time. If you fail to report a stolen debit card for more than 60 calendar days after receiving your account statement from the bank, you are liable for the entire loss. If your debit card is stolen, call the bank immediately to report the theft and then send a follow-up letter as well.

Another possible disadvantage of debit cards is that if you use your card for many transactions, you might forget to make a record of all transactions. As a result, you will have less money in your account than you think you have, and you could possibly overdraw your account and incur overdraft fees.

Recently, some financial institutions attempted to charge monthly fees to consumers who were using their debit cards. However, consumers protested and threatened to discontinue use of the cards if a monthly fee was charged. Financial institutions responded by dropping their plans to charge monthly fees.

Debit Cards for Teenagers

Some debit cards are available for teenagers. They are commonly structured so that parents can transfer funds from their account to their child's account, thus providing a convenient way for parents to ensure that their children have access to money when needed. A possible disadvantage is that the parents and the teenagers may have different ideas as to what constitutes a necessity. Some teenagers may become accustomed to spending beyond their means, with the expectation that their parents will cover any excess.

Parents may be able to use various tactics to influence their teenagers' spending behavior. The parents could try to specify the types of purchases that are acceptable or say that they will cover only charges due to emergency situations. Enforcing such rules can be difficult, however, especially because once the rules are broken, the parents will have to take actions that will not be popular with their teenagers.

Another possible solution is for the parents to set up debit cards with a spending limit. An advantage of this feature is that it may help teenagers become more disciplined with their spending. A disadvantage is that the teenagers may not have access to needed funds in an emergency. In addition, if the parents always replenish the funds when the account balance is low, the teenagers will not learn to budget their money.

Mobile Banking

Many financial institutions now offer mobile applications that enable you to bank via your smartphone. Using your phone, you can check your account balance and review recent transactions. If you're out shopping and need cash, you can find your bank's closest ATM. You may even be able to use your smartphone to deposit checks that you receive. You simply endorse the check on the back, photograph the front and back of the check, and transmit the photographs to your bank via your phone. Banks may charge a fee for mobile check deposits and may limit the number of checks that can be deposited per month. Other apps allow you to sign up for text alerts that let you know when your balance falls below a certain level.

You may also be able to use your smartphone to pay for purchases. Applications such as Apple Pay and Google Wallet allow you to simply wave your smartphone by a machine instead of swiping your debit card. More merchants are likely to accept this form of payment over time.

FREE APPS
for Personal Finance

Your Banking Services

Application:

The Chase Mobile app (by JPMorgan Chase & Co.) allows bank customers who have established an account to pay bills and credit cards, transfer money between accounts, and see their cash balance. Also check to see if any other financial institutions that you use offer apps like this.

To Find It:

Search for the "Chase Mobile" app on your mobile device.

PSYCHOLOGY
of Personal Finance

Paying Bills on Time Your checking account provides a quick and convenient means of paying bills. There are psychological forces that influence how people pay bills. Although no one enjoys paying bills, people deal with the process in different ways. Some people try to avoid the stress of bill paying by ignoring their bills. They defer payment, perhaps with the hope that their creditors will forget about the bills. But creditors tend to remember what they are owed, and, if you fail to pay by the deadline, you will receive a late notice and will be charged a late fee.

If you frequently incur late fees, consider keeping a schedule of your deadlines on your calendar. By avoiding these fees, you will have more money that you can use in other ways. You can avoid late payments by setting up an online payment system at your bank's Web site. This system allows payments to be made automatically from your checking account each month to cover bills before the due date. Automatic payments are especially useful for bills that are the same (or nearly the same) amount each month such as your Internet access or cable TV bill. If a bill varies considerably from month to month such as the heating bill for your apartment, you may not want to have it paid automatically.

Checking Account Fees Most financial institutions charge a monthly fee for a checking account, but there are usually ways to avoid the monthly fee or at least reduce it substantially. Because the fees can easily amount to more than $100 per year, you have an incentive to look for a way to avoid them. Most banks waive the monthly fee if you maintain a minimum balance in your account. Although the required minimum balance may be as much as $1,500 or higher, some banks require only $100 or so. Therefore, it pays to compare the required minimum balance among financial institutions before you select a financial institution.

Some banks also waive or reduce the fee if you authorize direct deposits to your account each month. Many companies will use direct deposit for your paycheck, so ask your employer if that can be arranged. If you are comfortable with online and mobile banking, you will find that many banks will not charge you a monthly fee if you do all your banking transactions through the Internet and ATMs, which cost the banks much less than if you require help from employees at the branches. Finally, some banks offer no-fee checking accounts for students or veterans, although these accounts may allow you to write only a small number of checks per month.

Monitoring Your Account Balance As you use funds from your checking account, you should record each transaction in your checkbook whether you're writing a check or using a debit card, a mobile app, or an automatic payment system. By doing this, you can always determine how much money is in your account. By keeping track of your account balance, you can make sure that there is money in your account when you want to use the funds. This is very important because you may be charged fees if you write a check that bounces or if there are insufficient funds in your account to make an automatic payment that you have requested. You may also be charged a monthly fee if your balance falls below the required minimum. Most financial institutions allow you to access your account at their Web site to check your balance online, but you should also keep a record of all of your transactions so that you can ensure that your balance according to your financial institution is accurate.

Reconciling Your Account Balance Financial institutions normally send a checking account statement once a month. If you have signed up for online banking, you may receive the statement by e-mail. When you receive your bank statement, you should make sure that the statement reconciles (agrees) with your record of transactions in your check register. Make sure that all deposits are listed, whether the deposits were made by direct deposit, via your smartphone, or at an ATM or bank branch. Then compare the checks in your register with those listed on the statement. Put a checkmark in your register beside the checks that the statement indicates have cleared (been deducted from your account). Next compare all your electronic transactions, debit card purchases, and ATM withdrawals with those on the statement. To reconcile the balance in your register with the balance on the statement, subtract any uncleared checks or unprocessed transactions from the statement balance. The result should equal the balance in your check register.

EXAMPLE

Last month the balance in your checking account was $800. This month you deposited $100 to your account. You wrote two checks that cleared, totaling $200, and used your debit card for three purchases, totaling $300. You did not withdraw any funds from the account, and no fees were charged this month. Your balance for this month is

Last month's balance	$800
+ Deposits	+ $100
− Checks that cleared	− $200
− Debit card purchases	− $300
= New balance	= $400

In a month when you had no fees or withdrawals, the balance in your register should be the same as the balance on your statement as long as all the checks that you wrote have cleared. But if you had written a check that has not yet cleared, the balance on your statement would exceed the balance in your register by the amount of that check. If you wrote a check for $100 that has not yet cleared, you can record that payment in your register immediately at the time of payment. Yet, the balance on your checking account statement would not include this payment until the check clears. This can cause some individuals to think that they have more money available than they really have and therefore might cause them to spend beyond the balance that is in their checking account. For this reason, do not rely on the monthly statement to determine your daily balance.

Many banks provide a worksheet that can be used to reconcile your account balance. An example of a reconciliation worksheet is shown in Exhibit 5.2. Your account balance can be compared with the balance shown on the bank statement. If there is a discrepancy, your balance may be wrong, or the bank's statement could be incorrect. The first step is to verify your math in your check register and then double-check your math on the reconciliation worksheet. If you still cannot resolve the discrepancy, contact the bank.

EXHIBIT 5.2	Example of a Worksheet to Reconcile Your Bank Statement

Beginning balance			**=$1,500**
Deposits	$100		
	$400		
	$500	→	+ $500
Withdrawals	$50		
	$150		
	$200	→	− $200
Checks that have cleared	$700		
	$100		
	$800	→	− $800
Debit card transactions	$25		
	$50		
	$125		
	$200	→	− $200
Automatic bill payments	$100		
	$100		
	$200	→	− $200
Bank fees	$0	→	−$0
Balance shown on bank statement			**$600**
Checks that have not yet cleared	$100		
	$100		
	$200	→	− $200
Adjusted bank balance **(your prevailing bank balance)**			**$400**

EXAMPLE

Your most recent checking account statement shows that you have a balance of $500. However, yesterday you wrote checks totaling $300 to pay bills. When these checks clear, your balance will be $200. Today, you received a credit card bill for $250. Even though this amount is less than the balance shown on your most recent statement, you do not have sufficient funds in your checking account to pay this bill.

If you write a check to cover the credit card bill or attempt to pay it online, you will create an overdraft because you really have only $200 in your account. By using the register to keep track of your transactions, you will always know the amount of funds available in your account.

You may think that reconciling your balance is a waste of time because you can easily check your balance online and review your recent transactions there, but the reconciliation is useful for several reasons. First, banks rarely make errors with checking accounts, but errors are possible, so you should always review your account. Second, you should check all the debit card transactions to make sure that all of them are valid and that no one has used your card without permission. Finally, reviewing all of your monthly transactions enables you to see where your money is going. When you realize that you spent more than $100 last month on your daily cappuccino, you may rethink your coffee habits.

Check Float

When you write a check, your checking account balance is not reduced until the check is cashed by the recipient and the check clears. The time from when you write a check until your checking account balance is reduced is referred to as the *float*. The float is partially due to the time it takes for the bank where the check is deposited to send information to your bank. Some individuals do not have sufficient funds in their account at the time that they write a check, expecting that the float will take a few days. This gives them time to deposit enough funds in their checking account before the check clears.

However, in October 2004, The Check Clearing for the 21st Century Act (referred to as Check 21) was implemented. This act allows banks to transmit electronic images of checks. Thus, if you make a payment to a person or company by check, the check may clear the same day. The float may be virtually eliminated, which means you should always make sure you have sufficient funds in your checking account before you write a check.

Another effect of Check 21 is that you may not receive the original canceled checks that you write. Because the banks that receive the checks may transmit electronic images of them to your bank, you may receive a copy of the electronic image (called a substitute check) instead of the original check with your statement.

Electronic checking deters fraud. When you write a check to a retail store for a purchase, the funds are electronically transferred from your account to the retail store's account. The cashier at the store stamps the back of the check, gives it back to you, and the check clears immediately. This system reduces fraud because the payee knows if there are sufficient funds in the customer's account to make a purchase. If there are not enough funds, the electronic transfer does not occur, and the check writer cannot make the purchase. Reducing fraud saves retail stores money and may make them more willing to accept checks.

Savings Accounts

In addition to checking accounts, financial institutions offer savings accounts, where you can deposit money that you do not intend to use for daily expenses. Unlike most checking accounts, savings accounts pay interest on the funds deposited there, although in recent years the interest rate has been quite low. Generally, you cannot write checks on the funds in your savings account or use the funds for purchases with a debit card. However, you can transfer funds from your savings account to your checking account. Most institutions allow you to make transfers at ATMs or by accessing the bank's Web site or by calling an automated phone system. Some institutions also offer mobile apps for transfers. The number of transfers that you can make in a month without being charged a fee may be limited. Therefore, make sure that you transfer enough funds to cover your monthly expenses so that you aren't charged a fee for excess transfers.

Credit Card Financing

Individuals use credit cards to purchase products and services on credit. At the end of each billing cycle, you receive a bill for the credit you used over that period. MasterCard and Visa cards allow you to finance your purchases through various financial institutions. Thus, if you are able to pay only the minimum balance on your card, the financial institution will finance the outstanding balance and charge interest for the credit that it provides to you.

safety deposit box
A box at a financial institution where a customer can store documents, jewelry, or other valuables.

Safety Deposit Boxes

Many financial institutions offer access to a **safety deposit box**, where a customer can store valuable documents, certificates, jewelry, or other items. Customers are charged an annual fee for access to a safety deposit box.

Automated Teller Machines (ATMs)

automated teller machine (ATM)
A machine where individuals can deposit and withdraw funds any time of the day.

Bank customers are likely to deposit and withdraw funds at an **automated teller machine (ATM)** by using their ATM card and entering their personal identification number (PIN). Located in numerous convenient locations, these machines allow customers access to their funds 24 hours a day, any day of the year. Some financial institutions have ATMs throughout the United States and in foreign countries. You can usually use ATMs from financial institutions other than your own, but you may be charged a service fee, which is often at least $1 per transaction.

FREE APPS
for Personal
Finance

Finding an ATM Nearby

Application:

Use the ATM Hunter app (by Mastercard) to find a nearby ATM. You can use your current location when searching or input an address or an airport.

To Find It:

Search for the "ATM Hunter" app on your mobile device.

cashier's check
A check that is written on behalf of a person to a specific payee and will be charged against a financial institution's account.

Cashier's Checks

A **cashier's check** is a check that is written on behalf of a person to a specific payee and will be charged against a financial institution's account. It is especially useful when the payee is concerned that a personal check may bounce.

EXAMPLE

You wish to buy a used car for $2,000 from Rod Simpkins, who is concerned that you may not have sufficient funds in your account. So you go to Lakeside Bank, where you have your checking account. You obtain a cashier's check from Lakeside Bank made out to Rod Simpkins. After verifying your account balance, the bank complies with your request and reduces your checking account balance by $2,000. It will likely charge you a small fee such as $10 or $15 for this service. Rod accepts the cashier's check from you because he knows that this check is backed by Lakeside Bank and will not bounce.

Money Orders

money order
A check that is written on behalf of a person for a fixed amount that is paid in advance.

A **money order** is a check that is written on behalf of a person for a fixed amount that is paid in advance. The U.S. Post Office and some financial institutions provide this service for a fee. A money order is a better alternative than cash when you need to mail funds.

Traveler's Checks

traveler's check
A check that is written on behalf of an individual and will be charged against a large well-known financial institution or credit card sponsor's account.

A **traveler's check** is a check that is written on behalf of an individual and will be charged against a large well-known financial institution or credit card sponsor's account. It is similar to a cashier's check, except that no payee is designated on the check. Traveler's checks are accepted around the world. If they are lost or stolen, the issuer will usually replace them without charge. The fee for a traveler's check varies among financial institutions.

Selecting a Financial Institution

Because financial institutions can provide many valuable services, you may want to select one financial institution that can provide all the services you need. Your selection of the proper financial institution can save you time and money.

Criteria Used to Select a Financial Institution

Your choice of a financial institution should be based on convenience, the ability to pay bills online, deposit rates and insurance, and fees.

Convenience You should be able to deposit and withdraw funds easily, which means the financial institution should be located close to where you live or work. You may also benefit if it has ATMs in convenient locations. In addition, a financial institution should offer most or all of the services you might need. Most financial institutions offer Internet banking, which allows you to keep track of your deposit accounts and even apply for loans online. You also usually can transfer funds online from one account to another within the institution. For added convenience, many institutions now offer mobile apps that allow you to deposit checks, check your account balance, and transfer funds. As mentioned earlier, many financial institutions allow you to pay bills online instead of writing and mailing checks.

Paying Bills Online Many financial institutions have established a system in which you can pay bills online instead of writing and sending checks. You establish an online account that is tied to your checking account. You are asked to register online, identify payees, and provide the payee's address. For each payee, you are prompted to indicate the amount of funds that you would like to have transferred to their account. The financial institution reduces (debits) your account balance by that amount and increases (credits) the account balance of the payee.

By paying bills online, you avoid the need to write checks and send them by mail. You can have payments sent automatically so that you do not need to worry about missing a payment. Your list of payees is stored in your online account so that you can pay your monthly bills quickly and not have to enter the payee information each time you pay bills. You can also track the payments and monitor the history of all bills paid online. You may also monitor the history per payee.

Some Web-based financial institutions do not have physical branches. For example, ING DIRECT (http://www.ingdirect.com) is a Web-based bank. Although Web-based banks allow you to keep track of your deposits online, they might not be appropriate for customers who prefer to deposit funds directly at a branch. For customers who prefer to make deposits at a branch but also want easy online access to their account information, the most convenient financial institutions are those with multiple branches and online access.

FREE APPS for Personal Finance

Paying Your Bills

Application:
The Mint Bills & Money app (by Intuit Mint Bills, Inc.) allows you to pay all your bills online, including bank bills and credit card bills.

To Find It:
Search for the "Mint Bills & Money" app on your mobile device.

Deposit Rates and Insurance The interest rates offered on deposits vary among financial institutions. You should comparison shop by checking the rates on the types of deposits that you might make. Financial institutions also vary on the minimum required balance. A lower minimum balance on savings accounts is preferable because it gives you more flexibility if you do not want to tie up your funds. Make sure that any deposits are insured by the FDIC or NCUSIF.

Web-based financial institutions tend to pay a higher interest rate on deposits than institutions with physical branches because they have lower expenses and can afford to pay higher deposit rates. Customers must weigh the trade-off of the higher deposit rates against the lack of access to branches.

Customers who prefer to make deposits through the mail may want to capitalize on the higher rates at Web-based financial institutions.

Fees Many financial institutions charge fees for various services. Determine what fees exist for writing checks or using ATMs. Avoid financial institutions that charge high fees on services you will use frequently, even if the institutions offer relatively high rates on deposits.

In recent years, many individuals have protested against banks that charge high fees, and they have closed their bank accounts. These protests against the banks are supported by the Occupy Wall Street movement, in which protestors are generally against large banks that they believe receive excessive support from the government. As an alternative, some people have established accounts at Walmart. While Walmart is not a bank and does not provide loans, it offers some bank services. Many Walmart stores have money centers where you can cash a paycheck of up to $1,000 for a fee and can buy a prepaid debit card called a MoneyCard. With this card, you can buy products online or withdraw funds from ATMs. Some Walmart stores without money centers offer financial services at customer service desks or kiosks. Because Walmart stores are typically open late, their banking services are accessible more hours per day than services at a typical bank.

Interest Rates on Deposits and Loans

The return you receive from your deposits at a financial institution and the cost of borrowing money from a financial institution are dependent on the interest rates. Therefore, your cash inflows and outflows are affected by the interest rates at the time of your transactions with the institution.

Most depository institutions issue **certificates of deposit (CDs)**, which specify a minimum investment, an interest rate, and a maturity date. For example, a bank may require a $500 minimum investment on all the CDs it offers. The maturities may include one month, three months, six months, one year, and five years. The money invested in a particular CD cannot be withdrawn until the maturity date, or it will be subject to a penalty for early withdrawal.

The interest rate offered varies among maturities. Interest rates on CDs are commonly reported on an annualized basis so that they can be compared among deposits. An annual interest rate of 6% on your deposit means that at the end of one year, you will receive interest equal to 6% of the amount that you originally deposited.

certificate of deposit (CD)
An instrument that is issued by a depository institution and specifies a minimum investment, an interest rate, and a maturity date.

Risk-Free Rate

A **risk-free rate** is a return on an investment that is guaranteed for a specified period. As an example, at a commercial bank you can invest in a CD with a maturity that matches your desired investment horizon. When you invest in a CD that has a maturity of one year, you are guaranteed the interest rate offered on that CD. Even if the bank goes bankrupt, the CD is insured for its full value up to $250,000 per customer by the federal government, so you will receive your deposit back at the time of maturity.

risk-free rate
A return on an investment that is guaranteed for a specified period.

Risk Premium

Rather than investing in risk-free deposits that are backed by the federal government, you could invest in deposits of some financial firms that offer a higher interest rate. These deposits are sometimes called certificates, but should not be confused with the CDs that are backed by government insurance. These certificates are subject to default risk, meaning that you may receive a lower return than you expected if the firm goes bankrupt. In fact, you could possibly lose your entire investment. These certificates are commonly advertised in newspapers. You can review the small print within the ads to determine if they are federally insured.

If you have accumulated only a small amount of savings, you should maintain all your savings in a financial institution where deposits are guaranteed by the government. It is not worthwhile to strive for a higher return because you could lose a portion or all of your savings.

If you have a substantial amount of money, however, you may consider investing a portion of it in riskier deposits or certificates, but you should expect to be compensated for the risk. Your potential return should contain a **risk premium**, or an additional return beyond the risk-free rate that you could earn from a deposit guaranteed by the government. The higher the potential default risk of an investment, the higher the risk premium you should expect.

If a particular risky deposit is supposed to offer a specific return (R) over a period and you know the risk-free rate (R_f) offered on a deposit backed by the government, you can determine the risk premium (RP) offered on the risky deposit:

$$RP = R - R_f$$

risk premium
An additional return beyond the risk-free rate that can be earned from a deposit guaranteed by the government.

EXAMPLE

Today, your local commercial bank is offering a one-year CD with an interest rate of 6%, so the existing one-year risk-free rate is 6%. You notice that Metallica Financial Company offers an interest rate of 10% on one-year certificates. The risk premium offered by this certificate is

$$RP = R - R_f$$
$$= 10\% - 6\%$$
$$= 4\%$$

You need to decide whether receiving the extra four percentage points in the annual return is worth the default risk. As you have a moderate amount of savings accumulated, you determine that the risk is not worth taking.

ECONOMIC IMPACT

Impact of the Economy on the Risk Premium As economic conditions change, the risk premium on various types of investments changes. When economic conditions weaken, firms that issue various types of debt securities must pay a higher risk premium to sell their securities. Investors become more concerned that these types of firms might go bankrupt and not repay their debt. Thus, you and other individuals would only consider investing in such debt securities during weak economic conditions if the premium was large enough to compensate for the risk. Conversely, under more favorable economic conditions, firms are in better financial health and are less likely to go bankrupt. Thus, investors are more willing to invest in debt securities issued by firms, and the risk premium is lower.

PSYCHOLOGY
of Personal
Finance

Twisted Perception of the Risk Premium When the economy weakens and the risk premium rises (for the reasons just explained), some investors are attracted to investments, but for the wrong reasons. They may decide to pursue investments with higher risk premiums in a weak economy to make up for limited income. However, their logic is irrational. The higher risk premium on investments during a weak economy is offered as compensation to investors for accepting more risk. Investors should not seek more risk on their investments as a substitute for limited job opportunities. In fact, if you have limited income because of a bad economy, a more rational strategy would be to focus on safe investments, even if they offer a lower return, so that you can avoid any losses in case you need the funds that you invested.

Comparing Interest Rates and Risk

When considering investments that have different degrees of risk, your choice depends on your risk tolerance. If you plan to use all your invested funds for necessities one year from now, you may need to avoid risk completely. In this case, you should choose a risk-free investment because other investments could be worth less in one year than they

Financial Planning
ONLINE

Go to:
The markets section of
http://www.bloomberg
.com

To get:
Updated quotations on
key interest rates and
charts showing recent
movements in these rates.

are worth today. The trade-off is that you will receive a relatively low rate of interest on your investment.

If you will need only a portion of your initial investment at the time the investment matures, you may be willing to take some risk. In this case, you may prefer an investment that offers a higher interest rate than the risk-free rate, but is exposed to the possibility of a loss. You can afford to take some risk because you would still have sufficient funds to pay for your necessities even if the investment results in a loss. However, you should still consider a risky investment only if the risk premium on the investment compensates you for the risk.

No single choice is optimal for all investors, as the proper choice varies with the investor's situation and willingness to tolerate risk. Some individuals are more willing to accept risk than others. The investment decision is based on your risk tolerance, which in turn is influenced by your financial situation.

EXAMPLE

Stephanie Spratt plans to invest $2,000. She will use these funds in one year as part of a down payment if she purchases a home. She is considering the following alternatives for investing the $2,000 over the next year:

1. A bank CD that offers a return of 6% (the risk-free rate) over the next year and is backed by government insurance

2. An investment in a deposit at a financial firm that offers an interest rate of 9% this year but is not backed by a government guarantee

Stephanie evaluates her possible investments. The 6% return from investing in the CD would result in an accumulated amount of:

Accumulated Amount = Initial Investment × (1 + Return)

$$= \$2,000 \times (1.06)$$

$$= \$2,120$$

The accumulated amount if Stephanie invests in the risky deposit is

Accumulated Amount = Initial Investment × (1 + Return)

$$= \$2,000 \times (1 + .09)$$

$$= \$2,180$$

Comparing the two accumulated amounts, Stephanie sees that she would earn an extra $60 from the risky deposit if the firm performs well over the next year. There is a risk that the return from the risky deposit could be poorer, however. If the risky deposit pays her only what she originally invested, she would earn zero interest. If the firm goes bankrupt, it might not have any funds at all to pay her. Although the chances that this firm will go bankrupt are low, Stephanie decides that the possibility of losing her entire investment is not worth the extra $60 in interest. She decides to invest in the bank CD.

Term Structure of Interest Rates

When considering investing in bank deposits or other debt securities, you must first determine your timeline for investing. When investors provide credit to financial markets, the relationship between the maturity of an investment and the interest rate on the investment is referred to as the **term structure of interest rates**. The term structure is often based on rates of return (or yields) offered by Treasury securities (which are debt securities issued by the U.S. Treasury) with different maturities. The rates of CDs and Treasury securities with a specific maturity are very similar at a given point in time, so this term structure looks very similar to one for deposit rates of financial institutions. The term structure is important to investors and borrowers because it provides the risk-free interest rates that you could earn for various maturities.

term structure of interest rates
The relationship between the maturities of risk-free debt securities and the annualized yields offered on those securities.

EXAMPLE

You are considering depositing $500 in a financial institution. You do not expect to need the funds for at least three years. You want to assess the term structure of interest rates so that you know the interest rate quoted for each maturity. The institution's rates as of today are shown in Exhibit 5.3.

The relationship between the maturities and annualized yields in Exhibit 5.3 is graphed in Exhibit 5.4. The term structure shown here for one specific point in time illustrates that annualized interest rates are higher on investments with longer terms to maturity. Thus, the longer the investment horizon you choose, the higher the annualized interest rate you receive.

If you invest in bank CDs, do not invest in a deposit that has a longer term to maturity than the three years (after which you may need the funds) because you will be subject to a penalty if you withdraw the funds before that date.

EXHIBIT 5.3 **Annualized Deposit Rates Offered on Deposits with Various Maturities**

Maturity	Annualized Deposit Rate (%)
1 month	0.20
3 months	0.24
6 months	0.45
1 year	0.70
2 years	1.00
3 years	1.25
4 years	1.60
5 years	1.70
10 years	3.80

EXHIBIT 5.4 **Comparison of Interest Rates Among Maturities**

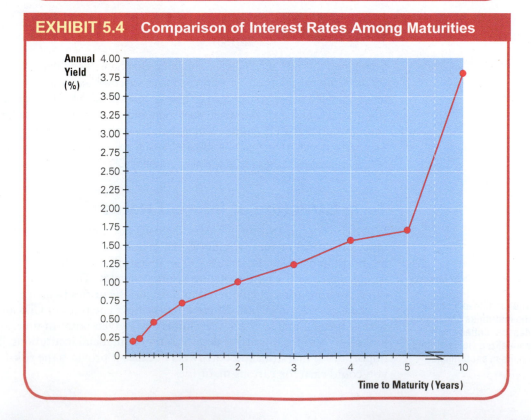

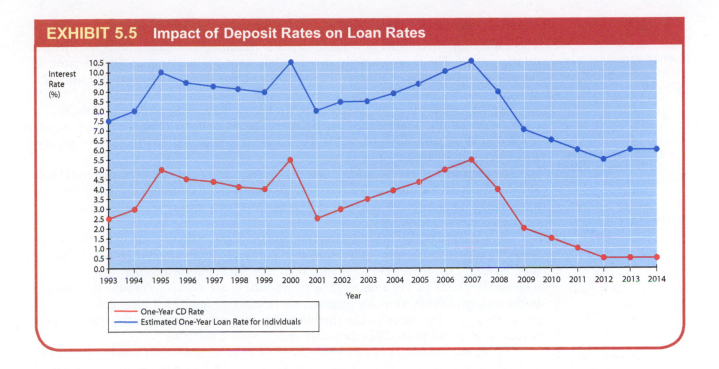

EXHIBIT 5.5   **Impact of Deposit Rates on Loan Rates**

Shifts in the Yield Curve The yield curve derived from annualized Treasury security yields appears every day in *The Wall Street Journal*. The current day's yield curve is compared to the curve from one week ago and four weeks ago. This allows you to easily see how the returns from investing in debt securities with different maturities have changed over time.

Loan Rates

Financial institutions obtain many of their funds by accepting deposits from individuals. They use the money to provide loans to other individuals and firms. In this way, by depositing funds, investors provide credit to financial markets. Financial institutions must charge a higher interest rate on the loans than they pay on the deposits to have sufficient funds to pay for their other expenses and earn a profit. Therefore, to borrow funds, you must normally pay a higher interest rate on the loan than the prevailing rate offered on deposits. The annual interest rate on loans to individuals is often three to seven percentage points above the annual rate offered on deposits. For example, if the prevailing annual interest rate on various deposits is 2%, the prevailing annual interest rate on loans to individuals may be 5% to 9%.

Exhibit 5.5 shows the relationship between the one-year CD rate and the average one-year rate on loans to individuals. Notice how the loan rate rises when financial institutions must pay a higher rate of interest on the CDs that they offer.

The interest rate a financial institution charges for a loan often varies among individuals. Higher rates of interest are charged on loans that are exposed to higher default risk. Therefore, individuals with poor credit histories or low incomes will likely be charged higher interest rates.

Why Interest Rates Change

A change in the risk-free interest rate causes other interest rates to change. Therefore, understanding why the risk-free interest rate changes allows you to understand why other interest rates change. Because the interest rate is influenced by the interaction between the supply and the demand for funds, a shift in supply or demand will cause a shift in the interest rate.

Shift in Monetary Policy

money supply
Demand deposits (checking accounts) and currency held by the public.

The **money supply** consists of demand deposits (checking accounts) and currency held by the public. The money supply is commonly used by investors as an indicator of the amount of funds that financial institutions can provide to consumers or businesses as loans.

The U.S. money supply is controlled by the Federal Reserve System (called "the Fed"), which is the central bank of the United States. The act of controlling the money supply is referred to as **monetary policy**. The Fed's monetary policy affects the money supply, which can influence interest rates.

monetary policy
The actions taken by the Federal Reserve to control the money supply.

The Federal Reserve Bank has funds that are not deposited in any commercial bank or other financial institution. The Fed most commonly conducts monetary policy through **open market operations**, which involve buying or selling Treasury securities (debt securities issued by the Treasury).

open market operations
The Fed's buying and selling of Treasury securities.

When the Fed wishes to reduce interest rates, it increases the amount of funds at commercial banks by using some of its reserves to purchase Treasury securities held by investors. Investors suddenly have more cash than they did before, which may cause them to increase their savings. The amount of funds supplied to the market increases. The increase in the supply of funds available increases the amount of funds that banks can lend and places downward pressure on the equilibrium interest rate. Consequently, interest rates decline in response to the Fed's monetary policy (see Exhibit 5.6).

During the financial crisis in 2008–2009, economic conditions weakened, and the Federal Reserve responded by lowering interest rates. Because the economy remained somewhat stagnant over the 2010–2014 period, the Fed maintained the lower interest rates. The Fed's goal was to encourage firms and individuals to borrow money and spend money to increase economic growth. In general, firms and individuals are more willing to borrow to spend money when interest rates are low because the cost of borrowing is lower.

When the Fed wishes to increase interest rates, it sells to investors some of the Treasury securities that it had previously purchased. The payments made by investors to the Fed for these transactions reduce the amount of funds that investors have for savings. The reduction in the supply of funds available at commercial banks reduces the amount of funds that banks can lend and causes interest rates to increase.

Financial Planning
ONLINE

Go to:
The markets section of http://www.bloomberg.com

To get:
Yields of Treasury securities with various maturities. This information is useful for determining how your return from investing funds in Treasury securities or bank deposits could vary with the maturity you choose.

Financial Planning
ONLINE

Go to:
http://www.bankrate.com and insert the search term "federal reserve."

To get:
Updated information about the Fed's recent actions and upcoming meetings, as well as forecasts of future policy decisions and the potential impact of these decisions.

Shift in the Government Demand for Funds

The U.S. government frequently borrows substantial amounts of funds. Any shift in the government's borrowing behavior can affect the aggregate demand for funds and affect the interest rate.

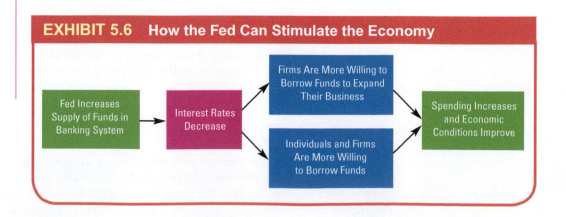

EXHIBIT 5.6   How the Fed Can Stimulate the Economy

Fed Increases Supply of Funds in Banking System → Interest Rates Decrease → Firms Are More Willing to Borrow Funds to Expand Their Business / Individuals and Firms Are More Willing to Borrow Funds → Spending Increases and Economic Conditions Improve

EXAMPLE

Assume that the U.S. government suddenly needs to borrow more funds than it normally borrows. The total amount of funds demanded will now be larger, which results in a shortage of funds at the original interest rate. This places upward pressure on the interest rate.

If the government reduces (instead of increases) the amount that it borrows, there will be a surplus of funds at the original interest rate, which will result in a lower interest rate.

Shift in the Business Demand for Funds

When economic conditions change, businesses review their spending plans and adjust their demand for funds. This shift in demand affects the interest rate.

ECONOMIC IMPACT

During the credit crisis in 2008–2009, economic conditions weakened substantially. Many firms reduced their expansion plans, which meant that they would not need to borrow as much money. This reflects a decrease in the demand for funds and results in lower interest rates.

Conversely, more favorable economic conditions have the opposite impact.

EXAMPLE

Assume that businesses have just become more optimistic about the economy and expect an increase in consumer demand for the products they produce. Consequently, they are more willing to expand and must borrow more funds to support their expansion. Their actions result in an increase in the aggregate demand for funds, similar to the effect of increased government borrowing. The shift results in a higher interest rate.

How Banking Services Fit Within Your Financial Plan

The key banking decisions for your financial plan are

- What banking service characteristics are most important to you?
- What financial institution provides the best banking service characteristics for you?

Interest rates will play a role in your decisions because you can compare rates among financial institutions to determine where you would earn the highest return on your deposits or pay the lowest rate on your loans. By making informed banking decisions, you can ensure that you receive the banking services that you need to conduct your financial transactions and that have the convenience that you desire, while at the same time reducing your fees. As an example, Exhibit 5.7 shows how banking service decisions apply to Stephanie Spratt's financial plan.

EXHIBIT 5.7   How Banking Services Fit Within Stephanie Spratt's Financial Plan

GOALS FOR BANKING SERVICES

1. *Identify the most important banking services.*
2. *Determine which financial institution will provide me with the best banking services.*

ANALYSIS

Characteristic	How It Affects Me
Interest rate offered on deposits	*This will affect the amount of interest income I earn on deposits.*
Interest rate charged on mortgages	*I could use the same financial institution if I buy a home in the future.*
Interest rate charged on personal loans	*I could use the same financial institution if I obtain a personal loan in the future.*
Fees charged for checking services	*I will be writing many checks, so I would prefer not to pay fees on a checking account if I maintain the minimum balance.*
Location	*The ideal financial institution would have a branch near my apartment building and near where I work.*
Online and mobile services available	*This would make my banking more convenient.*
ATMs	*Check locations for convenience and whether any fees are charged for using ATMs.*

DECISIONS

Decision Regarding Important Characteristics of a Financial Institution:

My most important banking service is the checking account because I will write many checks every month. I prefer a bank that does not charge fees for check writing if I maintain a minimum balance. I also value convenience, which I measure by the location of the financial institution's branches, and its online and mobile banking services. I would prefer a financial institution that offers reasonable rates on its deposit accounts, but convenience is more important to me than the deposit rate.

Decision Regarding the Optimal Financial Institution:

After screening financial institutions according to my criteria, I found three financial institutions that are desirable. I selected Quality Savings, Inc. because it does not charge for check writing if I maintain a minimum balance, has branches in convenient locations, and offers online and mobile banking. It also pays relatively high interest rates on its deposits and charges relatively low interest rates (compared to other financial institutions) on its loans. I may consider obtaining a mortgage there someday if I buy a home, as its mortgage rate was comparable to those of other financial institutions.

DISCUSSION QUESTIONS

1. How would Stephanie's banking service decisions be different if she were a single mother of two children?

2. How would Stephanie's banking service decisions be affected if she were 35 years old? If she were 50 years old?

SUMMARY

Types of Depository Institutions. Depository institutions (commercial banks, savings institutions, and credit unions) accept deposits and provide loans. Nondepository institutions include insurance companies (which provide insurance), securities firms (which provide brokerage and other services), and investment companies (which offer mutual funds). Financial conglomerates offer a wide variety of these financial services so that individuals can obtain all their financial services from a single firm.

Banking Services. Important services offered by financial institutions include checking and debit card services, savings accounts, credit card financing, automated teller machines, cashier's checks, money orders, and traveler's checks.

Selecting a Financial Institution. Financial institutions differ in the types of services that they offer, the interest rates that they pay for deposits or charge for loans, and the fees that they charge for providing services. You should compare the services offered, interest rates, and fees among financial institutions to identify the financial institution that would be most suitable and convenient for you.

Interest Rate Components. An interest rate is composed of the risk-free rate and the risk premium. The risk-free rate is the rate of interest paid on an investment that has no risk over a specific investment period (such as a bank deposit backed by government insurance). The risk premium is the additional amount above the risk-free rate that risky investments offer. The higher an investment's risk, the higher the risk premium it must offer to entice investors.

Why Interest Rates Change. Interest rates change in response to monetary policy. When the Fed pumps more money into the banking system, it increases the supply of funds that are available, and this reduces interest rates. It can also pull funds out of the banking system, which has the opposite effect. When the federal government or businesses borrow more funds, this places upward pressure on interest rates. When they reduce their borrowing, this reduces interest rates.

How Banking Services Fit Within Your Financial Plan. Banking services enable you to effectively execute financial transactions such as bill paying, saving, and borrowing. Thus, they help you to achieve your financial plan.

REVIEW QUESTIONS

All Review Questions are available in MyFinanceLab at http://www.myfinancelab.com.

1. **Types of Depository Institutions.** Describe and compare the three types of depository institutions.

2. **Types of Nondepository Institutions.** List and describe the four main types of nondepository financial institutions.

3. **Financial Conglomerate.** What is a financial conglomerate? List some services financial conglomerates provide. Give some examples of financial conglomerates.

4. **Banking Services.** List and describe some of the banking services offered by financial institutions.

5. **Debit versus Credit Card.** What is the difference between a debit card and a credit card?

6. **Special Services.** Name some special services that banks provide. How might you make use of them?

7. **Selecting a Bank.** Steve just received his first paycheck and wants to open a checking account. There are five banks in his hometown. What factors should Steve consider when choosing a bank?

8. **Influence of Interest Rates.** When making banking decisions, why should you be concerned about current interest rates?

9. **Risk-Free Rate.** What is a risk-free rate? Give an example of an investment with a risk-free rate. Why is there no risk?

10. **Risk Premium.** What is a risk premium? Who might take advantage of it?

11. **Calculating a Risk Premium.** How is the risk premium calculated?

12. **Interest Rates.** Where do financial institutions obtain funds for making loans? How are the interest rates for loans determined? Are the interest rates the same for all borrowers? Why or why not?

13. **Impact of Interest Rate Movements.** What effect would a general change in current interest rates have on you as a depositor or borrower?

14. **Assessing Investments.** In considering investments with different degrees of risk, what two factors will influence an investor's decision? What is an appropriate investment for an individual who needs funds in a short period of time for necessities?

15. **Term Structure of Interest Rates.** What is the term structure of interest rates? Why is this concept important to an investor?

16. **Monetary Policy.** What is monetary policy? What organization controls monetary policy in the United States?

17. **Change in Interest Rates.** Briefly discuss conditions that can cause a shift in the demand for funds and a change in the interest rate.

18. **Impact of Economy on Risk Premium.** Explain why a weak economy may cause the risk premium to rise.

19. **Risk Premiums Required by Investors.** Why is a high-risk premium an advantage for the investor? Why is a low-risk premium an advantage for an investor?

20. **Reconciling Your Account Balance.** Why is it important to reconcile your account balance every month?

21. **Check Float.** What is check float? How has check float changed due to electronic banking?

22. **Cashier's Checks and Money Orders.** What is the difference between a cashier's check and a money order?

23. **Paying Bills Online.** List the advantages of paying your bills online.

24. **Risk Premium.** What is the risk premium of Metallica Financial Company's 2-year interest rate of 12% given your local FDIC-insured bank only offers a 5% return for 2-year CDs? Why is Metallica offering a higher interest rate?

25. **Government Borrowing and Interest Rates.** What is the likely impact of increased government borrowing on market rates of interest?

26. **Risk and Return.** Why do some investors pursue higher-risk investments when their income falls during economic downturns? What is wrong with this strategy?

27. **Traveler's Checks.** When would you use a traveler's check? What are the advantages of using traveler's checks?

FINANCIAL PLANNING PROBLEMS

All Financial Planning Problems are available in MyFinanceLab *at http://www.myfinancelab.com.*

Refer to the following table when answering problems 1 through 4:

	Hillsboro Bank	First National	South Trust Bank	Sun Coast Bank
ATM Charges:				
Home bank	Free	Free	Free	Free
Other bank	4 free, then $1 per use	$1.25	$1.25	$1.25
Checking:				
Minimum deposit	$100	$25	$1	$1
Minimum balance required to avoid fees*	N/A	N/A	$500	N/A
Monthly fees	$6	$7	$11	$2.50
Check-writing charges	12 free, then $1 per check	7 free, then $1 per check	Unlimited	Each check 50 cents

*N/A means monthly fees apply irrespective of account balances.

1. **Selecting a Bank.** Jason wants to open a checking account with a $100 deposit. Jason believes he will write 15 checks per month and use other banks' ATMs 8 times a month. He will not be able to maintain a minimum balance. Which bank should Jason choose?

2. **Selecting a Bank.** Julie wants to open a bank account with $75. Julie estimates that she will write 20 checks per month and use her ATM card at the home bank. She will maintain a $200 balance. Which bank should Julie choose?

3. **Selecting a Bank.** Veronica plans to open a checking account with her $1,200 tax refund check. She believes she can maintain a $500 minimum balance. Also, she estimates that she will write 10 checks per month and will use other banks' ATMs as many as 15 times per month. Which bank should Veronica choose?

4. **Check Writing Fees.** Randy, a student, has $500 to deposit in a new checking account, but Randy knows he will not be able to maintain a minimum balance. He will not use an ATM card, but will write a large number of checks. Randy is trying to choose between the unlimited check writing offered by South Trust and the low per-check fee offered by Sun Coast. How many checks would

Randy have to write each month for the account at South Trust to be the better option?

5. **Checking Account Balance.** Paul has an account at St. Jerome Bank. He does not track his checking account balance in a checkbook register. Yesterday evening, he placed two checks in the mail for $156.66 and $238.94. Paul accesses his account online and finds that his balance is $568.40, and all the checks he has written except for the two checks from yesterday have cleared. Based on his balance, Paul writes a check for a new stereo for $241.00. Paul has no intention of making a deposit in the near future. What are the consequences of his actions?

6. **Adjusted Bank Balance.** Mary's last bank statement showed an ending balance of $168.51. This month, she deposited $600.00 in her account and withdrew a total of $239.00. Furthermore, Mary wrote a total of five checks, two of which have cleared. The two checks that have cleared total $143.00. The three remaining checks total $106.09. Mary pays no fees at her bank. What is the balance shown this month on Mary's bank statement? What is the adjusted bank balance?

7. **Selecting a CD.** Casey has $1,000 to invest in a certificate of deposit. Her local bank offers her 2.5% on a 12-month FDIC-insured CD. A nonfinancial institution offers her 5.2% on a 12-month CD.

What is the risk premium? What else must Casey consider in choosing between the two CDs?

8. **Ethical Dilemma.** Mike, a recent college graduate, opened a checking account with a local bank. He asked numerous questions before deciding on this bank, including inquiring about checking account fees and annual credit card fees. When Mike returns from his first international business trip he is surprised to see numerous fees on his credit card statement and his bank statement. When he calls the bank, they inform him that they recently added service charges on international transactions involving their checking and credit card accounts. When Mike protests, they state that his last bank statement included a flyer detailing these changes. In looking back, Mike realizes that he had, in fact, received the information, but had ignored it because it was included with considerable advertising information about car loan rate specials, and the lengthy document was in very small print.

a. Comment on the ethics of banks and other financial institutions' efforts to notify customers of fee changes. Should a letter be sent specifically dealing with these changes to ensure that customers are aware of the information?

b. Is there a lesson to be learned from Mike's experience?

FINANCIAL PLANNING ONLINE EXERCISES

1. Go to http://www.fdic.gov, and insert the search term "safe Internet banking." Read the article on "Safe Internet Banking." List three steps that you will take or are taking to ensure that your Internet banking is safe.

2. a. Conduct an online search for an Internet bank. Describe the services it offers. How do these services differ from the services offered by a "regular" commercial bank? Would you bank at an Internet bank? Why or why not?

b. Find some banks in your region, and study them. Do these banks offer any services your current bank does not offer? How do these other banks in your region compare to your current bank?

c. Locate a commercial bank located in a foreign country. How does this bank differ from your current bank? Would you consider banking with a foreign bank? Why or why not?

3. Go to the markets section of http://www.bloomberg.com.

a. How does the yield on Treasury securities with longer maturities differ from the yield on Treasury securities with shorter yields? Why do you think the yields vary with the maturity?

b. What is the yield on a 3-month T-bill? On a 6-month T-bill? If you needed funds in six months, you could invest in two consecutive 3-month T-bills or in one 6-month T-bill. Which strategy would you choose? Why?

c. What is the difference between the 10-year Treasury yield and the 10-year Municipal bond yield? Which do you think would be a better investment? Which would you feel more comfortable investing in considering your level of risk aversion?

4. Go to the news section of http://www.bloomberg.com. Locate an article related to recent market news. Write a brief summary of the article, and explain what impact it is likely to have on the economy and you as an individual.

PSYCHOLOGY OF PERSONAL FINANCE: Paying Your Bills

1. Some people purposely ignore a bill and put it out of their minds to avoid the stress associated with it. Other people pay their bills immediately because they worry that they might forget about paying them. What drives your behavior toward paying bills?

2. Read one practical article of how psychology can affect bill-paying behavior. You can easily retrieve possible articles by doing an online search using the terms "psychology" and "paying bills." Summarize the main points of the article.

WEB SEARCH EXERCISE

You can develop your personal finance skills by conducting an Internet search for related articles. Find a recent online article about personal finance that reinforces one or more concepts covered in this chapter. If your class has an online component, your professor may ask you to post your summary of the article there and provide a link to the article so that other students can access it. If your class is live, your professor may ask you to summarize your application of the article in class. Your professor may assign specific students to complete this assignment or may allow any student to do the assignment on a volunteer basis.

For recent online articles related to this chapter, consider using the following search terms (be sure to include the current year as a search term to ensure that the online articles are recent):

- Choosing your bank
- Paying your bills online
- Balancing your checkbook
- Your debit card
- Best bank deposit rates

VIDEO EXERCISE: Banking Tips

Go to one of the Web sites that contain video clips (such as http://www.youtube.com) and view some video clips about banking tips. You can use search phrases such as "banking tips." Select one video clip on this topic that you would recommend for the other students in your class.

1. Provide the Web link for the video clip.

2. What do you think is the main point of this video clip?

3. How might you change your use or selection of banking services as a result of watching this video clip?

BUILDING YOUR OWN FINANCIAL PLAN

The worksheets at the end of this chapter will guide you through the process of evaluating financial institutions, comparing interest rates on specific deposit types and loans, and reconciling your checking account balance. For the first worksheet, enter information about the specific services of interest to you and evaluate the offerings at several financial institutions that you visit in person or on the Internet. In addition to researching a commercial bank, a savings bank, and a credit union, research two other options, such as an online bank and an international bank. For the check-reconciling worksheet, you will need to refer to your bank statement and checkbook register.

Go to the worksheets at the end of this chapter, to continue building your financial plan.

THE SAMPSONS—A Continuing Case

Recall that the Sampsons have resolved to save a total of $800 per month. Dave and Sharon notice that their local bank offers the certificates of deposit listed in the following table; they now need to determine which CDs will best suit their savings goals. Each CD requires a minimum investment of $300. Recall that the Sampsons are saving $500 each month for a down payment on a new car that they will purchase within a year. They are also saving $300 each month for their children's college education, which begins 12 years from now.

Go to the worksheets at the end of this chapter to continue this case.

Maturity	Annualized Interest Rate (%)
1 month	1.0
3 months	1.2
6 months	1.6
1 year	2.0
3 years	2.5
5 years	2.8
7 years	3.0
10 years	3.2

NAME _____ DATE _____

CHAPTER 5: BUILDING YOUR OWN FINANCIAL PLAN

YOUR GOALS FOR CHAPTER 5

1. Identify the banking services that are most important to you.
2. Determine which financial institution will provide you with the best banking services.

ANALYSIS

1. Evaluate what banking services are most important to you with a score of "10" for the most important and "1" for the least important. Then evaluate five financial institutions with respect to the services offered and rate the institutions with "5" as the best for each service and "1" as the worst. The worksheet will calculate scores for each institution.

Banking Services Scorecard

Services Offered	Priority	Commercial Bank		Savings Institution		Credit Union		Institution 4		Institution 5	
		Rank	Score	Rank	Score	Rank	Score	Rank	Score	Rank	Score
1. Hours of operation—evenings, Saturdays											
2. Locations—proximity to work and home											
3. Fees/Minimum balance for checking accounts											
4. Fees for ATM usage											
5. Interest rate on savings accounts											
6. Interest rate on checking accounts											
7. VISA/MasterCard available and annual fee											
8. Interest rate on home loans											
9. Interest rate on car loans											
10. Safety deposit boxes and rental rates											
Total Score for Each Institution											

2. Use the following worksheet as a guide for reconciling your checking account balance by entering data from your bank statement and checkbook register. If the two balances do not match, carefully check your math and records. If there is still a discrepancy, contact the financial institution.

		Checkbook Register	
Bank Statement Balance	$	**Balance**	$
Plus Deposits in Transit *(Total of deposits that appear in your checkbook but do not appear on the bank statement)*	$	Plus Interest	$
Subtotal	$	Subtotal	$
Minus Outstanding Checks *(Total of any checks that you have written that do not appear on the bank statement; use the following worksheet to aid your computations)*	$	Minus Service Charge	$
Subtotal	$	Subtotal	$
Plus—Other *(Any items that appear in your checkbook but do not appear on the bank statement as well as any error that the bank has made)**	$	Plus—Other *(Including errors in your checkbook)* Description:	$
Description:			
Minus—Other*	$	Minus—Other *(Including errors in your checkbook)*	$
Description:		Description:	
Reconciled Balance	$	Reconciled Balance	$

Example: If you have ordered new checks and deducted the amount from your checkbook but the bank has not yet deducted the amount from your account

Outstanding Checks

CK# _____	$ _____
CK# _____	$ _____
CK# _____	$ _____
CK# _____	$ _____
CK# _____	$ _____
Total	$ _____

DECISIONS

1. Describe the services and characteristics that are of prime importance to you in a financial institution.

_____

_____

_____

_____

_____

_____

_____

_____

_____

_____

2. Which of the financial institutions you evaluated is most optimal for your needs? Why?

_____

_____

_____

_____

_____

_____

_____

_____

_____

_____

CHAPTER 5: THE SAMPSONS—A Continuing Case

CASE QUESTIONS

1. Advise the Sampsons on the maturity to select when investing their savings in a CD for a down payment on a car. What are the advantages or disadvantages of the relatively short-term maturities versus the longer-term maturities?

_____

_____

_____

_____

_____

_____

_____

_____

2. Advise the Sampsons on the maturity to select when investing their savings for their children's education. Describe any advantages or disadvantages of the relatively short-term maturities versus the longer-term maturities.

_____

_____

_____

_____

_____

_____

_____

3. If you thought that interest rates were going to rise in the next few months, how might this affect the advice that you give the Sampsons?

_____

_____

_____

_____

_____

_____

_____

chapter 6

Managing Your Money

Focus Pocus LTD/Fotolia

Jared lives from paycheck to paycheck. His checkbook register showed that he had a balance of $110, so he used his debit card for five transactions totaling $30, wrote a check for $20 to make the payment on his credit card, and had two automatic payments for utilities deducted from his account for a total of $50. Unfortunately, Jared had forgotten to list three debit card transactions in his check register, and instead of $110, his real balance was $35. As a result, the check to the credit card company bounced, and the automatic payments were not made. Each payee assessed a late fee of $15 for the late payment, and the bank charged Jared a nonsufficient funds fee of $35 for the check and each automatic payment. Thus, Jared was assessed a total of $150 in penalties.

Part of this expensive lesson for Jared could have been avoided if he had requested overdraft protection on his account. The overdraft protection would have saved him from the late fees, although he would still probably have had to pay overdraft fees and possibly interest on the overdraft loan. Some people fail to keep track of their balances and therefore may have insufficient funds to support their transactions. Consequently, they are charged penalty fees by their banks.

This chapter describes techniques for managing your checking account. It also identifies various types of money market investments and explains how the use of cash management can lead to increased liquidity within your financial plan.

MyFinanceLab helps you master the topics in this chapter and study more efficiently. Visit http://www.myfinancelab.com for more details.

The objectives of this chapter are to:

- Provide a background on money management
- Describe the most popular money market investments
- Identify the risk associated with money market investments
- Explain how to manage the risk of your money market investments
- Explain how money management fits within your financial plan

Background on Money Management

money management
A series of decisions made over a short-term period regarding cash inflows and outflows.

Money management describes the decisions you make over a short-term period regarding your cash inflows and outflows. It is separate from decisions about investing funds for a long-term period (such as several years) or borrowing funds for a long-term period. Instead, it focuses on maintaining short-term investments to achieve both liquidity and an adequate return on your investments, as explained next.

Liquidity

liquidity
Your ability to cover any cash deficiencies that you may experience.

As discussed in Chapter 1, **liquidity** refers to your ability to cover any short-term cash deficiencies. Recall that the personal cash flow statement determines the amount of excess or deficient funds that you have at the end of a period, such as one month from now. Money management is related to the personal cash flow statement because it determines how to use excess funds, or how to obtain funds if your cash inflows are insufficient. You should strive to maintain a sufficient amount of funds in liquid assets such as a checking account or savings account to draw on when your cash outflows exceed your cash inflows. In this way, you maintain adequate liquidity.

Liquidity is necessary because there will be periods when your cash inflows are not adequate to cover your cash outflows. But there are opportunity costs when you maintain an excessive amount of liquid funds. A portion of those funds could have been invested in less-liquid assets that could earn a higher return than, say, a savings account. In general, the more liquid an investment, the lower its return, so you forgo higher returns when maintaining a high degree of liquidity.

EXAMPLE

Stephanie Spratt's cash inflows are $2,500 per month after taxes. Her cash outflows are normally about $2,100 per month, leaving her with $400 in cash each month. This month she expects that she will have an extra expense of $600; therefore, her cash outflows will exceed her cash inflows by $200. She needs a convenient source of funds to cover the extra expense.

Using Credit Cards for Liquidity Some individuals rely on a credit card (to be discussed in detail in Chapter 8) as a source of liquidity rather than maintaining liquid investments. Many credit cards provide temporary free financing from the time you make purchases until the date when your payment is due. If you have insufficient funds to pay the entire credit card balance when the bill is due, you may pay only a portion of your balance and finance the rest of the payment. The interest rate is usually quite high, commonly ranging from 8% to 20%. Maintaining liquid assets that you can easily access when you need funds allows you to avoid using credit and paying high finance charges.

PSYCHOLOGY
of Personal
Finance

Many consumers initially obtain a credit card to serve liquidity needs, but then end up using it in other ways. Some consumers rely on the credit card for many of their purchases. Although their plan was to always pay off the credit card balance each month, they may be incapable of paying off the balance if the amount of their purchases is large. Paying the minimum payment on the credit card bill may seem painless, as most of the bill can just be deferred into the future. Some consumers feel the pleasure of putting off the payment and ignore that they will have to repay the debt as well as the interest later. Although credit cards can serve as an excellent source of liquidity, there is the danger that they are used as a permanent source of financing, which may result in credit repayment problems later.

Adequate Return

When you maintain short-term investments, you should strive to achieve the highest possible return. The return on your short-term investments is dependent on the prevailing risk-free rate and the level of risk you are willing to tolerate. Some assets that satisfy your liquidity needs may not necessarily achieve the return that you expect. For example, you could maintain a large amount of cash in your wallet as a source of liquidity, but it would earn a zero rate of return. Other investments may provide an adequate return, but are not liquid. To achieve both liquidity and an adequate return, you should consider investing in multiple money market investments with varied returns and levels of liquidity.

Money Market Investments

Common investments for short-term funds include the following money market investments:

- Checking account
- NOW account
- Savings deposit
- Certificate of deposit
- Money market deposit account (MMDA)
- Treasury bills
- Money market fund
- Asset management account

All these investments except Treasury bills and money market funds are offered by depository institutions and are insured for up to $250,000 in the event of default by the institution. In this section, we'll examine each of these investments in turn and focus on their liquidity and typical return.

Checking Account

Individuals deposit funds in a checking account at a depository institution to write checks or use their debit card to pay for various products and services. A checking account is a very liquid investment because you can access the funds (by withdrawing funds or writing checks) at any time.

overdraft protection
An arrangement that protects a customer who uses a debit card or writes a check for an amount that exceeds the checking account balance; it is a short-term loan from the depository institution where the checking account is maintained.

Overdraft Protection Some depository institutions offer **overdraft protection**, which protects a customer who engages in a transaction by using a debit card or writing a check for an amount that exceeds the checking account balance. The protection is essentially a short-term loan. For example, if you write a check for $300 but have a checking account balance of only $100, the depository institution will provide overdraft protection by making a loan of $200 to make up the difference. It will also likely charge you an overdraft fee. Without overdraft protection, checks written against an insufficient account balance bounce, meaning that they are not honored by the depository institution. In addition, a customer who writes a check that bounces may be charged a penalty fee by the financial institution. Overdraft protection's cost is the overdraft fee and the high interest rate charged on the loan.

Stop Payment If you write a check but believe that it was lost and never received by the payee, you may request that the financial institution **stop payment**, which means that the institution will not honor the check if someone tries to cash it. In some cases, a customer may even stop payment to prevent the recipient from cashing a check. For example, if you write a check to pay for home repairs, but the job is not completed, you may decide to stop payment on the check. Normally, a fee is charged for a stop payment service.

> **stop payment**
> A financial institution's notice that it will not honor a check if someone tries to cash it; usually occurs in response to a request by the writer of the check.

Direct Deposit You can set up a direct deposit system so that your paychecks go directly from your employer to your financial institution. Therefore, you will not need to deposit your paychecks. The direct deposits not only save you time but also could allow you to save money.

Some people find that the direct deposit system helps them save money because they tend to spend the money immediately if they cash their paycheck. When they have their paycheck sent directly to their checking account, they do not have excess cash to spend. Furthermore, their record of their spending by check or debit card allows them to monitor how they spend their money over time.

> **PSYCHOLOGY**
> of Personal Finance

Fees Depository institutions may charge a monthly fee such as $15 per month for providing checking services unless the depositor maintains a minimum balance in the checking account or a minimum aggregate balance in other accounts at that institution. Some financial institutions charge a fee per check written instead of a monthly fee. The specific fee structure and the rules for waiving the fee vary among financial institutions, so you should compare fees before you decide where to set up your checking account.

No Interest A disadvantage of investing funds in a checking account is that the funds do not earn any interest. For this reason, you should keep only enough funds in your checking account to cover anticipated expenses and a small excess amount in case unanticipated expenses arise. You should not deposit more funds in your checking account than you think you may need because you can earn interest by investing in other money market investments.

NOW Account

> **NOW (negotiable order of withdrawal) account**
> A type of deposit offered by depository institutions that provides checking services and pays interest.

Another deposit offered by depository institutions is a **negotiable order of withdrawal (NOW) account.** An advantage of a NOW account over a traditional checking account is that it pays interest, although the interest is relatively low compared with many other bank deposits. The depositor is required to maintain a minimum balance in a NOW account, so the account is not as liquid as a traditional checking account.

EXAMPLE

Stephanie Spratt has a checking account with no minimum balance. She is considering opening a NOW account that requires a minimum balance of $500 and offers an interest rate of 3%. She has an extra $800 in her checking account that she could transfer to the NOW account. How much interest would she earn over one year in the NOW account?

Interest Earned = Deposit Amount × Interest Rate

= $800 × .03

= $24

Stephanie would earn $24 in annual interest from the NOW account, versus zero interest from her traditional checking account. She would need to maintain the $500 minimum balance in the NOW account, whereas she has the use of all of the funds in her checking account. She decides to leave the funds in the checking account, as the extra liquidity is worth more to her than the $24 she could earn from the NOW account.

Savings Deposit

Traditional savings accounts offered by a depository institution pay a higher interest rate on deposits than offered on a NOW account. In addition, funds can normally be withdrawn from a savings account at any time. A savings account does not provide checking services. It is less liquid than a checking account or a NOW account because you cannot use the account to write checks. The interest rate offered on savings deposits varies among depository institutions. Many institutions quote their rates on their Web sites.

EXAMPLE

Stephanie Spratt wants to determine the amount of interest that she would earn over one year if she deposits $1,000 in a savings account that pays 4% interest.

Interest Earned = Deposit Amount × Interest Rate

$$= \$1,000 \times .04$$

$$= \$40$$

Although the interest income is attractive, she cannot write checks on a savings account. As she expects to need the funds in her checking account to pay bills in the near future, she decides not to switch those funds to a savings account at this time.

Automatic Transfer You may want to consider setting up an automatic transfer at your bank to move funds from one account to another. For example, you could request that your financial institution automatically transfer $50 from your checking account to your savings account every two weeks. This allows you to build your savings automatically, as you do not have to initiate the transfer. However, you should only set it up if you are sure that you will still have sufficient funds in your checking account to cover your spending needs.

PSYCHOLOGY of Personal Finance

The automatic transfer is not only convenient but can also ensure that you save a portion of your paycheck. You might not remember to request the transfer of funds from your checking account to your savings account if it is not done automatically. Therefore, your checking account will accumulate more funds, and this might encourage you to spend whatever funds you have. With the automatic transfer from your checking account to your savings account, you have less money available to spend when writing checks.

Certificate of Deposit

As mentioned in Chapter 5, a certificate of deposit (CD) offered by a depository institution specifies a minimum amount that must be invested, a maturity date on which the deposit matures, and an annualized interest rate. Common maturity dates for CDs are one month, three months, six months, one year, three years, and five years. CDs can be purchased by both firms and individuals. CDs that have smaller denominations (such as $5,000 or $10,000) are sometimes referred to as **retail CDs** because they are more attractive to individuals than to firms.

retail CDs
Certificates of deposit that have small denominations (such as $5,000 or $10,000).

Return Depository institutions offer higher interest rates on CDs than on savings deposits. The higher return is compensation for being willing to maintain the investment until maturity. Interest rates are quoted on an annualized (yearly) basis. The interest to be generated by your investment in a CD is based on the annualized interest rate and the amount of time until maturity. The interest rates offered on CDs vary among depository institutions.

EXAMPLE

A three-month (90-day) CD offers an annualized interest rate of 6% and requires a $5,000 minimum deposit. You want to determine the amount of interest you would earn if you invested $5,000 in the CD. Because the interest rate is annualized, you will receive only a fraction of the 6% rate because your investment is for a fraction of the year:

Interest Earned = Deposit Amount × Interest Rate

$$\times \text{ Adjustment for Investment Period}$$

$$= \$5,000 \times .06 \times 90/365$$

This process can be more easily understood by noting that the interest rate is applied for only 90 days, whereas the annual interest rate reflects 365 days. The interest rate that applies to your 90-day investment is for about one-fourth (90/365) of the year, so the applicable interest rate is

Interest Rate = .06 × 90/365

$$= .0148 \text{ or } 1.48\%$$

The 1.48% represents the actual return on your investment.

Now the interest can be determined by simply applying this return to the deposit amount:

Interest Earned = Deposit Amount × Interest Rate

$$= \$5,000 \times .0148$$

$$= \$73.97$$

Liquidity A penalty is imposed for early withdrawal from CDs, so these deposits are less liquid than funds deposited in a savings account. You should consider a CD only if you are certain that you will not need the funds until after it matures. You may decide to invest some of your funds in a CD and other funds in more liquid assets.

Choice Among CD Maturities CDs with longer terms to maturity typically offer higher annualized interest rates. However, CDs with longer maturities tie up your funds for a longer period of time and are therefore less liquid. Your choice of a maturity date for a CD may depend on your need for liquidity. For example, if you know that you may need your funds in four months, you could invest in a three-month CD and then place the funds in a more liquid asset (such as your checking account or savings account) when the CD matures. If you do not expect to need the funds for one year, you may consider a one-year CD.

Money Market Deposit Account (MMDA)

money market deposit account (MMDA)
A deposit offered by a depository institution that requires a minimum balance, has no maturity date, pays interest, and allows a limited number of checks to be written each month.

A **money market deposit account** (**MMDA**) is a deposit account offered by a depository institution that requires a minimum balance to be maintained, has no maturity date, pays interest, and allows a limited number of checks to be written each month. The specific details vary among financial institutions. For example, an account might require that a minimum balance of $2,500 be maintained over the month and charge a $15 per month fee in any month when the minimum balance falls below that level.

An MMDA differs from a NOW account in that it provides only limited checking services while paying a higher interest rate than that offered on NOW accounts. Many individuals maintain a checking account or NOW account to cover most of their day-to-day transactions and an MMDA to capitalize on the higher interest rate. Thus, they may maintain a larger amount of funds in the MMDA and use this account to write a large check for an unexpected expense. The MMDA is not as liquid as a checking account because it limits the number of checks that can be written.

Treasury Bills

Treasury securities
Debt securities issued by the U.S. Treasury.

As mentioned in Chapter 5, **Treasury securities** are debt securities issued by the U.S. Treasury. When the U.S. government needs to spend more money than it has received in taxes, it borrows funds by issuing Treasury securities. Individuals can purchase Treasury securities through a brokerage firm. Treasury securities are offered with various maturities, such as four weeks, three months, six months, one year, ten years, and thirty years. For money management purposes, individuals tend to focus on **Treasury bills (T-bills)**, which are Treasury securities that will mature in one year or less. T-bills are available with a minimum value at maturity (called the par value) of $100 and are denominated in multiples of $100 above that minimum (you can purchase T-bills at the U.S. Treasury's Web site). Many investors typically purchase T-bills with a value at maturity of at least $10,000.

Treasury bills (T-bills)
Treasury securities with maturities of one year or less.

Return Treasury bills are purchased at a discount from par value. If you invest in a T-bill and hold it until maturity, you earn a capital gain, which is the difference between the par value of the T-bill at maturity and the amount you paid for the T-bill. Your return on the T-bill is the capital gain as a percentage of your initial investment.

When measuring returns on investments, you should annualize the returns so that you can compare returns on various investments with different maturities. An investment over a one-month period will likely generate a smaller dollar amount of return than a one-year investment. To compare the one-month and one-year investments, you need to determine the annualized yield (or percentage return) on each investment.

EXAMPLE

An investor pays $9,400 to purchase a T-bill that has a par value of $10,000 and a one-year maturity. When the T-bill matures, she receives $10,000. The return from investing in the T-bill is

$$\text{Return on T-Bill} = \frac{\$10,000 - \$9,400}{\$9,400}$$

$$= 6.38\%$$

For an investment that lasts three months (one-fourth of a year), multiply by four to determine the annualized return. For an investment that lasts six months (one-half of a year), multiply by two to determine the annualized return. The most precise method of annualizing a return is to multiply the return by $365/N$, where N is the number of days the investment existed.

EXAMPLE

An investor pays $9,700 to purchase a T-bill with a par value of $10,000 and a maturity of 182 days. The annualized return from investing in the T-bill is:

$$\text{Return on T-Bill} = \frac{\$10,000 - \$9,700}{\$9,700} \times \frac{365}{182}$$

$$= 6.20\%$$

secondary market
A market where existing securities such as Treasury bills can be purchased or sold.

Secondary Market There is a **secondary market** for T-bills where they can be sold before their maturity with the help of a brokerage firm. This secondary market also allows individuals to purchase T-bills that were previously owned by someone else. The return on a T-bill is usually slightly lower than the return on a CD with the same maturity, but T-bills are more liquid because they have a secondary market, whereas CDs must be held until maturity. If you sell a T-bill in the secondary market, your capital gain is the difference between what you sold the T-bill for and what you paid for the T-bill. Your return is this capital gain as a percentage of your initial investment.

Quotations The prices of various T-bills and the returns they offer for holding them until maturity are quoted in financial newspapers and online sites.

EXAMPLE

An investor purchases a T-bill for $9,700 and sells the T-bill in the secondary market 60 days later for a price of $9,820. The annualized return is

$$\text{Return on T-Bill} = \frac{\$9,820 - \$9,700}{\$9,700} \times \frac{365}{60}$$

$$= 7.53\%$$

Money Market Funds (MMFs)

money market funds (MMFs)
Accounts that pool money from individuals and invest in securities that have a short-term maturity, such as one year or less.

Money market funds (MMFs) pool money from individuals to invest in securities that have a short-term maturity, such as one year or less. In fact, the average time remaining to maturity of debt securities held in an MMF is typically less than 90 days. Many MMFs invest in short-term Treasury securities or in wholesale CDs (in denominations of $100,000 or more). Investors can invest in MMFs by sending a check for the amount they wish to have invested for them. Some MMFs invest mainly in **commercial paper**, which consists of short-term debt securities issued by large corporations. Commercial paper typically generates a slightly higher interest rate than T-bills. Money market funds are not insured, but most of them invest in very safe investments and have a very low risk of default.

commercial paper
Short-term debt securities issued by large corporations that typically offer a slightly higher return than Treasury bills.

MMFs offer some liquidity in that individuals can write a limited number of checks on their accounts each month. Often the checks must exceed a minimum amount (such as $250). Individuals may use the checking account associated with an MMF to cover large expenditures, while maintaining a regular checking account to cover smaller purchases. Many individuals invest in an MMF so that they can earn interest until the money is needed. Some MMFs are linked with other accounts so that the money can earn interest until it is transferred to another account. For example, many brokerage accounts allow investors to place any unused funds in an MMF until the funds are used to purchase stock.

EXAMPLE

Assume that you set up an account with $9,000 to purchase stock at a brokerage firm on May 1. On that day, you purchase 100 shares of a stock priced at $50. To cover the purchase, the brokerage firm withdraws $5,000 ($50 × 100 shares) from your account. You still have $4,000 that you have not used, which is placed in a specific MMF account at the brokerage firm. This MMF offers the same limited check-writing services as other MMFs. The money will sit in that account until you use it to purchase stock or write checks against the account.

Assuming that the interest rate earned on the MMF is 6% annually (.5% per month), and you do not purchase any more stock until June 1, you will earn interest on that account over the month when the funds are not used:

Amount Invested in MMF × Interest Rate per Month = Interest Earned in 1 Month
$4,000 × .005   = $20

Therefore, the MMF account balance increases by $20 to $4,020 because the funds have earned interest. Any unused balance will continue to earn interest until you use it to purchase stock or write checks against the account.

EXHIBIT 6.1   Weekly Money Market Fund Yields

Fund	Average Maturity	7-Day Yield	Assets (millions of $)
Star Fund	43	3.28%	496

Financial Planning
ONLINE

Go to:
The data section of http://www.federalreserve.gov

To get:
Historical interest rate data.

Money Market Fund Quotations Financial newspapers such as *The Wall Street Journal* commonly publish the yields provided by numerous money market funds. An example of the typical information provided in the quotations is shown in Exhibit 6.1 for one money market fund. The first column lists the name of the MMF; the second column, the average maturity of the investments of that fund; the third column, the annualized yield generated by the fund; and the fourth column, the size of the fund (measured in millions of dollars). Review the quotation for Star Fund in Exhibit 6.1, which invests in government securities that have a short term remaining until maturity. This fund's investments have an average time to maturity of 43 days. It generated an annual yield of 3.28% for its investors over the last seven days. The fund presently manages $496 million in assets.

Asset Management Account

asset management account
An account that combines deposit accounts with a brokerage account and provides a single consolidated statement.

sweep account
An asset management account that sweeps any unused balance in the brokerage account into a money market investment at the end of each business day.

An **asset management account** combines deposit accounts with a brokerage account that is used to buy or sell stocks. The advantage of an asset management account is that it provides a single consolidated statement showing the ending balances and activity of all the accounts. Asset management accounts are available at some depository institutions and brokerage services. The financial institutions that offer these accounts require that the sum of all the accounts in the asset management account exceed some minimum amount, such as $15,000. A special type of asset management account is the **sweep account**, which sweeps any unused balance in the brokerage account into a money market investment at the end of each business day. The unused balance earns interest and remains available for writing checks.

Comparison of Money Market Investments

The various types of money market investments are compared in Exhibit 6.2. Notice that money market investments that offer a higher return tend to have less liquidity.

EXHIBIT 6.2   Comparison of Money Market Investments

Money Market Investment	Advantages	Disadvantages
Checking account	Very liquid	No interest
NOW account	Very liquid	Low interest rate; minimum balance required
MMDA	Liquid	Low interest rate
Savings account	Liquid	Low interest rate
Certificate of deposit (CD)	Relatively high interest rate	Less liquid
Treasury bill	Relatively high interest rate	High minimum purchase
Money market fund (MMF)	Liquid	Not as liquid as checking or NOW accounts
Asset management account	Convenient	High minimum balance required

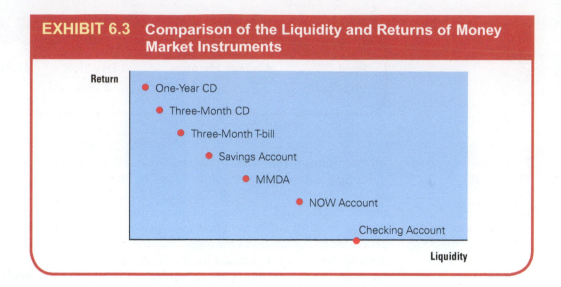

EXHIBIT 6.3   **Comparison of the Liquidity and Returns of Money Market Instruments**

The relationship between the returns and the liquidity of money market investments is illustrated graphically in Exhibit 6.3. Checking accounts offer the most liquidity but provide no return. At the other extreme, a one-year CD provides the highest return but has less liquidity than the other money market instruments.

Risk of Money Market Investments

Financial Planning
ONLINE

Go to:
The money section of CNN.com, and go to the personal finance section containing calculators.

To get:
Estimates of future savings that you will accumulate over time at different interest rates.

credit risk
The risk that a borrower may not repay on a timely basis.

default risk
The risk that a borrower may not repay on a timely basis.

interest rate risk
The risk that the value of an investment could decline as a result of a change in interest rates.

Before you consider investing short-term funds in various money market instruments, you must factor in your exposure to risk, or the uncertainty surrounding the potential return. Money market investments are vulnerable to three types of risk: (1) credit risk, (2) interest rate risk, and (3) liquidity risk.

Credit Risk

When you invest in money market securities, you may be exposed to **credit risk** (also referred to as **default risk**), which is the risk that the borrower will not repay on a timely basis. The borrower may make late payments or even default on the credit. In that event, you will receive only a portion (or none) of the money you invested. MMFs that invest in large deposits of financial institutions are insured only up to $250,000 by the Federal Deposit Insurance Corporation (FDIC). Treasury securities are backed by the federal government, but most other types of money market securities are subject to the possibility of default. However, although the potential for default is very low for some types of money market securities, it is important that you assess this risk before you invest money in money market securities.

Interest Rate Risk

Interest rate risk is the risk that the value of an investment could decline as a result of a change in interest rates. Investors who wish to limit their exposure to interest rate risk can invest in debt securities that fit the time frame in which they will need funds. That is, if you need funds in three months, you should consider an investment that has a maturity of three months, so that you do not have to worry about changes in interest rates. The following example illustrates how the value of an investment can be affected by interest rate movements.

EXAMPLE

Suppose that three months ago you purchased a one-year T-bill that offered a return of 5%. Interest rates have recently risen, and you are disappointed that you locked in your investment at 5% while more recently issued investments (including one-year T-bills) are now offering an annualized return of about 6%. You can sell your T-bill in the secondary market, but investors will pay a relatively low price for it because they can buy new securities that offer an annualized return of 6%. This explains why the value of a debt security decreases in response to an increase in interest rates.

Rather than selling your T-bill at a discounted price, you can simply hold it to maturity. However, the return on your investment over the entire one-year period will be only 5%, even though recently issued T-bills are offering higher returns. Neither of your two options is desirable.

Liquidity Risk

liquidity risk
The potential loss that could occur as a result of converting an investment into cash.

Recall that liquidity represents your ability to cover any short-term cash deficiencies. To be liquid, an investment should be easily converted to cash. **Liquidity risk** is the potential loss that could occur as a result of converting an investment to cash. For example, a retail CD has liquidity risk because it cannot be sold in the secondary market. You would incur a penalty if you tried to redeem it before maturity at the financial institution where you invested in the CD.

The liquidity risk of an investment is influenced by its secondary market. If a particular debt security has a strong secondary market, it can usually be sold quickly and at less of a discount than a debt security with an inactive secondary market. For example, you can easily sell a T-bill in a secondary market, which is why T-bills are more liquid than CDs.

Impact of Expected Economic Conditions on Liquidity Needs

ECONOMIC IMPACT

When economic conditions weaken, it can create some liquidity problems, as shown in Exhibit 6.4. For example, during the financial crisis in 2008–2009, some individuals lost their jobs. Other individuals who retained their jobs did not work as much as expected and therefore earned less income than they had anticipated. Many retired individuals relied on their investments for income, but their investments generated very poor returns over this period, which resulted in lower income than expected. As a result, their cash inflows were not always large enough to cover their cash outflows.

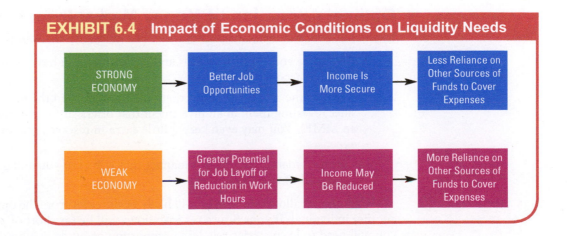

EXHIBIT 6.4   Impact of Economic Conditions on Liquidity Needs

If you suspect that economic conditions may weaken and may possibly result in lower income from your employer or your investments, you may wish to ensure that you maintain a greater degree of liquidity. You could allocate more funds to liquid money market securities and less to other types of investments. In this way, if economic conditions weaken and reduce your cash inflows, you can rely on your money market securities as a source of liquidity.

Risk Management

Risk management of money market investments involves (1) assessing the risk exhibited by the investments and (2) using your assessment of risk and your unique financial situation to determine the optimal allocation of your short-term funds among money market investments.

Risk Assessment of Money Market Investments

You must consider the risk-return trade-off before making investment decisions. The money market securities described in this chapter tend to be insulated from credit risk because they are insured or backed by the government. Treasury securities and small bank deposits are largely free from credit risk. One exception is MMFs that invest in commercial paper. If the commercial paper held by a particular MMF defaults, the return generated by the MMF will be adversely affected, and so will the return to investors who invested in that MMF.

As mentioned earlier, money market investments that have shorter maturities have less interest rate risk. In addition, investments in MMFs tend to have the least liquidity risk, especially when their investments focus on securities that will mature within the next month. Treasury securities that will mature in the next month or so also have very little liquidity risk.

Securities that are exposed to risk have to offer higher yields than less risky investments to attract funds from investors. The prospect of a higher return compensates investors for taking on a higher level of risk. Investors can earn a higher return by investing in MMFs that hold investments subject to credit risk and for securities that are particularly vulnerable to interest rate risk. Recall that debt securities with shorter maturities offer lower annualized yields. A three-month debt security typically offers a slightly lower annualized yield than a one-year security. However, the debt securities with longer maturities are more exposed to interest rate movements.

Yields are also higher for securities that are more exposed to liquidity risk. A retail CD must offer a slightly higher yield than a Treasury security with the same maturity because the Treasury security is more liquid.

Optimal Allocation of Money Market Investments

In general, your money management should be guided by the following steps:

1. Anticipate your upcoming bills and ensure that you have sufficient funds in your checking account.

2. Estimate the additional funds that you might need in the near future, and consider investing them in an investment that offers sufficient liquidity (such as an MMF). You may even keep a little extra in reserve here for unanticipated expenses.

3. Use the remaining funds in a manner that will earn you a higher return, within your level of risk tolerance.

The optimal allocation for you will likely be different from the optimal allocation for another individual. If your future net cash flows will be far short of upcoming expenses, you will need to keep a relatively large proportion of funds in a liquid investment (such

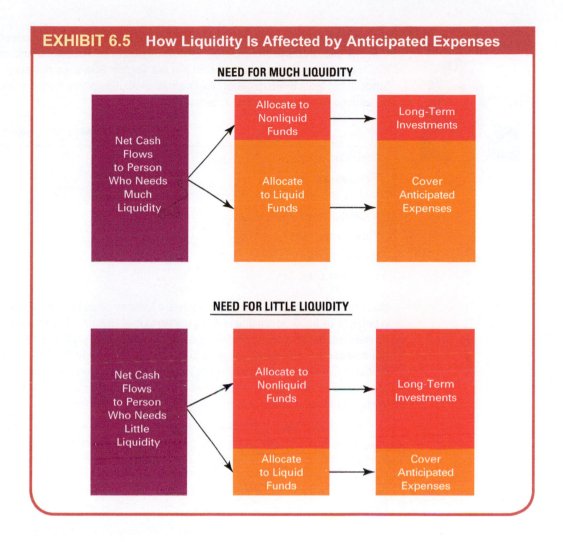

EXHIBIT 6.5   How Liquidity Is Affected by Anticipated Expenses

NEED FOR MUCH LIQUIDITY

Net Cash Flows to Person Who Needs Much Liquidity → Allocate to Nonliquid Funds → Long-Term Investments

Allocate to Liquid Funds → Cover Anticipated Expenses

NEED FOR LITTLE LIQUIDITY

Net Cash Flows to Person Who Needs Little Liquidity → Allocate to Nonliquid Funds → Long-Term Investments

Allocate to Liquid Funds → Cover Anticipated Expenses

as a checking account or a NOW account). Another person who has sufficient cash flows to cover expenses will not need much liquidity. The difference is illustrated in Exhibit 6.5. Even though the two individuals have the same level of net cash flows, one person must maintain more liquidity than the other.

Your decision on how to invest your short-term funds (after determining how much money to maintain in your checking account) should account for your willingness to tolerate risk. If you want to minimize all forms of risk, you may simply consider investing all your funds in an MMF that always focuses on Treasury securities maturing within a month or less. However, you will likely improve on the yield if you are willing to accept some degree of risk.

For example, if you know that you will not need your funds for at least six months and do not expect interest rates to rise substantially over that period, you might consider investing your funds in a six-month retail CD. A compromise would be to invest a portion of your short-term funds in the six-month retail CD and the remaining funds in the MMF that focuses on Treasury securities. The CD offers you a higher expected return (although less liquidity), while the MMF offers you liquidity in case you need funds immediately.

In recent years, interest rates on all money market investments have been very low, which means that your return on these investments is low. This creates a temptation to reduce such investments in favor of more exciting investments, such as stocks that have the potential to earn very high returns. Keep in mind, however, that the money market investments have a specific purpose. They create liquidity, so that you have easy access to funds. Stocks do not provide the same degree of liquidity.

PSYCHOLOGY of Personal Finance

EXAMPLE

Stephanie Spratt has $2,000 available to allocate to money market investments. She knows that she will need $400 to cover several small bills in the next week and may also need $600 in a month or so to pay for repairs on her car engine. She does not expect to need the other funds for at least three months. Her financial institution offers the following annualized yields on various money market instruments:

	Annualized Yield (%)
Checking account	0
Savings deposit	1.2
MMDA ($2,500 minimum balance)	2.0
MMF ($300 minimum balance)	1.5
Three-month CD	2.5
Six-month CD	2.7
One-year CD	3.0

Stephanie's existing checking account has a balance close to zero. She also has an MMF with a balance of $300, which she must maintain to meet the minimum balance. She will first focus on meeting her liquidity needs and then decide how to invest the remaining funds that are not needed to cover possible expenses. She decides to allocate $400 to her checking account so that she can make several payments to cover her upcoming bills. It is not worthwhile to invest these funds elsewhere as she will need the funds soon, and the checking account is the only investment that will allow her to make several small payments.

She knows that she might need another $600 in the near future for car repairs, but wants to earn as high a return as possible until she needs the money. She immediately eliminates the MMDA from consideration because it would require a minimum balance of $2,500. She decides to invest the $600 in her MMF. She can write a check from this account to cover the car repairs; meanwhile, the funds invested in the MMF will earn 1.5% interest on an annualized basis.

Stephanie now has $1,000 remaining to allocate and anticipates that she will not need the money for at least three months. She does not consider investing the $1,000 in a six-month CD or one-year CD, even though they offer slightly higher interest rates than the three-month CD, because she may need the funds in three months. She decides to invest the $1,000 in a three-month CD, so that she can increase liquidity while still earning a positive return.

Stephanie recognizes that other types of investments such as stocks can offer higher returns but their values can also decline. She does not consider using any of her $2,000 available for stocks because she expects that she will need this money in the near future. Although she could sell stocks at any time, she may have to accept a loss on her investment when selling the stock in some periods. She wants to focus on more liquid alternatives such as money market investments, so that she will have enough funds to pay her bills in the future.

If Stephanie had excess funds that she would not need for a few years, she would consider investing the residual in other investments (such as stocks) that offer a higher potential return. The potential return and risk on these other investments are discussed in Part 5.

How Money Management Fits Within Your Financial Plan

The following are the key money management decisions that you should include in your financial plan:

- How can you ensure that you can pay your anticipated bills on time?
- How can you maintain adequate liquidity in case you incur unanticipated expenses?
- How should you invest any remaining funds among money market investments?

By making proper decisions, you can minimize your use of credit and maximize the return on your liquid assets. As an example, Exhibit 6.6 shows how money market decisions apply to Stephanie Spratt's financial plan.

EXHIBIT 6.6   How Money Management Fits Within Stephanie Spratt's Financial Plan

GOALS FOR MONEY MANAGEMENT

1. Maintain sufficient liquidity to ensure that all anticipated bills are paid on time.
2. Maintain sufficient liquidity in case I incur unanticipated expenses.
3. Invest any excess funds in accounts that offer the highest return while ensuring adequate liquidity.

ANALYSIS

	Amount	Payment Method
Monthly cash inflows	$2,500	Direct deposited into checking account.
Typical monthly expenses	1,400	Make payments to pay these bills.
Other expenses for clothing or recreation	600	Use credit cards and then pay the credit card balance by check once a month.

DECISIONS

Decision on How to Ensure Adequate Liquidity to Cover Anticipated Expenses:

The two paychecks I receive each month amounting to $2,500 after taxes are direct deposited into my checking account. I can use this account to cover the $1,400 in anticipated bills each month. I can also use this account to write a check for the monthly credit card bill. I will attempt to leave about $400 extra in the checking account because my expenses may vary from month to month.

Decision on How to Ensure Liquidity to Cover Unanticipated Expenses:

I will also attempt to maintain about $2,500 in a money market fund (MMF) in case I need additional funds. I can earn interest on this money while ensuring liquidity.

Decision on How to Invest Remaining Funds to Achieve the Highest Return While Enhancing Liquidity:

As I accumulate additional savings, I will invest in certificates of deposit with short terms to maturity (such as one month). This money will not be as liquid as the MMF, but it will be accessible when the CD matures. The interest rate on the CD will be higher than the interest I can earn on my MMF.

DISCUSSION QUESTIONS

1. How would Stephanie's money management decisions be different if she were a single mother of two children?

2. How would Stephanie's money management decisions be affected if she were 35 years old? If she were 50 years old?

SUMMARY

Money Management. Money management involves the selection of short-term investments that satisfy your liquidity needs and also provide you with an adequate return on your investment. It is challenging because the short-term investments that offer relatively high returns tend to have less liquidity.

Popular Money Market Investments. Popular short-term investments considered for money management include checking accounts, NOW accounts, savings accounts, CDs, MMDAs, Treasury bills, money market funds, and asset management accounts. Checking accounts and NOW accounts offer the most liquidity. CDs and T-bills offer the highest return.

Risk of Money Market Investments. The risks related to money market investments are credit (default) risk, interest rate risk, and liquidity risk. The money market investments offered by depository institutions are insured and insulate you from the risk that the institution could default. Investments in T-bills have no default risk because they are backed by the federal government. Money market securities tend to have a low level of interest rate risk because they have short-term maturities. They also have relatively low liquidity risk because of the short-term maturities of their assets.

Risk Management. When applying money management, you should first anticipate your expenses in the next month and maintain enough funds in your checking account to cover those expenses. In addition, estimate the potential level of unanticipated expenses (such as possible car repairs) and maintain enough funds in a short-term investment such as a money market fund to cover these expenses. Finally, invest the remaining funds to earn a high return within your level of risk tolerance.

How Money Management Fits Within Your Financial Plan. Money management decisions can ensure that you have access to funds to pay your anticipated bills on time and that you maintain adequate liquidity in case you incur unanticipated expenses.

REVIEW QUESTIONS

All Review Questions are available in MyFinanceLab *at* http://www.myfinancelab.com.

1. **Money Management.** Define money management. How does it differ from long-term investment or long-term borrowing decisions?

2. **Liquidity.** What is liquidity? How is your personal cash flow statement used to help manage your liquidity? How does money management relate to the cash flow statement?

3. **Cash Flow Deficiency.** Name some ways an individual might handle a cash flow deficiency. Which way would be preferable? Why?

4. **Opportunity Cost of Liquid Funds.** What is the opportunity cost of having excessive amounts of liquid funds?

5. **Liquid Investments.** What two factors affect the return on short-term investments? What investments should you consider to achieve liquidity and an adequate return?

6. **Checking Accounts.** Why do individuals use checking accounts? What is the disadvantage of having funds in a checking account? Explain overdraft protection and stop payment orders. Are all bank fee structures the same?

7. **NOW Account.** What is a NOW account? How is it different from a regular checking account? How does a savings account compare with a NOW account?

8. **CDs.** What terms does a financial institution specify for certificates of deposit? Why are rates on CDs higher than those on savings accounts? What factor would most affect your choice of maturity date on a CD?

9. **MMDAs.** How does a money market deposit account (MMDA) differ from a NOW account? When might a depositor use an MMDA?

10. **Treasury Securities.** What are Treasury securities? What is a T-bill? How is it denominated? How do you earn a return on a T-bill? How is the return calculated?

11. **T-bills versus CDs.** Compare the interest rates offered on T-bills and CDs. Which type of investment is more liquid? Why?

12. **MMFs.** What are money market funds (MMFs)? What types of securities do they invest in? What is commercial paper? Are MMFs risky investments? Are MMFs liquid?

13. **Asset Management Account.** What is an asset management account? Discuss the advantages of such an account as well as its requirements.

14. **Money Market Investments.** Compare the return and liquidity of the various money market investments. Give specific examples.

15. **Risk of Money Market Investments.** What are the three types of risk that affect money market investments?

16. **Risk of Money Market Investments.** Generally compare the money market investments described in this chapter in terms of their vulnerability to credit risk, interest rate risk, and liquidity risk. Provide some examples of specific securities. What is the risk-return trade-off for these investments?

17. **Money Market Investments.** What steps should you take to determine the best allocation of your money market investments? What factors should you consider in determining your allocation?

18. **Liquidity During a Weak Economy.** Why is it important to have sufficient liquidity during a weak economy?

19. **Disadvantage of High Liquidity.** What is a disadvantage of maintaining a very high level of liquidity?

20. **Economic Impact on Liquidity Needs.** Assume that your monthly expenses will not change over the next three years, but you expect that the economy will be much weaker in about a year. Explain why you may need more liquidity even if your expenses do not change.

21. **Cost of Maintaining More Liquidity.** Explain why maintaining more liquidity during a weak economy is costly.

22. **Debit Cards.** How does a debit card transaction differ from writing a check?

23. **Overdraft Protection.** How will overdraft protection affect bounced checks? Should you take advantage of this feature if your bank offers overdraft protection?

24. **Automatic Transfer.** What is an automatic transfer? How can this tool help you save money?

25. **Risk Tolerance.** How does your individual tolerance for risk impact money management?

26. **Stocks and Liquidity.** Explain why you should not invest in the stock market if you expect to need the funds in the near future. Are stocks liquid?

27. **Credit Cards and Liquidity.** Explain the risks of using a credit card for your liquidity needs.

FINANCIAL PLANNING PROBLEMS

All Financial Planning Problems are available in MyFinanceLab *at* http://www.myfinancelab.com.

1. **Interest Earned.** Teresa has just opened a NOW account that pays 3.5% interest. If she maintains a minimum balance of $500 for the next 12 months, how much interest will she earn?

2. **Interest Earned.** Lisa is depositing $2,500 in a six-month CD that pays 4.25% interest. How much interest will she accrue if she holds the CD until maturity?

3. **Value of CD.** Travis has invested $3,000 in a three-month CD at 4%. How much will Travis have when the CD matures?

4. **Interest Earned.** Claire has invested $10,000 in an 18-month CD that pays 6.25%. How much interest will Claire receive at maturity?

5. **T-bill Return.** Troy paid $9,600 for a T-bill with a face value of $10,000. What is Troy's return if he holds the T-bill to maturity?

6. **MMF Value.** Bart is a college student who has never invested his funds. He has saved $1,000 and has decided to invest it in a money market fund with an expected return of 2.0%. Bart will need the money in one year. The MMF imposes fees that will cost Bart $20 at the time he withdraws his funds. How much money will Bart have in one year as a result of this investment?

7. **Return on T-bills.** Dave has $20,000 excess cash to invest. He can purchase a $20,000 T-bill for $19,400 or two $10,000 T-bills for $9,600 each. Which will give him the better return?

8. **Return on T-bills.** Lauren purchased a $40,000 T-bill for $38,400. A few months later, Lauren sold the T-bill for $39,000. What was Lauren's return on the T-bill?

9. **Annualized T-bill Rate.** Brenda purchased a $30,000, 90-day T-bill for $29,550. What will Brenda's return be when the T-bill matures? What will her annualized rate be?

10. **Interest Earned.** On June 1, Mia deposited $4,000 in an MMDA that pays 5% interest. On October 31, Mia invested $2,000 in a three-month CD that pays 6%. At the end of the year, how much interest will Mia have earned, assuming she hasn't taken anything out of the money market deposit account?

11. **Investment Return.** Thomas can invest $10,000 by purchasing a 1-year T-bill for $9,275, or he can place the $10,000 in a 12-month CD paying 8%. Which investment will provide a higher return? In addition to return, what else should Thomas consider when making his investment decision?

12. **Fractional Year Investment Return.** Jill placed $10,000 in a 90-day CD that offered an annualized return of 4%. How much interest will she earn on this CD?

13. **Ethical Dilemma.** Jason is in his mid-50s and was raised by parents of the Depression era. As a result, he is very risk adverse. He recently came into a very large amount of money, and he wants to put it where it will be safe, but where it will earn him some return. His banker tells him that he should put the money in a five-year CD. Jason asks if there is any way he can lose his money, and he is told that the federal government insures the deposit and will give him a higher return than a passbook savings account. Jason purchases a CD and goes home happy knowing that his money is safe and available whenever he needs it.

Four months later, the roof on Jason's barn collapses, and he needs the money to make repairs, but finds that he can only withdraw it at a substantial penalty.

a. Comment on the ethics of the banker in not fully discussing all the risks of a long-term certificate of deposit.

b. Is Jason correct in his thinking that he can find a totally risk-free investment?

FINANCIAL PLANNING ONLINE EXERCISES

1. Go to the bank rates section of http://www.bankrate.com, and answer the following questions:

   a. What bank in what city will pay you the highest rate on a money market account (MMA)?

   b. What bank in what city will pay you the highest rate on a one-year CD?

2. Go to the calculators section of http://www.bankrate.com to estimate how your savings will grow.

   a. By inputting an investment amount, the monthly deposit, the return, and the period of investment, you can calculate the value of your investment. Input $5,000 as the initial investment, $100 for the monthly deposit, and 6% for the return. How much will your investment be worth in 20 years?

   b. Now change the monthly deposit to $300. How much will your investment be worth in 20 years?

   c. Now change the period of investment to 30 years. How much more money will you be able to accumulate in 30 years as opposed to 20, using the original $100 monthly deposit amount?

   d. Now change the rate you can earn on your investment from 6% to 8% and evaluate the results.

3. Go to http://www.fdic.gov, and answer the following questions:

   a. List at least three types of bank accounts that are insured by the FDIC. Are money market deposit accounts insured and, if so, to what limit?

   b. List three types of consumer investment products that are not insured.

c. Are Treasury Securities insured by the FDIC? If Treasury Securities payments of interest and principal are deposited to your checking account, are they FDIC insured? Explain.

d. If you have a safety deposit box at an FDIC-insured bank, are the contents of the box insured by the FDIC? Explain fully.

PSYCHOLOGY OF PERSONAL FINANCE: Forced Savings

1. Some consumers force themselves to save money by depositing a portion of their paycheck into a savings account. They deposit the remainder into a checking account and then only spend the money in the checking account. Others motivate themselves to save by creating a special account that will have an intended purpose for the future, such as a vacation. They may be much more willing to save if they have a specified future reward as a result of their saving behavior. How do you motivate yourself to save?

2. Read one practical article of how psychology affects saving behavior. You can easily retrieve possible articles by doing an online search using the terms "psychology" and "saving." Summarize the main points of the article.

WEB SEARCH EXERCISE

You can develop your personal finance skills by conducting an Internet search for related articles. Find a recent online article about personal finance that reinforces one or more concepts covered in this chapter. If your class has an online component, your professor may ask you to post your summary of the article there and provide a link to the article so that other students can access it. If your class is live, your professor may ask you to summarize your application of the article in class. Your professor may assign specific students to complete this assignment or may allow any student to do the assignment on a volunteer basis.

For recent online articles related to this chapter, consider using the following search terms (be sure to include the current year as a search term to ensure that the online articles are recent):

- Managing your liquidity
- Managing your checking account
- Optimal savings deposit for you
- Optimal CD maturity for you
- Money market investments
- Money market yields

VIDEO EXERCISE: Investing in Money Markets

Go to one of the Web sites that contain video clips (such as http://www.youtube.com), and view some video clips about investing in money market securities. You can use search phrases such as "investing in money markets." Select one video clip on this topic that you would recommend for the other students in your class.

1. Provide the Web link for the video clip.

2. What do you think is the main point of this video clip?

3. How might you change your investment in money market securities as a result of watching this video clip?

BUILDING YOUR OWN FINANCIAL PLAN

Money market investments provide vehicles to assist you in accomplishing your short-term financial goals. Refer to the three short-term goals you established in Chapter 1. Then turn to the worksheets at the end of this chapter to continue building your financial plan.

Note: You may find it necessary to revisit some of the financial institutions involved in your analysis from Chapter 5 to gather the information necessary to select the most appropriate money market investment for each short-term goal.

THE SAMPSONS—A Continuing Case

Recall from Chapter 2 that the Sampsons currently have about $300 in cash and $1,700 in their checking account. This amount should be enough to cover upcoming bills. The Sampsons have just started saving $800 per month. This money will be placed in CDs every month, which they chose in Chapter 5. These funds, earmarked for a down payment on a car and their children's college education, are not available to the Sampsons until the CD matures. Review the Sampsons' recent cash flow statement and personal balance sheet. The monthly savings of $800 are not included in the cash flow statement.

The Sampsons' Personal Cash Flow Statement

Cash Inflows (Monthly)	**$4,000**
Cash Outflows (Monthly)	
Mortgage payment	$900
Internet	60
Electricity and water	80
Cellular	70
Groceries	500
Health care insurance and expenses	160
Clothing	180
Car expenses (insurance, maintenance, and gas)	300
School expenses	100
Partial payment of credit card balance	20
Recreation	1,000
Total Cash Outflows	**$3,370**
Net Cash Flows (Monthly)	**+ $630**

The Sampsons' Personal Balance Sheet

Assets	
Liquid Assets	
Cash	$300
Checking account	1,700
Savings account	0
Total liquid assets	**$2,000**
Household Assets	
Home	$100,000
Cars	9,000
Furniture	3,000
Total household assets	**$112,000**
Investment Assets	
Stocks	0
Total investment assets	**0**
Total Assets	**$114,000**
Liabilities and Net Worth	
Current Liabilities	
Credit card balance	$2,000
Total current liabilities	$2,000
Long-Term Liabilities	
Mortgage	$90,000
Car loan	0
Total long-term liabilities	$90,000
Total Liabilities	$92,000
Net Worth	**$22,000**

Go to the worksheets at the end of this chapter to continue this case.

CHAPTER 6: BUILDING YOUR OWN FINANCIAL PLAN

GOALS

1. Maintain sufficient liquidity to ensure that all your anticipated bills are paid on time.
2. Maintain sufficient liquidity so that you can cover unanticipated expenses.
3. Invest any excess funds in deposits that offer the highest return while ensuring liquidity.

ANALYSIS

1. Review the cash flow statement you prepared in Chapter 3 and assess your liquidity.
2. Evaluate the short-term goals you created in Chapter 1 as high, medium, or low with respect to liquidity, risk, fees/minimum balance, and return.

Short-Term Goal Prioritization of Factors

Short-Term Goal	Liquidity	Risk	Fees/Minimum Balance	Return

3. Rank each of the money market investments as good, fair, or poor with respect to liquidity, risk, fees/minimum balance, and return.

Money Market Investment	Liquidity	Risk	Fees/Minimum Balance	Return
Checking Account				
NOW Account				
Savings Account				
Money Market Deposit Account (MMDA)				
Certificate of Deposit				
Treasury Bill				
Money Market Fund				
Asset Management Account				

DECISIONS

1. Describe how you will ensure adequate liquidity to cover anticipated expenses.

_____

_____

_____

_____

_____

_____

_____

_____

2. Detail how you will ensure liquidity to meet unanticipated expenses.

_____

_____

_____

_____

_____

_____

_____

_____

3. Explain which money market investments will be most effective in reaching your short-term goals.

_____

_____

_____

_____

_____

_____

_____

_____

CHAPTER 6: THE SAMPSONS—A Continuing Case

CASE QUESTIONS

1. Based on the cash flow statement and personal balance sheet, do the Sampsons have adequate liquidity to cover their recurring cash flows and planned monthly savings in the long run? If not, what level of savings should they maintain for liquidity purposes?

_____

_____

_____

_____

_____

_____

_____

_____

_____

_____

_____

2. Advise the Sampsons on money market investments they should consider to provide them with adequate liquidity.

_____

_____

_____

_____

_____

_____

_____

_____

_____

_____

_____

_____

_____

Assessing and Securing Your Credit

Kim avoided using credit. She paid cash for everything, including two cars in the past. When it came time to buy her third car, Kim wanted to finance part of the cost. After applying for credit, she was treated to a rude awakening. The finance company used a three-tier credit rating system. An A-level credit rating was the highest, and the buyer received a 7% interest rate. The B-level buyer received a 9% rate. Kim only qualified for the C-level, at an 11% rate.

Daddy Cool/Fotolia

She was stunned. How could she have such a low rating when she had never been late paying any bills?

As it turns out, having no credit history looks as bad to a credit rating agency as having a bad credit history. You might think that not having to borrow money would demonstrate fiscal responsibility. Not so to a credit rating bureau.

The first part of this chapter focuses on obtaining credit. You'll discover that a good credit history is built by the proper use and control of credit, not the absence of credit. The second part of the chapter deals with identity theft: how it can affect your credit rating and how you can protect yourself from it.

MyFinanceLab helps you master the topics in this chapter and study more efficiently. Visit http://www.myfinancelab.com for more details.

The objectives of this chapter are to:

- Provide a background on credit
- Describe the role of credit bureaus
- Provide a background on identity theft
- Explain how to protect against identity theft
- Discuss how to respond to identity theft
- Explain how credit assessment and security fit within your financial plan

Background on Credit

credit
Funds provided by a creditor to a borrower that will be repaid by the borrower in the future with interest.

Credit represents funds a creditor provides to a borrower that the borrower will repay in the future with interest. The funds borrowed are sometimes referred to as the principal, so we segment repayment of credit into interest and principal payments. Credit is frequently extended to borrowers as a loan with set terms such as the amount of credit provided and the maturity date when the credit will be repaid. For most types of loans, interest payments are made periodically (such as every quarter or year), and the principal payment is made at the maturity date, when the loan is to be terminated.

Types of Credit

Credit can be classified as noninstallment, installment, or revolving open-end.

noninstallment credit
Credit provided for a short period, such as retail store credit.

Noninstallment Credit　**Noninstallment credit** is normally issued for a very short time, such as 30 days or less. It is provided by some retail stores to consumers who want to purchase products today and need credit for a very short period of time. The consumers are granted credit to make specific purchases and will have to repay the amount borrowed in the near future. Noninstallment credit is useful for consumers who expect to receive enough income in the near future to cover the amount of credit they are granted.

installment credit
Credit provided for specific purchases, with interest charged on the amount borrowed.

Installment Credit　**Installment credit** is also provided for specific purchases, but the borrower has a longer time (such as a few years) to repay the loan. Also referred to as an installment loan, interest is charged on the amount borrowed, and monthly payments of interest and principal must be made. Alternatively, monthly payments can be structured so that the borrower pays interest only until the maturity date, when the balance of the loan is due.

revolving open-end credit
Credit provided up to a specified maximum amount based on income and credit history; interest is charged each month on the remaining balance.

Revolving Open-End Credit　**Revolving open-end credit**, such as credit cards, allows consumers to borrow up to a specified maximum amount (such as $1,000 or $10,000). The credit limit is determined by the borrower's income level, debt level, and credit payment history. The consumer can pay the entire amount that is borrowed at the end of the month or pay a portion of the balance, and interest will be charged on the remaining balance. Typically, at least a minimum payment must be paid each month.

Should you use credit? Consider the advantages and disadvantages of credit.

Advantages of Using Credit

The appropriate use of credit helps you build a good credit history. Only by using credit wisely can you create the capacity to access credit in the future for large purchases such as a home or a car. This credit capacity allows individuals and families to avoid deferring large purchases until savings can be accumulated to make such purchases. Another advantage is that credit eliminates the need for carrying cash or writing checks.

Disadvantages of Using Credit

There can be a high cost to using credit. Access to credit can be a disadvantage because it may result in:

- Excessive spending
- A large accumulation of debt

PSYCHOLOGY
of Personal
Finance

Excessive Spending The behavior of some consumers is completely different when they pay with a credit card versus if they had to pull cash out of their wallet to make a payment. The credit card gives a feeling of freedom, as if it allows consumers to avoid the cost of purchases.

> **EXAMPLE**
>
> While at the mall today, Lisa saw a pair of Italian shoes that she liked. The shoes were priced at $300 and were not on sale. Lisa did not have any cash with her, so she used her credit card to pay for the shoes. Lisa did not need the shoes but decided to buy them because she did not see anything else at the mall that she wanted. Before purchasing the shoes, Lisa used her smartphone and determined that she could purchase the same shoes online for $100 less, but she would have to wait several days for them to be delivered, and she wanted them now. Lisa was also aware that the shoe store periodically has 40% off sales, and she could likely buy the shoes at the sale price if she would be willing to wait. Lisa's purchase decision was primarily influenced by her desire for immediate satisfaction. She knew that she could have waited until the shoes were on sale, but she went to the mall intending to purchase something today. Lisa's purchase decision was especially easy because she used credit instead of cash. Thus, she was able to make the purchase and still has all her cash that she can use for other future purchases.
>
> Now reconsider Lisa's purchase decision if she had just cashed her paycheck for $300 from working at her job over the last two weeks and if she did not have a credit card with her. She could pull $300 from her wallet to pay for the shoes. However, she is unwilling to use all her pay from two weeks of work to buy a pair of shoes that she does not need. She worked hard to earn that $300 and wants to get more out of her income than this pair of shoes. She might only consider using her cash to pay for the shoes if they were on sale, but even under those conditions, she would likely decide to use her cash for other purposes.

The point of this example is that some consumers have no control over their spending when using a credit card. They are tempted to purchase products they do not need and to overpay when purchasing products because the credit card makes them feel like they are not really paying for the products. Conversely, there is more psychological pain associated with using cash to make purchases than with using a credit card, even if the amount of the payment is exactly the same. Therefore, consumers make spending decisions more carefully when using cash. They tend to recognize that their cash was earned, that they have a limited amount of it, and that spending their cash now may prevent them from affording other products later. Thus, the use of cash imposes a limit on the amount of their spending.

Access to credit can also affect the types of purchases that consumers make. Consumers are more willing to select the more expensive options when they use credit instead of cash at the time they make their decision.

> **EXAMPLE**
>
> Dana and Nicole Thomas are twin sisters, and both pursued college degrees in education. Their parents provided each of them with $8,000 per year for their studies, and they had to obtain credit for any spending in excess of that amount. Each was faced with the following decisions:

- Pursue a college education at a private or a public university
- Live in an upscale apartment or in a college dormitory
- Buy a new car versus a used car

Dana chose to pursue her education at a public university, live in a college dormitory, and buy a used car. Nicole chose to pursue her education at a private university, live in an upscale apartment, and buy a new car. At the end of four years, Dana had outstanding debt of $11,000, which she planned to repay over the next two years. In contrast, Nicole had outstanding debt of $100,000. She will have to make payments over the next 20 years to pay off this credit. Because of her excessive use of credit during the last four years, she will have to restrict her spending over the next 20 years to repay what she borrowed.

Accumulation of Debt Another disadvantage of credit cards is that they can cause some consumers to accumulate too much debt. Some consumers frequently use credit cards for their purchases and pay the minimum amount required each month. Consequently, their debt accumulates. This problem is made worse because of the high interest rate they are paying on the balance owed.

Some years ago, college students received numerous offers of free credit cards, and many students accumulated thousands of dollars of credit card debt by the time they graduated. The Credit Card Accountability, Responsibility, and Disclosure Act of 2009 (also called the Credit CARD Act), which took effect in 2010, changed that. Now, to obtain a credit card, students under age 21 must either show proof of income or have a parent or other adult cosign the application and agree to be jointly liable for the debt. In addition, credit card companies may not offer students gifts such as T-shirts or other incentives for applying for a credit card. Colleges and universities were also encouraged to restrict credit card marketing on campus, and many have done so.

As a result of these reforms, today only about 30% of college students have a credit card, and the average balance, including those who have a zero balance, is about $500. Nevertheless, some students still manage to accumulate considerable credit card debt. The average balance for those who carry a balance every month is $925, and many of these students make only the minimum payment each month. Many students make minimum payments while in school with the expectation that they will be able to pay off their balance once they graduate and are working full-time. Yet the accumulating interest fees catch many by surprise, and the debt can quickly become difficult to manage. If you are unable to repay the credit you receive, you may not be able to obtain credit again or will have to pay a very high interest rate to obtain it.

Your spending decisions today can influence the amount of credit you need and therefore affect the amount of debt that you will have to repay in the future. Your ability to save money in the future is also affected by large credit payments, as illustrated in Exhibit 7.1. If your spending and credit card payments exceed your net cash flows, you will need to withdraw savings to cover the deficiency.

Warren Buffett, a successful billionaire investor, offered financial advice to some students. He told them that they will not make financial progress if they are borrowing money at 18% (a typical interest rate on credit cards). In recent years, more than 1 million people in the United States have filed for bankruptcy each year. A primary reason for these bankruptcies is that the individuals obtained more credit than they could repay. Even if obtaining credit at a high interest rate does not cause personal bankruptcy, it limits the potential increase in personal wealth.

Credit Rights

The Equal Credit Opportunity Act prohibits creditors from denying credit due to gender, age, race, national origin, religion, or marital status. It requires creditors to notify applicants within 30 days of a credit application whether they will receive credit. If credit is denied, creditors must explain the reason for the denial.

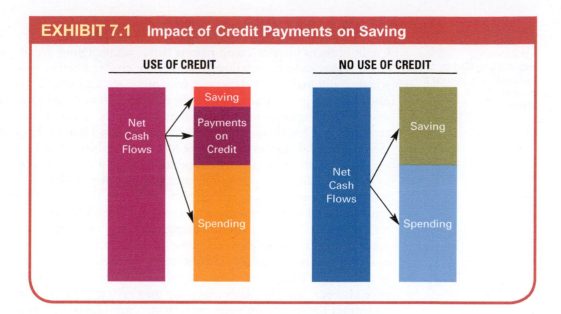

EXHIBIT 7.1   Impact of Credit Payments on Saving

The Financial Reform Act (also called the Dodd–Frank Wall Street Reform and Consumer Protection Act) of 2010 established the Consumer Financial Protection Bureau (CFPB) to regulate specific financial services for consumers, including online checking accounts, credit cards, and student loans. The CFPB can set rules to ensure that information regarding endorsements of specific financial products is accurate and to prevent deceptive practices. It may also regulate the credit rating bureaus (discussed in the next section).

Credit History

Your credit history is a record of how you have used credit, including whether your payments have ever been late. If you have a credit card or have obtained a bank loan, perhaps to purchase a car, the amount and timing of your payments will be in your credit history.

Even if you have never had a credit card or bank loan, you will have a credit history if you have rented an apartment. You receive credit when you use utilities such as water, electric power, and telephone services. The utility company extends credit by providing a service, and you are billed at the end of a period (such as one month). In this way, utility companies provide a form of short-term credit. To obtain this credit, you normally must make an initial deposit at the time the account is created. When you have accounts with utility companies, you develop a credit history that documents how timely you are in paying your bills. You can establish a favorable credit history by paying your utility bills on or before the due date. Doing so indicates to potential creditors that you may also repay other credit in a timely manner. Similarly, paying your rent on time each month will have a positive effect on your credit record.

Credit Insurance

Because access to credit is essential today, some consumers purchase credit insurance to make sure they will be able to keep making credit payments (and therefore maintain their credit rating) under adverse conditions. With credit insurance, an insurance company will cover their monthly credit payments if various conditions such as illness or unemployment occur. For instance, credit accident and health insurance ensures monthly credit payments for consumers during periods when they cannot work due to an accident or illness. Credit unemployment insurance ensures monthly payments for consumers during periods when they are unemployed.

Financial Planning ONLINE

Go to:
The consumer credit section of http://www.phil.frb.org

To get:
Information about how to establish, use, and protect credit.

Credit Bureaus

credit reports
Reports provided by credit bureaus to document a person's credit payment history.

Credit bureaus provide **credit reports** that document your credit payment history. Your credit report shows every time you apply for credit, whether you pay your bills on time, whether you maintain balances on your accounts, and whether you pay late fees. It may also contain information about public records such as bankruptcies and court judgments and identify inquiries made by various companies and potential employers about your credit rating. The three primary credit bureaus are Equifax, Experian, and TransUnion. (See Exhibit 7.4 later in this chapter for contact information.)

Your credit report is very important because it can determine whether you are able to obtain credit. It may also influence the interest rate that you pay when you borrow money. The better your credit report, the lower the interest rate you are charged for financing, and thus your interest payments to pay off loans will be lower. Because a better credit report reduces your financing costs, it allows you to use a larger proportion of your income for other purposes. Your credit report can affect other aspects of your life as well. Landlords may obtain your credit report when you apply to rent an apartment, and insurance companies commonly check your credit report when you apply for insurance on your car. The phone company may review your credit report when you obtain a contract for service for your smartphone. Individuals with poor credit reports may be charged higher rates. Furthermore, employers increasingly are obtaining credit reports on applicants for job positions, so it could even affect your career.

Because your credit report is so important, you should know what is in your report. Free credit reports are accessible to all U.S. consumers. You may order one free copy of your credit report from each of the nationwide consumer bureaus every 12 months. You must provide your name, address, Social Security number, and date of birth. (You might be asked for additional personal information for security reasons.) You can get immediate access to your credit report by requesting your report online at http://www.annualcreditreport.com. Phone and mail requests are processed and the report mailed to you within 15 days of receipt.

Many other Web sites advertise free credit reports. However, they may only provide the credit report if you subscribe to various types of credit services, for which they may charge fees.

Credit Reports Provided by Credit Bureaus

Exhibit 7.2 shows an example of a credit report. The precise format may vary among credit rating bureaus. In addition, the information about you may vary among the reports, although all three credit bureaus tend to focus on the same type of information. Review Exhibit 7.2, and notice the following six sections:

1. The report number and the date distinguish this report from other reports.
2. Identifying information such as your name, your spouse's name, your date of birth, your Social Security number, your current and previous addresses, your occupation, and your current or previous employers appears in this section.
3. Potentially negative information from public records, such as bankruptcy filings and tax liens, is included in your credit report.
4. If any unpaid accounts have been turned over to a collection agency, they will be listed in this part of the credit report. Note that the resolution is recorded as well.
5. All your accounts, both open and closed, are listed on your credit report. The report details when the accounts were opened, how long they have been open, the highest amount you have ever charged, and each account's current status. It also shows how many late payments you have made and how late they were.
6. The inquiries section lists the companies that have requested your credit report.

EXHIBIT 7.2 A Sample Credit Report

Credit Bureau

Report Number 716-80
08/28/13

Please address all future correspondence to:

Credit Bureau
P.O. Box 0000
City, State, Zip Code
(888) 000–0000

Personal Information

Cynthia Zubicki
120 Greenmeadow Drive
Durham, NC 27704

Social Security Number: 000-00-0000

Previous Addresses:
264 Concord Road
Gilbert, AZ 85296

Last Reported Employment: Architect

401 Brownell Road
Chandler, AZ 85226

Public Record Information

Bankruptcy filed 04/12; Durham District Court; Case Number 873JM34; Liabilities: $56,987; Assets: $672

Collection Agency Account Information

North Shore Collection Agency (888) 000–0000

Collection Reported 11/12; Assigned 1/12 to North Shore Collection Agency; Client: Gilbert Medical Center; Amount: $1,267; Paid Collection Account

Credit Account Information

Company Name Reported	Account Number	Date Opened	Individual or Joint	Months Review	Date of Last Activity	High Credit	Terms	Balance	Past Due	Status	Date
Durham Savings Bank	8762096	02/15	I	6	11/14	$4,897		$2,958		Paid as Agreed	04/15
Macy's	109–82-43176	06/15	I	36	01/15	$2,000		$0		Paid as Agreed	02/15
Chester Auto Finance	873092851	03/15	I	27	02/15	$2,400	$50	$300	$200	Paid 120 days past due date	03/15

Previous Payment History: 2 times 30 days late; 2 times 60 days late

Inquiries

05/27/04 Citibank; 10/15/15 Bloomingdale's; 03/21/15 Home Depot

Credit Score

A credit score is a rating that indicates a person's creditworthiness. The rating reflects the likelihood that an individual will be able to make payments on credit in a timely manner.

Lenders commonly assess the credit payment history provided by one or more credit bureaus when deciding whether to extend a personal loan. For example, financial institutions may rely on this information when they decide whether to approve your credit card application, provide you with a car loan, or provide you with a home (mortgage) loan. The credit score can also affect the interest rate that is quoted on the loan that you request. A high score could reduce your interest rate substantially, which may translate into savings of thousands of dollars in interest expenses over time. The credit bureaus rely on a model created by the Fair Isaac Corporation (FICO) for credit scoring. The FICO score is based on several factors. The exact weighting applied to each factor in determining a FICO score can vary among people depending on their credit history. In addition, the weighting of factors as applied to a specific person may change over time in response to changes in their credit reports. Nevertheless, some generalizations can be provided here about the most important factors for determining a person's FICO score.

Credit Payment History The most important factor determining your FICO score is your credit payment history, which makes up 35% of the score. If you have paid your bills on time over the last seven years, you will receive a high rating on that portion of your credit score. Measurements of your payment history may include your record of paying off credit in a timely manner, amounts past due on any delinquent accounts, the length of time that any accounts were delinquent, and the status of delinquent accounts (whether they have been paid off).

Credit Utilization Credit utilization, the amount of your available credit that you use each month, makes up 30% of the credit score on average. If you continue to rely on most of the credit that you were granted, you will receive a lower score. For example, if the limit on your credit card is $1,000, and you always run a balance of $900 and make only the minimum payment each month, you are utilizing 90% of your available credit. In contrast, if you have the same credit limit but charge only $200 per month and pay the bill in full when it arrives, you are not using much of your credit and will receive a higher score. This situation suggests that you have access to credit, but you have enough discipline not to use it.

Credit History Credit history makes up 15% of the FICO score on average. Measurement of your credit history may include the time since your accounts were opened and the length of your relationship with creditors. In general, longer-term relationships with your creditors are perceived to be more favorable.

New Credit New credit account information makes up 10% of the FICO score on average. Measurement of new credit may include the number of new accounts that you opened recently, the proportion of new accounts relative to your older accounts, the number of recent inquiries by credit card companies (which may be in response to your applications), and the time since any recent accounts were opened. In general, more new accounts and inquiries may result in a lower score because they suggest that you may be in need of additional credit, possibly because of financial problems.

Different Types of Credit The use of different types of credit makes up 10% of the FICO score on average. Types of credit include credit card loans, retail accounts, installment loans, mortgages, and finance company loans.

Overall, if you make your credit payments on time, maintain a low level of debt, and have demonstrated your ability to make timely credit payments for many years, you are likely to receive a very high credit score. The credit score is not allowed to reflect your gender, race, religion, national origin, or marital status.

VantageScore An alternative scoring system, VantageScore, was created in 2006 and has been refined since the financial crisis. The VantageScore can range from 501 to 990. Like the FICO score, the VantageScore is intended to measure the likelihood that the credit applicant will repay debt in a timely manner. VantageScore considers the same types of characteristics that are considered by FICO, such as credit utilization and credit history. Therefore, applicants with a very high FICO score would likely receive a very high VantageScore, and applicants with a very low FICO score would likely receive a very low VantageScore. However, the specific weighting of the characteristics is not exactly the same as that applied to derive the FICO scores, so it is possible that an applicant could earn a more favorable score from one scoring system than the other.

FREE APPS for Personal Finance

Monitoring Your Credit Score

Application:

The Credit Karma app (by Credit Karma, Inc.) provides your credit score, information to help you form a plan to raise your score, and monitoring tools for your credit accounts.

To Find It:

Search for the "Credit Karma" app on your mobile device.

Different Scores Among Bureaus

Although all three of the credit bureaus mentioned earlier rely on FICO to determine your credit score, you may be given a different score from each bureau. The reason for different scores is that the bureaus may not receive exactly the same information about you. Assume that Equifax received information from a utility company that you made a payment one month late, whereas that information was not made available to Experian and TransUnion. In this case, your credit score at Equifax would likely be lower than your credit score assigned by Experian and TransUnion.

The difference in credit scores among bureaus may cause some individuals to be approved for a loan based on the credit bureau that provided the highest credit score, but not receive approval for a loan based on the credit bureau that provided the lowest credit score. However, keep in mind that some financial institutions obtain information about a credit applicant from all three credit bureaus, so if any one of the three credit bureaus assigns a low credit score, the lender may be more cautious in providing credit.

Interpreting Credit Scores

Exhibit 7.3 shows the percentage of the population that falls into each credit score range. The scores range from 300 to 850. A score in the mid-to-high 700s not only ensures easy access to credit, but also may allow you to obtain credit at the lowest possible interest rate. A score of 600 or above is considered good and may indicate that you are worthy of credit. Bear in mind, though, that each financial institution sets its own criteria to determine whether to extend credit. Some financial institutions may require a minimum score of 580, whereas others require a minimum of 620. Ratings in the 570 to 600 range may cause some creditors to reject your application. Other creditors may be willing to extend credit in this range, but may charge a higher interest rate.

An acceptable credit score may vary with the type of credit (credit card, car loan, home loan, and so forth) that you are seeking. Although lenders commonly rely on credit information and a credit score from a credit bureau, they also consider other information not disclosed by credit bureaus. For example, a person with a high credit score from a credit bureau but a relatively low income may not be approved for a specific loan that would require very large payments each month.

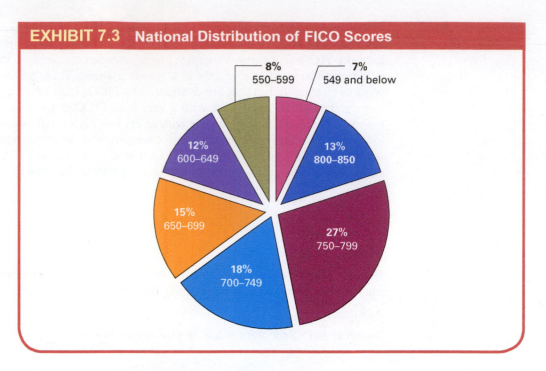

EXHIBIT 7.3   National Distribution of FICO Scores

Correcting Credit Report Mistakes

If you find inaccurate information in your credit report, send a letter to the credit bureau that issued the credit report. Send your letter by certified mail "return receipt requested" so that you will have a record that the company received your letter. Identify the specific information that you believe is incorrect. Explain why the information is incorrect. Include copies of any receipts you can use to support your claim. For example, if the credit report indicates that you did not pay a specific bill, include a copy of the receipt that proves you paid the bill.

A credit bureau is required to investigate your claim within 30 days. It will forward the proof you provided to the firm that initially filed the information with the consumer reporting company. This firm is required to review your claim and respond to the consumer reporting company about whether they agree with your claim. Then the credit bureau will decide whether your claim is justified. If so, it will remove the inaccurate information from the credit report and will send you a free copy of the revised credit report. In addition, you can ask the credit bureau to send the revised credit report to any person or company who requested and received this credit report within the last six months. If the problem is not resolved at this point, you can ask that a statement of the dispute be included in your credit report. The Consumer Financial Protection Bureau, described earlier in this chapter, can regulate the credit bureaus. This may ensure that any mistakes made on credit reports are quickly corrected.

EXAMPLE

Curious about her credit rating, last month Stephanie Spratt took advantage of her right to request a credit report from each of the credit bureaus. She was surprised to see how the reports varied. One of the bureaus recorded a late payment on a bill from a utility company about nine months ago. This single late payment did not severely affect her credit rating, but Stephanie did not want it on her record because she always pays her bills on time. She sent the credit bureau a letter with a copy of the check that proved her payment to the utility company was not late. The bureau removed the claim of a late payment from her record, and her credit score increased slightly. Stephanie learned from this experience that she should periodically check her credit rating, as it can affect her access to credit and the interest rate she may pay when obtaining credit.

Improving Your Credit Score

A low credit score is normally due to either missed payments or carrying an excessive amount of debt, both of which will be noted on your credit report. A poor credit history will appear on your credit report for seven years; filing for bankruptcy will remain on your record for ten years.

You can begin to improve your score immediately by catching up on late payments, making at least the minimum payments on time, and reducing your debt. You might also consider the following steps:

- Review your household budget, and cut back on all unnecessary expenditures.
- Destroy your credit cards so you won't be tempted to add to your debt. Keep your accounts open, however, because part of your credit rating is determined by how much credit you have and what percentage of it you use. If you reduce the amount of credit you have by closing accounts but maintain the same amount of debt, your percentage of use will increase, and your credit score could be negatively affected.
- Call your creditors immediately if you won't be able to make your payments on time. If you have missed payments in the past but can afford to make them now, ask your creditors if they will report your account "paid as agreed" to the credit bureau.

As you show a pattern of making payments on time and managing your credit responsibly, your credit score will improve. It may take a few years to completely rebuild your credit, however. Many companies advertise that they can improve your credit score. However, these companies cannot remove any accurate negative information from the credit report. And if the information in your credit report is not accurate, you can have that information removed without paying a company to do it for you.

There are some credit counseling organizations that can help you improve your credit score. They may help you establish a plan to repay existing debt over time. They may also help you establish a budget and develop a detailed financial plan for the future. Although some credit counselors are reputable and can be helpful, the Federal Trade Commission warns that others (even some claiming to be "nonprofit") charge high fees and provide little assistance. The commission suggests that you check with your state attorney general and local consumer protection agencies for help in finding a reputable counselor.

Identity Theft: A Threat to Your Credit

identity theft
Theft that occurs when an individual, without permission, uses your identifying information for his or her personal gain.

Identity theft occurs when any individual, without your permission, uses such personal identifying information as your Social Security number, driver's license number, credit card account numbers, bank account numbers, or any other information unique to you, including your name and date of birth, to obtain personal gain. Criminals use stolen account numbers to empty your bank accounts or charge purchases to your credit cards. They may also use stolen personal information to open accounts in your name. If you are a victim of identity theft, any purchases charged to the accounts appear under your name. When these accounts go unpaid, the delinquent accounts are reported on your credit report. Meanwhile, you are not even aware that these accounts exist. Your credit score may be reduced to the point at which you no longer have access to credit.

In some instances of identify theft, the criminal is not attempting to acquire money, goods, or services. The object instead is to obtain documents such as a driver's license, birth certificate, Social Security card, passport, visa, and other official government documents. These documents can be used to establish a new identity unknown to the authorities to facilitate various criminal activities. In one case, a known drug dealer used such documents to avoid detection when entering and leaving the United States. Although these actions do not result in financial loss to the victim, embarrassing situations can occur. The victim may be arrested or detained by customs or immigration authorities as a result of the identity thief's actions. In the case mentioned earlier, to make required business trips outside the country, the victim found it necessary to carry extensive government documentation proving that he was not, in fact, the drug dealer who had obtained a passport in his name.

According to the Federal Trade Commission, about 15 million people in the United States are subjected to identity theft each year, at an estimated cost of $50 billion. People of all ages and socioeconomic classes are at risk from this increasingly common crime. Consider the following cases:

- The credit card numbers of 40 million customers at Target and 56 million customers at Home Depot were compromised when hackers broke into databases at those companies. The credit card numbers were then sold online. Although the customers were not liable for purchases made with the stolen card numbers, many customers had to get new cards, and both companies faced considerable expenses in upgrading their systems and trying to restore their reputations.
- Hackers accessed information from 4 million federal employees.
- Identity theft burglars stole laptops and computer hard drives from a health care company serving as a Pentagon contractor in Phoenix. Personal information, including names, addresses, telephone numbers, birth dates, and Social Security numbers related to 562,000 troops, dependents, and retirees were among the stolen data.
- A ring of thieves in New York, New Jersey, and Connecticut stole credit card numbers from thousands of shoppers while serving as cashiers and clerks at pharmacies, shoe stores, and other retail businesses. The thieves used credit card information to manufacture fraudulent cards.
- A former H&R Block employee allegedly victimized at least 27 customers by using their personal information to obtain credit cards that were used to steal thousands of dollars in cash from ATMs and make merchandise purchases.

In these instances alone, millions of individuals were potentially affected, and some were victimized financially by the identity thieves.

The Cost of Identity Theft

The personal cost of identity theft is difficult to measure but easy to imagine, beginning with the victim's feeling of being violated and the resulting insecurity. Identity theft victims have been turned down for employment because of incorrect information found in background checks. They have been hounded for back taxes on income they did not earn or receive, and their accounts have been turned over to collection agencies for nonpayment of mortgages and student loans obtained by identity thieves. They have been refused loans for which they would normally have qualified, had their driver's licenses revoked for violations they did not commit, and have been enrolled for welfare benefits. One identity theft victim was even listed on a birth certificate as the mother of a child she didn't bear.

Calculating the financial costs of identity theft is an easier task. According to the Federal Trade Commission, the average individual loss due to identity theft is $1,500.

Financial losses are not the only costs incurred by an identity theft victim. Time is lost as well. Recent estimates suggest the average victim spends 600 hours dealing with the damage control necessitated by identity theft. The cost of the actual losses incurred and the additional expense of repairing the damage are substantial in both time and money to both individuals and businesses and, ultimately, to our economy.

Identity Theft Tactics

Aside from hacked databases, identity theft most commonly results from lost or stolen wallets. However, many other tactics can be used to obtain your personal data.

shoulder surfing
Tactic used when an identity thief stands close to you in a public place and reads the number of your credit card as you conduct business.

dumpster diving
Tactic used when an identity thief goes through your trash for discarded items that reveal personal information that can be used for fraudulent purposes.

skimming
Tactic used when a store employee steals your credit card number by copying the information contained in the magnetic strip on the card.

pretexting
Tactic used when an identity thief poses as an employee of a company with which you conduct business, to solicit your personal information.

phishing
Tactic used when pretexting happens online.

pharming
Similar to phishing, but targeted to larger audiences; tactic that directs users to bogus Web sites to collect their personal information.

Shoulder Surfing **Shoulder surfing** occurs in public places where you can be readily seen or heard by someone standing close. An example of shoulder surfing is someone standing near you in a hotel or other business establishment and reading the number off your credit card if it is left lying on the counter for too long.

Dumpster Diving As the name implies, **dumpster diving** occurs when the identity thief goes through your trash. The identity thief is looking for things such as credit card receipts, which contain your credit card number, and preapproved credit card solicitations. They contact the credit card company to change the address and then obtain a card in your name. Other targets include discarded information that might contain your Social Security number or bank account numbers.

The dumpster diver may also retrieve similar personal information from the dumpsters of places where you do business. For example, let us say that you complete a credit card application at a local store. If this credit card application, which contains substantial personal and financial information, is disposed of in the company's dumpster, it can be found and used by a dumpster diver. Other dumpsters that could provide usable information are those of your health care providers, your broker, your accountant, and even your bank.

Skimming **Skimming** occurs when identity thieves steal your credit or debit card number by copying the information contained in the magnetic strip on the card. Often, skimmers are employees in stores and restaurants who, when you are not looking, swipe your card through a reader that captures and stores the data. Skimmers also attach card readers to ATMs, so that when you swipe your card for access, they collect your information and use the data to create fake debit and credit cards.

Simple types of skimming may decline in the future, however. By October 2015, Europay, MasterCard, and Visa EMV technology will be widely used in the United States. EMV technology, which is already in use in Europe, replaces the magnetic strip on credit cards with an embedded chip. Every time an EMV card is used for payment or at an ATM, the chip creates a unique transaction code that cannot be used again. As a result, even if a thief or hacker manages to steal the chip information from one transaction, the information cannot be used for another transaction or to create a fake card. Thus, EMV technology can significantly reduce fraud involving credit and debit cards. All the credit card terminals in restaurants and stores will have to be replaced with new EMV terminals, however, and some older terminals may continue to be used after the October 2015 deadline that the credit card companies have established.

Pretexting, Phishing, and Pharming Another method of obtaining personal information is **pretexting**. This occurs when individuals access personal information under false pretenses. Many times the pretexter may use information obtained from dumpster diving to gain information about the companies with which you do business. The pretexter may pose as a survey taker or as an employee of a financial institution, insurance company, or other firm with which you have an account. You may be asked information such as your Social Security number or driver's license, bank, brokerage, or credit card numbers. The pretexter will say that the information is being solicited to update your file or for other routine business. Pretexters may use the information to steal your identity, or they may sell it to others for illegal use.

When pretexting happens online, it is called **phishing**. A phisher sends an e-mail message falsely claiming to be from a legitimate source that directs the recipient to a Web site where he or she is then asked to update account information such as passwords, credit card numbers, bank account numbers, and Social Security numbers. The Web site, in reality, is fake.

A practice that is similar to phishing but reaches many more targets with a single effort is known as **pharming**. By manipulating e-mail viruses and host files, pharmers redirect users, without their knowledge, from the legitimate commercial Web sites they thought they were visiting to bogus ones that look like the genuine sites. When users enter their login names and passwords, the pharmers collect the data.

Abusing Legitimate Access to Records Other sources of data are the employees of places where you work, bank, go to the doctor, and shop. In many cases these employees have easy and legitimate access to personal information that can be used to steal your identity.

For anyone who has gone through a divorce, most if not all personal financial information, including Social Security numbers, is included in the court records. In most states this information is considered part of the public record.

Crime Rings In some cases, the identity thieves may be part of a well-organized crime ring that has systematically infiltrated corporations and financial institutions for the sole purpose of obtaining information to facilitate large-scale identity thefts.

FREE APPS
for Personal
Finance

Identifying Permissions You Allowed in the Past

Application:

The MyPermissions app (by Online Permissions Technologies Ltd.) can identify all the permissions you have allowed due to your use of social media Web sites over time. These permissions can possibly expose your account to identity theft. You may find that you granted permissions for creating accounts that you no longer use, so you could eliminate these accounts to avoid exposure.

To Find It:

Search for the "MyPermissions" app on your mobile device.

Violating Your Mailbox A last source of information worth mentioning is your mailbox. Both incoming and outgoing mail may provide the information needed for your identity to be stolen. Outgoing mail can provide credit card and bank information if you leave letters in your mailbox for the postal carrier to pick up. Incoming mail can also provide your credit card account numbers, bank information, driver's license number, and Social Security number.

Protecting Against Identity Theft

There are many ways that you can safeguard your personal information and make it harder for an identity thief to prey on you. Most of these safeguards are relatively easy to install and inexpensive.

Shielding Personal Information at Home

Consider the following methods to safeguard your personal information:

- Go through your wallet or purse and remove anything that contains your Social Security number, including your Social Security card. Other items that you should not carry, unless absolutely necessary, are your passport, birth certificate, and rarely used credit cards. Also be sure that you are not carrying any account passwords or PINs in your wallet. Make a photocopy of the items that remain in your wallet or purse (both the front and back of the documents) and retain these records in a secure location, such as a safety deposit box or fireproof strong box.

- Document your accounts. For all credit cards that you have, whether or not you carry them in your wallet, keep a list of the name of the company, credit card number, and toll-free phone number in a secure location. Keep a list of all bank account numbers, brokerage account numbers, and their respective 800 numbers in a secure location as well.

- Buy a shredder and use it. When you receive preapproved credit card applications, shred them. When you dispose of out-of-date receipts from credit cards, shred them.

The best rule of thumb regarding what to shred is "when in doubt, shred it." You can purchase good shredders for less than $100; heavy-duty shredders are available in the $150–$200 range. Consider purchasing a shredder that crosscuts paper. Some even shred credit cards.

- Do not have your Social Security number printed on your checks.

- Remove your name and address from local phone directories and reverse directories (that is, directories listing phone numbers in numerical order with names and addresses attached). Install a locked mailbox or rent a P.O. box and pick up your mail at the post office.

- Shop online only when there is evidence of a secured Web site. An "s" at the end of the Web address (https://) and/or a padlock icon indicates a secure site.

- Be suspicious of any phone callers seeking to verify or update your personal information. If in doubt, tell the caller you will call back. Obtain the solicitor's name and phone number and then call the company to verify the caller's credentials.

- Mail all bills where remittance stubs contain account data in a U.S. Postal Service depository box. Do not leave them in your mailbox, even if it is a locked box. Some experts go so far as to recommend that such sensitive information be mailed only at a post office.

- Scrutinize every bank statement and credit card statement on the day you receive them. The earlier identity theft is detected, the less damage there will be to repair on your financial record.

- Take care when using smartphones to order merchandise. These calls usually require your giving a credit card account number for payment. There are devices available that allow people to scan and lock in on a signal and "overhear" your conversation.

- Be aware of delivery schedules. If you are expecting delivery of an item, whether it be a new credit card or a purchase you have made with a credit card, and it has not arrived at the expected time, contact the credit card issuer or merchant to determine its status. You will probably be able to track the delivery status online.

- Never have checks that you have ordered delivered to your house. Instead, have them sent to your P.O. box or pick them up at the financial institution. Some experts recommend that you restrict your use of personal checks to payment of bills via the U.S. mail. Do not use personal checks for everyday transactions, as they contain your account number, name, address, and phone number. Some merchants will also require your driver's license number. Remember that these checks will pass through many hands.

- Be careful what you post on social media. Identity thieves can gather a great deal of information about you from social media sites. In 2014, 25 members of an identity theft ring were arrested for forging checks. One of their sources of information was Instagram, where young people getting their first paycheck would post photos of themselves holding the check. By looking at the photos, the thieves could learn the name, address, and account number of the payor and the bank's routing number. With that information, they could forge checks.

- Protect your home computer from hackers and worms by installing a firewall and virus protection and updating both frequently. Don't download programs or open hyperlinks sent to you by people you don't know. Also, password-protect sensitive personal data. When disposing of a computer, obtain a strong "wipe" utility program to remove all personal, financial, or other sensitive data. The "Delete" function cannot be relied on to accomplish this task.

- When on vacation, have your mail held at the post office. Also, secure all personal information within your home to the best of your ability, and while on the road, do not leave credit card slips, PINs, or other sensitive information in unoccupied hotel rooms.

- File your income tax return as early as possible—don't wait until the April 15 deadline. Tax refund identity fraud has increased dramatically in recent years. Identity thieves who have your Social Security number, birth date, and other personal information can file a fraudulent income tax return in your name claiming a refund. Then the thieves keep the refund. When you file your return later, you receive a letter from the Internal Revenue Service (IRS) telling you that a return in your name has already been processed. Although the IRS will correct the mistake, doing so will likely take months, which could be a problem for you if you were counting on receiving a refund soon after filing.

Protecting Personal Information at Work

Consider the following safeguards you can take at your place of employment:

- If your employer requires that you wear a photo ID, be sure that it does not display your Social Security number. If it does, ask your employer to consider using another form of employee ID numbers.

- Examine your paycheck and stub. If either contains your Social Security number, request that your payroll office truncate this information.

- Examine your health insurance card. If it uses your Social Security number as an identifier, discuss the matter with your Human Resources department to determine if an alternative number can be used.

- Have a discussion with your employer's Human Resources department about the security measures in place to safeguard your records. Some questions you might consider asking are

  1. What personal data are maintained online?
  2. Who has access to the personnel records?
  3. Where are the hard copies of personnel records maintained?
  4. How secure is the area where records are maintained?
  5. Are temporary workers employed in the Human Resources department, and if so, how are they monitored and how is their access to files limited?
  6. Is a record of personnel who have accessed files maintained?

Also, you need to determine that your personal information is being properly safeguarded by your health care providers. Some of the same questions that you should address to your Human Resources department concerning the handling of your records should be asked of your health care providers. Safe record disposal, which you presume of your credit card issuer and banks, should also be expected of your health care providers.

Identity Theft Insurance

Identity theft insurance can be obtained as part of your homeowner's or renter's policy or as a stand-alone policy. Some credit card issuers add identity theft insurance as a cardholder benefit.

When obtaining identity theft insurance, low deductibles, reimbursement for lost wages, coverage for legal fees, and the cost associated with the denial of credit are items to consider in your policy selection. Some critics of identity theft insurance point out that the associated losses are seldom catastrophic, which is the reason we typically buy insurance. Still, for $25 to $60 per year (the typical cost of a $10,000 to $15,000 policy) a person may be able to obtain peace of mind in dealing with the cost of identity theft.

Response to Identity Theft

If you are a victim of identity theft, you must take action immediately to clean up your credit report. When doing so, it is essential to maintain a record of who you talk to and correspond with, the organization with which they are affiliated, the date of the conversation or correspondence, the phone number and/or address, and if it is a verbal conversation, notes on the nature of that conversation. If your communication is by mail, fax, or e-mail, keep a copy of the correspondence. If you correspond by certified mail, attach the verification of the receipt to the correspondence. Also, keep copies of all reports (credit, police) that you receive. You will be communicating with a large number of people, and it will be necessary to refer to previous conversations or correspondence to expedite the process. Maintaining a log will prove to be very helpful during this stressful period.

Contact the Police

Contact your local police or sheriff's department, and insist that a report be written. Be sure to obtain a copy of the report for your files.

Contact the FTC

Contact the FTC, which, as a result of the Identity Theft and Assumption Deterrence Act of 1998, has been designated to function as a central clearinghouse for all identity theft complaints. The Fair and Accurate Credit Transactions Act (FACTA), enacted in December 2003, requires the FTC to issue a standard form and procedures for use by consumers in informing creditors and credit bureaus that they are credit theft victims. Both are available on the FTC's Web site, http://www.ftc.gov.

Contact Credit Reporting Companies

Financial Planning ONLINE

Go to:
http://www.identitytheft
.gov

To get:
Information about identity theft and the tools to report identity theft.

Notify the major credit reporting companies, and request that a fraud alert be placed in your file. An initial fraud alert will stay on your report for up to 90 days. An extended alert will remain on your credit report for seven years if you provide the credit bureau with an identity theft report. This report consists of a copy of the report filed with your law enforcement agency when you initially reported the theft and any documentation beyond that verifying your identity to the satisfaction of the credit bureau. This alert will enable the company to contact you if there is any attempt to establish credit in your name. Also request a credit report for your review.

Contact Creditors

Contact all your creditors and any creditors with which unauthorized accounts have been opened in your name. Many creditors may request a copy of the police report that you obtained from your local law enforcement agency. While contacting your credit card companies and financial institutions, take the opportunity to change all your passwords. Do not use your mother's maiden name, the last four digits of your Social Security number, your birthday, street address, wedding anniversary, or any other readily available information that the identity thief may obtain.

Contact Others

If the identity thief has gained access to your bank accounts or created accounts in your name, you should also contact check verification companies. These companies maintain a database of individuals who have written bad checks and of accounts where there have been excessive or unusual transactions.

If you believe the identity thief has in any way obtained your data or illegally used your personal information involving the U.S. Postal Service, you should contact your local post office to make an appointment with the Postal Inspection Service. If the identity thief has compromised your Social Security number, immediately contact the Social Security Administration. It may be necessary that they issue you a new Social Security number.

You may be notified of pending lawsuits against you as a result of the identity theft. If this is the case, immediately seek the services of an attorney. In some cases of identity theft, the Federal Bureau of Investigation and the Secret Service may also need to be notified. Your local law enforcement agency should be able to advise you if these agencies need to be involved in your particular case.

This list of notifications is by no means exhaustive. Some cases of identity theft may necessitate the notification of your employer's Human Resources department, while others may involve corresponding with your health care providers and medical insurance companies. For victims who have extensive stock, bond, and mutual fund holdings, notifying brokers, mutual fund companies, and 401(k) administrators may also be advisable.

Exhibit 7.4 provides important contact information that you can use to prevent identity theft, report identity theft, or report related criminal activity.

EXAMPLE

Recently, Stephanie Spratt was shocked to receive a statement from Visa indicating that her credit card had been charged to its $5,000 limit. (The statement showed 18 unauthorized purchases, totaling $4,903.88, all made within a two-day time span.) Stephanie paid the balance in full last month, and the only thing she bought with the card this month was a pair of running shoes. Thinking she must have lost her Visa card, Stephanie quickly checked her wallet but it was in its usual compartment.

Stephanie keeps a list of all of her credit card numbers and toll-free phone numbers for the credit card companies in a fireproof box. She retrieves the information she needs and calls customer service at Visa to report the unauthorized charges, close the account, and request a new card. The customer service representative explains to Stephanie that had her card actually been stolen, she would have been liable under federal law for $50 of the $4,903.88 in charges. But, because the thief stole Stephanie's credit card number, she is not liable for unauthorized use.

Stephanie is relieved that she won't be held accountable for the charges, but she is also puzzled about how the thief accessed her credit card number. Also, she is worried that maybe the thief stole more than that. She recalls a recent e-mail from a popular online store, saying that her account would be terminated if she didn't update her credit information. A quick e-mail to the store confirms that no such e-mail was sent—Stephanie is a victim of a phishing scam.

As best she can recall, the information Stephanie provided to the phisher was her Visa account number, her name, and her address. To be safe, Stephanie's next step is to put an alert on her credit report. She decides to check her report in one month, and if there is fraudulent information, she will request corrections and fill out an identity theft report.

| EXHIBIT 7.4 | Useful Sources of Information to Protect Against Identity Theft |

Check Verification Companies

CheckRite	(800) 766-2748
ChexSystems	(800) 428-9623
Certigy/Equifax	(800) 437-5120
National Processing Systems	(800) 526-5380
Telecheck	(800) 710-9898

Federal Trade Commission
Web site Address: http://www.ftc.gov
Complaint About a Company or Business Practice: 877-382-4357
Identity theft: 877-438-4338

Equifax
Web site Address: http://www.equifax.com/
Credit Fraud Info: Insert the search term "credit fraud" at the Equifax Web site
Credit Report Information: 800-685-1111
Fraud Alert: 888-766-0088
Credit Reports and Scores: 866-493-9788

Experian
Web site Address: http://www.experian.com/
Credit Fraud Info: Insert the search term "credit fraud" at the Experian Web site
Credit Report Information: 888-397-3742
Credit Monitoring: 877-284-7942

TransUnion
Web site Address: http://www.transunion.com/
Credit Fraud Info: Insert the search term "credit fraud" at the TransUnion Web site
Credit Report Information: 800-888-4213
Credit Monitoring: 800-493-2392
Fraud Alert: 800-680-7289

Internal Revenue Service
Web site Address: http://www.irs.gov

Social Security Administration
Web site Address: http://www.ssa.gov

U.S. State Department
Passport Fraud: Go to http://www.state.gov and insert the search term "passport fraud"

How Credit Assessment and Security Fit Within Your Financial Plan

The following are the key credit assessment and security decisions that should be included within your financial plan:

1. Is your credit standing adequate so that you can use credit?
2. Is your credit and personal identity information secure?

EXHIBIT 7.5   How Credit Standing and Security Fit Within Stephanie Spratt's Financial Plan

GOALS

1. *Ensure that I always have easy access to credit, so that I can obtain personal loans or use credit cards whenever I desire.*
2. *Ensure that my credit and identity information is secure.*

DECISIONS

Decision Regarding My Credit Report

Contact the credit bureaus to request a copy of my credit report and ensure that my credit report is accurate. If there are any deficiencies listed on my report, correct them so that I can ensure easy access to credit in the future.

Decision Regarding the Security of My Credit and Identity

Leave most of my personal information at home. Carry only my Visa and MasterCard, and driver's license with me. Shred any documents I plan to discard that contain personal information.

By making proper decisions, you can ensure that you access credit only when your credit standing is adequate, and prevent others from using your credit or identity information. Exhibit 7.5 shows how credit standing and security apply to Stephanie Spratt's financial plan.

SUMMARY

Background on Credit. Credit, which consists of funds provided to a borrower that will be repaid in the future, has both advantages and disadvantages. An advantage is the convenience that credit provides in making day-to-day purchases without the necessity of carrying large amounts of cash. A disadvantage is that if not used properly, credit can result in bankruptcy.

Credit Bureaus. A complete history of your credit transactions is maintained by credit bureaus that numerically rate your credit score and report this information to interested parties.

Lenders commonly access the credit payment history provided by one or more credit bureaus when deciding whether to extend a personal loan. You can obtain a free credit report each year from each of the three credit bureaus to ensure that the report is accurate. The credit report contains potentially negative information from public records, such as bankruptcy filings. It also offers information about late payments, accounts in good standing, inquiries made about your credit history, and personal information.

Identity Theft. Identity theft, which involves the use of your personal identifying information

without your permission, is one of the fastest-growing crimes in our country. An identity thief may use your personal information to obtain goods, services, or money or to create a new identity. All these actions can have a negative effect on your credit history.

Common identity theft tactics include shoulder surfing, dumpster diving, skimming, pretexting, phishing, and pharming.

Protecting Against Identity Theft. You can protect against identity theft by shredding old financial information about your bank statements and mailing checks only in a U.S. Post Office mailbox. Take precautions where you work, bank, and receive medical care. Requesting the elimination of your Social Security number on health care insurance cards, identity badges, and paychecks is a necessary step in safeguarding your identity.

Obtain a copy of your credit report at least once a year. Carefully review your credit report for unusual account activity and the existence of accounts of which you are not aware.

Responding to Identity Theft. Should your identity be stolen, notify the police, and request a written report. Notify the FTC, credit bureaus, credit card companies, financial institutions, and when appropriate, the FBI and Secret Service.

How Credit Assessment and Security Fit Within Your Financial Plan. Access to credit can allow you to make purchases that you could not make if you had to rely on your cash and checking account. Thus, you can more easily achieve your financial plan by acquiring assets (such as a new car or a home) if you maintain a good credit standing. However, you should take steps to protect against identify theft so that you can continue to have access to credit.

REVIEW QUESTIONS

All Review Questions are available in MyFinanceLab *at* http://www.myfinancelab.com.

1. **Types of Credit.** Explain the three types of credit. Under what conditions might a consumer find each type useful?

2. **Using Credit.** What are the advantages and disadvantages of using credit?

3. **Credit Rights.** The Equal Credit Opportunity Act prohibits creditors from denying credit for what reasons? If you are denied credit, do you have the right to know the reason for the denial?

4. **Credit from Utilities.** How do utilities extend credit, and how can this credit help you establish a credit history?

5. **Impact of Credit Report.** Explain how a weak credit report can affect you.

6. **Credit Bureaus.** Name the three major credit bureaus. How do they score your credit rating? Will all three major credit bureaus always produce the same credit score?

7. **Credit Report.** What are the six major areas of information that may be included on your credit report?

8. **Credit Score.** What factors determine your credit score, and how are these factors weighted by FICO?

9. **VantageScore.** How does a VantageScore differ from a FICO score?

10. **Improving Your Credit Score.** How can you improve your credit score, and how long can it take to erase a poor credit history?

11. **Reviewing Your Credit Score.** How often should you review your credit report from each of the three major credit bureaus? Why is this review beneficial?

12. **Identity Theft.** What constitutes identity theft?

13. **Identity Theft.** Is identity theft only perpetrated to acquire money, goods, or services?

14. **Impact of Identity Theft.** Aside from the financial losses, what other negative impacts might a victim of identity theft encounter?

15. **Identity Theft Tactics.** Name and explain at least three tactics used by identity thieves to obtain information.

16. **Identity Theft.** Can identity theft occur through legitimate access to your personal information? Explain.

17. **Safeguarding Information.** Discuss steps you can take to safeguard your personal information.

18. **Responding to Identity Theft.** What steps should you take if you become a victim of identity theft?

19. **Credit CARD Act.** How did the Credit Card Accountability, Responsibility, and Disclosure Act of 2009 change credit card access to students under the age of 21? Why was this change deemed necessary?

20. **Credit History.** What is your credit history? How does it impact your ability to borrow money?

21. **Credit Score and Open Accounts.** Explain how closing a credit card account can negatively impact your credit score.

22. **Credit Counseling.** Explain the advantages and disadvantages of using a credit counseling organization.

23. **EMV Cards.** How will the new EMV technology help reduce identify theft?

24. **Social Media and Identity Theft.** What are some factors to consider when using social media with respect to identity theft?

FINANCIAL PLANNING PROBLEM

All Financial Planning Problems are available in MyFinanceLab *at http://www.myfinancelab.com.*

Ethical Dilemma. Rita is the office manager of a three-doctor practice. Her brother, Juan, a recent college graduate, recently started working for a large insurance company that specializes in health insurance. In attempting to build a client base, Juan asks Rita if she will provide him with a list of all the doctors' patients who do not currently have health insurance. Wishing to help her brother be successful in his new job, she runs the list, which includes names, addresses, telephone numbers, Social Security numbers, and brief medical histories.

1. Is Rita acting ethically? Explain.

2. What problems could Rita be creating for the practice's patients?

FINANCIAL PLANNING ONLINE EXERCISES

1. Go to the Web site of the Federal Reserve Bank of Philadelphia (http://www.phil.frb .org), and go to the section on consumer credit:

   a. What do lenders look for before lending money?

   b. After college, how will you go about establishing your credit?

   c. Select three of the common reasons for denying credit, and explain how you will avoid these issues.

   d. Explain what is meant by the "Rule of 78s."

2. Review the information at http://www.ftc.gov about free credit reports.

   a. What is the only authorized source for free credit reports under federal law?

   b. How do you request a free credit report?

   c. Why should you review your credit report?

   d. When reviewing your credit report, what should you look for?

3. Go to the Web site http://www.ftc.gov, and summarize what actions you should take if your identity is stolen.

PSYCHOLOGY OF PERSONAL FINANCE: Paying Off Credit Card Debt

1. Some consumers prefer putting off their credit card payments and don't think about having to repay the debt along with the interest later. At the other extreme, other consumers are obsessed with paying off the credit card balance each month because they dislike having any debt. What drives your behavior when using credit cards?

2. Read one practical article of how psychology affects paying credit card debt. You can easily retrieve possible articles by doing an online search using the terms "psychology" and "credit card debt." Summarize the main points of the article.

WEB SEARCH EXERCISE

You can develop your personal finance skills by conducting an Internet search for related articles. Find a recent online article about personal finance that reinforces one or more concepts covered in this chapter. If your class has an online component, your professor may ask you to post your summary of the article there and provide a link to the article so that other students can access it. If your class is live, your professor may ask you to summarize your application of the article in class. Your professor may assign specific students to complete this assignment or may allow any student to do the assignment on a volunteer basis.

For recent online articles related to this chapter, consider using the following search terms (be sure to include the current year as a search term to ensure that the online articles are recent):

- Benefits of credit
- Dangers of credit
- Your credit score
- Credit bureaus
- Protecting against identity theft

VIDEO EXERCISE: Improving Your Credit

Go to one of the Web sites that contains video clips (such as http://www.youtube.com), and view some video clips about improving your credit. You can use search phrases such as "improving your credit" or "assessing your credit." Select one video clip on this topic that is the most useful for you.

1. Provide the Web link for the video clip.
2. What do you think is the main point of this video clip?
3. How might you change your use of credit as a result of watching this video clip?

BUILDING YOUR OWN FINANCIAL PLAN

Credit is one of the most useful and dangerous elements of a personal financial plan. This case will assist you in reviewing your credit and safeguarding it from identity theft.

In the first part of the exercise, you will determine whether your credit history is being properly and accurately reported in the credit reports that banks and other lending institutions use to evaluate your creditworthiness. Then, you will determine your overall creditworthiness. Finally, you will establish practices that will help safeguard you against identity theft.

Go to the worksheets at the end of this chapter to continue building your financial plan.

THE SAMPSONS—A Continuing Case

The $2,000 credit card balance that the Sampsons are carrying, on which they are currently making the minimum payment due, has a credit limit of $10,000. The Sampsons have just received a letter from the credit card company offering to increase their credit limit to $20,000. The Sampsons have also read several articles on identity theft and are concerned with protecting themselves from this fast-growing crime. They currently receive their mail in a curbside mailbox, and they dispose of all junk mail in the trash.

Go to the worksheets at the end of this chapter to continue this case.

CHAPTER 7: BUILDING YOUR OWN FINANCIAL PLAN

GOALS

1. Evaluate your credit report.

2. Determine your overall creditworthiness.

3. Establish practices that will safeguard you from identity theft.

ANALYSIS

1. Obtain a copy of your credit report from http://www.annualcreditreport.com, scrutinize the report, and report any inaccuracies to the credit bureaus.

2. Go to the Web site http://www.wellsfargo.com, and insert the search term "evaluating your debt" so that you can evaluate your own debt situation.

3. Inventory your wallet/purse to determine if you can reduce your risk of identity theft by selectively removing certain items.

Item Description	Identity Theft Risk (High/Low)	Necessary to Carry? (Yes/No)	If Previous Column Is Marked "No," Where Should Item Be Stored?

DECISIONS

1. Are there any errors in your credit report you must correct? How can you improve your creditworthiness?

_____

_____

_____

_____

_____

_____

_____

_____

_____

_____

2. In addition to inventorying your wallet/purse and removing items, what other steps can you take in your life to reduce your exposure to identity theft?

_____

_____

_____

_____

_____

_____

_____

_____

_____

_____

CHAPTER 7: THE SAMPSONS—A Continuing Case

CASE QUESTIONS

1. Should the Sampsons accept the increase in the limit on their credit card, even if they do not anticipate using it?

_____

_____

_____

_____

_____

_____

_____

_____

_____

_____

_____

_____

_____

_____

_____

_____

2. Advise the Sampsons on steps that they can take to reduce their exposure to identity theft.

_____

_____

_____

_____

_____

_____

_____

_____

_____

_____

_____

_____

Managing Your Credit

When Tara graduated from college and started her first full-time job, she was on a tight budget. She determined that if she limited her spending, her salary would cover her expenses and allow her to save for a car. Tara decided to apply for a credit card so that she would be able to make emergency purchases, if necessary. Applying was easy, as every month or so she received notices from credit card companies offering her a credit card. When Tara received her card with a credit limit of $4,000, she promised herself that she would use it only for emergency purchases between paychecks and that she would pay the balance in full every month. But six months later, her friends suggested that they should all

Diego Cervo/Shutterstock

take a trip to Hawaii. Tara didn't have enough cash to pay for the trip, so she charged $3,800 on her credit card. She couldn't afford to pay the full balance on her card, but she didn't think that was a problem because she had received an offer of another credit card that would charge zero interest if she transferred her balance to it. She failed to read the fine print, which stated that the interest rate would rise to 18.5% after six months. Two years and three additional credit cards later, Tara has accumulated $11,500 in credit card debt. She frequently used her credit cards for unnecessary purchases. She believed that as long as she made a payment each month, it didn't matter that she quickly ran up charges to the limit because she could always get a new card and do a balance transfer. Each time she told herself that she would pay off the balance before the zero interest rate period expired, but each time she found it easier to just make the minimum payment, so soon she was paying 18.5% interest or higher on all her unpaid balances. She also failed to realize that a fee and substantially higher interest are associated with cash advances and that she would be charged $35 for every late payment. Improper use of credit cards can cause severe problems. Now Tara has a poor credit rating, which will affect her ability to get a loan for the car that she needs. In addition, it may take her several years to pay off her credit card debt.

This chapter focuses on effectively using credit. You'll see that a good credit history is built by the proper use and control of credit, not by the absence of credit.

MyFinanceLab helps you master the topics in this chapter and study more efficiently. Visit http://www.myfinancelab.com for more details.

209

The objectives of this chapter are to:

- Provide a background on credit cards
- Explain credit repayment
- Describe how to review the credit card statement
- Explain credit card regulations
- Offer tips on using credit cards
- Explain how managing your credit fits within your financial plan

Background on Credit Cards

The easiest way to establish credit is to obtain a credit card, which allows you to purchase products on credit wherever that card is honored. You receive a monthly statement that identifies the purchases you made with the credit card during that period. Normally, credit cards are not used for very large expenditures such as cars or homes, but they are very convenient for smaller purchases, such as meals at restaurants, gasoline, clothing, car repairs, and even groceries.

Obtaining a credit card is easy, perhaps too easy. Credit card companies frequently send unsolicited offers of credit cards to consumers. Often the cards are preapproved. More than 70% of all households in the United States have at least one credit card, and many have two or more cards. About 30% of all undergraduate students have credit cards. There are about 400 million credit card accounts in the United States, and more than 26 billion credit card transactions take place every year.

Advantages of Credit Cards

Credit cards offer three advantages. First, you can purchase products and services without carrying a large amount of cash or a checkbook. Second, as long as you pay off your balance each month, you receive free financing until the due date on your credit card statement. Third, you receive a monthly statement that contains a consolidated list of the purchases you made with the credit card, which enables you to keep track of your spending. In some cases, you receive an annual statement as well, detailing expenses by category, which can be useful in preparing your income tax return.

Disadvantages of Credit Cards

The main disadvantage of having a credit card is that it allows you to make purchases that you cannot afford and should not make. It gives you the opportunity to spend beyond your means.

EXAMPLE

Mia sees a new 55-inch television with exciting new features for $2,000. She already has a good TV, but it is smaller and lacks some of the new features. She does not have the cash to pay for the TV, but the store gives her a new credit card. The salesclerk tells Mia that she does not have to pay any money for one year and that the interest rate is 1.5% per month. In Mia's mind, 1.5% is close to zero, so she is very willing to obtain the TV on credit. She does not take time to read the application form, which states that the annual interest rate is 18%.

Exhibit 8.1 shows how the amount Mia owes on the TV will grow over the first 12 months. By the end of 10 months, Mia will owe $2,321, or $321 more than the price at the time she obtained the TV. Had she put off buying the TV for one year, she might have been able to save enough money to pay for it with cash. In addition, prices of televisions (like many high-tech products) tend to decline over time as new models are introduced, so she might have been able to purchase the TV for about $1,500 if she waited one year. By the time she starts making payments on this TV, she may even be tired of it and ready to buy another new TV.

The potential for excessive spending with credit cards is even more pronounced because of the financing available. As long as you make the minimum monthly payment, excessive spending can continue over time. Some consumers accumulate a large amount of debt and ultimately have to file for bankruptcy as a result.

Applying for a Credit Card

When you apply for a credit card, potential creditors obtain information from you, and from credit bureaus, so that they can assess your ability to repay credit.

Personal Information When you apply for credit, you are asked to complete an application that typically requests the following information:

- Cash inflows: What is your monthly income?
- Cash outflows: How much do you spend per month?
- Credit history: Have you borrowed funds in the past? Did you repay any previous loans in a timely manner?
- Capital: Do you have any funds in the form of savings or stocks that can be used if necessary to cover future debt payments?
- Collateral: Do you have any assets that can be used as collateral to secure the borrowed funds? (If you could not repay your debt, you could sell these assets to obtain the funds needed to repay the loans.)

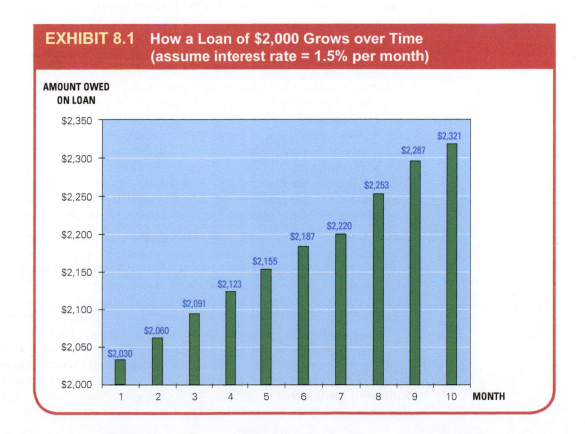

EXHIBIT 8.1   How a Loan of $2,000 Grows over Time (assume interest rate = 1.5% per month)

Creditors generally prefer that you have a high level of cash inflows, a low level of cash outflows, a large amount of capital and collateral, and a good credit history. Nevertheless, they commonly extend credit to individuals who do not have all of these attributes. For example, credit card issuers recognize that individuals starting their first job after college may not earn much income. Nevertheless, they may still provide a limited amount of credit if they believe that the individuals are likely to repay it. Some creditors also extend credit at higher interest rates to individuals who have a higher risk of defaulting.

Credit Check When you apply for credit, a credit card issuer typically conducts a credit check as part of the application review process. The company can obtain a credit report, discussed in Chapter 7, which indicates your creditworthiness based on information such as whether you have made late payments or have any current unpaid bills. A credit report summarizes your history of repaying credit with banks, retailers, credit card issuers, and other lenders. Recall that credit problems remain on a credit bureau's report for seven years. If you claim bankruptcy, this information normally remains on a credit bureau's report for 10 years.

Other Information That Creditors Evaluate Creditors also often ask an applicant to disclose income and any existing debt so that they can assess the existing debt level as a percentage of income. When the debt level is only a small fraction of the applicant's income, creditors are more willing to provide credit.

In addition to information about the applicant, creditors also consider existing economic conditions when they evaluate credit applications. If economic conditions weaken and you lose your job, you may be unable to repay your loan. Thus, creditors are less willing to extend credit when the economy is weak.

Types of Credit Cards

The most popular credit cards are MasterCard, Visa, and American Express. MasterCard and Visa allow your charges to be financed, as do some American Express cards. Other American Express cards require that the balance be paid in full each month. These three types of cards are especially convenient because they are accepted by most merchants. The merchants honor credit cards because they recognize that many consumers will make purchases only if they can use their credit cards. A credit card company receives a percentage (commonly between 2% and 4%) of the payments made to merchants with its credit card. For example, when you use your MasterCard to pay for a $100 car repair at a Shell Oil station, Shell will pay MasterCard a percentage, perhaps around $3.

Many financial institutions issue MasterCard and Visa credit cards to individuals. Each financial institution makes its own arrangements with credit card companies to do the billing and financing when necessary. The institution provides financing for individuals who choose not to pay their balance in full when they receive a billing statement. The financial institutions benefit by providing financing because they typically earn a high rate of interest on the credit extended. Some universities and charitable organizations also issue MasterCard and Visa credit cards and provide financing if needed.

retail (or proprietary) credit card
A credit card that is honored only by a specific retail establishment.

Retail Credit Cards An alternative to MasterCard, Visa, and American Express cards is a **retail (or proprietary) credit card** that is issued for use at a specific retail establishment. For example, many retail stores (such as JCPenney and Macy's) and gas stations (such as Shell Oil and ExxonMobil) issue their own credit card. If you use a Shell Oil credit card to pay for gas at a Shell station, Shell does not have to pay a small percentage of the proceeds to MasterCard or any other credit card company. You can usually obtain an application for a proprietary card while paying for products or services. You may be given instant credit when you complete the application. With most retail credit cards, you can pay a small portion of the balance owed each month, which means that the merchant finances your purchase. The interest rate you are charged when financing with retail credit cards is normally 18% or higher. Proprietary cards are less common than they used to be because many retail stores have established partnerships with the credit card companies to issue cobranded or affinity cards, which carry the store's name but can be used at other merchants like standard credit cards.

One disadvantage of a proprietary credit card is that it limits your purchases to a single merchant. However, you may find that the limit is an advantage if you are trying to restrict your use of credit so that you do not spend beyond your means. For example, you could use a Shell credit card to pay for gasoline and car repairs, but not to buy CDs, clothing, and many other products. Another disadvantage is that using many proprietary cards means you will have several credit card bills to pay each month; using one card for all purchases allows you to make only one online payment from your checking account or write only one check to cover all your credit card payments. In addition, keeping track of your spending is easier if you use only one card.

Secured and Prepaid Cards

If you have a poor credit history and have difficulty obtaining a standard credit card, you may be able to improve your credit record by obtaining a secured credit card, which is "secured" or backed by funds that you deposit. You can apply for a secured credit card at your financial institution, which will require you to make a deposit to a special account. The amount of funds that you deposit will be your credit limit, so if you deposit $500, you will have a limit of $500. You will receive a statement of your charges each month and be required to make a minimum payment. By making your payments on time and demonstrating that you can use credit wisely, you can repair your damaged credit history and may eventually qualify for a standard credit card.

Unlike secured cards, prepaid credit or debit cards will not improve your credit record. A prepaid card is not really a credit card because no credit is extended. The card can be used to spend the funds that are in your account.

Prepaid cards can be purchased at many retail stores and even gas stations. There is no application process—you simply pay the cashier and the funds are loaded into the account of the card. Once you have spent all the funds, the card can be reloaded. Although you should keep track of your purchases as you use the funds, there also is usually a Web site where you can check your balance online. Some cards allow you to have a personal identification number (PIN), which will enable you to use the card to withdraw cash from ATMs.

The advantage of prepaid cards is that they are convenient for people who do not have bank accounts. However, a major disadvantage of prepaid cards is the fees. You may have to pay an activation fee, a fee for reloading, a fee for withdrawing cash from an ATM, an inactivity fee if you don't use the card regularly, and even a fee for checking your balance online. Another disadvantage is that if your card is lost or stolen, you generally have less protection than with a standard credit card. Fees and theft protection vary substantially among card issuers, so always read the contract that comes with the card very carefully.

In recent years, a number of employers have begun paying their employees' wages with prepaid cards because issuing cards is considerably cheaper than issuing payroll checks. Although this practice can be convenient for employees without bank accounts, it has become controversial because of the fees associated with the cards. After receiving many complaints about prepaid payroll cards, the Consumer Financial Protection Bureau sent a notice to employers across the country reminding them that employees cannot be required to accept prepaid cards—they must be given at least one other option for receiving their wages, such as a check or direct deposit to a bank account. Employees are also entitled to receive a written explanation of all fees associated with the other cards and other protections.

Credit Limit

Credit card companies set a credit limit, which specifies the maximum amount of credit allowed. The credit limit varies among individuals. It may be a relatively small amount (such as $300) for individuals who have a low income. The credit limit can usually be increased for individuals who prove that they are creditworthy by paying their credit card bills on time. Some credit card companies may allow a large limit (such as $10,000 or more) to households that have made their credit payments consistently and have higher incomes.

A very high maximum may not be necessary, and it may tempt you to spend excessively. Make sure that the maximum limit is high enough to cover any necessary monthly purchases, but not so high that it encourages you to spend beyond what you can afford.

Although credit card companies may not charge an inactivity fee if you do not use your credit card for a specific period (such as one year), they may cancel your card. In addition, a card's annual fee may be linked to the level of spending. If you spend less, you pay a higher annual fee. Some rewards programs may also require a certain amount of spending during a given period.

Overlimit Protection

A few credit cards provide overlimit protection, which allows you to make purchases beyond your stated credit limit. This is similar to the overdraft protection that is provided on some checking accounts at financial institutions, in which checks can be written and will clear even if there are not enough funds in the checking account. The overlimit protection on credit cards prevents a situation in which you try to use your credit card, but it is rejected because you are over your credit limit.

Fees are charged, however, when overlimit protection is provided. The fees vary among credit card issuers, but can be as high as $39 or more each time the protection is used. Card issuers are prohibited from charging an overlimit fee unless the cardholder specifically requests overlimit protection. Even if the cardholder requests this protection, the card issuer may not charge more than one overlimit fee on any one billing statement. As a result of these rules, which went into effect in 2010, only a small number of credit cards now charge overlimit fees. Some issuers will process a few overlimit transactions for consumers with a long history of paying their bills. Other issuers simply reject the card if the individual is over the credit limit.

Annual Fee

Many credit cards charge an annual fee for the privilege of using the card. Annual fees range from $40 to $500 for cards with extensive rewards programs. The fee is sometimes waived for individuals who use their credit cards frequently and pay their credit card bills in a timely manner.

Incentives to Use the Card

Some credit card companies offer rewards to cardholders who frequently use their credit card. They may provide a cash reward to card users who reach a specific spending limit each month. Alternatively, they may award a point toward a free trip on an airline for every dollar spent. For example, after accumulating 20,000 points, you may qualify for a free flight. If you spend $20,000 over the year on purchases and use this particular credit card for all of them, you will accumulate enough points by the end of the year to earn a free round-trip flight on a designated airline to any destination in the United States. Some airlines issue their own credit cards, which provide similar benefits.

prestige cards
Credit cards issued by a financial institution to individuals who have an exceptional credit standing.

Prestige cards, which offer even more benefits, are available for individuals with high incomes and exceptional credit histories. These cards, which may carry annual fees of several hundred dollars, may offer rewards such as priority access to private jet programs and concierge service at luxury hotels.

Grace Period

Credit cards typically allow a grace period in which you are not charged any interest on your purchases. If a grace period is allowed, the card issuer must ensure that the bill is mailed or delivered at least 21 days before payment is due. Thus, the credit card issuer essentially provides you with free credit from the time you made the purchase until the bill is due.

EXAMPLE

On June 1, Stephanie Spratt paid a car repair bill of $200 with her credit card. The closing date for that month's billing statement is June 20. The card issuer mails the billing statement so that Stephanie receives it on June 30, and her payment is due on July 21. In this case, Stephanie receives about 51 days of free credit. On June 19, she purchased some clothing with her credit card. For that purchase, which is included on the billing statement, she receives about 40 days of free credit. On July 10, she purchased concert tickets with her credit card. This purchase occurs after the closing date of the billing statement and therefore will be listed on the next billing statement, which is due on August 21. For this purchase, credit is extended for about 41 days.

Late Fees Before the enactment of the Credit CARD Act of 2009, which took effect in 2010, card issuers often assessed substantial late fees for payments that were only a day or even a few hours late. Under the new rules, credit card bills must be due on the same date each month, and payments received by 5:00 p.m. on the due date must be considered timely. Late fees must be "reasonable," which in practice means no more than $25 for a first violation and $35 for a second violation within the next six months. A late fee may not be more than the minimum payment due. In the first six months after these rules took effect, the amount of late fees paid by consumers dropped by more than 50%.

Interest Rate

When you are granted credit and do not pay it off before the stated deadline, you will have to pay interest on that credit based on the interest rate imposed by the credit card company. About 34% of all households carry a balance on their credit cards, meaning that they do not immediately pay off the full amount of credit they are granted for their purchases each month. The interest rate charged on credit is commonly between 15% and 20% on an annualized basis and does not vary much over time. Although financing is convenient for individuals who are short on funds, it is expensive and should be avoided if possible.

Types of Interest Rates Charged on Credit Cards Credit cards can offer a fixed rate, a variable rate, or a tiered rate. A fixed rate does not change even if market interest rates are changing. The financial institution that provides financing on a credit card can change the fixed interest rate that it charges, but it must notify you if it does so.

A variable rate adjusts in response to a specified market interest rate, such as a one-year Treasury bill rate. For example, the credit card interest rate could be set equal to the one-year Treasury bill rate + 6%. The financial institution is required to disclose how that variable rate is determined.

Financial institutions may offer a tiered rate, such as a relatively low rate for balances below a specified balance and a higher rate above that balance. They can also revise the interest rate upward as a penalty if you make late payments.

Regulations on Interest Rates New regulations that took effect in 2010 provided clearer and more favorable financing rules for individuals who use credit cards. In particular, credit card companies are not allowed to increase the interest rate on one credit card if you miss a payment on another credit card. In addition, credit card companies must give 45 days of advance notice if they raise the interest rate on your credit card. Also, the rate on an existing credit balance cannot be increased unless the individual is at least 60 days late on payments.

Cash Advances

Many credit cards also allow cash advances at automated teller machines (ATMs). Because a cash advance represents credit extended by the sponsoring financial institution, interest is charged on this transaction. A transaction fee of 1% or 2% of the advance may also be charged. Credit card companies also sometimes provide "convenience checks" that you can use to make purchases that cannot be made by credit card. The interest rate applied to cash advances and convenience checks is generally higher than the interest rate charged on credit extended for specific credit card purchases. The interest rate is applied at the time of the cash advance; the grace period that applies to purchases with a credit card does not apply to cash advances and convenience checks. So, although cash advances and checks are convenient, they can also be extremely costly.

Repaying Credit

finance charge
The interest that you must pay as a result of using credit.

The **finance charge** is the interest that you must pay as a result of using credit. Purchases after the statement closing date are not normally considered when determining the finance charge because of the grace period, as they will appear on your next monthly statement. The finance charge applies only to balances that were not paid in full before their due date in the current billing period.

The following three methods are commonly used to calculate finance charges on outstanding credit card balances.

Average Daily Balance Method

Financial Planning
ONLINE

Go to:
The credit cards section of http://www.consumer finance.gov

To get:
Tips on selecting a credit card.

The most frequently used method is the average daily balance method. For each day in the billing period, the credit card company takes your beginning balance at the start of the day and then subtracts any payments made by you on that day to determine the balance at the end of the day. Then, it determines the average daily balance at the end of the day for every day in the billing period. This method takes into account the time that you pay off any part of the outstanding balance. Thus, if you pay off part of the outstanding balance during the billing period, your finance charges will be lower under this method than under the previous balance method (explained next). There are also variations of this method. The method may be adjusted to exclude any new purchases or to compute the average over two billing periods instead of one period.

Previous Balance Method

Under the previous balance method, interest is charged on the balance at the beginning of the new billing period. This method is the least favorable of the three to the cardholder because finance charges are applied even if part of the outstanding balance is paid off during the billing period.

Adjusted Balance Method

Under the adjusted balance method, interest is charged based on the balance at the end of the new billing period. This method is most favorable for you because it applies finance charges only to the outstanding balance that was not paid off during the billing period.

The following example illustrates the three methods for determining finance charges.

EXAMPLE

Assume that as of June 10, you have an outstanding credit card balance of $700 from purchases made over the last month. The new billing period begins on June 11. Assume that your outstanding balance for the first 15 days of this new billing period (from June 11 to June 25) is $700. Then, on June 25, the financial institution receives a payment of $200 from you, reducing the balance to $500. This is the balance for the remaining 15 days of the billing period.

- **Average Daily Balance Method.** Under this method the monthly interest rate is applied to the average daily balance. Because your daily balance was $700 over the first 15 days and $500 over the last 15 days, your average daily balance was $600 over the 30-day billing period. Using a monthly interest rate of 1.5%, your finance charge is

$$\$600 \times .015 = \$9.00$$

- **Previous Balance Method.** Under this method you will be subject to a finance charge that is calculated by applying the monthly interest rate to the $700 outstanding at the beginning of the new billing period. Using a monthly interest rate of 1.5%, your finance charge is

$$\$700 \times .015 = \$10.50$$

- **Adjusted Balance Method.** Under this method you will be subject to a finance charge that is calculated by applying the monthly interest rate to the $500 outstanding at the end of the new billing period. Using a monthly interest rate of 1.5%, your finance charge is

$$\$500 \times .015 = \$7.50$$

Notice from this example that the finance charge is lower if the credit card company uses the adjusted balance method. Individuals who frequently have financing charges can save a substantial amount of money over time by relying on a credit card that uses this method. The best way to reduce financing charges, however, is still to pay the entire credit card bill before the due date every month.

simple interest rate
The percentage of credit that must be paid as interest on an annual basis.

Estimating Credit Repayment

The percentage of the credit that you must pay as interest on your credit card on an annual basis is based on a **simple interest rate.**

EXAMPLE

If you borrow $10,000 and are charged a simple interest rate of 12%, the amount of interest you pay each year is

$$\text{Amount of Interest} = \text{Amount Borrowed} \times \text{Simple Interest Rate}$$
$$= \$10,000 \times .12$$
$$= \$1,200$$

annual percentage rate (APR)
The simple interest rate including any fees charged by the creditor.

The **annual percentage rate (APR)** on credit is the simple interest rate after including any fees (such as an application processing fee) imposed by the creditor. The APR is useful because it allows you to easily compare financing costs among various possible creditors.

Impact of Interest Rate on the Amount You Owe
The interest rate can have a major impact on the amount that you owe when using credit cards. A card with a higher interest rate can result in substantially higher interest expenses.

EXAMPLE

You plan to pursue credit card X because it has no annual fee, whereas credit card Y has an annual fee of $30. You typically have an outstanding credit balance of $3,000 each month. Credit card X charges an annual interest rate of 18% on balances carried forward, and credit card Y charges an interest rate of 12% on balances carried forward. The difference in the expenses associated with each credit card is shown here:

	Credit Card X	Credit Card Y
Average monthly balance	$3,000	$3,000
Annual interest rate	18%	12%
Annual interest expenses	18% × $3,000 = $540	12% × $3,000 = $360
Annual fee	$0	$30
Total annual expenses	$540	$390

The annual interest expenses can be determined from knowing the average monthly balance over the year. The higher the average monthly balance, the higher your interest expenses because you will have to pay interest on the balance.

Notice that credit card X results in $540 in annual interest expenses, which is $180 more than the annual interest expenses from credit card Y. Thus, although credit card X does not charge an annual fee, your interest expenses from using credit card X could be very high. The high interest expenses more than offset the advantage of no annual fee.

If you have always paid off your balance in the month that it occurred, you would not have any interest expenses. In this case, the interest rate on the credit card would not be important, and you may prefer credit card X because it does not have an annual fee. That is, you would benefit from no annual fee and would not be adversely affected by the high interest rate.

Exhibit 8.2 shows the amount of interest you would pay per year on a $10,000 loan at various simple interest rates, as well as the total amount of interest that would be paid over a four-year period. Notice how much larger the interest payments are when you pay a higher interest rate. When obtaining credit, it is important to seek out the lowest interest rate possible.

Impact of Financing Period on Credit Payments The total amount of interest paid on a credit card balance depends on the length of the financing period. Assume that you borrowed $10,000, and you only pay interest on the loan until you pay back the entire loan amount. Look at Exhibit 8.2, and compare the amount of interest that you would have to pay on a loan that lasts for one year versus four years for any particular interest rate shown. If you can pay off the loan at the end of one year, you would pay annual interest only one time, so your total interest paid is shown in the second column of Exhibit 8.2. However, if it takes you four years to pay off the loan, you have to pay the annual interest four times. Your total interest paid is shown in the third column; notice how much more interest you would have to pay if you allow the loan to last for four years.

Using Calculators to Estimate Repayment Your billing statement is required to show how many months (or years) it will take to pay off your balance if you make only the minimum payment each month. The statement will also tell you the total amount of money, including principal and interest, that you will pay if you pay only the minimum each month. In addition, the statement must show how much you would need to pay each month to pay off the balance in three years, the total cost of doing so, and the amount saved compared to making only the minimum payment. If you want to know more about paying off your balance, such as how long it would take if you paid $85 each month, you can go to various Web sites, such as http://www.federalreserve.gov, which will help you determine how much you will have to pay per month to pay off your balance over a specified number of months. These

EXHIBIT 8.2   How Interest Payments Are Influenced by Interest Rates (assume loan amount of $10,000)

Simple Interest Rate	Simple Interest Payment per Year	Total Simple Interest Payments over Four Years
6	$ 600	$2,400
8	800	3,200
10	1,000	4,000
12	1,200	4,800
14	1,400	5,600
16	1,600	6,400
18	1,800	7,200
20	2,000	8,000

calculators are very useful because they can help you achieve your goal of paying off your credit card balance within a particular period.

Reviewing Your Credit Card Statement

Individuals typically receive a credit card bill at the end of their billing cycle. This bill lists all the purchases that were made with that credit card during that period, as well as any balance carried over from the previous statement.

A credit card statement includes the following information:

- **Previous balance.** The amount carried over from the previous credit card statement
- **Purchases.** The amount of credit used this month to make purchases
- **Cash advances.** The amount of credit used this month by writing checks against the credit card account or making ATM withdrawals
- **Payments.** The payments that you made to the sponsoring financial institution this billing cycle

- **Finance charge.** The finance charge that is applied to any credit that exceeds the grace period or to any cash advances
- **New balance.** The amount that you owe the financial institution as of now
- **Minimum payment.** The minimum amount that you must pay
- **Paying off the balance.** The amount of time it will take to pay off the balance if only the minimum payment is made and the monthly payment required to pay off the balance in three years
- **Interest and fees.** The total amount of interest charged so far this year and the total amount of fees assessed

The credit card statement details why your new balance differs from the balance shown on your statement in the previous month. The difference between the previous balance and the new balance results from any new purchases, cash advances, or finance charges, which increase your balance, as well as any payments or refund credits, which reduce your balance. The statement also shows the method of calculating finance charges.

EXAMPLE

Suppose you have a credit card balance of $700 from purchases you made last month that you did not pay off. During that billing period, you send in $200 to pay off part of your outstanding balance. You also use the credit card for $100 worth of new purchases. Because you relied on the sponsoring financial institution to pay $500 of last month's bill, you owe a finance charge. Assuming the institution imposes a finance charge of 1.5% per month and uses the adjusted balance method to determine the finance charge (which results in a finance charge of $7.50), your credit card statement is as follows:

Previous Balance		$700.00
+ New Purchases	100.00	
+ Cash Advances	0	
− Payments	200.00	
+ Finance Charges	7.50	
= New Balance		$607.50

If you had paid the full amount of the previous balance ($700) during the billing period, the statement would be as follows:

Previous Balance		$700.00
+ New Purchases	100.00	
+ Cash Advances	0	
− Payments	700.00	
+ Finance Charges	0	
= New Balance		$100.00

Thus, if you had paid $700 instead of $200, you would not have borrowed from the sponsoring financial institution and would not have incurred a finance charge. The new balance at the end of this billing period would simply be the amount of purchases that occurred over this period.

When you receive your account statement, you should always scrutinize it for errors. There could be a math error, a double charge for a purchase, inappropriate charges due to someone else using your credit card, or an incorrect amount on a purchase. Under consumer protection laws, you have the right to dispute possible errors.

You can call the card issuer, but to protect your rights, you must also send a written notice within 60 calendar days after the charge appeared on your monthly statement.

Send your letter by certified mail to the address designated for billing inquiries on your statement. Do not send the letter to the address where payments are sent. Explain the problem and include copies of receipts if they are relevant. The card issuer must acknowledge receiving your letter within 30 days. The issuer then has 90 days to investigate the problem. You do not have to pay the disputed charges during this period, but you still must pay any undisputed charges on your bill. If the card issuer finds that there was an error, the charge will be removed from your bill. If the investigation indicates that the bill is correct, the issuer must send you a written explanation.

Regulation of Credit Cards

In the past, some credit card companies charged excessive fees or did not fully disclose the conditions under which fees would be assessed. Regulations have been instituted to ensure better treatment of consumers and that requirements in credit card agreements are transparent.

Credit CARD Act

The U.S. Congress passed the Credit Card Accountability, Responsibility, and Disclosure Act (also called the Credit CARD Act) of 2009 in an effort to ensure that consumers who use credit card services are treated fairly and have access to complete information about the fees and other provisions of the credit agreement. This act, which went into effect in 2010, contained numerous provisions that provide you with more protection. Several of these provisions have already been mentioned in this chapter, but the following are among the most important.

Conditions for Fees Credit card companies must clearly disclose the conditions under which fees will be charged to prospective cardholders. If a card issuer changes its fee structure, it must disclose this information at least 45 days in advance. Fees cannot exceed more than 25% of the initial credit limit. Fees charged for inactivity on credit cards were eliminated.

Advance Notice to Change Interest Rate Credit card companies may not increase the interest rate charged on credit that was provided for purchases made in the past. For example, if you made many purchases last year on a credit card and still owe much of the balance today, the credit card company cannot increase the interest rate applied to what you owe. If the credit card company decides to increase the interest rate, it must first notify you 45 days in advance, and then the higher interest rate only applies to credit provided for new purchases and does not apply to credit provided in the past.

Promotional Interest Rate Guidelines Promotional interest rates advertised to entice new cardholders must clearly disclose the details of the deal. In addition, the promotional rate must be offered for a period of at least six months.

Payment Period Cardholders must be given at least 21 days from the day on which the bill is mailed to make payment.

Credit Limit Cardholders may not be charged an overlimit fee for exceeding their credit limit unless they have specifically requested the card issuer's overlimit protection program. This provision prevents situations in which cardholders are charged fees for going beyond their credit limit without realizing that they had exceeded it.

Disclosure About Paying Balance Due Credit card statements must state how long it would take for a cardholder to pay off the existing balance due if only the minimum payment is made each month.

Restrictions for Cardholders Younger Than Age 21 Cardholders younger than the age of 21 must show proof of their income or have an adult cosigner to justify approval of credit. This is intended to ensure that young consumers are given a limited amount of credit that is in line with what they can afford. Gifts from credit card companies to college students who apply for credit cards are restricted.

Summary of Provisions The Credit CARD Act had a major impact on cardholders and the credit card companies. In general, it (1) ensures more complete disclosure of information so that cardholders understand the conditions, (2) reduces the fees paid by cardholders, and (3) limits the frequency with which credit card companies can increase their interest rates.

Consumer Financial Protection Bureau

During the 2008–2009 financial crisis, some consumers who borrowed money (in the form of mortgages, credit card debt, and other forms of credit) were misled by financial institutions about the terms of the financing arrangement. The Financial Reform Act (also called the Dodd–Frank Wall Street Reform and Consumer Protection Act) was passed in 2010 to prevent deceptive practices in the credit granting process. The Consumer Financial Protection Bureau (CFPB) was created in 2010 as part of the Financial Reform Act. Its primary goal is to enforce consumer finance laws (such as those imposed by the Credit CARD Act) to ensure that consumers who need financial services are treated fairly.

The CFPB also attempts to make sure that consumers receive full disclosure of information they need to make financial decisions. It has the authority to establish regulations that ensure consumers are treated properly and to prevent deceptive practices by financial institutions.

Tips on Using Credit Cards

Because you are likely to have one or more credit cards, consider the following tips to enjoy their use without incurring excessive costs.

Use a Credit Card Only If You Can Cover the Bill

Treat a credit card as a means of convenience, not a source of funds. Use a credit card only if you will have the cash to cover the payment when you receive your credit card statement. The use of this self-imposed credit limit is illustrated in Exhibit 8.3. The difference between your expected cash inflows and your expenses paid by online payment or check (such as rent) or by cash is the maximum amount of credit that you can use and still ensure full payment of the credit card balance.

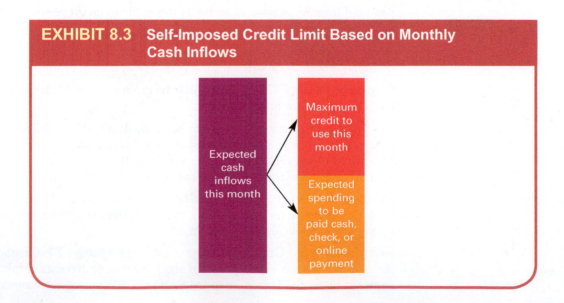

EXHIBIT 8.3   Self-Imposed Credit Limit Based on Monthly Cash Inflows

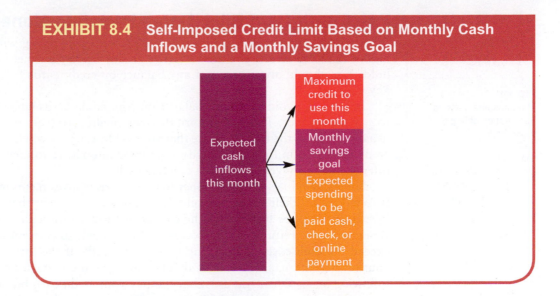

EXHIBIT 8.4   Self-Imposed Credit Limit Based on Monthly Cash Inflows and a Monthly Savings Goal

Impose a Tight Credit Limit

You may consider imposing a tighter credit limit as part of your budgeting process so that you can save or invest a specific amount every month. This limit is illustrated in Exhibit 8.4. You determine the maximum amount of credit you will use each month only after accounting for all spending to be paid by online payment, check, or cash, as well as a specified amount of saving.

You can also ask your credit card company to lower your credit limit to encourage you to restrict your spending. You might even consider using only credit cards sponsored by companies that sell necessities, such as a gas station or home repair store. You can cancel credit cards that could be used for discretionary spending. Remember, though, that reducing the amount of credit that you have available can lower your credit score if you have any debt because your debt-to-credit ratio will increase. Cutting up your cards so that you can't use them is preferable to canceling them as long as you don't order replacements.

Reduce Credit Limit When the Economy Weakens

ECONOMIC IMPACT

When the economy weakens, your cash inflows could be reduced. Your employer might cut your work hours, which would reduce your income. During the financial crisis in 2008 and 2009, many people lost their jobs. As a result, they not only needed to rely more on credit cards, but they also were not earning the income necessary to pay off the credit cards. In addition, their investments (if they had any) were generating less income during this period.

The obvious lesson is to reduce your reliance on credit so that you are not subjected to increased financial problems if economic conditions deteriorate. You can prepare for the possible reduction in your income by reducing your credit limit. That way, even if your income is reduced, you may still be capable of paying off your credit in a timely manner.

An extreme strategy would be to cancel all credit cards and pay for all expenses with cash, online payments, or check. Some people are more disciplined with their spending when they use cash to make payments because they recognize that they are giving up money to make purchases. When they use credit cards, they do not feel the pain of relinquishing their money because they only have to sign a piece of paper. Again, consider just cutting up your cards rather than canceling them so that your credit score will not be negatively affected.

**Financial Planning
ONLINE**

Go to:
The consumer information section of http://www.ftc.gov

To get:
Information about establishing, using, and protecting your credit.

PSYCHOLOGY
of Personal
Finance

Pay Credit Card Bills Before Investing Money

When you finance credit card balances, your cost of financing will normally be much higher than the return you are receiving on any money market investments that you hold. You should always pay off any balance on credit cards before you invest funds anywhere else.

In general, avoid carrying a balance on your credit cards when you have the money to pay the balance. The likely return that you might earn from investing your money is usually less than the financing rate that you will be charged when you delay paying your credit card bills in full. Debit cards are a good alternative to credit cards because they offer the same convenience of not carrying cash.

Some individuals use their money to invest in risky investments (such as stocks) rather than paying off their credit card bills. They apparently believe that their return from the investments will be higher than the cost of financing. Although some investments have generated large returns in specific years, it is difficult to earn returns that consistently exceed the high costs of financing with credit cards. If the thrill of a good return on your investment makes you think about delaying your credit card payment, consider the following logic. When you use money to pay your credit card bill immediately, you are preventing a charge of about 20% interest. Therefore, you have effectively increased your savings by 20% by using these funds to pay off the credit card debt.

EXAMPLE

Stephanie Spratt just received a credit card bill for $700. The sponsoring financial institution charges a 20% annual interest rate on the outstanding balance. Stephanie has sufficient funds in her checking account to pay the credit card bill, but she is considering financing her payment. If she pays $100 toward the credit card bill and finances the remaining $600 for one year, she will incur interest expenses of:

$$\text{Interest} = \text{Loan Amount} \times \text{Interest Rate}$$
$$= \$600 \times .20$$
$$= \$120$$

She could use the $600 to invest in savings rather than pay off her credit card bill. After one year, the $600 in a savings account will accumulate to $618 based on a 3% annual interest rate, as shown here:

$$\text{Interest Earned on Deposit} = \text{Initial Deposit} \times \text{Interest Rate}$$
$$= \$600 \times .03$$
$$= \$18$$

Her interest owed on the credit card loan ($120) exceeds the interest earned on the deposit ($18) in one year by $102. Stephanie decides that she would be better off using her cash to pay off the credit card bill immediately. By using her money to cover the credit card bill, she gives up the opportunity to earn 3% on that money, but she also avoids the 20% rate charged on the credit card loan. Thus, her wealth is $102 higher as a result of using funds to pay off the credit card bill rather than investing in a bank deposit. Although she could have used the funds to invest in a high-risk investment that might achieve a greater return, paying off the credit card guarantees that she can avoid a 20% financing rate.

If your cash inflows are not sufficient to cover your credit card bill, you should pull funds from savings (if there is no penalty for withdrawal) to cover the payment.

Pay Off Credit Card Debt Before Other Debt

If you cannot pay off your credit card balance in full each month with income or with savings, at least pay off this balance as soon as possible and cut back your discretionary spending. If you have other debt outstanding, you should pay off credit card debt first (assuming that the credit card debt has a higher interest rate). Even if you cannot pay your bill in full, you should still attempt to pay as much as possible so that you can minimize finance charges.

If possible, you may even consider taking out a home equity loan (discussed in Chapter 9) to pay any credit card bills so that you can avoid the high interest expenses. This strategy makes sense only if your credit card debt is substantial (such as several thousand dollars), and the interest rate on the home equity loan is less than that on your credit card.

Avoid Credit Repair Services

Companies that offer credit repair services claim to be able to solve your credit problems. For example, they may help you fix a mistake on your credit report. However, you could have done this yourself, without paying for the service. If you have made late credit payments or have defaulted on a loan, a credit repair service does not have the power to remove such credit information from your report.

Resolving an Excessive Credit Balance

If you find yourself with an excessive credit balance, there are several steps you can take. First, spend as little as possible. Then, consider how you can obtain funds to meet your monthly payment or to pay off your balance. Get a job if you don't have one, or work more hours at your current job. However, for students, additional work could disrupt your school schedule.

An alternative solution is to borrow funds from a family member. You will now have a monthly loan payment to a family member rather than credit card balances, but the payments may be lower. Another possibility is a debt consolidation loan from a financial institution. The structured schedule for paying off the loan in a set time period will instill more discipline in you than meeting a low minimum monthly payment on a credit card. If you do not choose to get a loan, you should still discipline yourself to make more than the minimum payment on your credit card.

You might even consider selling some assets to obtain cash, such as trading in a relatively new car for an old car. Also consider ways of reducing your everyday expenses. For example, if you have large monthly payments due to your smartphone, you could look for a less expensive contract. If you have your own apartment, you may consider getting a roommate.

personal bankruptcy
A plan proposed to the court in which you repay at least a portion of your debt and pay attorney and filing fees.

If all else fails, you may need to file for **personal bankruptcy**. In this case, you propose a plan to the court for repaying at least a portion of your debt and pay attorney and court filing fees. The two types of personal bankruptcy plans are known as Chapter 7 and Chapter 13. Chapter 7 allows the discharge of almost all debts, but you may also have to surrender assets to help satisfy the debt. Under Chapter 13, you keep your property but surrender control of your finances to the bankruptcy court. The court approves a three-to-five-year repayment plan based on your financial resources. You incur no interest charges on the indebtedness during the repayment period. Bankruptcy should only be considered if there is no other option.

How Credit Management Fits Within Your Financial Plan

The following are the key credit management decisions that should be included within your financial plan:

| EXHIBIT 8.5 | How Credit Management Fits Within Stephanie Spratt's Financial Plan |

GOALS FOR MANAGING CREDIT

1. Set my own limit on credit card purchases to ensure that I will always be able to pay off the credit balance in the same month.
2. Set a policy to avoid incurring high interest expenses on credit cards.

ANALYSIS

Monthly Cash Inflows	$2,500
− Typical Monthly Expenses (paid by checks)	− 1,400
= Amount of Funds Available	1,100

Liquid Assets	Balance	Annualized Interest Rate (%)
Cash	$100	0
Checking account balance	800	0
Money market fund	400	3.0
One-month CD	1,200	4.3
Credit card balance	600	20.0

DECISIONS

Decision on Credit Limit

Given that I have $1,100 each month left from my salary after paying typical expenses (by check), I have $1,100 remaining that can be used for credit card purchases if necessary. I will impose a maximum limit of $1,100 on my credit card spending. As my income rises over time, I may consider increasing my credit limit, but only up to some level that I can afford to pay off immediately when I receive the bill.

Decision on Paying Off Credit Balances

Given the interest rates that I can earn on deposit accounts versus the interest rate I would pay on a credit card balance, I will always pay off my credit card balance, even if I must withdraw funds from my savings account to do so.

- What limit should you impose on your credit card?
- When should you use credit?

By making proper decisions, you can avoid using credit and can maximize the return on your liquid assets. As an example, Exhibit 8.5 shows how credit decisions apply to Stephanie Spratt's financial plan.

DISCUSSION QUESTIONS

1. How would Stephanie's credit management decisions be different if she were a single mother of two children?
2. How would Stephanie's credit management decisions be affected if she were 35 years old? If she were 50 years old?

SUMMARY

Credit Cards. An advantage of using credit is that it enables you to obtain products and services that you cannot afford otherwise. A disadvantage of credit is that it is easier to obtain it than to pay it back. Some individuals use too much credit and are unable to make their credit payments, which may prevent them from obtaining credit in the future. When individuals apply for credit, they provide information about their cash inflows (income), cash outflows (spending habits), and collateral. Creditors also evaluate your credit report, which contains information on your credit history collected by a credit bureau.

Credit cards are distinguished by whether the sponsor is Visa, MasterCard, American Express, a proprietary merchant (such as JCPenney), or some other sponsor. They are also distinguished by the credit limit, the annual fee, the interest rate charged on credit not paid by the due date, whether they allow cash advances, and the rewards they offer.

Credit Repayment. By estimating credit repayment, you will notice the impact that a high interest rate has on the amount that you owe. In addition, delaying repayment for a longer period can substantially increase the total cost of credit.

Credit Card Statement. The credit card statement discloses your previous balance, a summary of your purchases and cash advances, recent payments that you made, finance charges (if any), the new balance, the minimum payment required, the time required to pay off the balance if you make only the minimum payment each month, and the amount you would have to pay each month to pay off the balance in three years.

Credit Card Regulation. The Credit Card Accountability, Responsibility, and Disclosure Act (also called Credit CARD Act) of 2009 was passed in an effort to ensure that consumers who use credit card services are treated fairly and have access to complete information about the fees and other provisions of the credit agreement.

Tips When Using Credit Cards. Credit cards should be used with discipline. You should impose your own credit limits rather than spend up to the limit granted by the card issuer. You should attempt to avoid financing costs, either by using income to cover the amount due or by withdrawing money from savings if necessary.

How Credit Management Fits Within Your Financial Plan. Although access to credit is beneficial, you need to discipline your use of credit by imposing limits. In this way, you will have greater access to credit in the future, which can help you to achieve your financial goals.

REVIEW QUESTIONS

All Review Questions are available in MyFinanceLab *at* http://www.myfinancelab.com.

1. **Credit Cards.** What are three advantages of using a credit card? Can you think of any disadvantages?

2. **Applying for Credit.** What information will you need to supply when applying for credit? What kinds of attributes are creditors looking for? Do you need to have all these attributes to get credit?

3. **Retail Credit Cards.** Describe the differences between a credit card like MasterCard or Visa and a retail (or proprietary) card. How do credit and retail cards generate revenue? What is the biggest disadvantage of a proprietary card?

4. **Credit Limit.** What is a credit limit? How can you increase your credit limit?

5. **Credit Card Fees.** How might you eliminate the annual fees that are charged by some credit cards?

6. **Credit Card Incentives.** Discuss how credit cards offer incentives to use the cards. How else might credit card companies reward cardholders with excellent credit ratings?

7. **Grace Period.** What is a grace period? How can you use it to your advantage?

8. **Finance Charge.** When is a finance charge applied to credit purchases? What is the common range of interest rates on credit cards?

9. **Cash Advance.** What is a cash advance? How are they commonly obtained? Discuss interest rates and grace periods with regard to cash advances.

10. **Simple Interest.** How does the interest rate affect your credit payments? What is meant by simple interest? What is the annual percentage rate (APR), and when is it used?

11. **Credit Card Statement.** List some items that appear on the credit card statement. What accounts for the difference between your previous balance and your new balance?

12. **Comparing Credit Cards.** What should you consider when comparing credit cards?

13. **Using Credit Cards.** List five tips for using credit cards wisely.

14. **Credit Cards as a Source of Funds.** Should you view credit cards as a source of funds? Why or why not? Why should you self-impose a tight credit limit?

15. **Credit Card Balance.** Why is paying your credit card balance in full so important? What should you do if you can't avoid credit card debt? Explain.

16. **Credit Management Decisions.** What credit management decisions should be included in your financial plan?

17. **Credit Card Use.** Discuss some ways that charging large amounts on your credit cards might affect your overall financial planning.

18. **Credit Card Finance Charges.** What are the three methods used by financial institutions to calculate finance charges on outstanding credit card balances? Briefly describe how interest is computed under each method.

19. **Credit Card Limit.** Explain how you can impose your own limits on credit card spending.

20. **Interest on Credit Cards.** Compare the amount of interest you earn on typical money market investments versus the amount of interest paid on credit cards.

21. **Dealing with an Excessive Credit Card Balance.** Propose possible solutions to reduce an excessive credit card balance.

22. **Credit CARD Act.** Describe some of the key provisions of the Credit CARD Act.

23. **Bureau of Consumer Financial Protection.** Describe the role of the Consumer Financial Protection Bureau.

24. **Secured Credit Cards.** How does a secured credit card differ from a standard credit card? Under what circumstances would you need a secured credit card?

25. **Prepaid Credit Cards.** What is a prepaid credit card? How does it differ from a secured credit card?

26. **Overlimit Protection.** What is overlimit protection? Explain why consumers should use this feature sparingly.

27. **Credit Card Incentives.** List some typical incentives credit cards issuers offer to encourage you to use their card.

28. **Late Fees.** Explain how the Credit CARD Act changed the way credit card issuers assess late fees.

29. **Cash Advances.** Explain why getting a cash advance on your credit card is a costly source of funds.

30. **Reviewing Your Statement.** Why should you review your credit card statement before paying the bill? What steps should you take if you discover an error?

31. **Cardholder Restrictions.** What credit restrictions apply to persons under age 21?

FINANCIAL PLANNING PROBLEMS

All Financial Planning Problems are available in MyFinanceLab *at http://www.myfinancelab.com.*

1. **Interest Charged.** You just borrowed $7,500 and are charged a simple interest rate of 8%. How much interest do you pay each year?

2. **Credit Card Fees and Financing.** Jarrod has narrowed his choice to two credit cards that may meet his needs. Card A has an APR of 21%. Card B has an APR of 14%, but also charges a $25 annual fee. Jarrod will not pay off his balance each month, but will carry a balance forward of about $400 each month. Which credit card should he choose?

3. **Credit Card Payment Terms.** Paul's credit card closes on the 3rd of the month, and his payment

is due on the 30th. If Paul purchases a stereo for $300 on June 12th, how many interest-free days will he have? When will he have to pay for the stereo in full in order to avoid finance charges?

4. **Credit Card Financing.** Chrissy currently has a credit card that charges 15% interest. She usually carries a balance of about $500. What will her total annual interest be with her current card?

5. **Credit Card Interest.** Margie has had a tough month. First, she had dental work that cost $700. Next, she had her car transmission rebuilt, which cost $1,400. She put both of these unexpected expenses on her credit card. If she does not pay her credit card balance when due, she will be charged 15% interest. Margie has $15,000 in a money market account that pays 5% interest. How much interest would she pay (annualized) if she does not pay off her credit card balance? How much interest will she lose if she pays the balance due out of her money market account? Should she pay off the balance?

6. **Credit Card Finance Charges.** Troy has a credit card that charges 18% on outstanding balances and on cash advances. The closing date on the credit card is the first of each month. Last month Troy left a balance on his credit card of $200. This month Troy took out a cash advance of $150 and made $325 in purchases. Troy made a payment of $220. What will the total of Troy's new balance be on his next credit card statement, taking into account finance charges?

7. **Credit Card Balance.** Eileen is a college student who consistently uses her credit card as a source of funds. She has maxed out her credit card at the $6,000 limit. Eileen does not plan on increasing her credit card balance any further, but has already

been declined for a car loan on a badly needed vehicle due to her existing credit card debt. Her credit card charges her 20% annually on outstanding balances. If Eileen does not reduce her credit card debt, how much will she pay annually to her credit card company?

Question 8 requires a financial calculator.

8. **Interest on Credit Cards.** Eileen (from question 7) wants a car that costs $12,000. How long would it have taken Eileen to save for the outright purchase of the car if she did not have any credit card debt and used the interest payments to save for the purchase of the car? Eileen can invest funds in an account paying 8% interest.

9. **Ethical Dilemma.** Chen recently graduated from college and accepted a job in a new city. Furnishing his apartment has proved more costly than he anticipated. To enable him to make purchases, he applied for and received a credit card with a $5,000 credit limit. Chen planned to pay off the balance over six months.

   Six months later Chen finds that other expenses incurred in starting a new career have restricted him to making only minimum payments. Not only that, he has borrowed on his card to the full extent of its credit limit. Upon returning from work today, Chen finds a letter from the credit card company offering to increase his limit to $10,000 because he has been a good customer and has not missed a payment.

   a. Discuss the ethics of credit card companies that offer to increase credit limits to individuals who make only minimum payments and who have maxed out their card.

   b. Should Chen accept the credit card company's offer?

FINANCIAL PLANNING ONLINE EXERCISES

1. Do an online search of credit card debt management, installment debt, and revolving credit.

   a. Is the total avoidance of debt an effective strategy to utilize in managing your debt and credit? Explain fully.

   b. Explain the difference between installment debt and revolving credit.

   c. Discuss the first step you would take if you had too much credit card debt.

   d. Explain the role of debt in today's society.

2. Go to the money section of CNN.com, and go to the personal finance section that includes calculators. Enter your information from your most recent credit card

statement(s) to determine when you will be debt free. If you have no credit card debt, give yourself a pat on the back and ask a friend if you can compute when he or she will be debt free.

3. Do an online search using the search term "Fair Credit Reporting Act." Explain how this law addresses credit report errors.

4. Do an online search of a few credit cards that are offered. Review the credit cards displayed by this search, and select the one that would best suit your needs. Identify the card you chose, and write a brief essay on the features of this card that caused you to select it.

5. Go to http://www.ftc.gov, and insert the search term "protecting your credit."

    a. Summarize what the Web site presents about the steps you should take to protect your credit.

    b. Discuss what steps you could take to improve your credit.

PSYCHOLOGY OF PERSONAL FINANCE: Using Your Credit Cards

For many people, less pain is associated with using a credit card to make purchases than with using cash, even if the amount of the payment is exactly the same. The use of the credit card almost feels like there is no payment, but the use of cash means that there is less cash available for other purchases. Therefore, spending decisions are made more carefully when using cash.

1. Describe your opinion on this topic. Do you feel less pain when using a credit card? Are your spending decisions made more carefully when you use cash as opposed to credit cards?

2. Read one practical article about how psychology affects the use of credit cards. You can easily retrieve possible articles by doing an online search using the terms "psychology" and "using credit cards." Summarize the main points of the article.

WEB SEARCH EXERCISE

You can develop your personal finance skills by conducting an Internet search for related articles. Find a recent online article about personal finance that reinforces one or more concepts covered in this chapter. If your class has an online component, your professor may ask you to post your summary of the article there and provide a link to the article so that other students can access it. If your class is live, your professor may ask you to summarize your application of the article in class. Your professor may assign specific students to complete this assignment or may allow any student to do the assignment on a volunteer basis.

For recent online articles related to this chapter, consider using the following search terms (be sure to include the current year as a search term to ensure that the online articles are recent):

- Credit card offers
- Using credit cards wisely
- Credit limit
- Avoiding finance charges
- Understanding your credit card statement
- Credit card fees
- Credit card debt

VIDEO EXERCISE: Tips on Using Credit Cards

Go to one of the Web sites that contain video clips (such as http://www.youtube.com) and view some video clips about using credit cards. You can use search phrases such as "credit cards." Select one video clip on this topic that you would recommend for the other students in your class.

1. Provide the Web link for the video clip.

2. What do you think is the main point of this video clip?

3. How might you change your use of credit cards as a result of watching this video clip?

BUILDING YOUR OWN FINANCIAL PLAN

Good credit decisions involve using credit properly and selecting the best sources of credit. The exercises in this case will assist you in the decisions regarding the use and selection of credit cards. They will help you determine how long it will take to pay off credit card debt you might have accrued and help you evaluate the many credit cards currently on the market.

Go to the worksheets at the end of this chapter to continue building your financial plan.

THE SAMPSONS—A Continuing Case

The Sampsons have been carrying a balance of about $2,000 on their credit card. They have been paying the minimum amount due and have been using any excess net cash flows to implement their new savings plan for a new car and their children's college education. To date, they have saved $2,000; they are currently earning 1% on the savings. Meanwhile, their credit card is charging them 18%. Dave and Sharon want to evaluate the return they are receiving from their savings versus the interest expenses they are accruing on their credit card.

Go to the worksheets at the end of this chapter to continue this case.

Part 2: Brad Brooks—A Continuing Case

Brad Brooks is pleased with your assistance in preparing his personal financial statements and your suggestions for improving his personal financial situation. He has called you for additional guidance. First, he wants to know what factors he should consider when selecting a bank and brokerage firm. He is mostly interested in financial institutions that will assist him in making investment and money management decisions. He finds savings accounts boring and has no desire to have one because the interest rate is so low.

Brad is also concerned about his liquidity. His credit card (with a $35 annual fee and 18% interest rate) is nearing its credit limit of $10,000. He is reluctant to sell his stocks to get cash to pay off part of the credit balance; he thinks that his stock investment could generate a return of 10% per year over the next few years. He does not want to give up this return to pay off his credit card balance.

Go to the worksheets at the end of this chapter to continue this case.

CHAPTER 8: BUILDING YOUR OWN FINANCIAL PLAN

GOALS

1. Establish a credit limit that will enable you to pay credit card balances in full each month.

2. Select credit cards that will provide the most favorable terms at the lowest cost.

ANALYSIS

1. Referring to your personal cash flow statement, determine how much excess cash inflows you have each month. Based on this amount, set a self-imposed credit limit each month so that you can pay off your balance in full. If you have existing credit card debt, use the following worksheet to determine how many months it will take you to pay off your balance at three different monthly payment amounts. (The Excel worksheet will perform the calculations for you.) Revise your cash flow statement based on your decisions.

	Alternative 1	Alternative 2	Alternative 3
Credit Card Debt	_____	_____	_____
Monthly Payment	_____	_____	_____
Interest Rate per Year	_____	_____	_____
Months to Pay Off Debt	_____	_____	_____

2. Use the following worksheet to select a credit card with favorable terms. Rate the cards from 5 being the best in a category to 1 being the worst.

Bank Credit Card Scorecard

Question	Credit Card Issuer				
	1	2	3	4	5
1. Annual fee					
2. Interest rate on purchases					
3. Interest rate on cash advances					
4. Transaction fee for cash advances					
5. Insurance on purchases					
6. Credit earned toward purchases at selected businesses					
7. Frequent flyer miles					
8. Credit limit available					
Total					

DECISIONS

1. What is your self-imposed credit limit each month for future credit card purchases? How much of your cash inflows do you need to allot each month to paying off existing credit card debt?

   _____

   _____

   _____

   _____

   _____

   _____

   _____

   _____

   _____

   _____

   _____

   _____

2. What credit cards offer the most favorable terms for your needs?

   _____

   _____

   _____

   _____

   _____

   _____

   _____

   _____

   _____

   _____

   _____

CHAPTER 8: THE SAMPSONS—A Continuing Case

CASE QUESTIONS

1. Advise the Sampsons on whether they should continue making minimum payments on their credit card or use money from their savings to pay off the credit balance.

_____

_____

_____

_____

_____

_____

_____

_____

_____

_____

_____

_____

2. Explain how the Sampsons' credit card decisions are related to their budget.

_____

_____

_____

_____

_____

_____

_____

_____

_____

_____

_____

_____

PART 2: BRAD BROOKS—A Continuing Case

CASE QUESTIONS

1. Assuming that you could convince Brad to maintain checking, savings, and retirement accounts, discuss the pros and cons of various types of financial institutions where Brad could maintain his

   a. checking account

   b. savings account

   c. retirement accounts

   Be sure to comment on Brad's idea to find financial institutions that can give him advice on his financial decisions.

   _____

   _____

   _____

   _____

   _____

   _____

2. Even if Brad's stock investments earn a return of 10% per year, is that better than using the funds to pay off the credit card balance? Recall that the credit card interest rate is 18%. Based on his projected annualized return, would it be advisable to sell the stocks to pay off his credit card? Should Brad consider shopping for a new credit card?

   _____

   _____

   _____

   _____

   _____

   _____

3. Would your advice change if Brad were

   a. 45 years old?

   _____

   _____

   b. 60 years old?

   _____

   _____

4. In talking to Brad, you mentioned the increasing threat of identity theft. Brad seems concerned, and after asking him several questions, you determine the following:

   a. For convenience, Brad has his driver's license number printed on his checks. He also uses checks to make virtually all payments, including transactions with local merchants. Brad has a debit card, but seldom uses it.

   b. Because Brad drives past the post office to and from work each day, he maintains a post office box and mails all letters and payments at the post office.

   c. Brad has several credit cards in his wallet, but uses only one regularly. He also carries his Social Security card, as he can never remember the number.

   d. Brad recycles, including old invoices, credit card statements, and bank statements after retaining them for the appropriate legal time period.

   e. Brad uses his smartphone for virtually all his telephone calls, including ordering merchandise and paying by credit card.

   Comment on each of these points in terms of the risk of identity theft, and make recommendations to Brad for appropriate changes that will reduce his risk of exposure to identity theft.

   _____

   _____

   _____

   _____

   _____

   _____

5. Prepare a written or oral report on your findings and recommendations for Brad.

   _____

   _____

   _____

   _____

   _____

   _____

   _____

   _____

   _____

   _____

   _____

   _____

   _____

Personal Financing

The chapters in this part explain how you can use credit to obtain funds to support your spending. Chapter 9 describes the process of obtaining a personal loan for a large purchase such as a car and the types of decisions that you need to make when considering a personal loan. Chapter 10 describes the process of obtaining a mortgage and the types of decisions that you need to make when considering a mortgage loan. Your decisions regarding whether to borrow, how much to borrow, and how to borrow will affect your cash flows and wealth.

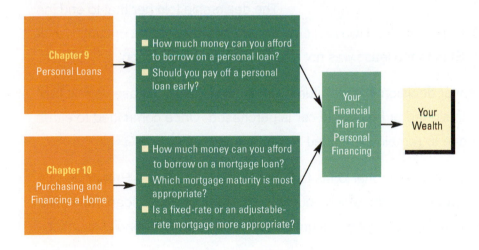

Chapter 9
Personal Loans

- How much money can you afford to borrow on a personal loan?
- Should you pay off a personal loan early?

Chapter 10
Purchasing and Financing a Home

- How much money can you afford to borrow on a mortgage loan?
- Which mortgage maturity is most appropriate?
- Is a fixed-rate or an adjustable-rate mortgage more appropriate?

Your Financial Plan for Personal Financing

Your Wealth

Personal Loans

A and N photography/Shutterstock

Karen realized that her car was facing some serious maintenance issues, and she decided to lease a new car. The monthly lease payment was $499.35, and she was allowed to drive 15,000 miles per year with extra miles charged at $0.25 per mile. After 18 months, however, Karen began to tire of the large monthly payments. She went back to the auto dealer to explore ending the lease early. The dealership told her that to end the lease, she must pay $7,350. Karen only had two real choices: buy the car outright or continue the lease for its three-year term. Ending the lease was not a financially attractive option.

You may be faced with a similar decision in your future. The time to make a "lease versus buy" decision is before the lease is signed or before the car is purchased. Once committed to either action, you most likely will have to remain committed to your course.

This chapter focuses on your use of personal loans to finance large purchases. Proper decisions on whether to obtain a personal loan, which source to use for a personal loan, how much to borrow, and what terms to arrange can have a significant impact on your financial situation.

MyFinanceLab helps you master the topics in this chapter and study more efficiently. Visit http://www.myfinancelab.com for more details.

The objectives of this chapter are to:

- Provide a background on personal loans
- Outline the types of interest rates that are charged on personal loans
- Discuss car loans
- Explain how to decide between financing the purchase of a car and leasing a car
- Describe the key features of student loans
- Describe home equity loans
- Describe payday loans
- Describe how personal loans fit within your financial plan

Background on Personal Loans

Consumers commonly obtain a personal loan to finance a large purchase such as a car or a home improvement project. A personal loan is different from access to credit (from a credit card) in that a personal loan is normally used to finance one large purchase and has a specific repayment schedule. The loan is provided at the time of your purchase and is used along with your cash down payment to cover the entire purchase price. You can pay off the personal loan on an installment basis, for example, by making a payment each month for the next 48 months.

Sources of Personal Loans

The first step in obtaining a personal loan is to identify possible sources of financing and evaluate the possible loan terms. Common sources of personal loans are financial institutions, family members, and peer-to-peer lending. Before you attempt to obtain any type of loan, you should check your credit report to make sure that it does not contain any incorrect information.

Financial Institutions The most common source of financing for a personal loan is a financial institution. Commercial banks, savings institutions, and credit unions provide personal loans. They pool the deposited funds that they receive from savers to create loans for borrowers.

Finance companies also provide personal loans. Some finance companies are subsidiaries of automobile manufacturers that finance car purchases.

Family Members or Friends An alternative source of financing is one or more family members or friends. If they trust that you will repay the loan on time and in full, they may be willing to provide you with a loan that earns the same interest rate as their savings account. You could also offer to pay an interest rate on the loan that is a few percentage points above the savings rate. By borrowing funds from family and friends, you can often get a more favorable rate than financial institutions offer. The loan agreement should be in writing and signed by all parties to avoid any possible misinterpretations.

Peer-to-Peer Lending Another source of financing, especially for those with good credit histories, is peer-to-peer (P2P) lending, which is done through online platforms. The two most important are Lending Club and Prosper, which together facilitate lending amounting to more than $1 billion per year. In P2P lending, the funds are provided by individual investors, not by financial institutions. Individuals may borrow amounts ranging from $1,000 to $35,000 at interest rates that may be lower than the interest charged by a financial institution. Although the borrower must pay a loan origination fee, it may also be less than a financial institution would charge. Loans are issued for three- or five-year terms and require monthly payments.

To obtain a loan, you apply at a P2P lending Web site, which will obtain your credit report and FICO score. Your FICO score will largely determine the amount of money that you will be offered and the interest rate that you will be charged. The average FICO score for P2P borrowers is around 700. The majority of P2P borrowers use their loans to pay off existing loans from other lenders or to pay off credit card debt.

Determining Whether a Loan Is Sensible

Before pursuing a loan, first you should decide if a loan is sensible. Even if you can obtain a loan, it might not be a good idea. The loan will require you to make periodic payments over time. Consider the sacrifice you may have to make in the future as you use a portion of your monthly income to pay off the loan rather than use the money for some other purpose. For example, a loan of $2,000 to buy a used car so that you can commute to your workplace and to school may be sensible. However, a loan of $30,000 so that you can purchase a new car with a big engine is questionable. Such a large loan will require very large monthly payments and might leave you with very little income to cover necessities such as food or rent.

You should avoid a loan if your source of income to repay the loan is questionable. When economic conditions are weak, job layoffs are common. Consider the consequences of having a personal loan if there are no job opportunities. How would you repay the loan? Do you have alternative sources of funds to repay the loan?

The Personal Loan Process

The process of applying for a personal loan from a financial institution involves filling out the application, negotiating the loan contract, and negotiating the interest rate. A sample loan application is shown in Exhibit 9.1.

Application Process When applying for a loan, you need to provide information from your personal balance sheet and personal cash flow statement to document your ability to repay the loan.

- **Personal Balance Sheet.** Recall from Chapter 2 that your financial condition is partially measured by a personal balance sheet. The personal balance sheet indicates your assets, liabilities, and net worth at a specific point in time. The assets are relevant because they may serve as possible collateral to back a loan. The liabilities are relevant because they represent your existing debts.

- **Personal Cash Flow Statement.** Your financial condition is also represented by your personal cash flow statement, as discussed in Chapter 2. This statement indicates your cash inflows and cash outflows and therefore suggests how much free cash flow you have on a periodic basis. Lenders use this cash flow information to determine whether you qualify for a loan and, if so, the maximum size of the loan that you warrant. An individual with existing loans or credit card debt may have insufficient cash flows to cover the payments on any additional loans.

The key component of the personal cash flow statement of most prospective borrowers is their income. Lenders require income documentation, such as a Form W-2, which indicates annual earnings, or pay stubs, which indicate recent salary.

Loan Contract If the lender approves your loan application, it will work with you to develop a **loan contract**, which specifies the terms of the loan, as agreed to by the borrower and the lender. Specifically, the loan contract identifies the amount of the loan, interest rate, repayment schedule, maturity, and collateral.

- **Amount of the Loan.** The amount of the loan is based on how much the lender believes you can pay back in the future. You should borrow only the amount of

EXHIBIT 9.1   An Example of a Loan Application

LOAN APPLICATION

I. INFORMATION ABOUT LOAN REQUESTED

Purpose of Loan:

_____

Amount of Loan: _____

Term of Loan (number of years or months): _____

II. INFORMATION ABOUT APPLICANT

Name: _____

Address: _____

_____

Phone Number: _____

Social Security Number: _____

III. FINANCIAL INFORMATION OF APPLICANT

Primary Bank: _____

Occupation: _____

Monthly Income: _____

Name of Employer: _____

Address of Employer: _____

_____

Assets	**Dollar Value**
_____	_____
_____	_____
_____	_____
_____	_____
Total Value of Assets	_____

Liabilities	
_____	_____
_____	_____
_____	_____
_____	_____
_____	_____
Total Value of Liabilities	_____

funds that you will need because you will be charged interest on the entire amount that you borrow.

- **Interest Rate.** The interest rate is critical because it determines the cost incurred on a personal loan. It must be specified in a loan contract. More information about interest rates is provided in a later section.

- **Loan Repayment Schedule.** Personal loans are usually **amortized**, which means that the principal (original amount loaned out) is repaid through a series of equal payments. Each loan repayment includes both interest owed and a portion of the principal. As more of the principal is paid down, the amount of interest is reduced, and a larger portion of the payment is used to repay principal.

amortize
To repay the principal of a loan (the original amount loaned out) through a series of equal payments. A loan repaid in this manner is said to be amortized.

maturity
With respect to a loan, the life or duration of the loan.

- **Maturity.** A loan contract specifies the **maturity**, or life of the loan. A longer maturity for a loan results in lower monthly payments and therefore makes it easier to cover the payments each month. For example, the monthly payment on a five-year loan for $16,000 may be $100 less than the payment on a four-year loan for the same amount. With the five-year loan, however, you are in debt for an additional year, and you pay more interest over the life of the loan than you would on the four-year loan. In general, you should select a maturity on personal loans that is as short as possible, as long as you allow yourself sufficient liquidity. If you have extra funds during the time you have a loan, you should consider paying off the loan early for two reasons. First, you can reduce the total amount of interest by paying off the loan early. Second, you will be able to save the money that you would otherwise have used to make the loan payments. Before you pay off the loan early, however, you should check the loan contract to make sure that it does not impose a prepayment penalty. Lenders sometimes impose a penalty if a loan is paid off early because they are receiving less interest. When you obtain a loan, you should always ask if there is a prepayment penalty. If there is, you may want to try to negotiate to have it removed or look for other lenders.

collateral
Assets of a borrower that back a secured loan in the event that the borrower defaults.

secured loan
A loan that is backed or secured by collateral.

unsecured loan
A loan that is not backed by collateral.

- **Collateral. Collateral** is the assets of the borrower (if any) that back the loan in the event that the borrower defaults. A loan that is backed or secured by collateral is referred to as a **secured loan**; a loan that is not backed by collateral is an **unsecured loan**. In general, you will receive more favorable terms (such as a lower interest rate) on a secured loan because the lender has less to lose in the event that the loan is not repaid.

If the loan is secured, the loan agreement describes the collateral. When a loan is used to purchase a specific asset, that asset is commonly used as collateral. For example, if your purchase of a boat is partly financed, the boat would serve as collateral. That is, the lender could repossess the boat if you were unable to make the loan payments. Some loans are backed by assets other than those purchased with the loan. For example, a boat loan could be backed by stocks that you own.

Some personal loans are backed by the equity in a borrower's home, and these loans are commonly referred to as home equity loans. The proceeds of the loan can be used for any purpose. Home equity loans are described later in this chapter.

Cosigning Some borrowers are only able to obtain a personal loan if someone with a stronger credit history cosigns. The cosigner is responsible for any unpaid balance if the borrower does not repay the loan. If the borrower defaults and the cosigner does not repay the loan, the lender has the right to sue the cosigner or to try to seize that person's assets, just as if the cosigner were the borrower. As a result, the cosigner's credit report will be negatively affected. In addition, cosigning on a loan can restrict the amount that the cosigner is able to borrow. Therefore, you should only be willing to cosign a loan if you trust the borrower and will not need to borrow funds for yourself in the near future.

There are several steps you can take to protect yourself when applying for a loan. Be wary of any lenders who pursue you with high-pressure tactics. Short-term offers and up-front application fees also indicate a disreputable lender. Always make sure you understand the loan terms before signing a loan agreement. If you cannot obtain reasonable loan terms, reconsider whether you truly need a loan at this time.

Interest Rates on Personal Loans

The three most common types of interest rates financial institutions use to measure the interest due on personal loans are the annual percentage rate, simple interest, and add-on interest.

annual percentage rate (APR)
A rate that measures the finance expenses (including interest and other expenses) on a loan annually.

Annual Percentage Rate

As a result of the Truth-in-Lending Act (1969), lenders are required to disclose a standardized loan rate with directly comparable interest expenses over the life of the loan. This makes it easier for you to compare loans offered by different lenders and select the best loan. The **annual percentage rate (APR)** measures the finance expenses (including interest and all other expenses) on a loan annually.

EXAMPLE

Suppose that you have a choice of borrowing $2,000 over the next year from Bank A, Bank B, or Bank C. Bank A offers an interest rate of 10% on its loan. Bank B offers an interest rate of 8%, but also charges a fee of $100 at the time the loan is granted. Bank C offers an interest rate of 6%, but charges a loan fee of $200 at the time the loan is granted. Exhibit 9.2 shows the APRs.

In this example, Bank A offers the lowest APR for a one-year loan. Even though its interest rate is higher, its total financing costs are lower than those charged by the other banks because it does not have any fees. Thus, the APR on its loan is equal to the interest rate charged on the loan. In contrast, the APRs on the loans provided by Banks B and C are much higher than the interest rate charged on their loans because of the fees.

Simple Interest

simple interest
Interest on a loan computed as a percentage of the existing loan amount (or principal).

Simple interest is the interest computed as a percentage of the existing loan amount (or principal). It is measured using the principal, the interest rate applied to the principal, and the loan's time to maturity (in years). The loan repayment schedule is easily determined by a computer or a calculator, or you can use various Web sites. If you input the loan amount, the interest rate, and the loan maturity, the loan repayment schedule will provide you with the following information:

- The monthly payment
- The amount of each monthly payment applied to pay interest
- The amount of each monthly payment applied to pay down the loan principal
- The outstanding loan balance that remains after each monthly payment

The size of the monthly payment is dependent on the size of the loan, the interest rate, and the maturity. The larger the loan amount, the larger the monthly payment. The higher the interest rate, the larger the monthly payment. For a given loan amount and interest rate, the longer the period over which the loan is repaid (e.g., 36 months versus 24 months), the smaller the monthly payment. As mentioned earlier, however, the longer the maturity, the more you will pay in interest expenses.

EXHIBIT 9.2 Measurement of the Annual Percentage Rate

	Interest Expenses	Other Finance Expenses	Total Finance Expenses	Number of Years	Average Annual Finance Expenses	Annual Percentage Rate (APR)*
Bank A	$200	0	$200	1	$200	$200/$2,000 = 10%
Bank B	160	$100	260	1	260	$260/$2,000 = 13%
Bank C	120	200	320	1	320	$320/$2,000 = 16%

*The APR is calculated by dividing the average annual finance expenses by the average annual loan balance.

EXHIBIT 9.3	Example of Loan Repayment Schedule: One-Year Loan, 12% Interest Rate (Monthly Payment = $177.70)		
Month	**Interest Payment**	**Payment of Principal**	**Outstanding Loan Balance**
			$2,000.00
1	$20.00	$157.70	1,842.30
2	18.42	159.28	1,683.02
3	16.83	160.87	1,522.16
4	15.22	162.48	1,359.68
5	13.60	164.10	1,195.58
6	11.96	165.74	1,029.84
7	10.30	167.40	862.44
8	8.63	169.07	693.37
9	6.94	170.76	522.61
10	5.23	172.47	350.13
11	3.50	174.20	175.94
12	1.76	175.94	0

EXAMPLE

You obtain a loan of $2,000 that is based on the simple interest method with an annual interest rate of 12% (1% per month) and 12 equal monthly payments. Given this information, a computer generates the loan repayment schedule in Exhibit 9.3. Notice at the top of the exhibit that each monthly payment is $177.70. Each payment consists of an interest payment and a portion that goes to repay the loan principal. At the end of the first month, the interest owed on $2,000 based on a monthly interest rate of 1% is

$$\text{Interest Owed} = \text{Outstanding Loan Balance} \times \text{Interest Rate}$$
$$= \$2,000 \times .01$$
$$= \$20$$

Because the total payment is $177.70 and the interest payment is $20, the remainder ($157.70) is applied to pay down the principal. The outstanding loan balance after one month is

$$\text{Outstanding Loan Balance} = \text{Previous Balance} - \text{Principal Payment}$$
$$= \$2,000 - \$157.70$$
$$= \$1,842.30$$

At the end of the second month, the interest rate of 1% is applied to the outstanding balance to determine the interest payment:

$$\text{Interest Owed} = \$1,842.30 \times .01$$
$$= \$18.42$$

This same process is followed to determine the amount of interest that is paid each month. The remainder of each payment is applied to pay off the principal. As each month passes, the outstanding loan balance is reduced, so the interest payment in the following month is reduced. The total monthly payment remains the same for all months, so the principal payment increases over time.

add-on interest method
A method of determining the monthly payment on a loan; involves calculating interest that must be paid on the loan amount, adding together the interest and loan principal, and dividing by the number of payments.

Add-On Interest

With the **add-on interest method,** the amount of the monthly payment is determined by calculating the interest that must be paid on the loan amount, adding the interest and loan principal together, and dividing by the number of payments.

EXAMPLE

Reconsider the example in which you receive a loan of $2,000 to be repaid over one year, but assume that you are charged 12% interest based on the add-on method. You would first determine the amount of interest that is owed by applying the annual interest rate to the loan amount:

$$\text{Interest Owed} = \$2,000 \times .12$$
$$= \$240$$

Next, determine the total payment owed by adding the interest to the loan amount:

$$\text{Total Payment} = \$2,000 + \$240$$
$$= \$2,240$$

Finally, divide the total payment by the number of monthly payments:

$$\text{Monthly payment} = \$2,240/12$$
$$= \$186.67$$

Notice that your monthly payment with the add-on method is about $9 per month more than your payment with the simple interest method. Even though the same interest rate is used for both methods, the add-on method is more costly. The reason is that the interest payment is not reduced over time as you pay off the loan.

FREE APPS
for Personal
Finance

Estimating the Time to Repay Your Debt

Application:

The Debts Break app (by LINKSLINKS LTD) allows you to estimate how long it will take you to pay off your debt based on input you provide about the amount of debt you have, the interest rate, and the amount of funds you will have per period to repay debt.

To Find It:

Search for the "Debts Break" app on your mobile device.

Car Loans

A common type of personal loan is a car loan. There are many decisions to make when you get a car: how much money to spend on it, what type to purchase, how to get the best price, whether to finance it or purchase it with cash, and whether to buy or lease the car. All these decisions are discussed in this chapter. The initial focus is on how much money to spend for a car because this decision can influence all the remaining decisions about the car you'll get.

How Much Money to Spend on a Car?

Your decision about much money you should spend on a car is critical because it can affect your budget as well as your lifestyle. When making this decision, carefully consider how your choices could affect your spending on other needs, and your lifestyle in general.

> **EXAMPLE**
>
> Evan just started college and lives on campus. He spends all his time on campus or in the nearby college town, but he needs a car to go to work at his part-time job. Evan will earn about $500 per month from his job, which he hopes will cover his various college expenses over the next four years. The dealer advises Evan that with an income of $500 per month, he could buy a new car for about $22,000, and he could obtain financing over a four-year period in which he would pay $500 per month. Evan is excited about the idea of having a new car. However, the purchase of this car would use all the money that he would earn on the job. Therefore, he would have no money left to cover his monthly expenses, and his reason for getting a part-time job was to cover college expenses. Evan realizes that purchasing a new car is not rational. He would be better off without the part-time job if the purchase of a car would require him to use all his income to make car payments. He decides that he will only purchase a car and keep his job if he can purchase a reliable car for less than $4,000. This would require about $100 in monthly payments over a four-year period, so that he could use the remaining $400 in income per month from his job for other purposes.

One of the most common reasons why college students like Evan are tempted to spend much more money on a car than they need to is because credit is so easily available. Some students make decisions based on whether they can cover the monthly payment rather than what they need. They receive immediate satisfaction from having a new car, but do not feel the pain from paying off the large car loan until after the purchase. They also face peer pressure and may want to have a new car because their friends do, without thinking about how the large monthly car payments may absorb all their monthly budget. It is natural for college students or any consumers to assess what their peers have when making decisions. If all your friends have borrowed excessively to buy expensive cars, you may convince yourself that this is normal, without realizing how it might constrain other forms of spending.

Consider How Your Decision Affects Your Personal Budget Before buying an expensive new car, consider how your personal cash flow statement (explained in Chapter 2) would be affected by large monthly car payments. If you do not have money saved to buy the car, and your car payment would be $500 per month, identify all the purchases in your typical monthly budget that you will no longer be able to make. You may need to cancel your spring break vacation, stop going out to restaurants, and stop going to movies. Alternatively, you might need to move into a smaller apartment so that you can reduce your rent expense to make your car payment. When considering the sacrifices you may need to make to buy a new car, you may decide not to, so that you have spending money to enjoy life in other ways.

Adding Credit Card Debt to Car Loan Debt Some consumers might consider purchasing a new car with a car loan and avoid restricting their other spending by using credit cards and making only the minimum required payments on the cards each month. This solution provides immediate satisfaction because it initially allows them to buy a new car while living a lifestyle beyond what they can really afford. However, they will have to sacrifice in the future when the debt accumulates and they have to pay it off. They will not only have the burden of the large car payment every month for the next four years, but also will have to make large payments to cover credit card debt in the future. They will also be forced to pay high interest rates on credit card debt.

Many consumers who could not stay within a reasonable budget in their younger years have difficulty adjusting in future years when they need to start paying off debt. They were accustomed to spending beyond their income when they were younger, and they do not want to sacrifice now to make up for their excessive spending in earlier years. Thus, their lack of discipline might lead them to a long-term trend of excessive spending that could ultimately end in their credit being cut off by their creditors. If they had been willing to sacrifice in their younger years by staying within their budget and buying a cheap used car, they might have avoided the accumulation of debt over time.

Some consumers who spend excessively on a car might believe that if they find they cannot afford to make the monthly car payments, they can easily correct the situation by selling their car. However, this solution is limited. New cars lose at least 10% and sometimes as much as 20% of their value as soon as they are driven off the lot. Consider the new car that Evan could have purchased for $22,000 with borrowed money in the example presented earlier. If Evan purchased the car and tried to sell it a month later, he might receive about $18,000, or $4,000 less than what he owed on the car. In other words, the use of the new car for one month cost him $4,000. The point here is that consumers should not rush into purchasing a new car until they have carefully considered whether they can really afford it.

The No-Debt Solution

Some consumers avoid the debt problems described earlier by limiting the amount of money they will spend on a car (or on any purchases) to whatever they can afford to pay with cash. This strategy forces them to purchase an inexpensive used car when they are younger because that is all that they can afford. In addition to avoiding debt, this approach might allow them to save much more of their income over time because they can save some or all the money each month that they would have needed to make debt payments. This may enable them to save enough money over time so that they can purchase a new car with cash. Their decision to stay within a limited budget at an early age may be easier to accept when they realize that it will allow them to spend more money in the future.

The Limited-Debt Solution

There are many variations of the no-debt solution that are not as extreme but still very effective. Some consumers might use cash to purchase a used car and use credit cards for other purchases, but they may limit these purchases to what they can afford to pay off when they receive the credit card bill each month. In this way, they avoid the accumulation of debt. Alternatively, some consumers might be willing to borrow to purchase a car, but may structure the loan so that they pay it off within a short-term period. The payments on a short-term loan (such as one year) would be much higher than the payments on a four-year car loan, so this would reduce the amount that they could spend on the car. However, this restriction might be beneficial because it prevents them from spending an excessive amount of money on the car.

FREE APPS for Personal Finance

Estimating Your Monthly Car Loan Payment

Application:

The RoadLoans app (by RoadLoans.com) estimates your monthly payment on a car loan based on the amount of the loan, loan maturity, and interest rate. You can easily adjust your input to determine how your monthly payment would change based on a different loan amount, maturity, or interest rate.

To Find It:

Search for the "RoadLoans" app on your mobile device.

Once you have decided how much money you will spend on a car, you can focus on the other related decisions, which are discussed next.

Selecting the Car

When selecting a car, consider the following factors.

Personal Preferences Determine the car that fits your needs. Do you want a small car that is easy to park and gets good gas mileage? Or do you need a minivan to hold your children and their sports equipment? You can always screen the cars on your list further by deciding on the size of the engine.

Price While you have already determined the amount that you are willing to spend, you should compare the prices of the cars that fit your preferences and are within your price range. There will likely be more than one car within your price range that could satisfy your needs and preferences, and one of these cars might have a lower price because the dealer has a larger inventory of that car and is more willing to sell it at a lower price.

Condition When buying a used car, be sure to assess the condition of the car beginning with the exterior. Has some of the paint worn off? Is there rust? Are the tires in good shape? Are the tires worn on one side (which may indicate that a wheel alignment is needed)? Next, check the interior. Are the seats worn? Do the electric devices work? Now look under the hood. Is there any sign of leaks? If you are still seriously considering the vehicle, ask to see the repair and maintenance records. Has the car been properly maintained and serviced over time? Has the oil been changed periodically?

All these checks can help you assess a car's condition, but none replaces the expertise of a qualified mechanic. The cost of having a mechanic evaluate the car is worthwhile because it may enable you to avoid buying a car that will ultimately result in large repair expenses.

The Federal Trade Commission's Used Car Rule requires dealers to post a Buyers Guide in every used car offered for sale (a few states require their own similar guide). The guide must tell you whether the car is being sold "as is" or with a warranty and what percentage of the repair costs the dealer will pay under the warranty if there is one. If the Buyers Guide indicates that there is a warranty, the dealer must give you a written warranty indicating what the warranty covers. Sometimes the guide will indicate that the car is being sold "as is," but the dealer will give you an oral promise to repair the vehicle or cancel the sale if you're not satisfied with the car. Do not rely on an oral promise; insist that the dealer's promises be written on the Buyers Guide.

Insurance Some cars are subject to significantly higher insurance costs because they are more difficult to repair after accidents, are higher priced, or are common theft targets. Obtain insurance estimates on any car before making the purchase. Be aware that to obtain a loan to purchase a car, you will have to have insurance to cover the car. If you let your insurance lapse, the lender has the right to obtain insurance on the car and charge you for it. This is called force-placed insurance, and it is usually much more expensive than insurance that you obtain yourself.

Resale Value Some cars have a much higher resale value than others. For example, you can expect that an Acura will have a higher resale value than a Hyundai. Although you cannot perfectly predict the future resale value of a car, you can look at today's resale value of similar cars that were sold years ago. Numerous sites on the Internet, such as http://www.edmunds.com, provide the market values of used cars, which you can use to determine the resale value as a proportion of the original sales price.

Repair Expenses Some cars are subject to much higher repair bills than others. To compare potential repair expenses, review *Consumer Reports* magazine, which commonly estimates the typical repair expenses for various cars.

Financial Planning
ONLINE

Go to:
http://www.ftc.gov, and search for "Are Car Ads Taking You for a Ride?"

To get:
Questions that you should ask when you are offered unusually low financing rates.

Financing Rate If you plan to finance your car purchase through the car dealer, you should compare financing rates among dealers. One dealer may charge a lower price for the car but charge higher financing costs for the loan. Other dealers may offer an unusually low financing rate, but charge a higher price on the car. When financing through a car dealer, beware of a dealer markup, in which the dealer arranges the loan and then marks up the lender's interest rate without disclosing the markup to the customer. For example, a dealer may obtain financing for your car at 10%, but charge you 12%. If you obtain financing from a financial institution rather than the dealer, you can easily compare financing rates of various financial institutions on the Internet.

In some cases, you may wish to determine how much you can borrow before you decide which car to purchase. You can use auto loan Web sites to estimate the maximum amount you can borrow, based on the financial information you provide.

FREE APPS for Personal Finance

Searching for Cars in Your Location

Application:

The AutoTrader app (by Autotrader.com, Inc) allows you to search for new and used cars that are for sale near you. A listing of used cars for sale near your location includes the price, mileage, a photo, and seller contact information.

To Find It:

Search for the "AutoTrader" app on your mobile device.

Revised Car Loan Contracts Some car dealers will allow a car buyer to write a check for the down payment, fill out a car loan application, and drive the car home. If the application is not approved, the car buyer may have to reapply for a car loan that is set at a higher rate. At this point, the buyer may not have much choice except to accept the less-favorable terms set by the lender.

EXAMPLE

Stephanie Spratt has been working full-time for about a year and has saved enough money to afford a down payment on a new car. She considers which car to buy based on the following criteria:

- **Price.** Stephanie's favorite cars are priced in the $35,000 to $45,000 range, but she does not want to borrow such a large amount of money. She hopes to buy a home within a few years (which will require another loan) and therefore wants to limit the amount she borrows now.

  Next, Stephanie reviews her current assets to determine her down payment amount. She can sell her existing car for $1,000. She has accumulated about $4,000 in savings, which she would like to maintain for liquidity. She also still has her stock, which is worth about $3,000 at this time. She would prefer to keep her stock rather than sell it. She decides to use the $1,000 from the sale of her used car to make the down payment.

  Stephanie wants to borrow no more than $17,000 to buy a car, so she considers cars in the $16,000 to $20,000 price range. She identifies eight cars that are within that range, but she does not like three of them and therefore focuses on the remaining five cars. Next, she obtains more detailed information on the prices of the five cars online.

- **Resale Value, Repair Expenses, and Insurance.** Stephanie also uses the Internet to obtain ratings on the resale value, repair expenses, and insurance rates for each of the five cars. She recognizes that some dealers attempt to attract customers by offering unusually low financing rates, but then price the car higher to offset the low financing rate. She prefers to avoid these types of dealers, so she plans to obtain her financing from a car-financing Web site. She inputs information about her salary and loan history and is quickly able to determine the financing rate she would pay.

Using the Internet, Stephanie easily obtains the information shown in Exhibit 9.4. Car A has a relatively low resale value after two years. Car D has relatively high repair expenses and service maintenance. Cars A and C have relatively high insurance rates. Therefore, she eliminates Cars A, C, and D. She will choose between Cars B and E.

Negotiating the Price

When shopping for a car, you have a choice between dealers that negotiate and dealers that offer one set price for a specific car to all customers. Any dealer that negotiates will purposely price its cars well above the price for which it is willing to sell the car. For example, the dealer may initially quote a price that represents the manufacturer's suggested retail price (MSRP). This price is also referred to as the sticker price. The strategy of some dealers is to make you think that you are getting a great deal as a result of the negotiations. If any customer is naïve enough to pay the full price, the car dealer earns a much larger profit at the customer's expense.

The salespeople are trained to act as if they are almost giving the car away to the customer by reducing the price by 5% to 20%. During the negotiations, they will say that they must discuss the price you offer with the sales manager. They already know the price at which they can sell the car to you, but this creates the appearance that they are pleading with the sales manager. During the negotiations, the dealer may offer you "free" rustproofing, a DVD system, leather seats, or other features. These features are usually priced very high to make you believe that you are getting a good deal.

If you intend to purchase a new car, consider ordering it if you don't see what you want on the dealer's lot. The cars on the lot may have many features that you don't want. Thus, they will have a higher price. Sometimes, however, dealers want to sell their current inventory to make room for new models, and, in that case, you may be able to negotiate a better price.

Negotiating by Phone When purchasing a new car, it may be beneficial to negotiate by phone. After deciding on the type of car that you want, call a dealer and describe the car and options you desire. Explain that you plan to call other local car dealers, and that you will select the dealer that offers the lowest price. You may also want to emphasize that you will only call each dealer once.

Some dealers may not have the exact car that you want, so you may still have to compare features. For example, one dealer may quote a price that is $200 lower than the

EXHIBIT 9.4	**Stephanie Spratt's Car Analysis**		
Car	**Expected Resale Value After Two Years (as a proportion of original sales price)**	**Repair Expenses and Service Maintenance**	**Insurance**
A	Low	Moderate	High
B	Moderate	Low	Low
C	Moderate	Moderate	High
D	Moderate	High	Moderate
E	Moderate	Low	Moderate

next-lowest quote, but the car may not be the specific color you requested. Nevertheless, the process described here can at least minimize the negotiation process.

Trade-In Tactics If you are trading a car in, some dealers will pay a relatively high price for your trade-in, but charge a high price for the new car. For example, they may pay you $500 more than your used car is worth, but then charge you at least $500 more than they would have charged for the new car if you did not have a car to trade in. Attempt to negotiate the price on the new car first, before even mentioning that you have a car to trade in.

If you purchase a car from a typical dealer, many of the salespeople will congratulate you as if you had just won the lottery. This is also part of their strategy to make you feel that you got a great deal.

No-Haggle Dealers Some car dealerships advertise that they do not haggle on the price. Buying a car from these dealers is not only less stressful but far less time-consuming. They set one price for a car, so you do not have to prepare for a negotiating battle. Some of these car dealerships still negotiate, however, so before you buy the car, you should make sure the price is no higher than that quoted by other dealers.

The Value of Information Some car dealers attempt to make a higher profit from customers who are not well informed about the price that they should pay for a car. One way to avoid being taken advantage of when purchasing a car is to be informed. Shop around and make sure that you know the typical sales price for the car you want. You can obtain this information from *Consumer Reports* and various Web sites that will provide you with a quote based on the car model and features you want. You can do all your shopping from your computer or your smartphone. For example, you may be able to obtain the dealer invoice price, which is the price that the dealer pays the manufacturer for the car. The difference between the price quoted by the dealer and the invoice price is the dealer markup. Be aware that manufacturers commonly provide dealers a rebate (referred to as a hold back), but dealers do not normally provide this information to their customers. A dealer could possibly charge a price that is only $200 above its dealer invoice, but if it received an $800 rebate from the manufacturer, the price is really marked up $1,000.

Purchasing a Car Online You can buy a car online directly from some car manufacturers or from car referral services such as Autobytel Inc. or Carpoint. Car referral services forward your price quotation request to specific dealerships, which then respond by sending you a quote. CarsDirect at http://www.carsdirect.com provides you with quotes based on deals it has made with various dealerships. That is, it receives guarantees from some dealerships on the prices for various types of cars. When a customer requests a quote, the car-buying service provides quotations that include a markup for its service. In other words, it is serving as the middleman between you and the dealership. If a customer agrees to the price, the car-buying service instructs one of its dealerships to deliver the car.

Buying a new car online is not as efficient as buying an airline ticket or a book online. A car is not as standardized as a book, and the many options available can make the online correspondence more difficult. At a dealership, a customer can see the actual difference in the design of two models of a particular car. It is not as easy to detect the differences on a Web site. Unlike a Web site, a dealership can anticipate your questions and arrange for a test drive. It is also more difficult to force an online service to meet its delivery promise to you. For example, an online car seller may guarantee you a price for a specific car, but not necessarily meet the delivery date. You have limited ability to enforce the deal because you may only be able to reach them by e-mail or voice mail. You can place more pressure on a local dealership to meet its promise by showing up at the dealership and expressing your concerns.

You can also buy used cars online, through eBay. However, the purchase of a used car online is subject to the same limitations as the purchase of a new car online. Given the limitations of buying a car online, many customers still prefer to buy a car at a dealership.

EXAMPLE

Stephanie Spratt has decided to use the Internet to shop for her car. Several Web sites state the price for each of the two new cars she is considering (Cars B and E from the previous example). She reviews specific details about each car, including which car has more value relative to its price, the options, available colors, and the delivery dates. She believes that although Car B is cheaper, its value will depreciate more quickly than Car E's. In addition, she can get the exact options and color she desires for Car E, and it can be delivered soon. She is almost ready to purchase Car E, which is priced at $18,000 including taxes. But first, she wants to consider the financing costs per month and whether to lease the car or purchase it.

Financing Decisions

If you consider purchasing a new car and plan to finance the purchase, you should estimate the dollar amount of the monthly payment. By evaluating your typical monthly cash inflows and outflows, you can determine whether you can afford to make the required payments to finance the car. You should conduct the estimate before shopping for a car so that you know how much you can afford. The more money needed to cover the car payments, the less you can add to your savings or other investments.

EXAMPLE

Stephanie Spratt wants to compare her monthly car payments if she borrows $15,000 versus $17,000 to buy a car. She must also decide whether to repay the loan over three years, four years, or five years. The larger the down payment she makes, the less she will need to borrow. However, she wants to retain some of her savings to maintain liquidity and to use for a future down payment on a house.

Stephanie goes to a car-financing Web site where she is asked to input the approximate amount she will borrow. The Web site then provides the available interest rate and shows the payments for each alternative loan amount and repayment period, as shown in Exhibit 9.5. The interest rate of 7.6% at the top of the exhibit is a fixed rate that Stephanie can lock in for the loan period. The possible loan amounts are shown at the top of the columns, and each row shows a different loan repayment period.

Notice how the payment decreases if Stephanie extends the loan period. If she borrows $17,000, her payment would be $530 for a three-year loan, $412 for a four-year loan, or $341 for a five-year loan. Alternatively, she can lower her monthly payments by reducing her loan amount from $17,000 to $15,000. Notice that if she takes out a four-year loan for $15,000, her monthly payment is less than if she borrows $17,000.

Stephanie selects the $17,000 loan with a four-year term and a $412 monthly payment. The four-year term is preferable because the monthly loan payment for a three-year term is higher than she wants to pay. Because the purchase price of the car is $18,000, she will use the proceeds from selling her old car to cover the $1,000 down payment.

EXHIBIT 9.5	Stephanie Spratt's Possible Monthly Loan Payments (7.6% interest rate)	

	Loan Amount	
Loan Maturity	**$15,000**	**$17,000**
36 months (3 years)	$467	$530
48 months (4 years)	363	412
60 months (5 years)	301	341

Some auto dealerships provide financing for up to seven years. The advantage of such a long period to repay the loan is that for a given loan amount, your monthly payment will be lower. However, the disadvantage of such a long period is that by the time you pay off the loan, the car may be worthless. Even if you sell the car after a few years, the car is likely to be worth less than the amount you still owe on the car. Conversely, if you pay off a car loan in a short amount of time, you are relieved of car payments until you purchase another car.

Purchase Versus Lease Decision

A popular alternative to buying a car is leasing one. An advantage of leasing is that you do not need a substantial down payment. In addition, you return the car to the car dealer at the end of the lease period, so you do not need to worry about finding a buyer for the car. In addition, you will always be driving a relatively new car.

Leasing a car also has disadvantages. Because you do not own the car, you have no equity investment in it, even though the car still has value. You are also responsible for maintenance costs while you are leasing it. Keep in mind that you will be charged for any damage to the car over the lease period. Note, too, that if you always lease another car when the lease period ends, you will be making lease payments indefinitely and will never actually own a car. Constantly leasing a car is almost always more expensive than purchasing a car. Some car dealers impose additional charges beyond the monthly lease payments. You will be charged if you drive more than the maximum number of miles specified in the lease agreement. You may be assessed a fee if you end the lease before the period specified in the contract. You may also have to purchase more car insurance than you already have. Some of these charges may be hidden within the lease agreement. Thousands of customers have filed legal claims, alleging that they were not informed of all possible charges when they leased a car. If you ever seriously consider leasing, make sure that you read and understand the entire lease agreement.

Your Decision to Lease a Car

Application:

The Leasify app (by Level Software LLC) allows you to assess your cost of leasing a car. This can help you calculate payments and can serve as a useful guide in your decision.

To Find It:

Search for the "Leasify" app on your mobile device.

EXAMPLE

Stephanie Spratt now wonders if she should lease the car she selected, rather than purchasing it for $18,000. If she purchases the car, she can invest $1,000 as a down payment today, and the remaining $17,000 will be financed by a car loan. She will pay $412 per month over four years to cover the financing. She expects that the car will be worth $10,000 at the end of four years. By purchasing instead of leasing, she forgoes interest that she could have earned from investing the $1,000 down payment over the next four years. If she invests the funds in a bank, she would earn 4% annually after considering taxes paid on the interest.

Alternatively, she could lease the same car for $300 per month over the four-year period. The lease would require an $800 security deposit, which she would receive back at the end of the four-year period. However, she would forgo interest she could have earned if she had invested the $800 instead. And, at the end of a lease, she would have no equity and no car.

Stephanie's comparison of the cost of purchasing versus leasing is shown in Exhibit 9.6. Stephanie estimates the total cost of purchasing the car to be $10,936 while the total cost of leasing is $14,528. Therefore, she decides to purchase the car.

EXHIBIT 9.6　**Stephanie Spratt's Comparison of the Cost of Purchasing Versus Leasing**

Cost of Purchasing the Car

		Cost
1.	Down payment	$1,000
2.	Down payment of $1,000 results in forgone interest income:	
	Forgone Interest	
	Income per Year　=　Down Payment × Annual Interest Rate	
	=　$1,000 × .04	
	=　$40	
	Forgone Interest over Four Years =　$40 × 4	
	=　$160	160
3.	Total monthly payments are:	
	Total Monthly Payments =　Monthly Payment × Number of Months	
	=　$412 × 48	
	=　$19,776	$19,776
	Total	$20,936
	Minus: Expected amount to be received when car is sold in four years	10,000
	Total cost	$10,936

Cost of Leasing the Car for Four Years

		Cost
1.	Security deposit of $800 results in forgone interest income (although she will receive her deposit back in four years):	
	Forgone Interest	
	Income per Year　=　Down Payment × Annual Interest Rate	
	=　$800 × .04	
	=　$32	
	Forgone Interest over Four Years　=　$32 × 4	
	=　$128	$128
2.	Total monthly payments are:	
	Total Monthly Payments =　Monthly Payment × Number of Months	
	=　$300 × 48	
	=　$14,400	14,400
	Total cost	$14,528

The decision to purchase versus lease a car is highly dependent on the estimated market value of the car at the end of the lease period. If the expected value of the car in the previous example were $6,000 instead of $10,000 after four years, the total cost of purchasing the car would have been $4,000 more. Substitute $6,000 for $10,000 in Exhibit 9.6 and recalculate the cost of purchasing to verify this. With an expected market value of $6,000, the total cost of purchasing the car would have been higher than the total cost of leasing, so leasing would have been preferable. Remember that some dealers may impose additional charges for leasing, such as a charge for driving more than the maximum miles allowed. Include any of these expenses in your estimate of the leasing expenses.

Student Loans

student loan
A loan provided to finance part of the expenses a student incurs while pursuing a degree.

The largest personal loan for many students is the **student loan**, which is a loan to finance a portion of a student's expenses while pursuing an undergraduate or graduate degree. About 70% of students graduate with at least some student loan debt. The average amount is $28,400. There are two types of student loans: federal loans, which are provided by the U.S. government, and private loans, which are provided by financial institutions. For most students, federal loans are preferable to private loans because the interest rate is lower, and it is fixed, not variable. In addition, many federal loans are subsidized, which means that the government pays the interest on the loans while you are in school. Federal loans include Perkins Loans, which are subsidized and awarded based on financial need; Subsidized Direct Loans, which are based on financial need; and Unsubsidized Direct Loans, for which everyone is eligible. The amount of money available through these loans is limited, however, and many students find that they also need to obtain private loans.

You can borrow larger amounts of money with private loans than with federal loans, but private loans are also generally more expensive. Private loans charge a higher interest rate than federal loans, and interest is charged while you are in school. In addition, these loans often have a variable interest rate, so your monthly payment could increase over time if market interest rates rise. The terms of private loans vary considerably among lenders, so it is worth shopping around. Most lenders require that undergraduates have a cosigner for the loan.

Even if you don't graduate from college, you still have to pay back your student loans. Failure to do so will damage your credit history. The interest is tax-deductible up to a maximum of $2,500, but the tax benefits are phased out for individuals in high tax brackets. In certain circumstances, teachers and those working in certain public service jobs can have at least part of their student loan debt forgiven.

If you find yourself in a situation when you cannot repay your loans, such as being unemployed, you can ask your lender for a deferment, which means that your payments are temporarily delayed. During the deferment period, interest will continue to be charged on private loans and unsubsidized federal loans. It will be added to your principal, so a long period of deferment could substantially increase the amount that you will ultimately have to repay. When you are taking out student loans, you should also be aware that unlike other types of debt, student loans are not dischargeable in bankruptcy except in very rare circumstances. Thus, unless you fit into one of the few exceptions, you will have to repay all the money that you borrow with interest.

Student loan programs can be quite complex because there are so many types of loans. You should investigate the options carefully before taking out loans. Your school's financial aid office can be a good source of information. Several U.S. government Web sites can also be helpful: http://www.ed.gov and http://studentloans.gov (both from the Department of Education) and http://www.consumerfinance.gov (the Consumer Financial Protection Bureau).

Home Equity Loans

home equity loan
A loan where the equity in a home serves as collateral for the loan.

equity of a home
The market value of a home minus the debt owed on the home.

One of the most popular types of personal loans is a **home equity loan**, which allows homeowners to borrow against the equity in their home. The home serves as collateral to back the loan. The borrowed funds can be used for any purpose, including a vacation, tuition payments, or health care expenses.

The **equity of a home** is determined by subtracting the amount owed on the home from its market value. If a home has a market value of $100,000 and the homeowner has a mortgage loan (discussed in the next chapter) with a balance of $60,000, the equity value is $40,000.

There are two ways to borrow against your home's equity. With a simple home equity loan, you receive the money you are borrowing in a lump sum. The loan usually will have a fixed interest rate. With a home equity line of credit (HELOC), the lender provides you with a line of credit that you can draw against over a period, such as 10 years. That is, the HELOC allows you to borrow various amounts up to a specific credit limit. Some plans require you to borrow a minimum amount such as $300 each time you draw on the line of credit or to keep a certain balance outstanding. You may also be required to make an initial withdrawal when the HELOC is set up. HELOCs typically have variable interest rates, but you pay interest only on the amount of funds that you borrow. You can typically pay the interest owed per month on the amount you borrow and then pay the principal at a specified maturity date. You may also be allowed to pay off the principal before the HELOC's term ends and still have access to the funds if you need them in the future.

Setting up either type of home equity loan will entail fees in addition to the interest charged. These fees may include an appraisal fee so that the lender can determine the value of the home, an application fee that may not be refunded even if your loan request is turned down, up-front charges that may amount to 2% or 3% or more of the credit limit, and closing costs including fees for attorneys and a title search. In addition, some HELOC plans charge annual maintenance fees or transaction fees whenever you draw on the line of credit.

Credit Limit on a Home Equity Loan

Financial institutions provide home equity loans of up to 80% (or more in some cases) of the value of the equity in a home.

Financial institutions define the market value of your equity as the market value of your home minus the mortgage balance (amount still owed on the home). When the market value of a home rises, they are willing to provide more credit than if the market value remains the same.

If you default on a home equity loan, the lender can claim your home, use a portion of the proceeds to pay off the mortgage, and use the remainder to cover your home equity loan. If the market price of the home declines, the equity that you invested is reduced. For this reason, lenders do not like to lend the full amount of the equity when extending a home equity loan.

The following example illustrates how to determine the maximum amount of credit that can be provided on a home equity loan.

EXAMPLE

Suppose that you own a home worth $100,000 that you purchased four years ago. You initially made a down payment of $20,000 and took out an $80,000 mortgage. Over the last four years, your mortgage payments have added $10,000 in equity. Thus, you have invested $30,000 in the home, including your $20,000 down payment. Assume that the home's market value has not changed. Also, assume that a creditor is willing to provide you with a home equity loan of 70% based on the market value of equity in the home. In this example, the market value of equity is equal to the amount of equity you invested in the home.

$$\text{Maximum Amount of Credit Provided} = \text{Market Value of Equity in Home} \times .70$$
$$= \$30,000 \times .70$$
$$= \$21,000$$

EXAMPLE

Use the information in the previous example, except now assume that the market value of your home has risen from $100,000 to $120,000 since you purchased it. Recall that you paid off $10,000 of the $80,000 mortgage loan, so your mortgage balance is $70,000. The market value of the equity in the home is

$$\text{Market Value of Equity in Home} = \text{Market Value of Home} - \text{Mortgage Balance}$$
$$= \$120,000 - \$70,000$$
$$= \$50,000$$

The market value of the equity is $50,000, while the amount of equity that you invested in the home is $30,000. The difference between these two amounts is the $20,000 increase in the value of the home since you purchased it. The credit limit based on the market value of the equity is

$$\text{Maximum Amount of Credit Provided} = \text{Market Value of Equity in Home} \times .70$$
$$= \$50,000 \times .70$$
$$= \$35,000$$

ECONOMIC IMPACT

Impact of the Economy on the Credit Limit When the economy improves, job opportunities improve, consumers receive more income, and they increase their demand for homes. The market values of homes rise in response to the strong demand. As the market value of a home rises while the existing debt on the home mortgage has not changed, the home equity value rises.

However, when the economy weakens, there are fewer job opportunities, consumers receive less income, and they reduce their demand for homes. The market values of homes declines in response to the weak demand. As the market value of a home declines while the existing debt on the home mortgage has not changed, the home equity value decreases. In many cases, the market value of the home may decline below the mortgage balance, which means that there is no equity in the home. Consequently, there is no collateral that could be used to back a loan, and homeowners will not be able to obtain a home equity loan under these conditions.

Interest Rate

A home equity line of credit typically has a variable interest rate that is tied to a specified interest rate index that changes periodically (such as every six months). The loan contract specifies how the interest rate will be determined. For example, it may be set equal to the average deposit rates across financial institutions within a particular district plus three percentage points. Because the home serves as collateral for the loan, the lender faces less risk than with an unsecured loan so the interest rate is lower.

EXAMPLE

You borrow $10,000 with a HELOC and pay $1,000 in interest on the loan in a particular year. Assuming that you can deduct this amount from your taxable income and that your marginal income tax rate is 25%, your tax savings in that year are

$$\begin{aligned}\text{Tax Savings in One Year} \\ \text{from Home Equity Loan} &= \text{Amount of Interest Paid} \times \text{Marginal Tax Rate} \\ &= \$1,000 \times .25 \\ &= \$250 \end{aligned}$$

Tax-Deductible Interest Interest that is paid on a home equity loan of up to $100,000 is tax-deductible. Borrowers can therefore reduce their taxes by using a home equity loan instead of other types of loans or credit cards.

Thus, when you use a home equity loan, not only do you benefit from a relatively low interest rate, but you also generate tax savings.

Payday Loans

payday loan
A short-term loan provided in advance of a paycheck.

A **payday loan** is a short-term loan provided to you if you need funds in advance of receiving your paycheck. To obtain a payday loan, you write a check to the lender for the amount of the loan plus the interest. You date the check for the date in the future when you will receive your paycheck. The payday loan firm will hold the check until that time and will cash it then because your checking account will have sufficient funds. After you provide this check to the payday loan firm, it provides you with your loan in cash or by transmitting funds into your checking account.

EXAMPLE

Assume that you need $400 for some immediate purpose, but will not have any money until you receive your paycheck one week from today. You provide the payday loan firm a check dated one week from today. Be aware that firms such as Cash King, Cash One, CheckMate, and EZLoans, which provide payday loans, charge a high rate of interest on these short-term loans. The payday loan firm may request that your payment be $440, which reflects the loan of $400 and $40 interest and/or fees. You are paying $40 more than the loan you received, which reflects 10% of the loan amount. The cost of financing a payday loan follows:

$$\text{Cost of Financing} = 10\% \times (\text{number of days in a year}/ \text{number of days in which you have the loan})$$
$$= 10\% \times (365/7)$$
$$= 521\%$$

This is not a misprint. It is within the typical range of the cost of financing charged for payday loans.

Although states have usury laws that place a limit on the maximum interest rate that can be charged, the payday loan firms have circumvented that limit by referring to the interest as fees. Some states recognize that the fees are really interest payments and prevent payday firms from establishing businesses. However, payday loan firms can be based in the states that allow them and still reach residents in any state via the Internet.

Financial Planning
ONLINE

Go to:
The consumer section of
http://www.ftc.gov and
insert the search term
"personal loan scam"

To get:
Warnings about some
personal loan scams.

Reasons to Avoid Payday Loans

You should avoid payday loans for the following reasons. First, by using your next paycheck to cover a loan payment, you may not have sufficient cash available to make normal purchases after covering the loan. Thus, you may need another loan to cover your purchases in that period, and this can create a continual cycle in which your paycheck is always needed to repay short-term loans.

Second, as we have seen, the cost of financing with a payday loan is outrageous. Consider how much you would have paid in interest on $400 if you were able to get a loan that charged you a more reasonable rate such as 10% annually.

$$\text{Interest rate for a 7-day period} = 10\% \times (7/365)$$
$$= .192\%$$

The interest to be paid $= \$400 \times .192\% = \$0.76$. Thus, you would pay less than $1 interest on a seven-day loan if you were charged a 10% annualized interest rate. This is substantially less than the interest you would be charged by a payday loan firm. The payday loan firms are able to charge excessive rates because some people who need money quickly may not be creditworthy and therefore have difficulty obtaining funds from other sources. Alternatively, some borrowers do not realize how high the cost of financing is when they borrow money from a payday loan firm.

In 2014, the Consumer Financial Protection Bureau released a study showing that more than 80% of payday loans are renewed within two weeks. Furthermore, the study found that the majority of payday borrowers renew their loans so many times that they end up owing more in fees than they originally borrowed.

Alternatives to Payday Loans

The simple solution is to avoid borrowing money until you have the funds to spend. But if you have to borrow, there are alternative ways of financing that are not as expensive. For example, perhaps you can borrow funds from a friend or family member for a week. Or you may be able to obtain credit through your credit card. Although relying on credit card financing is not recommended, it is substantially wiser than financing through a payday loan. To illustrate, assume that you could have used a credit card to make your $400 purchase. Also assume that the rate on your credit card is 18% annually, or 1.5% over one month. In this case, your cost of financing would be $400 \times 1.5\% = \$6$. This financing cost for one month is much lower than the cost of financing when using a payday loan, and in this example the credit card financing lasts three weeks longer than the payday financing period.

How Personal Loans Fit Within Your Financial Plan

The following are the key personal loan decisions that should be included within your financial plan:

1. How much money can you afford to borrow on a personal loan?
2. If you obtain a personal loan, should you pay it off early?

By making sound decisions, you can avoid accumulating an excessive amount of debt. Exhibit 9.7 provides an example of how personal loan decisions apply to Stephanie Spratt's financial plan. The exhibit shows how Stephanie reviews her typical monthly cash flows to determine whether she can cover her monthly loan payments.

EXHIBIT 9.7   How Personal Loan Management Fits Within Stephanie Spratt's Financial Plan

GOALS FOR PERSONAL FINANCING

1. *Limit the amount of financing to a level and maturity that I can pay back on a timely basis.*
2. *For any personal loan, I will consider paying off the loan balance as soon as possible.*

ANALYSIS

Monthly Cash Inflows	$2,500
− Typical Monthly Expenses	1,400
− Monthly Car Loan Payment	412
= Amount of Funds Available	**$688**

DECISIONS

Decision on Affording a Personal Loan:

The financing of my new car requires a payment of $412 per month. This leaves me with $688 per month after paying typical monthly expenses. I can afford to make the payments. I will not need additional personal loans for any other purpose.

Decision on Paying Off Personal Loan Balances:

The car loan has an interest rate of 7.6 percent. I expect that my stock investment will earn a higher rate of return than this interest rate. Once I have accumulated more savings, however, I will seriously consider using my savings and invested funds to pay off the balance of the loan early.

DISCUSSION QUESTIONS

1. How would Stephanie's personal loan decisions be different if she were a single mother of two children?

2. How would Stephanie's personal loan decisions be affected if she were 35 years old? If she were 50 years old?

SUMMARY

Personal Loans. When applying for a personal loan, you need to disclose your personal balance sheet and cash flow statement so that the lender can evaluate your ability to repay a loan. A loan contract specifies the amount of the loan, interest rate, repayment schedule, maturity, and collateral.

Interest Rates on Personal Loans. The common types of interest rates charged on personal loans are the annual percentage rate (APR), simple interest, and add-on interest. The APR measures the interest and other expenses as a percentage of the loan amount on an annualized basis. Simple interest measures the interest as a percentage of the existing loan amount. Add-on interest calculates interest on the loan amount, adds the interest and principal, and divides by the number of payments.

Financing a Car. Your decision to purchase a car may require financing. You can reduce your monthly payments on the car loan if you make a higher down payment, but doing this may reduce your liquidity. Alternatively, you can reduce your monthly payments by extending the loan period.

Car Loan versus Lease. The decision of whether to purchase a car with a car loan or lease a car requires an estimation of the total cost of each alternative. The total cost of purchasing a car consists of the down payment, the forgone interest income from the down payment, and the total monthly loan payments. The total cost of leasing consists of the forgone interest income from the security deposit and the total monthly lease payments.

Student Loans. Student loans are provided by the federal government and by financial institutions that participate in student loan programs.

Home Equity Loans. A home equity loan or home equity line of credit commonly has more favorable terms than other personal loans. It has a relatively low interest rate because of the collateral (the home) that backs the loan. In addition, the interest paid on a home equity loan is tax deductible up to a limit.

Payday Loans. A payday loan is a short-term loan that provides funds in advance of receiving a paycheck. Payday loans typically have a very high interest rate. Therefore, consider various alternative ways of borrowing money before obtaining a payday loan.

How Personal Loans Fit Within Your Financial Plan. Personal loans allow you to obtain assets that you could not obtain if you did not have access to funding. They can enable you to achieve your financial goals, such as buying a car or a home.

REVIEW QUESTIONS

All Review Questions are available in MyFinanceLab *at* http://www.myfinancelab.com.

1. **Sources of Personal Loans.** List some possible sources of personal loans. What precautions should be taken with loans from family members or friends?

2. **Personal Loan Process.** What does the personal loan process involve?

3. **Loan Amortization.** What does it mean if a loan is amortized? What do the loan payments represent?

4. **Loan Application Process.** What information must borrowers supply to lenders in the loan application process? Why is this information important to lenders?

5. **Loan Contract.** What information is included in a loan contract? How is the amount of the loan determined?

6. **Collateral.** Explain how collateral works. Do all loans have collateral? What is the relationship between collateral and interest rates?

7. **Loan Maturity.** How does the maturity of a loan affect the monthly payments? What should you consider when selecting the maturity?

8. **Payday Loan.** Explain the difference between a 10% rate charged on a payday loan and a 10% rate charged by a bank on a personal loan.

9. **Cosigning a Loan.** What are your responsibilities if you cosign a loan? What are the potential consequences of failing to live up to your responsibilities as a cosigner?

10. **APR.** What is the purpose of the annual percentage rate measurement? Could lenders with the same interest rates report different APRs?

11. **Simple Interest.** What is simple interest? What information is needed to compute it? What information is contained in a loan repayment schedule?

12. **Add-On Interest.** How are payments calculated under the add-on interest method?

13. **Simple versus Add-On Interest.** Why are loan payments under the simple interest method usually lower than loan payments under the add-on interest method?

14. **Buying a Car.** List the steps in buying a car. What financial criteria should be considered? Discuss each briefly.

15. **Buying a Car Online.** Why is purchasing a new car online not as efficient as buying a new car at a dealership?

16. **Car Sales Tactics.** Describe some techniques that car salespeople might use in negotiating the price of the car. What should you be aware of at "no-haggle" dealerships?

17. **Financing.** What should be the first step in financing a purchase of a car? Aside from the interest rate, what two factors will have the largest impact on the size of your monthly payment?

18. **Leasing a Car.** What are the advantages and disadvantages of leasing a car? Give some advice for someone considering leasing.

19. **Student Loan.** Who extends student loans? What are the characteristics of student loans?

20. **Home Equity.** What is home equity? Describe how home equity loans work.

21. **Credit Limits.** Discuss the two ways financial institutions might define equity to set credit limits. What happens if you default on a home equity loan?

22. **Home Equity Loan.** How are interest rates calculated for the two types of home equity loans? Why do borrowers prefer home equity loans to other loans?

23. **Home Equity Loan.** How can borrowers enjoy tax savings by using a home equity loan? How are these tax savings computed?

24. **Impact of Economy on Home Equity Line of Credit.** Why may a weak economy cause the limit on your home equity line of credit to decline? Why may a strong economy cause the limit on your home equity line of credit to rise?

25. **Peer-to-Peer Lending.** What is peer-to-peer lending? What are the advantages of a peer-to-peer loan?

26. **Prepayment Penalty.** How does a prepayment penalty impact your decision to pay a loan off early?

27. **New Cars.** Explain the advantages and disadvantages of buying a new car instead of a used car.

28. **Buyers Guide.** What type of information is contained in the Buyers Guide?

29. **Student Loan Deferment.** Explain when you might use a deferment on student loans. What are the disadvantages of deferring student loans?

30. **Payday Loans.** What are payday loans? Why should you avoid payday loans as a source of funds?

31. **Alternatives to Payday Loans.** What are some viable alternatives to payday loans?

FINANCIAL PLANNING PROBLEMS

All Financial Planning Problems are available in MyFinanceLab *at http://www.myfinancelab.com.*

1. **Origination Fees.** Jack needs to borrow $1,000 for one year. Bank South will give him the loan at 9%. SunCoast Bank will give him the loan at 7% with a $50 loan origination fee. First National will give him the loan at 6% with a $25 loan origination fee. Determine the total interest and fees Jack will be charged in each case. Which loan should Jack choose?

2. **Amortization.** Beth has just borrowed $5,000 on a four-year loan at 8% simple interest. Complete the amortization table at the bottom of the page for the first five months of the loan.

3. **Add-On Interest Loan.** If Beth had taken the same loan as an add-on interest loan, how would her payments differ? Why is there a difference?

4. **Loan Payments.** Tracy is borrowing $8,000 on a six-year, 11%, add-on interest loan. What will Tracy's monthly payments be?

5. **Loan Interest.** Sharon is considering the purchase of a car. After making the down payment, she will finance $15,500. Sharon is offered three maturities. On a four-year loan, Sharon will pay $371.17 per month. On a five-year loan, Sharon's monthly payments will be $306.99. On a six-year loan, they will be $264.26. Sharon rejects the four-year loan, as it

is not within her budget. How much interest will Sharon pay over the life of the loan on the five-year loan? On the six-year loan? Which should she choose if she bases her decision solely on total interest paid?

6. **Loan Interest.** Refer to question 5. If Sharon had been able to afford the four-year loan, how much interest would she have saved compared to the five-year loan?

7. **Finance Charges.** Bill wants to purchase a new car for $45,000. Bill has no savings, so he needs to finance the entire purchase amount. With no down payment, the interest rate on the loan is 13%, and the maturity of the loan is six years. His monthly payments will be $903.33. Bill's monthly net cash flows are $583.00. Bill also has a credit card with a $10,000 limit and an interest rate of 18%. If Bill uses all his net cash flows to make the monthly payments on the car, how much will he add each month to his credit card balance if he uses it to finance the remainder of the car? What will the finance charges be on his credit card for the first two months that finance charges apply? (Assume that Bill makes no payments on his credit card.)

Payment Number	Beginning Balance	Payment Amount	Applied to Interest	Applied to Principal	New Balance
1	$5,000.00	$122	$33.33	$88.67	$4,911.33
2	a	122	32.74	b	4,822.07
3	4,822.07	c	d	89.85	4,732.22
4	4,732.22	122	e	90.45	f
5	4,641.77	122	30.95	g	h

8. **Credit Limit.** Mary and Marty are interested in obtaining a home equity line of credit. They purchased their house five years ago for $125,000, and it now has a market value of $156,000. Originally, Mary and Marty paid $25,000 down on the house and took out a $100,000 mortgage. The current balance on their mortgage is $72,000. The bank uses 70% of equity in determining the credit limit. What will their credit limit be if the bank bases their credit limit on equity invested and will loan 70% of the equity?

9. **Credit Limit.** Refer to question 8. What will Mary and Marty's credit limit be if the bank uses the market value of equity to determine their credit limit and will loan 70% of the equity?

10. **Tax Savings.** John and Cheryl just borrowed $30,000 on a home equity line of credit. The interest rate for the loan is 6.75% for the entire year, and they took out the loan on May 1. John and Cheryl are in the 28% tax bracket. What will be their tax savings for the first year ending December 31?

11. **Tax Savings.** Noel has a 15% marginal tax rate. If he pays $1,400 in interest on a home equity loan in the first year, what are his tax savings?

12. **Ethical Dilemma.** Fritz and Helga work for a local manufacturing company. Since their marriage five years ago, they have been working extensive overtime, including Sundays and holidays. Fritz and Helga have established a lifestyle based on their overtime earnings. Recently, the company lost two major contracts, and all overtime has been eliminated. As a result, Fritz and Helga are having difficulty paying their bills. Several months ago they began using a local payday loan company so that they could pay their bills on time. The first week they borrowed only a small amount to cover some past due bills. The next week, however, to pay back the loan plus interest, they were left with an even smaller amount to pay bills resulting in a higher payday loan the second week. In paying back the second week's loan, their remaining available funds were further reduced. This cycle continued until they were no longer able to borrow because the repayment plus interest would have exceeded their paychecks. Now Fritz and Helga's cars have been repossessed, their home has been foreclosed on, and they are preparing to file for bankruptcy.

a. Was the payday loan company being ethical in continuing to lend more and more to Fritz and Helga each week?

b. What could Fritz and Helga have done to avoid ultimate financial ruin?

FINANCIAL PLANNING ONLINE EXERCISES

1. Access a new car calculator, and enter the information identifying the make, model, and features of your dream car. Are there any available in your area? What are the price ranges?

2. Access car price quotations online. Determine the trade-in value of your existing car. How does the value differ from the price you paid for it?

PSYCHOLOGY OF PERSONAL FINANCE: Your Car Loan

1. People are tempted to spend much more money on a car than they need to because credit is so easily available. Some students make decisions based on whether they can cover the monthly payment rather than what they need. Describe your own behavior toward financing the purchase of a car.

2. Some consumers might consider purchasing a new car (with a car loan), while using credit cards to cover other purchases, and making only the minimum required payment to the credit card company each month. What is your opinion of this strategy?

WEB SEARCH EXERCISE

You can develop your personal finance skills by conducting an Internet search for related articles. Find a recent online article about personal finance that reinforces one or more concepts covered in this chapter. If your class has an online component, your professor may ask you to post your summary of the article there and provide a link to the article so that other students can access it. If your class is live, your professor may ask you to summarize your application of the article in class. Your professor may assign specific students to complete this assignment or may allow any student to do the assignment on a volunteer basis.

For recent online articles related to this chapter, consider using the following search terms (be sure to include the current year as a search term to ensure that the online articles are recent):

- Applying for a personal loan
- Understanding the personal loan contract
- Car loan
- Buying a car
- Financing a car
- Leasing a car
- Obtaining a student loan
- Obtaining a home equity loan

VIDEO EXERCISE: Applying for a Personal Loan

Go to one of the Web sites that contains video clips (such as http://www.youtube.com), and view some video clips about personal loan applications. You can use search phrases such as "personal loans." Select one video clip on this topic that you would recommend for the other students in your class.

1. Provide the Web link for the video clip.

2. What do you think is the main point of this video clip?

3. How might you change your personal loan application process as a result of watching this video clip?

BUILDING YOUR OWN FINANCIAL PLAN

Loans to finance purchases such as automobiles and homes may be obtained from a variety of sources, each of which has advantages and disadvantages. For example, automobile purchases may be financed through the dealer, a local bank, a credit union, or a finance company. Review all loans that you currently have or anticipate having on graduation, and identify as many sources of these loans as possible. Evaluate the advantages and disadvantages of each source to assist you in determining where to best meet your various borrowing needs.

Go to the worksheets at the end of this chapter to continue building your financial plan.

THE SAMPSONS—A Continuing Case

Assume that the Sampsons have paid off their credit card debt and have also achieved their goal of saving $5,000 that they will use as a down payment on a new car. (They have also been saving an additional $300 per month over the last year for their children's college education.) Sharon's new car is priced at $25,000 plus 5% sales tax. She will receive a $1,000 trade-in credit on her existing car and will make a $5,000 down payment on the new car. The Sampsons would like to allocate a maximum of $500 per month to the loan payments on Sharon's new car. The annual interest rate on a car loan is currently 7%. They would prefer to have a relatively short loan maturity, but cannot afford a monthly payment higher than $500.

Go to the worksheets at the end of this chapter to continue this case.

CHAPTER 9: BUILDING YOUR OWN FINANCIAL PLAN

GOALS

1. Limit your personal financing to a level and maturity that you can pay back on time.
2. For loans you anticipate needing in the future, evaluate the advantages and disadvantages of lenders.
3. Compare the cost of buying and leasing a car.

ANALYSIS

1. Review your personal cash flow statement. How much can you afford to pay each month for personal loans?
2. Identify several prospective lenders for personal loans you may need in the future. What are the advantages and disadvantages of each source with respect to the interest rates offered, method of calculating interest, and other criteria of importance to you?

Loan Evaluation

Loan One:

Description of Loan	Sources for Loan	Advantages of Source	Disadvantages of Source
	1.		
	2.		
	3.		

Loan Two:

Description of Loan	Sources for Loan	Advantages of Source	Disadvantages of Source
	1.		
	2.		
	3.		

Loan Three:

Description of Loan	Sources for Loan	Advantages of Source	Disadvantages of Source
	1.		
	2.		
	3.		

3. Compare the cost of purchasing a car versus leasing a car over a four-year period.

Cost of Purchasing versus Leasing a Car

Cost of Purchasing a Car

Down payment	
Interest rate	
Number of months	
Annual forgone interest on down payment	
Monthly payment on car loan	
Total monthly payments	
Total	
Expected amount to be received when car is sold	
Total cost of purchasing	

Cost of Leasing a Car

Security deposit	
Forgone interest	
Monthly lease payments	
Total monthly payments	
Total cost of leasing	

If you enter this information in the Excel worksheet, the software will create a graphic comparison of purchasing versus leasing.

DECISIONS

1. Report how much you can afford to spend each month on personal loans.

_____

_____

_____

_____

_____

_____

_____

_____

2. Report which lenders you may consider using in the future and why.

_____

_____

_____

_____

_____

_____

_____

_____

3. Is purchasing or leasing a vehicle a better choice for your needs?

_____

_____

_____

_____

_____

_____

_____

_____

CHAPTER 9: THE SAMPSONS—A CONTINUING CASE

CASE QUESTIONS

1. Advise the Sampsons on possible loan maturities. Access an online loan payment calculator. Input information to determine the possible monthly car payments for a three-year (36-month) payment period, a four-year (48-month) payment, and a five-year (60-month) period. Enter the results in the following table:

	Three-Year (36-month) Period	Four-Year (48-month) Period	Five-Year (60-month) Period
Interest rate	7%	7%	7%
Monthly payment			
Total finance payments			
Total payments including the down payment and the trade-in			

2. What are the trade-offs among the three alternative loan maturities?

_____

_____

_____

_____

_____

_____

_____

_____

3. Based on the information on finance payments that you retrieved from the loan payment Web site, advise the Sampsons on the best loan maturity for their needs.

_____

_____

_____

_____

_____

_____

_____

_____

Purchasing and Financing a Home

Andrey Popov/Fotolia

Two years ago, Brian Menke purchased a small home that he could easily afford near the firm where he works. His coworker, Tim Remington, also bought a home. Unlike Brian, Tim would need most of his paycheck to cover the mortgage and expenses of his home, but he thought the purchase would be a good investment.

Because his mortgage payment was relatively low, Brian was able to save money during the next year. Tim, however, was unable to save any money, and when interest rates increased, his mortgage payment increased. Tim suddenly realized he could not afford his home. Because the demand for homes had weakened, housing prices had declined since Tim purchased his home. Tim sold his home, but for $20,000 less than he paid for it. He also had to pay the real estate broker a commission of $16,000. Thus, Tim received $36,000 less from the sale of his home than his purchase price in the previous year.

During the following year, the economy improved and home prices increased. Brian's home was now worth $12,000 more than he had paid for it. But the improved economy did not help Tim, who no longer owned a home.

Financial planning made the difference. Brian's strategy was more conservative, which allowed for the possibility that the economy and market conditions could weaken temporarily. Conversely, Tim did not consider that his mortgage payment could increase and also wrongly assumed that home prices would never decline.

Buying your first home is an important personal financial decision due to the long-term and costly nature of the investment. Your decision on how much to spend and how much to finance will affect your cash flows for years. This chapter describes the fundamentals of purchasing a home and will help you evaluate your first home purchase.

MyFinanceLab helps you master the topics in this chapter and study more efficiently. Visit http://www.myfinancelab.com for more details.

The objectives of this chapter are to:

- Describe the factors that determine how much you can afford when buying a home
- Explain how to select a home to purchase
- Explain how to conduct a valuation of a home
- Describe the transaction costs of purchasing a home
- Describe the characteristics of a fixed-rate mortgage
- Describe the characteristics of an adjustable-rate mortgage
- Show how to compare the costs of purchasing versus renting a home
- Describe special types of mortgages
- Explain the mortgage refinancing decision
- Explain how a mortgage fits within your financial plan

How Much Can You Afford?

Before you go shopping for a home, you first need to determine how much you can afford to spend on a home based on your financial situation. This can save you time, because you can remove homes from consideration if they are beyond what you can afford.

Most individuals pay for a home with a down payment (perhaps 10% to 20% of the purchase price) and obtain a mortgage loan to finance the rest. A mortgage loan is most likely the biggest loan you will ever obtain in your lifetime. You will pay monthly mortgage payments over the life of the loan. The terms for mortgages vary. You will need to decide whether to obtain a fixed-rate or adjustable-rate mortgage and what the maturity of the mortgage should be. Traditionally, mortgages had a fixed interest rate and a maturity of 30 years. Mortgage loan lenders determine how much money they will lend you based on your financial situation and credit history. Various Web sites can estimate the maximum value of a home you can afford based on your financial situation (such as your income and your net worth).

Financial planners suggest that a home price should be no more than 2.5 times the total gross annual household income and that monthly mortgage payments should not exceed 28% of gross monthly income. They also suggest that all the household's monthly debt payments (including the mortgage) should be no more than about 40% of the total monthly gross income. However, these generalizations do not apply to everyone, as other financial information and spending habits of the homeowners should also be considered.

Affordable Down Payment

You can determine your maximum down payment by estimating the market value of the assets that you are willing to convert to cash for a down payment and for transaction costs (such as closing costs) when obtaining a mortgage. Be sure to maintain some funds for liquidity purposes to cover unanticipated bills.

Affordable Monthly Mortgage Payments

How large a mortgage payment can you afford? Refer to your cash flow statement to determine how much net cash flow you have to make a mortgage payment. If you purchase a home, you will no longer have a rent payment, so that money can be used as part of the mortgage payment. You should also be aware, however, that owning a home entails some periodic expenses (such as property taxes, homeowner's insurance, and home repairs). You should not plan to purchase a home that will absorb all your current excess cash inflows. The larger your mortgage payments, the less you can add to your savings or other investments.

PSYCHOLOGY of Personal Finance

Lessons Learned from Others' Mistakes Once some home buyers determine the maximum that they can afford, they tend to view that maximum as the amount that they should spend. But by spending the maximum, they may have no funds available for unanticipated expenses that could occur.

In fact, another behavioral characteristic of home buyers is that they tend to buy a home for more money than they originally planned to spend. This occurs because as they start looking at homes for sale, they commonly see a home with desirable features that is priced beyond the amount they had planned to spend. They may use the following reasoning to justify spending more than they had intended to purchase the house:

- The more expensive house may not require any additional down payment if they just obtain a larger mortgage.

- They can possibly obtain a second job to afford the higher mortgage payment.

- They will benefit from buying the more expensive home because if prices rise over time, more expensive homes will likely rise in value by a greater degree.

Each of these reasons is questionable. First, the home buyers may be able to obtain a larger mortgage, but that means more debt, and that they will need to make larger monthly mortgage payments. Second, obtaining an extra job just to afford a more expensive home might reduce the enjoyment of that home. Third, home values might rise over time, but they could also decline over time, and if the values drop, the more expensive homes will likely suffer a larger decline in value.

Like many purchasing decisions, the buying of a home provides immediate satisfaction, and the pain of paying for it is not felt until later. Therefore, home buyers can find many reasons to spend more money on a home than what they can afford. By the time home buyers feel the pain from paying off the debt that was needed to make the initial purchase, it is too late to reverse their decision. Normally, home buyers cannot easily sell a home that they just purchased, and even if they could, the transaction costs (discussed later in this chapter) are substantial. Therefore, home buyers should carefully assess how much they can afford to spend on a home and should use that amount as a maximum when reviewing homes for sale.

EXAMPLE

Stephanie Spratt just received an unexpected bonus and a promotion from her employer. After assessing her financial situation, she decides that she may want to purchase a home in the near future. She has about $15,000 in liquid assets for use toward a down payment and transaction costs. She evaluates her personal cash flows. Because she would no longer need to pay rent for her apartment, she can afford to allocate $900 a month to monthly mortgage payments plus home insurance. She begins to look at homes for sale in the range of $90,000 to $110,000. Once she identifies a home that she may want to purchase, she will obtain estimates of the required down payment, the transaction costs, and the mortgage payment.

ECONOMIC IMPACT

When you consider how much you can afford, consider the economic conditions and stability of your job situation. If economic conditions weaken, will your job be affected? Your mortgage payments extend for a long period of time, so you should assess the likelihood that you will continue to earn sufficient income each month over the life of the mortgage to make mortgage payments. Although you could obtain another job if you are laid off, you might not be able to earn the same level of income. Thus, you may want to use a conservative estimate of your future income when determining the mortgage payment you can afford, just to make sure that you can afford the home even if economic conditions deteriorate.

Selecting a Home

Buying a home may be the single biggest investment you will ever make, so the decision should be taken very seriously. You should carefully consider several factors. Evaluate the homes for sale in your target area to determine the typical price range and features. Once you decide on a realistic price range, identify a specific home that you desire. You can compare the cost of buying that home to the cost of renting. This way, you can weigh the extra costs against the benefits of home ownership.

An alternative to purchasing a house is to purchase a condominium. In a condominium, individuals own units of a housing complex, but jointly own the surrounding land and common areas (such as parking lots) and amenities (such as a swimming pool). The benefits of a condominium are somewhat different from those of a house. Whereas a house is detached, units in a condominium are typically attached, so there is less privacy. Condominium expenses are shared among unit owners, but the owners of a house pay for expenses on their own. Nevertheless, the factors to be considered when selecting or financing a house are also relevant when purchasing a condominium. Thus, the following discussion will use *home* rather than *house* to indicate that it also applies to a condominium.

Relying on a Real Estate Agent

You may consider advice from a real estate broker when you assess homes, decide whether to buy a home, or determine which home to purchase. Yet you should not rely completely on the advice of real estate brokers because they have a vested interest: They earn a commission only if you purchase a home through them. You should consider their input, but make decisions that meet your needs and preferences. A good real estate broker will ask you about your preferences and suggest appropriate homes.

Financial Planning
ONLINE

Go to:
http://www.calculatorweb
.com

To get:
An estimate of how much money you could borrow to finance a home, based on your income and other financial information.

Financial Planning
ONLINE

Go to:
The real estate section of Yahoo.com

To get:
Sales prices of homes on a street in a city that you specify over a recent period. It can also provide a list of homes in the city you specify that sold within a certain price range.

Using Online Realtor Services

Increasingly, online services are being used to facilitate home purchases. Web sites such as http://www.ziprealty.com allow sellers to present detailed information about their home in a database that is made accessible to potential home buyers. These types of Web sites are sometimes limited to particular cities. The realty company sponsoring the Web site may provide services to complete a contract, and the commission for using the online service is less than the traditional commission charged by real estate agents.

Other online services allow sellers to list their home in a database, without providing other real estate–related services. The contract would have to be completed by the buyer and seller without the help of a real estate agent. The advantage of this type of service is that it charges lower commissions than a traditional full-service real estate company. Some of these online services are actually subsidiaries of the traditional full-service real estate companies.

Criteria Used to Select a Home

The following list identifies the most important factors to consider when selecting a home.

- **Home Price Relative to Your Budget.** Stay within your budget. Avoid purchasing a home that you cannot afford. Although your favorite home may have expensive new appliances and a large yard, it may not be worth the stress of struggling to make the mortgage payments.

    If you have a poor credit rating, you should think carefully before purchasing a home. Even if you are able to obtain a mortgage, you might be better off paying down the debts that have caused you to have a poor credit rating. Then, after you have paid off your debts and saved enough to make a larger down payment, you can consider purchasing a home.

- **Convenient Location.** Focus on homes in a convenient area so that you can minimize commuting time to work or travel time to other activities. You may save 10 or more hours of travel time a week as well as saving on gasoline costs.

- **Maintenance.** Some homes built by well-known construction companies have lower repair bills than others. In addition, newer homes tend to need fewer repairs than older homes. A home with a large yard requires more maintenance.

  In condominiums, residents share common areas, such as a swimming pool or tennis court. Normally, the residents pay a fixed monthly fee to cover the costs of maintaining the common areas. In addition, they may be assessed an extra fee to maintain the structure of the condominium, such as a new roof or other repairs.

- **School System.** If you have children, the reputation of the school system is very important. Even if you do not have children, the resale value of your house benefits from a good school system.

- **Insurance.** When you own a home, you need to purchase homeowner's insurance, which covers the home in case of burglary or damage. The cost of insurance varies among homes. It is higher for more expensive homes and for homes in high-risk areas (such as flood zones) because it costs the insurer more to replace parts of the home that are damaged.

- **Taxes.** Taxes are imposed on homes to pay for local services, such as the local school system and the local park system. Taxes vary substantially among locations. Annual property taxes are often between 1% and 2% of the market value of the home. Thus, the tax on a $100,000 home is typically between $1,000 and $2,000 per year. Property taxes are tax-deductible if you itemize deductions on your income tax return. You can deduct them from your income when determining your federal income tax.

- **Homeowner's Association.** Some homes are connected with homeowner's associations, which set guidelines for the homes and may even assess fees that are used to hire security guards or to maintain common grounds within the area. The monthly fees charged by some homeowner's associations are very high and should be considered when buying a home.

- **Resale Value.** The resale value of a home is highly dependent on its location. Most homes with similar features within a specific subdivision or neighborhood are in the same range. Although home prices in a given subdivision tend to move in the same direction, the price movements can vary substantially among homes. For example, homes in a subdivision that are within walking distance of a school may be worth more than comparable houses several miles from the school.

  You cannot perfectly predict the future resale value of a home, but you can evaluate today's resale value of similar homes in that location that were sold years ago. Information about home prices is provided on numerous Web sites. Be aware, however, that the rate of increase in home prices in previous years does not necessarily serve as a good predictor of the future.

  Keep in mind that when you use a real estate agent to sell a home (as most people do), you will pay the agent a commission that is usually about 6% of the selling price. Thus, if you resell your home for $100,000, you will probably pay a commission of about $6,000 and therefore receive $94,000. The buyer of a home does not pay a commission.

- **Personal Preferences.** In addition to the general criteria just described, you will have your own personal preferences regarding features such as the number of bedrooms, size of the kitchen, and size of the yard.

Searching for a Home

Application:

The Real Estate by Zillow app (by Zillow.com) allows you to review homes for sale at your present location and displays photos of homes, sales prices, and other details. You can also review homes for sale in other remote locations that you identify.

To Find It:

Search for the "Zillow" app on your mobile device.

Valuation of a Home

You should use the criteria described previously to screen your list of desirable homes so that you can spend time analyzing the advantages and disadvantages of three or four particular homes. You will probably find some homes that meet all your criteria, but are simply overpriced and therefore should not be considered.

Market Analysis

You can conduct a market analysis, in which you estimate the price of a home based on the prices of similar homes in the area. The market value can be estimated by multiplying the number of square feet in a home by the average price per square foot of similar homes in the area. A real estate broker or appraiser may also provide you with a valuation.

EXAMPLE

Stephanie Spratt has identified a house that she is interested in purchasing. She finds the selling prices of three other homes that were just sold in the same area, with a similar lot size, and about the same age as the home that she is considering. The purchase prices are shown in the second column of Exhibit 10.1.

She recognizes that homes in an area vary in price due to their size. She determines the price per square foot by dividing each home's price by the square feet, as shown in the third column. Then she determines that the average price per square foot of the three homes is $88, as shown at the bottom of the exhibit. Because the home that Stephanie wants to purchase has 1,300 square feet, she estimates its market value to be:

$$\text{Market Value of Home} = \text{Average Price per Square Foot} \times \text{Square Feet of Home}$$
$$= \$88 \times 1,300$$
$$= \$114,400$$

She estimates the price of this home at $114,400. Although she will consider other factors, this initial analysis gives her some insight into what the home is worth. For example, the real estate broker told her that the owner of the home has already moved and wants to sell it quickly. Stephanie decides that she would be willing to purchase the home at a price of $108,000. But before negotiating the price with the seller, she needs to determine the costs that she would incur as a result of purchasing the home.

EXHIBIT 10.1   Using a Market Analysis to Purchase a Home

House Size	Price	Price per Square Foot
1,300 square feet	$120,000	$120,000/1,300 = $92
1,200 square feet	$104,100	$104,100/1,200 = $87
1,100 square feet	$94,000	$94,000/1,100 = $85
Average price per square foot = ($92 + $87 + $85)/3 = $88		

Economic Impact on Home Values

ECONOMIC IMPACT

Economic conditions affect the valuations of homes that are estimated by market valuations. When economic conditions improve, people are more confident that their income will be stable or may even grow over time, and they are more willing to purchase homes. As the demand for homes increases, the prices of homes rise. The average price per square foot of homes rises, and so the market analysis of a home results in higher valuations. Conversely, when economic conditions weaken, people become more concerned that their income might be eliminated (due to layoffs) or reduced over time. They are less willing to purchase homes, and the decline in demand for homes causes the prices of homes to decline. The average price per square foot of homes declines, and so the market analysis of a home results in lower valuations.

The impact of the economy on home prices is illustrated in Exhibit 10.2. The initial momentum is the higher income levels during a strong economy, which can encourage some renters to purchase homes. In addition, a strong economy makes people feel more confident that their jobs are secure and that they will be able to afford mortgage payments over a long period of time. It is also easier for buyers to obtain financing in a strong economy because financial institutions are more willing to provide mortgage loans, as they are more confident that the borrowers will earn sufficient income to repay their mortgage loans. The strong desire to purchase homes causes the total demand for homes to exceed the number of homes that are for sale. Homeowners are less willing to sell their homes under favorable conditions when they are confident that they can still afford to make mortgage payments. The homeowners who are willing to sell their homes can ask relatively high prices and are still likely to sell their homes.

During a weak economy, the opposite effects occur. The initial momentum is the lower income levels during a weak economy, which causes people to spend their money more conservatively. Renters may not consider purchasing homes under these conditions, as layoffs commonly occur when the economy is weak. Because their jobs are not secure, they are less confident that they could afford mortgage payments over a long period of time. Financial institutions are less willing to provide mortgage loans, as they are less confident that the borrowers will earn sufficient income to repay their mortgage loans over time. Some homeowners need to sell their homes because their income has been reduced or because they were laid off.

Financial Planning ONLINE

Go to:
http://www.realtor.com

To get:
A listing of homes for sale in an area that you specify and homes in the price and size range that you specify.

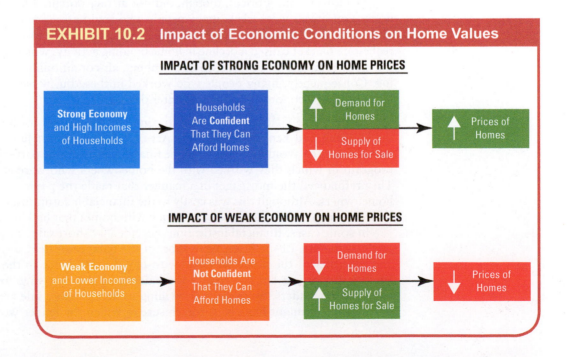

EXHIBIT 10.2   Impact of Economic Conditions on Home Values

IMPACT OF STRONG ECONOMY ON HOME PRICES

Strong Economy and High Incomes of Households → Households Are **Confident** That They Can Afford Homes → ↑ Demand for Homes / ↓ Supply of Homes for Sale → ↑ Prices of Homes

IMPACT OF WEAK ECONOMY ON HOME PRICES

Weak Economy and Lower Incomes of Households → Households Are **Not Confident** That They Can Afford Homes → ↓ Demand for Homes / ↑ Supply of Homes for Sale → ↓ Prices of Homes

Impact of the Financial Crisis on Home Values

During 2003–2006, economic conditions were favorable, and home builders were building many new homes. Mortgage lenders were aggressively attempting to find buyers for these homes because not only could they earn interest on the loans provided, but they also could earn fees from the mortgage application process. Some mortgage lenders were providing subprime mortgages, which are mortgage loans to borrowers without sufficient income or a down payment to qualify for prime mortgages. Mortgage lenders were willing to provide these mortgages because they could charge a higher interest rate and additional upfront fees to compensate for the higher level of risk. If the borrowers defaulted on the mortgage loans, the mortgage lender could take ownership of the homes. Mortgage lenders were optimistic that home prices would rise or at least not decline, and therefore that the homes would serve as effective collateral in the event that a borrower defaulted on the loan. Thus, they were willing to take the risk of extending subprime loans.

Mortgage Defaults As interest rates increased in 2006, the interest rate on variable-rate mortgages increased, and some home buyers could no longer afford their payments. Many others defaulted on their subprime mortgages because they could not afford the homes; in fact, many should not have qualified for a mortgage in the first place. Some mortgages that were insured against default by a private insurer defaulted because some insurance companies that insured mortgages did not have sufficient funds to cover their obligations. By January 2009, about 10% of all homeowners were late on their mortgage payments or had defaulted on their loans. About 25% of all outstanding subprime mortgages had late payments of at least 30 days. Many financial institutions were involved in providing these mortgage loans, and they experienced large losses or even bankruptcy.

Impact on Home Prices These conditions resulted in the financial crisis of 2008–2009. Many homeowners who could not afford the homes they were living in were trying to sell their homes. In some cases, the lenders who provided the mortgages repossessed the homes because the homeowners were no longer making their mortgage payments. These lenders, however, were also struggling to sell the homes that they had repossessed. The supply of homes for sale was very large, but the demand for homes was low. Consequently, the only way that homeowners could sell their homes was by lowering their price to a level that might attract a potential buyer. These conditions caused home prices to decline substantially. In some areas, home prices declined by more than 50%.

The lower homes prices, though, did not attract potential buyers. Because the economic conditions were weak, many people who could afford to buy a home were afraid that home prices might decline even more or that they might lose their jobs. This slower real estate market caused a decline in home building activity, which decreased the demand for many related businesses, such as plumbing, air-conditioning, roofing, and landscaping. Consequently, many people who worked in these businesses lost their jobs, which weakened the economy to an even greater degree.

Resolving the Crisis In an effort to stimulate the market for homes and mortgages, the Housing and Economic Recovery Act of 2008, passed in July 2008, allowed some homeowners to avoid foreclosure. Some financial institutions participated in a voluntary program in which they worked with the homeowners who were at risk of foreclosure. They refinanced the mortgages in a manner that made the payments more affordable to homeowners. Although this was costly to the financial institutions, it was less costly than if foreclosure occurred and they were stuck with homes that had lost much of their value.

In some cases, financial institutions accepted a "short sale" arrangement—the proceeds of the sale of the home were short of the balance of debt owed on the mortgage, and the seller of the home was unable to pay the difference to the lender. That is, the lending institution did not receive the balance of the mortgage loan that it had provided. Some lenders, however, were willing to accept short sale arrangements because the alternative might have been foreclosure in which the lender would have to reclaim the home and sell it. The costs to the financial institutions associated with the process of foreclosure and selling the home might be greater than the loss incurred by accepting a short sale arrangement. The U.S. government also created several programs to help financial institutions that suffered major losses due to the large number of defaults on their mortgage loans.

Lessons from the Crisis Even with the government's efforts to help financial institutions and homeowners, the housing market remained very weak in 2008 and 2009. Many homeowners who had purchased homes during the 2007 peak of the housing boom never recovered the losses they incurred. Overall, the financial crisis illustrated how allowing unqualified mortgage applicants to qualify for mortgages could ultimately hurt the mortgage market. Second, it illuminated the risk of owning a home, as real estate prices can decline substantially under some conditions. Third, it showed how economic conditions have a strong impact on the demand for homes and therefore on the prices of homes. Fourth, it demonstrated how housing conditions have a strong impact on the economy because so many jobs are connected to the construction of new homes.

Correcting the Mortgage Application Process The government implemented the Financial Reform Act (also called the Dodd–Frank Wall Street Reform and Consumer Protection Act) of 2010 to stabilize the mortgage markets. One of the provisions of the act requires that financial institutions granting mortgages verify the income, job status, and credit history of mortgage applicants before approving mortgage applications. This provision is to ensure that mortgage applicants show proof that they qualify for a mortgage before a mortgage loan is granted.

In 2014, the Consumer Financial Protection Bureau (CFPB) issued new rules to strengthen the provisions of the 2010 act. The rules define a new class of mortgages called Qualified Mortgages, which are designed to be safer and easier to understand than many of the loans extended before the financial crisis. To issue Qualified Mortgages, lenders must assess a borrower's ability to repay the loan and must ensure that the borrower's total monthly debt-to-income ratio, including mortgage payments, is not higher than 43%. Qualified Mortgages cannot have risky features such as interest-only payments (such loans were common before the financial crisis). The rules also limit the fees that lenders can charge on Qualified Mortgages. In addition, the rules provide more safeguards for borrowers who fall behind in their mortgage payments. Lenders have an incentive to make loans that meet the requirements of Qualified Mortgages because they receive certain legal protections if the borrower fails to repay the loan.

Effects of Business Activity and Zoning Laws

The value of a home is also dependent on the demand for homes in that area or subdivision, which can vary in response to business activity or zoning laws.

Business Activity Nearby When a large firm moves into an area, people hired for jobs at that firm search for homes nearby. As a result, demand for homes in the area increases, and home prices may rise as well. Conversely, when a large firm closes its facilities, home prices in that area may decline as homeowners who worked there attempt to sell their homes. The large supply of homes for sale relative to demand may cause homeowners to lower their price to find a willing buyer.

Zoning Laws Locations are zoned for industrial use or residential use. When zoning laws for a location change, its desirability may be affected. Homes near areas that have just been zoned for industrial use become less desirable. Therefore, the demand for homes in these areas may decline, causing prices of homes to decline as well.

Zoning laws also change for school systems. The value of a subdivision can change substantially in response to a change in the public schools that the resident children would attend. Proximity to schools can increase home values, whereas increased distance from schools often lowers home values.

Obtaining a Second Opinion on Your Valuation

If your valuation leads you to believe that a particular home is undervalued, you may want to get a second opinion before you try to purchase that home. If you are using a real estate broker to help you find a home, that broker may conduct a valuation of the home and offer suggestions about the price that you should be willing to offer. Be aware, however, that although brokers are experienced at valuing homes, some brokers provide a valuation that is intended to serve the seller rather than the buyer. That is, they may overestimate the value so that potential buyers are convinced that the home is worth buying. In this way, the brokers can ensure that a home will sell and that they will receive a commission. Although many real estate brokers are honest and will provide an unbiased estimate, you should always conduct your own valuation and carefully assess the broker's valuation.

Negotiating a Price

Once you have finished your valuation and are convinced that you should buy a particular home, you need to negotiate a price with the seller of the home by making an offer. Some homes are initially priced above the price that the seller will accept. As with any investment, you want to make sure that you do not pay more than you have to for a home.

You may consider the advice of your real estate broker on the offer that you should make. Most sellers are willing to accept less than their original asking price. Once you decide on an offering price, you can submit an offer in the form of a contract to buy the home, which must be approved by the seller. Your real estate broker takes the contract to the seller and serves as the intermediary between you and the seller during the negotiation process.

The seller may accept your offer, reject it, or make a counteroffer. If the asking price is $100,000 and you offer $90,000, the seller may reject that offer but make a counteroffer of, say, $96,000. Then the decision reverts to you. You can agree, reject that offer, or revise the contract again. For example, you may counter by offering $94,000. The contract negotiation can go back and forth until the buyer and seller either come to an agreement or decide that it is no longer worthwhile to pursue a possible agreement. The contract stipulates not only the price, but also other conditions that are requested by the buyer, such as repairs to be completed by the seller and the date when the buyer will be able to move into the home.

An offer is commonly contingent on an inspection of the home. You should always have the home inspected, even if it is a newly constructed house. The inspector will determine the condition of the plumbing; the electrical, cooling, and heating systems; and the roof, siding, and other aspects of the house. An inspection for termites and other pests may also be needed. If the inspection discovers some major problems, you may want to withdraw your offer or negotiate a lower price to enable you to pay for repairs. Lenders may require a certificate of inspection before they will extend a loan.

Transaction Costs of Purchasing a Home

Once you have started the offer process, you should begin applying for a mortgage from a financial institution, or you may even start this process before making the offer so that you are sure that the financing will be available. The loan application process requires that you summarize your financial condition, including your income, your assets, and your liabilities. You will need to provide proof of income, such as recent paycheck stubs and bank statements. The lender will check your financial condition by contacting your employer to verify your employment and to learn your present salary.

In addition to applying for a mortgage, you will need to plan to cover the transaction costs of purchasing the home. These include the down payment and closing costs.

Down Payment

When you purchase a home, you use your own money to make a down payment and pay the remaining amount owed with financing. Your down payment represents your equity investment in the home.

For a conventional mortgage, a lender typically requires a down payment of 10% to 20% of the home's selling price. The lender expects you to cover a portion of the purchase price with your own money because the home serves as collateral to back the loan. The lending institution bears the risk that you may possibly default on the loan. If you are unable to make your mortgage payments, the lender can take ownership of the home and sell it to obtain the funds that you owe.

If the home's value declines over time, however, a creditor may not obtain all the funds that it initially lent. Your down payment provides a cushion in case the value of the home declines. The lender could sell the home for less than the original purchase price and still recover the entire mortgage loan.

With government-backed loans, a traditional lender extends the loan, but the government insures it in the event of default. Government-backed mortgages may require lower down payments and may even specify lower interest rates than conventional mortgages. Government-backed mortgages are often backed by the Federal Housing Administration (FHA) or the Veterans Administration (VA). To qualify for federally insured mortgages, borrowers must satisfy various requirements imposed by the guarantors. The FHA loans enable low- or middle-income individuals to obtain mortgage financing. The VA loans are extended to military veterans. Both FHA and VA loans are assumable by the buyer in the event that the homeowner who initially qualified for the mortgage loan decides to sell the home.

The FHA will guarantee loans where the borrower makes a down payment as small as 3.5% of the purchase price. It also will guarantee loans where the borrower has a FICO score lower than 580, although a larger down payment is required. Without the FHA guarantee, a lender would probably require a FICO score of at least 620, depending on the borrower's other characteristics and the amount to be borrowed. Even if the FHA will guarantee a loan for a borrower with a low FICO score, the lender makes the final decision of whether to extend the loan.

If you obtain an FHA or VA loan, you will need to maintain an escrow account. Your monthly mortgage payment will include an additional payment for your home insurance and your property taxes. The mortgage lender that receives your monthly mortgage payment will place these extra additional payments in your escrow account so that it can pay for your insurance and property taxes on an annual basis.

Private Mortgage Insurance If your down payment is less than 20% of the selling price of the home you are buying, you will very likely have to purchase private mortgage insurance (PMI). PMI insures the lender in the event that the borrower (homeowner) does not repay the loan. PMI is always required for FHA-guaranteed loans when the down payment is less than 20%. PMI can add substantially to the cost of a mortgage. Its cost typically ranges from 0.5% to 1% of the amount borrowed, which represents an annual cost between $500 and $1,000 for a $100,000 mortgage. The FHA frequently revises the rates for PMI on loans it guarantees, so check for the current rates if you are considering obtaining an FHA-guaranteed loan. Recent FHA rates were 0.85% of the loan amount for the annual premium plus a 1.75% upfront fee added to the loan amount. Thus, a person who obtained a mortgage of $100,000 would actually have to repay that amount plus the $1,750 upfront fee, or $101,750, in addition to paying the premium of about $850 per year ($71 per month). The cost of PMI for homeowners was tax-deductible in some periods and could be tax-deductible in the future if Congress renews that law.

You have to pay PMI until the principal balance of your mortgage has been reduced to 80% of the original loan (the equivalent of making a 20% down payment). For some FHA-guaranteed loans, PMI is required for the duration of the loan. If your home increases substantially in value in the years after you purchase it, you may be able to have

PMI terminated based on the new appraised value of your home. If you refinance your loan at a lower interest rate, you may also be able to shorten the period in which PMI payments are required.

When you consider purchasing a home, you should include PMI in your calculations if your down payment will be less than 20% of the selling price of the home. You may decide to cut back on your vacation plans or other discretionary spending so that you can make a larger down payment.

In some cases, a financial institution that grants a mortgage will cover the private mortgage insurance fee itself rather than charge the homeowner. It might charge a slightly higher interest rate on the mortgage to compensate for paying the private mortgage insurance itself. Thus, a financial institution that offers a mortgage rate of 5% when covering the private mortgage insurance itself might alternatively offer a slightly lower rate to homeowners if they pay the private mortgage insurance themselves.

Closing Costs

A borrower incurs various fees in the mortgage loan application process. These fees are often referred to as closing costs. The most important fees are identified here. Under the CFPB's new rules, a loan over $100,000 cannot be a Qualified Mortgage if the fees associated with it exceed 3% of the loan amount.

Loan Application Fee
When applying for a mortgage loan, you may be charged an application fee by the lender. The fee typically ranges from $100 to $500.

points
A fee charged by the lender to reduce the interest rate when a mortgage loan is provided; stated as a percentage of the mortgage loan amount.

Points
Lenders sometimes charge a fee commonly referred to as discount points or **points** to reduce the interest rate on a loan. The more points you pay, the lower the interest rate on the loan. Points are stated as a percentage of the loan amount and often are between 1% and 2% of the mortgage loan. If you are charged 2 points when you obtain a mortgage in the amount of $100,000, a fee of $2,000 (computed as 2% × 100,000) is charged at the time the loan is granted. Points are tax-deductible, so the expense can be deducted from your income when determining your taxable income. Lenders do not always charge points, so you should shop around to see if you can find a lender who will offer you a similar interest rate without charging points.

Loan Origination Fee
Lenders may also charge a loan origination fee, which is usually 1% of the mortgage amount. If you are charged a 1% origination fee on a $100,000 mortgage, the fee is $1,000 (computed as 1% × $100,000). Many lenders allow homeowners to select among different fee structures, so you may be able to pay a lower loan origination fee if you accept a slightly higher interest rate. Some lenders may not charge an origination fee, but they charge a higher interest rate on the mortgage instead.

Appraisal Fee
An appraisal is used to estimate the market value of the home and thus protects the financial institution's interests. If you are unable to make your monthly payments, the financial institution can sell the home to recoup the mortgage loan that it provided. The appraisal fee commonly ranges between $200 and $500.

Title Search and Insurance
An agreement to purchase a home from a current owner (as opposed to a new home from a developer) typically involves various transaction costs for a title search and insurance. A title search is conducted by the mortgage company to ensure that the home or property is owned by the seller. Title insurance provides you with protection in the event that persons other than the seller show evidence that they hold the actual deed of ownership to the property. It also protects you in the event that there are other liabilities attached to the home that were not discovered during the title search.

Both the closing costs and the down payment are due at the time of the closing. Closing costs can be added to the mortgage amount. During the closing, the title for the home is transferred to the buyer, the seller is paid in full, and the buyer takes possession of the home.

EXAMPLE

Recall that Stephanie Spratt considers making an offer of $108,000 on a house. She wants to determine the transaction costs. She is planning to make a down payment of $8,000 and borrow $100,000. She called York Financial Institution for information about obtaining a mortgage loan. She learned that if she applied for a $100,000 mortgage, York would charge the following:

- 1 point
- 1% origination fee
- $300 for an appraisal
- $200 application fee
- $400 for a title search and title insurance
- $200 for other fees

York's offer also acknowledges that it is willing to cover the private mortgage insurance payments.

Based on the details above, Stephanie would incur the following closing costs:

Points	(1% of mortgage)	$ 1,000
Origination Fee	(1% of mortgage)	1,000
Appraisal Fee		300
Application Fee		200
Title Search and Insurance		400
Other Fees		200
Total		$3,100

Stephanie will need a down payment of $8,000 and $3,100 in closing costs to purchase the home.

Financing with Fixed-Rate Mortgages

fixed-rate mortgage
A mortgage in which a fixed interest rate is specified until maturity.

A **fixed-rate mortgage** specifies a fixed interest rate that is constant for the life of the mortgage. When homeowners expect that interest rates will rise, they tend to prefer fixed-rate mortgages because their mortgage payments will be sheltered from the rising market interest rates. Many other types of mortgages are available, but the traditional fixed-rate 30-year mortgage is still popular. The interest rate charged on 30-year fixed-rate mortgages is typically related to other long-term interest rates (such as the 30-year Treasury bond rate) at the time that the mortgage is created. You can access various Web sites to obtain a general summary of prevailing mortgage rates, but rates vary among financial institutions. If you sell a home before the mortgage is paid off, you can use a portion of the proceeds from selling the home to pay off the mortgage. Alternatively, it may be possible for the buyer to assume your mortgage under some conditions.

Financial Planning
ONLINE

Go to:
The mortgage rate section of Yahoo.com (located within the Finance section)

To get:
Average mortgage rates for specific regions and states.

Amortization Table

Your monthly mortgage payment for a fixed-rate mortgage is based on an amortization schedule. This schedule discloses the monthly payment that you will make, based on a specific mortgage amount, a fixed interest rate level, and a maturity.

Allocation of the Mortgage Payment Each monthly mortgage payment represents a partial equity payment that pays a portion of the principal of the loan and an interest payment.

EXAMPLE

Stephanie Spratt decides to review mortgage Web sites to estimate her monthly mortgage payments. One Web site asks her to input the mortgage amount she desires and the interest rate that she expects to pay on a 30-year mortgage. She inputs $100,000 as the mortgage amount and 5% as the interest rate. The Web site then provides her with an amortization schedule, which is summarized in Exhibit 10.3. This exhibit shows how her mortgage payments would be allocated to paying off principal versus interest. Notice how the initial payments are allocated mostly to interest, with a relatively small amount used to pay off the principal. For example, for month 2, $121 of her payment is applied to the principal, while $416 goes to pay the interest expense. Initially, when the amount of principal is large, most of her payment is needed to cover the interest owed. Exhibit 10.3 shows that as time passes, the proportion of the payment allocated to equity increases. Notice that by month 360 (which represents the last month of the 30-year mortgage period), $534 of the payment is applied to principal and $3 to interest.

Notice, too, that her balance after 100 months is $87,086. This means that over a period of more than eight years, Stephanie would pay off less than $13,000 of the equity in her home, or less than 13% of the original mortgage amount. After 200 months (two-thirds of the life of the 30-year mortgage), her mortgage balance would be almost $66,000, which means she would have paid off only about $34,000 of the $100,000 mortgage (just slightly more than one-third of the original mortgage amount).

The amount of Stephanie's annual mortgage payments that would be allocated to paying off the principal is shown in Exhibit 10.4. In the first year, she would pay off only $1,475 of the principal, while the rest of her mortgage payments ($4,967) in the first year would be used to pay interest. This information is very surprising to Stephanie, so she reviews the mortgage situation further to determine if it is possible to build equity in the home more quickly.

EXHIBIT 10.3   Amortization Schedule for a 30-Year (360-Month) Fixed-Rate Mortgage for $100,000 at a 5% Interest Rate

Month	Payment	Principal	Interest	Balance
1	$537	$120	$417	$99,880
2	537	121	416	99,343
10	537	125	412	98,775
⋮				
25	537	133	404	96,841
⋮				
49	537	147	390	93,483
⋮				
100	537	173	364	87,086
⋮				
200	537	263	275	65,822
⋮				
360	537	534	3	0

Note: Numbers are rounded to the nearest dollar.

EXHIBIT 10.4   Allocation of Principal Versus Interest Paid per Year on a $100,000 30-Year Mortgage

Year	Principal Paid in That Year	Interest Paid in That Year
1	$1,475	$4,967
2	1,551	4,890
3	1,631	4,812
4	1,713	4,728
6	1,894	4,548
8	2,092	4,350
10	2,312	4,131
12	2,555	3,888
15	2,966	3,191
17	3,278	3,164
20	3,807	2,635
22	4,207	2,235
24	4,629	1,793
26	5,136	1,286
28	5,675	767
30	6,271	171

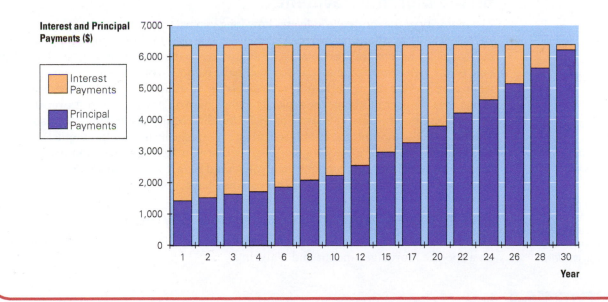

Impact of the Mortgage Amount on the Monthly Payment

The larger the mortgage amount, the larger your monthly payments will be for a given interest rate and maturity. Exhibit 10.5 shows the monthly payment based on a 30-year mortgage and a 5% interest rate for different mortgage amounts. Notice the change in the mortgage payment for larger mortgage amounts. For example, the monthly mortgage payment for an $80,000 mortgage is $429, while the monthly payment for a $120,000 mortgage is $644.

EXHIBIT 10.5	Monthly Mortgage Payments Based on Different Mortgage Amounts (30-Year Fixed-Rate Mortgage; 5% Interest Rate)
Mortgage Amount	**Monthly Mortgage Payment**
$60,000	$322
80,000	429
100,000	537
120,000	644
140,000	751
160,000	859
180,000	966

Impact of the Interest Rate on the Monthly Payment

Given the large amount of funds that you may borrow to finance a home, you should make every effort to obtain a mortgage loan that has a low interest rate. The lower the interest rate on the mortgage, the smaller the monthly mortgage payment. Even a slight increase (such as 0.5%) in the interest rate increases your monthly mortgage payment.

Impact of the Mortgage Maturity on the Monthly Payment

The maturity of the mortgage indicates how long you will take to complete your financing payments and pay off the mortgage. At that point, you own the home outright. The 15-year mortgage has become very popular as an alternative to the 30-year mortgage. The advantage of a 15-year mortgage is that you will have paid off your mortgage after 15 years, whereas a 30-year mortgage requires payments for an additional 15 years. Monthly payments on a 15-year mortgage are typically higher, but you pay less interest over the life of the loan and build equity at a faster pace. By building equity faster, you may also be able to terminate the monthly premiums for private mortgage insurance more quickly.

The advantage of a 30-year mortgage is that you have smaller monthly payments for a given mortgage loan amount than you would for a 15-year mortgage. The monthly payments may be more affordable, and you may have more liquidity.

Estimating the Monthly Mortgage Payment

You can use mortgage loan Web sites to obtain estimates of your monthly payments based on a specific mortgage amount and maturity.

Financial Planning
ONLINE

Go to:
The consumer interest rates section of http://www.bloomberg.com (in the markets section)

To get:
The monthly payment of a fixed-rate mortgage based on the loan amount, interest rate, and the loan maturity.

EXAMPLE

Stephanie Spratt wants to estimate her monthly mortgage payment on a $100,000 fixed-rate mortgage based on several interest rate scenarios for 15- and 30-year maturities, as shown in Exhibit 10.6. At an interest rate of 5%, the monthly payment on the 30-year mortgage would be $537. At an interest rate of 6%, the monthly payment on the 30-year mortgage would be $600, or $63 more per month. Next, Stephanie evaluates the payments for a 15-year term. She believes she can obtain a loan at a 5% interest rate on either maturity, so she focuses on the difference in monthly payments pertaining to that rate.

Although the monthly payment is more for the 15-year mortgage, the difference is not as large as Stephanie had expected. Given the interest rate of 5%, the 15-year mortgage requires a monthly payment of $791, which is $254 more than the $537 payment on the 30-year mortgage. This is the obvious disadvantage of a 15-year mortgage.

The advantage is that she would pay down the mortgage sooner, meaning that she would accumulate a larger equity investment in the home more quickly. To gain more insight on this advantage, she reviews a Web site to compare the remaining loan balance for each of the two mortgage maturities on a year-by-year basis. This comparison is summarized in Exhibit 10.7. Notice that after six years, she would still owe $89,935 on the 30-year mortgage, versus $68,661 on the 15-year mortgage. At this point, she would owe $21,274 more on the 30-year mortgage than she would on the 15-year mortgage. After 10 years, she would owe almost $40,000 more on the 30-year mortgage than on the 15-year mortgage. After 15 years, she would still owe about $68,000 on the 30-year mortgage, while the 15-year mortgage would be paid off.

The Web site also shows the total payments over the life of the mortgage for both types of mortgages if the mortgage is not paid off until maturity.

	30-Year Mortgage	15-Year Mortgage
Total Principal Payments	$100,000	$100,000
Total Interest Payments	93,256	42,343
Total Payments	$193,256	$142,343

Stephanie would pay about $51,000 more in interest with the 30-year mortgage than with the 15-year mortgage. The total payments on the 30-year mortgage are much larger than the total payments that would be made over the life of the 15-year mortgage.

Weighing the advantages of the 15-year mortgage against the disadvantage of paying the extra $254 per month, Stephanie decides she prefers the 15-year mortgage. If she stays in the home, she will have no mortgage debt in 15 years. Even if she decides to sell this home before she pays off the 15-year mortgage, she will have paid down a larger amount of the mortgage. Because she will have a larger equity investment (from paying off more of the principal) with the 15-year mortgage, she will increase her net worth to a greater degree.

EXHIBIT 10.6	Comparison of Monthly Payments for a 30-Year versus a 15-Year Mortgage of $100,000 Based on Different Interest Rates

	Monthly Payment on a:	
Interest Rate	30-Year Mortgage	15-Year Mortgage
4%	$477	$740
5	537	791
6	600	844
7	665	899
8	734	956

Note: Payments are rounded to the nearest dollar.

EXHIBIT 10.7   Comparison of Mortgage Balance for a 30-Year versus a 15-Year Mortgage ($100,000 Initial Mortgage Amount; 5% Interest Rate)

End of Year	Balance on 30-Year Mortgage	Balance on 15-Year Mortgage
1	$98,525	$95,406
2	96,974	90,577
3	95,343	85,500
4	93,630	80,166
5	91,829	74,577
6	89,935	68,661
7	87,945	62,464
8	85,853	55,950
9	83,654	49,103
10	81,342	41,905
11	78,912	34,385
12	76,357	26,385
13	73,673	18,025
14	70,850	9,237
15	67,884	0

Note: Balances are rounded to the nearest dollar.

FREE APPS
for Personal
Finance

Generating an Amortization Schedule

Application:

The Zillow Mortgages app (by Zillow.com) allows you to input information such as the price of a home and mortgage interest rate so that you can generate an amortization schedule. This schedule shows the monthly payment, proportion of payment representing interest, and the balance remaining on the mortgage loan.

To Find It:

Search for the "Zillow Mortgages" app on your mobile device.

Financing with Adjustable-Rate Mortgages

adjustable-rate mortgage (ARM)
A mortgage where the interest owed changes in response to movements in a specific market-determined interest rate.

An alternative to a fixed-rate mortgage is an **adjustable-rate mortgage (ARM)**, in which the interest owed changes in response to movements in a specific market-determined interest rate. An ARM is sometimes referred to as a variable-rate mortgage. ARMs should definitely be considered along with fixed-rate mortgages. Like a fixed-rate mortgage, an ARM can be obtained for a 15-year or a 30-year maturity. ARMs have various characteristics that must be stated in the mortgage contract.

The advantage of an adjustable-rate mortgage is that the interest rate you pay on your mortgage declines when market interest rates decline. This reduces your monthly mortgage payment, so that you have more money to spend or to invest. The disadvantage of an adjustable-rate mortgage is that the interest rate you pay on your mortgage increases when market interest rates increase. This increases your monthly mortgage payment, so that you have less money to spend or invest. In fact, some homeowners have defaulted on their loans when interest rates increased because they could not afford to pay the higher monthly payment.

Initial Rate

Many ARMs specify a relatively low initial mortgage rate over the first year or so. This initial rate is beneficial to homeowners in that it results in a low monthly mortgage payment over the first year. Recognize, however, that this rate is only temporary, as the mortgage rate will be adjusted. Under the CFPB's new rules, in determining the borrower's ability to repay the loan, the lender will generally have to consider the payment due based on the highest interest rate that could be charged under the mortgage contract.

Interest Rate Index

The initial mortgage rate will be adjusted after a period (such as one year) in line with a specified interest rate index. The interest rate index to which the mortgage rate is tied must be included in the mortgage contract. Many ARMs use a rate that is tied to the average cost of deposits of financial institutions. For example, the interest rate charged on an ARM might be set at 3 percentage points above that benchmark. Thus, if the benchmark is 4% in a given year, the ARM will apply an interest rate of 7% (computed as 4% + 3%). If the interest rate index has risen to 5% by the time of the next mortgage rate adjustment, the new mortgage rate will be 8% (computed as 5% + 3%).

Frequency of Rate Adjustments

The mortgage contract also specifies how frequently the mortgage rate will be adjusted. Some ARMs specify that the rate will be adjusted once a year. Thus, the mortgage rate is set based on the specified interest rate index and then remains the same for the next 12 months. This means that the monthly payments will be constant for the next 12 months. At the end of the 12-month period, the mortgage rate is revised based on the prevailing interest rate index and is held constant for the following 12 months.

Some ARMs allow for less frequent adjustments, such as every three years or every five years. Others allow a single adjustment at the end of the fifth year, and the adjusted rate is then held constant over the next 25 years of a 30-year mortgage. Before an ARM adjusts, the CFPB requires the lender to give the borrower sufficient notice so that the borrower can attempt to refinance with another mortgage that is more desirable.

Other ARMs offer the following alternatives:

- An interest rate that is fixed for the first three years, but converts to an ARM (and adjusts annually) after three years
- An interest rate that is fixed for the first five years, but converts to an ARM (and adjusts annually) after five years
- An interest rate that adjusts for the first five years and then is fixed (based on an interest rate index at that time) for the next 25 years

With so many alternatives available, you can easily find a mortgage that fits your preferences. For example, if you expect that interest rates will decline consistently over time, you may prefer an ARM that is adjusted every year. If your expectations are correct, your mortgage rate will decline over time with the decline in market interest rates. It is difficult to forecast the direction of interest rates accurately, however, which means that your future mortgage payments are uncertain. When considering a particular adjustable-rate mortgage, you should estimate what the monthly payments would be under the adverse conditions in which market rates rise substantially over time. Make sure that you can afford the monthly payments if interest rates increase.

Caps on Adjustable-Rate Mortgages

caps
Maximum and minimum fluctuations in the interest rate on an adjustable-rate mortgage.

The adjustable-rate mortgage contract also typically specifies **caps**, or a maximum and minimum fluctuation in the interest rate. For example, an ARM may have a cap of 2% per year, which prevents the mortgage rate from being adjusted upward by more than 2 percentage points from its existing level in each year. Assume the market interest rate increases by 3 percentage points from one year to the next. Without a cap, the mortgage rate on the ARM would increase by 3 percentage points. With a 2% cap, however, only an increase of 2 percentage points is allowed in that year. This cap is useful because it limits the potential increase in the mortgage payments that may result from an increase in interest rates.

In addition to a cap on the annual increase in the mortgage rate, there is usually a lifetime cap, which represents the maximum amount of the increase in the mortgage rate over the life of the mortgage. A lifetime cap of 5% is commonly used. Thus, if an ARM has an initial mortgage rate of 7% and a 5% cap, the maximum mortgage rate over the life of the mortgage would be 12%.

Financing with a Fixed- versus an Adjustable-Rate Mortgage

Your decision to use a fixed- versus an adjustable-rate mortgage to finance the purchase of a home is dependent on your expectations of future interest rates. The primary advantage of an ARM is that the initial interest rate is lower than that of a fixed-rate mortgage. However, if interest rates rise, you may end up paying a higher interest rate on your mortgage than if you had obtained a fixed-rate mortgage.

EXAMPLE

Stephanie Spratt has already determined that if she finances with a 15-year fixed-rate mortgage, she would pay a 5% interest rate. Alternatively, she could obtain an adjustable-rate mortgage that specifies an initial rate of 4%, with the interest rate adjusted each year to an index reflecting the average cost of bank funds plus 3 percentage points.

Stephanie notices that financial experts have predicted an increase in interest rates in the near future. She is uncomfortable with uncertainty about her mortgage rate and how it could affect her mortgage payment. Although an ARM would result in a lower mortgage payment in the first year, it would result in a higher mortgage payment in the following years if interest rates increase. Thus, Stephanie decides to choose a fixed-rate mortgage instead of an ARM.

Decision to Own Versus Rent a Home

When considering the purchase (and therefore ownership) of a home, you should compare the cost of purchasing a home with the cost of renting. People attribute different advantages and disadvantages to owning a home versus renting because preferences are subjective. Some individuals value the privacy of a home, while others value the flexibility of renting, which allows them to move without much cost or difficulty. The financial assessment of owning a home versus renting can be performed objectively. Once the financial assessment is conducted, personal preferences can also be considered.

Estimating the Total Cost of Renting and Owning

The main cost of renting a home is the monthly rent payment. There is also an opportunity cost of tying up funds in a security deposit. Those funds could have been invested if you did not need to provide the security deposit. Another possible cost of renting is the purchase of renter's insurance.

The primary costs of purchasing a home are the down payment and the monthly mortgage payment. The down payment has an opportunity cost because the funds could have been invested to earn interest if they were not tied up in the purchase of the home. Closing costs are incurred at the time the home is purchased, although a portion of these costs is tax-deductible. Owning a home also involves some additional costs, such as maintenance and repair. Property taxes are assessed annually as a percentage of the home's value. Homeowner's insurance is paid annually and is primarily based on the value of the home.

FREE APPS
for Personal
Finance

Searching for an Apartment

Application:

The Zillow Rentals app (by Zillow.com) allows you to search for a home or apartments for rent near your location. The listing provides the location, the rent price per month, and details of the home or apartment available for rent.

To Find It:

Search for the "Zillow Rentals" app on your mobile device.

EXAMPLE

Stephanie Spratt has found a home she likes and has obtained financing. Before making a final decision, she wants to compare the cost of the home to the cost of remaining in her apartment. Although she would prefer a home, she wants to determine how much more expensive the home is compared to the apartment. If she purchases the home, she expects to live in it for at least three years. Therefore, she decides to compare the cost of owning a home to the cost of renting over the next three years. First, Stephanie calculates the cost of renting:

- **Cost of Rent.** Her estimated cost of renting is shown in the top panel of Exhibit 10.8. Her rent is currently $600 per month, so her annual rent is $7,200 (computed as $600 × 12). She does not expect a rent increase over the next three years and therefore estimates her cost of renting over this period to be $7,200 × 3 = $21,600. (If she had expected an increase in rent, she would have simply added the extra cost to the estimated rent over the next three years.)

- **Cost of Renter's Insurance.** She does not have renter's insurance at this time, as the value of her household assets is low.

- **Opportunity Cost of Security Deposit.** She provided a security deposit of $1,000 to the apartment complex. Although she expects to get this deposit back when she stops renting, there is an opportunity cost associated with it. She believes she might earn 2% (after considering tax effects) annually if she had been able to invest those funds, which would have generated annual interest of $20 (computed as $1,000 × .02). The opportunity cost over three years is three times the annual cost, or $60.

- **Total Cost of Renting.** Stephanie estimates the total cost of renting as $7,220 per year and $21,660 over the next three years, as shown in Exhibit 10.8.

Stephanie determines the total cost of purchasing a home by adding up expenses, subtracting any tax savings, and subtracting the value of the equity:

- **Mortgage Payment.** The primary cost of buying a home is the mortgage payment, which she expects to be $791 per month or $9,492 per year (not including payments for property taxes or home insurance).

- **Down Payment.** Stephanie would make a down payment of $8,000 to buy the home.

EXHIBIT 10.8   **Comparing the Total Cost of Renting Versus Buying a Home over a Three-Year Period**

Cost of Renting	Amount per Year	Total over Next Three Years
Rent ($600 per month)	$7,200	$21,600
Renter's insurance	0	0
Opportunity cost of security deposit	20	60
Total cost of renting	$7,220	$21,660

Cost of Purchasing	Amount per Year	Total over Next Three Years
Mortgage payment ($791 per month)	$9,492	$28,476
Down payment	8,000	8,000 (first year only)
Opportunity cost of down payment	160	480
Property taxes	1,500	4,500
Home insurance	600	1,800
Closing costs	3,100	3,100 (first year only)
Maintenance costs	1,000	3,000
Total costs before tax benefits		**$49,356**
Total tax savings		$325
Equity investment		$23,000
Cost of purchasing home over three years		**$26,031**

- **Opportunity Cost of the Down Payment.** If Stephanie did not buy a house, she believes could have invested the $8,000 and earned 2% per year after considering tax effects. Therefore, the annual opportunity cost (what she could have earned if she invested the funds) is $160 (computed as $8,000 × .02).

- **Property Taxes.** Stephanie assumes that the annual property tax will be $1,500 based on last year's property tax paid by the current owner of the home. Thus, the expected property tax payments over the next three years are estimated to be $4,500 (computed as 3 × $1,500).

- **Home Insurance (including private mortgage insurance).** Insurance on this home is expected to cost a total of $600 per year or a total of $1,800 over a three-year period (computed as 3 × $600).

- **Closing Costs.** Closing costs (transaction costs) associated with buying a home must be included, although those costs are incurred only in the first year for a mortgage. The closing costs are estimated to be $3,100, as shown earlier.

- **Maintenance Costs.** Stephanie expects maintenance costs on the home to be $1,000 per year.

- **Utilities.** She will pay for utilities such as water and electricity and will incur a cable TV bill if she buys the home. She already incurs those costs while renting an apartment, so she does not need to include them in her analysis.

- **Tax Savings.** Stephanie must also consider the tax savings that a home provides. She believes that her income will likely be taxed at a rate of about 25% in the future. Because the home mortgage interest is tax-deductible, she estimates that her taxes will be reduced by 25% of the amount by which her taxable income is reduced. The amount of mortgage interest changes every year and therefore so do her tax savings from interest expenses. She can estimate her interest expenses over three years by using an amortization table based on her mortgage amount, mortgage maturity, and mortgage rate. She estimates that her mortgage interest expense over the next three years will be about $14,700.

Note that Stephanie will generate tax savings from property taxes because they are tax-deductible. Given an annual property tax of $1,500, she will have a $4,500 tax deduction over the next three years. Stephanie will also generate tax savings from the points that she would pay (a one-time fee of $1,000) as part of the closing costs because the points are tax-deductible.

The total itemized deductions resulting from the purchase of the house over the next three years are:

	Deduction
Interest	$14,700
Property Taxes	$4,500
Points	$1,000
Total	$20,200

However, keep in mind that individuals without significant tax deductions can receive their standard deduction, as explained in Chapter 4. Stephanie expects that she would be able to take a standard deduction of about $6,300 each year if she does not itemize her deductions. If she does not buy the home, she would take the standard deduction each year, which she expects would be worth $18,900 over three years. The tax savings from buying the home occur because the value of itemized deductions exceeds the expected value of standard deductions over the three-year period by $1,300 (computed as $20,200 − $18,900). When considering Stephanie's marginal tax rate, extra deductions result in a tax savings of:

$$\text{Tax Savings} = \text{Value of Extra Deductions} \times \text{Marginal Tax Rate}$$
$$= \$1,300 \times .25$$
$$= \$325.$$

- **Value of the Equity Investment.** Another advantage of owning a home is that Stephanie will have an equity investment in it. Her down payment will be $8,000, and she will pay about $15,000 in principal on her 15-year mortgage over the three-year period. The value of this equity investment could be higher in three years if the market value of the home increases. If Stephanie assumes that the home's value will not change, the value of the equity investment will be $23,000 (computed as $8,000 + $15,000).

- **Total Cost of Purchasing a Home.** The total cost of purchasing a home is determined by adding all the expenses, subtracting the tax savings, and then subtracting the equity investment. As shown in Exhibit 10.8, Stephanie estimates that the total cost of purchasing the home over the three-year period will be $26,031.

The total cost of purchasing a home over three years is about $4,371 more than the cost of renting. Stephanie believes this is a relatively low cost when considering that she would rather live in a home than an apartment. She also believes that the home's value may rise over time. If the value of the home increased by 2% per year, the market value of her equity in the home would increase by more than $6,000 in three years.

Now that Stephanie has decided that she wants to purchase a home and can afford it, she negotiates with the seller, and she ultimately submits an offer of $108,000, which is accepted by the seller.

Special Types of Mortgages

In some cases, prospective buyers do not qualify for a traditional fixed-rate mortgage or an adjustable-rate mortgage. Some special types of mortgages are available that can make a home more affordable.

Graduated Payment Mortgage

graduated payment mortgage
A mortgage where the payments are low in the early years and then rise to a higher level over time.

A **graduated payment mortgage** sets relatively low monthly mortgage payments when the mortgage is first created and then gradually increases the payments over the first five or so years. The payments level off after that time. This type of mortgage may be useful for someone whose income will increase over time because the mortgage payments will increase as the homeowner's income increases. A graduated payment mortgage would not be desirable for people who are not certain that their income will rise.

Balloon Payment Mortgage

balloon payment mortgage
A mortgage where the monthly payments are relatively low, but one large payment is required after a specified period to pay off the mortgage loan.

A **balloon payment mortgage** sets relatively low monthly payments and then requires one large payment (called a balloon payment) after a specified period (such as five years) to pay off the remainder of the mortgage loan. A balloon payment mortgage is sometimes offered by the seller of a home to the buyer, especially when the buyer cannot afford to make large monthly payments and does not qualify for a more traditional mortgage. In this situation, the seller might provide a mortgage for five years. The expectation is that the buyer's income will rise, enabling the buyer to obtain a traditional mortgage from a financial institution before the end of the five-year period. Then, the buyer will have enough cash to make the balloon payment to the seller. Under the CFPB's new rules, a balloon payment mortgage generally cannot be a Qualified Mortgage unless the lender qualifies as a "small creditor" (the seller of the home would likely qualify) and other criteria are met.

Interest-Only Mortgage

Interest-only mortgages are adjustable-rate mortgages that allow home buyers to pay only interest on the mortgage during the first few years. These mortgages were popular in the years before the financial crisis when house prices were rising rapidly. Some buyers liked them because no principal was paid in the first years, so the mortgage payments seemed more affordable. However, the mortgage payment increased abruptly when the homeowner had to begin making principal payments. Some mortgage payments increased by 30% or more, and many homeowners were unable to make their payments. Under the CFPB's new rules, interest-only mortgages cannot be Qualified Mortgages, and they are rarely offered today.

Mortgage Refinancing

mortgage refinancing
Paying off an existing mortgage with a new mortgage that has a lower interest rate.

Mortgage refinancing involves paying off an existing mortgage with a new mortgage that has a lower interest rate. You may use mortgage refinancing to obtain a new mortgage if market interest rates (and therefore mortgage rates) decline. One disadvantage of mortgage refinancing is that you will incur closing costs again. Nevertheless, it may still be advantageous to refinance because the savings on your monthly mortgage payments (even after considering tax effects) may exceed the new closing costs. Mortgage refinancing is more likely to be worthwhile when the prevailing mortgage interest rate is substantially below the interest rate on your existing mortgage. It is also more likely to be worthwhile when you expect to be living in the home for a long time because you will reap greater benefits from the lower monthly mortgage payments that result from refinancing. If you have an FHA-guaranteed mortgage, you may be eligible for the FHA's "streamline refinance" program, which can be a faster and less expensive way to refinance for some borrowers.

Rate Modification

When interest rates decline, some mortgage lenders may be willing to allow a "rate modification" to existing mortgage holders with a fixed-rate mortgage. They may charge a one-time fee that is typically between $500 and $1,500. Your fixed-rate mortgage may be revised to reflect the prevailing mortgage rate. You can benefit because you receive the lower interest rate. You would not need to go through the process of refinancing through another mortgage lender or incur costs associated with a new mortgage application. Some mortgage lenders are willing to allow rate modifications because they realize that if they do not provide you with an opportunity to pay the lower interest rate, you will likely obtain a new mortgage from another lender and will pay off your existing mortgage. In this case, you will no longer make payments at the high interest rate, and your existing mortgage lender will lose you as a customer. By allowing a rate modification, your existing mortgage lender retains you as a customer by offering you a mortgage that is similar to what it is presently offering to other new customers, and it earns a one-time fee from you for modifying the mortgage rate that you are charged.

Refinancing Analysis

To determine whether you should refinance, you can compare the advantage of monthly savings of interest expenses to the cost of refinancing. If the benefits from reducing your interest expenses exceed the closing costs incurred from refinancing, the refinancing is feasible.

The advantages of refinancing (lower interest payments) occur each year, whereas the disadvantage (closing costs) occurs only at the time of refinancing. Therefore, refinancing tends to be more beneficial when a homeowner plans to own the home for a longer period. The savings from a lower interest payment can accumulate over each additional year the mortgage exists.

EXAMPLE

Stephanie Spratt decides that if interest rates decline in the future, she may refinance. If interest rates decline to 4% a year from now, Stephanie would save about $51 on her monthly mortgage payment by refinancing her 15-year mortgage. Stephanie needs to determine the potential savings in the monthly interest payments over the time that she expects to remain in the home.

A monthly reduction in interest payments of $51 reflects an annual reduction of $612 (computed as $51 × 12). But because interest on the mortgage is tax-deductible, the reduction in interest payments by $612 interest means that her taxable income would be $612 higher. Because she expects that her marginal tax rate would be about 25%, her taxes would increase:

Annual Increase in Taxes = Annual Increase in Taxable Income × Marginal Tax Rate
= $612 × .25
= $153

Her annual savings due to refinancing at a lower interest rate would be:

$612 − $153 = $459

The disadvantage of refinancing is that Stephanie may incur about the same closing costs that she incurred from purchasing the home ($3,100). Before comparing this cost to the benefits of refinancing, she accounts for the tax savings. Because the points are tax-deductible, she determines the tax savings from these costs:

Tax Savings on Points = Cost of Points × Marginal Tax Rate
= $1,000 × .25
= $250

$$\text{After-tax Closing Costs} = \text{Closing Costs} - \text{Tax Savings}$$
$$= \$3,100 - \$250$$
$$= \$2,850$$

The after-tax closing costs ($2,850) due to refinancing would exceed the savings on the interest payments ($918) even if Stephanie lives in the home for several years. Stephanie is now aware that even if the mortgage interest rates decrease by 1 percentage point over the next year, it would not be worthwhile for her to refinance her home. She will reassess this decision after she has a better guess of the number of years in which she will live in the home. The longer the period that she plans to be in the home after refinancing, the greater are the benefits due to the lower interest rate, and the greater the likelihood that refinancing would be worthwhile.

How a Mortgage Fits Within Your Financial Plan

The following are the key mortgage loan decisions that should be included within your financial plan:

- What mortgage amount can you afford?
- What maturity should you select?
- Should you consider a fixed-rate or an adjustable-rate mortgage?

By making informed decisions, you can avoid accumulating an excessive amount of debt. Exhibit 10.9 provides a summary of how Stephanie Spratt's mortgage loan decisions apply to her financial plan.

EXHIBIT 10.9   How Mortgage Financing Fits Within Stephanie Spratt's Financial Plan

GOALS FOR MORTGAGE FINANCING

1. *Limit the amount of mortgage financing to a level that is affordable.*
2. *Select a short loan maturity if possible, assuming that the payments are affordable.*
3. *Select the type of mortgage loan (fixed- or adjustable-rate) that is more likely to result in lower interest expenses.*

ANALYSIS

	15-Year Mortgage (5% interest rate)	30-Year Mortgage (5% interest rate)
Monthly payment	$791	$537
Total interest payments	$42,343	$93,256
Advantages	Pay off mortgage in half the time of a 30-year mortgage; pay lower interest expenses on the loan	Smaller monthly payment
Difference between mortgage payment and rent payment	$791 – $600 = $191	$537 – $600 = –$63

DECISIONS

Decision on Affording a Mortgage:

The monthly interest payment on a $100,000 mortgage loan with a 15-year maturity is $791. My rent is $600 per month, so the difference is $191 per month. Since my monthly cash flows (from my salary) exceed my typical monthly expenses (including my car loan payment) and my purchases of clothes by almost $600, I can afford that difference. I will not save as much money as I planned if I buy a home, but I will be building equity.

Decision on the Mortgage Maturity:

I prefer the 15-year mortgage because I will pay off a larger portion of the principal each year.

Decision on the Type of Mortgage Loan:

I prefer the fixed-rate mortgage because I know with certainty that the monthly payments will not increase. I am worried that interest rates may increase in the future, which would cause interest expenses to be higher on the adjustable-rate mortgage.

DISCUSSION QUESTIONS

1. How would Stephanie's mortgage financing decisions be different if she were a single mother of two children?

2. How would Stephanie's mortgage financing decisions be affected if she were 35 years old? If she were 50 years old?

SUMMARY

Affording a Home. When considering the purchase of a home, you should evaluate your financial situation to determine how much you can afford. To determine the amount you can afford when purchasing a home, consider the down payment that you can make. In addition, consider the amount of your income that you can use each month to cover the mortgage payment.

Selecting a Home to Purchase. When shopping for a home, some of the key criteria used in the selection process are price, convenience of the location, the school system, and the potential resale value.

Valuation of a Home. You can conduct a valuation of a home with a market analysis. Homes in the same area that were recently sold can be used to determine the average price per square foot. Then, this price per square foot can be applied to the square footage of the home you wish to value.

Transaction Costs. The transaction costs of purchasing a home include the down payment and closing costs. The key closing costs are points and the origination fee.

Financing with a Fixed-Rate Mortgage. A fixed-rate mortgage specifies a fixed interest rate to be paid over the life of the mortgage. Because most of the monthly mortgage payment on a 30-year mortgage is allocated to cover the interest expense in the early years, a relatively small amount of principal is paid off in those years. A 15-year fixed-rate mortgage is a popular alternative to the 30-year mortgage. It requires a larger monthly payment, but a larger proportion of the payment is allocated to principal in the early years.

Financing with ARMs. An adjustable-rate mortgage (ARM) ties the interest rate to an interest rate index, so the mortgage interest rate changes over time with the index. Homeowners who expect interest rates to decline in the future are especially likely to choose ARMs.

Buying a Home versus Renting. Before making a final decision to buy a home, you can compare the total cost of owning a home versus renting over a particular period to determine which choice will enhance your financial position more. The total cost of owning a home is estimated by adding up the expenses associated with the home, subtracting the tax savings from owning the home, and subtracting the expected value of the equity of the home at the end of the period.

Special Types of Mortgages. When prospective buyers do not qualify for a traditional mortgage, they may consider special types of mortgages that can make a home more affordable, such as a graduated payment mortgage, a balloon payment mortgage, or an interest-only mortgage.

Mortgage Refinancing. You may consider mortgage refinancing when quoted interest rates on new mortgages decline. When refinancing, you will incur closing costs. Thus, you should consider refinancing only if the benefits (expected reduction in interest expenses over time) exceed the closing costs.

How Mortgage Financing Fits Within Your Financial Plan. Mortgage financing allows you to obtain a home, and therefore it may be necessary for you to complete your financial plan.

REVIEW QUESTIONS

All Review Questions are available in MyFinanceLab *at* http://www.myfinancelab.com.

1. **Steps in Buying a Home.** What is your first task when considering buying a home? Why is this step important? How can a real estate broker help you?

2. **Purchasing a Home.** What are the two financial components you must consider before purchasing a home? Why should you consider them?

3. **Affordable Payments.** What should you consider when determining an affordable down payment and monthly mortgage payments?

4. **Selection Criteria.** List the criteria you should use when selecting a home.

5. **Selection Criteria.** How do price, convenience of the location, and maintenance affect your home-buying decisions?

6. **School System Influence.** Why is the reputation of the school system in the area of the home you are buying important?

7. **Home Insurance and Taxes.** Why do insurance costs and taxes vary among homes?

8. **Home Resale Value.** What is the main factor in determining a home's resale value? How can you predict a home's resale value? Who pays commissions when a home is sold?

9. **Market Analysis.** Once you have reduced your list of three or four homes down to one home, what is your next step? Should you offer the price the seller is asking? Describe how you would conduct a market analysis of the home.

10. **Demand for Homes.** Why does the value of a home depend on the demand for homes? What factors influence the demand for homes?

11. **Loan Programs.** How do lenders protect their interest in a home? Describe two government-backed home loan programs.

12. **Closing Costs.** What are closing costs? List and briefly describe the different closing costs you might incur when applying for a mortgage.

13. **Fixed-Rate Mortgage.** Describe the characteristics of a fixed-rate mortgage. Why do certain homeowners prefer a fixed-rate mortgage to an adjustable-rate mortgage?

14. **Amortization Table.** What is an amortization table? What does each mortgage payment represent?

15. **Monthly Mortgage Payments.** List the three things that determine the amount of the monthly mortgage payment. Explain how each affects the payment.

16. **Adjustable-Rate Mortgage.** Discuss the characteristics of an adjustable-rate mortgage. What influences your choice of a fixed- or adjustable-rate mortgage?

17. **Costs of Renting.** What are the costs of renting a home?

18. **Costs of Buying a Home.** Describe some of the costs of buying a home. Are there potential tax savings associated with buying a home?

19. **Features of Graduated Payment.** Describe the features of graduated payment and balloon payment mortgages.

20. **Mortgage Refinancing.** What is mortgage refinancing? Are there any disadvantages to refinancing?

21. **Impact of a Weak Economy on Home Values.** Explain how a weak economy affects the values of homes.

22. **Impact of Strong Economy on Home Values.** Explain how stronger economic conditions affect the values of homes.

23. **Private Mortgage Insurance.** What is private mortgage insurance? How does it impact the cost of your mortgage?

24. **Home Buyer Risks.** What are some of the risks associated with buying a home?

25. **Qualified Mortgage.** What is a Qualified Mortgage?

26. **Home Inspection.** What is a home inspection? Why is it important for you to have a home inspected before purchase?

27. **FHA Loans.** What is an FHA loan? How does the FHA or VA help lower-income individuals buy homes?

28. **Escrow Accounts.** What is an escrow account? How do escrow accounts help protect the lender?

29. **Balloon Payment Mortgage.** What is a balloon payment mortgage? When is this type of mortgage useful?

FINANCIAL PLANNING PROBLEMS

All Financial Planning Problems are available in MyFinanceLab at http://www.myfinancelab.com.

1. **Mortgage Payment.** Dorothy and Matt are ready to purchase their first home. Their current monthly cash inflows are $4,900, and their current monthly cash outflows are $3,650. Their rent makes up $650 of their cash flows. They would like to put 10% of their cash inflows in savings and put another $200 in their checking account for emergencies. How much of a mortgage payment can they manage under these conditions?

2. **Home Price Offer.** Denise and Kenny are ready to make an offer on an 1,800-square-foot home that is priced at $135,000. They investigate other homes on lots of similar size and find the following information:
   - A 2,400-square-foot home sold for $168,000.
   - A 1,500-square-foot home sold for $106,500.
   - An 1,100-square-foot home sold for $79,000.

   What offer should they make on the home?

3. **Closing Costs.** Larry and Laurie have found a home and made a $125,000 offer that has been accepted. They make a down payment of 10%.

Their bank charges a loan origination fee of 1% of the loan and points of 1.5% (both are based on the loan amount). Other fees include a $25 loan application fee, a $250 appraisal fee, and $350 for title search and insurance. How much cash will Larry and Laurie need at closing?

4. **Total Interest Paid.** Lloyd and Jean are considering purchasing a home requiring a $75,000 mortgage. The payment on a 30-year mortgage for this amount is $498.97. The payment for a 15-year maturity is $674.12. What is the difference in the total interest paid between the two different maturities?

5. **Tax Savings.** This month you made a mortgage payment of $700, of which $600 was an interest payment and $100 a payment of the loan principal. You are in the 25% marginal tax bracket. What are the tax savings as a result of this payment?

6. **Annual Costs of Renting.** Teresa rents her apartment for $650 per month, utilities not included. When she moved in, she paid a $700 security

deposit using money from her savings account that was paying 3% interest. Her renter's insurance costs her $60 per year. What are Teresa's total annual costs of renting?

7. **Cost of Condo.** Matt has found a condominium in an area where he would enjoy living. He would need a $5,000 down payment from his savings and would have to pay closing costs of $2,500 to purchase the condo. His monthly mortgage payments would be $520 including property taxes and insurance. The condominium's homeowner's association charges maintenance fees of $400 per year. Calculate the cost of Matt's condo during the first year if he currently has the $5,000 down payment invested in an account earning 5% interest.

8. **Tax Savings.** Matt (from problem 7) paid mortgage interest of $4,330 during his first year in the condo. His property taxes were $600, and his homeowner's insurance was $460. If Matt is in a 25% marginal tax rate bracket, what were his tax savings for his first year?

9. **Refinancing.** Doug and Lynn bought their home three years ago. They have a mortgage payment of $601.69. Interest rates have recently fallen, and they can lower their mortgage payments to $491.31 if they refinance. What would their annual savings be if they refinance? They are in a 15% marginal tax rate bracket. (*Hint*: Consider the reduction in tax savings.)

10. **Refinancing.** If the cost of refinancing their house is $3,860, how long would Doug and Lynn (from problem 9) have to remain in their home to recover the cost? (Ignore any interest on the savings in answering this question.)

11. **Accumulating the Down Payment.** Paul wants to purchase his own home. He currently lives in an apartment, and his rent is being paid by his parents. Paul's parents have informed him that they would not pay his mortgage payments. Paul has no savings, but can save $400 per month. The home he desires costs $100,000, and his real estate broker informs him that a down payment of 20% would be required. If Paul can earn 4% on his savings, how long will it take him to accumulate the required down payment?

12. **Mortgage Affordability.** Paul (from problem 11) will be able to save $400 per month (which can be used for mortgage payments) for the indefinite future. If Paul finances the remaining cost of the home (after making the $20,000 down payment) at a rate of 5% over 30 years, what are his resulting monthly mortgage payments? Can he afford the mortgage?

13. **Private Mortgage Insurance.** Justin's new FHA mortgage is for $131,500. How much will his overall mortgage increase with an upfront fee of 1.5%? How much will his total mortgage be with the upfront PMI fee added? Will Justin always pay PMI on this loan?

14. **Ethical Dilemma.** Mia would like to purchase a specific home and knows that she can afford the home, but her income is slightly lower than the amount needed to qualify for the mortgage. She is a waitress and makes much of her income from tips, so she can exaggerate her estimated income. Should she increase her estimated income on the mortgage application?

FINANCIAL PLANNING ONLINE EXERCISES

1. Go to a Web site such as http://www.bankrate.com that has calculators to derive an amortization table.

   a. Determine the monthly payment on a $200,000 15-year mortgage with a 5% interest rate.

   b. Now change the interest rate to 6%. What is the difference in monthly payments on the loan?

   c. Now change the loan term to 30 years, and assume a 5% interest rate. What is the difference in monthly payments on the loan?

2. Go to http://www.realtor.com. Enter the ZIP Code of your current home or the ZIP Code of where you plan to live after graduation, the price range of houses you are interested in, the number of bedrooms and baths, and click "Search."

   a. How many houses meet your criteria in the designated area?

   b. What is the range of prices, highest to lowest?

   c. Of the houses listed, identify the one that you are most interested in, and explain why.

3. Go to http://www.mortgageloan.com and search using the terms "refinance" and "mortgage."

   a. What are the current national refinance rates for a 30-year fixed mortgage? For a 15-year fixed mortgage?

   b. Discuss the benefits of home refinancing.

4. Go to http://www.bankrate.com or to another Web site that contains amortization schedule calculators to answer the following questions:

   a. Assume you have a mortgage of $150,000 for 30 years at 5%. What are (1) the monthly payment, (2) the total payments, and (3) the total interest payment?

   b. Assume the same data as in "a" except for a term of 15 years. What are (1) the monthly payment, (2) the total payments, and (3) the total interest payment?

   c. Assume the same facts as in "a" except the interest rate is 6%. What are (1) the monthly payment, (2) the total payments, and (3) the total interest payment?

5. Access http://www.lendingtree.com or another Web site that has information on FHA loans and answer the following questions:

   a. What is an FHA loan, and how long have they been in existence?

   b. What are the key components of an FHA loan?

   c. What are the five eligibility requirements?

PSYCHOLOGY OF PERSONAL FINANCE: Buying Your Home

1. Home buyers tend to buy a home for more money than they originally planned to spend. This occurs because as they start looking at homes for sale, they commonly see a home with desirable features that is priced beyond the amount they had planned to spend. Describe your behavior if you were going to buy a home. Does the behavior described in this question reflect your behavior, or would you be more disciplined?

2. Read one practical article of how psychology affects decisions when buying a home. You can easily retrieve possible articles by doing an online search using the terms "psychology" and "buying home." Summarize the main points of the article.

WEB SEARCH EXERCISE

You can develop your personal finance skills by conducting an Internet search for related articles. Find a recent online article about personal finance that reinforces one or more concepts covered in this chapter. If your class has an online component, your professor may ask you to post your summary of the article there and provide a link to the article so that other students can access it. If your class is live, your professor may ask you to summarize your application of the article in class. Your professor may assign specific students to complete this assignment or may allow any student to do the assignment on a volunteer basis.

For recent online articles related to this chapter, consider using the following search terms (be sure to include the current year as a search term to ensure that the online articles are recent):

- Purchasing a home
- Choosing a realtor
- Pricing a home
- Financing a home
- Selecting a mortgage
- Managing mortgage payments
- Buy versus rent home

VIDEO EXERCISE: Purchasing a Home

Go to one of the Web sites that contain video clips (such as http://www.youtube.com) and view some video clips about purchasing a home. You can use search phrases such as "buying a home." Select one video clip on this topic that you would recommend for the other students in your class.

1. Provide the Web link for the video clip.

2. What do you think is the main point of this video clip?

3. How might you change your process of purchasing a home as a result of watching this video clip?

BUILDING YOUR OWN FINANCIAL PLAN

The purchase of a home is the largest expenditure that most individuals will make in their lifetime. For this reason, you should approach this decision with as much information as possible. This exercise will familiarize you with various information sources and will alert you to what you can and cannot expect from a real estate agent.

Go to the worksheets at the end of this chapter to continue to build your financial plan.

THE SAMPSONS—A Continuing Case

When the Sampsons purchased a home, they obtained a 30-year mortgage with a fixed interest rate of 8.6%. Their monthly mortgage payment (excluding property taxes and insurance) is about $700 per month. Today, they could obtain a 30-year mortgage with an interest rate of 5%. Dave and Sharon want to determine how much they can lower their monthly payments by refinancing. If they refinance their home, they would incur transaction fees of $2,400 after considering any tax effects. The Sampsons are in the 25% tax bracket.

Go to the worksheets at the end of this chapter to continue this case.

PART 3: BRAD BROOKS—A Continuing Case

Brad Brooks listened to your advice about reducing the use of his smartphone (which saves him $250 per month) and reducing his entertainment expenses by $200 per month. He still rents the condo for $1,000 per month. However, now Brad has the urge to upgrade his car and housing situations. He is interested in purchasing an SUV for $35,000. He still owes $10,000 on his two-year-old sedan (which has 57,000 miles) and has found a buyer who will pay him $15,000 cash. This would enable him to pay off his current car loan (loan balance is presently $10,000 on his existing car) and still have $5,000 for a down payment on the SUV. He would finance the remaining $30,000 of the purchase price for four years at 8%.

Brad would also like to purchase his condo. He knows that he will enjoy tax advantages with ownership and is eager to reduce his tax burden. He can make the purchase with 10% down; the total purchase price is $90,000. A 30-year mortgage is available with a 5% rate. Closing costs due at signing will total $3,100. The property taxes on his condo will be $1,800 per year, his Property Owners' Association (POA) fee is $70 per month, and his household insurance will increase by $240 a year if he buys the condo. Turn to the worksheets at the end of this chapter to continue this case.

CHAPTER 10: BUILDING YOUR OWN FINANCIAL PLAN

GOALS

1. Assess whether you should purchase a home.
2. Determine the costs associated with buying a home.

ANALYSIS

1. Use a Web site to search listings of local homes for sale in your price range. Record information on homes of interest below.

	From	**To**
Price Range:		
ZIP Code:		

Potential Homes

Address	List Price	MSN Price Estimate	Monthly Payment	Real Estate Agent

2. Referring to your cash flow statement and personal balance sheet, compare the monthly payment estimates to the rent you are currently paying. Determine the amount of a down payment you can afford to make.

Down payment $ _____

3. Gather current information on loan rates and record it below.

Mortgage Type	Rate

4. Create an amortization table for the fixed-rate mortgage that is most affordable. (The Excel worksheet will calculate the monthly payment based on your input and create the amortization table.)

Loan Amount   _____

Number of Years   _____

Annual Interest Rate   _____

Monthly Payment   _____

Amortization Schedule for Year 1

Monthly Payment	Payment	Principal	Interest	Balance

Compare the allocation of principal versus interest paid per year on the loan. (The Excel worksheet will create a bar graph based on your input.)

  DATE

Amortization Schedule (Annual Totals)

Year	Annual Payments	Principal	Interest	Balance
1				
2				
3				
4				
5				
6				
7				
8				
9				
10				
11				
12				
13				
14				
15				
16				
17				
18				
19				
20				
21				
22				
23				
24				
25				
26				
27				
28				
29				
30				

5. Select the mortgage with the best terms. Compare the cost of purchasing a home with these mort-gage terms to renting over a three-year period.

Renting Versus Owning a Home

Cost of Renting	Per Month	Amount per Year	Total over Three Years
Rent			
Renter's insurance			
Opportunity cost of security deposit			
Total cost of renting			

Cost of Purchasing	Per Month	Amount per Year	Total over Three Years
Mortgage payment			
Down payment			
Opportunity cost of down payment			
Property taxes			
Home insurance			
Closing costs			
Maintenance costs			
Total costs before tax benefits			
Total tax savings			
Equity investment			
Increase in home value			
Value of equity			
Cost of purchasing home over three years			

If you enter this information in the Excel worksheet, the software will create a chart comparing the cost of renting versus purchasing.

DECISIONS

1. What is the mortgage amount and down payment that you can afford?

   _____
   _____
   _____
   _____
   _____
   _____
   _____

2. Is a fixed-rate or adjustable-rate mortgage better suited to your financial situation? What maturity, interest rate, and monthly payment can you afford?

   _____
   _____
   _____
   _____
   _____
   _____
   _____

3. Describe whether buying or renting a home is preferable for you.

   _____
   _____
   _____
   _____
   _____
   _____

CHAPTER 10: THE SAMPSONS—A Continuing Case

CASE QUESTIONS

1. Use a Web site or a financial calculator to determine the monthly mortgage payment (excluding property taxes and insurance) on a $90,000 mortgage if the Sampsons obtain a new 30-year mortgage at the 5% interest rate.

Mortgage loan	$90,000
Interest rate	5%
Years	30
Loan payment	

2. The Sampsons expect that they will not move for at least three years. Advise the Sampsons on whether they should refinance their mortgage by comparing the savings of refinancing with the costs.

Current mortgage payment	
New mortgage payment	
Monthly savings	
Annual savings	
Marginal tax rate	
Increase in taxes	
Annual savings after tax	
Years in house after refinancing	
Total savings	

3. Why might your advice about refinancing change in the future?

PART 3: BRAD BROOKS—A Continuing Case

CASE QUESTIONS

1. Refer to Brad's personal cash flow statement that you developed in Part 1, with the revisions based on Brad's giving up the smartphone and reducing his entertainment expenses by $200 per month. Based on his revised personal cash flow statement, offer your opinion about whether Brad can afford to purchase the SUV and still achieve his goals of paying off his credit card balance and increasing his savings over the next 4 years.

Personal Cash Flow Statement

Cash Inflows	This Month
Total Cash Inflows	

Cash Outflows	
Total Cash Outflows	
Net Cash Flows	

Protecting Your Wealth

The chapters in this part focus on insurance, which is critical for protecting you and your personal assets against damages and liability. Chapter 11 focuses on decisions about auto and homeowner's insurance. Chapter 12 presents key considerations regarding health and disability insurance, and Chapter 13 explains the provisions of life insurance.

Auto and Homeowner's Insurance

Monkey Business Images/Shutterstock

Matt was recently in a major accident that caused extensive damage to his eight-year-old sedan. When his insurance company asked Matt to get an estimate of the cost of repairs, he took it to a well-respected repair shop. They quoted a total repair bill of $5,250.

Matt was prepared to pay his $250 deductible as long as the insurance company paid the rest.

Because the book value of a car of his make and model, in good condition, is only $3,240, the insurance company "totaled" his car, declaring it a total loss and reimbursing him only to the extent of the book value. Matt must either repair the car using the insurance company reimbursement plus over $2,000 out of his own pocket or accept the loss and buy another car.

Understanding your insurance needs is important when determining the type and amount of coverage you need to shield you from financial loss and protect you against liability.

MyFinanceLab helps you master the topics in this chapter and study more efficiently. Visit http://www.myfinancelab.com for more details.

The objectives of this chapter are to:

- Explain insurance and risk management
- Describe the role of insurance companies
- Provide a background on auto insurance
- Identify the factors that affect your auto insurance premium
- Explain how to respond if you are in an auto accident
- Describe the key provisions of homeowner's insurance
- Describe financial coverage provided by homeowner's insurance
- Describe the use of renter's insurance
- Describe the use of umbrella personal liability insurance policies
- Explain how insurance fits within your financial plan

Insurance and the Management of Risk

liability
The amount that you may be required to pay other individuals for damage that you caused to them or their property.

Property insurance ensures that any damages to your auto and home are covered, and that your personal assets are protected from any liability. In the context of insurance, the term **liability** is used to mean that you may be required to pay other individuals for damage that you caused to them or to their property. Health insurance can ensure that most of your medical bills will be covered and therefore can also protect your personal assets from any liability. Life insurance can ensure financial support for your dependents, other individuals, or charities when you die.

The primary function of insurance is to maintain your existing level of wealth by protecting you against potential financial losses or liability as a result of unexpected events. It can ensure that your income continues if an accident or illness prevents you from working, or it can prevent others from taking away your personal assets.

You benefit from having auto insurance even when you do not receive any payments from the insurance company because you have the peace of mind of knowing that your assets are protected if you are in a collision. Insurance is costly, but it may be well worth the cost to ensure that your wealth will not be taken away from you. However, you do not want to waste money by overinsuring. It is important, therefore, that you carefully identify your exposure to possible losses, so that you can purchase insurance that properly protects you against the possible losses that could occur.

risk
Exposure to events or perils that can cause a financial loss.

risk management
Decisions about whether and how to protect against risk.

In the context of insurance, the term **risk** can be defined as exposure to events (or perils) that can cause a financial loss. **Risk management** represents decisions about whether and how to protect against risk. The first step in risk management is to recognize the risks to which you are exposed. Then you must decide whether to protect against risk. When determining whether to protect against risk, your alternatives include avoiding risk, reducing risk, and insuring against risk. If you decide to insure against risk, you can select the amount of coverage as well as policy provisions.

Avoid Risk

Consider your actions that expose you to a financial loss. Owners are exposed to a financial loss if their property is damaged. You can avoid the risk of property damage by not owning any property. However, you cannot completely avoid risk by avoiding ownership of property. If you lease a car, you are still exposed to liability and financial loss if the car is in an accident. Other types of risk are unrelated to property. For example, you are exposed to a financial loss if you require medical attention or become disabled.

Reduce Risk

One method of managing risk is to reduce your exposure to financial loss. For example, you can purchase a small home rather than a large home to reduce the maximum possible financial loss due to property damage. You can purchase an inexpensive car to limit the possible financial loss due to property damage. You may reduce the risk of losses on your home due to a fire by installing a fire alarm or smoke detector. You may be able to reduce your exposure to an illness or a disability by getting periodic health checkups.

However, these steps do not fully block your exposure to financial loss. If you drive a car, you are not only subject to property damage for your own car but also liability for damage to other vehicles and their drivers if you are found to be at fault for an accident. Your financial loss could be large even if the car you drive has little value.

Accept Risk

A third alternative when managing risk is to accept risk and not seek to limit your exposure to a financial loss. This alternative may be feasible when the likelihood of an event that could cause a financial loss is very low and the potential financial loss due to the event is small. For example, if you seldom drive your car and live in a town with little traffic, you are relatively unlikely to get into an accident. You are also more likely to accept risk when the possible financial loss resulting from the event is limited. For example, if you drive an inexpensive old car, you may be willing to accept your exposure to financial loss due to property damage. However, you are still subject to liability, which could put all your personal assets in jeopardy.

PSYCHOLOGY
of Personal
Finance

Psychology Behind Accepting Risk Many people opt to accept risk rather than pay for insurance because they do not feel much satisfaction from buying insurance. When they make a payment, they may feel that they receive nothing in return. Buying insurance is different from buying many other products or services that provide immediate benefits. In fact, some people might argue that they only benefit from insurance if an unfortunate event occurs that causes them to need it. Otherwise, they may perceive insurance as a waste of money. They should, however, consider their potential liability if an adverse event happens and they do not have insurance. In many cases, people do not make an informed decision to accept risk, but simply defer the decision to buy insurance because they do not want to spend the money. Or they may have a mind-set that they will be careful and will therefore avoid any undesirable event that would require insurance.

However, people do not have complete control over whether adverse events occur. Careful drivers can have a major car accident. Prudent homeowners can be subject to major house damage due to weather. People with healthy diets can suffer from a major illness. The cost of an adverse event could completely wipe out one's savings.

Insure Against Risk

A final alternative is to insure against risk. If you cannot avoid a specific type of risk, you cannot reduce that risk, and you do not wish to be exposed to financial loss as a result of the risk, you should consider insurance.

premium
The cost of obtaining insurance.

The decision to obtain insurance is determined by weighing the costs and the benefits. The cost of obtaining insurance is the **premium** that is paid for a policy each year. The benefit of obtaining insurance is that it can protect your assets or your income from events that otherwise might cause a financial loss. Consequently, you protect your existing net worth and also increase the likelihood that you will be able to increase your net worth in the future. Without insurance, you could lose all your assets if you are involved in an accident that causes major repair expenses or liability.

You cannot insure against all types of risk, as some types of insurance are either unavailable or too expensive. Your risk management will determine which types of risk you wish to insure against. When there is a high likelihood that an event will cause a financial loss, and the potential financial loss from that event is large, insurance should be considered. You may choose to accept the types of risk that might only result in small financial losses. In this chapter and the following two, you will learn the key provisions of auto, homeowner's, health, disability, and life insurance. With this background, you can determine your own risk management plan.

Your risk management decisions are also affected by your degree of risk tolerance. For example, you and your neighbor could be in the same financial position and have the same exposure to various types of risk. Yet, you may obtain more insurance than your neighbor because you are more concerned about exposure to financial loss. Although you incur annual insurance expenses from insurance premiums, you are protected from financial losses resulting from covered perils.

Economic Impact on the Decision to Insure Against Risk

ECONOMIC IMPACT

Your decision to insure against risk may be influenced by economic conditions. When economic conditions are favorable and incomes are higher, people are willing to purchase insurance or increase their insurance coverage. When economic conditions are weak, people tend to reduce their insurance so that they can use their funds for other purposes. However, consider the possible danger in reducing your own insurance coverage in a weak economy. You might not have alternative ways to cover unexpected expenses, especially if your future income is uncertain. Insurance should not be viewed as an optional purchase that is dropped whenever your income declines. Some level of insurance is necessary, just like food and shelter. Insurance can help you cover major expenses due to specific events (such as a car accident or health care problem) that could otherwise cause considerable financial problems for you.

Role of Insurance Companies

Insurance companies offer insurance policies that can protect you against financial loss. They charge premiums to the insured in return for the insurance they provide.

Because there are many different types of risk that could cause financial losses, there are many different types of insurance that can protect you from those risks. Exhibit 11.1 describes the common events that can cause a major financial loss and the related insurance that can protect you from these events. The most popular forms of insurance for individuals are property and casualty insurance, life insurance, and health insurance. Property and casualty insurance is used to insure property and therefore consists primarily of auto insurance and home insurance. Some insurance companies specialize in a particular type of insurance, whereas others offer all types of insurance for individuals. Companies that offer the same type of insurance vary in terms of the specific policies that they offer.

Some insurance companies are stand-alone operations, but other insurance businesses are associated with financial institutions such as commercial banks, savings institutions, or securities firms. Some financial institutions have insurance centers within their branches to enable customers to take care of their insurance needs where they receive other financial services.

Insurance Company Operations

When an insurance company sells an insurance policy to you, it is obliged to cover claims as described in the insurance policy. For example, if your car is insured by a policy, the insurance company is obligated to protect you from financial loss due to an accident. If an accident occurs, the insurance company provides payments (subject to limits specified in the contract) to cover any liability to the driver and passengers and to repair property damage resulting from the accident.

EXHIBIT 11.1   Common Events That Could Cause a Financial Loss

Event	Financial Loss	Protection
You have a car accident and damage your car	Car repairs	Auto insurance
You have a car accident in which another person in your car is injured	Medical bills and liability	Auto insurance
You have a car accident in which another person in the other driver's car is injured	Medical bills and liability	Auto insurance
Your home is damaged by a fire	Home repairs	Homeowner's insurance
Your neighbor is injured while in your home	Medical bills and liability	Homeowner's insurance
You become ill and need medical attention	Medical bills	Health insurance
You develop an illness that requires long-term care	Medical bills	Long-term care insurance
You become disabled	Loss of income	Disability insurance
You die while family members rely on your income	Loss of income	Life insurance

In general, insurance companies generate their revenue from receiving payments for policies, and from earning a return from investing the proceeds until the funds are needed to cover claims. They incur costs from making payments to cover policyholder claims. The majority of policyholders do not need to file claims during the coverage period. When an insurance company makes payments due to a claim, the payments are commonly more than the annual premium that was paid by the policyholder. For example, consider a policyholder who pays $1,000 in auto insurance for the year. Assume that he is in an accident, and the insurance company has to pay $20,000 to cover liability and to repair the car. The payout by the insurance company is 20 times the premium received. In other words, it would take a total of 20 auto insurance policy premiums to generate enough revenue to cover the cost of the one claim.

When you buy insurance, you are relying on the insurance company to provide you with adequate coverage over a future period. However, if the insurance company mismanages its operations, it could experience large losses and not be able to cover your claim. In addition, you would probably lose the premium that you had already paid. Thus, it is important that you select an insurance company that is financially strong. There are several services that rate the financial strength of insurance companies, including A. M. Best (http://www.ambest.com), Demotech, Inc. (http://www.demotech.com), Moody's Investors Service (http://www.moodys.com), and Standard & Poor's Financial Services (http://www.standardandpoors.com). The ratings indicate if the insurance companies are in good financial shape and therefore should be able to cover any claims filed in the future.

Relationship Between Insurance Company Claims and Premiums Because insurance companies rely mostly on their premiums to cover claims, they price their insurance policies to reflect the probability of a claim and the size of the claim. For an event that is very unlikely and could cause only minor damage, the premium would be relatively low. For an event that is more likely and could cause major damage, the insurance premium would be relatively high.

Financial Planning
ONLINE

Go to:
http://www.ambest.com

To get:
Information about how insurance companies are rated.

underwriters
From an insurance perspective, underwriters are hired to calculate the risk of specific insurance policies, decide what policies to offer, and what premiums to charge.

Insurance Underwriters An insurance company relies on **underwriters**, who calculate the risk of specific insurance policies, to decide what insurance policies to offer and what premiums to charge. Underwriters recognize that their insurance company must generate revenue that is greater than its expenses to be profitable, so they set premiums that are aligned with anticipated payouts.

Group Insurance Company Policies for Employers Insurance companies commonly offer group insurance policies to employers, so that their employees can obtain discounts, especially for health insurance and disability insurance. Check with your employer to determine if you can obtain the insurance you desire through them. In most cases, the premium you are charged through your employer's insurance plan will be less expensive than if you attempt to obtain the insurance on your own.

insurance agent
Recommends insurance policies for customers.

captive (or exclusive) insurance agent
Works for one particular insurance company.

independent insurance agent
Represents many different insurance companies.

Role of Insurance Agents and Brokers When contacting an insurance company, it is likely that you will communicate with an insurance agent or broker. An **insurance agent** represents one or more insurance companies and recommends an insurance policy that fits the customer's needs. **Captive (or exclusive) insurance agents** work for one particular insurance company, whereas **independent insurance agents** (also called insurance brokers) represent many different insurance companies. They are linked online to various insurance companies and therefore can quickly obtain quotations for different policies. In addition to helping customers with various types of insurance, insurance agents may also offer financial planning services, such as retirement planning and estate planning. Some insurance agents are also certified to serve as a broker for mutual funds or other financial products.

The best insurance companies provide quick and thorough claims service. Sources of information on service by insurance companies include the Better Business Bureau, *Consumer Reports* magazine, and state insurance agencies.

Auto Insurance

Auto insurance insures against damage to an automobile and expenses associated with accidents. In this way, it protects one of your main assets (your car) and also limits your potential liabilities (expenses due to an accident). If you own or drive a car, you need auto insurance. Policies are purchased for a year or six months at property and casualty insurance companies. Your policy specifies the amount of coverage if you are legally liable for bodily injury, if you and your passengers incur medical bills, and if your car is damaged as the result of an accident or some other event (such as a tree falling on the car).

The amount spent on auto insurance has remained fairly stable over the last few years, as shown in Exhibit 11.2. One reason for the size of auto insurance premiums is auto insurance fraud, whereby people submit false claims to get reimbursed by insurance companies. Common forms of fraud include faking an accident, injury, theft, or arson to collect money illegally. The RAND Institute of Civil Justice estimates that one-third of all people injured in accidents exaggerate their injuries, which results in an additional $13 to $18 billion per year in insurance expenses.

Much insurance abuse stems from attorneys who aggressively seek out anyone who has been in an accident. Personal injury attorneys may encourage accident victims to embellish their circumstances to create grounds for a lawsuit, since the attorneys could receive a third or more of the award. The awards granted by the courts for "pain and suffering" combined with the attorney's fees cost insurance companies a substantial amount of the insurance premiums they collect. Some states have implemented **no-fault insurance programs**, which do not hold a specific driver liable for causing the accident. The intent is to avoid costly court battles in which each driver attempts to blame the other. No-fault provisions vary among the states that have imposed no-fault laws. In general, the insurance companies in these states provide coverage (up to specified limits) to their respective policyholders for direct costs incurred due to bodily injury, medical bills, replacement of lost income due to

no-fault insurance programs
Do not hold a specific driver liable for causing the accident.

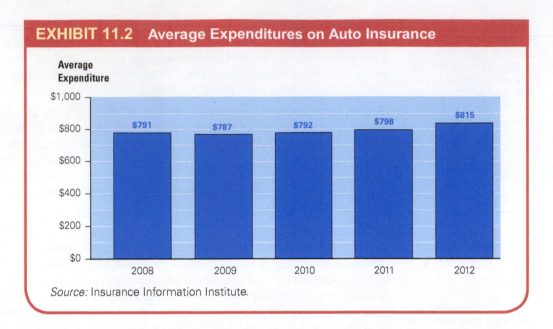

EXHIBIT 11.2   Average Expenditures on Auto Insurance

Average Expenditure

$1,000
$800 — $791 (2008), $787 (2009), $792 (2010), $798 (2011), $815 (2012)
$600
$400
$200
$0

2008   2009   2010   2011   2012

Source: Insurance Information Institute.

the insured's inability to work, and funeral expenses. However, they do not pay for indirect expenses such as emotional distress or pain and suffering due to an accident.

Insurance companies in some no-fault states have been subjected to fraud, especially in New York and New Jersey. For example, some medical professionals charge individuals in accidents for more medical care than is really provided or necessary, knowing that the insurance company will cover the bill. According to the Insurance Research Council, one in five claims for medical payments in New York between 2007 and 2011 was at least partially fraudulent. In response, New York has enacted new regulations governing its no-fault insurance.

Auto Insurance Policy Provisions

insurance policy
Contract between an insurance company and the policyholder.

auto insurance policy
Specifies the coverage provided by the insurance company for a particular individual and vehicle.

An **insurance policy** is a contract between the insurance company and the policyholder. An **auto insurance policy** specifies the coverage (including dollar limits) provided by an insurance company for a particular individual and vehicle. The contract identifies the policyholder and family members who are also insured if they use the insured vehicle. You should have insurance information such as your policy number and the name of a contact person at the insurance company with you when you drive. If you are in an accident, exchange your insurance information with that of the other driver and also fill out a police report.

Every auto insurance policy explains what is covered in detail. Review your own auto insurance policy as you read on, so that you understand your coverage.

Coverage A: Liability Coverage

bodily injury liability coverage
Protects against liability associated with injuries caused by the policyholder.

Liability coverage consists of two key components: (1) bodily injury liability and (2) property damage liability. **Bodily injury liability coverage** protects you against liability associated with injuries that you (or family members listed on the policy) cause. You or your family members are also covered if you cause injuries to others while driving someone else's car with the owner's permission. Bodily injury expenses include medical bills and lost wages as a result of an accident that you cause. The coverage is designed to protect you if you cause an accident and the driver of the other car sues you.

Given the large awards granted in lawsuits in the United States, it is critical to have adequate liability coverage. Any legal expenses incurred by an insurance company when defending you against a lawsuit are not considered when determining the limits on liability coverage. For example, if a person sues you and is awarded an amount that is less than the liability limit in your contract, it is covered by your policy regardless of the legal expenses incurred by the insurance company. If the award granted in a lawsuit against you exceeds the limit on your policy's liability coverage, you will be required to pay the difference and therefore could lose your other assets. At a minimum, you should have coverage of $50,000 for any individual and $100,000 to cover all persons who are injured. A more common recommendation is $100,000 for any individual and $300,000 to $400,000 to cover all injured persons.

property damage liability coverage
Protects against losses that result when the policyholder damages another person's property with his car.

Property damage liability coverage protects you from losses that result when you damage another person's property with your car. Examples include damage to a car, a fence, a lamppost, or a building. Note that property damage liability does not cover your own car or other property that you own. A common recommendation for property damage liability coverage is between $40,000 and $50,000.

Policy Limits   The auto insurance policy specifies monetary limits on the coverage of the bodily injury per person, bodily injury for all people who are injured, and property damage. The policy's limits are often presented as a set of three numbers, split by slashes that are referred to as split liability limits. For example, the split liability limit of 100/300/50 means that the coverage is limited to $100,000 per person injured in an accident, $300,000 for all people combined, and $50,000 to cover damage to the car or other property. If one person suffers bodily injury that results in a liability of $80,000, the entire amount of the liability is covered. If one person's bodily injury results in a liability of $120,000, the coverage is limited to $100,000. If four people suffer bodily injuries amounting to a total of $400,000, $300,000 of that amount is covered.

financial responsibility laws
Laws that require individuals who drive cars to purchase a minimum amount of liability insurance.

Almost all states have **financial responsibility laws** that require individuals who drive cars to purchase a minimum amount of liability insurance. States that do not require liability insurance may require you to show that you can cover damage that you cause. State governments recognize that if an uninsured driver causes an accident, he or she would avoid financial responsibility for any individuals harmed in the accident. These important state laws tend to require a very low level of insurance, which would not cover the liability in many accidents.

There are two types of financial responsibility laws. The first type requires that drivers show proof of auto insurance when they register the car in order to receive their license plates. This law is not always effective because some drivers obtain insurance and then cancel it after they receive their license plates. The second type requires that drivers show proof of their auto insurance when they are in an accident. If they are caught without insurance, they may lose their driver's license. However, the uninsured driver still escapes his financial responsibility at the expense of other individuals who are harmed in the accident.

The minimum liability coverage varies by state, but is usually at least $10,000 to cover each person injured in an accident, $30,000 to cover all persons injured in an accident, and at least $10,000 to cover property damage to the car. Exhibit 11.3 shows the minimum insurance required by all states. Look at the minimum level for your state. Because there are drivers in your state who are underinsured, you will need adequate insurance in case you are in an accident with a driver who has minimal auto insurance, even if the accident is his or her fault.

Coverage B: Medical Payments Coverage

medical payments coverage
Insures against the cost of medical care for you and other passengers in your car when you are at fault in an accident.

Medical payments coverage insures against the cost of medical care for you and other passengers in your car when you are deemed to be at fault in an accident. The medical coverage applies only to the insured car. If you were driving someone else's car, the owner of that car would be responsible for the medical coverage for passengers in that car. You can also obtain medical insurance that covers you if you ride in a car driven by an uninsured driver.

Some advisers may suggest that a minimal amount of medical payments coverage is adequate for your car if you have a good health insurance plan. However, medical

EXHIBIT 11.3	Minimum Auto Insurance Liability Limits				
State	**Liability Limits**	**State**	**Liability Limits**	**State**	**Liability Limits**
Alabama	25/50/25	Kentucky	25/50/10	North Dakota	25/50/25
Alaska	50/100/25	Louisiana	15/30/25	Ohio	25/50/25
Arizona	15/30/10	Maine	50/100/25	Oklahoma	25/50/25
Arkansas	25/50/25	Maryland	30/60/15	Oregon	25/50/20
California	15/30/05	Massachusetts	20/40/5	Pennsylvania	15/30/5
Colorado	25/50/15	Michigan	20/40/10	Rhode Island	25/50/25
Connecticut	20/40/10	Minnesota	30/60/10	South Carolina	25/50/25
Delaware	15/30/5	Mississippi	25/50/25	South Dakota	25/50/25
D.C.	25/50/10	Missouri	25/50/10	Tennessee	25/50/15
Florida	10/20/10	Montana	25/50/10	Texas	30/60/25
Georgia	25/50/25	Nebraska	25/50/25	Utah	25/65/15
Hawaii	20/40/10	Nevada	15/30/10	Vermont	25/50/10
Idaho	25/50/15	New Hampshire	25/50/25	Virginia	25/50/20
Illinois	20/40/15	New Jersey	15/30/5	Washington	25/50/10
Indiana	25/50/10	New Mexico	25/50/10	West Virginia	20/40/10
Iowa	20/40/15	New York	25/50/10	Wisconsin	25/50/10
Kansas	25/50/10	North Carolina	30/60/25	Wyoming	25/50/20

Source: Data from Insurance Information Institute.

payments coverage can be valuable even if you have health insurance because your health insurance policy would not cover nonfamily passengers in your car who could be injured. The coverage may even include funeral expenses.

If the driver of the other car in the accident is determined to be at fault, the medical payments may be covered by that driver's policy. However, if that driver's insurance provides insufficient coverage, your policy can be applied. Some states require that drivers obtain a minimal amount of medical payments coverage, such as $1,000 per person. However, insurance professionals recommend a higher level of coverage, such as $10,000 per person.

Coverage C: Uninsured or Underinsured Motorist Coverage

uninsured motorist coverage
Insures against the cost of bodily injury when an accident is caused by another driver who is not insured.

Uninsured motorist coverage insures against the cost of bodily injury when an accident is caused by another driver who is not insured. Given the large number of uninsured drivers, this coverage is needed.

The coverage also applies if you are in an accident caused by a hit-and-run driver or by a driver who is at fault but whose insurance company goes bankrupt. This coverage applies to bodily injury when you are not at fault, while the liability coverage from Part A applies to bodily injury when you are at fault. Like the insurance on bodily injury in Part A, there are policy limits that you specify, such as $100,000 per person and $300,000 for all persons. The higher the limits, the higher the insurance premium. At a minimum, you should have coverage of $40,000 per accident. Some financial planners recommend coverage of $300,000 per accident.

underinsured motorist coverage
Insures against bodily injury and drivers who have insufficient coverage.

You can also obtain **underinsured motorist coverage** to insure you against bodily injury and drivers who have insufficient coverage. Suppose that there is bodily injury to you as a result of an accident caused by an underinsured driver. If the damages to you are $40,000 and the insurance policy of the underinsured driver only covers $30,000, your insurance company will provide the difference of $10,000.

Coverage D: Collision and Comprehensive Coverage

collision insurance
Insures against costs of damage to your car resulting from an accident in which the policyholder is at fault.

comprehensive coverage
Insures you against damage to your car that results from floods, theft, fire, hail, explosions, riots, and various other events.

Collision and comprehensive coverage insure against damage to your car. **Collision insurance** insures you against costs of damage to your car resulting from an accident in which you are at fault. **Comprehensive coverage** insures you against damage to your car that results from floods, theft, fire, hail, explosions, riots, vandalism, or various other events.

Collision and comprehensive coverage is optional. Car loan providers, however, may require the borrower to maintain insurance that will cover any property damage to the car to protect the lender in the event that the car owner has an accident and stops making the loan payments on the car loan. The car that serves as collateral on the loan may be worthless if it is damaged in an accident. More than 70% of all insured people purchase collision and comprehensive coverage.

Collision and comprehensive coverage is especially valuable if you have a new car that you would likely repair if it were damaged. The coverage may not be so valuable if you have an old car because you may not feel the need to repair damage as long as the car can still be driven. Note that the coverage is limited to the cash value of the car. For example, if your car was worth $2,000 before the accident and $1,200 after the accident, your insurance company will pay no more than $800. The insurance company will not incur extremely high repair expenses to replace cars that have little value.

Collision coverage can be valuable even if you do not believe you were at fault in an accident. If the other driver claims that you were at fault, you and your insurance company may need to take the matter to court. Meanwhile, you can use the collision coverage to have the car repaired. If your insurance company wins the lawsuit, the other driver's insurance company will be required to pay the expenses associated with repairing your car.

Collision coverage is normally limited to the car itself and not to items that were damaged while in the car. For example, if you were transporting a new computer at the time of an accident, the damage to the computer would not be protected by comprehensive coverage.

deductible
A set dollar amount that you are responsible for paying before any coverage is provided by your insurer.

Deductible The **deductible** is the amount of damage that you are responsible for paying before any coverage is provided by the insurance company. For example, a deductible of $250 means that you must pay the first $250 in damages due to an accident. The insurance company pays any additional expenses beyond the deductible. The deductible is normally between $250 and $1,000.

Other Provisions

You can elect coverage for expenses not covered in the standard policy. Specifically, a policy can cover the cost of a rental car while your car is being repaired after an accident. You can also elect coverage for towing, even if the problems are not the result of an accident. Your premium will increase slightly for these provisions.

You can also include a provision on your auto insurance policy to cover any car that you rent. If you do not have such a provision, the rental car agency will typically offer to sell you collision damage coverage, liability insurance, medical coverage, and even coverage for theft of personal belongings from the car. If rent-a-car insurance is not covered by your policy, some credit cards provide you with collision and comprehensive insurance benefits when you use that card to pay for the rental services.

An auto insurance policy also specifies exclusions and limitations of the coverage. For example, coverage may not apply if you intentionally damage a car, if you drive a car that is not yours without the permission of the owner, or if you drive a car that you own

EXHIBIT 11.4 Summary of Auto Insurance Provisions

Financial Damages Related to Your Car in an Accident

	Auto Insurance Provision
Liability due to passengers in your car when you are at fault	Bodily injury liability
Liability due to passengers in your car when you are not at fault but driver of other car is uninsured or underinsured	Uninsured/Underinsured Motorist
Damage to your own car	Collision
Treatment of injuries to driver and passengers of your car	Medical

Financial Damages Related to the Other Car or Other Property in an Accident

Liability due to passengers in the other car	Bodily injury liability
Liability due to damage to the other car	Property damage liability
Liability due to damage to other property	Property damage liability

Financial Damages Related to Your Car When Not in an Accident

Damage to your car as a result of theft, fire, vandalism, or other non-accident events	Comprehensive

but that is not listed on your insurance policy. It also explains how you should comply with procedures if you are in an accident.

Summary of Auto Insurance Provisions

The most important types of coverage identified earlier are included in a standard insurance policy. They are summarized in Exhibit 11.4. Notice that the exhibit classifies the potential financial damages as: (1) related to your car in an accident, (2) related to the other car or other property in an accident, and (3) related to your car when not in an accident.

In general, the liability coverage is the most expensive and represents about 60% of the total premium on average. Note that the limits for bodily injury are specified. The cost of collision and comprehensive insurance commonly represents about 30% of the total premium, but it varies with the car. The cost of collision insurance represents a higher proportion of the total premium for new cars than for older cars.

FREE APPS for Personal Finance

Managing Your Insurance Policy

Application:

The GEICO Mobile app (by GEICO) allows you to pay your insurance bill, access your insurance policy, and manage your insurance policy. Although this app is exclusively for GEICO customers, some other insurance companies also provide similar apps for their customers.

To Find It:

Search for the "GEICO" app on your mobile device.

Auto Insurance Premiums

Your insurance premium is influenced by the likelihood that you will submit claims to the insurance company and the cost to the insurance company for covering those claims. As explained earlier, your auto insurance premium will be higher for a policy that specifies a greater amount of liability coverage and a lower deductible. However, there are other factors that can also affect your premium.

**Financial Planning
ONLINE**

Go to:
http://www.insweb.com

To get:
A recommendation on the amount of car insurance coverage that is appropriate for you.

Characteristics of Your Car

The type of car you drive and the amount of coverage provided by your insurance policy affect the premium that you pay. The typical annual auto insurance premium paid for some cars is about $1,000, whereas the typical annual auto insurance premium paid for other cars can be as high as $3,500. Such a large difference should motivate you to obtain quotes on auto insurance premiums before purchasing a particular car.

Value of Car Insurance premiums are more expensive when the potential financial loss is greater. The collision and comprehensive insurance premiums are high for new cars. In addition, the premium is normally more for an expensive car than an inexpensive car of the same age. The insurance on a new Mercedes is higher than the insurance on a new Ford Fiesta. For more information, do an online search of the most expensive or least expensive cars to insure. Many Web sites offer much information on this topic.

Repair Record of Your Car Some car models require more repair work for the same type of damage. For example, replacing a door on a Toyota may be easier than on some other cars, which reduces the repair bill. When a car can be repaired easily and inexpensively, its insurance premium is lower.

FREE APPS
for Personal
Finance

Auto Insurance Information

Application:

The Go—Compare Car Insurance app (by Go Inc.) helps you compare quotations from several major insurance companies, based on personalized information that you enter.

To Find It:

Search for the "Go—Compare Car Insurance" app on your mobile device.

Your Personal Characteristics

Other factors that characterize you personally affect your insurance premium.

Your Age Insurance companies often base their premiums on personal profiles, and age is one of the most important characteristics. Younger drivers are more likely to get into accidents, and therefore they pay higher insurance premiums. In particular, drivers between the ages of 16 and 25 are considered to be high risk. Insurance companies incur higher expenses from covering their claims and offset the higher expenses by charging higher premiums. Another important characteristic is gender, as male drivers tend to get into more accidents than female drivers. For these reasons, male teenagers are charged very high auto insurance premiums.

Your Mileage You are more likely to get into an accident the more miles you drive. Thus, your premium will be higher if you drive more. Many insurance companies classify drivers in two or more mileage groups. For example, if you drive less than 10,000 miles per year, you may qualify for the low-mileage group, which entitles you to a lower premium.

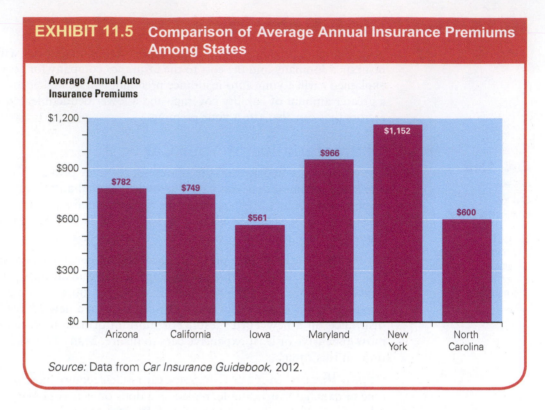

EXHIBIT 11.5   Comparison of Average Annual Insurance Premiums Among States

Average Annual Auto Insurance Premiums

State	Premium
Arizona	$782
California	$749
Iowa	$561
Maryland	$966
New York	$1,152
North Carolina	$600

Source: Data from *Car Insurance Guidebook,* 2012.

Your Driving Record If you have an excellent driving record, including no accidents and no traffic tickets for a year or longer, you may be charged a lower premium than other drivers. No one purposely creates a bad driving record, but some drivers do not realize how much their insurance premium will increase if they establish a poor driving record. Because most insurance companies attempt to avoid drivers with a history of causing accidents, these drivers cannot comparison shop effectively. They may have to accept the premium of any insurance company that is willing to insure their car. Once drivers are labeled as high risk, it will take several years of safe driving to prove that they have improved their driving habits. Thus, they will pay relatively high insurance premiums for several years.

Your Location Auto insurance is more expensive in large cities, where the probability of being involved in an accident is higher. The expenditures also vary among states for a given year, as you can see in Exhibit 11.5. The premiums tend to be higher in highly populated, highly urban states with much traffic such as Connecticut, New Jersey, and New York, and lower in less populated, largely rural states such as Iowa, Kansas, Maine, and Wyoming. Within each state, insurance expenditures vary. For example, insurance in Los Angeles is much higher than insurance in other parts of California.

Your Driver Training Insurance companies recognize that driver training can improve driver performance and can reduce the likelihood of accidents in the future. They encourage drivers to take driver training programs. If you have completed a driver training program, you may qualify for a discount.

Your School Performance Insurance companies recognize that good students also appear to be safer drivers. Therefore, they may charge good students lower premiums.

Your Credit History Insurance companies have found that persons with poor credit histories tend to make more insurance claims. Therefore, the insurance company will probably look at your credit history and charge you a higher premium if your record is poor and you have a low credit rating. A few states do not allow insurance companies to base premiums on the applicant's credit history, but in most states this has become a common practice.

Your Insurance Company

One final factor that affects your auto insurance premium is the insurance company that you select. The largest companies for providing auto insurance are Allstate, Farmers, GEICO, Progressive, and State Farm. These five companies account for more than half of all auto insurance provided in the United States.

Auto insurance premiums can vary substantially among insurance companies, so always obtain several quotes before you select an insurance company. Several Web sites (such as http://www.insweb.com and http://www.esurance.com) provide auto insurance quotes online. Some Web sites even allow you to buy insurance online.

If you have specific questions about the coverage and want to speak to an insurance salesperson, you can call some insurance companies directly. A comparison of quotes online might at least help you determine which insurance companies to call for more information. Alternatively, you can call an independent insurance agent, who can help you purchase insurance from one of several insurance companies.

When comparing prices, recognize that the price comparison may vary with the type of policy desired. For example, an insurance company may have relatively low premiums compared to its competitors for a policy involving substantial coverage for bodily injury liability, but relatively high premiums for a policy involving collision coverage. Therefore, you should not select a company based on advice you receive from friends or family members. If their policy is different from the policy you desire, another company may offer a better deal. In addition, companies change their premiums over time, so a company may charge relatively low premiums in one period, but relatively high premiums in the following period for the same policy.

Comparing Prices at the Time of Renewal Once an auto insurance policy has been in effect for 60 days, an insurance company can only cancel your policy if you provided fraudulent information on your application, if your driver's license is suspended, or if you do not pay your insurance premium. However, an insurance company may decide not to renew your policy when it expires if you had a poor driving record over the recent policy period. For example, it is unlikely to renew your contract if you caused an accident as a result of drunk driving. Federal law also allows a company to deny renewal if your credit rating has declined, although state law may restrict a company's ability to do this.

If an insurance company is willing to renew your policy, it may raise the premium in the renewal period even if your driving record has been good. You can switch to a different insurance company when the policy expires if you are not satisfied with your present insurance company or think that the premium is too high. You should compare auto insurance prices among companies before renewing your policy. However, recognize that your driving record will follow you. If you recently caused one or more accidents, you will likely be charged a higher premium whether you continue with your existing insurance company or switch to a new company.

EXAMPLE

Stephanie Spratt is about to renew her car insurance policy. She is considering two policies. Policy A is 100/300/50, which means that the liability coverage is limited to $100,000 per person injured in an accident, $300,000 maximum per accident, and $50,000 to cover damage to the other vehicle or other property. The policy has collision and comprehensive coverage with a deductible of $200. The annual premium for this policy is $1,240. Policy B has liability coverage of 60/100/20 and an annual premium of $800. Stephanie prefers Policy A, because Policy B subjects her to a high level of risk due to liability. Although Policy B is less expensive, the potential savings are not worth the extra risk that would result from having lower liability coverage.

Stephanie's insurance agent tells her that if she increases her deductible from $200 to $400, her premium will fall to $1,100, which is $140 less than the $1,240 premium quoted for a policy with a $200 deductible. She decides to raise her deductible so that she can reduce next year's premium by $140. The policy Stephanie chose is shown in Exhibit 11.6.

EXHIBIT 11.6   Stephanie Spratt's Auto Insurance Policy

Insured Policyholder:	Stephanie Spratt	**License Number:**	ZZ QQZZ
Policy Number:	WW77-QG22-999	**Amount Due:**	$1,100
Coverage Begins On:	April 6 for one year	**Drivers of Car in Your Household:**	One driver, age 25.
Insured Car:	Honda Civic	**Ordinary Use of Car:**	Less than 10,000 miles
Due Date:	April 6		per year.

COVERAGE

Liability	
Bodily Injury ($100,000/$300,000 limit)	
Property Damage ($50,000 limit)	
Total Liability	$480
Medical Expenses and Income Loss	$170
Uninsured/Underinsured Motorist ($100,000/$300,000 limit)	$210
Collision ($400 Deductible)	$270
Comprehensive ($400 Deductible)	$86
Emergency Road Service	$4
Total	**$1,220**
Discounts in the Premium	
Antilock Brakes	$30
Accident-free last seven years	$90
Total Discounts	$120
Amount Due	**$1,100**

If You Are in an Auto Accident

If you are in an auto accident, contact the police immediately. Request information from the other driver(s) in the accident, including their insurance information. You may also obtain contact information (including license plate numbers) from witnesses, just in case they leave before the police arrive. Make sure that you can validate whatever information other drivers provide. Some drivers who believe they are at fault and do not have insurance may attempt to give you a fake name and leave before police arrive. Take pictures of any evidence that may prove that you were not at fault. Write down the details of how the accident happened while they are fresh in your mind. Ask for a copy of the police report.

File a claim with your insurance company immediately. Your insurance company will review the police report and may contact witnesses. It will also verify that your insurance policy is still in effect, and determine whether the repairs and medical treatment will be covered based on your policy's provisions. The insurance policy may specify some guidelines for having your car repaired, such as obtaining at least two estimates before you have repairs done. A claims adjuster employed by the insurance company may investigate the accident details and attempt to determine how much you should be paid.

Once you incur expenses, such as car repair or medical expenses, send this information along with receipts to the insurance company. The insurance company will respond by reimbursing you for the portion of the expenses covered under your policy. It may provide full or partial reimbursement. Alternatively, it may state that some or all of your expenses are not covered by your policy.

If your insurance company believes that the other driver is at fault, it should seek damages from the other driver's insurance company. If the other driver is not insured, your insurance company will pay your claim if you have uninsured or underinsured motorist insurance. If your claim is denied by your insurance company and you still believe that the other driver is at fault, you may need to file a claim against the other driver or the other driver's insurance company. This is also the case when an injured party seeks damages greater than those offered by his or her policy.

Homeowner's Insurance Provisions

homeowner's insurance
Provides insurance in the event of property damage, theft, or personal liability relating to your home.

Homeowner's insurance provides insurance in the event of property damage, theft, or personal liability relating to home ownership. It not only protects the most valuable asset for many individuals, but also limits their potential liabilities (expenses) associated with the home. Premiums on homeowner's insurance are commonly paid yearly or may be included in your mortgage payment.

Financial loss due to the ownership of a home could occur due to a wide variety of adverse events, ranging from a flood to burglary. The cost of covering claims due to fire, lightning, wind, hail, and water damage represent almost half of all expenses incurred by homeowner's insurance companies.

Homeowner's insurance is structured in six different packages, distinguished by the degree of coverage. After selecting the package that you prefer, you can request additional provisions for the policy to fit your particular needs. Eight packages are summarized in Exhibit 11.7. Notice that HO-1, HO-2, HO-3, HO-5, and HO-8 focus on insurance for the home. The higher the number, the greater the coverage, and the higher the premium that would be paid for a given home. Two packages, HO-4 and HO-6, provide renter's insurance and insurance for condominium owners, respectively. HO-7 provides insurance for mobile homes.

A homeowner's insurance policy typically provides coverage of property damage and protection from personal liability. As shown in Exhibit 11.7, the specific details regarding the coverage vary among homeowner's insurance policies. Most homeowner's insurance policies focus on the following types of coverage.

EXHIBIT 11.7   Types of Perils Protected by Homeowner's (HO) Insurance Policies

HO-1: Protects against fire, lightning, explosions, hail, riots, vehicles, aircraft, smoke, vandalism, theft, malicious mischief, glass breakage.

HO-2: Protects against the events identified in HO-1, along with falling objects, the weight of ice, snow, or sleet, the collapse of buildings, overflow of water or steam, power surges, and the explosion of steam or hot-water systems, frozen plumbing, heating units, air-conditioning systems, and domestic appliances.

HO-3: Protects the home and any other structures on the property against all events except those that are specifically excluded by the homeowner's policy. The events that are typically not covered by this insurance are earthquakes, floods, termites, war, and nuclear accidents. It may be possible to obtain additional insurance to protect against floods or earthquakes. This policy also protects personal assets against the events that are listed in HO-2.

HO-4: Renter's insurance. Protects personal assets from events such as theft, fire, vandalism, and smoke.

HO-5: Protects the home, other structures on the property, and personal assets against all events except those that are excluded by the specific homeowner's policy. This policy provides coverage of the home similar to that provided by HO-3, but slightly more coverage of personal assets.

HO-6: Condominium owner's insurance. Protects personal assets from events such as theft, fire, vandalism, and smoke (review the specific policy to determine which events are covered).

HO-7: Is intended to cover mobile homes and house trailers.

HO-8: Protects the home from the same events identified in HO-1, except that it is based on repairs or cash values, not replacement costs.

Property Damage

cash value policy
Pays you for the value of the damaged property after considering its depreciation.

replacement cost policy
Pays you for the actual cost of replacing the damaged property.

The homeowner's policy covers damage to the home. The specific provisions of the policy explain the degree of coverage. A **cash value policy** pays you for the value of the damaged property after considering its depreciation (wear and tear). A **replacement cost policy** pays you for the actual cost of replacing the damaged property. A replacement cost policy is preferable because the actual cost of replacing damaged property is normally higher than the assessed value of property. For example, assume a home is completely destroyed and was valued at $90,000 just before it was destroyed. A cash value policy would provide insurance coverage of $90,000, even though the cost of rebuilding (replacing) the home could be $100,000 or more. In contrast, the replacement cost policy would insure the home for its replacement cost and therefore would cover the entire cost of repairing the damage up to a limit specified in the homeowner's policy. A policy typically specifies a deductible, or an amount that you would need to pay for damage before the insurance coverage is applied.

Minimum Limit Many insurers require that your homeowner's insurance policy cover at least 80% of the full replacement cost. The financial institution that provides your mortgage loan will likely require homeowner's insurance coverage that would at least cover your mortgage. In most cases, you would want more insurance than is required by the mortgage lender. You should have sufficient insurance not only to cover the mortgage loan balance, but also to replace the property and all personal assets that are damaged.

Other Structures on Property

The homeowner's insurance policy also specifies whether separate structures such as a garage, shed, or swimming pool are covered, and the maximum amount of coverage. Trees and shrubs are usually included with a specified maximum amount of coverage. A deductible may be applied to these other structures.

Personal Property

home inventory
Contains detailed information about your personal property that can be used when filing a claim.

A policy normally covers personal assets such as furniture, computers, or clothing up to some specified maximum amount. For example, a policy may specify that all personal assets such as furniture and clothing are covered up to $40,000. Standard homeowner's insurance policies limit the coverage of personal property to no more than one-half of the coverage of the dwelling. A deductible may also be applied to the personal property.

A **home inventory** includes detailed information about your personal property that can be used when filing a claim. Create a list of all your personal assets, and estimate the market value of each of them. Use a video camera to film your personal assets in your home for proof of their existence. Keep the list and the video in a safe place outside your home, so that you have access to them even if your home is destroyed.

Personal Property Replacement Cost Coverage Many homeowner's policies cover personal property for their cash value. For example, if a home entertainment system priced at $2,500 three years ago is assumed to have a life of five years, it would have used up three-fifths of its life. Based on this amount of depreciation, the insurer will pay you the cash value of $1,000. Yet, if this home entertainment system was destroyed in a fire, you might need to spend $3,000 to replace it.

Just as the dwelling can be insured at replacement cost rather than cash value, so can personal assets. This provision will increase your insurance premium slightly, but it may be worthwhile if you have personal assets that have a high replacement cost.

personal property floater
An extension of the homeowner's insurance policy that allows you to itemize your valuables.

Personal Property Floater Some personal assets are very valuable but are not fully covered by your homeowner's policy. You may need to obtain a **personal property floater** (also called personal articles floater), which is an extension of the homeowner's insurance policy that allows you to itemize your valuables. For example, if you have very expensive computer equipment or jewelry in your home, you may purchase this additional insurance to protect those specific assets. An alternative type is an unscheduled personal property floater, which provides protection for all of your personal property.

Home Office Provision Assets in a home office such as a personal computer are not covered in many standard homeowner's policies. You can request a home office provision, which will require a higher premium. Alternatively, you could purchase a separate policy to cover the home office.

Liability

The policy specifies coverage in the event that you are sued as the result of an event that occurs in your home or on your property. Normally, you are responsible for an injury to other persons while they are on your property. For example, if a neighbor falls down the steps of your home and sues you, your policy would likely cover you. Your exposure to liability is not tied to the value of your home. Even if you have a small home with a low value, you need to protect against liability. Some insurance companies provide minimum coverage of $100,000 against liability. However, a higher level of coverage, such as $300,000, is commonly recommended. The coverage includes the court costs and awards granted as a result of lawsuits against you due to injuries on your property.

Other Types of Provisions

There are many other possible provisions that could be included in a policy to cover a wide variety of circumstances. For example, if an event such as a fire forces you to live away from home, you will incur additional living expenses. A loss-of-use provision specifies whether your policy covers these expenses and the maximum amount of coverage.

Homeowner's Insurance Premiums

Homeowner's insurance premiums have risen in recent years. This section describes the factors that influence the premium charged, and explains how you can reduce your premium.

Factors That Affect Homeowner's Insurance Premiums

Your homeowner's insurance premium is influenced by the likelihood that you will submit claims to the insurance company and the cost to the insurance company of covering those claims. The premium you pay for homeowner's insurance is primarily dependent on the following factors:

- **Value of Insured Home.** Insurance premiums reflect the value of the insured home and therefore are higher for more expensive homes.
- **Deductible.** A higher deductible reduces the amount of coverage provided by the homeowner's insurance and therefore results in a lower insurance premium.
- **Location.** The potential for damage due to weather conditions is greater in some areas, and therefore the premiums are higher as well. For example, homes along the Gulf Coast are more likely to be damaged by a hurricane than homes located 40 miles inland. Home insurance rates are therefore much higher along the coast. Similarly, premiums will be higher for homes in locations prone to tornadoes, floods, or earthquakes. Exhibit 11.8 illustrates how average insurance premiums can vary among states. Notice that coastal states that are most exposed to hurricanes (Florida and Texas), and states with a high likelihood of tornadoes (Oklahoma) have higher premiums than other states.

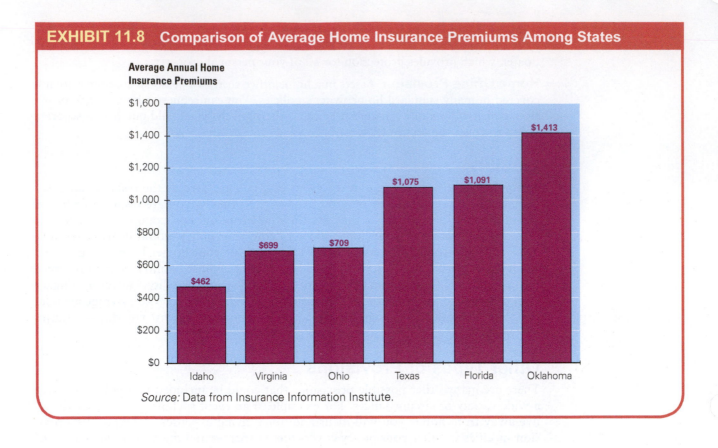

EXHIBIT 11.8   Comparison of Average Home Insurance Premiums Among States

Average Annual Home Insurance Premiums

Idaho: $462
Virginia: $699
Ohio: $709
Texas: $1,075
Florida: $1,091
Oklahoma: $1,413

Source: Data from Insurance Information Institute.

- **Degree of Protection.** If you want protection against an earthquake on a home in California, you must pay a higher premium. If you want protection against a flood, you may need to buy an additional insurance policy.
- **Discounts.** You may obtain discounts on your insurance by maintaining a smoke detector system in your home, paying for your insurance in one lump sum, or purchasing multiple types of insurance (such as auto, health, and life) from the same insurer.

Reducing Your Homeowner's Insurance Premium

Consider the following actions you can take to reduce your homeowner's insurance premium.

Increase Your Deductible If you are willing to pay a higher deductible, you can reduce your premium. For example, if you use a deductible of $1,000 instead of $100, you may be able to reduce your premium by about 20% or more.

Improve Protection If you improve the protection of your home, your insurance premium will decline. For example, you could install storm shutters to protect against bad weather or a security system to protect against burglary.

Use One Insurer for All Types of Insurance Some insurance companies offer lower premiums to customers who purchase more than one type of insurance from them.

Stay with the Same Insurance Company When you stay with the same insurance company, you may be rewarded with a lower insurance premium.

Shop Around As with auto insurance, you may be able to reduce your homeowner's insurance premium by obtaining quotations from various insurance companies. The insurance premium can vary substantially among insurers.

EXHIBIT 11.9   Stephanie Spratt's Homeowner's Insurance Policy

Coverages and Limits	
Dwelling	$110,000
Personal Property ($1,000 deductible)	$25,000
Personal Liability	$100,000
Damage to Property of Others	$500
Medical Payments to Others (per person)	$1,000
Discounts	$25 for House Alarm
Annual Premium	$600

EXAMPLE

Stephanie Spratt is reviewing her homeowner's insurance policy, which is shown in Exhibit 11.9, to determine whether she should change her homeowner's insurance policy once her existing policy expires. She may consider increasing her deductible because this would allow her to incur a lower insurance premium. When her homeowner's policy is near expiration, she plans to obtain a home insurance quote from her auto insurance company because that company also provides home insurance. She hopes that she might be able to receive a discount if she obtains both types of insurance from one insurance company.

Filing a Claim

If your property is damaged, you should contact your insurance company immediately. A claims adjuster from your insurance company will come to estimate the damage. Present your home inventory to the adjuster. Her estimate will include the cost of repairing the damage done to your home and compensation for damaged property. The company may be willing to issue a check so that you can hire someone to do the repairs. You should consider obtaining an independent estimate on the repairs to ensure that the amount the insurance company offers you is sufficient. If the insurance company's estimate is too low, you can appeal it.

Renter's Insurance

renter's insurance
An insurance policy that covers your possessions within a house, condo, or apartment that you are renting.

Renter's insurance insures your possessions within a house, condo, or apartment that you are renting. It does not insure the structure itself because the insurance is for the renter only, not the owner of the property. It covers personal assets such as furniture, televisions, computer equipment, and audio equipment. The insurance protects against damage due to weather or the loss of personal assets due to burglary. It can cover living expenses while the rental property is being repaired. It also covers liability in the event that a friend or neighbor is injured while on the rental property.

Renters whose personal assets have a high market value need renter's insurance to protect those assets. Even renters without valuable personal assets may desire renter's insurance to protect against liability.

Renter's Insurance Policy Provisions

Renter's insurance specifies the maximum amount of coverage for your personal assets. It may also specify maximum coverage for specific items such as jewelry. The insurance premium is dependent on the amount of coverage you desire. Your renter's insurance may also cover liability resulting from injury to a person while on your premises. For example, if your pet injures a neighbor in your yard, your renter's insurance may cover your liability up to a limit. Because renter's insurance policies vary, you should closely review any policy to ensure that the insurance coverage is appropriate.

Umbrella Personal Liability Policy

umbrella personal liability policy
A supplement to auto and homeowner's insurance that provides additional personal liability coverage.

You can supplement your auto and homeowner's insurance with an **umbrella personal liability policy**, which provides additional personal liability coverage.

This type of policy is intended to provide additional insurance, not to replace the other policies. In fact, the insurance will not be provided unless you show proof of existing insurance coverage. Umbrella policies are especially useful when you have personal assets beyond a car and home that you wish to protect from liability. You may be able to purchase an umbrella policy for about $200 per year for coverage of $1 million.

How Insurance Fits Within Your Financial Plan

The following are the key decisions about auto and homeowner's insurance that should be included within your financial plan:

- Do you have adequate insurance to protect your wealth?
- How much insurance should you plan to have in the future?

Exhibit 11.10 provides an example of how auto and homeowner's insurance decisions apply to Stephanie Spratt's financial plan.

EXHIBIT 11.10   How Auto and Homeowner's Insurance Fit Within Stephanie Spratt's Financial Plan

GOALS FOR AUTO AND HOMEOWNER'S INSURANCE PLANNING

1. *Maintain adequate insurance for my car and my home.*
2. *Determine whether I should increase my auto and homeowner's insurance levels in the future.*

ANALYSIS

Type of Insurance	Protection	Status
Auto	*Protects one of my main assets and limits my potential liabilities.*	*Already have insurance, but I'm considering more liability coverage.*
Homeowner's	*Protects my largest asset and limits my potential liabilities.*	*Recently purchased homeowner's insurance as a result of buying a home.*

DECISIONS

Decision on Whether My Present Insurance Coverage Is Adequate:

I may increase my auto insurance liability coverage to 100/300/40. While more costly, the increased liability coverage could be worthwhile. I will also consider raising my deductible, which would reduce the insurance premium.

I currently have sufficient homeowner's insurance, but I will consider switching my policy over to my auto insurance company when the present policy expires. I will receive a discount on the insurance premium as a result of having multiple insurance contracts with the same insurance company. I will create a home inventory. I might also consider increasing my deductible on my home in order to pay a lower insurance premium.

Decision on Insurance Coverage in the Future:

If I buy a more expensive car, I will need additional insurance. However, I will not be buying a new car in the near future. If I buy a more expensive home or if the value of my existing home rises substantially, I will need to increase my homeowner's coverage.

DISCUSSION QUESTIONS

1. How would Stephanie's auto and homeowner's insurance purchasing decisions be different if she were a single mother of two children?

2. How would Stephanie's auto and homeowner's insurance purchasing decisions be affected if she were 35 years old? If she were 50 years old?

SUMMARY

Risk Management. The term *risk* can be defined as exposure to events (or perils) that can cause a financial loss. Your risk management decisions determine whether and how to protect against risk. Your alternatives are to avoid risk, reduce risk, accept risk, or insure against risk. There are some types of risk that are difficult to avoid and dangerous to accept. For these types of risk, insurance is needed. Once you decide whether to obtain a particular type of insurance, you must decide on the amount of coverage and where to purchase the insurance.

Role of Insurance Companies. Insurance companies provide insurance that can protect you from major financial losses. Property and casualty insurance is used to insure property and therefore consists primarily of auto insurance and home insurance. Some insurance companies specialize in a particular type of insurance, while others offer all types of insurance for individuals.

Auto Insurance. Automobile insurance insures against damage to your automobile and expenses associated with an accident. It includes liability coverage, medical payments coverage, uninsured or underinsured motorist coverage, and collision and comprehensive coverage (damage to your car).

Auto Insurance Premium. The higher the value of your car and the lower your deductible, the higher your auto insurance premium will be. In addition, personal characteristics such as a young age, more mileage driven, a highly populated location, and a poor credit history result in a higher auto insurance premium.

If You Are in an Auto Accident. If you are in an auto accident, contact the police immediately, and obtain insurance information from the other driver(s). Ask for a copy of the police report. File a claim with your insurance company immediately.

Homeowner's Insurance. A homeowner's insurance policy provides coverage of property damage and protection from personal liability. Policies specify whether the property coverage is based on a cash value versus the cost of replacement, and whether other structures on the property are covered.

Homeowner's Insurance Premium. The premium paid for homeowner's insurance is dependent on the home's value, the deductible, and the likelihood of damage to the home. In general, the higher the value of the home and the lower your deductible, the higher your home insurance premium will be.

Renter's Insurance. Renter's insurance insures your possessions within a house, condo, or apartment that you are renting. It covers personal assets and protects against damage due to weather or the loss of personal assets due to burglary.

Umbrella Personal Liability Policy. You can supplement your auto and homeowner's insurance with an umbrella personal liability policy, which provides additional personal liability coverage. Umbrella policies are especially useful when you have personal assets beyond a car and home that you wish to protect.

How Insurance Fits Within Your Financial Plan. Many people identify a home and a car as key purchases to be made within their financial plan. You need insurance to protect these assets against major losses that could occur, so you can ultimately complete your financial plan and achieve your financial goals.

REVIEW QUESTIONS

All Review Questions are available in MyFinanceLab *at* http://www.myfinancelab.com.

1. **Purpose of Insurance.** What is the purpose of insurance? What is meant by the term *liability*? How can individuals benefit from insurance?

2. **Risk Management.** What is risk? What is risk management? How does insurance fit into risk management?

3. **Insurance Company Claims.** What is the responsibility of the insurance company that sells you a policy? What is the relationship between insurance company claims and premiums paid by policyholders?

4. **Insurance Underwriters.** What is the role of insurance underwriters? What is the role of insurance agents? Describe the two different types of insurance agents.

5. **Liability Coverage.** Describe the two components of liability coverage in an auto insurance policy.

6. **Policy Limits.** What do policy limits of 25/50/25 mean? Do you think the minimum amounts of liability insurance required by your state are suitable for all drivers? Explain your answer.

7. **Financial Responsibility Laws.** Describe the two types of financial responsibility laws most states have. Are these laws always effective?

8. **Medical Payments Coverage.** How does medical payments coverage under an auto insurance policy work? Why is medical payments coverage valuable even if you have a good health insurance plan?

9. **Auto Insurance Coverage.** Describe collision and comprehensive coverage. Is this type of coverage required by most states? Who may require this type of coverage?

10. **Auto Insurance Premium.** List and briefly discuss factors that will affect your auto insurance premium.

11. **No-Fault Insurance.** What is the intent of no-fault insurance? How does no-fault insurance generally work? What is a disadvantage of no-fault insurance?

12. **Car Accident.** What steps should you take if you are in a car accident?

13. **Homeowner's Insurance.** What is homeowner's insurance? How are the premiums normally paid?

14. **Types of Homeowner's Insurance.** List and briefly describe the four packages of homeowner's insurance that focus on insurance for the home.

15. **Cash Value Insurance.** What is a "cash value" homeowner's policy? What is a "replacement cost" homeowner's policy?

16. **Personal Property Insurance.** Is personal property typically insured under a homeowner's insurance policy? If so, are there limits to the coverage of personal property? What is a home inventory?

17. **Personal Property Floater.** What is a personal property floater? What is the difference between scheduled and unscheduled floaters?

18. **Homeowner Insurance Premium.** List and briefly describe some of the factors that affect homeowner's insurance premiums.

19. **Reducing Home Insurance Premiums.** What are some steps you could take to reduce your homeowner's insurance premium?

20. **Filing a Claim.** Describe the steps you would take to file a claim on your homeowner's insurance.

21. **Renter's Insurance.** How is renter's insurance different from homeowner's insurance? Who should consider purchasing renter's insurance? Briefly describe some of the provisions of a renter's insurance policy.

22. **Umbrella Policy.** What is the purpose of an umbrella personal liability policy? Who might need one?

23. **Financial Strength of the Insurance Company.** How can you determine the financial strength of an insurance company? Why is this important to you as a consumer?

24. **Risk Reduction.** List some ways you can reduce risk and limit your overall exposure to loss.

25. **Psychology and Risk.** Why do some people choose to accept risk rather than purchase insurance? Why is this mind-set problematic?

26. **Geographic Location and Insurance Costs.** Why does your geographic location impact the cost of homeowner's insurance? Why does it impact the cost of your automobile insurance?

27. **Credit History and Insurance.** How does your credit history impact your insurance costs?

28. **Home Inventory.** Why is it important to keep a detailed inventory of your household possessions outside your home?

29. **Policy Coverages.** Why is it important to carefully review the types of perils covered by your

homeowner's insurance policy? What are some common perils that are not covered by many homeowner's policies?

30. **Ethical Dilemma.** You teach Personal Finance at a local community college. The state in which you teach requires proof of liability insurance to renew your license plates.

During the discussion of this topic in class, several students admit that they obtain a liability policy just prior to the renewal of their license plates and then cancel it immediately thereafter. They do this because they know that the state has no system for following up on the cancellation of the liability policies once the license plates are issued. These students, who are out of work as a result of a local plant shutdown, say that they cannot afford to maintain the insurance, but they must have access to cars for transportation.

a. Discuss whether you consider the conduct of the students to be unethical.

b. How does the conduct of these students potentially affect other members of the class who maintain liability insurance on their vehicles?

FINANCIAL PLANNING ONLINE EXERCISES

1. Answer the following questions using the information found at http://www.ambest.com. Describe the information that you can access about insurance ratings and why this information may be useful to you.

2. Go to http://www.insweb.com or to any Web site where you can obtain a quote on auto insurance.

   a. Obtain an auto insurance quote for the vehicle that you drive. Compare that quote to the insurance premium that you presently pay.

   b. Assume you could purchase a new vehicle that you desire. Obtain an insurance quote for that vehicle. How does the insurance on this new vehicle compare to the insurance quote on the vehicle that you presently drive? Why do you think the quotes are different?

PSYCHOLOGY OF PERSONAL FINANCE: Your Auto Insurance

1. Consumers commonly focus on the price when buying auto insurance. They feel less pain from buying auto insurance when they pay as little as possible. However, this strategy can backfire because the insurance they receive may reflect the low price they paid. Describe your own behavior when purchasing auto insurance. Do you request specific insurance coverage or pursue the cheapest possible policy?

2. Read one practical article of how psychology affects decisions when buying auto insurance. You can easily retrieve possible articles by doing an online search using the terms "psychology" and "buying auto insurance." Summarize the main points of the article.

WEB SEARCH EXERCISE

You can develop your personal finance skills by conducting an Internet search for related articles. Find a recent online article about personal finance that reinforces one or more concepts covered in this chapter. If your class has an online component, your professor may ask you to post your summary of the article there and provide a link to the article so that other students can access it. If your class is live, your professor may ask you to summarize your application of the article in class. Your professor may assign specific students to complete this assignment or may allow any student to do the assignment on a volunteer basis.

For recent online articles related to this chapter, consider using the following search terms (be sure to include the current year as a search term to ensure that the online articles are recent):

- How auto insurance protects you
- Auto insurance coverage
- Auto insurance premium
- Selecting auto insurance
- How home insurance protects you
- Home insurance coverage
- Home insurance premium
- Selecting home insurance

VIDEO EXERCISE: Selecting Auto Insurance

Go to one of the Web sites that contain video clips (such as http://www.youtube.com) and view some video clips available about selecting auto insurance. You can use search phrases such as "auto insurance tips." Select one video clip on this topic that you would recommend for the other students in your class.

1. Provide the Web link for the video clip.
2. What do you think is the main point of this video clip?
3. How might you change your process of selecting auto insurance as a result of watching this video clip?

BUILDING YOUR OWN FINANCIAL PLAN

Referring to the balance sheet that you prepared in Chapter 2, identify assets that you believe require insurance coverage from an auto or homeowner's policy. Do not overlook risk exposures that can be covered by insurance for less obvious items such as clothing and other personal property.

Go to the worksheets at the end of this chapter to continue building your financial plan.

THE SAMPSONS—A Continuing Case

As the next step in reviewing their finances, the Sampsons are assessing their insurance needs related to their vehicles and home. They indicated the amount of money they spend on insurance on their personal balance sheet in Chapter 2.

They currently have auto insurance on their two cars. Each insurance policy has a $1,000 deductible and specifies limits of 100/200/20 ($100,000 per person injured in an accident, $200,000 for all people combined, and $20,000 to cover other damage to the car or to other property). Dave and Sharon live in a no-fault state.

Their homeowner's insurance covers the market value of their home and has a deductible of $10,000. Their policy does not cover floods, which periodically occur in their area. Their house has never been flooded, though, so Dave and Sharon are not concerned.

Go to the worksheets at the end of this chapter to continue this case.

CHAPTER 11: BUILDING YOUR OWN FINANCIAL PLAN

GOALS

1. Ensure that your car and dwelling are adequately insured.

2. Prepare a home inventory.

3. Determine whether you should increase your auto and homeowner's or renter's insurance in the future.

ANALYSIS

1. Review the personal balance sheet you created in Chapter 2. Which assets require coverage from an auto or homeowner's/renter's policy? What risks should you insure against?

_____

_____

_____

_____

2. Using Web sites such as http://www.insurance.com and http://www.insweb.com, obtain a quote for auto insurance based on a bodily injury limit of $100,000/$300,000 limit.

Coverage

Liability

Bodily Injury ($100,000/$300,000 limit)	$	
Property Damage ($50,000 limit)	$	
Subtotal Liability		$
No-Fault Medical Expenses and Income Loss	$	
Uninsured/Underinsured Motorist ($100,000/$300,000 limit)	$	
Collision ($ _____ Deductible)	$	
Comprehensive ($ _____ Deductible)	$	
Emergency Road Service	$	
Subtotal		$

Additional Charges (List):	$	
	$	
	$	
	$	
	$	
	$	
	$	
Subtotal		$

Discounts in the Premium

Antilock Brakes	$	
Accident-Free Last Seven Years	$	
Other Discounts (List):	$	
	$	
	$	
	$	
	$	
Minus Total Discounts		$
Total Amount Due		$

3. Complete your home inventory using the following worksheet. If you input this information in the Excel worksheet, the software will perform calculations and present pie charts showing the purchase cost of your property versus the replacement cost. Based on your inventory, how much personal property coverage should you have? Is replacement cost or cash value a better policy option? Do you need a personal property floater for any high-ticket items?

   In addition to facilitating the process of settling insurance claims and verifying losses, a home inventory helps you determine the amount of insurance you need. The complexity of your inventory depends on your stage in life and family situation. It's a good idea to include copies of sales receipts and purchase contracts with your inventory. After completing your home inventory, print multiple copies and file them in secure locations (safety deposit box, fireproof box, at your parents' home, and so on). You should also consider taking pictures of individual items or videotaping entire rooms as further documentation.

NAME _____ **DATE** _____

Home Inventory

	Item Description	Make and Model	Date Acquired	Estimated Purchase Cost	Estimated Replacement Cost
Electronics					
Computer Equipment (PC, Laptop, Tablet)					
Television					
Audio Equipment					
DVD Player					
Smartphone					
Camera/Video Camera					
Major Appliances					
Refrigerator/Freezer					
Stove					
Dishwasher					
Washer/Dryer					
Microwave					
Coffeemaker					
Vacuum					
Blender/Food Processor					
Clothing and Accessories					
Pants					
Shirts					
Sweaters					
Coats					
Dresses					
Skirts					
Shoes					
Accessories (Belts, Ties, etc.)					
Watches					
Rings					
Earrings					
Necklaces					
Bracelets					

Home Inventory (continued)

	Item Description	Make and Model	Date Acquired	Estimated Purchase Cost	Estimated Replacement Cost
Clothing and Accessories (continued)					
Cufflinks					
Linens					
Towels					
Bedding					
Furniture					
Living Room Set					
Dining Room Set					
Bedroom Sets					
Kitchen Set					
Bookshelves					
Lamps					
Rugs					
Patio Set					
Art and Music					
Books					
CDs/Records					
DVDs					
Artwork					
Kitchen Equipment					
Dishes					
Glassware					
Silverware					
Pots and Pans					
Utensils					

Home Inventory (continued)

	Item Description	Make and Model	Date Acquired	Estimated Purchase Cost	Estimated Replacement Cost
Athletic Equipment					
Collectibles					
Other					

4. Using a Web site that provides homeowner's or renter's insurance, obtain a quote for your homeowner's/renter's insurance policy. Complete the worksheet below.

Coverage and Limits

Dwelling	$
Personal Property ($ _____ Deductible)	$
Personal Liability	$
Damage to Property of Others	$
Medical Payments to Others (per Person)	$
Discounts	$
Annual Premium	$

DECISIONS

1. What are the key risks related to auto and homeowner's/renter's insurance that you will insure against?

_____
_____
_____
_____
_____
_____
_____
_____
_____

2. What coverage levels will you maintain for your auto policy? Which of the policy quotes you requested is most attractive? What actions can you take to receive policy discounts in the future?

_____
_____
_____
_____
_____
_____
_____
_____

3. What coverage levels will you maintain for your homeowner's/renter's policy? Which of the policy quotes you requested is most attractive? What actions can you take to receive policy discounts in the future?

_____
_____
_____
_____
_____
_____
_____
_____

CHAPTER 11: THE SAMPSONS—A Continuing Case

CASE QUESTIONS

1. Advise the Sampsons regarding their car insurance. Do they have enough insurance? Do they have too much insurance? How might they be able to reduce their premium?

2. Consider the Sampsons' homeowner's insurance. Do they have enough insurance? Do they have too much insurance? Should they increase their deductible?

Health and Disability Insurance

While out of town, Ruby felt chest pains, so she went to the nearest hospital and was required to stay the night for tests. One week later, Ruby received a bill of $15,000 from the hospital. Even though she had medical insurance, she would have to pay over $5,000 out of pocket. It could have been worse. Had Ruby not had insurance, the entire $15,000 bill would have been hers to pay.

Torwaiphoto/Shutterstock

Health care can be very expensive. The health insurance policy that you select will determine how much of your health care expenses are covered. Proper health insurance decisions can protect your net worth.

MyFinanceLab helps you master the topics in this chapter and study more efficiently. Visit http://www.myfinancelab.com for more details.

The objectives of this chapter are to:

- Provide a background on health insurance
- Compare the types of private health care plans
- Describe the contents of health care plans
- Describe government health care plans
- Describe federal regulations in health care
- Describe long-term care insurance
- Explain the benefits of disability insurance
- Explain how health and disability insurance fit within your financial plan

Background on Health Insurance

health insurance
Insurance offered by private insurance companies or the government that covers health care expenses incurred by policyholders for necessary medical care.

Health insurance covers health care expenses incurred by policyholders. It limits your potential liabilities and ensures that you will receive necessary medical care. Many more options are available for health insurance than for auto or homeowner's insurance. Health insurance is offered by private insurance companies and by the government. Some private insurance companies provide only health insurance, while other companies offer it along with other types of insurance.

The nation's largest health care insurer, Blue Cross and Blue Shield, serves many employers with a group participation plan. Blue Cross and Blue Shield contracts with doctors and hospitals on the types of services it will cover and the amount it will pay for each service. Individuals insured by Blue Cross and Blue Shield are then covered up to the agreed-on specific dollar amount for each service.

Depending on the type of contract between a health care provider and the insurance company, the provider may be paid a discount on charges, a per diem rate, or a case rate. Health care providers employ billing and reimbursement specialists to ensure that they have been paid correctly after submitting a claim for payment. Health care providers are required to comply with complex billing procedures to receive payments for services rendered. Hospitals and physicians' offices employ medical coders to analyze patient accounts and attach the proper billing codes to the accounts before submitting them for payment. The coding often determines the amount of the payment.

Policyholders are responsible for their share of the agreed-upon amount between their insurance company and the medical provider. For example, if their policy calls for a co-payment of $500, and the insurance company has agreed to pay a total of $5,000 for their hospital stay, the insurance company will pay $4,500, and the policyholder is responsible for $500, regardless of the total charges. The medical provider cannot charge the insurance company or the patient any more than the contracted amount, even if the charges exceed $5,000. Without health insurance, the high expenses of health care could quickly eliminate most of your wealth. Therefore, health insurance is a critical component of your financial planning.

Cost of Health Insurance

Health insurance has received much attention in recent years because it has become very expensive. The need for health care is greater for individuals who are older, and the average age of the population has increased in recent years. Because older individuals require more health care, the cost of providing health care is rising. People are living longer, partly due to effective health care; therefore, they require medical attention for a longer period of time.

FREE APPS
for Personal
Finance

Your Health Insurance

Application:

The Florida Blue app (by Blue Cross and Blue Shield of Florida) provides information such as your deductible, a summary of your claims, and the doctors who are participating in your plan. It also allows you to compare drug prices and identify the pharmacy closest to your location. Blue Cross and Blue Shield offers similar types of apps to individuals in other states.

To Find It:

Search for the "Florida Blue" app on your mobile device.

Currently, about one in every five workers is uninsured. This ratio has increased over time as many workers can no longer afford to be insured. Many of these workers can become more susceptible to a serious illness because they do not receive regular preventive health care. When they receive emergency health care that they cannot afford, the cost must be covered by others. This cost must be covered by raising the prices charged for health care services, which results in higher costs of insurance, and this causes more workers to remain uninsured.

The health insurance industry relies on technology for improvements. Technological advances have been achieved that can save or extend lives, but these innovations are costly. Recent examples include digital mammography, which provides a much better image than film mammography; tomosynthesis, which provides a three-dimensional mammography image; and improved chemotherapy drugs that result in much better responses by many types of cancers.

Although health insurance is expensive, it is necessary. Your health insurance decision is not whether to obtain it, but which health plan to purchase and how much coverage to purchase. By understanding your health insurance options, you can select health insurance that is within your budget and offers adequate protection.

Federal regulations allow you to continue your employer's insurance plan for 18 months after you stop working for the employer. Workers can continue their health insurance coverage even if they have switched jobs, even if they have preexisting medical problems. However, although your previous employer might have been paying a large proportion of your insurance premium while you were an employee, you will have to pay the entire premium once you are no longer an employee. In addition, health insurance now allows you to maintain your health as a means of preventing serious health problems. Under most conditions, health insurance now allows insured people to receive preventive medical services. Recent developments in health insurance are covered near the end of this chapter.

Private Health Insurance

private health insurance
Health insurance that can be purchased from private insurance companies to provide coverage for health care expenses.

Private health insurance refers to health insurance that can be purchased from private insurance companies to provide coverage for health care expenses. You can purchase this insurance directly from private health insurance companies or through your employer. Most large employers offer their employees the opportunity to participate in a health insurance plan as part of their benefits package. The employer and employee typically share the cost of the health insurance. The employees' portion of the premium is deducted from their pay, and the employer pays the remainder. Some employers pay a large portion of the premium to attract and retain good employees. Employers tend to obtain all their health insurance from one company.

Private insurance is usually less expensive when provided under an employer's plan. Information about health insurance premiums is available at http://www.insweb.com and http://www.insure.com.

Types of Private Health Insurance Coverage

The most common types of private health insurance plans can be classified as fee for service (sometimes known as indemnity plans) or managed care plans (health maintenance organizations and preferred provider organizations). Each of these plans cover common health care costs, including physician office visits, inpatient hospital stays, outpatient surgery, emergency room, and other outpatient services, such as physical therapy or lab work. However, there are significant differences between the types of plans. To decide which plan serves your needs best, you need to understand the differences among plans.

fee for service plan
Health insurance that reimburses individuals for part or all of the expenses they incur from health care providers; individuals are free to decide whether to seek care from a primary care physician or a specialist.

Fee for Service (Indemnity) Plans
A **fee for service plan** (also known as an indemnity plan) reimburses individuals for part or all of the health care expenses they incur from health care providers (such as doctors or hospitals). Individuals are free to decide whether to seek care from a primary care physician or a specialist. Many fee for service plans have a coinsurance provision in which the insurance company pays a percentage of the bill. For example, a provision may specify that the insurance company pays 80% of the bill and that you pay the remaining 20%. After you reach the policy's out-of-pocket limit, the insurance company pays 100% of covered medical expenses.

The advantage of a fee for service plan is that you can choose your own health care provider. If having that flexibility is important to you, then a fee for service plan might be your best choice. Although indemnity plans offer more flexibility than managed care plans, they also charge higher premiums. Normally, you must pay a deductible, although most of the bill will be reimbursed by the insurer.

managed health care plan
A health insurance policy under which individuals receive services from specific doctors or hospitals that are part of the plan.

Managed Health Care Plans
Managed health care plans require individuals to receive health care services from specific doctors or hospitals that are part of the plan or network. You are billed only for services not covered by your insurance.

Managed health care plans charge lower premiums than indemnity plans, but they impose more restrictions on the specific health care providers (e.g., doctors and hospitals) that individuals can use. Managed health care plans are normally classified as health maintenance organizations or preferred provider organizations.

health maintenance organization (HMO)
A health insurance plan that covers health care services approved by doctors; a primary care physician provides general health services and refers patients to a specialist as necessary.

Health Maintenance Organizations
Each **health maintenance organization (HMO)** establishes an agreement with select health care providers (such as doctors and hospitals) that are obligated to provide services to the HMO members. The health care providers involved in the agreement are paid a predetermined amount of compensation per month. Their compensation is referred to as "per member per month" (PMPM) for each patient who participates in the plan. Even though the fee is prearranged, the cost to the health care provider varies with the demand for services. For example, if the patients of a particular HMO require minimal health care, a hospital will incur limited costs to take care of those patients. If the patients of a particular HMO require substantial health care, however, a hospital will incur higher costs as they take care of more patients. The hospital is more profitable when the demand for health care services by the HMO participants is relatively low because the reimbursement is a fixed amount, regardless of how many patients they see.

Patients participating in an HMO normally choose what is called their "primary care physician." They will need to see their primary care physician to get a referral before they can see a specialist or other health care provider. The HMO philosophy is that the primary care physician can reduce overall health care costs by eliminating unnecessary patient visits to specialists. For example, some patients might feel ill and think they are having cardiac issues and see a cardiologist only to find out that they have the flu. Such appointments with a specialist can be avoided if the patient is required to see their primary care physician before seeing a specialist.

An advantage of HMOs is that they offer health care services at a low cost. Because HMOs emphasize the early detection and treatment of illnesses, they can keep the premiums relatively low. Individuals also typically pay a small fee (such as $10) for a visit to a physician who participates in an HMO or for a prescription. An HMO also typically covers a portion of prescription expenses.

A disadvantage of HMOs is that individuals must choose among the primary care physicians and specialists who participate in the plan. Thus, they cannot select a physician who is not approved by the HMO. HMO members typically pay lower premiums in exchange for less flexibility.

preferred provider organization (PPO)
A health insurance plan that allows individuals to select a health care provider and covers most of the fees for services; a referral from a doctor is not required to visit a specialist.

Preferred Provider Organizations A **preferred provider organization** (PPO) is a combination of a fee for service policy and an HMO policy. A PPO allows individuals to select their health care providers and have most of the fee covered. A PPO also uses a primary care physician, but there are usually more physicians available for each area of specialization than in an HMO. The premiums and fees for health care services are higher in a PPO than an HMO. For example, individuals may be charged 20% of the bill for specific health care services provided by a PPO versus a small flat fee such as $15 for the same services provided by an HMO. Patients are still given a listing of in-network providers, but, in a PPO, they also have the flexibility to see providers outside the PPO network. They will likely incur higher out-of-pocket costs if they choose a provider that is out of the PPO network, but they have that flexibility under a PPO plan.

discount on charge arrangement
An arrangement in which the preferred provider organization (PPO) pays a specific percentage of the health care provider's charges.

A common payment arrangement between health care providers and PPOs is the **discount on charge arrangement**, in which the PPO agrees to pay a specific percentage of the provider's charges. For example, if the agreement between the PPO and the provider is a 30% discount on charges and the provider charged $1,000, the PPO would pay a total of $700 (70% of $1,000, representing a discount of 30%). Under this arrangement, the provider receives $300 less than what it normally charges for this type of service. A portion of the $700 payment to the provider would be made by the patient, and the rest of the payment would be made by the PPO. The specific breakdown of the payments is dictated by the contract between the PPO and the patient.

per diem rate arrangement
An arrangement in which the preferred provider organization (PPO) pays the provider a specific sum for each day a patient is hospitalized.

A second type of arrangement between the PPO and the provider is the **per diem rate arrangement**, in which the provider is paid a specific amount for each day the patient is hospitalized. If the PPO arrangement is a $650 per diem rate and the hospital charges $1,000 for a one-day stay in the hospital, the total amount owed to the hospital would be $650. The payment by the patient to the hospital is determined by the contract between the patient and the PPO.

A patient's contract with the PPO typically specifies that the PPO pays 80% of the amount owed, and the patient pays the remaining 20%. If the total amount owed to the provider is $700, the PPO would pay 80% of the $700, or $560. The patient would be required to pay 20% of $700, or $140. The patient's payment is often referred to as a co-payment. Patients receive an Explanation of Benefits (EOB) form from the PPO after receiving health care services. The EOB lists the total charges, the total amount that is owed to the provider, and the amount owed by the patient. You should always make sure that the amount you are billed by the provider agrees with the amount shown as your responsibility on your EOB.

Premiums for Private Health Care Insurance

Employers may offer individual coverage or family coverage. Higher premiums are charged for family coverage. A married couple without children should compare the premiums if each of them purchases individual insurance versus if one person buys family insurance. Individuals or couples who have children or plan to have children in the near future need a family plan.

Individuals who are unemployed, self-employed, or whose employer does not offer a health plan can obtain managed care or other types of health insurance directly from private insurance companies. However, the insurance premiums are normally higher if insurance is purchased individually rather than through an employer-sponsored plan.

You can obtain insurance quotes and go through the application process online. Some Web sites provide general quotes on the premiums charged by various insurance companies for health care. The quotes may also include information on the deductible, the coinsurance rate, and the fee you would pay for a visit to a doctor. If you want to obtain more information about any specific quote, the Web site provides a link to the

EXHIBIT 12.1	Comparison of Private Health Insurance Plans	
Type of Private Health Plan	**Premium**	**Selection of Physician**
Indemnity Plan	High	Flexibility to select physician or specialist
Managed Care: HMOs	Relatively low	Primary care physician refers patients to specialist
Managed Care: PPOs	Low, but usually higher than HMOs	There is a greater number of physicians to choose from in PPOs than HMOs

Financial Planning
ONLINE

Go to:
http://www.individual-health-plans.com

To get:
Information about different types of plans, including PPOs and HMOs.

insurance company providing that quote. When you submit an application online, the initial quote of the premium may be changed after you provide information such as your medical history and present health condition.

Comparison of Private Health Insurance Plans

A comparison of private health insurance plans is provided in Exhibit 12.1. This exhibit illustrates the trade-off between the flexibility that individuals have in selecting their physician and the premium that they are charged for health insurance.

HMOs and PPOs offer brochures that provide the comparative information you need to review before you decide which plan to select. Exhibit 12.2 lists the questions that you should ask before you make your selection. If these questions are not answered in the brochure, contact a representative who can provide the answers.

EXAMPLE

When Stephanie Spratt started working for her present employer, she was offered the opportunity to participate either in an HMO, or in a fee for service plan in which she would be able to seek whatever health care provider she preferred. She is now reviewing her health care choice. The premium for the indemnity plan is $100 higher per month than her HMO. She also has the opportunity to switch to a PPO, but her premium would be $75 per month higher than her HMO. An advantage of this PPO over her HMO is that there are more physicians available in each health care specialization. At this time, Stephanie does not have a need for any specialists. She decides that she will continue to participate in the HMO because she does not think that the advantages of the fee for service plan or the PPO are worth the extra premium.

Contents of Health Care Plans

Health care plans (insurance policies) contain the following information.

Identification of Insured Persons

A health insurance contract identifies who is covered, such as an individual or a family.

Location

Some U.S. insurance companies provide coverage for health care in the United States only, while others provide coverage in non-U.S. countries too. Typically, full health insurance benefits are confined to the local area of the beneficiary. Benefits are reduced or eliminated for nonemergency health care received out of the area.

EXHIBIT 12.2   Questions to Ask When Considering a Particular HMO or PPO

Questions Regarding Your Cost

1. Monthly premium?

2. Deductible?

3. Coinsurance/Co-pay amounts?

4. Limits on coverage?

5. Maximum out-of-pocket expenses per year?

Questions Regarding the Doctors/Health Care Providers

1. How many doctors are in the plan?

2. Who are the doctors in the plan?

3. Which doctors are accepting new patients?

4. How long in advance must you schedule a routine visit to the doctor?

5. Where are the doctors located?

6. What health care services do the doctors provide?

7. What hospitals/labs/diagnostic centers are in the plan?

General Questions

1. Is access to specialists only allowed with a referral from a primary care physician?

2. What coverage is provided if the patient receives services out of the primary network (for example, a visit to an emergency room while out of town)?

3. If a physician is accessed outside of the plan, are there out-of-network benefits?

Cancellation and Renewability Options

Your health insurance contract should specify if the insurance company can cancel the contract at any time, or if it guarantees continuous coverage as long as the policyholders pay the premiums on time. In addition, it should specify if you are given the option to renew your contract up to a specified age level. If you renew the contract, the insurance company can charge you a higher premium if your health conditions diminished since you last applied for health insurance.

Other Coverage

Health insurance policies can cover a wide variety of health care needs. Policies specify the types of health care covered and the limitations for each. The following are some common types of health care that may be included within health insurance policies.

Rehabilitation Health insurance policies may provide coverage for rehabilitation, including physical therapy sessions and counseling. Many policies set an upper limit on the number of visits for physical therapy, occupational therapy, and speech therapy. When a physician determines that a policyholder who has had therapy for an injury is healed, or when the policyholder has had the number of sessions allowed under the policy, the insurance company will not pay for any further rehabilitative services.

Mental Health   Some policies cover mental health conditions to a limited degree. They may provide partial reimbursement for expenses associated with the treatment of mental disorders. They may also specify a maximum period or lifetime amount in which such treatments are covered.

Pregnancy   A health insurance policy may provide coverage of direct expenses and may even pay for sick leave during the last weeks of pregnancy.

dental insurance
Insurance that covers part or all of the fees imposed for dental services, including annual checkups, orthodontics, and oral surgery.

Dental Insurance   A health insurance policy may provide **dental insurance**, which covers part or all of the fees imposed for dental services, including annual checkups, orthodontics, and oral surgery.

Vision Insurance   Some health insurance policies provide **vision insurance**, which covers part or all of the fees imposed for optician, ophthalmologist, and optometrist services, including annual checkups, glasses, contact lenses, and surgery.

vision insurance
Insurance that covers part or all of the fees imposed for optician and optometrist services, including annual checkups, glasses, contact lenses, and surgery.

Determinants of Unreimbursed Medical Expenses

For a given health care service, the insurance policy specifies the criteria used to ascertain the amount of the bill that you must pay. This amount is determined by the deductible, coinsurance, stop-loss provision, coverage limits, and coordination of benefits, as explained next.

Deductible   A deductible requires that the insured bear the cost of the health care up to a level that is specified in the policy. If a policy specifies a deductible of $500 for specific health care, and the bill is $475, you will have to pay the entire amount. If the bill is $900, you will pay the first $500, and the policy will cover the remaining $400. The deductible in health care is similar to the deductible in auto insurance, in that it reduces the potential liability to the insurance company. Therefore, the premiums charged for a particular policy are generally lower when the deductible is higher.

Coinsurance   A coinsurance clause specifies the proportion of health care expenses that will be paid by the insurance company. For example, for a $1,000 bill that is subject to a 20% co-pay, you will pay $200 (20% of $1,000).

Stop-Loss Provision   A stop-loss provision sets a maximum amount that you must pay for one or more health care services.

Coverage Limits   Many policies have limits on the amount of coverage that the insurance company will provide for particular health care services. The limits may be applied to hospital expenses, surgery procedures, outpatient services, and nursing services. Thus, if policyholders select health care services costing more than what is covered by the policy, they will have to pay the difference themselves. These limits may be imposed even if the total health care expenses due to a specific illness or injury are not subject to a maximum limit. This policy is intended to discourage excessive utilization of services by policyholders. For example, many policies have a limit on coverage for outpatient physical therapy, occupational therapy, and speech therapy.

Coordination of Benefits   When a policy has a coordination of benefits provision, it means that the benefits are dependent on what benefits would be paid by other policies that you have. The benefits that would be paid by multiple policies could possibly overlap, but this provision limits the total reimbursement to no more than your expenses. This provision can be beneficial to you because your insurance premiums and coinsurance will be lower if the insurance benefits are coordinated among policies to limit the reimbursement amount.

Expenses Not Covered by Private Insurance Plans

Regardless of the private health insurance plan used, there will likely be some health care expenses that are not covered. You should budget for the possibility of some health care expenses that may not be included in your coverage.

flexible spending account
An account established by the employer for the employee to use pretax income to pay for medical expenses.

A **flexible spending account** is an account established by an employer for employees to use pretax income to pay for medical expenses. The amount that you set aside each pay period for your flexible spending account is not subject to federal, state, and local income taxes, or to FICA taxes. If you have unreimbursed medical or dental expenses, you can draw from this account to pay these expenses. By using this account, you are not taxed on the income that you used to pay these health care expenses.

A recent ruling allows up to $500 of unused funds to be rolled over to the next year without reducing the contribution limits for the next year. This change may encourage increased usage of the account. For this reason, some individuals allocate a minimal amount to the account. If you budget properly, you can take advantage of the tax savings by setting up a flexible spending account, while also making sure that you have enough funds to pay your out-of-pocket medical bills during the year.

Government Health Care Plans

The government-sponsored health care plans are Medicare and Medicaid.

Medicare

Financial Planning
ONLINE

Go to:
http://www.medicare.gov

To get:
An overview of services offered by Medicare, including the specific benefits that are available.

Recall from Chapter 4 that the Medicare program provides health insurance to individuals who are 65 years of age or older and qualify for Social Security benefits, or who are disabled. Medicare also provides payments to health care providers in the case of illness. Medicare is composed of various parts. Part A consists of hospital insurance and is used to cover expenses associated with inpatient care (including surgeries) in hospitals or nursing facilities and a limited amount of home health care. There is no additional premium required for Part A coverage for individuals who qualify because they (or their spouse) paid sufficient Medicare taxes while working.

Part B represents optional medical insurance and covers some expenses that are not covered by Part A, such as outpatient hospital care, physical therapy, and some home health services. You must pay a monthly premium to receive Part B coverage.

Part C of Medicare represents a combination of Parts A and B, provided through private insurance companies that are approved by Medicare. In many cases, the Part C plans identify specific doctors or hospitals that you must use.

Part D provides coverage for prescription drugs. The Part D component can vary among insurance plans in terms of the specific drugs that are covered, the amount of coverage per type of drug, and the deductible. You must have Parts A and B of Medicare to qualify for Part D.

medigap insurance
Insurance provided by private insurance companies to cover medical expenses that are not covered by Medicare.

Medigap Insurance Some individuals want supplemental insurance that offers more coverage than Medicare provides. **Medigap insurance** is provided by private insurance companies to cover medical expenses that are not covered by Medicare. There are various types of Medigap policies. In most states, there are 11 standardized policies, which are classified as Medigap plans. These plans vary in terms of the premium that you pay and the benefits that you receive. Plan A is the most basic and includes coverage of hospitalization expenses that are not covered by Medicare. The other plans provide additional coverage beyond Plan A, each differentiated by the amount of medical care covered. Insurance companies can select whatever plans they wish to offer to individuals. The premiums that they charge are higher for the policies that provide more coverage.

Financial Planning
ONLINE

Go to:
http://www.medigapchoice.com

To get:
An overview of services offered by Medigap.

Medicare Prescription Act The Medicare Prescription Drug Improvement and Modernization Act of 2003 allows coverage for senior citizens and people with disabilities. Medicare now covers some prescription drugs that were not covered before, which may prevent some illnesses and therefore eliminate the need for other high-cost health care services.

The act allows seniors to purchase various forms of coverage for prescription drugs. The coverage is provided through private firms, either by itself or as a part of managed care plans. The premium and the deductible will change over time to reflect costs.

The standard coverage is 75% of prescription expenses for the first $2,000 spent after the $250 deductible for the year. Thus, an individual would have to pay the entire cost of the first $250 that was spent and would then pay only 25% of the next $2,000 in prescription expenses, after accounting for the coverage. Additional coverage is provided only if a senior's expenses exceed $3,600 for the year. Low-income seniors are not charged a premium and are not subject to a deductible.

The act also allows individuals to establish a **health savings account**, which shelters income from taxes and can be used to pay health care expenses. The health savings account is set up with pretax dollars, similar to some college savings accounts and retirement accounts that have been created by the U.S. government to encourage saving. It differs from those accounts in that it is designed to ensure that individuals save sufficient money to cover their annual health care expenses. Because this money is not taxed, individuals have an incentive to create an account and thus reduce their taxes. If individuals have more money in their account than they need in a given year, the money remains in the account and can be used in the following year. In addition, money in the account earns interest until it is spent on health care.

Businesses can set up health savings accounts for their employees and can contribute to their accounts (up to the $4,500 maximum). People must be under age 65 to qualify for the plan and have a high-deductible health plan, which is defined as a minimum $1,300 deductible for individuals and $2,600 deductible for family plans.

Medicaid

The **Medicaid** program provides health insurance for individuals with low incomes and those in need of public assistance. It is intended to provide health care to the aged, blind, disabled, and needy families with dependent children. To qualify, individuals must meet some federal guidelines, but the program is administered on a state-by-state basis. Individuals who qualify for Medicare may also be eligible for Medicaid if they need public assistance; in this case, they will receive more health benefits.

Health Care Insurance Regulations

Federal regulations ensure that individuals can maintain continuous health care coverage, despite their employment status. In particular, the following acts have played a major role.

Consolidated Omnibus Budget Reconciliation Act (COBRA)

As a result of the Consolidated Omnibus Budget Reconciliation Act (COBRA) of 1986, you can continue your health insurance provided through an employer's plan for 18 months after you stop working for the employer. The act applies to private firms and state government agencies, but not to federal government agencies. If you retire, COBRA allows you to continue your health insurance (within the 18-month maximum period) up to the point at which you qualify for government health care. However, as mentioned earlier, you will usually be responsible for the full cost of coverage because your previous employer no longer covers a portion of the premium that you owe.

Health Insurance Portability and Accountability Act (HIPAA)

The Health Insurance Portability and Accountability Act (HIPAA) of 1996 ensures that workers can continue their health insurance coverage even if they have switched jobs. Specifically, the act prohibits insurance companies from denying health insurance coverage based on an applicant's health status, medical condition or history, previous health insurance claims, or disability. The act is especially important for workers who have preexisting medical problems. For example, consider a woman employed by a firm in Kansas who has an existing medical condition. She wants to move to Dallas and is searching for work with a new employer there. Before HIPAA, she may not have been able to obtain health insurance in Texas because the insurance company would have been concerned that she might need to file many claims given her existing medical condition. However, as a result of HIPAA, she cannot be denied health insurance because of her existing medical condition.

To remain eligible for protection under HIPAA, a person must maintain continuous enrollment in a health care plan. This provision is intended to prevent individuals from participating in a health insurance plan only when they have a medical condition or illness for which they want treatment.

HIPAA also established a set of national standards for the protection of health information. The use of computers and automation has resulted in more health insurance fraud and threatens the privacy of information about health care recipients. Therefore, The U.S. Department of Health and Human Services issued the Privacy Rule as part of HIPAA to protect this information. The Privacy Rule applies to health plans, health care clearinghouses, and any health care provider who transmits health information in electronic format. The rule protects all individually identifiable health information held or transmitted by a covered entity. This information is referred to as "protected health information" (PHI). PHI includes any past, present, or future physical or mental health condition, the provision of health care to the individual, and any payment for the provision of health care. The purpose of the Privacy Rule is to define and limit the instances in which an individual's protected health information may be used or disclosed to others.

Affordable Care Act

The Patient Protection and Affordable Care Act (PPACA), also called the Affordable Care Act (ACA), was passed in 2010. The provisions of this law require that U.S. citizens obtain health insurance and use the insurance so that they maintain their health, in an effort to prevent serious health problems. At the time the law was passed, more than 50 million people in the United States did not have health insurance.

The PPACA covers far-ranging health care issues. It allows people covered by Medicare Part B and some other plans to receive preventive medical services such as annual health exams, mammograms, and screenings for high cholesterol, diabetes, and some types of cancer at no cost. However, many are unaware of what preventive services are covered and therefore are not taking advantage of this benefit. The law allows people with Medicare Part D to receive substantial discounts on drugs.

The law allows young adults who cannot participate in an employer's health insurance plan to continue on a parent's health insurance until age 26. It requires that at least 85% of the health insurance premiums received by insurers for large employer plans must be used to pay for health care services and health care quality improvement. This is intended to limit the proportion of the premium that insurers use to pay for executive salaries or advertising. If insurance companies do not meet these goals, they will be required to provide rebates to consumers. Health care providers must meet specific standards before they can bill insurance companies for the services provided. These standards are intended to prevent health insurance fraud, which has become a serious problem. Companies have engaged in fraud by providing unnecessary health care services to receive reimbursement and by requesting reimbursement for services that they never provided. During 2009, efforts to fight fraud returned more than $2.5 billion to the Medicare trust fund. The law invests new resources and requires new screening procedures for health care providers to boost these efforts and reduce fraud and waste in Medicare and Medicaid.

Since 2014, health insurers can no longer deny applicants based on preexisting conditions, such as disease, disability, or other health problems that exist at the time of the application for health care insurance.

Twenty-six states challenged the constitutionality of the PPACA in court, and this case went to the U.S. Supreme Court. The states' concern was that many people who were healthy and presently did not have health insurance might attempt to avoid buying health insurance. Although states could fine these people according to the PPACA, the fine would be less than the health insurance premium. People could claim the requirement to buy health insurance to be a violation of constitutional rights. In a 5–4 decision, in June 2012 the Supreme Court upheld the constitutionality of the PPACA.

The enactment of PPACA remains a contentious political issue. Some politicians have suggested an alternative plan in which health care insurance would be optional, and any taxpayer who purchased health insurance would receive a large tax credit. This plan would provide an incentive for everyone to have health insurance, without the requirement that causes a constitutional challenge. Updates on this issue will be provided on the text's Web site.

Finding a Health Insurance Plan

Application:

The onpatient PHR app (by drchrono Inc.) allows you to review your personal health record (PHR) with your smartphone.

To Find It:

Search for the "onpatient PHR" app on your mobile device.

Long-Term Care Insurance

Many people who are elderly or have long-term illnesses need some assistance with everyday tasks such as eating or dressing. Others need around-the-clock medical assistance. According to the Americans for Long-Term Care Security (ALTCS), 20% of individuals in the United States aged 50 and older will need long-term care services. In addition, more than half of all individuals in the United States will need long-term care at some period during their life, and long-term care can be very expensive. The cost of having an aide provide basic care at home such as feeding or dressing each day can easily exceed $1,000 per week. The cost of care by a nurse is higher. For individuals who enter a nursing home, the cost of a private room is about $77,000 per year on average.

Government health care plans offer little assistance. Medicare does not cover the costs of long-term care. Although Medicaid might cover some of these expenses for qualifying individuals, the coverage is limited.

long-term care insurance
Insurance that covers expenses associated with long-term health conditions that cause individuals to need help with everyday tasks.

Long-term care insurance covers expenses associated with long-term health conditions that cause individuals to need help with everyday tasks. It is provided by many private insurance companies, and it typically covers care in a nursing home, assisted living facility, or at home. However, given the high expenses associated with long-term care, the premiums for long-term care insurance are very high. Premiums of $3,000 or more per year for long-term care are quite common.

Long-Term Care Insurance Provisions

Like other insurance policies, you can design a long-term care policy that fits your needs. Some of the more common provisions are listed here.

Eligibility to Receive Benefits Policies include the range of benefits for which policyholders can file claims. For example, a policy may specify that the long-term care be restricted to medical health care services, while a more flexible policy may also allow for other care such as feeding or dressing.

Types of Services Long-term care insurance policies specify the types of medical care services that are covered. A policy that covers nursing home care or assisted living will have higher premiums than a policy that covers nursing home care only. For individuals who prefer a more flexible long-term care policy that covers the cost of home health aides, premiums will be higher.

Amount of Coverage Policies also specify the maximum amount of coverage provided per day. If you want the maximum amount of coverage that a company will provide, you will pay a high premium. If you are willing to accept a lower maximum amount of daily coverage, your premium can be reduced. A policy with less coverage may not completely cover the daily costs that you could incur. In that case, you would need to cover a portion of your expenses.

A policy can contain a coinsurance provision that requires the policyholder to bear a portion of the health care expense. For example, a policyholder can select a policy in which the insurance company pays 80% of the health care expenses specified in the policy, while the policyholder pays the remaining 20%. Because the potential expense to the insurance company is lower as a result of the coinsurance provision, the premium will be lower.

Elimination Period to Receive Benefits A policy may specify an elimination (or waiting) period before policyholders are eligible to have their long-term care costs covered. An elimination period of between 60 and 90 days is common. The policyholder is responsible for covering expenses until the elimination period is completed. If the health care is needed over a period that is shorter than the elimination period, it will not be covered by the long-term care insurance.

Maximum Period to Receive Benefits You can choose to receive insurance benefits for the entire period in which you need long-term care, even if the period is 30 years or longer. If you choose to receive insurance benefits for a limited period, you would be charged a lower premium. For example, your long-term care could be covered for up to three years.

Continued Coverage A policy may contain a *waiver of policy premium* provision that allows you to stop paying premiums once you need long-term care. There are some alternative provisions that may also allow a limited amount of coverage after you have a policy for a specified number of years, without having to pay any more premiums. In general, any provision that provides additional benefits in the future will require higher premiums today.

Inflation Adjustment Some policies allow for the coverage to increase in line with inflation over time. Thus, the maximum benefits will rise each year with the increase in an inflation index. You will pay a higher premium for a long-term health care policy that contains this provision.

Stop-Loss Provision The insurance covering a long-term illness may also specify a stop-loss provision, which sets a maximum limit on the health care expense to be incurred by the policyholder. Reconsider the previous example in which the policyholder was required to pay 20% of expenses associated with his long-term illness. If the related health care expenses are $600,000 over time, the policyholder would have to pay $120,000 (20% of $600,000). However, if the policyholder has a stop-loss provision specifying a $30,000 limit, the policyholder would only owe $30,000. The lower the stop-loss limit, the higher the premium.

Factors That Affect Long-Term Care Insurance Premiums

The insurance premium charged for long-term care insurance is influenced by the likelihood that the insurance company will have to cover claims and the size of those claims.

Provisions of Policy Because the long-term care policy provisions described earlier affect the likelihood and size of claims, they affect the premiums on long-term care insurance. In addition to the provisions of the policy, the following characteristics of the policyholder also affect the premiums on long-term care insurance.

Age Individuals who are older are more likely to need long-term care insurance, so they are charged higher premiums. Policy premiums are especially high for individuals who are 60 years of age or older.

Health Condition Individuals who have an existing long-term illness are more likely to need to file a claim, so they are charged higher premiums.

Reducing Your Cost of Long-Term Care Insurance

When comparing long-term care insurance offered by insurance companies, recognize that a higher premium will be charged for various provisions that provide more comprehensive coverage. You can save money by selecting a policy that is only flexible on the provisions that are most important to you. For example, if you can tolerate a longer elimination period before the policy goes into effect, you can reduce your premium. If you think the continued coverage or the inflation-adjustment provisions are not very beneficial to you, select a policy that does not contain these provisions.

Insurance companies charge varying premiums for long-term care insurance policies. You should shop around and compare premiums. Internet quotes are one option. Also, review how insurance premiums charged by the insurance companies have changed over time because they may serve as an indication of future premiums.

Determining the Amount of Coverage

To determine whether you need long-term care insurance, consider your family's health history. If there is a history of long-term illnesses, then you are more likely to need coverage. In addition, consider your financial situation. If you can afford substantial coverage for long-term insurance, it may be worthwhile. Individuals who are under age 60 and have no serious illnesses can obtain long-term care insurance at reasonable rates.

Disability Insurance

disability income insurance
Insurance that provides income to policyholders in the event that they become disabled.

Disability income insurance provides income to policyholders in the event that they become disabled. The probability of becoming disabled in a given year is less than 4% for individuals under age 40 and less than 8% for individuals under age 50. However, the probability is about 15% at age 60, and it increases with age. Thus, disability insurance is especially important for older individuals who rely on their income. However, younger individuals should also consider disability insurance because it provides peace of mind, and the premiums are low. Disability insurance can ensure that you will still be able to support yourself and your dependents if you become disabled.

One of the most important aspects of disability insurance is the definition of disability. Benefits are paid to you only if you meet the definition of disability as defined by your policy. The most liberal definition (easiest to qualify for) of disability is the "own occupation" definition. The disability insurance policy will provide benefits if you are unable to do the duties required of your occupation. A more restrictive definition of disability is the "any occupation" definition. The "any occupation" coverage will only provide benefits if you cannot do the duties of any job that fits your education and experience. Because the coverage provided by this type of policy is more restrictive, it has a lower premium than "own occupation" policies. Some policies offer coverage if you are unable to do your job in your own occupation for an initial period, such as two years. After that point, they only offer coverage if you are unable to do the duties of any job that fits your education and experience. The Social Security Administration will consider you disabled only if you are disabled for a period of at least 5 months with the expectation that the disability will last at least 12 months or is likely to result in death.

Sources of Disability Income Insurance

Some of the more common sources of disability income insurance are discussed here.

Individual Disability Insurance You can purchase individual disability insurance and specify the amount of coverage that you desire. The insurance premium varies with your type of job. For example, workers in a steel plant are more at risk than workers in an office building.

Employer Disability Insurance About half of all large and medium-sized firms offer an optional disability plan through an insurance company. Employees at some firms either are provided the insurance at no cost or participate in a plan by paying for the coverage. The premiums charged through group plans are normally low. A typical disability policy offered through employers covers about 60% of the employee's salary. The maximum time that disability benefits are provided varies substantially among policies.

Insurance from Social Security If you are disabled, you may receive some income from the Social Security Administration. The income is determined by the amount of Social Security contributions you have made over time. The guidelines to qualify for disability benefits from Social Security are strict, meaning that you may not necessarily receive benefits even if you believe that you are disabled. In addition, the income provided by Social Security may not be sufficient to maintain your lifestyle. Therefore, you will probably need disability income insurance to supplement the possible disability benefits that you would receive from Social Security.

Insurance from Worker's Compensation If you become disabled at your workplace, you may receive some income through worker's compensation from the state where you reside. The income you receive is influenced by your prevailing salary level. Disability income insurance may supplement any benefits that you would receive from worker's compensation.

Disability Insurance Provisions

The specific characteristics of disability insurance vary among insurance companies, as explained here.

Amount of Coverage The disability insurance contract specifies the amount of income that will be provided if you become disabled. The amount may be specified as a maximum dollar amount or as a percentage of the income that you were earning before being disabled. The higher your coverage, the more you will pay for disability insurance.

You should have enough coverage so that you can maintain your lifestyle and still support your dependents if you become disabled. You can determine the disposable (after-tax) income that you would normally need to support your lifestyle and your dependents.

EXAMPLE

Stephanie Spratt receives some disability insurance coverage from her employer, but she is considering purchasing additional disability insurance. She wants to determine how much more coverage she would need to cover her typical expenses. Normally, she needs about $2,100 per month to cover her typical expenses. About $100 of those monthly expenses are attributed to work, such as clothing and commuting expenses. Because Stephanie would not be going to work if she were disabled, she need not consider those expenses. Her normal monthly expenses when excluding work-related expenses are $2,000 per month, as shown in Panel A of Exhibit 12.3. This is the amount of disability coverage that she would need.

The next step is to determine how much disability coverage she already has. To be conservative, she assumes that there will be no Social Security benefits, as she may have a disability that is not covered by its guidelines. Her employer-provided disability policy's coverage is $800 per month. She presumes that any disability that she might have someday will not result from her work, so that worker's compensation does not apply.

The final step is comparing the coverage that she needs (Panel A of Exhibit 12.3) with the coverage that she has from sources other than her individual disability insurance. In this example, the difference is: $2,000 − $800 = $1,200. If she buys additional disability insurance, she will purchase coverage of $1,200 per month. Because her present salary is $38,000, the amount of extra coverage reflects about 32% of her salary ($1,200/$3,800 = .32). The disability income that she would receive is normally not subject to federal tax. Disability income is subject to a state income tax, but this tax does not apply to Stephanie because she resides in a state in which taxes are not imposed.

Stephanie decides that she will buy the extra $1,200 disability insurance coverage through her employer. At $10 per month, the premium is affordable.

probationary period
The period extending from the time your disability income application is approved until your coverage goes into effect.

waiting period
The period from the time you are disabled until you begin to receive disability income benefits.

Probationary Period
You may be subject to a **probationary period,** which extends from the time your application is approved until your coverage goes into effect. A common probationary period is one month.

Waiting Period
The disability insurance contract should specify if there is a **waiting period** (such as three months or six months) before you would begin to receive any income benefits. You would have to cover your expenses during the waiting period. For example, if you become disabled today, and your policy specifies a three-month waiting period, you will receive benefits only if your disability lasts beyond the three-month period. One reason for the waiting period is that it eliminates many claims that would occur if people could receive benefits when they were disabled for just a few days or weeks because of a sore neck or back. The premiums for disability insurance would be higher if there were no waiting period or a very short waiting period.

Length of Time for Disability Benefits
Disability benefits may be limited to a few years or may last for the policyholder's lifetime. The longer the period in which your policy provides disability income, the more you will pay for disability insurance.

Non-Cancelable Provision
A non-cancelable provision gives you the right to renew the policy each year at the same premium, with no change in the benefits. In exchange, you pay a higher premium now to ensure that it will not be increased in the future.

EXHIBIT 12.3   Determining Stephanie Spratt's Disability Insurance Needs

Panel A: Total Coverage Needed

Typical monthly expenses	$2,100
– Expenses related to work	–100
= Typical monthly expenses after excluding work expenses	$2,000

Panel B: Coverage That You Expect to Receive from:

Employer Disability Insurance	$800
Social Security	$0
Worker's Compensation	$0
Total	$800
Amount Needed from Individual Disability Insurance	$1,200

Renewable Provision A renewable provision gives you the right to renew the policy with the same benefits. The insurance company can increase your premium if it is increasing the premium for all of its insured customers with the same profile.

Deciding on Disability Insurance

You can contact insurance companies about disability insurance rates or ask your employer's benefits department whether the insurance is available.

How Health and Disability Insurance Fit Within Your Financial Plan

The following are the key decisions about health and disability insurance that should be included within your financial plan:

- Do you have adequate insurance to protect your wealth?
- How much insurance should you plan to have in the future?

Exhibit 12.4 provides an example of how health and disability decisions apply to Stephanie Spratt's plan.

EXHIBIT 12.4   How Health and Disability Insurance Fit Within Stephanie Spratt's Financial Plan

GOALS FOR HEALTH AND DISABILITY INSURANCE PLANNING

1. Ensure that my exposure to health problems or a disability is covered by insurance.
2. Determine whether I should increase my health and disability insurance in the future.

ANALYSIS

Type of Insurance	Protection	Status
Health	Protects my assets and wealth.	I have a good health insurance plan through work.
Disability	Protects my income if I become disabled.	My employer-provided disability policy offers some coverage, but I am buying a policy that offers additional coverage.

DECISIONS

Decision on Whether My Present Health and Disability Insurance Coverage Is Adequate:

I presently rely on the HMO offered through my employer. This plan offers adequate insurance at an affordable premium. Because I am in my twenties and in good health, I do not need long-term care insurance at this time.

I presently have $800 of disability insurance coverage per month that is provided by my employer. I have decided to purchase a policy specifying an additional $1,200 of coverage per month to cover my monthly expenses of $2,000 if I'm disabled. The premium charged to me for disability insurance is only $10 per month. The insurance will provide adequate coverage for me if I become disabled.

Decision on Health and Disability Insurance Coverage for the Future:

I may switch to a PPO someday if I want more flexibility to select specialists. I will consider long-term care insurance in the future. I will also increase my disability insurance if my income or expenses increase over time.

DISCUSSION QUESTIONS

1. How would Stephanie's health and disability insurance purchasing decisions be different if she were a single mother of two children?

2. How would Stephanie's health and disability insurance purchasing decisions be affected if she were 35 years old? If she were 50 years old?

SUMMARY

Health Care Plans. Health insurance covers health care expenses incurred by policyholders. Health care plans can be classified as private plans or managed care plans. Private plans allow much flexibility in your choice of the health care provider, but they require a reimbursement process. Managed care plans include health maintenance organizations (HMOs) and preferred provider organizations (PPOs), which bill only the amount that is not covered by the plan. This avoids the reimbursement process. HMOs require the use of a specified primary care physician who refers the individual to a specialist when necessary; PPOs allow more flexibility in the choice of the health care provider but require much higher premiums.

Types of Private Health Care Plans. Private health care plans are commonly classified as fee for service (sometimes known as indemnity plans) or managed care plans. A fee for service plan reimburses individuals for part or all of the health care expenses they incur from health care providers (such as doctors or hospitals). Individuals are free to decide whether to seek care from a primary care physician or a specialist. They are billed directly by the health care providers and then must complete forms to request reimbursement for the services rendered and prescriptions. Managed health care plans (which include health maintenance organizations and preferred provider organizations) allow individuals to receive health care services from specific doctors or hospitals that are part of the plan, and they are billed only for services not covered by insurance. The plans charge lower premiums than fee for service plans, but impose more restrictions on the specific health care providers (doctors, hospitals) that individuals can use.

Contents of Health Care Plans. Health care plans (insurance policies) identify the insured persons, describe the location (in the United States only or outside the United States as well) where coverage is provided, whether the policy excludes coverage for preexisting conditions, whether there are options to cancel the contract, the coverage for rehabilitation, mental health, and pregnancy,

whether the contract can be renewed, and the criteria used to determine the amount of the bill that you must pay. This amount is determined by the deductible, coinsurance, stop-loss provisions, coverage limits, and coordination of benefits.

Government Health Care Plans. There are also government health plans. The Medicare program provides health insurance to individuals who are over 65 years of age and qualify for Social Security or who are disabled. The Medicaid program provides health insurance to individuals with low incomes.

Health Care Insurance Regulations. The Consolidated Omnibus Budget Reconciliation Act (COBRA) of 1986 allows you to continue your health insurance provided through an employer's plan for 18 months after you stop working for the employer. The Health Insurance Portability and Accountability Act (HIPAA) of 1996 allows you to continue health insurance coverage even if you switch jobs. The act is especially important if you have preexisting medical problems. The Patient Protection and Affordable Care Act (PPACA) of 2010 allows you to receive preventive medical services such as annual health exams, mammograms, and screenings for high cholesterol, diabetes, and some types of cancer at no cost under some conditions.

Long-Term Care Insurance. Long-term care insurance covers expenses associated with long-term illnesses, including care by a nursing home, assisted living facility, or at home. The premiums for long-term care insurance is very high but can be reduced by accepting a longer elimination period.

Disability Insurance. Disability insurance provides income to you if you become disabled. It can replace a portion of the income that you would have received had you been able to continue working.

How Health and Disability Insurance Fit Within Your Financial Plan. Health care can be very expensive and could disrupt your progress toward achieving your financial plan. Therefore, you need insurance to protect yourself so that you can continue to achieve your financial goals.

REVIEW QUESTIONS

All Review Questions are available in MyFinanceLab *at* http://www.myfinancelab.com.

1. **Health Insurance.** How do individuals benefit from having health insurance? Why has health insurance received a lot of attention recently?

2. **Private Health Insurance.** What is private health insurance? Briefly describe some types of private health insurance coverage.

3. **Health Insurance Providers.** Who offers health insurance? Do employers offer health insurance?

4. **Fee for Service versus Managed Plans.** Compare and contrast private health care fee for service plans and managed health care plans.

5. **HMO.** Describe how an HMO works. What are the advantages and disadvantages of this type of health care coverage?

6. **HMO versus PPO.** What questions should you ask when considering an HMO or PPO?

7. **PPO.** What is a preferred provider organization (PPO)? How does it operate?

8. **PPO Charges.** Compare and contrast the discount on charge arrangement and the per diem arrangement associated with PPOs.

9. **Continuous Health Care Coverage.** Briefly describe two federal regulations intended to ensure that individuals can maintain continuous health care coverage if their employment status changes.

10. **Flexible Spending Account.** What is a flexible spending account? Why do some individuals allocate a minimal amount to this account?

11. **Medicare.** What is Medicare? Describe Parts A and B of Medicare.

12. **Medicare Prescription Act.** Briefly describe the provisions of the Medicare Prescription Act.

13. **Medigap Insurance.** What is Medigap insurance?

14. **Medicaid.** What is Medicaid? How do individuals qualify for Medicaid?

15. **Long-Term Care Insurance.** What is the purpose of long-term care insurance? What factors influence long-term care insurance premiums? What factors should be considered when purchasing long-term care insurance?

16. **Health Insurance.** What are some other types of health insurance that might be offered by an employer?

17. **Disability Income Insurance.** What is the purpose of disability income insurance? Why might younger individuals consider purchasing disability insurance?

18. **Source of Disability Insurance.** Briefly describe some of the sources of disability income insurance.

19. **Provisions of Disability Insurance.** Briefly describe some of the provisions of disability income insurance.

20. **Affordable Care Act.** Briefly describe some of the significant features of the Affordable Care Act.

21. **Health Savings Account.** What is a health savings account, or HSA? Why is this account often preferable to a flexible spending account?

22. **Vision Insurance.** What types of services are typically covered by vision insurance? Why should some individuals consider buying a separate vision insurance policy?

23. **High-Deductible Health Plan.** What is a high-deductible health plan? How is this type of plan related to an HSA?

24. **Preexisting Conditions.** How did the PPACA change the way insurance companies treat persons with preexisting conditions?

25. **Health Insurance and Wealth.** How are health insurance and disability insurance related to your wealth?

FINANCIAL PLANNING PROBLEMS

All Financial Planning Problems are available in MyFinanceLab *at* http://www.myfinancelab.com.

1. **PPO Charges.** A PPO uses a discount on charge arrangement. Marie incurred total charges by a hospital of $20,000, and the percentage paid to the provider is 70%. Marie's contract with the PPO specifies her co-pay as 20%. How much does Marie have to pay?

2. **Stop-Loss Provision.** Pete's health insurance policy specifies that he should pay 30% of expenses associated with a long-term illness, and he has a stop-loss provision of $35,000 in his policy. If Pete incurs expenses of $70,000, how much would he owe?

3. **Disability Insurance.** Christine's total monthly expenses typically amount to $1,800. About $50 of these expenses are work related. Christine's employer provides disability insurance coverage

of $500 per month. How much individual disability insurance should Christine purchase?

4. **COBRA.** Susan recently quit working for a local firm and has yet to find a new job. She knows she can maintain her health insurance from her old employer due to COBRA. How much will it likely cost her for health insurance if she previously paid $100 per month and her employer paid an additional $350 per month for her health coverage?

5. **Ethical Dilemma.** Vera is an 85-year-old widow and retiree from a large corporation. Her former employer recently changed the health care coverage for retirees to an HMO. Vera is having difficulty with her knees and has requested a referral to an orthopedist. After ordering X-rays, her primary care physician informs her that her knees are not serious enough to warrant knee replacement, and he gives her a prescription to alleviate the pain. Several weeks later Vera reads an article that doctors in her HMO are rewarded for keeping utilization costs down.

a. Discuss the ethics of HMOs rewarding physicians for keeping utilization costs down.

b. Does Vera have any options?

FINANCIAL PLANNING ONLINE EXERCISES

1. Go to the Web site http://www.healthcare.gov, and answer the following questions:

   a. Click the dropdown menu "Get Answers" and then "Why health coverage is important." List some of the reasons cited regarding the importance of health insurance.

   b. Go back to the "Get Answers" page and click on "Get New Coverage" and then "Fees and Exemptions." How much will you have to pay if you do not obtain coverage?

   c. Now click on "What plans cover," which is also on the "Get New Coverage" page. List a few of the covered health benefits required by law.

4. Go to http://www.medicare.gov, click on "Sign Up/Change Plans", and then click on "Your Medicare coverage choices" to review the section on Medicare plans.

   a. Describe some choices for Medicare plans. Which plan do you find more attractive? Why?

   b. Search this Web site or alternative Web sites on "Medigap (Supplemental Insurance)." Describe Medigap. How many policies are available?

PSYCHOLOGY OF PERSONAL FINANCE: Your Health Insurance

1. Consumers tend to feel less pain when buying health or disability insurance by paying as little as possible. However, this strategy can backfire because the insurance they receive may reflect the low price they paid. Describe your own behavior when purchasing health or disability insurance. Do you request specific insurance coverage or pursue the cheapest possible policy?

2. Read one practical article about how psychology affects decisions when buying health insurance. You can easily retrieve possible articles by doing an online search using the terms "psychology" and "buying health insurance." Summarize the main points of the article.

WEB SEARCH EXERCISE

You can develop your personal finance skills by conducting an Internet search for related articles. Find a recent online article about personal finance that reinforces one or more concepts covered in this chapter. If your class has an online component, your professor may ask you to post your summary of the article there and provide a link to the article so that other students can access it. If your class is live, your professor may ask you to summarize your application of the article in class. Your professor may assign specific students to complete this assignment or may allow any student to do the assignment on a volunteer basis.

For recent online articles related to this chapter, consider using the following search terms (be sure to include the current year as a search term to ensure that the online articles are recent):

- How health insurance protects you
- Health insurance coverage
- Health insurance premium
- Selecting health insurance
- Health care plans
- Selecting disability insurance

VIDEO EXERCISE: Selecting Health Insurance

Go to one of the Web sites that contain video clips (such as http://www.youtube.com) and view some video clips about selecting health insurance. You can use search phrases such as "selecting health insurance." Select one video clip on this topic that you would recommend for the other students in your class.

1. Provide the Web link for the video clip.

2. What do you think is the main point of this video clip?

3. How might you change your process of selecting health insurance as a result of watching this video clip?

BUILDING YOUR OWN FINANCIAL PLAN

Health and disability income insurance do not depend on tangible assets but rather on your perceived need for this type of insurance and your general well-being.

Health insurance has become quite expensive in recent years. The first step in researching health insurance options is to evaluate offerings from your employer.

Go to the worksheets at the end of this chapter to continue building your financial plan.

THE SAMPSONS—A Continuing Case

Dave and Sharon Sampson are assessing the amount of health insurance and disability income insurance they have.

The Sampsons' health insurance is provided by a health maintenance organization (HMO). Recently, Dave and Sharon have heard about preferred provider organizations (PPOs) and are wondering whether they should switch to a PPO. Upon hearing that PPOs are more expensive than HMOs, Dave and Sharon are hesitant to switch, but they have not yet made up their minds. Dave and Sharon are both happy with their primary care physician and any specialists they need to consult under their HMO plan.

Dave and Sharon currently do not have disability income insurance because they do not believe that they are at risk of becoming disabled. Recall from Chapter 2 that Dave and Sharon have about $3,400 a month in expenses, none of which are work related. Their net cash flow in recent months is about $600 a month, but they are attempting to save that money. Dave's employer provides $200 in disability insurance coverage.

The Sampsons have also recently heard about long-term care insurance and are wondering whether they should purchase this type of insurance.

Go to the worksheets at the end of this chapter to continue this case.

NAME _____   DATE _____

CHAPTER 12: BUILDING YOUR OWN FINANCIAL PLAN

YOUR GOALS FOR CHAPTER 12

1. Ensure that your health and disability insurance adequately protects your wealth.
2. Develop a plan for your future health insurance needs, including long-term care.

ANALYSIS

1. Complete the following worksheet to aid your evaluation of information provided by your employer for your health insurance options. Which type of policy (fee for service, HMO, or PPO) is best suited to your needs and budget?

Health Insurance Coverage Comparison

Fee for Service

Premium Co-Pay	☐ Yes	☐ No	
If Yes, Amount of Premium Co-Pay	$		
Coverage Eligibility	☐ Self	☐ Two-person	☐ Family
Coverage:			
In State	☐ Yes	☐ No	
Out of State	☐ Yes	☐ No	
Out of the Country	☐ Yes	☐ No	
Prescription Coverage	☐ Yes	☐ No	
If Yes, Amount of Co-Pay	$		
Office Visits:			
Co-Pay Amount	$		
Annual Deductible	☐ Yes	☐ No	
If Yes, Amount of Deductible	$		
Hospital Benefits:			
Maximum Days of Hospital Care	Days		
Maximum Days for Mental Health or Substance Abuse	Days		
Co-Pay	☐ Yes	☐ No	
If Yes, Amount of Co-Pay	$		
Annual Deductible	☐ Yes	☐ No	
If Yes, Amount of Deductible	$		

Outpatient Care:

Emergency Room Care	☐ Yes	☐ No
Physical Therapy	☐ Yes	☐ No
Occupational Therapy	☐ Yes	☐ No
Speech Therapy	☐ Yes	☐ No

Dental Coverage: ☐ Yes   ☐ No

If Yes, Co-Pay for Regular Checkups	☐ Yes	☐ No
If Yes, Amount of Co-Pay	$	

Orthodontic Coverage: ☐ Yes   ☐ No

If Yes, Co-Pay for Regular Checkups	☐ Yes	☐ No
If Yes, Amount of Co-Pay	$	

Vision Coverage: ☐ Yes   ☐ No

Frequency of Regular Eye Exams	
Co-Pay for Regular Eye Exams	$
Frequency for New Lenses	
Co-Pay for New Lenses	$
Frequency for New Frames	
Co-Pay for New Frames	$

HMO

Premium Co-Pay	☐ Yes	☐ No	
If Yes, Amount of Premium Co-Pay	$		
Coverage Eligibility	☐ Self	☐ Two-person	☐ Family

Coverage:

In State	☐ Yes	☐ No
Out of State	☐ Yes	☐ No
Out of the Country	☐ Yes	☐ No
Prescription Coverage	☐ Yes	☐ No
If Yes, Amount of Co-Pay	$	

Office Visits:

Co-Pay Amount	$	
Annual Deductible	☐ Yes	☐ No
If Yes, Amount of Deductible	$	

Hospital Benefits:

Maximum Days of Hospital Care	Days
Maximum Days for Mental Health or Substance Abuse	Days
Co-Pay	☐ Yes ☐ No
If Yes, Amount of Co-Pay	$
Annual Deductible	☐ Yes ☐ No
If Yes, Amount of Deductible	$

Outpatient Care:

Emergency Room Care	☐ Yes ☐ No
Physical Therapy	☐ Yes ☐ No
Occupational Therapy	☐ Yes ☐ No
Speech Therapy	☐ Yes ☐ No

Dental Coverage:

Dental Coverage:	☐ Yes ☐ No
If Yes, Co-Pay for Regular Checkups	☐ Yes ☐ No
If Yes, Amount of Co-Pay	$

Orthodontic Coverage:

Orthodontic Coverage:	☐ Yes ☐ No
If Yes, Co-Pay for Regular Checkups	☐ Yes ☐ No
If Yes, Amount of Co-Pay	$

Vision Coverage:

Vision Coverage:	☐ Yes ☐ No
Frequency of Regular Eye Exams	
Co-Pay for Regular Eye Exams	$
Frequency for New Lenses	
Co-Pay for New Lenses	$
Frequency for New Frames	
Co-Pay for New Frames	$

PPO

Premium Co-Pay	☐ Yes ☐ No		
If Yes, Amount of Premium Co-Pay	$		
Coverage Eligibility	☐ Self	☐ Two-person	☐ Family

Coverage:

In State	☐ Yes ☐ No
Out of State	☐ Yes ☐ No

Out of the Country	☐ Yes	☐ No
Prescription Coverage	☐ Yes	☐ No
If Yes, Amount of Co-Pay	$	

Office Visits:

Co-Pay Amount	$	
Annual Deductible	☐ Yes	☐ No
If Yes, Amount of Deductible	$	

Hospital Benefits:

Maximum Days of Hospital Care	Days	
Maximum Days for Mental Health or Substance Abuse	Days	
Co-Pay	☐ Yes	☐ No
If Yes, Amount of Co-Pay	$	
Annual Deductible	☐ Yes	☐ No
If Yes, Amount of Deductible	$	

Outpatient Care:

Emergency Room Care	☐ Yes	☐ No
Physical Therapy	☐ Yes	☐ No
Occupational Therapy	☐ Yes	☐ No
Speech Therapy	☐ Yes	☐ No
Dental Coverage:	☐ Yes	☐ No
If Yes, Co-Pay for Regular Checkups	☐ Yes	☐ No
If Yes, Amount of Co-Pay	$	

Orthodontic Coverage:

Orthodontic Coverage:	☐ Yes	☐ No
If Yes, Co-Pay for Regular Checkups	☐ Yes	☐ No
If Yes, Amount of Co-Pay	$	

Vision Coverage:

Vision Coverage:	☐ Yes	☐ No
Frequency of Regular Eye Exams		
Co-Pay for Regular Eye Exams	$	
Frequency for New Lenses		
Co-Pay for New Lenses	$	
Frequency for New Frames		
Co-Pay for New Frames	$	

2. If you are under age 60, long-term care insurance has probably not been a major concern to date. Based on your family health history, your financial situation, and any long-term illnesses that you have, should you look into getting a policy? Why or why not?

_____

_____

_____

_____

_____

_____

_____

_____

3. Referring to the personal cash flow statement you developed in Chapter 2, complete the following worksheet to determine your disability insurance needs. If you input this information in the Excel worksheet, the software will create a chart showing your sources of disability income.

Disability Insurance Needs

Cash Inflows	$	
Minus Work-Related Cash Inflows*	$	
Cash Inflows if Disabled		$
Total Cash Outflows	$	
Minus Work-Related Cash Outflows*	$	
Cash Outflows if Disabled		$
Cash Inflows Minus Outflows—Net Cash Flows if Disabled		$
Employer Disability Insurance	$	
Social Security	$	
Worker's Compensation	$	
Total Insurance Cash Inflows		$
Net Cash Flows if Disabled Minus Total Insurance Cash Inflows**		$

 * These are cash flows that will discontinue if you are not working.

** A negative number indicates the amount of disability insurance coverage that you need per month. If the number is positive, it indicates that you have no need for disability insurance.

DECISIONS

1. What steps have you taken or will you take to ensure that your health insurance needs are being met? Which type of health insurance plan will you seek from your employer?

_____

_____

_____

_____

_____

_____

_____

2. Does your age, personal health history, or family health history indicate that you should consider long-term care insurance?

_____

_____

_____

_____

_____

_____

_____

_____

3. What are your disability insurance needs? What amount of additional coverage, if any, do you require?

_____

_____

_____

_____

_____

_____

_____

CHAPTER 12: THE SAMPSONS—A Continuing Case

CASE QUESTIONS

1. Make suggestions to the Sampsons regarding their health insurance. Do you think they should switch from the HMO to a PPO? Why or why not?

_____

_____

_____

_____

_____

_____

_____

2. Do you think the Sampsons should purchase disability insurance? Why or why not?

_____

_____

_____

_____

_____

_____

_____

3. Should the Sampsons purchase long-term care insurance? Why or why not?

_____

_____

_____

_____

_____

_____

_____

Life Insurance

Maria quit her job to care for her young children. Shortly after she stopped working, her husband, Diego, was killed in an auto accident. It was only then that Maria fully appreciated the benefit of a $400,000 life insurance policy. Shortly after their first child was born, their neighbor, an insurance agent, approached Maria and Diego. The agent convinced them that because he was the sole provider

Halfpoint/Fotolia

for the family, Diego needed a sizable insurance policy to replace his income in the event of his death. The insurance is enough to cover expenses until well after the children are in school and Maria reenters the workforce.

Without life insurance, the death of a breadwinner eliminates some or all of the household's employment income forever. Life insurance can provide financial protection for members of a household.

MyFinanceLab helps you master the topics in this chapter and study more efficiently. Visit http://www.myfinancelab.com for more details.

The objectives of this chapter are to:

- Provide a background on life insurance
- Describe the types of life insurance that are available
- Identify the factors that influence life insurance needs
- Review the contents of a life insurance policy
- Discuss how to select a life insurance company
- Explain how life insurance fits within your financial plan

Background on Life Insurance

life insurance
Insurance that provides a payment to a specified beneficiary when the policyholder dies.

Life insurance provides a payment to a specified beneficiary when the policyholder dies. In this way, it allows you to provide financial support to specified beneficiaries in the event of your death. A $100,000 policy means that if you die, the beneficiary named in your policy will receive $100,000. The amount received by the beneficiary is not taxed.

Life insurance is provided by life insurance companies, which may be independent firms or subsidiaries of financial conglomerates. Many financial institutions that provide banking and brokerage services also have a subsidiary that provides life insurance. You pay a premium on a periodic (such as quarterly) basis for life insurance.

Role of Life Insurance

Before deciding whether to buy life insurance or how much life insurance to buy, you need to consider your financial goals. The most common financial goal related to life insurance is to maintain financial support for your dependents. Life insurance is critical to protect a family's financial situation in the event that a breadwinner dies. It provides the family with support to cover burial expenses or medical expenses not covered by health insurance. Life insurance can also maintain the family's lifestyle in the future, even without the breadwinner's income. In addition, it may help dependents pay off any accumulated debt. If you are the breadwinner and have others who rely on your income, you should have life insurance.

If no one else relies on your income, life insurance may not be necessary. For example, if you and your spouse both work full-time and your spouse could be self-sufficient without your income, life insurance is not as important. If you are single and are not providing financial support to anyone, life insurance may not be needed.

However, many individuals without dependents still want to leave money to their heirs. For example, you may decide that you want to finance your nephew's college education. If you die before your nephew attends college, a life insurance policy can achieve your goal. Alternatively, you may want to provide financial support for your parents. In this case, you can designate your parents as the beneficiaries in a life insurance policy. You can even set up a life insurance policy that designates your favorite charity as the beneficiary.

As time passes, rethink your life insurance decisions. Even if you decide not to purchase life insurance now, you may require life insurance in the future. If you already have a life insurance policy, you may need to increase the coverage or add a new or different beneficiary at a future point in time.

Psychology Behind the Life Insurance Decision

PSYCHOLOGY
of Personal
Finance

Psychology can discourage people from making the decision to buy life insurance. It is natural human behavior to focus on more enjoyable events such as a wedding or a vacation instead of death. Thus, people tend to defer the decision to buy life insurance because they do not want to think about it. In addition, the decision to buy life insurance will result in periodic payments, and people may feel that there is no immediate benefit or satisfaction in return. People would rather spend their money on products or services that provide an immediate benefit. This psychological effect might explain why about one-third of all households in the United States do not have any life insurance. In fact, one-half of all households in the United States admit that they do not have a sufficient amount of life insurance.

To overcome these obstacles, parents should consider what would happen to their children if they died. If they confront the possibility of death and purchase life insurance, they should recognize that they do receive an immediate benefit: They can ensure that if they die, their children will receive sufficient support.

Although your decision to buy life insurance is not as enjoyable as buying clothes or stocks, it can be even more rewarding. The first step is to invest time by reading this chapter on life insurance and then deciding whether you should consider buying life insurance to protect the financial future of your loved ones.

Role of Life Insurance Companies

Many insurance companies can provide you with life insurance coverage. They can explain the different types of life insurance that are available and help you determine the type of life insurance that would satisfy your needs. They can also help you determine the amount of coverage that you need. Many people who purchase life insurance will be alive 40 or more years after they purchase the policy, and they rely on the life insurance company to provide the benefits on their death in the future. Thus, it is important that the company is financially sound so that it will continue to exist and fulfill its insurance contracts for its policyholders in the distant future.

Applying for Life Insurance

To apply for life insurance, you fill out a detailed application form with information about your medical history and lifestyle that is used to determine your eligibility and premium. If you suffer from a chronic illness such as diabetes or heart disease or are a smoker, your premium will be higher. You may be tempted to omit some information so that you can pay a lower premium. As part of the application process, you will most likely go through a medical exam. Between the exam and information available from the Medical Information Bureau, a clearinghouse of medical information that insurers share, the insurer will most likely uncover any inaccuracies in your application.

If your application does slip through with inaccuracies, your insurance benefits could be eliminated. The policy is a legal contract between you and the insurance company, so you must be truthful. It is not worth jeopardizing the peace of mind that life insurance brings by trying to save a relatively small amount on premiums.

Types of Life Insurance

Although the needs for life insurance are straightforward, there are many options for policies. Term insurance, whole life insurance, and universal life insurance are the most popular types of life insurance.

Term Insurance

term insurance
Life insurance that is provided over a specified time period and does not build a cash value.

Term insurance is life insurance provided over a specified time period. The term is typically from 5 to 20 years. Term insurance does not build a cash value, meaning that the policy does not serve as an investment. It is intended strictly to provide insurance to a beneficiary in the event of death. If the insured person remains alive over the term, the policy expires at the end of the term and has no value.

Consider the case of a single mother with three young children. She plans to provide financial support for her children until they complete their college education. Although her income is sufficient to provide that support, she wants backup support if she dies. She decides to purchase 20-year term insurance. If she dies during this period, her children will receive the coverage specified in the policy. If she is still living at the end of the term, the policy will expire. Even under these conditions, the policy would have served its purpose, giving her peace of mind over the period by ensuring sufficient financial support for her children. Once the term expires, the children will be old enough to support themselves financially.

Premiums on Term Insurance Insurance companies may require that the premium on term insurance be paid monthly, quarterly, semi-annually, or annually. If the premium is not paid by the due date, the policyholder is given a grace period. If the premium is not paid during the grace period, the policy will be terminated.

Determinants of Term Insurance Premiums The annual insurance premiums for term insurance vary based on a number of factors. First, the longer the term of the policy, the longer the period in which the insurance company must provide coverage and the higher the annual premium.

Second, the older the policyholder, the higher the policy premium. Older people are more likely to die within a given term. Exhibit 13.1 provides a sampling of quoted annual premiums (based on a policyholder with no unusual medical problems). The actual premiums will vary among life insurance companies, but the general comparison described here still holds. Notice from Exhibit 13.1 that the annual premium for a 45-year-old is more than twice that of a 25-year-old. In addition, the annual premium for a 60-year-old is more than four times that of a 45-year-old.

Third, the greater the insurance coverage (benefits upon death), the higher the insurance premiums. Exhibit 13.2 illustrates the annual premiums for two profiles based on various coverage levels. Notice that the annual premium for a $500,000 policy is more than twice that of a $100,000 policy.

Fourth, the annual premium is higher for a male than for a female of the same age. Because women tend to live longer than men, the probability of a male dying during a

Financial Planning
ONLINE

Go to:
http://www.lifeinsurance
hub.net

To get:
Information about the advantages and disadvantages of term insurance.

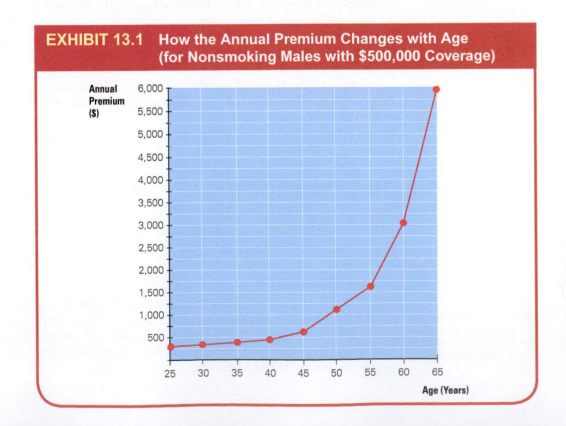

EXHIBIT 13.1 How the Annual Premium Changes with Age (for Nonsmoking Males with $500,000 Coverage)

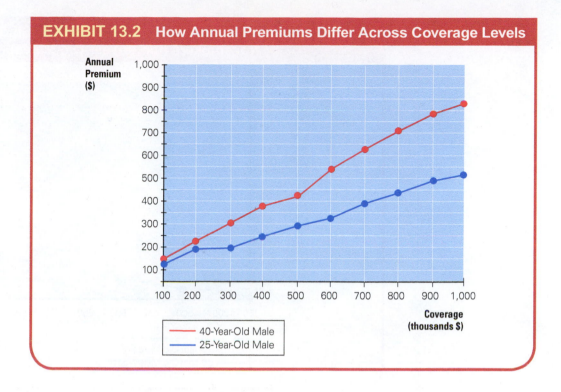

EXHIBIT 13.2   How Annual Premiums Differ Across Coverage Levels

specified term is higher than that of a female of the same age. Exhibit 13.3 shows the difference in quoted annual premiums between males and females for various levels of insurance coverage. In general, the quoted annual premiums for men are between 10% and 25% higher than for women.

Fifth, the annual premium is substantially larger for smokers than for nonsmokers. Exhibit 13.4 shows the difference in annual premiums of male smokers versus male

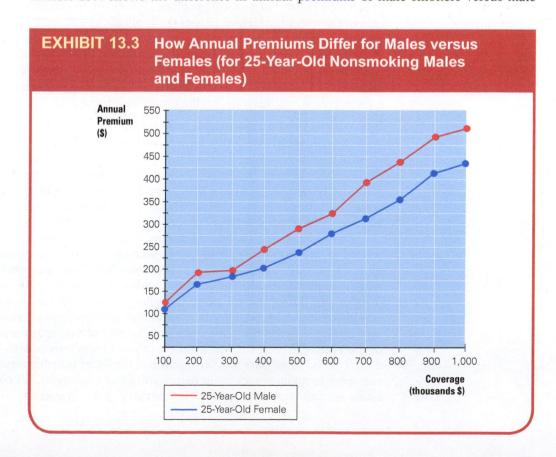

EXHIBIT 13.3   How Annual Premiums Differ for Males versus Females (for 25-Year-Old Nonsmoking Males and Females)

EXHIBIT 13.4   How Annual Premiums Differ for Smokers versus Nonsmokers (for 25-Year-Old Males)

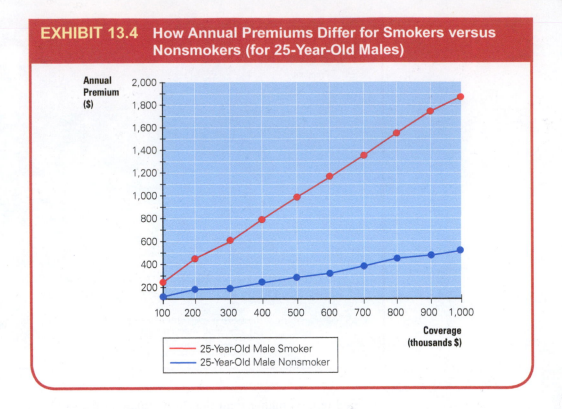

nonsmokers for various coverage levels. The annual premiums for smokers are more than twice that of nonsmokers, regardless of the coverage level. This general relationship holds regardless of the age or gender of the applicant.

Sixth, the annual premium may be much larger for policyholders whose family members have a history of medical problems. For example, the annual premium quoted may be more than doubled if members of the applicant's immediate family have diabetes, heart disease, or kidney disease prior to age 60.

The size of the premium on term insurance is dependent on the likelihood of death over the specified term and the length of the term in which insurance is desired. The likelihood of death is affected by health, age, and gender. A term insurance premium for a given person will vary among life insurance companies.

Reviewing Premiums on Term Insurance Using the Internet   Some life insurance companies provide quotes for term insurance on their Web sites. You need to provide information such as your date of birth, your state of residency, the amount of coverage, the length of the term of insurance, and answer some general questions about your health. Within a minute of providing this information, you will receive quotes. You can even adjust the amount of insurance coverage if you want to determine how the premium is affected by alternative levels of coverage.

Visit Web sites such as http://www.insure.com, http://www.insweb.com, or the finance section of Yahoo.com, and insert the search term "insurance quotes" in order to obtain quotes from various life insurance companies based on your specified needs. First they request some information as described earlier, and then they list various quotes on term insurance by different companies. This allows you to select the company that you believe would accommodate your needs. You can link to the policy contract of that company and may be able to access the name and phone number of a company representative. The value of this type of Web site is that it may help you obtain quotes without being subjected to a sales pitch. Then, once you have screened the list of possible insurance companies, you can speak to an insurance agent before you select a company. Of course, you should also assess the financial soundness of the company that you select.

decreasing-term insurance
A form of term insurance in which the benefits that will be paid to the beneficiary are reduced over time and the premium remains constant.

mortgage life insurance
Life insurance that pays off a mortgage in the event of the policyholder's death.

Financial Planning ONLINE

Go to:
http://www.intelliquote.com/

To get:
Quotes from various insurance companies for a specific term insurance policy based on information that you specify.

group term insurance
Term insurance with generally lower than typical premiums that is available to people within a defined group.

whole life insurance (permanent insurance)
Life insurance that continues to provide insurance as long as premiums are paid; it not only provides benefits to the beneficiary but also has a cash value.

Financial Planning ONLINE

Go to:
http://www.calculatorweb.com

To get:
An opinion about whether you should purchase whole life insurance or term insurance based on the premiums and other information.

Decreasing-Term Insurance A common type of term insurance is **decreasing-term insurance**, in which the insurance benefits to the beneficiary are reduced over time. The premium paid for the insurance remains constant over the term. This type of insurance is popular for families because it provides a relatively high level of insurance in the earlier years when it is most needed. As time passes, a family can accumulate savings, pay off part of a mortgage, and increase their investments, so smaller life insurance benefits are needed. Several forms of decreasing-term insurance are available, with different terms and different degrees to which the insurance benefits decrease over the term. The same factors that affect the premium of term insurance also affect the premium of decreasing-term insurance.

Mortgage Life Insurance Mortgage life insurance pays off a policyholder's mortgage in the event of his death. It is commonly purchased to ensure that a family can afford to continue living in their home even if the breadwinner dies. Mortgage insurance is a special form of decreasing-term insurance. In fact, individuals can achieve the same goal (and possibly save money) by purchasing a term insurance policy that provides benefits large enough to pay off the mortgage.

Group Term Insurance Group term insurance is term insurance provided to a designated group of people with a common bond, such as the same employer. Group term insurance premiums are usually lower than the typical premiums an individual would pay because the insured receive a group discount. Some companies that have a group plan may pay for term insurance for their employees as a benefit.

Whole Life Insurance

Whole life insurance (sometimes referred to as **permanent insurance**) continues to provide insurance as long as premiums are paid; the policy accumulates savings for the policyholder over time. In this way, it not only provides benefits to a beneficiary if the policyholder dies, but also creates a form of savings with a cash value. For this reason, whole life insurance is sometimes referred to as cash-value life insurance.

The cash value is typically specified on a schedule. Your whole life insurance premium is a fixed amount that is used for two purposes: life insurance and savings. A portion of the premium pays for the life insurance provided by the policy, so that the beneficiaries you identify in the policy will be covered if you die. The remainder of the premium is invested for you as a form of savings that builds a cash value over time. If you withdraw the cash, the amount by which the cash value exceeds the premiums that were paid is subject to taxes.

You can change your policy by using your cash value to make a one-time payment for a new policy. The death benefit of the new policy is dependent on the cash value amount of the policy that you exchange.

A whole life insurance policy can serve as a source of liquidity. You can borrow against the cash value at an interest rate specified in the policy. However, recognize that this type of loan reduces the cash value of your insurance policy.

Whole Life Insurance Premiums Many insurance policies allow the premium to be paid monthly, quarterly, or annually. The premium on whole life insurance is constant for the duration of the policy. In the earlier years, a portion of the premium paid for the insurance reflects the potential payout to a beneficiary someday, and the remainder is invested by the insurance company as a form of savings. The portion of the premium dedicated to savings is high in the earlier years when the policyholder is young because the portion of the premium needed to insure against the possibility of death is relatively low. In the later years, the premium required to insure against possible death is relatively high, as the likelihood of death is greater. Because the insurance premium is constant, it is not sufficient to cover the amount needed to insure against possible death in the later years. Thus, a portion of the policy's cash value is used to supplement the premium paid in these years.

If you do not pay a premium on a whole life policy, the insurance company will (with your consent) draw from the cash value of your policy to cover the premium.

Determinants of Whole Life Insurance Premiums

The premiums among whole life policies can vary substantially. Because a whole life policy provides life insurance coverage, the annual premiums are also influenced by the same factors that affect the amount of term insurance premiums. In particular, the quoted annual premiums are higher when the applicant is a male who smokes, is over 60 years old, and requires a larger amount of insurance coverage.

Forms of Whole Life Insurance

limited payment policy
Allows you to pay premiums over a specified period but remain insured for life.

Many alternative forms of whole life insurance are available, so you can structure the premium payments in a manner that fits your needs. One such policy is a **limited payment policy** that allows you to pay premiums over a specified period but remain insured for life. For example, you could make payments until you retire, but continue to be insured after retirement. If you are 45 years old and plan to retire at age 65, this means you would request a payment period of 20 years. The insurance premiums are larger than if you were required to pay premiums continuously, but you build a large cash value during the payment period. Once the payment period ends, your savings accumulated within the whole life policy are used to cover your future premiums.

Alternatively, a whole life policy can be structured to provide a higher level of death benefits to the beneficiaries in the earlier years of the policy. For example, it may specify insurance coverage of $300,000 over the next 10 years and $100,000 of coverage after 10 years. This type of policy may be useful for policyholders who have young children. The coverage is higher in the years when the children are young and unable to take care of themselves.

Comparison to Term Insurance

Premiums for whole life insurance are higher than premiums for term insurance. The advantage of whole life insurance over term insurance is that it not only provides insurance against possible death, but it also accumulates savings over time. Note, though, that you can accumulate savings on your own by purchasing term insurance with lower premiums and then investing the difference.

Some people may prefer whole life insurance because it forces them to save money and accumulate funds. However, it is a relatively inefficient way to save money. They may be better off by establishing a routine to automatically deposit a portion of each paycheck in a bank account, to force some level of savings over time.

The choice of term insurance versus whole life insurance is dependent on your particular needs. If you only have life insurance to insure beneficiaries in the event of your death, term insurance is probably more appropriate.

If you live beyond the term stated in a term insurance policy, you would have to pay a higher annual premium when establishing a new term insurance policy. Conversely, the premium for the basic whole life policy remains constant. Nevertheless, term insurance is typically a less expensive way to meet your life insurance needs.

EXAMPLE

Stephanie Spratt has a close relationship with her two young nieces, who come from a broken home. Although Stephanie is presently focused on building her own wealth, she hopes that someday she will have sufficient funds to pay for her nieces' college education. She is considering purchasing life insurance that would provide benefits of $100,000 and naming her nieces as beneficiaries. She will either invest in a 20-year term life insurance policy for $120 per year or in a whole life policy for $500 per year.

The whole life premium is higher, but the policy builds a cash value over time. If she buys a term insurance policy for $120 per year, she can invest the difference on her own. If she invests the money in a manner similar to the whole life policy, she will likely be able to accumulate savings more quickly on her own. A whole life insurance policy generally generates low returns on the cash that is invested because part of the premium is used to cover administrative fees. Stephanie decides to purchase the term life policy.

Universal Life Insurance

universal life insurance
Life insurance that provides insurance over a specified term and accumulates savings for the policyholder over this time.

Universal life insurance provides insurance over a specified term and accumulates savings for policyholders over this time. It is a combination of term insurance and a savings plan. Because it allows policyholders to build savings, it is classified as a cash-value life insurance policy.

Universal life insurance policies allow "term riders" so you can temporarily increase the level of insurance for a particular period. For example, if you needed an extra $100,000 of insurance coverage over the next five years, you could purchase a term rider to provide the additional coverage.

Universal life insurance allows policyholders to alter their payments over time. It specifies the premium needed to cover the term insurance portion. When policyholders pay more than that amount, the extra amount is invested in savings on which policyholders earn interest.

Unlike whole life insurance policies where the insurance company makes the investment decisions, policyholders are given a set of alternative investments that are administered by the insurance company and can decide how the savings plan funds are to be invested. If policyholders skip premium payments, the amount needed to cover the term insurance portion or any administrative expenses will be withdrawn from their savings plan.

variable life insurance
Life insurance that provides insurance over a specified term and allows policyholders to invest residual funds, after the premium on the term portion is paid, in various types of investments.

Variable Life Insurance One type of universal life insurance is called **variable life insurance**, which allows policyholders to invest the residual funds after the premium payment on the term portion is paid in various types of investments, some of which are similar to mutual funds. Variable life insurance differs from whole life insurance in that it allows policyholders to make their own investment decisions.

An advantage of variable life insurance is that it provides policyholders with some flexibility in making their payments and in deciding how the savings should be invested. However, the fees on variable life insurance can be high. You can achieve the same benefits by simply purchasing term insurance and investing other funds in the manner you prefer, without incurring the high administrative fees that you pay for variable life insurance.

Because variable life policyholders can choose to have their savings plan invested in stocks, their cash value can rise substantially during favorable stock market conditions. In the late 1990s, variable life insurance became very popular as the stock market performed well. However, in the 2000–2002 period stock market conditions were very poor, causing major reductions in the cash values of individual policies.

Determining the Amount of Life Insurance

Once you identify the policy type that best suits your needs, your next decision is the policy amount. You can determine the amount of life insurance you need by applying the income method or the budget method, as explained next.

Income Method

income method
A method that determines how much life insurance is needed based on the policyholder's annual income.

The **income method** is a general formula for determining how much life insurance you should maintain based on your income. This method normally specifies the life insurance amount as a multiple of your annual income, such as 10 times your annual income. For example, if you have an annual income of $40,000, this formula would suggest that you need $400,000 in life insurance. This method is very easy to use. The disadvantage is that it does not consider your age and your family circumstances (including your annual household expenses). Thus, it does not differentiate between a household with no children and one with children, which will likely need more life insurance because its expenses will be higher.

EXAMPLE

The Trent household earns $50,000 per year. The Carlin household also earns $50,000. Both households rely on a neighbor who sells insurance for advice and were told that they should have coverage of 10 times their annual income. However, the Trent household financial situation is completely different from that of the Carlin household. The Trents are in their early 30s and they have two very young children. Daren Trent is the present breadwinner, and Rita Trent plans to stay at home for several more years. The Trents have discussed having more children. They have large credit card balances, two car loans, and a mortgage loan. Their $50,000 income barely covers their existing expenses, and they have very little savings. They tend to overspend on their children and will likely continue to do so. They have a goal of sending their children to private universities, and they would like to purchase a bigger home in the future.

The Carlins do not have any children. They are in their late 50s and both work part-time. They have established a very large amount of savings and a substantial retirement account, so that they could retire now if they had to. They have completely paid off their mortgage and do not have any other debt.

Given the distinct differences in their financial conditions, the insurance coverage should not be the same for both households. The Trents should apply a higher multiple of their annual income, while the Carlins should apply a lower multiple. Some insurance agents would likely suggest that the Trents use a multiple such as 20, so their life insurance would be 20 × $50,000 = $1,000,000. The Carlins may use a much smaller multiple such as 6, so their life insurance coverage would be 6 × $50,000 = $300,000. ●

The difference in the appropriate amount of coverage in the preceding example is due to the difference in future funds that would be needed in the event of death. The adjustments here are arbitrary, however, and may not provide proper coverage. Thus, the income method is limited, even if it allows for some adjustments to account for differences in financial situations.

Budget Method

budget method (needs method)
A method that determines how much life insurance is needed based on the household's expected future expenses.

An alternative method is the **budget method** (also referred to as the **needs method**), which determines your life insurance needs by considering your future budget based on your household's expected future expenses and your current financial situation. This method requires a little more effort than the income method to determine the necessary insurance coverage. However, it provides a better estimate than the income method. The main reason for having life insurance is to ensure that a household's needs are covered in the event of death, not just to replace lost income. The budget method estimates the amount of future funds that will be needed, so that the insurance coverage will be adequate. Some important factors that should be considered when determining needs follow:

- **Annual Living Expenses.** You should have sufficient insurance so that your family can live comfortably without your income. Your family's future expenses will be higher if you have children. Younger children will need financial support for a longer period of time.

- **Special Future Expenses.** If you want to ensure a college education for your children, you need adequate life insurance to cover the expected future expenses.

- **Debt.** If your family relies on your income to cover debt, you may want to ensure that your life insurance can pay off credit card bills and even a mortgage.

- **Job Marketability of Your Spouse.** If your spouse has very limited job marketability, you may need more life insurance so that your spouse can receive job training.

- **Value of Existing Savings.** If you have accumulated a large amount of savings, your family may possibly draw interest or dividends from these savings to cover a portion of their periodic expenses. The more savings your household has accumulated, the less life insurance you need.

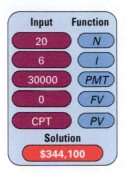

EXAMPLE

You wish to purchase a life insurance policy that generates a pretax income of at least $30,000 per year for the next 20 years to cover living expenses (excluding the mortgage payment) for your spouse and two children in the event that you die. You have just enough savings to cover burial expenses, and you anticipate no unusual expenses for the household in the future.

To determine your insurance needs, you must estimate the amount of insurance today that will cover your household's future living expenses. You can use the time value of money concepts from Chapter 3 to determine the amount of funds today that can provide an annuity equal to $30,000 over each of the next 20 years.

First, assume that you expect your spouse will be able to earn at least 6% annually by investing the money received from the life insurance policy. Next, estimate the present value of an annuity (see Table C.4 in Appendix C) that can provide your household with a $30,000 annuity over 20 years if it generates an annual return of 6%:

$$\text{Amount of Insurance Needed} = \text{Annuity Amount} \times PVIFA\,(i = 6\%, n = 20)$$

$$= \$30,000 \times 11.47$$

$$= \$344,100$$

Based on the following additional information about your household, you then adjust the amount of insurance needed:

- **Other Special Future Expenses.** You also want to allocate an extra $50,000 in life insurance to pay for your two children's college expenses. Although college expenses will rise in the future, the money set aside will accumulate interest over time, so it should be sufficient.

- **Job Training.** You want to have additional insurance of $20,000 to ensure that your spouse can pay for job training in the event of your death.

- **Debt.** You have a $60,000 mortgage and no other loans or credit card debt outstanding. You decide to increase the life insurance amount so that the mortgage can be paid off in the event that you die. Therefore, you specify an extra $60,000 in life insurance.

By summing up your preferences, you determine you need a total of $474,100 in life insurance. You round off the number and obtain quotes for policies with coverage of $475,000 or $500,000.

Using the Internet to Determine Your Insurance Coverage Some insurance companies' Web sites allow you to determine your beneficiary's needs, so that you can decide on the amount of insurance coverage necessary. They ask you to provide basic information such as your total amount of debt, how much annual income you want your family to receive on your death, and how many years you want the income to last. These sites may even allow you to specify the amount of funds that you wish to provide for the education of your family members.

FREE APPS
for Personal
Finance

Estimating the Amount of Life Insurance Needed

Application:

The Life Happens Needs Calculator app (by Life and Health Insurance Foundation for Education) provides you with recommendations regarding how much life insurance you need based on your situation.

To Find It:

Search for the "Life Happens Needs" app on your mobile device.

ECONOMIC IMPACT

Limitations in Estimating Needs When using the budget method to decide needs, keep in mind that the amount of funds you will need is subject to much uncertainty. Here are some common reasons why you may underestimate the life insurance coverage that you need:

- Someone within your household could experience an unanticipated major illness or disability.

- The income level of your household may not rise over time as expected. It could even decline due to layoffs. Many individuals lost their jobs or were assigned fewer work hours during the financial crisis in 2008–2009. In addition, their investments declined in value. Thus, their income was less than expected. When estimating expected income, recognize that economic conditions could weaken over time.

- Inflation could cause you to underestimate the cost of some needs. For example, you may have identified a home as one of your future needs and estimated that the home would cost $120,000 based on existing home prices. However, the price of a home could possibly double within 10–20 years. If the insurance policy only allowed for $120,000 for a home, it might not be sufficient to purchase the kind of home that you desire.

- The insurance policy that you purchase today may not provide coverage until many years from now. For households that save money between purchasing a policy and the death of the policyholder, the funding needed from an insurance policy is reduced. However, for households that accumulate more debt every year, the funding needed from an insurance policy increases. Households should consider the potential change in their debt level over time so that they can more accurately estimate the insurance coverage they will need.

As you attempt to determine your needs, account for the uncertainty by recognizing how the values of these needs may be higher under some conditions. For example, allow for the possibility of higher home prices or tuition when you estimate the values of these needs.

Overestimating your future needs means that you will have more insurance benefits than you really need. Underestimating your future needs means you will have less insurance than you really need. The insurance benefits would not be adequate to provide the desired standard of living for your family. When accounting for this uncertainty, it is better to overestimate your family's future needs than to underestimate them.

Distinguishing Between Needs and Dreams

Before you estimate your needs, distinguish between needs and dreams. To illustrate, consider a young couple that presently has no savings, but has dreams that the breadwinner's career path will generate a substantial amount of income and savings over the years, so that they can retire by age 55 and live in a large home in a mountain resort town. To achieve their dreams, they will likely need about $3 million by the time they are 55 years old. However, if the breadwinner dies, the spouse's life and aspirations may change completely. The dream of a large home in a mountain resort may no longer exist if the couple cannot live there together. The needs to be covered by life insurance should be separated from dreams.

To guide a household in determining needs, the following logic may be applied. First, decide what necessities must be covered for the household to survive and continue its normal standard of living if the breadwinner dies. This exercise can help to determine the minimal desired life insurance coverage.

Next, the household may wish to consider some additional preferences beyond necessities, such as having enough money to ensure that the children's college education is covered. There is an obvious trade-off: The greater the total value of needs if the breadwinner dies, the greater the necessary life insurance coverage, and the higher the life insurance premiums. A higher level of life insurance premiums today results in a smaller amount of funds that could be used for other purposes.

In general, households attempt to strike a compromise when identifying their life insurance needs. The breadwinner may desire that the family could enjoy an even higher standard of living than is possible today. However, life insurance is not normally viewed as a means by which the surviving family members can suddenly become rich. Ideally, life insurance can provide the financial support for family members to continue with their lives and pursuit of goals, just as if the breadwinner were still alive.

Contents of a Life Insurance Policy

A life insurance policy contains the following information.

Beneficiary

beneficiary
Person named to receive the benefits of an insurance policy.

The named **beneficiary** receives the benefits when the policyholder dies. When you name a beneficiary on your life insurance policy, keep the following points in mind. First, you can name multiple beneficiaries and specify how you want the death benefits to be divided. You can also name a contingent beneficiary who would receive the benefits in the event that your primary beneficiary is no longer living. You can change the beneficiary any time you wish, but until you do, the existing contract will be enforced. If you name a person rather than your estate as your beneficiary, the benefits can be paid to the person directly and avoid probate and related expenses.

Grace Period

The insurance policy specifies the grace period allowed beyond the date when payment is due. The typical grace period is 30 days.

Living Benefits

living benefits (accelerated death benefits)
Benefits that allow the policyholder to receive a portion of death benefits before they die.

Some whole life insurance policies allow **living benefits** (also referred to as **accelerated death benefits**), in which policyholders can receive a portion of the death benefits under special circumstances including terminal illness or long-term care needs of the insured.

Nonforfeiture Clause

nonforfeiture clause
Allows you to receive the savings you accumulated if you terminate your whole life policy.

A key provision of the whole life policy is a **nonforfeiture clause,** which allows you to use the accumulated cash value if you terminate your whole life policy. You can elect to receive the cash or may be able to direct the funds to purchase a term life insurance contract with a one-time payment. The coverage of the new policy is dependent on the amount of cash value available.

Loans

You can borrow cash from your whole life policy once it has an accumulated cash value. The loan rates are usually lower than rates offered on personal loans, and interest is paid back into the cash value of the policy.

Incontestability Date

Policies specify a date after which the provisions are incontestable. Until that date, an insurance company can cancel a policy if it determines that some of the information provided by the policyholder is inaccurate.

Renewability Option

renewability option
Allows you to renew your policy for another term once an existing policy expires.

A **renewability option** allows you to renew your term insurance policy for another term (up to an age limit specified in the policy) once the existing term expires. The premium for the next term will be higher than that for the prevailing term because you will be older.

In addition, the premium charged in the next term can increase to reflect any change in your health. The advantage of the renewability option is that your renewal is guaranteed. Without a renewability option, you may not be able to renew your insurance if your health has deteriorated. Many term insurance policies include the renewability option at no extra charge. Make sure that this option is available in any term insurance policy that you consider.

Conversion Option

conversion option
Allows you to convert your term insurance policy into a different type of policy (called a whole life policy) that will be in effect the rest of your life.

A **conversion option** allows you to convert your term insurance policy into a whole life policy that will be in effect the rest of your life. An insurance policy with a conversion option specifies the period in which the conversion can occur. At the time of this conversion, the premium will be increased, but it will then stay constant for the rest of your life.

Settlement Options

settlement options
The alternative ways a beneficiary can receive life insurance benefits in the event that the insured person dies.

Settlement options are the alternative ways beneficiaries can receive life insurance benefits in the event that the insured person dies. Normally, the benefits are not taxed, although there are some exceptions beyond the scope of this text. When you purchase a life insurance policy, you select the settlement option that is most appropriate for your beneficiaries. The appropriate option is dependent on the needs and other characteristics of the beneficiaries. Some of the common options are identified next.

lump-sum settlement
A single payment of all the benefits owed to a beneficiary under a life insurance policy.

Lump Sum A **lump-sum settlement** provides all the benefits to the beneficiary in a single payment on the death of the insured. A $250,000 life insurance policy would provide $250,000 to the beneficiary in a lump sum. This settlement is often used if the beneficiary is disciplined and will use the proceeds wisely. If the beneficiary does not have sufficient discipline, however, an alternative settlement option may be more appropriate.

installment payments settlement
The payment of life insurance benefits owed to a beneficiary as a stream of equal payments over a specified number of years.

Installment Payments The policyholder can elect to use an **installment payments settlement,** which means that the beneficiary will receive a stream of equal payments over a specified number of years. For example, instead of paying $300,000 to the beneficiary in a lump sum, the policy may specify that the beneficiary will receive annual payments starting at the time of the policyholder's death and lasting for 10 years. By spreading the amount over time, this settlement option ensures that the beneficiary will not immediately spend the total amount to be received.

interest payments settlement
A method of paying life insurance benefits in which the company retains the amount owed for a specified number of years and pays interest to the beneficiary.

Interest Payments The policyholder can also elect to use an **interest payments settlement,** which means that the amount owed to the beneficiary will be held by the life insurance company for a specified number of years. Until the amount is distributed, the beneficiary will receive periodic interest payments on the amount. Like the installment payments option, this settlement option prevents the beneficiary from quickly spending all of the policy proceeds.

Selecting a Life Insurance Company

All life insurance companies are not the same. For this reason, you should research multiple life insurance companies before you select one. Keep the following criteria in mind when you choose a life insurance company.

The Specific Policy That You Want

Although all life insurance companies offer some forms of term insurance and whole life insurance, make sure the company offers the specific policy that you want. For example, you may want a 10-year term policy with a settlement option that provides installment payments.

Relatively Low Insurance Premiums

The cost of insurance is an important factor to consider when selecting a particular life insurance policy. As you compare the premiums across insurance companies, make sure that the quotes you receive are for comparable policies.

Life Insurance Quotations

Application:

The i-Illustrate Lite app (by John Hancock) provides quick life insurance quotes based on the information that you input.

To Find It:

Search for the "John Hancock" app on your mobile device.

Strong Financial Condition

**Financial Planning
ONLINE**

Go to:
http://www.prudential
.com and insert the term
"life insurance needs
estimator"

To get:
A recommendation for
the amount of life insur-
ance that you should
have, based on your
financial situation.

As mentioned earlier, policyholders rely on a life insurance company to survive in the long run so that it can serve them on their death. If a life insurance company fails, it will not pay the benefits of its policyholders in the future. People who paid life insurance premiums in the past will not receive the benefits that they deserve. Thus, it is important to assess the financial condition of the life insurance company before you purchase an insurance policy.

Some people believe that insurance companies that focus only on life insurance coverage are safer because they would not be exposed to potential liability resulting from health insurance or liability claims. For example, assume that you have a life insurance policy with a small company that also provides liability coverage. Assume that one of its customers is sued and the court system awards $50 million to the plaintiff. Consequently, the insurance company may go bankrupt because it cannot afford to cover the claim, and therefore it cannot provide any life insurance benefits in the future. Companies that focus only on life insurance can avoid this type of exposure. Life insurance benefits that must be paid out in the future are more predictable than future benefits payable for liability or health insurance claims.

Many people who are not qualified to judge the financial condition of an insurance company rely on ratings assigned by rating services such as A.M. Best, Moody's, and Standard & Poor's. The Web site http://www.insure.com provides ratings of many insurance companies at no charge. Only consider insurance companies that are rated highly.

Services

Make sure that the insurance company will provide you with the type of service that you can expect. For example, you may want to ensure that the insurance company can supply convenient online services. If you want to discuss possible changes to your life insurance policy in person, you may consider choosing an insurance company that has a branch close to your residence. You may want to make sure that you are comfortable with the agent employed by the insurance company. Some agents receive certifications when they have completed specialized training, such as the Chartered Life Underwriter (CLU) certificate. However, keep in mind that although your policy may be in place at a specific company for many years, the agent may leave the company tomorrow. Your policy does not leave with the agent.

Other Types of Insurance

Some life insurance companies offer all types of insurance, including liability insurance and health insurance. You may want to select a life insurance company that can also provide these other types of insurance, assuming that this company satisfies all other criteria. It is more convenient to have all types of insurance at one company. In addition, you may receive a discount on your life insurance premium if you purchase other types of insurance from the same company.

How Life Insurance Fits Within Your Financial Plan

The following are the key decisions about life insurance that should be included within your financial plan:

- Do you need life insurance?
- What type of life insurance is most appropriate for you?
- How much life insurance should you plan for in the future?

Exhibit 13.5 provides an example of how life insurance decisions apply to Stephanie Spratt's financial plan.

EXHIBIT 13.5   How Life Insurance Fits Within Stephanie Spratt's Financial Plan

GOALS FOR LIFE INSURANCE PLANNING

1. Determine whether I need to purchase life insurance.
2. If so, determine what type of life insurance to buy.
3. Determine whether I should purchase or add to my life insurance in the future.

ANALYSIS

Type of Insurance Plan	Benefits	Status
Term insurance	Insurance benefits provided to beneficiary.	Not needed at this time since I do not have a spouse or dependents.
Whole life insurance	Insurance benefits provided to beneficiary, and policy builds a cash value over time.	Not needed at this time.
Universal life insurance	Insurance benefits provided to beneficiary, and policy builds a cash value over time.	Not needed at this time.

DECISIONS

Decision on Whether I Need Life Insurance and Type of Insurance:

I decided to purchase term life insurance to provide my two nieces with a college education if I die. The policy is small, and so the premium I pay is $120 per year, or only $10 per month. My reason for buying life insurance is simply to have insurance, not to build a cash value. Term insurance serves my purpose and is much cheaper than whole or universal policies.

Decision on Insurance Coverage in the Future:

In the future, I will need to ensure proper life insurance coverage if I have a family. I would want to ensure that my children have sufficient funds to support them and possibly even pay for their college education if I die. If I have a child, I will obtain a 20-year term life insurance policy for $300,000.

DISCUSSION QUESTIONS

1. How would Stephanie's decisions regarding purchasing life insurance be different if she were a single mother of two children?

2. How would Stephanie's decisions regarding purchasing life insurance be affected if she were 35 years old? If she were 50 years old?

SUMMARY

Role of Life Insurance. Life insurance is needed to maintain financial support for your dependents. It can protect a family's financial situation in the event that a breadwinner dies.

Types of Life Insurance. Life insurance provides payments to specified beneficiaries if the policyholder dies. Term insurance is strictly intended to provide insurance in the event of the death of the policyholder, whereas whole life insurance and universal life insurance use a portion of the premium to build cash value. The premiums for whole life and universal life insurance are higher than the premiums for term insurance to account for the portion distributed into a savings plan and for the administrative fees.

Amount of Life Insurance Needed. The amount of life insurance that you need can be measured by the income method, in which you attempt to replace the income that would be discontinued due to death. The amount of life insurance can be more precisely measured by the budget method, which considers factors such as your household's future annual living expenses and existing debt.

Cost of Life Insurance Premiums. The cost of the life insurance premium is dependent on the amount of life insurance coverage, on whether the life insurance policy has a cash value, and on personal characteristics such as age and health.

Life Insurance Policy Provisions. A life insurance policy specifies provisions regarding the rights of the insured policyholder and the settlement options available to the beneficiaries.

Selecting a Life Insurance Company. When selecting a life insurance company, consider whether it offers other types of insurance that you might need, offers the specific provisions in its policy that you desire, charges relatively low premiums on its policies, and has a strong financial condition (is likely to remain in business).

How Life Insurance Fits Within Your Financial Plan. Part of your financial plan may be to financially support your family. Life insurance can ensure that financial support is provided for your family in the event of your death. Therefore, life insurance can help you achieve your financial plan.

REVIEW QUESTIONS

All Review Questions are available in MyFinanceLab at http://www.myfinancelab.com.

1. **Purpose of Life Insurance.** What is the purpose of life insurance? Do you think everyone needs life insurance? Explain.

2. **Term Insurance.** What is term insurance? What factors determine the premium for term insurance? What is decreasing-term insurance?

3. **Mortgage Life Insurance.** What is mortgage life insurance? Is mortgage life insurance a good buy? Why or why not?

4. **Term Insurance Options.** Briefly describe some of the term insurance options.

5. **Whole Life Insurance.** What is whole life insurance? What benefit does it provide that term life insurance does not?

6. **Loan Clauses.** Describe the nonforfeiture and loan clauses of whole life insurance policies.

7. **Whole Life Premium.** Why is the premium paid for whole life higher than the premium for term life? What alternative approach to purchasing life insurance might provide the same benefits as whole life?

8. **Universal Life Insurance.** What is universal life insurance? How does it differ from term life and whole life?

9. **Variable Life Insurance.** What is variable life insurance? What are the advantages and disadvantages of variable life policies? How can individuals avoid the high fees of variable life insurance?

10. **Income Method.** Describe the income method to determine the amount of life insurance needed. What is the disadvantage of this method?

11. **Life Insurance Needs.** Discuss why life insurance needs should not be based on a family's dreams for the future.

12. **Budget Method.** Describe the budget method to determine the amount of life insurance needed. What elements must be considered in making this calculation?

13. **Factors Affecting Premiums.** List and briefly discuss the factors that affect an individual's life insurance premium.

14. **How the Internet Facilitates Insurance Quotes.** Explain how use of the Internet can expedite the purchase of life insurance. Why do many customers prefer this method?

15. **Settlement Options.** What are settlement options? Which option should you choose?

16. **Lump-Sum Settlement.** What is a lump-sum settlement? What kind of beneficiary would benefit the most from this option?

17. **Installment Payments Settlement.** What is an installment payments settlement? When would an insured individual choose this option?

18. **Interest Payments Option.** What is the interest payments option? How does it differ from the installment payments option?

19. **Beneficiary.** What is a beneficiary? Why is it important to periodically review your beneficiaries?

20. **Psychology and Life Insurance.** Why do some people postpone buying life insurance even when they need it?

21. **Group Term Life Insurance.** What is group term life insurance? What are the advantages of group term life insurance?

22. **Limitations in Estimating Life Insurance Needs.** What are some factors that make estimating life insurance needs difficult?

23. **Living Benefits.** What are living benefits? When might a policyholder use this option?

24. **Conversion Option.** What is a conversion option? What are the benefits of having this option?

25. **Financial Condition of Insurance Company.** Why is it important to evaluate the financial condition of a life insurance company?

FINANCIAL PLANNING PROBLEMS

All Financial Planning Problems are available in MyFinanceLab *at http://www.myfinancelab.com.*

1. **Income Method.** Nancy is a widow with two teenage children. Nancy's gross income is $3,000 per month, and taxes take about 30% of her income. Using the income method, Nancy calculates she will need to purchase about eight times her disposable income in life insurance to meet her needs. How much insurance should Nancy purchase?

2. **Purchasing Additional Insurance.** Nancy's employer provides her with two times her annual gross salary in life insurance. How much additional insurance should Nancy purchase based on the information in the previous problem?

3. **Amount of Insurance Needed.** Peter is married and has two children. He wants to be sure that he has sufficient life insurance to take care of his family if he dies. Peter's wife is a homemaker but attends college part-time pursuing a law degree. It will cost approximately $40,000 for her to finish her education. Because the children are teenagers, Peter feels he will only need to provide the family with income for the next 10 years. He further calculates that the household expenses run approximately $35,000 per year. The balance on the home mortgage is $30,000. Peter set up a college fund for his children when they were babies, and it currently contains sufficient funds for them to attend college. Assuming that Peter's wife can invest the insurance proceeds at 8%, calculate the amount of insurance Peter needs to purchase.

4. **Amount of Insurance Needed.** Marty and Mary have jobs and contribute to the household expenses according to their income. Marty contributes 75% of the expenses, and Mary contributes 25%. Currently, their household expenses are $30,000 annually. Marty and Mary have three children. The youngest child is 12, so they would like to ensure that they could maintain their current standard of living for at least the next eight years. They feel that the insurance proceeds could be

invested at 6%. In addition to covering the annual expenses, they would like to make sure that each of their children has $25,000 available for college. If Marty were to die, Mary would go back to school part-time to upgrade her training as a nurse. This would cost $20,000. They have a mortgage on their home with a balance of $55,000. How much life insurance should they purchase for Marty?

5. **Amount of Insurance Needed.** Considering the information in the previous problem, how much life insurance should they purchase for Mary?

6. **Decision to Purchase Insurance.** Bart is a college student. Because his plan is to get a job immediately after graduation, he determines that he will need about $250,000 in life insurance to provide for his future wife and children (Bart is not married yet and does not have any children). Bart has obtained a quote over the Internet that would require him to pay $200 annually in life insurance premiums. As a college student, this is a significant expense for Bart, and he would likely have to borrow money to pay for the insurance premiums. Advise Bart on the timing of his life insurance purchase.

7. **Ethical Dilemma.** Shortly after Steve graduated from college, he considered a whole life insurance policy that would provide $10,000 in life insurance protection and accumulate a cash value of twice his current annual income by age 65. Two years later, after Steve's marriage, he bought a second policy. Through his working years he paid the $280 annual premium per policy. Steve kept remembering what the agent had told him many years before about each policy having a cash value double his annual income.

Steve was nearing age 65 and dug out the policies from his safety deposit box so that he could begin to put numbers together to plan his retirement. As he opened the two policies, he was appalled to see that the cash value on the older policy was $17,000 and on the newer policy was only $15,000. The two policies together amounted to only one-third his current annual earnings, far from the figure promised him by the agent.

a. Was the agent being unethical in not showing Steve the potential impact of inflation on the policies' cash value?

b. Taking just the first policy, would Steve have been better off to invest the $280 annual premium in a mutual fund that would have given an annual return of 8% per year (assume a 30-year investment period)?

FINANCIAL PLANNING ONLINE EXERCISES

1. Go to http://www.bankrate.com and insert the search term "life insurance."
   a. What are some differences between term and permanent life insurance?
   b. Why is permanent life insurance more expensive than term life insurance?
   c. Obtain a quote on term insurance of $100,000 for 10 years.
   d. Go to the calculator that allows you to determine how much life insurance you need. Input the data based on your personal situation, and let the calculator determine how much life insurance you need.
   e. Go to the calculator that allows you to compare whole life versus term insurance. Notice the input that you need to provide to make this decision. Input the data based on your personal situation, and let the calculator determine which type of insurance would be better for you.

PSYCHOLOGY OF PERSONAL FINANCE: Your Life Insurance

1. People tend to put off the decision to purchase life insurance. They might argue that they cannot afford it. They do not want to sacrifice any other type of spending so that they could afford to pay for life insurance. Describe your own behavior when purchasing life insurance. If you do not have life insurance, why not?

2. Read one practical article about how psychology affects decisions when buying life insurance. You can easily retrieve possible articles by doing an online search using the terms "psychology" and "buying life insurance." Summarize the main points of the article.

WEB SEARCH EXERCISE

You can develop your personal finance skills by conducting an Internet search for related articles. Find a recent online article about personal finance that reinforces one or more concepts covered in this chapter. If your class has an online component, your professor may ask you to post your summary of the article there and provide a link to the article so that other students can access it. If your class is live, your professor may ask you to summarize your application of the article in class. Your professor may assign specific students to complete this assignment or may allow any student to do the assignment on a volunteer basis.

For recent online articles related to this chapter, consider using the following search terms (be sure to include the current year as a search term to ensure that the online articles are recent):

- How life insurance protects your family
- Whole life insurance
- Term insurance
- Life insurance premium
- Selecting a life insurance company

VIDEO EXERCISE: Selecting Life Insurance

Go to one of the Web sites that contain video clips (such as http://www.youtube.com) and review some video clips about selecting life insurance. You can use search phrases such as "life insurance tips." Select one video clip on this topic that you would recommend for the other students in your class.

1. Provide the Web link for the video clip.
2. What do you think is the main point of this video clip?
3. How might you change your process of selecting life insurance as a result of watching this video clip?

BUILDING YOUR OWN FINANCIAL PLAN

Life insurance is the most controversial and hard-to-select form of insurance. It is controversial because no entity requires that you have life insurance in the way that you are required to insure an auto or home. It is also the one form of insurance for which you, the policyholder, will not be the one to file the claim. Selection is difficult because the insurance industry has numerous policy options for term and whole life insurance.

Insurance needs should be reviewed when major changes occur in your life. Specifically, this review should take place if you marry, divorce, or become a parent.

Go to the worksheets at the end of this chapter to continue building your financial plan.

THE SAMPSONS—A Continuing Case

The Sampsons have one remaining insurance need: life insurance. They have decided to purchase term life insurance. They want a life insurance policy that will provide for the family in the event of Dave's death because he is the major breadwinner. The Sampsons do not know how much insurance to purchase, but their goal is to have enough money for general expenses over the next 15 years.

Recall that Dave's salary after taxes is about $40,000. He wants to ensure that the family would have insurance benefits that could provide $40,000 for the next 15 years. By the end of this period, the children would have completed college. Dave also wants to add an additional $330,000 of insurance coverage to provide support for Sharon through her retirement years because they have not saved much money for retirement.

Go to the worksheets at the end of this chapter to continue this case.

PART 4: BRAD BROOKS—A Continuing Case

Brad tells you about his plans to upgrade his auto insurance. Specifically, he would like to add several types of coverage to his policy, such as uninsured motorist coverage and rental car coverage. Recall that Brad is 30 years old. He also has a driving record that contains several speeding tickets and two accidents (one of which he caused). He realizes that adding coverage will increase the cost of his insurance. Therefore, he is thinking about switching insurance companies to a more inexpensive carrier.

Brad says that he is generally happy with the HMO insurance plan he has through the technology company where he works. However, Brad mentions that he does not particularly like to see his primary care physician each time he requires a consultation with a specialist. He tells you that his company also offers a PPO, but that he did not choose that plan because he knows little about it.

Brad is trying to decide between term life insurance and whole life insurance. He likes whole life insurance, as he believes that the loan feature on that policy will give him an option for meeting his liquidity needs.

Go to the worksheets at the end of this chapter to continue this case.

CHAPTER 13: BUILDING YOUR OWN FINANCIAL PLAN

YOUR GOALS FOR CHAPTER 13

1. Determine whether you need to purchase life insurance, and if so, how much.

2. Determine the most appropriate types of life insurance.

3. Decide whether you should purchase or add to your life insurance in the future.

ANALYSIS

1. Your life insurance needs are dependent on several factors. The following worksheet employs the budget method discussed in the text. Complete the worksheet by filling in the appropriate information to determine your life insurance needs.

1. Annual living expenses (*Refer to your personal cash flow statement developed in Chapter 2 to determine this figure.*)	$		
2. Minus spouse's disposable "after-tax" income	$		
3. Minus interest or dividends from savings*	$		
4. Minus other income	$		
5. Annual living expenses to be replaced by insurance (line 1 minus lines 2, 3, and 4)		$	
6. Assuming a 6% rate of return and the number of years of expenses for which you will need coverage, determine the present value (line 5 times *PVIFA* for _____ years at 6%)		×	
7. Insurance needs for annual living expenses (line 5 times line 6)			$
8. Special future expenses		$	
9. The number of years until line 8 occurs and multiply by the present value of a dollar assuming 6% (line 8 times *PVIF* _____ years at 6%)		×	
10. Insurance needs for special future expenses (line 8 times line 9)			$
11. Current debt to be repaid by insurance proceeds			$
12. Educational/training expenses for spouse to be paid by insurance proceeds			$
13. Value of existing savings			$

14. Final expenses (funeral and other related items)			$
15. Life insurance provided by employer			$
Total Insurance Needs (Add lines 7, 10, 11, 12, and 14 and subtract lines 13 and 15.)			$

* This number should be adjusted if savings are to be liquidated and included in line 13. Only the interest and dividends from those savings not counted in line 13 should be included here.

2. Review the following information about types of life insurance plans. Indicate how suitable each type is for your situation in the third column.

Type of Insurance Plan	Benefits	Suitability
Term Insurance	Insurance benefits provided to beneficiary	
Whole Life Insurance	Insurance benefits provided to beneficiary and policy builds a cash value over time	
Universal Insurance	Insurance benefits provided to beneficiary and policy builds a cash value over time; policy-holders can choose among alternative investment plans	

3. If you have determined that you need life insurance, obtain premiums for the policy type and amount you desire at http://www.prudential.com. Click the "Products & Services" tab. Under "Planning Guides," click "All Guides, Tutorials, & Calculators." Under "Calculators," click "Life Insurance Quotes," and enter the premiums in the following worksheet.

Policy Type			
Name of Insurance Company			
Total Premium	$	$	$

4. Make any necessary changes to your personal cash flow statement to reflect premiums for life insurance.

Personal Cash Flow Statement

Cash Inflows	This Month
Disposable (after-tax) income	
Interest on deposits	
Dividend payments	
Other	
Total Cash Inflows	

NAME   **DATE**

Cash Outflows	This Month
Rent	
Internet/Cable	
Electricity and water	
Mobile phone	
Groceries	
Health care insurance and expenses	
Life insurance	
Clothing	
Car expenses (insurance, maintenance, and gas)	
Recreation	
Other	
Total Cash Outflows	
Net Cash Flows	

DECISIONS

1. Do you need life insurance? If so, how much and what type of policy will suit your needs?

_____

_____

_____

_____

_____

_____

2. What do you anticipate your life insurance coverage needs to be in the future?

_____

_____

_____

_____

_____

_____

CHAPTER 13: THE SAMPSONS—A Continuing Case

CASE QUESTIONS

1. Determine the present value of the insurance benefits that could provide $40,000 per year over the next 15 years for the Sampson family. Assume that the insurance payment could be invested to earn 3% interest over time.

Annual Amount	$40,000
Number of Years	15
Annual Interest Rate	3%
Present Value	$

2. Considering the insurance benefits needed to provide $40,000 per year over the next 15 years, plus the additional $330,000 of insurance coverage, what amount of insurance coverage is needed?

3. Given the total amount of insurance coverage needed and Dave's present age (30 years old), estimate the premium that the Sampsons would pay using an insurance Web site that provides quotes (such as http://www.insure.com or the finance section of Yahoo.com; search for "insurance quotes."

4. Dave Sampson is a social smoker. Because he only smokes occasionally, he would like to omit this information from his life insurance application. Advise Dave on this course of action.

PART 4: BRAD BROOKS—A Continuing Case

CASE QUESTIONS

1. Regarding Brad's auto insurance decision, comment on the following:

   a. His plan to add different types of coverage to his auto insurance policy

   _____

   _____

   _____

   b. The associated costs of adding different types of coverage to his auto insurance policy

   _____

   _____

   _____

   c. Any resulting negative consequences of switching to a more inexpensive auto insurance company

   _____

   _____

   _____

   d. Any other factors Brad should consider before switching insurance companies

   _____

   _____

   _____

2. Describe to Brad how he could benefit from a PPO. Are there any negative factors Brad needs to know about if he seriously considers switching to a PPO? Consider Brad's cash flow situation from the previous parts when answering this question.

   _____

   _____

   _____

3. Concerning Brad's life insurance decision, comment on the following:

   a. His need for life insurance

   _____

   _____

   _____

b. If you think he needs life insurance, is whole life his best choice?

_____

_____

_____

c. His plan to use the whole life policy's loan feature as a means for maintaining liquidity

_____

_____

_____

Personal Investing

The chapters in this part explain the various types of investments that are available, how to value investments, and how to determine which investments to select. Chapter 14 provides a background on investing, and Chapter 15 explains how to decide which stocks to buy. Chapter 16 focuses on investing in bonds. Chapter 17 on mutual funds explains the advantages and disadvantages of investing in a portfolio of securities rather than individual stocks and bonds. Chapter 18 stresses the importance of allocating your money across various types of investments. Your decisions regarding whether to invest, how much to invest, and how to invest will affect your cash flows and wealth.

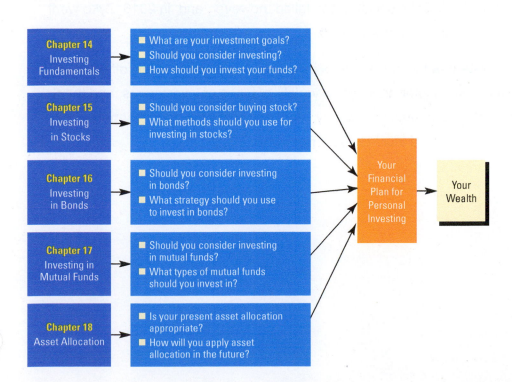

Investing Fundamentals

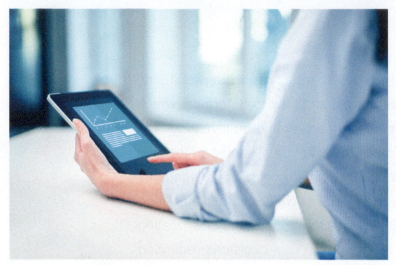

Syda Productions/Shutterstock

Anita is a patient investor. In 2002 she invested $3,000 in stocks of well-known companies. By 2016, her original investment was worth $10,000.

Meanwhile, Lisa invested $3,000 in stock of Zyko Company because Zyko claimed that its new technology would change the world. Lisa wanted to earn higher returns on her investment than she might earn on stock of well-established firms. Zyko's technology failed, however, and, in 2016, Zyko went bankrupt. Consequently, Lisa's stock was worthless.

These examples demonstrate that the same type of investment can have entirely different outcomes. As you will learn in this chapter, there are a variety of types of investments, and the risk and return of these different investments vary widely. Your ability to analyze investments can enhance your investment income and increase your net worth.

MyFinanceLab helps you master the topics in this chapter and study more efficiently. Visit http://www.myfinancelab.com for more details.

The objectives of this chapter are to:

- Describe the common types of investments available to investors
- Explain how to measure the return on investments
- Identify the risks of investments
- Explain the trade-off between the return and risk of investments
- Describe common investment mistakes that should be avoided
- Explain how personal investing fits within your financial plan

Types of Investments

PSYCHOLOGY
of Personal Finance

Before considering how to invest money, review your personal balance sheet. If you have any existing loans, you should consider paying off those loans before investing any money. Some individuals receive a much larger psychological boost from using money to make investments rather than to pay off existing loans. However, such behavior can backfire, as illustrated here.

EXAMPLE   Jared just received an expected bonus of $10,000 from his job. He has an existing car loan of $10,000 on which he is paying an interest rate of 8%. If he pays off the existing loan, he will no longer have to make monthly payments on this loan. However, Jared wants to generate a much larger return on his money than just paying off the loan. He decides to invest the entire $10,000 in a very risky investment that could rise substantially over the next year under ideal conditions, but which could also become worthless under less-favorable conditions. Over the next several months, adverse conditions occurred, which caused the investment to become worthless. Consequently, Jared not only lost his entire investment, but he still has a $10,000 loan outstanding that he could have paid off. Jared feels like a victim because his investment failed, but in truth his investment was a gamble: He chose to ignore information that suggested the investment could fail because he decided that luck was on his side.

In many cases, your best use of funds is to pay off liabilities before you consider investing in assets, especially when the loan rate is as high as or higher than the expected return on the investment. Assuming that you do not have existing liabilities that should be paid off, you can review the possible ways to invest any money that you have. Your first priority should be to ensure adequate liquidity. You can satisfy your liquidity needs by depositing funds in financial institutions or by investing in money market securities such as certificates of deposit. Because these types of investments are primarily focused on providing liquidity, they offer a relatively low return. If you have additional funds beyond your liquidity needs, you have a wide variety of investments to consider.

Money Market Securities

Recall from Chapter 6 that there are several different money market securities available, including certificates of deposit, money market deposit accounts, and money market funds. Most money market securities provide interest income. Even if your liquidity needs are covered, you may invest in these securities to maintain a low level of risk. However, you can also consider some alternative securities that typically provide a higher rate of return but are more risky.

Stocks

As mentioned in Chapter 2, stocks are financial instruments representing partial ownership of a firm. Traditionally, stocks were issued in certificate form, and investors received a certificate representing their shares. Today, however, stocks are commonly issued in book entry form, and investors simply receive a statement indicating how many shares of stock they own in a particular company. Stock investors become shareholders of the firm. Firms issue stocks to obtain funds to expand their business operations. Investors invest in stock when they believe that they may earn a higher return than alternative investments offer. Because stocks are a popular type of investment for individuals, they are the focus of Chapter 15.

Common versus Preferred Stock Stock can be classified as common stock or preferred stock. **Common stock** is a financial instrument issued by a firm to raise funds that represents partial ownership in the firm. Investors who hold common stock normally have the right to vote on key issues such as the sale of the company. They elect the board of directors, which is responsible for ensuring that the firm's managers serve the interests of its shareholders. **Preferred stock** is a financial instrument issued by a firm to raise funds that entitles shareholders to first priority (ahead of common stockholders) in receiving dividends. Corporations issue common stock more frequently than preferred stock. The price of preferred stock is not as volatile as the price of common stock and does not have as much potential to increase substantially. For this reason, investors who strive for high returns typically invest in common stock.

Primary and Secondary Stock Markets Stocks can be traded in a primary or a secondary market. The **primary market** is a market in which newly issued securities are traded. Firms can raise funds by issuing new stock in the primary market. The first offering of a firm's stock to the public is referred to as an **initial public offering (IPO)**. A **secondary market** facilitates the trading of existing securities by enabling investors to sell their shares at any time. These shares are purchased by other investors who wish to invest in that stock. Thus, even if a firm is not issuing new shares of stock, investors can easily obtain shares of that firm's stock by purchasing them in the secondary market. On a typical day, more than 1 million shares of any large firm's stock are traded in the secondary market. The price of the stock changes each day in response to changes in supply and demand.

Types of Investors Investors in stock can be classified as institutional investors or individual investors. **Institutional investors** are professionals employed by a financial institution who are responsible for managing money on behalf of the clients they serve. They attempt to select stocks or other securities that will provide a reasonable return on investment. The employees of financial institutions who make investment decisions are referred to as **portfolio managers** because they manage a portfolio of securities (including stocks). More than half of all trading in financial markets is attributable to institutional investors.

Individual investors commonly invest a portion of the money earned from their jobs. Like institutional investors, they invest in stocks to earn a reasonable return on their investment. In this way, their money can grow by the time they wish to use it to make purchases. The number of individual investors had increased substantially before the financial crisis of 2008–2009, but this number has declined since then. Approximately, 65% of Americans owned some stocks in 2007 but only 52% owned stocks in 2013.

Many individual investors hold their stocks for periods beyond one year, but some individual investors called **day traders** buy stocks and then sell them on the same day. They hope to capitalize on very short-term movements in security prices. In many cases, their investments last for only a few minutes. Many day traders conduct their investing as a career, relying on their returns from investing as their main source of income. This type of investing is very risky because the stock prices of even the best-managed firms periodically decline. Day trading is not recommended for most investors.

In addition to receiving dividends, shareholders can earn a return if the price of the stock increases by the time they sell it. The market value of a firm is based on the number

common stock
A financial instrument issued by a firm to raise funds that represents partial ownership in the firm.

preferred stock
A financial instrument issued by a firm to raise funds that entitles shareholders to first priority to receive dividends.

primary market
A market in which newly issued securities are traded.

initial public offering (IPO)
The first offering of a firm's stock to the public.

secondary market
A market in which existing securities are traded.

institutional investors
Professionals responsible for managing money on behalf of the clients they serve.

portfolio managers
Employees of financial institutions who make investment decisions.

individual investors
Individuals who invest funds in securities.

day traders
Investors who buy stocks and then sell them on the same day.

FREE APPS for Personal Finance

Customized Financial News on Your Stocks

Application:

The Yahoo! Finance app (by Yahoo! Inc.) provides customized news articles on the companies that you select. It also provides stock quotations and additional research on stocks.

To Find It:

Search for the "Yahoo Finance" app on your mobile device.

Financial Planning
ONLINE

Go to:
http://www.renaissance
capital.com

To get:
Information about firms that are about to engage in an IPO fund; also summarizes the performance of recent IPOs.

Financial Planning
ONLINE

Go to:
The finance section of Yahoo.com

To get:
Historical price movements for stock that you specify.

publicly traded stock indexes
Securities whose values move in tandem with a particular stock index representing a set of stocks.

of shares of stock outstanding multiplied by the price of the stock. The price of a share of stock is determined by dividing the market value of the firm by the number of shares of stock outstanding. Thus, a firm that has a market value of $600 million and 10 million shares of stock outstanding has a value per share of:

$$\text{Value of Stock per Share} = \text{Market Value of Firm/Number of Shares Outstanding}$$
$$= \$600{,}000{,}000/10{,}000{,}000$$
$$= \$60$$

The market price of a stock is dependent on the number of investors who are willing to purchase the stock (the demand for the stock) and the number of investors who wish to sell their holdings of the stock (the supply of stock for sale). There is no limit to how high a stock's price can rise. The demand for the stock and the supply of stock for sale are influenced by the respective firm's business performance, as measured by its earnings and other characteristics. When the firm performs well, its stock becomes more desirable to investors, who demand more shares of that stock. In addition, investors holding shares of this stock are less willing to sell it. The increase in the demand for the stock and the reduction in the number of shares of stock for sale by investors results in a higher stock price.

Conversely, when a firm performs poorly (has low or negative earnings), its market value declines. The demand for shares of its stock also declines. In addition, some investors who had been holding the stock will decide to sell their shares, thereby increasing the supply of stock for sale and resulting in a lower stock price. The performance of the firm depends on how well it is managed.

Investors benefit when they invest in a well-managed firm because the firm's earnings usually will increase, and so will its stock price. Under these conditions, investors may generate a capital gain, which represents the difference between their selling price and purchase price. In contrast, a poorly managed firm may have lower earnings than expected, which could cause its stock price to decline.

Bonds

Recall from Chapter 2 that bonds are long-term debt securities issued by government agencies or corporations. Treasury bonds are issued by the Treasury and backed by the U.S. government. Corporate bonds are issued by corporations.

Mutual Funds

Recall as well from Chapter 2 that mutual funds sell shares to individuals and invest the proceeds in a portfolio of investments such as bonds or stocks. They are managed by experienced portfolio managers. They are attractive to investors who have limited funds and want to invest in a diversified portfolio. Because a stock mutual fund typically invests in numerous stocks, it enables investors to achieve broad diversification with an investment as low as $500. There are thousands of mutual funds from which to choose.

Publicly Traded Indexes Another option for investors who want a diversified portfolio of stocks is to invest in **publicly traded stock indexes**, which are securities whose values move in tandem with a particular stock index representing a set of stocks. These indexes are also known as exchange-traded funds (ETFs) because they trade on the stock exchanges like individual stocks.

Much research has shown that sophisticated investors (such as well-paid portfolio managers of financial institutions) are unable to outperform various stock indexes on average. Thus, by investing in an index, individual investors can ensure that their performance will match that index.

One of the most popular publicly traded indexes is the Standard & Poor's Depository Receipt (SPDR, called "Spider"), for the S&P 500 index. The S&P 500 Spider is a basket of stocks that matches the S&P 500 index and is traded on the New York Stock Exchange. Additional exchange-traded funds have been created to match other stock indexes. You can buy Spiders through a broker, just like stocks. When investors expect that the large U.S. stocks represented by the S&P 500 will experience strong performance, they can capitalize on their expectations by purchasing shares of the S&P 500 Spider. Spiders provide investors with a return not only in the form of potential share price appreciation, but also dividends in the form of additional shares to the investors. Any expenses incurred by the Spiders from creating the index are deducted from the dividends.

Investors can also invest in specific sector indexes as well as in market indexes. There are publicly traded indexes that represent a variety of specific sectors, including the Internet, energy, technology, and financial sectors. Because an index represents several stocks, you can achieve some degree of diversification by investing in an index.

Real Estate

One way of investing in real estate is to buy a home. The value of a home changes over time, in response to supply and demand. When the demand for homes in your area increases, home values tend to rise. The return that you earn on your home is difficult to measure because you must take into account the financing, real estate agent commissions, and tax effects. However, a few generalizations are worth mentioning. For a given amount invested in the home, your return is dependent on how the value of your home changes over the time that you own it. Your return is also dependent on your original down payment on the home. The return will be higher if you made a smaller down payment when purchasing the home. Because the value of a home can decline over time, there is the risk of a loss (a negative return) on your investment. If you are in a hurry to sell your home, you may have to lower your selling price to attract potential buyers, which will result in a lower return on your investment.

You can also invest in real estate by purchasing rental property or land. The price of land is based on supply and demand. There is little open land, and with dense populations along the coasts of the United States, open land along the coasts typically has a high price.

Investment Return

When individuals make an investment, they typically assess the performance of the investment based on its return. The means by which various types of investments generate returns to investors are described here.

Return from Investing in Stock

Stocks can offer a return on investment through dividends and stock price appreciation. Some firms distribute quarterly income to their shareholders in the form of dividends rather than reinvest the earnings in the firm's operations. They tend to keep the dollar amount of the dividends per share fixed from one quarter to the next, but may periodically increase the amount. They rarely reduce the dividend amount unless they experience relatively weak performance and cannot afford to make their dividend payment. The amount of dividends paid out per year is usually between 1% and 3% of the stock's price.

A firm's decision to distribute earnings as dividends, rather than reinvesting all of its earnings to support future growth, may depend on the opportunities that are available to the firm. In general, firms that pay high dividends tend to be older, established firms that have less chance for substantial growth. Conversely, firms that pay low dividends tend to be younger firms that have more growth opportunities. The stocks of firms with substantial growth opportunities are often referred to as **growth stocks**. An investment in these younger firms offers the prospect of a very large return because they have not reached their full potential. At the same time, an investment in these firms is exposed to much higher uncertainty because young firms are more likely to fail or experience very weak performance than mature firms.

The higher the dividend paid by a firm, the lower its potential stock price appreciation. When a firm distributes a large proportion of its earnings to investors as dividends, it limits its potential growth and the potential degree to which its value (and stock price) may increase. Stocks that provide investors with periodic income in the form of large dividends are referred to as **income stocks**.

growth stocks
Stocks of firms with substantial growth opportunities.

income stocks
Stocks that provide investors with periodic income in the form of large dividends.

Return from Investing in Bonds

Bonds offer a return to investors in the form of coupon payments and bond price appreciation. They pay periodic interest (coupon) payments and therefore can provide a fixed amount of interest income per year. Thus, they are desirable for investors who want to have their investments generate a specific amount of interest income each year.

A bond's price can increase over time and therefore may provide investors with a capital gain, representing the difference between the price at which it was sold by an investor versus the price at which it was purchased. However, a bond's price may decline, which could cause investors to experience a capital loss. Even the prices of Treasury bonds decline in some periods. More details about bonds are provided in Chapter 16.

Return from Investing in Mutual Funds

The coupon or dividend payment generated by the mutual fund's portfolio of securities is passed on to the individual investor. Because a mutual fund represents a portfolio of securities, its value changes over time in response to changes in the values of those securities. Therefore, the price at which an investor purchases shares of a mutual fund changes over time. A mutual fund can generate a capital gain for individual investors because the price at which investors sell their shares of the fund may be higher than the price at which they purchased the shares. However, the price of the mutual fund's shares may also decline over time, which would result in a capital loss. Mutual funds are discussed in more detail in Chapter 17.

Return from Investing in Real Estate

Real estate that can be rented (such as office buildings and apartments) generates income in the form of rent payments. In addition, investors may earn a capital gain if they sell the property for a higher price than they paid for it. Alternatively, they may sustain a capital loss if they sell the property for a lower price than they paid for it.

The price of land changes over time in response to real estate development. Many individuals may purchase land as an investment, hoping that they will be able to sell it in the future for a higher price than they paid for it.

Measuring the Return on Your Investment

For investments that do not provide any periodic income (such as dividends or coupon payments), the return (R) can be measured as the percentage change in the price (P) from the time the investment was purchased (time $t-1$) until the time at which it is sold (time t):

$$R = \frac{P_t - P_{t-1}}{P_{t-1}}$$

For example, if you pay $1,000 to make an investment and receive $1,100 when you sell the investment in one year, you earn a return of:

$$R = \frac{\$1,100 - \$1,000}{\$1,000}$$

$$= .10, \text{ or } 10\%$$

Incorporating Dividend or Coupon Payments If you also earned dividend or coupon payments over this period, your return will be even higher. For a short-term period such as one year or less, the return on a security that pays dividends or interest can be estimated by adjusting preceding the equation. Add the dividend or coupon amount to the numerator. The return on your investment in stocks accounts for any dividends or coupon payments you received as well as the change in the investment value over your investment period. For stocks that pay dividends, the return is

$$R = \frac{(P_t - P_{t-1}) + D}{P_{t-1}}$$

where R is the return, P_{t-1} is the price of the stock at the time of the investment, P_t is the price of the stock at the end of the investment horizon, and D represents the dividends earned over the investment horizon.

EXAMPLE

You purchased 100 shares of stock from Wax, Inc., for $50 per share one year ago. During the year, the firm experienced strong earnings. It paid dividends of $1 per share over the year, and you sold the stock for $58 at the end of the year. Your return on your investment was

$$R = \frac{(P_t - P_{t-1}) + D}{P_{t-1}}$$

$$= \frac{(\$58 - \$50) + \$1}{\$50}$$

$$= .18, \text{ or } 18\%$$

Differing Tax Rates on Returns Income received as a result of interest payments or bond coupon payments is classified as ordinary income for tax purposes. In addition, capital gains resulting from the sale of investments held for one year or less are taxed at ordinary income tax rates. Capital gains resulting from the sale of investments held for more than one year are subject to a long-term capital gains tax. Given the difference in tax rates applied to short- and long-term capital gains, some investors may achieve a higher after-tax return by holding on to investments for more than one year.

EXAMPLE

As in the previous example, you purchased 100 shares of Wax stock, except that instead of selling the stock after one year, you sell the stock after 366 days (one day over a year). Because you have held the stock for one more day, your capital gain shifts from a short-term gain to a long-term gain (currently taxed at 15% for most taxpayers). Assume that your marginal tax rate (tax rate charged on any additional ordinary income) is 35%. The tax effects of the previous example involving a short-term capital gain are shown in the second column of Exhibit 14.1, whereas the tax effects of the long-term capital gain are shown in the third column. The taxes on dividends are as follows:

$$\text{Tax on Dividends Received} = \text{Amount of Dividend} \times \text{Dividend Tax Rate}$$

$$= \$100 \times .15$$

$$= \$15$$

The tax on capital gains depends on whether the gain is short term or long term. The short-term capital gains tax is

$$\text{Tax on Short-Term Capital Gain} = \text{Amount of Short-Term Capital Gain}$$
$$\times \text{Marginal Income Tax Rate}$$

$$= \$800 \times .35$$

$$= \$280$$

The long-term capital gains tax is

$$\text{Tax on Long-Term Capital Gain} = \text{Amount of Long-Term Capital Gain}$$
$$\times \text{Long-Term Capital Gain Tax Rate}$$

$$= \$800 \times .15$$

$$= \$120$$

The long-term capital gains tax is $160 lower than the short-term capital gains tax. Thus, your after-tax income from holding the stock one extra day is $160 higher. There are proposals to raise the long-term capital gains rate for some taxpayers in the future, but even then the long-term capital gains tax rate would be lower than the tax rate on short-term capital gains. Thus, even if the tax rates are changed over time, the example illustrates how you should consider the taxes you would pay on your short-term versus long-term capital gains because the tax rate could influence your decision of how long to keep your investment.

EXHIBIT 14.1   Comparing the Tax Effects on Short- and Long-Term Capital Gains

	If Stock Is Held for One Year	If Stock Is Held for More Than One Year
Dividends	$100	$100
Short-term capital gain	800	0
Long-term capital gain	0	800
Total income	$900	$900
Tax on dividends (15%)	$15	$15
Short-term capital gains tax (35%)	280	0
Long-term capital gains tax (15%)	0	120
Total taxes	$295	$135
After-tax income	$605	$765

How Your Wealth Is Influenced by Your Return

When an investment provides income to you, any portion of that income that you save will increase the value of your assets. For example, if you receive a coupon payment of $100 this month as a result of holding a bond and deposit the check in your savings account, your assets will increase by $100. If the value of your investments increases and your liabilities do not increase, your wealth increases.

The degree to which you can accumulate wealth is partially dependent on your investment decisions. You can estimate the amount by which your wealth will increase from an investment based on an assumed rate of return.

EXAMPLE

Stephanie Spratt hopes to invest $4,000 at the end of the year. If her investments appreciate by 6% annually, the value of her investment will be $7,163 in 10 years. If she earns an annual return of 10%, the value of those investments will be $10,375 in 10 years. The higher the rate of return, the higher the future value interest factor (*FVIF*), and the larger the amount of funds that she will accumulate.

If you can invest a specific amount in the stock market every year, the future value of these annual investments can be estimated as an annuity.

EXAMPLE

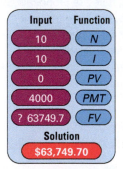

Input	Function
10	N
10	I
0	PV
4000	PMT
? 63749.7	FV

Solution

$63,749.70

Stephanie Spratt believes that she can save $4,000 to invest in stocks at the end of each year for the next 10 years. If she expects the investment value to increase by 10% annually, she can use the future value interest factor of an annuity at 10% over 10 years, which is 15.937 (see Table C.3 in Appendix C). Based on her annual investment of $4,000 and the future value interest factor of an annuity (*FVIFA*), she will accumulate

$$\text{FV of Annual Stock Investments} = \text{Annual Investment} \times FVIFA_{i,n}$$

$$= \$4,000 \times 15.937$$

$$= \$63,748$$

The input for the financial calculator is shown at the left. Any difference is due to rounding.

If Stephanie's investment value increases by 5% per year, the *FVIFA* is 12.578, and the value of her annual investments in 10 years will be

$$\text{FV of Annual Stock Investments} = \text{Annual Investment} \times FVIVA_{i,n}$$

$$= \$4,000 \times 12.578$$

$$= \$50,312$$

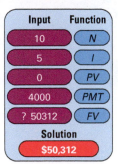

Input	Function
10	N
5	I
0	PV
4000	PMT
? 50312	FV

Solution

$50,312

The input for the financial calculator is shown at the left.

Notice how the increase in Stephanie's wealth is sensitive to the rate of return earned on her annual investment. An annual increase in investment value of 10% would allow her to accumulate $13,436 more than if the annual increase is 5%.

Risk from Investing

The risk of an investment comes from the uncertainty surrounding its return. The return that you will earn on a specific stock is uncertain because its future dividend payments are not guaranteed, and its future price (when you sell the stock) is uncertain. The return that you will earn on a bond is uncertain because its coupon payments are not guaranteed, and its future price (when you sell the bond) is uncertain. The return that you will earn from investing in a stock mutual fund is uncertain too, both because its dividend payments are uncertain and the future values of the stocks contained within the mutual fund when you sell the mutual fund shares are uncertain. The return that you will earn from investing in real estate is also uncertain because its value when you sell it is uncertain. Chapters 15, 16, and 17 discuss specific risks associated with stock, bond, and mutual fund investments.

Illustration of Risk

PSYCHOLOGY *of Personal Finance*

If investors gamble at a casino, they recognize that they may lose money because of uncertainty surrounding whatever they bet on. They can place other types of bets that are long shots, meaning that these bets are unlikely to be correct. If they are correct, they will win a large amount of money. But if they are wrong, they will lose money. They may feel a special satisfaction from the act of gambling to win a large amount of money, even though the odds of winning are very low.

Some types of investments are similar to gambling in that they will generate a large gain under perfect conditions, but they will perform poorly under unfavorable conditions. As with gambling, these types of investments attract investors because the potential of a large gain is appealing. However, many investors are in denial about the risk that is involved when pursuing investments that have the potential for very large returns.

EXAMPLE

You have $5,000 to invest and plan to invest this money for one year. You consider an investment in a business that produces smartphones. You expect to generate a return on your investment of 15% over one year under the following ideal conditions:

- The president of the company remains healthy.
- The key employees in the company continue to work there.
- The business creates a new type of smartphone that becomes popular with consumers during the next year.

These three ideal conditions are subject to uncertainty, as there is no guarantee that the ideal conditions will occur. If the president of the company becomes ill, there may be a lack of leadership, and the business may not perform well. If key employees in the company decide to leave to work for another firm, the business may not perform well. If the smartphone created by the business does not appeal to customers, the firm's sales will be low and business performance may be weak.

Overall, if any one of the ideal conditions does not occur, the performance of the business may be much weaker than what you expected, and the return on your investment will be less than what you expected. Thus, the uncertainty surrounding these conditions causes uncertainty surrounding the return that you will earn on your investment. In fact, conditions could possibly be bad enough to cause the business to perform very poorly. In this case, the return on your investment may be negative, so that you end up with less money in one year than you initially invested, or you might even lose your entire investment. The greater the uncertainty surrounding the conditions that affect the return on your investment, the greater is the risk that the return on your investment will be worse than what you expected. Although it is impossible to anticipate changes in all conditions, it is possible to at least recognize how various types of unfavorable conditions could occur that might cause losses in some investments.

Risk Due to Uncertainty Surrounding Economic Conditions

ECONOMIC IMPACT

A key reason for uncertainty surrounding the return on an investment is the uncertainty surrounding the economic conditions that influence the performance of an investment. The future values of investments are dependent on the demand by investors. When economic conditions are favorable, the income levels of investors are high, the earnings levels of firms are high, and there is a strong demand for most types of investments. When economic conditions are weak, the income levels of investors are low, the earnings levels of firms are low, and there is a weak demand for most types of investments. However, future economic conditions are uncertain, so it is difficult to predict the level of demand for various investments and therefore the future values of these investments.

To appreciate how the values of investments are sensitive to the economy, consider the period from 2005 to 2009, in which there were two extreme phases of the economy. In the 2005–2007 period, the economy was very strong. Some financial institutions attempted to benefit from the strong housing market by granting mortgages to applicants who did not qualify because of insufficient income or credit history. Because the economy was so strong, financial institutions had confidence that these applicants would be able to make enough income to make their loan payments. Construction of new homes was increasing substantially and was stimulating the economy by creating new jobs. The strong demand for real estate caused an increase in home prices, which resulted in a high return on real estate investments. The economy continued to strengthen, and as consumers spent much of their high incomes on products and services, this created strong sales and profits for businesses. Thus, the values of firms increased and so did the values of their stocks. Investors who invested in stocks earned a high return on their investments.

However, in the 2008–2009 period, the economy was very weak. Many people who had been granted mortgages but had not really qualified were unable to make their mortgage payments. This triggered a financial crisis, as these homeowners could not afford the homes they had purchased. In general, there was a massive supply of homes for sale, without much demand for the homes. This caused a substantial decline in home prices, as homeowners trying to sell their homes could only find a willing buyer if they lowered their price to attract buyers. Prices of some homes declined by more than 50% from 2007. Thus, most homeowners who purchased a home in 2006 or 2007 suffered a major loss on their home.

Many investors who made investments in real estate such as homes and office buildings in 2007 and sold them in 2009 suffered major losses. The financial crisis not only affected the real estate investments, but many other types of investments as well. Because of the excess of homes available for sale in the market, there was no need for any more new homes. The construction of new homes stopped, and many construction workers in the housing industry lost their jobs. As people lost their jobs, they no longer had income, and their amount of spending declined in response. Consequently, the businesses that relied on high consumer spending experienced a major decline in their sales and profits.

Many firms went bankrupt during the financial crisis in 2008–2009, including Circuit City and Lehman Brothers. Numerous investors who invested in these stocks lost 100% of their investment. Even firms that have normally performed well over time can experience weak performance in particular periods. Thus, it is not unusual for the stock or bond prices of even the most well-known firms to decline by more than 10% within a particular month or year. Many stocks of large well-known companies experienced price declines of 40% or more during the financial crisis.

Stocks and bonds of smaller firms tend to be even more risky, as they commonly experience pronounced fluctuations in their performance level. Some firms are more stable than others and are therefore less likely to experience a major decline in performance. Nevertheless, some investors prefer investments that have a higher growth potential, and they tolerate the higher level of risk. Before you select an investment, you should assess the risk.

Measuring an Investment's Risk

Investors measure the risk of investments to determine the degree of uncertainty surrounding their future returns. Two common measures of an investment's risk are its range of returns and the standard deviation of its returns. These measures can be applied to investments whose prices are frequently quoted over time and are explained next.

range of returns
Returns of a specific investment over a given period.

Range of Returns By reviewing the monthly returns of a specific investment over a given period, you can determine the **range of returns**, from the smallest (most negative) to the largest return. Compare an investment that has a range of monthly returns from 0.2% to 1.4% over the last year with another investment that has a range of −3.0% to 4.3%. The first investment is less risky because its range of returns is smaller, and therefore it is more stable. Investments with a wide range have more risk because they have a higher probability of experiencing a large decline in price.

standard deviation
The degree of volatility in the stock's returns over time.

Standard Deviation of Returns A second measure of risk is the **standard deviation** of a stock's monthly returns, which measures the degree of volatility in the stock's returns over time. A large standard deviation means that the returns deviate substantially from the mean over time. The more volatile the returns, the greater the chance that the stock could deviate far from its mean in a given period. Thus, an investment with a high standard deviation is more likely to experience a large gain or a large loss in a given period. The investment's return is subject to greater uncertainty, and for this reason it is perceived as riskier.

Although these two measures differ, they tend to rank the risk levels of stocks rather consistently. That is, a very risky stock will normally have a relatively wide range of returns and a high standard deviation of returns.

Subjective Measures of Risk The use of the range and standard deviation is limited because these measures of risk are not always accurate predictors of the future. For example, an investment that had stable returns in the past could experience a substantial decline in price in the future in response to poor economic conditions. Because of this limitation, the risk of some investments is commonly measured subjectively. For instance, the risk of a bond may be measured by a subjective assessment of the issuing firm's ability to repay its debt. The assessment may include an estimate of the firm's future monthly revenue to determine whether the firm will have sufficient funds to cover its interest and other expenses. Investors may rely on experts to offer their risk assessment of a particular type of investment. Bond rating agencies offer risk assessments of various bonds, as explained in Chapter 16.

Trade-Off Between Return and Risk

Every individual investor would like investments that offer a very high return and have no risk. However, such investments do not exist. Investors must weigh the trade-off between the potential return of an investment and the risk. If you want an investment that may generate a higher return, you have to tolerate the higher degree of uncertainty (risk) associated with that investment.

EXAMPLE

Stephanie Spratt has $1,000 that she could invest for the next three months in a three-month bank CD or in a stock. The bank CD offers a guaranteed return of 2% over the three-month period. Alternatively, she thinks the price of the stock will rise by 5% over the next three months. Yet, because the future price of the stock is uncertain, her return from investing in this stock is also uncertain. The return could be less than 5% and might even be negative. Stephanie decides to invest in the CD rather than the stock.

The preceding example illustrates the trade-off between a risk-free investment and a risky investment. There are also trade-offs between assets with varying degrees of risk, as explained next for each type of investment.

Return-Risk Trade-Off Among Stocks

Some firms have the potential to achieve a much higher performance level than others. But to do so, they take on more risk than other firms. That is, they may try to operate with less funding and pursue long-shot opportunities. Investors who invest in one of these firms may earn very high returns if the firm's strategies are successful. However, they could lose most or all of their investment if the firm's strategies fail.

In general, smaller firms have more potential for fast growth, and their stocks have the potential to increase in value to a greater degree. Yet, their stocks are risky because many small firms never reach their potential. The more mature firms that have already achieved high growth have less potential for future growth. However, these firms tend to be less risky because their business is more stable.

Initial public offerings (IPOs) are another stock investment option. You may have heard that IPO returns often exceed 20% over the first day. However, there is much risk to this type of investment. Individual investors rarely have access to IPOs at the initial price. Institutional investors (such as mutual funds or insurance companies with large amounts of money to invest) normally have the first shot at purchasing shares of an IPO. Most individual investors can invest (if there are any shares left) only after the institutional investors have had a chance to purchase shares. By the time individual investors are able to invest in a newly issued stock, the price has already risen. Thus, individual investors commonly obtain the shares only after the price has reached its peak and can incur large losses as the stock price declines over the following several months. For example, Groupon, Inc., which runs a popular Web site where consumers can obtain discounted gift certificates for restaurants and other businesses, went public in 2011 at a price of $20 per share. The stock price reached a high of $31 on the day of the IPO, but it has not been that high since. In early 2015, the price was below $10. In fact, many IPOs have performed poorly. On average, the long-term return on IPOs is weak compared to typical returns of other stocks in aggregate. Many firms (such as Pets.com) that engaged in IPOs failed within a few years, causing investors to lose all of their investment.

Return-Risk Trade-Off Among Bonds

You may invest in a bond issued by a firm to earn the high coupon payment. The risk of your investment is that the firm may be unable to pay its coupon payment if its financial condition deteriorates. If you purchase a bond of a large, well-known, and successful firm, there is minimal risk that the firm will default on its payments. If you purchase a bond issued by a firm that is struggling financially, there is more risk that this firm will default on its payments. If this firm defaults on the bond, your return will be very poor. During the financial crisis in 2008–2009, many bonds defaulted.

High-risk bonds tend to offer higher coupon payments. Thus, you must weigh the trade-off between the potential return and the risk. If you are willing to tolerate the higher risk, you may consider investing in the bond issued by a weak firm. Alternatively, if you prefer less risk, you can purchase a bond issued by a successful and established firm, as long as you are willing to accept a lower return on your investment.

Return-Risk Trade-Off Among Mutual Funds

When you invest in a mutual fund composed of stocks, you earn a return from the dividend payments and the increase in the prices of stocks held by the mutual fund. The risk of a stock mutual fund is that the prices of stocks can decline in any particular period. Because the mutual fund is composed of numerous stocks, the adverse impact caused by any single stock is reduced. However, when economic conditions weaken, most stocks tend to perform poorly. Just as smaller stocks tend to be riskier than larger stocks, mutual funds that contain mostly small stocks are riskier than mutual funds containing larger stocks. Yet, some investors still prefer mutual funds consisting of small stocks because they expect a higher return from these stocks.

When you invest in a mutual fund composed of bonds, your primary risk is that the bonds held by the mutual fund could default. Because a bond mutual fund contains numerous bonds, the adverse effect of a single bond default within a mutual fund is reduced. Yet, when economic conditions deteriorate, many firms that issued bonds can experience financial problems and have difficulty making their coupon payments. Some bond mutual funds are not highly exposed to risk because they invest only in corporate bonds issued by the most creditworthy corporations. Others are highly exposed because they invest in bonds issued by relatively weak corporations that pay high coupon rates. Investors who prefer risky bond mutual funds because of their potential to offer a high return must tolerate the high level of risk.

Return-Risk Trade-Off Among Real Estate Investments

When you invest in real estate, your risk depends on your particular investment. If you buy rental property, it may not generate your anticipated periodic income if you cannot find renters or if your renters default on their rent payment. In addition, there is a risk that the property's value will decline over time. The degree of risk varies with the type of real estate investment. If you purchase an office building that is fully occupied, the risk is relatively low, although the value of the building could decline over time. Conversely, if you purchase a piece of open land in New Mexico because you hope that you will someday discover oil on the land, there is much risk in this investment.

Comparing Different Types of Investments

As a prudent investor, you must choose investments that suit your personal objectives. If you want to achieve a fixed return over a short-term period without any risk, you should consider investing in a certificate of deposit. The disadvantage of this investment is that it offers a relatively low return. If you want to achieve a stable return over a long-term period, you should consider Treasury bonds or mutual funds that contain Treasury bonds. At the other extreme, if you desire a very high return, you could consider investing in land or in some small stocks.

Many investors fall in between these two extremes. They prefer a higher return than is offered by CDs or Treasury bonds but want to limit their risk. There is no formula that can determine your ideal investment because the choice depends on how much risk you want to take, and on your financial situation.

To illustrate, consider the following situations and the possible solutions shown in Exhibit 14.2. In general, you are in a better position to take some risk when you know that you will not need to sell the investment in the near future. Even if the value of the investment declines, you have the flexibility to hold on to the investment until the value increases. Conversely, individuals investing for the short term should play it safe. Because the prices of risky investments fluctuate substantially, it is dangerous to invest in a risky investment when you know that you will be selling that investment in the near future. You could be forced to sell it when the investment has a low value. Investors who decide

EXHIBIT 14.2   How Investment Decisions Vary with Your Situation

Situation	Decision
You have $1,000 to invest but will need the funds in one month to pay bills.	You need liquidity. You should only consider money market securities.
You have $3,000 to invest but will need the funds in a year to make a tuition payment.	You should consider safe money market securities such as a one-year insured CD.
You have $5,000 to invest and will likely use the funds in about three years when you buy a home.	Consider a three-year insured CD or stocks of relatively stable firms that have relatively low risk.
You have $10,000 to invest and have no funds set aside for retirement in 20 years.	Consider investing in a diversified stock mutual fund.
You have $5,000 to invest. You expect that you will be laid off from your job within the next year.	You should probably invest the funds in money market securities so that you will have easy access to the funds if you lose your job.

to pursue higher potential returns must be willing to accept the high risk associated with these investments.

By keeping a variety of investments, you can find a tolerable risk level. You can diversify your investments among many different stocks, thereby reducing your exposure to any particular investment. If you divide your money equally among five investments and one investment performs poorly, your exposure is limited.

Even if you diversify your portfolio among various investments, you are still exposed to general economic conditions, as the values of all investments can decline during periods in which economic conditions are weak. For this reason, you should consider diversifying among various types of investments that are not equally sensitive to economic conditions. The strategy of diversification is crucial for investors, and is given more attention in Chapter 18.

Learning from Investment Mistakes

Many individual investors learn from their own mistakes or from the mistakes of others. Consider the following investment mistakes, so that you can avoid them.

Making Decisions Based on Unrealistic Goals

One of the most common mistakes is letting unrealistic goals dictate your investment decisions. These goals may force you to take more risk than you should and can result in major losses.

EXAMPLE   Laurie Chen has $4,000, which should cover her school expenses next year. She is considering investing the money in a one-year CD that would earn about 6%, or about $240 in interest before next year. However, she would like to earn a higher return on her money within the next year so that she can buy a used car. She decides to invest in a small stock that earned a return of 50% last year. If the stock's value increases by 50% again, her investment would generate a gain of $2,000, which would allow her to buy a used car. Unfortunately, the stock's value declines by 30% over the year. At the end of the year, her investment is worth $2,800, a $1,200 loss. She does not have sufficient funds to buy the car or cover her school expenses. She did not view her investment as a gamble, as the money was invested in the stock of a firm. However, her investment in one small stock was just as risky as gambling, especially because she had no information to support her decision except for the fact that the stock performed well in the previous year.

Borrowing to Invest

Another common mistake is to invest money that could have been used to pay off an existing loan. The potential to earn a high return on an investment can tempt individuals to take more risk than they should.

EXAMPLE   Charles Krenshaw recently took out a $5,000 loan to cover this year's college expenses. His parents gave him $5,000 so that he could pay off the loan. Rather than pay off the loan, Charles invested the $5,000 from his parents in a stock. He had hoped that he could earn a large return on the $5,000, so that he could sell the investment at the end of the year, pay off the loan, and have enough funds to travel through Europe during the summer. During the year, he had to make interest payments on the existing loan. The stock that he purchased declined in value by 90%, leaving him with just $500 at the end of the year. He now has insufficient funds to take a vacation or to pay off the loan.

Taking Risks to Recover Losses

Another common mistake is taking excessive risks to recover your losses. This can lead to additional losses and may even push individuals toward bankruptcy.

EXAMPLE   Sarah Barnes lost 10% of her investment in the last year from investing in a diversified mutual fund. She needs the money before next winter to purchase a new furnace for her home. Yet she wants to make up for her loss and has shifted her money into a risky mutual fund that will likely generate a higher return if economic conditions are favorable, but will perform poorly if economic conditions are unfavorable. She experiences a 20% loss on this investment because economic conditions weakened. She no longer has sufficient funds to pay for the furnace.

In some periods, many investors bid up the prices of stocks because of their unrealistic expectations about how well these stocks would perform in the future. The media hype adds to the investors' irrational exuberance. These actions create a so-called speculative bubble, meaning that once the prices are blown up to a certain level, the speculative bubble will burst, and stock prices will decline to where they should be. One reason for the generally poor stock performance in some periods was that the speculative bubble burst. Although there may be periods in the future during which stocks or other investments earn abnormally high returns, you should be realistic when making investment decisions. An investment that has the potential to rise substantially in value also has the potential to decline substantially in value. If you cannot afford the possible loss, you should not make that investment.

How Personal Investing Fits Within Your Financial Plan

The following are the key investment decisions that should be included within your financial plan:

- What are your investment goals?
- Given your existing budget, should you make investments?
- Based on your risk tolerance, how should you invest funds?

Exhibit 14.3 provides an example of how these decisions apply to Stephanie Spratt's financial plan.

EXHIBIT 14.3 How Investments Fit Within Stephanie Spratt's Financial Plan

GOALS FOR INVESTING

1. *Determine my investment goals.*
2. *Determine whether to make investments.*
3. *Determine the types of investments that would achieve my investment goals.*

ANALYSIS OF FUNDING

Monthly Cash Inflows	$2,500
– Typical Monthly Expenses	1,488
– Monthly Car Loan Payment	412
= Amount of Funds Available	$600

ANALYSIS OF POSSIBLE INVESTMENTS

Type of Investment	Assessment
1. CDs and Other Money Market Securities	*Many money market securities provide good liquidity and are safe, but they typically offer low returns.*
2. Stocks	*Can provide high returns, but are risky given the limited amount of funds I anticipate I will have for investing.*
3. Bonds	*Some bonds have low risk, but they offer lower potential returns than stocks.*
4. Real Estate	*The value of my home may increase over time. Additional real estate investments can generate high returns but are usually risky.*
5. Stock Mutual Funds	*Can provide high returns, and offer more diversification than investing in individual stocks, but can generate losses if stock market conditions are weak.*
6. Bond Mutual Funds	*Offer more diversification than investing in individual bonds, but can generate losses if bond market conditions are weak.*

DECISION

My primary investment goal is to maintain sufficient liquidity in any funds that I invest to cover any unanticipated expenses. However, I would like to earn a return on any funds that I have until they are needed to cover expenses.

After paying for my typical monthly expenses (not including recreation), I have $600 left each month. I am not in a financial position to make long-term investments at this time because I will use some of these funds each month for recreation and will deposit the remaining funds in liquid accounts such as a money market fund. I need to increase my liquidity since I might incur unexpected home repair expenses periodically. Beyond maintaining liquidity, I hope to save enough money to pay off my car loan early. Once I pay off that loan, I will reconsider whether to invest in riskier investments that have the potential to offer a higher return. My salary should also increase over time, which will make investments more affordable.

When I start long-term investing, I will consider stock mutual funds and bond mutual funds rather than individual stocks or bonds. I can periodically invest in mutual funds with small amounts of money and achieve diversification benefits. Since I already own a home, I do not want to invest in additional real estate.

DISCUSSION QUESTIONS

1. How would Stephanie's investing decisions be different if she were a single mother of two children?

2. How would Stephanie's investing decisions be affected if she were 35 years old? If she were 50 years old?

SUMMARY

Common Types of Investments. Common types of investments include money market securities, stocks, bonds, mutual funds, and real estate. Each type of investment is unique in how it provides a return to its investors.

Measuring Return on Investment. The return on an investment is determined by the income that the investment generates and the capital gain of the investment over the investment horizon. Some stocks offer periodic income in the form of dividends, whereas bonds offer periodic income in the form of coupon payments.

Risk of Investments. The risk from making an investment varies among types of investments. In particular, money market securities tend to have lower risk, and many stocks and real estate investments have higher risk. However, the risk also varies within a particular type of investment. Some money market securities have more risk than others. Some stocks have more risk than others. Investors measure the risk of investments to determine the degree of uncertainty surrounding their future returns. Two common measures of an investment's risk are its range of returns and the standard deviation of its returns. When an investment has a very large range or standard deviation of returns, its possible future returns are more dispersed or unpredictable. This implies more risk or uncertainty surrounding its future return.

Return-Risk Trade-Off. Investors weigh the trade-off between return and risk when making investments. When they select investments that have the potential to offer high returns, they must accept a higher degree of risk. Alternatively, they can select investments with lower risk, but they must accept a relatively low return. The proper choice is dependent on the investor's willingness to accept risk, which is influenced by the investor's financial position. Some investors are not in a financial position in which they can afford to take much risk, and should therefore select investments with little or no risk.

Common Investment Mistakes. You can learn from investment mistakes made by others. In particular, do not make investments that are driven by unrealistic goals. Do not invest when the funds could be more properly used to pay off existing debt. Do not attempt high-risk investments as a means of recovering recent losses. Recognize the risk of making investments that may be experiencing a speculative bubble.

How Personal Investing Fits Within Your Financial Plan. Personal investing allows you to accumulate more wealth to achieve various future spending or retirement goals, and therefore it can help you complete your financial plan.

REVIEW QUESTIONS

All Review Questions are available in MyFinanceLab at http://www.myfinancelab.com.

1. **Investing Priorities.** What should your first priority of investing be? What is the disadvantage of investments that satisfy that priority?

2. **Stocks.** What are stocks? How are stocks beneficial to corporations? Why do investors invest in stocks?

3. **Secondary Markets.** Distinguish between the primary and secondary stock markets. Why does the price of a stock change each day in the secondary market?

4. **Types of Investors.** Classify and describe the two types of investors. What are day traders?

5. **Return on Stocks.** How do shareholders earn returns from investing in stocks? How is the market value of a firm determined? What determines the market price of a stock?

6. **Dividends.** What type of firm typically pays dividends? What are growth stocks? What are income stocks?

7. **Dividends.** What are dividends? Do all firms pay them?

8. **Preferred Stock.** Discuss the differences between common stock and preferred stock.

9. **Bonds.** What are bonds? How do bonds provide a return to investors?

10. **Mutual Funds.** How do mutual funds operate? Who manages mutual funds? How are coupon or dividend payments handled by the mutual fund? Can investors incur capital losses with mutual funds?

11. **Real Estate Investment.** In what geographic areas is the price of land relatively high? What components make up the return from investing in real estate?

12. **Dividend-Paying Stocks.** What is the formula for estimating returns on dividend-paying stocks? Describe each element of the formula. How do you calculate the dollar amount of your returns?

13. **Capital Gains Taxes.** What is the difference in tax rates on long-term versus short-term capital gains?

14. **Investments in Stocks.** How can investments in stock increase your wealth? How would you calculate the value of a stock investment of a single sum over time? How would you calculate the value of a stock investment of a specific amount over several periods?

15. **Risk of Investments.** Define the risk of an investment. What types of firms are particularly risky?

16. **Measuring Risk.** Why do investors measure risk? Describe the two common measures of risk.

17. **Return-Risk Trade-Off.** What is the return-risk trade-off? What types of stock investments are particularly tempting for stock investors? What other factors must individual investors consider before making this type of investment?

18. **Risk Among Investments.** Describe the return-risk trade-offs among bonds, mutual funds, and real estate investments.

19. **Diversification.** How can you limit your risk through diversification?

20. **Investment Mistakes.** Describe common investment mistakes made by individuals.

21. **Economic Conditions and Investments.** Describe how economic conditions might affect certain investments.

22. **Investing and Liquidity.** How is investing related to liquidity? Give some examples of liquid investments.

23. **Exchange-Traded Funds.** What is an exchange-traded fund? How does it differ from a mutual fund?

24. **Growth Stocks and Income Stocks.** What is a growth stock? What is an income stock? Why would investors prefer one type over the other?

25. **IPOs.** What is an IPO? What are the risks associated with buying IPOs?

26. **Investing and Personal Financial Goals.** How is investing related to your personal financial goals?

27. **Personal Risk Tolerance.** How does your personal tolerance for risk impact your investment decisions?

28. **Real Estate Investing Risks.** What are some of the risks associated with investing in real estate?

FINANCIAL PLANNING PROBLEMS

All Financial Planning Problems are available in MyFinanceLab *at* http://www.myfinancelab.com.

1. **Return on Stock.** Joel purchased 100 shares of stock for $20 per share. During the year, he received dividend checks amounting to $150. Joel recently sold the stock for $32 per share. What was Joel's return on the stock?

2. **Dollar Amount of Return.** What is the dollar amount of Joel's return (see problem 1)?

3. **Capital Gains Tax.** Joel (from problem 1) is in the 25% tax bracket. What amount of taxes will he pay on his capital gain if he held the stock for less than a year?

4. **Capital Gains Tax.** How much would Joel (from problem 1) save in taxes if he held the stock for more than a year, assuming he sold it for the same amount?

5. **Return on Stock.** Emma bought a stock a year ago for $53 per share. She received no dividends on the stock and sold the stock today for $38 per share. What is Emma's return on the stock?

6. **Value of Investment.** Tammy has $3,500 that she wants to invest in stock. She believes she can earn a 12% annual return. What would be the value of Tammy's investment in 10 years if she is able to achieve her goal?

7. **Value of Investment.** Dawn decides to invest $2,000 each year in stock at the end of each of the next five years. She believes she can earn a 9% return over that time period. How much will Dawn's investment be worth at the end of five years?

8. **Value of Investment.** Bob purchased stock in a new social media company for $40 per share shortly after the stock's IPO. The stock had been heavily publicized on the Internet. Over the next three years, the stock price declined by 15% each year. What is the company's stock price after three years?

9. **Value of Investment.** Floyd wants to invest the $15,000 he received from his grandfather's estate. He wants to use the money to finance his education when he pursues his doctorate in five years. What amount will he have in five years if he earns a 9% return? If he receives a 10% return? A 12% return?

10. **Value of Investment.** Morris will start investing $1,500 a year in stocks. He feels he can average a 12% return. If he follows this plan, how much will he accumulate in 5 years? In 10 years? In 20 years?

11. **Capital Gains Tax.** Thomas purchased 400 shares of stock A for $23 a share and sold them more than a year later for $20 per share. He purchased 500 shares of stock B for $40 per share and sold them for $53 per share after holding them for more than a year. Both of the sales were in the same year. If Thomas is in a 25% tax bracket, what will his capital gains tax be for the year?

12. **Capital Loss.** Charles recently sold 500 shares of stock A for $12,000. In addition, he sold 600 shares of stock A for $6,000. Charles had paid $20 per share for all his shares of stock A. What amount of loss will he have, assuming both sales were on stocks held for more than one year?

13. **Real Estate Returns.** Jenna purchased a 5-acre parcel of land for $28,000 and sold it two years later for $41,000. What was her return on that investment?

14. **Ethical Dilemma.** Carlo and Rita's daughter just celebrated her 16th birthday, and Carlo and Rita realize they have accumulated only half the money they will need for their daughter's college education. With college just two years away, they are concerned about how they will save the remaining amount in such a short time.

Carlo regularly has lunch with Sam, a coworker. While discussing his dilemma of financing his daughter's education, Sam tells Carlo about an investment that he made based on a tip from his cousin Leo that doubled his money in just over one year. Sam tells Carlo that Leo assured him there was very little risk involved. Carlo asks Sam if he will contact Leo to see if he has any additional hot tips that could double his daughter's college savings in two years with virtually no risk.

The next day at lunch Sam gives Carlo the name of a stock that Leo recommended. It is a small start-up company that Leo believes will double within the next 24 months with virtually no risk. Carlo immediately invests his daughter's college fund in the stock of the company. Six months later, Carlo receives a letter from the company announcing that it is going out of business and closing its doors. Upon calling his broker, Carlo finds the stock is now worthless.

a. Comment on Leo's ethics when assuring his friends and relatives that the investments he recommends can produce major rewards with virtually no risk.

b. What basic investing principle did Carlo forget in his desire to fund his daughter's college education?

FINANCIAL PLANNING ONLINE EXERCISES

1. Go to http://www.renaissancecapital.com.
   a. Describe what type of information is available to investors.
   b. Summarize in general how IPOs have performed recently.

2. Go to the Finance section of Yahoo.com where you can obtain stock quotes, and insert the stock symbol of a stock in which you are interested.

   a. What was the last price of the stock you looked up?

   b. What is the P/E ratio of the stock?

   c. Does the stock pay a dividend? If so, how much?

3. Go to the Finance section of Yahoo.com to determine how stocks are correlated with various indexes.

   a. Enter "GE," the symbol for General Electric, in the box where you can obtain stock quotes. The Yahoo Finance Web site can generate a chart that shows historical stock price movements of GE or any stock you specify. It can also allow you to compare the stock's price movements to a stock index. Determine how GE stock performed relative to the stock index. You can choose various time periods from one day to five years. Repeat the exercise for various time periods.

   b. Repeat part (a) except replace GE stock with a stock in which you are interested. Determine how your stock performed relative to the stock index. You can choose various time periods from one day to five years. Repeat the exercise for various time periods.

PSYCHOLOGY OF PERSONAL FINANCE: Your Investments

1. Some investors get a bigger thrill from gambling with money than from paying off a loan. Thus, they invest in stocks hoping to make a larger return than whatever interest rate they are paying on their loan. Describe your behavior of investing. Do you use money to invest that could have been used to pay off a credit card loan? If so, why? Do you think there is any risk associated with such a strategy?

2. Read one practical article about how psychology affects decisions when investing in stocks. You can easily retrieve possible articles by doing an online search using the terms "psychology" and "investing in stocks." Summarize the main points of the article.

WEB SEARCH EXERCISE

You can develop your personal finance skills by conducting an Internet search for related articles. Find a recent online article about personal finance that reinforces one or more concepts covered in this chapter. If your class has an online component, your professor may ask you to post your summary of the article there and provide a link to the article so that other students can access it. If your class is live, your professor may ask you to summarize your application of the article in class. Your professor may assign specific students to complete this assignment or may allow any student to do the assignment on a volunteer basis.

For recent online articles related to this chapter, consider using the following search terms (be sure to include the current year as a search term to ensure that the online articles are recent):

- Understanding stocks
- Understanding bonds
- Risk of investing
- Investing in mutual funds
- Investing in real estate

VIDEO EXERCISE: Investing

Go to one of the Web sites that contain video clips (such as http://www.youtube.com) and review some video clips about investing. You can use search phrases such as "tips on investing." Select one video clip on this topic that you would recommend for the other students in your class.

1. Provide the Web link for the video clip.

2. What do you think is the main point of this video clip?

3. How might you change your process of investing as a result of watching this video clip?

BUILDING YOUR OWN FINANCIAL PLAN

Very likely, some of the goals you established in Chapter 1 can best be met through investing. Before taking the plunge into investing, however, you need to address a few questions. The first of these is to determine your risk tolerance. Not all investors have the "stomach" for the uncertainty surrounding returns on investments.

The next issue to be addressed is how different investments are suited to different goals. For example, a growth stock might be desirable if your goal is to build savings for a retirement that is 30 years away, while a certificate of deposit might be better suited to provide the down payment for a house within the next five years.

The decision of what kind of investment is right for a particular goal should be reviewed annually. The closer a goal comes to fulfillment, the more likely it is that a change in investing strategy will be necessary.

Go to the worksheets at the end of this chapter to continue building your financial plan.

THE SAMPSONS—A Continuing Case

Recall that the Sampsons have a goal of saving about $300 per month ($3,600 per year) for their children's college education. They want to estimate how this money would grow over time if they invest it in stock. Dave and Sharon have never owned stock before.

The Sampsons guess that under normal conditions, the stocks would generate a return of about 5% per year over time. However, they recognize that there is uncertainty surrounding the return. They believe that the stock will generate an annual return of only 2% if stock market conditions are weak in the future, but it could generate an annual return of 9% if stock market conditions are strong.

Go to the worksheets at the end of this chapter to continue this case.

CHAPTER 14: BUILDING YOUR OWN FINANCIAL PLAN

GOALS

1. Identify your investment goals.
2. Determine whether to invest, given your current cash flows.
3. Determine what kinds of investments you should purchase to meet your financial goals.

ANALYSIS

1. Review your cash flow statement to determine how much you can afford to invest in stocks each month.
2. Evaluate your risk tolerance to see if your temperament is suited to the uncertainty of stock investments.

Risk Tolerance Quiz

Answer True or False by entering an X in the appropriate box.
(The Excel worksheet will offer an assessment based on your input.)

		TRUE	FALSE
1.	If I own stock, I will check its price at least daily if not more often.	☐	☐
2.	When driving on an interstate, and traffic and weather permit, I never drive in excess of the posted speed limit.	☐	☐
3.	If the price of my stock declines, my first reaction is to sell.	☐	☐
4.	Another stock market crash similar to 1929 could occur very unexpectedly.	☐	☐
5.	When I fly in less than perfect weather, I tend to get nervous and concerned about my safety.	☐	☐
6.	If I sold a stock at a loss of more than 25%, it would greatly shake my confidence in my ability to invest.	☐	☐
7.	I intensely dislike blind dates.	☐	☐
8.	When I travel, I write down a packing list to be sure that I don't forget anything.	☐	☐
9.	When traveling with others, I prefer to do the driving.	☐	☐
10.	Before buying a stock I would want to talk to at least two other people to confirm my choice.	☐	☐

Results

0–3   True: You have the risk tolerance to invest in individual common stocks.

4–6   True: You would be a nervous investor, but with more knowledge and a few successes, you could probably raise your risk tolerance to a suitable level. Mutual funds might prove a good starting point for your level of risk tolerance.

7–10   True: You are probably a very conservative and risk-intolerant investor who is probably better suited to a bond portfolio.

3. Determine whether investments will help you achieve your short-, intermediate-, and long-term goals. Complete the worksheet below for the short-, intermediate-, and long-term goals that you have established and reviewed throughout the course. In determining whether investing is suitable for each goal, take into consideration the timeline for accomplishing the goal, the critical nature of the goal, and, of course, the results of your risk tolerance test. For those goals that you determine investments are not suitable, enter "No" in column two, and leave the rest of the line blank for that goal. If, however, you enter "Yes" in column two, think about the kind of investment that is appropriate and justify your selection as a risk-appropriate means to accomplish this goal.

Short-Term Goals	Suitable? Yes or No	Type of Investment	Justification
1.			
2.			
3.			

Intermediate-Term Goals	Suitable? Yes or No	Type of Investment	Justification
1.			
2.			
3.			

Long-Term Goals	Suitable? Yes or No	Type of Investment	Justification
1.			
2.			
3.			

DECISIONS

1. Summarize your reasoning for either investing or not investing to meet your goals.

_____

_____

_____

2. If you decide to invest, how much will you invest each month? What types of investments will you purchase? Why?

_____

_____

_____

CHAPTER 14: THE SAMPSONS—A Continuing Case

CASE QUESTIONS

1. Compare the returns from investing in stock over the next 12 years by filling in the following worksheet.

Savings Accumulated over the Next 12 Years

	Normal Stock Market Conditions	Weak Stock Market Conditions	Strong Stock Market Conditions
Amount Invested per Year	$3,600	$3,600	$3,600
Annual Return	5%	2%	9%
FVIFA (n = 12 Years)			
Value of Investments in 12 Years			

2. Explain to the Sampsons why there is a trade-off when investing in bank CDs versus stock to support their children's future college education.

_____

_____

_____

_____

3. Advise the Sampsons on whether they should invest their money each month in bank CDs, in stocks, or in some combination of the two, to save for their children's college education.

_____

_____

_____

_____

4. The Sampsons are considering investing in an IPO of a high-tech firm because they have heard that the return on IPOs can be very high. Advise the Sampsons on this course of action.

_____

_____

_____

_____

Investing in Stocks

PathDoc/Shutterstock

Lynn owned 500 shares of a stock that she had bought at $40 per share. As the price rose steadily over the course of several months to over $48, Lynn decided to implement a sell strategy that would take the uncertainty out of the sales transaction. She called her broker and placed a limit order to sell her stock if and when it reached $50 per share. A $50 per-share price would allow Lynn to earn at least a 25% return on her investment and result in a $5,000 gain before subtracting the commissions.

Over the next few days, the price slipped to the mid-40s and then drifted lower still. Lynn didn't sell because she was sure the dip in price was only temporary. Finally, when the price reached $30 per share, she called her broker and sold all of her shares. Lynn ultimately suffered a $5,000 loss on her investment.

When investing in stocks, your investment decisions depend on your risk tolerance, investing knowledge, and experience. You should approach any potential stock purchase with an investment strategy that will guide you in your stock selection. That investment strategy is the focus of this chapter.

MyFinanceLab helps you master the topics in this chapter and study more efficiently. Visit http://www.myfinancelab.com for more details.

The objectives of this chapter are to:

- Identify the functions of stock exchanges
- Describe how to interpret stock quotations
- Explain how to execute the purchase and sale of stocks
- Explain how to analyze a stock
- Explain how investing in stocks fits within your financial plan

Stock Exchanges

stock exchanges
Facilities that allow investors to purchase or sell existing stocks.

Now that you understand how to value and evaluate stocks, you can start to make stock investments. **Stock exchanges** are facilities that allow investors to purchase and sell existing stocks. They facilitate trading in the secondary market so that investors can sell stocks that they have previously purchased. An organized securities exchange occupies a physical location where trading occurs. A stock has to be listed on a stock exchange to be traded there, meaning that it must fulfill specific requirements of the exchange. For example, to list its stock, a firm may have to be a minimum size and have a minimum number of shares of stock outstanding. The requirements ensure that there will be an active market for stocks in which shares are commonly traded.

New York Stock Exchange

The most popular organized exchange in the United States is the New York Stock Exchange (NYSE), which handles transactions for approximately 2,800 stocks. In 2007, the NYSE merged with Euronext (which represented various European exchanges) to form NYSE Euronext, the first global exchange. In 2013, NYSE Euronext was acquired by Intercontinental Exchange (ICE). Today, the NYSE and Euronext operate as divisions of ICE. The transactions on the NYSE are conducted by the traders who have been authorized to trade stocks listed on the exchange for themselves or others.

floor traders
Traders at a stock exchange who execute trades to fill orders placed by other investors.

Floor Traders and Specialists Traditionally, some traders (called **floor traders**) executed trades to accommodate requests by other investors (such as individual investors like you), and other traders executed trades for themselves. When floor traders executed trades for other investors, they earned a commission in the form of a bid–ask spread, which reflected the difference between the price at which they were willing to buy a stock and the price at which they were willing to sell it. For example, suppose a trader executed an order where one investor bid $20.12 per share to buy a stock while the seller received $20.00 per share. The bid–ask spread of $.12 per share went to the floor trader. In this example, a trade of 1,000 shares cost $120 because of the bid–ask spread.

specialists
Traders who help to create a market in one or more stocks by taking an opposite position to the orders placed by clients.

Some traders, traditionally called **specialists** but now generally known as designated market makers (DMMs), helped to create a market in one or more stocks by taking an opposite position to the orders placed by clients. That is, they might have been willing to buy the stocks that an investor wanted to sell or sell holdings of their stocks that an investor wanted to buy.

Today, the trading volume on the NYSE generally exceeds a billion shares of stock per day, so most trades are executed electronically, not by human beings. Only about 15% of the transactions on the NYSE now take place on the floor of the exchange by the method just described. Floor traders and specialists still exist, but their numbers have declined, and so has their importance. There were about 3,000 floor traders in 2007, but by 2014 there were only a few hundred. Yet, during periods of extreme imbalances in the market, floor traders and specialists can still play a role in promoting stability and orderly trading.

A Typical Stock Transaction on the NYSE To buy a stock that is listed on the NYSE, you tell your brokerage firm the name of the stock and the number of shares you want to purchase. If the transaction is one of the minority that go to the floor of the exchange as described earlier, the order is sent to a floor trader or specialist who communicates your desire to purchase the specific stock and negotiates the price. Once the trade is complete, the floor trader at the NYSE sends confirmation to the brokerage firm that the trade has been made, and the brokerage firm informs you that the trade has been completed.

More likely, however, the brokerage firm will submit your request to purchase the stock electronically, with an indication of the price you are willing to pay. Meanwhile, other investors who own the stock and wish to sell it submit their preferences electronically to the NYSE, with an indication of the prices at which they are willing to sell the stock. A computer matches up buy and sell orders and communicates your executed order to the brokerage firm.

Other Stock Exchanges

The NYSE MKT LLC is also based in New York and focuses on the trading of stocks of smaller firms and exchange-traded funds. These stocks are less actively traded than those on the NYSE. The NYSE MKT LLC was formerly known as the American Stock Exchange (AMEX), which was acquired by NYSE Euronext in 2008. There are also some regional securities exchanges located in large U.S. cities. These regional exchanges tend to have less stringent listing requirements and therefore list stocks from smaller firms that may be well known in that specific region. Stocks are traded on the NYSE MKT LLC and the regional stock exchanges in much the same way as on the NYSE.

Over-the-Counter (OTC) Market

over-the-counter (OTC) market
An electronic communications network that allows investors to buy or sell securities.

The **over-the-counter (OTC) market** is an electronic communications network that allows investors to buy or sell securities. It is not a visible facility like the organized exchanges. Trades are communicated through a computer network by **market makers**, who execute the trades on the OTC and earn commissions in the form of a bid–ask spread. Trades in the OTC market are conducted over a computer network between two dealers sitting in their respective offices who may be hundreds or thousands of miles apart.

market makers
Traders who execute trades on the OTC market and earn commissions in the form of a bid–ask spread.

The listing requirements for the OTC market are generally less stringent than those for the NYSE. More than 3,000 stocks are listed on the OTC market. A key part of the OTC market is the NASDAQ, or the National Association of Securities Dealers Automated Quotation system. The NASDAQ provides continually updated market price information on OTC stocks that meet its requirements on size and trading volume. In 2008, NASDAQ acquired OMX (which controls eight European stock exchanges) to become NASDAQ OMX Group.

Electronic Communications Networks (ECNs)

electronic communications networks (ECNs)
Computer systems that match desired purchases and sales of stocks.

Electronic communications networks (ECNs) are computer systems that match desired purchases and sales of stocks. For example, the ECN receives orders from investors to buy shares of a stock at a specified price and matches them with orders from investors to sell the stock at that price. A person is not needed to perform the match. ECNs now make up about 60% of all trading of NASDAQ stocks. ECNs enable investors to bypass the market makers and therefore avoid the transaction costs (bid–ask spread) they charge.

ECNs are also being used to execute some transactions on the NYSE and the NYSE MKT LLC. They can match orders any time, so they are especially valuable at night after the exchanges are closed.

At many online brokerage firms, if an order comes in after the stock exchanges are closed (during so-called after-hours trading), the firm will send the order to the ECNs, where the trade will be executed. However, at night there may not be sufficient trading volume in some stocks, especially those of small companies, to enable all transactions to be executed. An investor who wants to sell a thinly traded stock may not be able to find a willing buyer. As more investors have learned that they can have orders executed at night, however, the trading volume has increased, making ECNs even more popular.

Stock Quotations

If you consider investing in stocks, you will need to learn how to obtain and interpret stock price quotations. Fortunately, price quotations are readily available for actively traded stocks. The most up-to-date quotes can be obtained online. Price information is available from stockbrokers and is widely published by the news media. Popular sources of stock quotations are financial newspapers (such as the *The Wall Street Journal*), business sections of many local newspapers, financial news television networks (such as CNBC), and financial Web sites.

Stock quotations provide information about the price of each stock over the previous day or a recent period. An example of stock quotations is shown in Exhibit 15.1 for Zugle Company. Notice that the name of the stock is in the third column. To the left (the first and second columns), the high (HI) price and low (LO) price of the stock are provided. Those stocks that are subject to more uncertainty tend to have a wider range in prices over time. Some investors use this range as a simple measure of the firm's risk.

The annual dividends (if any) paid on the stock commonly appear just to the right of the name of the stock. The dividend yield (annual dividends as a percentage of the stock price) is shown in the fourth column. This represents the annual return that you would receive solely from dividends if you purchased the stock today and if the dividend payments remain unchanged.

In the fifth column is the price-earnings (PE) ratio, which is the stock price divided by the firm's annual earnings per share. Some investors closely monitor the PE ratio when attempting to value stocks.

The remaining information summarizes the trading of the stock on the previous day. The sixth column shows the volume of trading (in 100s of shares). For some widely traded stocks, more than a million shares may trade per day, while 20,000 or fewer shares may trade per day for smaller stocks.

The seventh column shows the closing price (CLOSE), which is the price at the end of the day when the stock market closes. The last column discloses the net change (NET CHG) in the price of the stock, which is measured as the change in the closing price from the previous day. Investors review this column to determine how stock prices changed from one day to the next.

Review the stock quotations of Zugle Company in Exhibit 15.1. Its stock price has traded between $49.40 and $62.10 per share over the last year. It pays annual dividends of $1.00 per share ($.25 per share per quarter). The annual dividend reflects a dividend yield of 2.0%, meaning that investors purchasing the stock at the time of this

EXHIBIT 15.1　Example of a Daily Stock Quotation

| 52-Week | | | | | | | |
Hi	Lo	Stock (Div.)	Yield (%)	PE	Vol. (100s)	Close	Net Change
62.10	49.40	Zugle ($1.00)	2.00%	14	9000	50.00	+.27

quotation would earn an annual return of 2.0% on their investment if the dividend remains unchanged over the next year. The price-earnings ratio is 14, which means that the prevailing stock price of Zugle is 14 times its annual earnings per share. Its volume of trading for the day was 900,000 shares. At the close of trading in the stock market, its stock price was $50.00. The net change in the price shows that the stock price increased by $.27 per share from the day before.

FREE APPS
for Personal
Finance

Obtain Real-Time Stock Quotes

Application:

The Stock Tracker app (by Wei Tang) provides quotes that are in real time for investors who wish to access up-to-the-minute stock prices.

To Find It:

Search for the "Stock Tracker" app on your mobile device.

Purchasing and Selling Stocks

When trading stocks, you need to begin by selecting a brokerage firm and placing an order. These functions are discussed next.

Selecting a Broker

When selecting a broker, consider the following characteristics.

Analyst Recommendations A full-service broker can provide you with investment advice. You also have access to stock ratings that are assigned by stock analysts employed by brokerage firms.

Financial Planning ONLINE

Go to:
The finance section of Yahoo.com

To get:
Price quotes or analyst recommendations about a stock that you specify.

Recommendations from brokers and analysts have limitations, however. Some brokerage firms may advise you to buy or sell securities frequently, rather than holding on to your investment portfolio over time because for each transaction, you must pay a commission to that brokerage firm. In addition, frequent trading may cause you to hold on to stocks less than one year, so the capital gain is treated as ordinary income for federal income tax purposes (unless the gain occurs as a result of trading stocks in your retirement account). If your marginal tax rate on ordinary income is higher than 15% (the current maximum long-term capital gains tax rate for most taxpayers), you will be subject to a higher tax rate because you did not hold the stocks for at least one year. Many studies have shown that the recommendations made by brokers or analysts do not lead to better performance than the stock market in general. Some advisers have very limited experience in analyzing and valuing securities. Even those who are very experienced will not necessarily be able to help you achieve unusually high performance.

Brokers and analysts tend to be overly optimistic about stocks. They prefer not to mention negative opinions about stocks because they do not want to offend any firms with which their own investment firm might do business in the future.

In response to much criticism, some analysts have recently been more willing to issue sell recommendations on some stocks. However, there is still a tendency for analysts to be generally optimistic about most stocks, and some conflicts of interest may occur. For example, analysts may own the stocks they are recommending, so it is in their best interests to create a demand for the stock so that its price will rise. Today, analysts have to disclose ownership of stocks that they recommend.

Individual Broker Skills Brokers within a brokerage firm have unique skills and personalities. Your preference for a specific firm might be heavily influenced by the individual broker who serves you. You can obtain information about individual brokers on the Internet.

Brokerage Commissions You can choose a discount or full-service brokerage firm. A **discount brokerage firm** executes your desired transactions but does not offer investment advice. A **full-service brokerage firm** offers investment advice and executes transactions. Full-service brokerage firms tend to charge higher fees for their services than discount brokers. For example, a full-service firm may charge a commission of $100 for a transaction, whereas a discount firm will likely charge you between $8 and $30 for the same transaction.

Placing an Order

Whenever you place an order to buy or sell a stock, you must specify the following:

- Name of the stock
- Buy or sell
- Number of shares
- Market order or limit order

Name of the Stock It is important to know the **ticker symbol** for your stock. The ticker symbol is the abbreviated term that is used to identify a stock for trading purposes. For example, Microsoft's symbol is MSFT, and Nike's symbol is NKE. A symbol is shorter and simpler than the formal name of a firm and easily distinguishes between different firms with similar names.

Buy or Sell Brokerage firms execute buy and sell transactions. Therefore, it is necessary to specify whether you are buying or selling a security at the time you place the order. Once you place your order and it is executed, you are bound by the instructions you gave.

Number of Shares Shares are typically sold in multiples of 100, referred to as **round-lot** transactions. An order to buy or sell less than 100 shares is referred to as an **odd-lot** transaction.

Market Order or Limit Order You can buy or sell a stock by placing a **market order**, which is an order to execute the transaction at the stock's prevailing market price. The advantage of a market order is that you are assured that your order will be executed quickly. A disadvantage is that the stock price could change abruptly just before you place your order, causing you to pay much more for the stock than you expected.

discount brokerage firm
A brokerage firm that executes your desired transactions but does not offer investment advice.

full-service brokerage firm
A brokerage firm that offers investment advice and executes transactions.

ticker symbol
The abbreviated term that is used to identify a stock for trading purposes.

round lot
Shares bought or sold in multiples of 100.

odd lot
Less than 100 shares of stock.

market order
An order to buy or sell a stock at its prevailing market price.

EXAMPLE

You want to buy 100 shares of Trendy stock, which had a closing price of $40. You assume that you will pay about $40 per share when the market opens this morning, or $4,000 ($40 × 100 shares), for the shares not including the commission. However, your order is executed at $43, which means that you pay $4,300 ($43 × 100 shares). Unfortunately for you, many other investors wanted to buy Trendy stock this morning, creating increased demand for the stock. The strong demand relative to the small number of shares available for sale caused the stock price to increase to $43 before your broker could find a willing seller of Trendy stock.

limit order
An order to buy or sell a stock only if the price is within limits that you specify.

Alternatively, you can buy or sell stock by placing a **limit order**, which is an order to execute the transaction only if the price is within the limits that you specify. A limit order sets a maximum price at which the stock can be purchased and can be good for one day or until canceled (normally canceled in six months if a transaction has not been executed by then). Your limit order will specify whether you are willing to accept a portion of the shares desired (normally, in round lots of 100); alternatively, you can specify that you want the full number of shares to be traded or none at all.

> **EXAMPLE**
>
> Using the information in the previous example, you place a limit order on Trendy stock, with a maximum limit of $41, good for the day. When the stock opens at $43 this morning, your order is not executed because the market price exceeds your limit price. Later in the day, the stock price declines to $41, at which time your order is executed.

A disadvantage of a limit order when buying stock is that you may miss out on a transaction that you desired. If the price of Trendy stock had continued to rise throughout the day after opening at $43, your order would not have been executed at all.

Limit orders can also be used to sell stocks. In this case, a limit order specifies a minimum price at which the stock should be sold.

> **EXAMPLE**
>
> You own 100 shares of Zina stock, which is currently worth $18 per share. You would be willing to sell it at $20 per share. You do not have time to monitor the market price so that you can sell the stock when its price is at least $20 per share. Therefore, you place a limit order to sell 100 shares of Zina stock at a minimum price of $20, good until canceled. A few months later, Zina's price rises to $20 per share. You soon receive confirmation from your brokerage firm that the transaction has been executed.

stop order
An order to execute a transaction when the stock price reaches a specified level; a special form of limit order.

buy stop order
An order to buy a stock when the price rises to a specified level.

sell stop order
An order to sell a stock when the price falls to a specified level.

Stop Orders A **stop order** is a special form of limit order; it is an order to execute a transaction when the stock price reaches a specified level. A **buy stop order** is an order for the brokerage firm to buy a stock for the investor when the price rises to a specified level. Conversely, a **sell stop order** is an order for the brokerage firm to sell a stock when the price falls to a specified level.

Placing an Order Online

Individuals who wish to buy or sell stocks are increasingly using online brokerage services such as TD Ameritrade and E*TRADE. One advantage of placing orders online is that the commission charged per transaction is very low, such as $8 or $20, regardless of the size of the transaction (up to a specified maximum level). A second advantage is the convenience. In addition to accepting orders, online brokers provide real-time stock quotes and financial information. To establish an account with an online brokerage service, go to its Web site and follow the instructions to set up an account. Then you'll need to send the online broker a check, and once the check has cleared, your account will show that you have funds you can use to invest online. Generally, you are required to maintain a minimum balance in your account such as $500 or $1,000.

Recall from Chapter 5 that many online brokerage firms have a money market fund where your cash is deposited until it is used to make transactions. Consequently, you can earn some interest on your funds until you use them to purchase securities. Once you place an order, the online brokerage firm will use the money in your money market fund to pay for the transaction. You may even receive blank checks so that you can write checks against your money market account.

As many investors have shifted to online brokerage, traditional brokerage firms (such as Merrill Lynch), now offer online services. You can place an order from your computer in less than a minute, and the order will be executed just as quickly.

Financial Planning
ONLINE

Go to:
http://www.etrade.com

To get:
Information that you can use when making investment decisions. It also illustrates how you can trade stocks online, which typically reduces your transaction costs.

Manage Your Stocks

Application:

The Fidelity Investments app (by Fidelity Investments) allows you to monitor your investments, transfer funds within your account, buy and sell stocks or mutual funds, and check the status of orders.

To Find It:

Search for the "Fidelity Investments" app on your mobile device.

Buying Stock on Margin

on margin
Purchasing a stock with a portion of the funds borrowed from a brokerage firm.

Some investors choose to purchase stock **on margin**, meaning that a portion of their purchase is funded with money borrowed from their brokerage firm. Buying a stock on margin enables you to purchase stocks without having the full amount of cash necessary.

The Federal Reserve limits the margin to 50%, so a maximum of 50% of the investment can be borrowed from the brokerage firm. For example, for a $2,000 purchase of stock, you and the brokerage firm would each pay $1,000. If the value of investments made with partially borrowed funds declines, you may receive a **margin call** from your brokerage firm, meaning that you have to increase the cash in your account to bring the margin back up to the minimum level.

margin call
A request from a brokerage firm for the investor to increase the cash in the account in order to bring the margin back up to the minimum level.

When you buy a stock on margin, the gain on your investment is magnified because you are able to create a larger investment with the borrowed funds. However, if the stock experiences a decline in price, your loss will be magnified. For example, if you invest $1,000 of your own money but do not borrow any funds, your maximum loss is $1,000. Conversely, if you invest $1,000 of your own money and borrow an additional $1,000 to invest, your maximum loss is now $2,000. You still need to repay the funds you borrowed, regardless of the performance of your investment.

Some investors achieve high returns from buying stocks on margin. However, they commonly use the proceeds to make more investments in stocks. With their confidence boosted from their recent investment performance, they make riskier investments. Ultimately, some of these investors end up losing much of the money they invested because of taking excessive risk.

Short Selling Stock

short selling (shorting)
A process by which investors sell a stock that they do not own.

Short selling (or "**shorting**") a stock is the process by which investors sell a stock that they do not own. Investors consider short selling a stock when the stock is overvalued in their opinion. In the short selling process, they borrow the stock from another investor and will ultimately have to return that stock to the brokerage firm from which they borrowed it. Their goal is to sell the stock while the price is relatively high. Then, they will purchase the stock at a future point in time after the price has declined, so that they can return the stock to the brokerage firm from which they initially borrowed the stock. Like any investor, short sellers attempt to buy low (buy the stock at a low price) and sell high (sell the stock at a high price). The only difference from the normal investing process is that they sell the stock first (before they even own it) and then buy it later.

Like any investment in stock, the risk to short selling is that the return is uncertain because the future conditions that affect the stock price are uncertain. Investors who expect that the stock price will decline may be wrong. If the stock price rises following their short sale, they will ultimately have to pay a higher price than the price at which they initially sold the stock. Consequently, they would suffer a loss on their investment.

Analyzing Stocks

The price of a stock is based on the demand for that stock versus the supply of stock for sale. The demand for shares is determined by the number of investors who wish to purchase shares of the stock. The supply of stock for sale is determined by the number of investors who decide to sell their shares.

The valuation process involves identifying a firm that you think may perform well in the future and determining whether its price is overvalued, undervalued, or on target. You buy a stock when you think that it is undervalued and that you can therefore achieve a high return from investing in it. Yet your purchase of the stock means that some other investor was willing to sell it. So, although you believe the stock is undervalued, others apparently think it is overvalued. This difference in opinion is what causes a high volume of trading. When valuing stocks, investors may use technical analysis or fundamental analysis. **Technical analysis** is the valuation of stocks based on historical price patterns. For example, you might purchase a stock whenever its price rises for three consecutive days because you expect that a trend in prices indicates future price movements. Alternatively, you may decide to sell a stock if its price declines for several consecutive days because you expect that the trend will continue.

Fundamental analysis is the valuation of stocks based on an examination of fundamental characteristics such as revenue or earnings. There are many different ways to apply fundamental analysis, as explained next.

technical analysis
The valuation of stocks based on historical price patterns.

fundamental analysis
The valuation of stocks based on an examination of fundamental characteristics such as revenue or earnings, or the sensitivity of the firm's performance to economic conditions.

Analyzing a Firm's Financial Condition

One firm can outperform another in the same industry because its managers make better decisions about how to finance its business, market its products, and manage its employees. By conducting an analysis of a firm, you can assess its future performance. Firms that are publicly traded publish an annual report that contains standardized financial information. Specifically, the report includes a letter summarizing the firm's recent performance and its expected performance in the future. The report also contains financial statements measuring the firm's financial condition, which you can examine in the same manner that you evaluate your personal financial statements to determine your financial health. You can download annual reports for most companies from their Web sites. Prospective investors typically focus on the balance sheet and income statement.

Balance Sheet The firm's **balance sheet** indicates its sources of funds and how it has invested its funds as of a particular point in time. The balance sheet is segmented into two parts: (1) assets and (2) liabilities and shareholder's equity. These two parts must balance.

The firm's assets indicate how it has invested its funds and what it owns. Assets are often classified as short-term and long-term assets. Short-term assets include cash, securities purchased by the firm, accounts receivable (money owed to the firm for previous sales), and inventories (materials used to produce products and finished products waiting to be sold). Long-term assets (sometimes called fixed assets) include machinery and buildings purchased by the firm.

The liabilities and shareholder's equity indicate how the firm has obtained its funds. Liabilities represent the amount owed to creditors or suppliers and are classified as short term or long term. Shareholder's equity is the net worth of the firm. It represents the investment in the firm by investors.

balance sheet
A financial statement that indicates a firm's sources of funds and how it has invested its funds as of a particular point in time.

Income Statement The firm's **income statement** measures its revenues, expenses, and earnings over a particular period of time. Investors use it to determine how much income (earnings) the firm generated over a particular period or what expenses the firm incurred. An annual report may include an income statement for the year and for the four quarters within that year.

The income statement starts with revenues generated by the firm over the year. Then the cost of goods sold (which includes the cost of materials used in production) is

income statement
A financial statement that measures a firm's revenues, expenses, and earnings over a particular period of time.

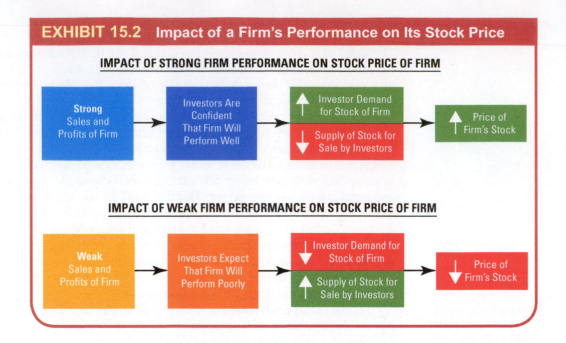

subtracted to derive the gross profit. Operating expenses (such as salaries) are subtracted from the gross profit to determine earnings before interest and taxes (also referred to as operating profit). Finally, interest payments and taxes are subtracted to determine the earnings after taxes (also referred to as the net profit).

The impact of the firm's financial condition on its value and stock price (for firms that have publicly traded stock) is summarized in Exhibit 15.2. When a firm's sales and profits are strong, investors have confidence that the firm will perform well in the future, and they are willing to invest in the firm's stock. Because the firm's prospects look bright, only a few investors will be willing to sell its stock. Thus, the demand for the stock is much larger than the supply of stock for sale by investors, and the price at which sellers can sell the stock rises.

When a firm's sales and profits are weak, the opposite effects occur. Investors become concerned that the firm will perform poorly in the future and might even go bankrupt. They are not willing to invest in the firm's stock because the stock might become worthless if the firm fails. When only a few investors want to buy a stock being sold by investors, and many investors want to sell that stock because of its recent poor performance, the price at which sellers can sell the stock falls. In other words, sellers must be willing to accept a very low price to entice another investor to buy their stock.

FREE APPS
for Personal
Finance

Financial Data Analysis

Application:

The CNNMoney Business and Finance News app (by CNNMoney.com) provides business news, financial data analysis, and financial news video coverage for investors.

To Find It:

Search for the "CNNMoney" app on your mobile device.

Accounting Fraud In the early 2000s, scandals at several large companies including Enron and WorldCom brought attention to the accounting practices of certain firms. One of the problems that led to the scandals was the conflict of interest that may occur between a firm's top managers and investors who purchase its stock. A firm's top managers are commonly evaluated according to how the firm's value (as measured by stock price) changes over time. These managers may receive shares of the firm's stock as part of their compensation. Thus, if the value of the firm increases, the managers can sell their shares at a high price and earn a high level of compensation.

Consequently, the managers may seek to use an accounting method that will either inflate the firm's revenue or deflate its expenses, causing the firm's reported earnings to appear higher than they actually are. Investors who rely on those reported earnings to derive the stock value will buy the stock when they believe that the firm's earnings have risen. Their actions push the value of the stock higher. Ultimately, however, investors recognize that the firm's financial statements are not accurate, and the stock price falls. Many investors, however, may lose most or all the money that they invested because they trusted the firm's financial statements. Although legislation was enacted after these scandals to curb the worst abuses and reform the accounting methods used by companies, managers at many firms continue to have an incentive to make their companies look more profitable than they actually are.

Analyzing Economic Conditions

A firm's future revenue and earnings are influenced by demand for its products, which is typically influenced by economic and industry conditions. An economic analysis involves assessing any economic conditions that can affect a firm's stock price, including economic growth, the impact of international economies, interest rates, and inflation. Each of these conditions is discussed in turn.

Economic Growth In the United States, **economic growth** is the growth in the U.S. economy over a particular period. It is commonly measured by the amount of production in the United States, or the **gross domestic product (GDP)**, which is the total market value of all products and services produced in the United States. The production level of products and services is closely related to the aggregate (overall) demand for products and services. When consumers have more money to spend, there is additional aggregate demand for products and services. The firms that provide products and services experience higher sales (revenue) and earnings, and their stock prices may rise.

When economic conditions are weak, the aggregate demand for products and services declines. Firms experience a lower level of sales and earnings, and their stock prices may decline as a result.

During the financial crisis in 2008–2009, economic conditions weakened substantially. Home prices plummeted. Many firms went bankrupt. Others had to reduce their workforce because their sales had declined substantially. Many individuals were laid off or were assigned fewer work hours. Thus, their income declined. Firms experienced a decline in demand for their products and services, a decline in profitability, and a decline in value (stock price).

Given the potential impact of economic growth on stock prices, investors also monitor the U.S. government's **fiscal policy**, or the means by which the government imposes taxes on individuals and corporations and by which it spends its money. When corporate tax rates are increased, the after-tax earnings of corporations are reduced, which means there is less money for shareholders. When individual tax rates are increased, individuals have less money to spend and therefore consume fewer products. The demand for products and services declines as a result, reducing firms' earnings.

Impact of International Economies When assessing a country's economic conditions, it is important to recognize how a country's economy may be influenced by international conditions. Some of the products sold in the United States are produced by firms in other countries such as China. Firms in China are major producers of electronics, clothing, children's toys, and many other products that are sold in the United States. When the U.S. economy strengthens, consumers in the United States purchase more products, including those produced in China. Thus, the firms based in China may

economic growth
A measure of growth in a country's economy over a particular period.

gross domestic product (GDP)
The total market value of all products and services produced in a country.

ECONOMIC IMPACT

fiscal policy
The means by which the U.S. government imposes taxes on individuals and corporations and by which it spends its money.

hire more employees so that they can increase production to satisfy the increased demand by U.S. consumers. As more employees are hired in China, income of Chinese workers rises, which will allow them to increase their spending. Thus, a strong U.S. economy can strengthen the economy in China. The same concept applies to other countries that produce products purchased by U.S. consumers.

Consumers in foreign countries purchase some products that are produced in the United States, so their economies can influence the U.S. economy. For example, consumers in China purchase some products produced in the United States, so when China's economy is strong, this can be beneficial to the United States. European consumers commonly purchase U.S. products as well, so their economy is closely linked to the U.S. economy.

Just as one country's strong economy can improve another country's economy, a weaker economy has an influence as well, but in the opposite direction. As an economy weakens, consumer spending declines, which means that the demand for products produced to satisfy those consumers declines. Thus, firms in those countries might lay off some workers because they do not need to produce as many products, and income declines in those countries. During the 2008–2009 financial crisis in the United States, the weak economy in the United States had an adverse effect on economic conditions in many countries. In 2014, many European countries experienced weak economic conditions, and this had an adverse effect on U.S. companies that sold many products to Europe.

Interest Rates Interest rates can affect economic growth and therefore have an indirect impact on stock prices. In general, stocks perform better when interest rates are low because firms can obtain financing at relatively low rates. Firms tend to be more willing to expand when interest rates are low, and their expansions stimulate the economy. When interest rates are low, investors also tend to shift more of their funds into stock because the interest earned on money market securities is relatively low. The general shift into stocks increases the demand for stocks, which places upward pressure on stock prices.

Lower interest rates may enable more consumers to afford cars or homes. Car manufacturers and homebuilders then experience higher earnings, and their stock prices tend to increase as well. Financial publications often refer to the Federal Reserve Board ("the Fed") when discussing interest rates, because the Fed uses **monetary policy** by adjusting the supply of funds in the financial system to influence interest rates. When the Fed affects interest rates, it influences the amount of spending by consumers with borrowed funds and therefore influences economic growth.

Inflation Stock prices are also affected by **inflation**, or the increase in the general level of prices of products and services over a specified period. One of the most common measures of inflation is the **consumer price index (CPI)**, which represents prices of consumer products such as groceries, household products, housing, and gasoline. An alternative measure of inflation is the **producer price index (PPI)**, which represents prices of products that are used to produce other products, such as coal, lumber, and metals. Inflation can cause an increase in the prices that firms pay for materials or equipment.

The main publications providing information about inflation and other economic conditions are listed in Exhibit 15.3. These publications commonly provide historical data for inflation, economic growth, interest rates, and many other economic indicators.

Industry Conditions

A firm's stock price is also susceptible to industry conditions. The demand for products or services within an industry changes over time. For example, the popularity of the Internet increased the demand for computers, disks, printers, and Internet guides in the 1990s. Producers of these products initially benefited from the increased demand. However, as other firms notice the increased demand, they often enter an industry.

---

monetary policy
The policy established by the Federal Reserve to adjust the supply of funds in the financial system in order to influence interest rates.

inflation
The increase in the general level of prices of products and services over a specified period.

consumer price index (CPI)
A measure of inflation that represents prices of consumer products such as groceries, household products, housing, and gasoline.

producer price index (PPI)
A measure of inflation that represents prices of products that are used to produce other products, such as coal, lumber, and metals.

Financial Planning
ONLINE

Go to:
http://www.oecd.org

To get:
Information about economic conditions that can affect the values of investments.

EXHIBIT 15.3   Sources of Economic Information

Published Sources

- **Federal Reserve Bulletin:** provides data on economic conditions, including interest rates, unemployment rates, inflation rates, and the money supply.

- **Federal Reserve District Bank publications:** provide information on national and regional economic conditions.

- **Survey of Current Business:** provides data on various indicators of economic activity, including national income, production levels, and employment levels.

Online Sources

- **Bloomberg (http://www.bloomberg.com):** provides reports on interest rates, other economic conditions, and news announcements about various economic indicators.

- *Federal Reserve Meeting Information* is also available online at http://www.federalreserve.gov.

- *Federal Reserve District Bank publications* are also online at http://www.frbsf.org.

- **Federal Reserve System (http://www.federalreserve.gov):** provides detailed statistics on economic conditions.

- **St. Louis Federal Reserve District (http://www.stlouisfed.org):** provides updated information about U.S. economic conditions.

- *Survey of Current Business* is also online at http://www.bea.gov.

- **Yahoo! Finance:** provides information and news about economic conditions.

Competition is another industry factor that frequently affects sales, earnings, and therefore the stock price of a firm. Competition has intensified for many industries as a result of the Internet, which has reduced the costs of marketing and delivering products for some firms.

Industry Indicators Numerous financial Web sites also provide information on specific industries. Another indicator of industry performance is the industry stock index, which measures how the market value of the firms within the industry has changed over a specific period. The prevailing stock index for a particular industry indicates the general expectations of investors about that industry.

Integrating Your Analyses

By conducting an analysis of the firm itself, the economy, and the industry, you can assess a firm's future performance. This process enables you to determine whether to purchase the firm's stock. Exhibit 15.4 summarizes the potential impact of economic, industry, and firm-specific conditions on a firm's stock price.

Limitations of Stock Analysis

Many investors enjoy analyzing stocks, especially when their analysis leads to good investment decisions that result in high returns. However, some of the limitations of analyzing stocks are described here.

Financial Planning
ONLINE

Go to:
The markets section of
http://www.bloomberg.com

To get:
A summary of recent
stock performance.

EXHIBIT 15.4   Factors That Increase and Decrease a Stock's Price

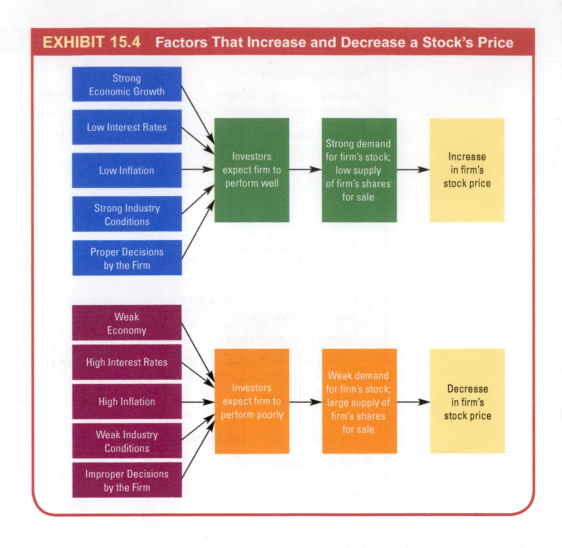

Difficulty in Forecasting Future Conditions Although you may be able to determine which firms are most sensitive or least sensitive to economic or industry conditions, it is difficult to forecast future economic or industry conditions. You might correctly determine that a specific stock is highly sensitive to industry conditions and therefore purchase the stock because the industry's conditions appear to be favorable. However, the industry might suffer from conditions that were completely unexpected, such as an environmental crisis, labor strikes, weather conditions, or other factors. In this case, the stock you selected may actually perform worse than most other stocks because of its high degree of sensitivity to industry conditions.

Favorable Attributes Are Reflected in the Stock Price When analyzing stocks, one obvious goal is to identify companies that have favorable attributes that may lead to strong profits and a higher stock price in the future. However, companies with favorable attributes attract investors, and the strong demand for those stocks may have caused those stocks to become expensive before you purchase them. For example, the stock of a company that is expected to perform very well in the future probably has been in demand in recent weeks, which caused a higher price. Thus, if you decide to buy the stock now because of the expectations of high future profits, you have to pay a high price for that stock. Even if the company achieves the high profits that are expected, the return on your investment in this stock might be no better than that of most other stocks because you purchased the stock at a high price that already reflected the favorable attributes.

The obvious lesson here is to purchase stocks before their prices already reflect their favorable attributes. However, this requires you to anticipate the favorable attributes about a company before other investors do so that you can purchase the stock before it experiences a large increase in price. Although it is possible to anticipate favorable attributes of a company before other investors, your assessment is subject to uncertainty. If you guess wrong, the return on your investment may be poor. If you recognize your limitations, it should encourage you to limit the amount of your investments in risky stocks just in case your expectations are wrong.

FREE APPS
for Personal
Finance

Investing Game

Application:

The Stock Wars app (by Continuous Integration Inc.) allows you to simulate investing in a stock portfolio and monitoring the performance of your portfolio over time. You can see how you would have performed from investing without risking any money.

To Find It:

Search for the "Stock Wars" app on your mobile device.

How Stock Investment Methods Fit Within Your Financial Plan

The following are key decisions about investing in stock that should be included within your financial plan:

- Should you consider buying stock?
- What methods should you use for investing in stocks?

The first decision was discussed in Chapter 14, while the second decision about how to conduct stock transactions has been examined in this chapter. Exhibit 15.5 provides an example of how this decision applies to Stephanie Spratt's financial plan.

EXHIBIT 15.5   How Stock Investment Methods Fit Within Stephanie Spratt's Financial Plan

GOALS FOR INVESTING IN STOCK

1. Determine if I could benefit from investing more money in common stock.
2. If I consider investing in stocks, determine how to execute stock transactions.

ANALYSIS

Type of Brokerage Firm

Full-service	Guidance on stock selection; higher commissions charged on transactions.
Discount	No guidance on stock selection; lower commissions charged on transactions.

Type of Order When Purchasing Stock

Market Order	A buy order is executed at the market price.
Limit Order	A buy order is only executed if the price is at or below a price that I may specify.
Buy Stop Order	A buy order is executed if the price rises to a price that I may specify.

Whether to Borrow

Pay with Cash	Need cash to pay for the entire investment. My return will be equal to the return on the stock itself.
Buying on Margin	Can make investment with less money (by borrowing a portion of the funds needed). My return will be larger than the return on the stock itself. My return (whether it is a gain or loss) is more pronounced if I borrow to buy the stock, which increases the risk of my investment.

DECISION

In the future when I invest in stocks, I will use a discount broker instead of a full-service broker because I prefer to make my own investment decisions and the commissions charged by a discount broker are low. I will use only limit orders to buy stocks, so that I can set the maximum price that I am willing to pay. I will only invest in a stock if I have sufficient funds to cover the entire investment because it is a less risky method of executing a stock transaction. Buying on margin magnifies the return (whether positive or negative) on the stock, and causes the investment to be more risky than I desire.

DISCUSSION QUESTIONS

1. How would Stephanie's decisions concerning conducting stock transactions be different if she were a single mother of two children?

2. How would Stephanie's decisions concerning conducting stock transactions be affected if she were 35 years old? If she were 50 years old?

SUMMARY

Stock Exchange. Stocks are listed on stock exchanges, where they can be purchased or sold. You can relay your order to a brokerage firm, which sends the order to an exchange where the stock is listed. The order is executed electronically by a computer or by traders at the exchange. Some orders are executed through electronic communications networks (ECNs), which are computer systems that match desired purchases and sales of stocks.

Stock Quotations. A stock's price quotations are provided in financial newspapers and online. These quotations should be considered when deciding whether to purchase a stock.

Stock Transactions. To buy or sell, you can contact a brokerage firm. You may use an online brokerage firm, which can be more convenient and less costly than a traditional full-service brokerage firm. Upon receiving your order, the firm will send the order to the stock exchange where the trade is executed.

Analyzing Stocks. An analysis of a firm involves reviewing the annual report and the financial statements (such as the balance sheet and income statement), along with other financial reports. This analysis includes an assessment of the firm's profitability.

An economic analysis involves assessing how a stock's price can be affected by economic conditions. The most closely monitored economic factors that affect stock prices are economic growth, interest rates, and inflation. In general, stocks are favorably affected by economic growth, favorable international conditions, a decline in interest rates, and a decline in inflation.

An industry analysis involves assessing how a stock's price can be affected by industry conditions. Two closely monitored industry characteristics are consumer preferences within an industry and industry competition. Stocks are favorably affected when the firms recognize shifts in consumer preferences and when the firms face a relatively low degree of competition.

How Investing in Stocks Fits Within Your Financial Plan. In general, stocks have generated a high return on investment over long periods. Therefore, they can allow you to accumulate wealth in order to accommodate your future spending preferences that will satisfy your financial plan. However, they must be managed with care to limit the risk.

REVIEW QUESTIONS

All Review Questions are available in MyFinanceLab *at* http://www.myfinancelab.com.

1. **Stock Exchanges.** What are stock exchanges? How do they facilitate the trading of stocks?

2. **NYSE.** Describe a typical stock transaction at the New York Stock Exchange (NYSE). What are floor traders? What are specialists? What other exchanges trade stocks in a similar manner to the NYSE?

3. **ECNs.** What are electronic communications networks (ECNs)? How are ECNs used?

4. **Brokerage Firms.** How is the market for a stock created? How do brokerage firms expedite this process? Compare the two types of brokerage services.

5. **Online Brokerage Services.** What are some advantages of using online brokerage services? Describe how an investor would set up and use an online brokerage account.

6. **Placing Orders.** What information must you provide when placing an order to buy or sell stock? What is a ticker symbol, and why is it important?

7. **Round versus Odd Lot.** What do the terms *round lot* and *odd lot* mean in stock transactions?

8. **Types of Orders.** Discuss the differences between a market order, a limit order, and a stop order.

9. **Buying on Margin.** What is buying a stock on margin? What may happen if the value of the stock bought on margin declines? What are the advantages to investors and brokerage firms when stocks are bought on margin?

10. **Annual Report.** Why is it necessary to analyze a firm? What is an annual report? What information does it contain to aid the analysis?

11. **Financial Statements.** List the characteristics of a firm that investors analyze by using the balance sheet and the income statement.

12. **Misleading Information.** Why may the top managers of a firm be tempted to use misleading estimates of revenues and expenses? How may managers be able to boost the reported earnings of their firm?

13. **Economic Analysis.** When performing an economic analysis of stocks, what economic factors are most closely watched?

14. **Economic Growth.** Explain how economic growth is measured. How does economic growth affect stock prices? What are some popular indicators of economic growth? How does the government's fiscal policy affect economic growth?

15. **Interest Rates.** How do interest rates affect economic growth? Why do interest rates affect some stock prices more than others? Which federal agency influences interest rates?

16. **Inflation.** What is inflation? How is inflation measured? How does inflation affect stock prices?

17. **Industry Analysis.** Why is an industry analysis of stocks important? List some sources of information about firms and their industry.

18. **Short Sales.** What is a short sale? When would this strategy be used?

19. **Global Impact on Investments.** How can another country's economic conditions affect a U.S. firm and therefore its stock price?

20. **OTC.** What is the OTC? What is the role of a market maker?

21. **Selecting a Broker.** What factors should you consider when selecting which stockbroker to use?

22. **Stock Price.** What determines stock price? How do investors use this information to make buy or sell decisions?

23. **Technical Analysis versus Fundamental Analysis.** What is technical analysis? What is fundamental analysis?

24. **Limitations of Stock Analysis.** What are some limitations of stock analysis?

25. **Stock Investment and Your Financial Plan.** Why should young people have investments in stocks as part of their portfolio?

26. **Ethical Dilemma.** The top managers of a publicly traded manufacturing company are reviewing the projected fourth quarter financial results in late November. Based on the projected sales, the company will fall short of its yearly profit goals. This will result in the company's executives and managers not receiving their year-end bonuses. The managers discuss how sales can be increased sufficiently to produce results that will qualify them for year-end bonuses. A decision is made to notify all customers that if they will agree to accept shipments for first-quarter orders before the end of the fourth quarter, the company will agree to pick up the shipping costs. The company's controller and CFO review the plan and agree that it is within acceptable guidelines of Generally Accepted Accounting Principles (GAAP).

The plan results in a significant increase in both sales and net income despite the company's increased shipping costs. The increase is sufficient to warrant payment of bonuses to the executives and managers and also results in a significant increase in the company's stock price.

a. Was the incentive plan devised by the company's management for the purpose of increasing sales and profits to a level justifying bonuses ethical?

b. Discuss any negative impact that this incentive program could have for the company and its shareholders in the future.

FINANCIAL PLANNING ONLINE EXERCISES

1. Go to the finance section of Yahoo.com to review analysts' stock recommendations.

   a. Enter the stock symbol NOK, for Nokia Corporation, and click "Get Quotes." Then click the link for "Analyst Opinion." Information on analysts' recommendations and various earnings-related information will be provided. What is the average broker recommendation? What is your opinion of Nokia after reviewing the analysts' comments and earnings estimates?

   b. Now enter the symbol XRX, for Xerox. Click "Get Quotes" and then "Research Reports." What is the average broker recommendation? What is your opinion of Xerox after reviewing the analysts' comments and estimates?

   c. What are the major differences between Nokia and Xerox, based on the information on each company provided by analysts?

   d. Now enter the symbol T, for AT&T. Click "Get Quotes" and "Research Reports." What is the average broker recommendation? What is your opinion of AT&T after reviewing the analysts' comments and estimates?

2. Go to the http://www.etrade.com. Go to the section "Investor Education." Summarize the general advice that is available to you about investing in stocks.

3. Go to the finance section of Yahoo.com to assess the recent performance of stock indexes. Summarize the performance of stocks in the last year.

PSYCHOLOGY OF PERSONAL FINANCE: Buying Stocks on Margin

1. Some investors are naive and are overconfident that the stocks in which they invest will perform well. They know that they might achieve high returns from buying stocks on margin, but they ignore the risk that they could incur large losses. What is your behavior toward buying stocks on margin? What is the risk associated with this strategy?

2. Read one practical article about how psychology affects decisions when buying stocks on margin. You can easily retrieve possible articles by doing an online search using the terms "psychology" and "buying stocks on margin." Summarize the main points of the article.

WEB SEARCH EXERCISE

You can develop your personal finance skills by conducting an Internet search for related articles. Find a recent online article about personal finance that reinforces one or more concepts covered in this chapter. If your class has an online component, your professor may ask you to post your summary of the article there and provide a link to the article so that other students can access it. If your class is live, your professor may ask you to summarize your application of the article in class. Your professor may assign specific students to complete this assignment or may allow any student to do the assignment on a volunteer basis.

For recent online articles related to this chapter, consider using the following search terms (be sure to include the current year as a search term to ensure that the online articles are recent):

- Selecting a broker
- Buying stock on margin
- Short selling
- Valuing a stock
- Impact of economy on stocks

VIDEO EXERCISE: Investing in Stocks

Go to one of the Web sites that contain video clips (such as http://www.youtube.com) and review some video clips about investing in stocks. You can use search phrases such as "tips on investing in stocks." Select one video clip on this topic that you would recommend for the other students in your class.

1. Provide the Web link for the video clip.

2. What do you think is the main point of this video clip?

3. How might you change your process of investing in stocks as a result of watching this video clip?

BUILDING YOUR OWN FINANCIAL PLAN

Selecting the right stock investment method is an important decision for any investor. This case walks you through a list of questions designed to assist you in making the important decision of whether a full-service broker or online/discount broker better suits your needs. Carefully consider the types of investments you will be making, how frequently you will make transactions, and how important one-on-one advice from a broker is to you. When comparing brokerage firms' offerings, be sure to consider at least one online or discount broker.

As you get older and your portfolio grows in size and possibly in complexity, you need to review the suitability of your broker periodically, just as you do your tax preparer as we discussed in Chapter 4.

Go to the worksheets at the end of this chapter to continue building your financial plan.

THE SAMPSONS—A Continuing Case

Recall that one of the Sampsons' goals is to invest for their children's future college education. To become more educated investors, they have been reviewing analyst and brokerage firm recommendations. Dave and Sharon are ready to invest in several stocks that are rated highly by analysts. Before they purchase the stock, they ask you to weigh in with an opinion.

Go to the worksheets at the end of this chapter to continue this case.

CHAPTER 15: BUILDING YOUR OWN FINANCIAL PLAN

GOAL

1. Determine a method to use for investing in stocks.

ANALYSIS

1. Respond to each of the following statements by checking the appropriate box.

	Yes	No
a. I will feel better if I have a specific person to talk to about my account.	☐	☐
b. I will require professional research assistance to make investment decisions.	☐	☐
c. I will utilize banking-type services such as check writing and debit cards.	☐	☐
d. I will feel more comfortable if I have a broker who calls me from time to time with suggestions about how to improve the performance of my portfolio.	☐	☐
e. I will have a relatively complex portfolio that is designed to minimize taxes.	☐	☐
f. I will use my portfolio to meet a variety of goals with varying time horizons (short-, intermediate-, and long-term).	☐	☐
g. I will require advice on the tax implications of my investments.	☐	☐
h. My portfolio is large enough to require an annual review and rebalancing.	☐	☐
i. I will sleep better if I know who is watching my money.	☐	☐
j. I will feel better doing business with people who know my name.	☐	☐

If you answered "Yes" to five or more of the above statements, you should seriously consider a full-service broker.

2. What type of orders—market, limit, or buy stop—do you intend to use when purchasing stocks? Do you intend to pay with cash or buy on margin? Why?

_____

_____

_____

_____

_____

_____

_____

_____

_____

_____

_____

DECISIONS

1. What type of brokerage firm will you work with—full-service or discount/online? Why?

   _____

   _____

   _____

   _____

   _____

   _____

   _____

   _____

   _____

   _____

   _____

   _____

   _____

2. Summarize your decision on the type of orders you will place to purchase stocks and your preference for using cash versus buying on margin.

   _____

   _____

   _____

   _____

   _____

   _____

   _____

   _____

   _____

   _____

CHAPTER 15: THE SAMPSONS—A Continuing Case

CASE QUESTIONS

1. Offer advice to the Sampsons about whether they should buy stocks that are rated highly by analysts.

_____

_____

_____

_____

_____

_____

_____

_____

_____

_____

_____

_____

_____

_____

2. Some Web sites identify firms that were top performers the previous day. Should the Sampsons buy these stocks? Explain.

_____

_____

_____

_____

_____

_____

_____

_____

_____

_____

_____

_____

Investing in Bonds

Neal wanted to invest in bonds because he knew that they could provide periodic interest payments that would serve as a source of income. He knew that he could buy bonds issued by the U.S. Treasury. However, these bonds only offered a yield of 5%. Neal wanted to earn a higher yield. His broker suggested that he invest in junk bonds, which are issued by companies whose financial condition

Stephen VanHorn/Shutterstock

is weak. Neal noticed that some of these bonds offer a yield of 10%, double the yield provided by Treasury bonds. He also noticed that over the previous five years when the economy was strong, these bonds provided very high returns to investors—much higher than U.S. Treasury bonds. He decided to invest in junk bonds issued by one particular company that were offering a yield of 11%. During the following year, the U.S. economy weakened, and this company could not afford to cover its debt. It filed for bankruptcy, and Neal's bonds became worthless. Although many other companies also had poorer performance while the U.S. economy was weak, their financial condition was strong enough to enable them to cover their debt payments. Neal realized the potential adverse consequence of investing in risky bonds.

Like other investments, bonds have unique characteristics. As with stocks, the return and risk vary depending on their issuer as well as current and expected economic conditions. Understanding the different types of bonds and various bond investment strategies can help you build your own investment portfolio and enhance your wealth.

MyFinanceLab helps you master the topics in this chapter and study more efficiently. Visit http://www.myfinancelab.com for more details.

The objectives of this chapter are to:

- Provide a background on bonds
- Identify the different types of bonds
- Identify factors that affect the return (yield) from investing in a bond
- Describe how bonds are valued
- Discuss why some bonds are risky
- Describe common bond investment strategies
- Explain how investing in bonds can fit within your financial plan

Background on Bonds

bonds
Long-term debt securities issued by government agencies or corporations.

Recall that investors commonly invest some of their funds in **bonds,** which are long-term debt securities issued by government agencies or corporations. Bonds commonly offer more favorable returns than bank deposits. In addition, they typically provide fixed interest payments (called coupon payments) that represent additional income each year. The **par value** of a bond is its face value, or the amount returned to the investor at the maturity date when the bond is due.

par value
For a bond, its face value, or the amount returned to the investor at the maturity date when the bond is due.

Most bonds have maturities between 10 and 30 years, although some bonds have longer maturities. Investors provide the issuers of bonds with funds (credit). In return, the issuers are obligated to make interest (or coupon) payments and to pay the par value at maturity. When a bond has a par value of $1,000, a coupon rate of 6% means that $60 (.06 × $1,000) is paid annually to investors. The coupon payments are normally paid semiannually (in this example, $30 every six months).

Some bonds are sold at a price below par value; in this case, investors who hold the bonds until maturity will earn a return from the difference between par value and what they paid. This income is in addition to the coupon payments earned.

You should consider investing in bonds rather than stock if you wish to receive periodic income from your investments. As will be explained in Chapter 18, many investors diversify among stocks and bonds to achieve their desired return and risk preferences.

Bond Characteristics

Bonds that are distributed by a particular type of issuer can offer various features such as a call feature or convertibility.

call feature
A feature on a bond that allows the issuer to repurchase the bond from the investor before maturity.

Call Feature A **call feature** on a bond allows the issuer to buy back the bond from the investor before maturity. This feature is desirable for issuers because it allows them to retire existing bonds with coupon rates that are higher than the prevailing interest rates.

Investors are willing to purchase bonds with a call feature only if the bonds offer a slightly higher return than similar bonds without a call feature. This premium compensates the investors for the possibility that the bonds may be called before maturity.

> **EXAMPLE** Five years ago, Cieplak, Inc., issued 15-year callable bonds with a coupon rate of 9%. Interest rates have declined since then. Today, Cieplak can issue new bonds at a rate of 7%. It decides to retire the existing bonds by buying them back from investors and to issue new bonds at a 7% coupon rate. By calling the old bonds, Cieplak has reduced its cost of financing.

convertible bond
A bond that can be converted into a stated number of shares of the issuer's stock if the stock price reaches a specified price.

Financial Planning
ONLINE

Go to:
http://www.calculatorweb.com, and then go to the section on bond calculators.

To get:
An estimate of the yield to maturity of your bond based on its present price, its coupon rate, and its maturity. Thus, you can determine the rate of return that the bond will generate for you from today until it matures.

yield to maturity
The annualized return on a bond if it is held until maturity.

Treasury bonds
Long-term debt securities issued by the U.S. Treasury.

municipal bonds
Long-term debt securities issued by state and local government agencies.

Convertible Feature A **convertible bond** allows the investor to convert the bond into a stated number of shares of the issuer's stock if the stock price reaches a specified price. This feature enables bond investors to benefit when the issuer's stock price rises. Because convertibility is a desirable feature for investors, convertible bonds tend to offer a lower return than nonconvertible bonds. Consequently, if the stock price does not rise to the specified trigger price, the convertible bond provides a lower return to investors than alternative bonds without a convertible feature. If the stock price does reach the trigger price, however, investors can convert their bonds into shares of the issuer's stock, thereby earning a higher return than they would have earned on nonconvertible bonds.

A Bond's Yield to Maturity

A bond's **yield to maturity** is the annualized return on the bond if it is held until maturity. Consider a bond that is priced at $1,000, has a par value of $1,000, a maturity of 20 years, and a coupon rate of 10%. This bond has a yield to maturity of 10%, which is the same as its coupon rate because the price paid for the bond equals the principal.

As an alternative example, if this bond's price were lower than the principal amount, its yield to maturity would exceed the coupon rate of 10%. The bond would also generate income in the form of a capital gain because the purchase price would be less than the principal amount to be received at maturity. Conversely, if this bond's price were higher than the principal amount, its yield to maturity would be less than the 10% coupon rate because the amount paid for the bond would exceed the principal amount to be received at maturity.

Bond Trading in the Secondary Market

Investors can sell their bonds to other investors in the secondary market before the bonds reach maturity. Bond prices change in response to interest rate movements and other factors. Some bonds are traded on stock exchanges such as the New York Stock Exchange. Other bonds are traded in the over-the-counter market. Many investors sell their bonds in the secondary market so that they can obtain funds to cover upcoming expenses or to invest in other more attractive types of securities. Brokerage firms take orders from investors to buy or sell bonds and execute the transactions for investors.

Types of Bonds

Bonds can be classified according to the type of issuer as follows:

- Treasury bonds
- Municipal bonds
- Federal agency bonds
- Corporate bonds

Treasury Bonds

Treasury bonds are long-term debt securities issued by the U.S. Treasury, a branch of the federal government. Because the payments are guaranteed by the federal government, they are not exposed to the risk of default by the issuer. The interest on Treasury bonds is subject to federal income tax, but it is exempt from state and local taxes. Treasury bonds are very liquid because they can easily be sold in the secondary market.

Municipal Bonds

Municipal bonds are long-term debt securities issued by state and local government agencies; these agencies generate fees from some municipal projects or use tax revenues to repay the debt. Because a state or local government agency might possibly default on its coupon payments, municipal bonds are not free from the risk of default. In recent years, for example, several local governments, including Stockton (California), Harrisburg (Pennsylvania), and Detroit (Michigan), have defaulted and were unable to make all the coupon payments on their bonds. In some instances, insurance covered part of the payments, but investors still suffered losses. Nevertheless, most municipal bonds have a very low default risk. To entice investors, municipal bonds that are issued by a local government with a relatively high level of risk offer a higher yield than other municipal bonds with a lower level of risk.

The interest on municipal bonds is exempt from federal income tax, which is especially beneficial to investors who are in a high tax bracket. The interest is also exempt from state and local taxes when the investor resides in the same state as the municipality that issued the bonds. Municipal bonds tend to have a lower coupon rate than Treasury bonds issued at the same time. However, the municipal bonds may offer a higher after-tax return to investors.

EXAMPLE

Mike Rivas lives in Florida, where there is no state income tax. For federal income tax, however, he faces a 35% marginal rate, meaning that he will pay a tax of 35% on any additional income that he earns this year. Last year, Mike invested $100,000 in Treasury bonds with a coupon rate of 4% and $100,000 in municipal bonds with a coupon rate of 3%. His annual earnings from these two investments are shown here:

	Treasury Bonds	Municipal Bonds
Interest income before taxes	$4,000 (.04 × $100,000)	$3,000 (.03 × $100,000)
Federal taxes owed	$1,400 (.35 × $4,000)	0
Interest income after taxes	$2,600	$3,000

Notice that even though Mike received more interest income from the Treasury bonds, he must pay 35% of that income to the federal government. Therefore, he keeps only 65% of that income, or a total of $2,600. In contrast, none of the interest income of $3,000 from the municipal bonds is taxed. Consequently, every year Mike receives $400 more in after-tax interest income from the municipal bonds with the 3% coupon rate than from the Treasury bonds with the 4% coupon rate.

Federal Agency Bonds

federal agency bonds
Long-term debt securities issued by federal agencies.

Federal agency bonds are long-term debt securities issued or guaranteed by federal government agencies or government-sponsored entities (GSEs). The Government National Mortgage Association (called Ginnie Mae or abbreviated as GNMA), for example, guarantees mortgage-backed securities that are issued by the Federal Housing Administration (FHA) and by the Department of Veteran Affairs (VA). The Federal Home Loan Mortgage Association (called Freddie Mac) is a GSE that commonly issues bonds and uses the proceeds to purchase conventional mortgages. Another GSE that commonly issues bonds is the Federal National Mortgage Association (Fannie Mae).

Bonds issued by government agencies such as Ginnie Mae are taxed in the same way as Treasury bonds. The interest is taxed at the federal level but is exempt from state and local taxes. The interest on bonds issued by GSEs such as Fannie Mae and Freddie Mac is subject to federal, state, and local taxes.

Because Ginnie Mae is a government agency, its securities are backed by the full faith and credit of the U.S. government. The GSEs, however, are government sponsored but privately owned by shareholders. Therefore, some investors were concerned that their bonds might be riskier than those of other agencies. During the financial crisis in 2008, Fannie Mae and Freddie Mac suffered massive losses because they had invested in many

EXHIBIT 16.1 An Example of Corporate Bond Quotations

Company	Coupon	Maturity	Price	Yield	Estimated Volume (in $1,000s)
Zugle Co.	5.00%	Dec. 1, 2018	100.00	5.00%	4,000

so-called subprime mortgages that were not repaid. In September 2008, the U.S. government took over the management of Fannie Mae and Freddie Mac, which eliminated any concerns about default risk of the debt securities issued by these agencies.

Corporate Bonds

corporate bonds
Long-term debt securities issued by large firms.

Corporate bonds are long-term debt securities issued by large firms. The repayment of debt by corporations is not backed by the federal government, so corporate bonds are subject to default risk. At one extreme, bonds issued by corporations such as Coca-Cola and IBM have very low default risk because of the companies' proven ability to generate sufficient cash flows for many years. At the other extreme, bonds issued by smaller, less-stable corporations are subject to a higher degree of default risk. These bonds are referred to as **high-yield bonds** or **junk bonds**. Many investors are willing to invest in junk bonds because they offer a relatively high rate of return. However, they are more likely to default than other bonds, especially if economic conditions are poor.

high-yield (junk) bonds
Bonds issued by smaller, less-stable corporations that are subject to a higher degree of default risk.

Corporate Bond Quotations Corporate bond quotations are provided in financial newspapers, including *The Wall Street Journal*, and online at numerous financial Web sites. The quotations typically include the following information:

- Coupon rate
- Maturity
- Current yield
- Volume
- Closing price
- Net change in price from the previous trading day

To illustrate how the bond quotation information can be used, review the information disclosed for Zugle Company in Exhibit 16.1. The bonds pay an annual coupon rate of 5.00%, which reflects a payment of $50.00 per $1,000 par of value. The maturity date of these bonds is December 1, 2018. The last price at which these bonds were traded on the previous day was 100.00, which means that the bonds are selling at par value. The yield (5.00%) represents the yield that will be earned by investors who purchase the bond at the latest price and hold it until maturity. The estimated trading volume of the bonds is $4,000,000.

Return from Investing in Bonds

If you purchase a bond and hold it until maturity, you will earn the yield to maturity specified when you purchased the bond. However, as mentioned earlier, many investors sell bonds in the secondary market before they reach maturity. Because a bond's price changes over time, your return from investing in a bond is dependent on the price at the time you sell it.

Impact of Interest Rate Movements on Bond Returns

Your return from investing in a bond can be highly influenced by the interest rate movements over the period you hold the bond. To illustrate, suppose that you purchase a bond at par value that has a coupon rate of 6%. After one year, you decide to sell the bond. At this time, new bonds being sold at par value are offering a coupon rate of 8%. Because investors can purchase a new bond that offers coupon payments of 8%, they will not be willing to buy your bond unless you sell it to them for less than par value. In other words, you must offer a discount on the price to compensate for the bond's lower coupon rate.

If interest rates had declined over the year rather than increased, you would see the opposite effects. You could sell your bond for a premium above par value because the coupon rate of your bond would be higher than the coupon rate offered on newly issued bonds. Thus, interest rate movements and bond prices are inversely related. Your return from investing in bonds will be more favorable if interest rates decline over the period you hold the bonds.

Analysis of Interest Rates

Application:

The Fed app (by the Federal Reserve Bank of Chicago) provides information about the Federal Reserve's monetary policy actions, which can affect interest rates and bond values.

To Find it:

Search for the "Federal Reserve Bank" app on your mobile device.

Tax Implications of Investing in Bonds

When determining the return from investing in a bond, you need to account for tax effects. The interest income that you receive from a bond is taxed as ordinary income for federal income tax purposes (except for tax-exempt bonds, as explained earlier). Selling bonds in the secondary market at a higher price than the price you originally paid for them results in a capital gain. The capital gain (or loss) is the difference between the price at which you sell the bond and the initial price that you paid for it. Recall from Chapter 4 that a capital gain from an asset held one year or less is a short-term capital gain and is taxed as ordinary income. A capital gain from an asset held for more than one year is subject to a long-term capital gains tax.

EXAMPLE

You purchase 10 newly issued bonds for $9,700. The bonds have a total par value of $10,000 and a maturity of 10 years. The bonds pay a coupon rate of 8%, or $800 (.08 × $10,000) per year. The coupon payments are made every six months, so each payment is $400. Exhibit 16.2 shows your return and the tax implications for four different scenarios. Notice how taxes incurred from investments in bonds are dependent on the change in the bond price over time and the length of time the bonds are held.

Valuing a Bond

Before investing in a bond, you may wish to determine its value using time value of money analysis. A bond's value is determined as the present value of the future cash flows to be received by the investor, which are the periodic coupon payments and the principal payment at maturity. The present value of a bond can be computed by discounting the future cash flows (coupon payments and principal payment) to be received from the bond. The discount rate used to discount the cash flows should reflect your required rate of return.

EXHIBIT 16.2 Potential Tax Implications from Investing in Bonds

Scenario	Implication
1. You sell the bonds after eight months at a price of $9,800.	You receive one $400 coupon payment six months after buying the bond, which is taxed at your ordinary income tax rate. You also earn a short-term capital gain of $100, which is taxed at your ordinary income tax rate.
2. You sell the bonds after two years at a price of $10,200.	You receive coupon payments (taxed at your ordinary income tax rate) of $800 in the first year and in the second year. You also earn a long-term capital gain of $500 in the second year, which is subject to the long-term capital gains tax for that year.
3. You sell the bonds after two years at a price of $9,500.	You receive coupon payments (taxed at your ordinary income tax rate) of $800 in the first year and in the second year. You also incur a long-term capital loss of $200 in the second year.
4. You hold the bonds until maturity.	You receive coupon payments (taxed at your ordinary income tax rate) each year over the 10-year life of the bond. You also receive the bond's principal of $10,000 at the end of the 10-year period. This reflects a long-term capital gain of $300, which is subject to the long-term capital gains tax for that year.

Financial Planning ONLINE

Go to:
The markets section of http://www.bloomberg.com

To get:
A summary of recent financial news related to the bond market, which you may want to consider before selling or buying bonds.

Thus, the value of a bond consists of the present value of the future coupon payments, along with the present value of the principal payment. If you pay the price that is obtained by this valuation approach and hold the bond to maturity, you will earn the return that you require.

The market price of any bond is based on investors' required rate of return, which is influenced by the interest rates available on alternative investments at the time. If bond investors require a rate of return of 8% as Victor does in the following example, the bond will be priced in the bond market at the value he has derived. However, if the bond market participants use a different required rate of return, the market price of the bond will be different. For example, if most investors require a 9% return on this bond, the bond will have a market price below the value derived by Victor (conduct your own valuation using a 9% discount rate to verify this).

EXAMPLE

Victor is planning to purchase a bond that has seven years remaining until maturity, a par value of $1,000, and a coupon rate of 6% (let's assume the coupon payments are paid once annually at the end of the year). He is willing to purchase this bond only if he can earn a return of 8% because he knows that he can earn 8% on alternative bonds.

The first step in valuing a bond is to identify the coupon payments, principal payment, and required rate of return:

- Future cash flows:
  Coupon payment (C) = .06 × $1,000 = $60
  Principal payment ($Prin$) = $1,000
- Discount rate:
  Required rate of return = 8%

The next step is to use this information to discount the future cash flows of the bond with the help of the present value tables in Appendix C:

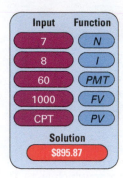

Input	Function
7	N
8	I
60	PMT
1000	FV
CPT	PV

Solution

$895.87

$$\text{Value of Bond} = \text{Present Value of Coupon Payments} + \text{Present Value of Principal}$$

$$= [C \times (PVIFA, 8\%, 7 \text{ yrs})] + [Prin \times (PVIF, 8\%, 7 \text{ yrs})]$$

$$= [\$60 \times 5.2064] + [\$1,000 \times .5835]$$

$$= \$312.38 + \$583.50$$

$$= \$895.88$$

Note that slight differences from using the tables in the appendix occur because those numbers are rounded.

When using a financial calculator to determine the value of the bond, the future value will be $1,000 because this is the amount the bondholder will receive at maturity.

Based on this analysis, Victor is willing to pay $895.88 for this bond, which will provide the annualized return of 8%. If he can obtain the bond for a lower price, his return will exceed 8%. If the price exceeds $895.88, his return will be less than 8%, so he will choose not to buy the bond.

Risk from Investing in Bonds

Bond investors are exposed to the risk that the bonds may not provide the expected return. The main sources of risk are default risk, call risk, and interest rate risk.

Default Risk

If the issuer of the bond (a local government or a firm) defaults on its payments, investors do not receive all the coupon payments that they are owed and will not receive the principal. Investors will invest in a risky bond only if it offers a higher yield than other bonds to compensate for the risk. The extra yield required by investors to compensate for default risk is referred to as a **risk premium**. Treasury bonds do not contain a risk premium because they are free from **default risk**. This means that the return on a risky bond to an investor will be higher than the return on bonds with less risk.

Many investors purposely invest in the riskier bonds because of the higher return offered on these bonds. They avoid investing in the safer bonds such as Treasury bonds because the return is relatively low. They like the thrill of the gamble when investing in risky bonds—and when these bonds perform well. However, if these bonds default, investors could lose most or all of their investment.

risk premium
The extra yield required by investors to compensate for the risk of default.

default risk
Risk that the borrower of funds will not repay the creditors.

Use of Risk Ratings to Measure the Default Risk Investors can use ratings (provided by agencies such as Moody's Investors Service or Standard & Poor's) to assess the risk of corporate bonds. The ratings reflect the likelihood that the issuers will repay their debt over time. The ratings are classified as shown in Exhibit 16.3. Investors can select the corporate bonds that fit their degree of risk tolerance by weighing the higher potential return against the higher default risk of lower-grade debt securities. The lower (weaker) the risk rating, the higher the risk premium offered on a bond. Ratings are commonly lowered during weak economic conditions, because risky bonds are more susceptible to default under these economic conditions. Some investors shift to investing in Treasury bonds when the economy weakens because they become more concerned that other types of bonds may default.

The Financial Crisis and Default Risk During the financial crisis in 2008–2009, many firms experienced financial problems and were unable to make payments on their bonds. Investors who purchased these bonds lost most or all of their investments. When the investors purchased these bonds, they probably viewed the bonds as a good investment because they offered a higher rate of return than Treasury bonds. However, these investors did not anticipate the financial crisis.

EXHIBIT 16.3   Bond Rating Classes

Risk Class	Standard & Poor's	Moody's
Highest quality (least risk)	AAA	Aaa
High quality	AA	Aa
High-medium quality	A	A
Medium quality	BBB	Baa
Medium-low quality	BB	Ba
Low quality	B	B
Poor quality	CCC	Caa
Very poor quality	CC	Ca
Lowest quality	DDD	C

ECONOMIC IMPACT

During the financial crisis, some investors alleged that the ratings agencies had misled investors by assigning high ratings to risky securities. In a number of cases, the ratings did not truly reflect the default risk. A problem with the rating system is that the ratings agencies are paid by the companies that issue the securities. Because bonds with lower ratings must pay higher interest rates to attract investors, issuers want their bonds to have high ratings. If a ratings agency assigns a low rating, the issuing company may take its future business to another agency. Legislation enacted after the crisis tried to address this problem, and, in 2014, the Securities and Exchange Commission issued new rules to try to prevent the conflict of interest that exists at the ratings agencies. Under the new rules, the ratings agencies' methods are to be more transparent, and the ratings part of their business is to be strictly separated from sales and marketing. If analysts at a ratings agency leave to work for a company they rated, all their ratings of that company's securities will be reviewed.

EXAMPLE

Stephanie Spratt reviews today's bond yields as quoted in financial newspapers for bonds with a 10-year maturity, as shown in the second column:

Type of Bond	Bond Yield Offered	Risk Premium Contained Within Bond Yield
Treasury bonds	5.0%	0.0%
AAA-rated corporate bonds	5.5	0.5
A-rated corporate bonds	5.8	0.8
BB-rated corporate bonds	6.8	1.8
CCC-rated corporate bonds	7.5	2.5

Based on the bond yields, she derives the risk premium for each type of bond, shown in the third column. Notice that because the Treasury bonds are risk-free, they have no risk premium. However, the other bonds have a risk premium, which is the amount by which their annualized yield exceeds the Treasury bond yield. Although the other bonds are appealing because they offer a higher yield than the Treasury bonds, they could default, causing investors to lose all of their investment.

Stephanie decides that she prefers Treasury bonds or AAA-rated bonds to other types of bonds because she believes the risk premium is not enough compensation for the risk. However, at this time she cannot afford to buy any type of bond.

Call Risk

Bonds with a call feature are subject to **call risk** (also called **prepayment risk**), which is the risk that the bond will be called. If issuers of callable bonds choose to redeem these bonds under certain conditions, the bondholders must sell them back to the issuer.

> **EXAMPLE**
>
> Two years ago, Christine Ramirez purchased 10-year bonds that offered a yield to maturity of 7%. She planned to hold the bonds until maturity. Recently, interest rates declined and the issuer called the bonds. Christine could use the proceeds to buy other bonds, but the yield to maturity offered on new bonds is lower because interest rates have declined. The return that Christine will earn from investing in new bonds is likely to be less than the return that she would have earned if she could have retained the 10-year bonds until maturity.

Interest Rate Risk

All bonds are subject to **interest rate risk,** which is the risk that the bond's price will decline in response to an increase in interest rates. A bond is valued as the present value of its future expected cash flows. Most bonds pay fixed coupon payments. If interest rates rise, investors will require a higher return on a bond. Consequently, the discount rate applied to value the bond is increased, and the market price of the bond will decline.

> **EXAMPLE**
>
> Three months ago, Rob Suerth paid $10,000 for a 20-year Treasury bond that has a par value of $10,000 and a 5% coupon rate. Since then, interest rates have increased. New 20-year Treasury bonds with a par value of $10,000 are priced at $10,000 and offer a coupon rate of 7%. Thus, Rob would earn 2 percentage points more in coupon payments from a new bond than from the bond he purchased three months ago.
>
> He decides to sell his Treasury bond and use the proceeds to invest in the new bonds. He quickly learns that no one in the secondary market is willing to purchase his bond for the price he paid. These investors avoid his bond for the same reason that he wants to sell it; they would prefer to earn 7% on the new bonds rather than earn 5% on his bond. The only way that Rob can sell his bond is by lowering the price to compensate for the bond's lower coupon rate (compared to new bonds).

Impact of a Bond's Maturity on its Interest Rate Risk Bonds with longer terms to maturity are more sensitive to interest rate movements than bonds with short terms remaining until they mature. To understand why, consider two bonds. Each has a par value of $1,000 and offers a 7% coupon rate, but one bond has 20 years remaining until maturity, whereas the other has only one year remaining. If market interest rates suddenly decline from 7% to 5%, which bond would you prefer to own? The bond with 20 years to maturity becomes very attractive because you could receive coupon payments reflecting a 7% return for the next 20 years. Conversely, the bond with one year remaining until maturity will provide the 7% payment only over the next year. Although the market price of both bonds increases in response to the decline in interest rates, it increases more for the bond with the longer term to maturity.

Now assume that, instead of declining, interest rates have risen from their initial level of 7% to 9%. Which bond would you prefer? Each bond provides a 7% coupon rate, which is less than the prevailing interest rate. The bond with one year to maturity will mature soon, however, so you can reinvest the proceeds at the higher interest rates at that time (assuming the rates are still high). Conversely, you are stuck with the other bond for 20 more years. Although neither bond would be very desirable under these conditions, the bond with the longer term to maturity is less desirable. Therefore, its price in the secondary market will decline more than the price of the bond with a short term to maturity.

Bond Investment Strategies

Most bond investment strategies involve investing in a diversified portfolio of bonds rather than in one bond. Diversification reduces your exposure to possible default by a single issuer. If you cannot afford to invest in a diversified portfolio of bonds, you may consider investing in a bond mutual fund with a small minimum investment (such as $1,000). Additional information on bond mutual funds is provided in Chapter 17. Whether you focus on individual bonds or bond mutual funds, the bond investment strategies summarized here apply.

Interest Rate Strategy

interest rate strategy
Selecting bonds for investment based on interest rate expectations.

With an **interest rate strategy**, you select bonds based on interest rate expectations. When you expect interest rates to decline, you invest heavily in long-term bonds whose prices will increase the most if interest rates fall. Conversely, when you expect interest rates to increase, you shift most of your money to bonds with short terms to maturity to minimize the adverse impact of the higher interest rates.

Investors who use the interest rate strategy may experience poor performance if their guesses about the future direction of interest rate movements are incorrect. In addition, this strategy requires frequent trading to capitalize on shifts in expectations of interest rates. Some investors who follow this strategy frequently sell their entire portfolio of bonds so that they can shift to bonds with different maturities in response to shifts in interest rate expectations. The frequent trading results in high transaction costs (in the form of commissions to brokerage firms). In addition, the high turnover of bonds may generate more short-term capital gains, which are taxed at the ordinary federal income tax rate. This rate is higher for most investors than the tax on long-term capital gains.

Passive Strategy

passive strategy
Investing in a diversified portfolio of bonds that are held for a long period of time.

With a **passive strategy**, you invest in a diversified portfolio of bonds that are held for a long period of time. The portfolio is simply intended to generate periodic interest income in the form of coupon payments. The passive strategy is especially valuable for investors who want to generate stable interest income over time and do not want to incur costs associated with frequent trading.

A passive strategy does not have to focus on very safe bonds that offer low returns; it may reflect a portfolio of bonds with diversified risk levels. The diversification is intended to reduce the exposure to default from a single issuer of bonds. To reduce exposure to interest rate risk, a portfolio may even attempt to diversify across a wide range of bond maturities.

One disadvantage of this strategy is that it does not capitalize on expectations of interest rate movements. Investors who use a passive strategy, however, are more comfortable matching general bond market movements than trying to beat the bond market and possibly failing.

Maturity Matching Strategy

maturity matching strategy
Investing in bonds that will generate payments to match future expenses.

The **maturity matching strategy** involves selecting bonds that will generate payments to match future expenses. For example, parents of an 8-year-old child may consider investing in a 10-year bond so that the principal can be used to pay for the child's college education.

Alternatively, they may invest in a bond portfolio just before retirement so that they will receive annual income (coupon payments) to cover periodic expenses after retirement. The matching strategy is conservative, in that it is simply intended to cover future expenses, rather than to beat the bond market in general.

How Investing in Bonds Fits Within Your Financial Plan

The following are the key decisions about bonds that should be included within your financial plan:

- Should you consider buying bonds?
- What strategy should you use for investing in bonds?

Exhibit 16.4 provides an example of how bond decisions apply to Stephanie Spratt's financial plan. Stephanie's first concern is maintaining adequate liquidity and making her existing loan payments. She is not in a position to buy bonds right now, but will consider bonds once her financial position improves.

EXHIBIT 16.4 How Bonds Fit Within Stephanie Spratt's Financial Plan

GOALS FOR INVESTING IN BONDS

1. Determine if I could benefit from investing in bonds.
2. If I decide to invest in bonds, determine what strategy to use to invest in bonds.

ANALYSIS

Strategy to Invest in Bonds	Opinion
Interest rate strategy	I cannot forecast the direction of interest rates (even experts are commonly wrong on their interest rate forecasts), so this strategy could backfire. This strategy would also complicate my tax return.
Passive strategy	May be appropriate for me in many situations, and the low transaction costs are appealing.
Maturity matching strategy	Not applicable to my situation, since I am not trying to match coupon payments to future expenses.

DECISIONS

Decision on Whether to Invest in Bonds:

I cannot afford to buy bonds right now, but I will consider purchasing them in the future when my financial position improves. Bonds can generate a decent return, and some bonds are free from default risk. I find Treasury or AAA-rated bonds to be most attractive.

Decision on the Strategy to Use for Investing in Bonds:

I am not attempting to match coupon payments with future anticipated expenses. I may consider expected interest rate movements according to financial experts when I decide which bond fund to invest in, but I will not shift in and out of bond funds frequently to capitalize on expected interest rate movements. I will likely use a passive strategy of investing in bonds and will retain bond investments for a long period of time.

DISCUSSION QUESTIONS

1. How would Stephanie's bond investing decisions be different if she were a single mother of two children?

2. How would Stephanie's bond investing decisions be affected if she were 35 years old? If she were 50 years old?

SUMMARY

Background on Bonds. Bonds are issued to borrow long-term funds. Issuers are obligated to make interest (or coupon) payments and to pay the par value at maturity. You should consider investing in bonds rather than stock if you wish to receive periodic income from your investments.

Types of Bonds. The common issuers are the U.S. Treasury, municipalities, federal government agencies and government-sponsored entities (GSEs), and corporations.

Yield on Bonds. A bond's yield to maturity is the annualized return that is earned by an investor who holds the bond until maturity. This yield is composed of interest (coupon) payments and the difference between the principal value and the price at which the bond was originally purchased.

Bond Valuation. A bond's value is determined as the present value of the future cash flows to be received by investors. The future cash flows represent periodic coupon payments and the principal payment at maturity. The discount rate at which the cash flows are discounted reflects the required rate of return by investors.

Risk of Bonds. Bonds can be exposed to default risk, which reflects the possibility that the issuer will default on the bond payments. Some bonds are exposed to call risk, or the risk that the bond will be called before maturity. Bonds are also subject to interest rate risk, or the risk of a decline in price in response to rising interest rates.

Bond Investment Strategies. A popular bond investment strategy is the interest rate strategy, in which bonds are selected based on the expectation of future interest rates. An alternative strategy is a passive strategy, in which a diversified portfolio of bonds is maintained. A third bond strategy is the maturity matching strategy, in which the investor selects bonds that will mature on future dates when funds will be needed.

How Investing in Bonds Fits Within Your Financial Plan. Investing in bonds can generate periodic income and therefore can help support your future spending or saving. In this way, investing in bonds can allow you to achieve your financial plan.

REVIEW QUESTIONS

All Review Questions are available in MyFinanceLab at http://www.myfinancelab.com.

1. **Bond Characteristics.** What is a bond? What is a bond's par value? What are coupon payments, and how often are they normally paid? What happens when investors buy a bond below par value? When should you consider investing in bonds?

2. **Call Feature.** What is a call feature on a bond? How will a call feature affect investor interest in purchasing the bond?

3. **Convertible Bond.** What is a convertible bond? How does a bond's convertibility feature affect its return?

4. **Yield to Maturity.** What is a bond's yield to maturity? How does the price paid for a bond affect its yield to maturity?

5. **Secondary Market.** Discuss how bonds are sold on the secondary market.

6. **Treasury Bonds.** What are Treasury bonds? Describe their key characteristics.

7. **Municipal Bonds.** What are municipal bonds? Why are they issued? Are all municipal bonds free from default risk? What characteristic makes municipal bonds especially attractive to high-income investors?

8. **Federal Agency Bonds.** What are federal agency bonds? Compare and contrast the three most common federal agency bonds.

9. **Corporate Bonds.** What are corporate bonds? Are corporate bonds subject to default risk? What are junk bonds? Why would investors purchase junk bonds?

10. **Corporate Bond Quotations.** List the information provided in corporate bond quotations.

11. **Return on a Bond.** When an investor sells a bond in the secondary market before the bond reaches maturity, what determines the return on the bond? How do interest rate movements affect bond returns in general?

12. **Tax Effects.** Discuss the effect of taxes on bond returns.

13. **Default Risk.** Discuss default risk as it relates to bonds. How may investors use risk ratings? What is the relationship between the risk rating and the risk premium? How do economic conditions affect default risk?

14. **Call Risk.** What is the risk to investors on bonds that have a call feature?

15. **Interest Rate Risk.** What is interest rate risk? How does a rise in interest rates affect a bond's price?

16. **Interest Rate Risk.** How is interest rate risk affected by a bond's maturity? How can investors use expectations of interest rate movements to their advantage?

17. **Interest Rate Strategy.** Describe how the interest rate strategy for bond investment works. What are some of the potential problems with this strategy?

18. **Passive Strategy.** How does the passive strategy for bond investment work? What is the main disadvantage of this strategy?

19. **Maturity Matching.** Describe the maturity matching strategy of investing in bonds. Give an example. Why is this strategy considered conservative?

20. **Bond Value.** How is the value of a bond determined? What information is needed to perform the calculation?

21. **Impact of Weak Economy on Bond Prices.** Explain why prices of risky bonds may decline when economic conditions weaken.

22. **Bond Price Sensitivity to Economic Conditions.** Why are prices of some bonds more sensitive to economic conditions than others?

23. **Federal Agency Bonds and Taxes.** What types of tax incentives are offered by federal agency bonds?

24. **GSE Bonds.** What is a GSE bond? How is interest income from a GSE bond treated for tax purposes?

25. **Junk Bond.** What is a junk bond? Why would an investor buy a junk bond?

26. **Bond Values.** Describe the process of valuing a bond.

27. **Conflict of Interest and Rating Agencies.** Why do bond rating agencies have a possible conflict of interest when issuing bond ratings? What is a possible outcome of this conflict of interest? How have regulators attempted to resolve this issue?

28. **Bonds and Your Financial Plan.** What benefits do bonds provide in an investment portfolio?

FINANCIAL PLANNING PROBLEMS

All Financial Planning Problems are available in MyFinanceLab *at http://www.myfinancelab.com.*

1. **Bond Payments.** Bernie purchased 20 bonds with par values of $1,000 each. The bonds carry a coupon rate of 9% payable semiannually. How much will Bernie receive for his first interest payment?

2. **Annual Interest.** Paul has $10,000 that he wishes to invest in bonds. He can purchase Treasury bonds with a coupon rate of 7% or municipal bonds with a coupon rate of 5.5%. Paul lives in a state with no state income tax and has a marginal tax rate of 25%. Which investment will give Paul the higher annual interest after taxes are considered?

3. **Tax Consequences.** Bonnie paid $9,500 for corporate bonds that have a par value of $10,000 and a coupon rate of 9%, payable annually. Bonnie received her first interest payment after holding the bonds for 11 months and then sold the bonds for $9,700. If Bonnie is in a 35% marginal tax bracket for federal income tax purposes, what are the tax consequences of her ownership and sale of the bonds?

4. **Tax Consequences.** Katie paid $9,400 for a Ginnie Mae bond with a par value of $10,000 and a coupon rate of 6.5%. Two years later, after having

received the annual interest payments on the bond, Katie sold the bond for $9,700. What are her total tax consequences if she is in a 25% marginal tax bracket?

5. **Return on Bonds.** Timothy has an opportunity to buy a $1,000 par value municipal bond with a coupon rate of 7% and a maturity of five years. The bond pays interest annually. If Timothy requires a return of 8%, what should he pay for the bond?

6. **Bond Valuation.** Mia wants to invest in Treasury bonds that have a par value of $20,000 and a coupon rate of 4.5%. The bonds have a 10-year maturity, and Mia requires a 6% return. How much should Mia pay for her bonds, assuming interest is paid annually?

7. **Bond Valuation.** Emma is considering purchasing bonds with a par value of $10,000. The bonds have an annual coupon rate of 8% and six years to maturity. The bonds are priced at $9,550. If Emma requires a 10% return, should she buy these bonds?

8. **Bond Valuation.** Mark has a Treasury bond with a par value of $30,000 and a coupon rate of 6%. The bond has 15 years to maturity. Mark needs to sell the bond and new bonds are currently carrying coupon rates of 8%. At what price should Mark sell the bond?

9. **Bond Valuation.** What if Mark's Treasury bond in the previous problem had a coupon rate of 9% and new bonds still had interest rates of 8%? For what price should Mark sell the bond in this situation?

10. **Risk Premium.** Sandy has a choice between purchasing $5,000 in Treasury bonds paying 7% interest or purchasing $5,000 in BB-rated corporate bonds with a coupon rate of 9.2%. What is the risk premium on the BB-rated corporate bonds?

11. **Ethical Dilemma.** John is a relatively conservative investor. He has recently come into a large inheritance and wishes to invest the money where he can get a good return, but not worry about losing his principal. His broker recommends that he buy 20-year corporate bonds in the country's largest automobile company, United General. His broker assures him that the bonds are secured by the assets of the company and the interest payments are contractually set. The broker explains that although all investments carry some risk, the risk that John will lose his investment with these bonds is minimal.

John buys the bonds and over the next two years enjoys the steady stream of interest payments. During the third year, United General posts the largest quarterly loss in its history. Although the company is far from bankruptcy, the bond rating agencies downgrade the company's bonds to junk status. John is horrified to see the decline in the price of his bonds as he is considering selling a large portion of them to buy a home. When he discusses his dissatisfaction with his broker, the broker points out that John is still receiving his interest payments and if he holds the bonds until maturity he will not sustain a loss. The broker reiterates that in their initial meeting John's concerns were safety of principal and interest payments and the investment still offers both of these.

a. Was the broker being ethical by not informing John of the other risks involved in the purchase of bonds? Why or why not?

b. What could John have done differently with his bond investments if he anticipated buying a home in the next three to five years?

FINANCIAL PLANNING ONLINE EXERCISES

1. Go to http://www.calculatorweb.com and to the Bond Calculator. Describe what this calculator allows you to do.

2. Go to the markets section of http://www.bloomberg.com. You will see information about municipal bond yields for various maturities. The yields observed during the last two trading days are shown along with the percentage change in yields. The yields from a week ago and six months ago are also provided. The equivalent yield on a taxable bond for an investor with a federal marginal tax rate of 28% is shown for comparison, as the interest received on municipal bonds is exempt from federal income taxes. Why are the yields different for the various maturities?

3. Go to the news section of http://www.bloomberg.com. Summarize a recent news event that could have an impact on bond prices.

PSYCHOLOGY OF PERSONAL FINANCE: Buying Risky Bonds

1. Investors expect that the return on a risky bond to an investor will be higher than the return on bonds with less risk. They enjoy the thrill of the gamble of investing in risky bonds and when these bonds perform well. However, investors must understand that risky bonds are more likely to default than safer bonds. Describe your behavior toward buying risky bonds.

2. Read one practical article about how psychology affects decisions when buying bonds on margin. You can easily retrieve possible articles by doing an online search using the terms "psychology" and "buying risky bonds." Summarize the main points of the article.

WEB SEARCH EXERCISE

You can develop your personal finance skills by conducting an Internet search for related articles. Find a recent online article about personal finance that reinforces one or more concepts covered in this chapter. If your class has an online component, your professor may ask you to post your summary of the article there and provide a link to the article so that other students can access it. If your class is live, your professor may ask you to summarize your application of the article in class. Your professor may assign specific students to complete this assignment or may allow any student to do the assignment on a volunteer basis.

For recent online articles related to this chapter, consider using the following search terms (be sure to include the current year as a search term to ensure that the online articles are recent):

- Types of bonds
- Valuing bonds
- Risk of bonds
- Strategies to invest in bonds

VIDEO EXERCISE: Investing in Bonds

Go to one of the Web sites that contain video clips (such as http://www.youtube.com), and review some video clips about investing in bonds. You can use search phrases such as "tips on investing in bonds." Select one video clip on this topic that you would recommend for the other students in your class.

1. Provide the Web link for the video clip.

2. What do you think is the main point of this video clip?

3. How might you change your process of investing in bonds as a result of watching this video clip?

BUILDING YOUR OWN FINANCIAL PLAN

Based on an investor's risk tolerance and/or timeline for goal achievement, bonds may prove to be a useful investment instrument. Referring to the risk tolerance test that you took in Chapter 14 and the goals that you established in Chapter 1, consider the extent to which bonds may play a role in your overall financial planning. Carefully consider whether any of your financial goals can be met with bond investing; revise your goals and personal cash flow statement to reflect any decision you make.

Bonds, like stocks, need to be reviewed as market conditions change, although bonds are far less volatile than stocks and therefore do not require daily monitoring.

Go to the worksheets at the end of this chapter to continue building your financial plan.

THE SAMPSONS—A Continuing Case

The Sampsons are considering investing in bonds as a way of saving for their children's college education. They learn that there are bonds with maturities between 12 and 16 years from now, which is exactly when they need the funds for college expenses. Dave and Sharon notice that some highly rated municipal bonds offer a coupon rate of 2%, while some highly rated corporate bonds offer a coupon rate of 4%. The Sampsons could purchase either type of bond at its par value.

The income from the corporate bonds would be subject to tax at their marginal rate of 25%. The income on the municipal bonds would not be subject to federal income tax. Dave and Sharon are looking to you for advice on whether bonds are a sound investment and, if so, what type of bond they should purchase.

Go to the worksheets at the end of this chapter to continue this case.

CHAPTER 16: BUILDING YOUR OWN FINANCIAL PLAN

YOUR GOALS FOR CHAPTER 16

1. Determine if you could benefit from investing in bonds.

2. If you decide to invest in bonds, determine what strategy to use.

ANALYSIS

1. Briefly summarize your financial goals, and then consider whether any of your financial goals could be met with bond investing. Indicate the bond type (Treasury, corporate, municipal, government agency) and maturity.

Short-Term Goals	Use Bonds (Yes or No)	Type of Bond	Maturity (Years)	Reasoning (Factoring in Risk Exposure)
1.				
2.				
3.				
Intermediate-Term Goals				
1.				
2.				
3.				
Long-Term Goals				
1.				
2.				
3.				

2. Consider the suitability of the following bond investment strategies for your financial situation. Enter your conclusions in the second column.

Strategy to Invest in Bonds	Opinion
1. Interest Rate Strategy	
2. Passive Strategy	
3. Maturity Matching Strategy	

DECISIONS

1. Describe your rationale for investing or not investing in bonds.

   _____
   _____
   _____
   _____
   _____
   _____
   _____
   _____
   _____
   _____
   _____
   _____
   _____
   _____
   _____

2. If you decide to invest in bonds, what strategy will you use?

   _____
   _____
   _____
   _____
   _____
   _____
   _____
   _____
   _____
   _____
   _____
   _____
   _____
   _____

CHAPTER 16: THE SAMPSONS—A Continuing Case

CASE QUESTIONS

1. Should the Sampsons consider investing a portion of their savings in bonds to save for their children's education? Why or why not?

   _____

   _____

   _____

   _____

   _____

   _____

2. If the Sampsons should purchase bonds, what maturities should they consider, keeping in mind their investment goal?

   _____

   _____

   _____

   _____

   _____

   _____

3. If the Sampsons should consider bonds, should they invest in corporate bonds or municipal bonds? Factor into your analysis the return they would receive after tax liabilities, based on the bonds having a $1,000 par value and the Sampsons being in a 25% marginal tax bracket.

   _____

   _____

   _____

   _____

   _____

   _____

After-Tax Rate Computation

Corporate Bond Yield	
Marginal Tax Rate	
After-Tax Rate	
Annual After-Tax Interest ($)	

4. The Sampsons learn that many corporate bonds have recently been downgraded due to question-able financial statements. However, the Sampsons are not concerned because the corporate bond they are considering is highly rated. Explain the possible impact of a downgrade of the corporate bond to the Sampsons, given their financial goals.

_____

_____

_____

_____

_____

_____

_____

_____

_____

_____

_____

_____

Investing in Mutual Funds

chapter 7

Rob bought 200 shares of a mutual fund for $25 per share in late September. By December, his mutual fund shares were priced at $23.50, but he was not terribly disappointed, as this was a long-term investment.

What surprised Rob, however, was the capital gains distribution that he received in December. Although the value of his investment was $300 less than the purchase price,

Goodluz/Shutterstock

the mutual fund distributed $3.95 per share, a total distribution of $790 that Rob must report as taxable income. What Rob failed to realize at the time of his purchase was that the fund he had selected was sitting on accumulated capital gains from stocks that it had purchased in previous years. After five years of good returns, the fund managers had sold some of the stocks within the fund to lock in gains. Rob, as a current shareholder, received his share of the gains. Too late, Rob realized that most mutual funds distribute their gains, as they are required to do by law, near the end of the year. Rob has more to learn about mutual funds and their tax implications.

This chapter explains how to invest in stock mutual funds and bond mutual funds to diversify your investment portfolio. An understanding of mutual funds can help you make proper investment decisions and can enhance your wealth.

MyFinanceLab helps you master the topics in this chapter and study more efficiently. Visit http://www.myfinancelab.com for more details.

The objectives of this chapter are to:

- Provide a background on mutual funds
- Identify types of stock and bond mutual funds
- Explain the return-risk trade-off among mutual funds
- Discuss how to choose among mutual funds
- Describe quotations of mutual funds
- Explain how to diversify among mutual funds
- Explain how investing in mutual funds fits within your financial plan

Background on Mutual Funds

stock mutual funds
Funds that sell shares to individuals and invest the proceeds in stocks.

bond mutual funds
Funds that sell shares to individuals and invest the proceeds in bonds.

Mutual funds can be broadly distinguished according to the securities in which they invest. **Stock mutual funds** sell shares to individuals and invest the proceeds in stocks. **Bond mutual funds** sell shares to individuals and invest the proceeds in bonds. Mutual funds employ portfolio managers who decide what securities to purchase. Therefore, individual investors who invest in mutual funds do not have to select securities themselves. The minimum investment in a mutual fund is usually between $500 and $3,000, depending on the fund. Many mutual funds are subsidiaries of other types of financial institutions.

Mutual funds are popular with investors. In total, U.S. mutual funds have more than $15 trillion in assets. Stock funds account for about 52% of the assets, and bond funds account for about 22%. In recent years, net cash inflows to mutual funds (purchases of mutual fund shares minus redemptions) have exceeded $150 billion per year.

Motives for Investing in Mutual Funds

One motive for investing in mutual funds is that you can invest in a broadly diversified portfolio with a small initial investment. If you have $1,000 to invest, you (along with other investors) can own a portfolio of 100 or more stocks through a mutual fund. If you had attempted to buy stocks directly with your $1,000, however, you might not have enough money to buy even 100 shares of a single stock.

A second motive for investing in mutual funds is the expertise of the portfolio managers. Your investments reflect the decisions of experienced professionals who have access to the best research available.

A third motive for investing in mutual funds is that they can meet specific investment goals. For example, some mutual funds are designed to satisfy investors who desire potential appreciation in their investments, whereas other mutual funds are designed to provide periodic income to investors.

Net Asset Value

net asset value (NAV)
The market value of the securities that a mutual fund has purchased minus any liabilities owed.

Each mutual fund's value can be determined by its **net asset value** (**NAV**), which represents the market value of the securities that it has purchased minus any liabilities owed. For example, suppose that a mutual fund owns 100 different stocks including 10,000 shares of Nike that are currently worth $60 per share. This mutual fund's holdings of Nike are worth $600,000 ($60 × 10,000 shares) as of today. The values of the other 99 stocks owned by the fund are determined in the same manner, and all the values are summed. Then, any liabilities such as expenses owed to the mutual fund's managers are subtracted to determine the NAV.

The NAV is commonly reported on a per-share basis by dividing the NAV by the number of shares in the fund. Each day, the market value of all the mutual fund's assets is determined. Any interest or dividends earned by the fund are added to the market value of the assets, and any expenses (such as mailing, marketing, and portfolio management) that are charged to the fund or any dividends distributed to the fund's shareholders (investors) are deducted. As the value of the mutual fund's portfolio increases or decreases, so does the fund's NAV.

Open-End versus Closed-End Funds

Mutual funds are classified as either open-end funds or closed-end funds.

open-end mutual funds
Funds that sell shares directly to investors and repurchase those shares whenever investors wish to sell them.

Open-End Funds Open-end mutual funds sell shares directly to investors and repurchase those shares whenever investors wish to sell them. The funds are managed by investment companies that are commonly subsidiaries of a larger financial conglomerate. Bank of America, Citigroup, Wells Fargo, and many other financial institutions have investment company subsidiaries that operate open-end mutual funds. Many investment companies operate a **family**, or group, of separately managed open-end mutual funds. For example, Fidelity, T. Rowe Price, and Vanguard manage several different open-end funds, each of which has its own investment objective. By offering a diverse set of mutual funds, these investment companies satisfy investors with many different investment preferences.

family
A group of separately managed open-end mutual funds held by one investment company.

Consider an open-end stock mutual fund that receives $10 million today as new investors purchase shares of the fund. In addition, today some investors who had previously purchased shares decide to sell those shares back to the fund, resulting in $6 million in redemptions. In this example, the stock mutual fund has a net inflow of $4 million of new money that its portfolio managers will invest.

On some days, the value of redemptions may exceed the value of new shares purchased. Mutual fund managers typically maintain a small portion of the fund's portfolio in the form of cash or marketable securities so that they have sufficient liquidity when redemptions exceed new share purchases. Otherwise, they can sell some stocks in their portfolio to obtain the necessary money for redemptions.

closed-end funds
Funds that sell shares to investors but do not repurchase them; instead, fund shares are purchased and sold on stock exchanges.

Closed-End Funds Closed-end funds issue shares to investors when the funds are first created, but they do not repurchase shares from investors. Unlike an open-end fund, shares of a closed-end fund are purchased and sold on stock exchanges. Thus, the fund does not sell new shares on demand to investors and does not allow investors to redeem shares. The market price per share is determined by the demand for shares versus the supply of shares that are being sold, similar to how stocks are priced in the market. The price per share of a closed-end fund can differ from the fund's NAV per share. A closed-end fund's share price may exhibit a **premium** (above the NAV) in some periods and a **discount** (below the NAV) in other periods.

premium
The amount by which a closed-end fund's share price in the secondary market is above the fund's NAV.

discount
The amount by which a closed-end fund's share price in the secondary market is below the fund's NAV.

Load versus No-Load Funds

Open-end mutual funds can be either load funds or no-load funds. **No-load mutual funds** sell directly to investors and do not charge a fee. Conversely, **load mutual funds** charge a fee (or load) when you purchase them. In most cases, the fee goes to stockbrokers or other financial service advisers who execute transactions for investors in load mutual funds. Because no-load funds do not pay a fee to brokers, brokers are less likely to recommend them to investors.

Investors should recognize the impact of loads on their investment performance. In some cases, the difference in loads is the reason one mutual fund outperforms another.

no-load mutual funds
Funds that sell directly to investors and do not charge a fee.

load mutual funds
Funds whose shares are sold by a stockbroker who charges a fee (or load) for the transaction.

EXHIBIT 17.1 Comparison of Returns from a No-Load Fund and a Load Fund

No-Load Fund

Invest $5,000 in the mutual fund	$5,000
Less: Load (fee)	− $0
Amount of funds invested	$5,000
	÷ $20
$5,000/$20 per share = 250 shares	250 shares
End of Year 1: You redeem shares for $22 per share	× $22
Amount received = 250 shares × $22 = $5,500	$5,500
Return = ($5,500 − $5,000)/$5,000 = 10%	10%

Load Fund

Invest $5,000; 4% of $5,000 (or $200) goes to the broker	$5,000
Less: Load (fee)	− $200
The remaining 96% of $5,000 (or $4,800) is used to purchase 240 shares	$4,800 ÷$20
$4,800/$20 per share = 240 shares	240 shares
You redeem shares for $22 per share	× $22
Amount received = 240 shares × $22 = $5,280	$5,280
Return = ($5,280 $5,000)/$5,000 = 5.6%	5.6%

EXAMPLE

You have $5,000 to invest in a stock mutual fund. You have a choice of investing in a no-load fund by sending your investment directly to the fund or purchasing a mutual fund that has a 4% load and has been recommended by a broker. Each fund has a NAV of $20 per share, and their stock portfolios are very similar. You expect each fund's NAV to be $22 at the end of the year, which would represent a 10% return from the prevailing NAV of $20 per share (assuming there are no dividends or capital gain distributions over the year). You plan to sell the mutual fund in one year. If the NAVs change as expected, your return for each fund will be as shown in Exhibit 17.1.

Notice that you would earn a return of 10% on the no-load fund versus 5.6% on the load fund. Although the load fund's portfolio generated a 10% return, your return is less because of the load fee. Based on this analysis, you decide to purchase shares of the no-load fund.

Studies on mutual funds have found that no-load funds perform at least as well as load funds on average, even when not including the fees paid on a load fund. When considering the fee paid on load funds, no-load funds have outperformed load funds, on average.

So why do some investors purchase load funds? They may believe that specific load funds will generate high returns and outperform other no-load funds, even after considering the fee that is charged. Some investors may purchase load funds because they do not realize that there are no-load funds or do not know how to invest in them. To invest in no-load funds, you can submit an application online.

Expense Ratios

As mentioned earlier in this chapter, mutual funds incur expenses, including administrative, legal, and clerical expenses and portfolio management fees. Some mutual funds have much higher expenses than others. These expenses are incurred by the fund's shareholders because the fund's NAV (which is what investors receive when redeeming their shares) accounts for the expenses incurred. Investors should review the annual expenses of any mutual funds in which they invest. In particular, they should focus on the fund's **expense ratio**, which measures the annual expenses per share divided by the NAV of the fund. An expense ratio of 1% means that shareholders incur annual expenses amounting to 1% of the value of the fund. The higher the expense ratio, the lower the return for a given level of portfolio performance. Mutual funds that incur more expenses are worthwhile only if they offer a high enough return to offset the extra expenses.

expense ratio
The annual expenses per share divided by the net asset value of a mutual fund.

On average, mutual funds have an expense ratio of about 1.5%. The expense ratios of mutual funds can be found in various financial newspapers and on many financial Web sites.

Reported Components of Expense Ratios Many mutual funds break their expense ratios into three categories: management, 12b-1 fee, and "other." The management fee represents the fee charged for managing the mutual fund's portfolio and is typically the largest component of the expense ratio. It includes the cost of researching various securities and compensating the employees who manage the mutual fund's portfolio. The 12b-1 fee is charged by some mutual funds to pay brokers who invest in the mutual fund on behalf of customers. A mutual fund may be called "no-load" but still compensate brokers. Some mutual funds have this arrangement with brokers because it enables them to attract more investors. Therefore, the shareholders who invest in the mutual fund incur a higher expense ratio than if the fund did not charge such a fee. The 12b-1 fee can be as high as 1% of assets. The third category of the expense ratio ("other" expenses) includes general business expenses such as mailing and customer service.

Some mutual funds do not include the commissions that they pay brokers within their reported expense ratio. This expense may be 0.5% or more for some mutual funds. Thus, the exclusion of the commissions from the expense ratio is misleading and allows some mutual funds to understate the expenses that are charged to shareholders. Until regulators require clearly standardized reporting by mutual funds, investors must recognize the differences in the reporting process among mutual funds.

Relationship Between Expense Ratios and Performance Research has shown that mutual funds with relatively low expenses tend to outperform other funds with similar objectives. This finding suggests that the mutual funds with higher expenses cannot justify them.

Types of Mutual Funds

Investors can select from a wide array of mutual funds, including stock mutual funds and bond mutual funds. Each category includes many types of funds to suit the preferences of individual investors.

Types of Stock Mutual Funds

Open-end stock mutual funds are commonly classified according to their investment objectives. If you consider investing in a stock mutual fund, you must decide on the type of fund in which you wish to invest. Some of the more common investment objectives are described here.

growth funds
Mutual funds that focus on stocks with potential for above-average growth.

Growth Funds **Growth funds** focus on stocks that have potential for above-average growth.

Capital Appreciation Funds Capital appreciation funds focus on stocks that are expected to grow at a very high rate. These firms tend to pay low or no dividends so that they can reinvest all of their earnings to expand.

Small Capitalization (Small-Cap) Funds Small capitalization (small-cap) funds focus on firms that are relatively small. Small-cap funds and capital appreciation funds overlap somewhat because smaller firms tend to have more potential for growth than larger firms.

Midsize Capitalization (Mid-Cap) Funds Midsize capitalization (mid-cap) funds focus on medium-size firms. These firms tend to be more established than small-cap firms, but may have less growth potential.

Equity Income Funds Equity income funds focus on firms that pay a high level of dividends. These firms tend to exhibit less growth because they use a relatively large portion of their earnings to pay dividends rather than reinvesting earnings for expansion. The firms normally have less potential for high returns and exhibit less risk.

Balanced Growth and Income Funds Balanced growth and income funds contain both growth stocks and stocks that pay high dividends. This type of fund distributes dividends periodically, while offering more potential for an increase in the fund's value than an equity income fund.

Sector Funds Sector funds focus on stocks in a specific industry or sector, such as technology stocks. Investors who expect a specific industry to perform well may invest in a sector fund. Sector funds enable investors with small amounts of funds to invest in a diversified portfolio of stocks within a particular sector.

An example of a sector fund is a **technology fund**, which focuses on stocks of technology-based firms. Most of these firms are relatively young. They have potential for very high returns, but also exhibit a high degree of risk because they do not have a consistent record of strong performance.

Index Funds Index funds are mutual funds that attempt to mirror the movements of an existing stock index. Investors who buy shares in an index fund should earn returns similar to what they would receive if they actually invested in the index. For example, Vanguard offers a mutual fund containing a set of stocks that moves in the same manner as the S&P 500 index. It may not contain every stock in the index, but it is still able to mimic the index's movement.

Other index funds mimic broader indexes such as the Wilshire 5000 for investors who want an index that represents the entire stock market. In addition, there are small market capitalization index funds that are intended to mirror movements in the small-cap index. Other index funds mimic foreign stock indexes, such as a European index and a Pacific Basin index. Investors who want to invest in a particular country, but do not want to incur excessive expenses associated with foreign stock exchanges, can invest in an index fund targeted to that country.

Index funds have become very popular because of their performance relative to other mutual funds. They incur lower expenses than a typical mutual fund because they are not actively managed. The index fund does not incur expenses for researching various stocks because it is intended simply to mimic an index. In addition, the fund's portfolio is not frequently revised. Consequently, index funds incur very low transaction costs, which can enhance performance. Some index funds have expense ratios of between 0.20% and 0.30%, which is substantially lower than the expense ratios of most other mutual funds.

In addition to having lower expense ratios, index funds may offer another benefit. Much research has found that the performance of portfolios managed by portfolio managers is frequently lower than the performance of an existing stock index. Thus, investors may be better off investing in an index fund than in an actively managed portfolio. Many investors are choosing index funds. Almost a third of all households that invest in mutual funds own shares in at least one index fund.

Note, however, that some index funds have expense ratios that are 1.25% or higher, even though their portfolio management expenses are low. You should ensure that the expense ratio is low before selecting a fund.

EXAMPLE

You consider investing in either a no-load mutual fund that focuses on growth stocks or an index mutual fund. When not including expenses incurred by the mutual funds, you expect that the growth fund will generate an annual return of 9% versus an annual return of 8% for the index fund. The growth fund has an expense ratio of 1.5%, versus an expense ratio of 0.2% for the index fund. Based on your expectations about the portfolio returns, your returns would be:

	Growth Fund	Index Fund
Fund's portfolio return (before expenses)	9.0%	8.0%
Expense ratio	1.5%	0.2%
Your annual return	7.5%	7.8%

The comparison shows that the index fund can generate a higher return for you than the other fund even if its portfolio return is lower. Based on this analysis, you should invest in the index fund.

international stock funds
Mutual funds that focus on firms that are based outside the United States.

International Stock Funds International stock funds focus on firms that are based outside the United States. Some of these funds focus on firms in a specific country, whereas others focus on a specific region or continent. Funds with a country or regional concentration are attractive to investors who want to invest in a specific country, but prefer to rely on an experienced portfolio manager to select the stocks. The expenses associated with managing a portfolio are higher for international mutual funds than for other mutual funds because monitoring foreign firms from the United States is expensive. In addition, transaction costs from buying and selling stocks of foreign firms are higher. Nevertheless, many international stock funds have expense ratios that are less than 1.8%.

Some mutual funds invest in stocks of both foreign firms and U.S. firms. These are called "global mutual funds" to distinguish them from international mutual funds.

socially responsible stock funds
Mutual funds that screen out firms viewed by some as offensive.

Socially Responsible Stock Funds Socially responsible stock funds focus on firms that have high standards of corporate governance and avoid firms viewed as offensive by some investors. For example, a socially responsible fund likely would not invest in firms that produce cigarettes or guns or fossil fuels. It might invest in a solar energy company or one producing electric cars.

Hybrid Funds In recent years, hybrid funds, which include both stocks and bonds in their portfolios, have become increasingly popular. Many investors like the idea of combining the potential for growth of stocks with the relative stability and income of bonds.

There are several types of hybrid funds. Asset allocation funds (also called balanced funds) have relatively fixed percentages of stocks and bonds in their portfolios. Thus, a fund's portfolio might generally contain about 60% stocks and 40% bonds, and the fund manager would make small adjustments as market conditions change. Another type of hybrid fund is the life-cycle fund (also called an age-based or target-date fund), which has become a popular choice for retirement accounts. In a life-cycle fund, the allocation between stocks and bonds changes automatically as the investor grows older. Thus, the allocation for a young investor would be weighted toward stocks, but, as the investor aged and neared retirement, the allocation would shift toward bonds to provide retirement income.

Other Types of Stock Funds The types of mutual funds described here can be further subdivided, as new fund types have been created to satisfy the preferences of investors. As an example, some growth stock funds have been designed to focus specifically on small firms, whereas others have been created to focus on large firms. Investors who desire large firms that are expected to grow would consider investing in large-cap growth funds. Investors who desire small firms that are expected to grow would consider investing in small-cap growth funds.

Since the financial crisis of 2008–2009, some investors have been attracted by so-called alternative funds, whose investments and strategies differ considerably from those of standard mutual funds. Alternative funds may purchase nontraditional investments such as foreign currencies, gold, or even rare coins, or they may use aggressive strategies such as short selling. Although some alternative funds performed relatively well when the stock market declined dramatically during the financial crisis, these funds can be very risky, and investors should be aware that they could lose much of their investment.

Exchange-Traded Funds as Substitutes for Mutual Funds Exchange-traded funds (ETFs) are designed to mimic particular stock indexes (like index funds), but they are traded on a stock exchange just like closed-end funds, and their share price changes throughout the day. There are ETFs representing many different sector indexes, such as technology and banking. Therefore, ETFs appeal to investors who want to invest in a particular sector but do not have strong opinions about which stocks to purchase within that sector. ETFs also appeal to investors who want to invest in a particular country's stock market, but do not have strong opinions about which stocks to purchase within the stock market. ETFs have a fixed number of shares, like closed-end funds. ETFs differ from most open-end and closed-end funds, however, in that they are not actively managed. Exchange-traded funds have become very popular in recent years because they are an efficient way for investors to invest in a particular stock index. Today, there is more than $1 trillion invested in ETFs, and there are numerous ETFs available.

exchange-traded funds (ETFs)
Funds that are designed to mimic particular stock indexes (like index funds), but they are traded on a stock exchange just like closed-end funds, and their share price changes throughout the day.

FREE APPS for Personal Finance

Monitoring Exchange-Traded Funds

Application:

The Vanguard app (by The Vanguard Group, Inc.) allows you to conduct an analysis of exchange-traded funds.

To Find It:

Search for the "Vanguard" app on your mobile device.

Types of Bond Mutual Funds

Investors can also select a bond fund that satisfies their investment objectives. The more popular types of bond funds are identified here.

Treasury bond funds
Mutual funds that focus on investments in Treasury bonds.

Treasury Bond Funds Treasury bond funds focus on investments in Treasury bonds. Recall that these bonds are backed by the federal government, so they are free from default risk.

Ginnie Mae funds
Mutual funds that invest in bonds issued by the Government National Mortgage Association.

Ginnie Mae Funds Ginnie Mae funds invest in bonds issued by the Government National Mortgage Association. These bonds have a low degree of default risk because they are issued by a government agency.

corporate bond funds
Mutual funds that focus on bonds issued by high-quality firms that tend to have a low degree of default risk.

Corporate Bond Funds Corporate bond funds focus on bonds issued by high-quality firms. Thus, they tend to have a low degree of default risk.

high-yield (junk) bond funds
Mutual funds that focus on relatively risky bonds issued by firms that are subject to default risk.

High-Yield (Junk) Bond Funds High-yield (junk) bond funds focus on relatively risky bonds issued by firms that are subject to default risk. These bond funds tend to offer a higher expected return than corporate bond funds, however, because of the high yields offered to compensate for the high default risk.

municipal bond funds
Mutual funds that invest in municipal bonds.

Municipal Bond Funds Municipal bond funds invest in municipal bonds. Recall from Chapter 16 that the interest income on these bonds is exempt from federal taxes. Consequently, municipal bond funds are attractive to investors in high income tax brackets.

index bond funds
Mutual funds that are intended to mimic the performance of a specified bond index.

Index Bond Funds

Index bond funds are intended to mimic the performance of a specified bond index. For example, Vanguard offers several different bond index funds, including

- A total bond index fund that tracks an aggregate (broad) bond index
- A short-term bond index fund that tracks an index representing bonds with 1 to 5 years to maturity
- An intermediate bond index fund that tracks an index representing bonds with 5 to 10 years to maturity
- A long-term bond fund that tracks an index representing bonds with 15 to 25 years to maturity

international bond funds
Mutual funds that focus on bonds issued by non-U.S. firms or governments.

exchange rate risk
Risk realized when the value of a bond drops because the currency denominating the bond weakens against the dollar.

global bond funds
Mutual funds that invest in foreign bonds as well as U.S. bonds.

International Bond Funds

International bond funds focus on bonds issued by non-U.S. firms or governments. Some international bonds are attractive to U.S. investors because they offer a higher yield than is offered on U.S. bonds. They are subject to **exchange rate risk**—if the currency denominating the foreign bonds weakens against the dollar, the value of the foreign bonds is reduced, and the international bond fund's performance is adversely affected. Also, expenses incurred by international bond funds tend to be higher than those of domestic bond funds because of costly international transactions.

Some bond funds focus on investments within a specific country or region. These funds are attractive to investors who want to invest in a foreign country but do not want to select the bonds themselves. Some bond funds invest in both foreign bonds and U.S. bonds. They are referred to as **global bond funds** to distinguish them from the international bond funds that concentrate solely on non-U.S. bonds.

Like other bond funds, international and global bond funds are exposed to interest rate movements. Foreign bond prices are influenced by the interest rate of the currency denominating the bond in the same way that U.S. bond prices are influenced by U.S. interest rate movements. When the interest rate of the currency denominating the bonds increases, bond prices decline. Conversely, when the interest rate of the currency decreases, prices of bonds denominated in that currency increase.

Maturity Classifications

Each type of bond fund can be segmented further by the range of maturities. For example, some Treasury bond funds are classified as medium term (8–12 years) or long term (13–30 years). Other bond funds are also segmented in this manner.

Return and Risk of a Mutual Fund

Before investing in a mutual fund, set your objectives in terms of expected return and the risk (the degree of uncertainty surrounding the expected return) that you can tolerate.

Return from Investing in a Mutual Fund

You can receive a return on your investment in a mutual fund in three different ways: dividend distributions, capital gain distributions, and capital gains from redeeming your shares.

Dividend Distributions

A mutual fund that receives dividend payments must distribute these dividends to its investors in the same year. Mutual funds normally allow their investors to choose whether to receive dividends in the form of cash payments or as additional shares (which means the dividends are reinvested to buy more shares of the fund). Regardless of the manner by which dividends are distributed, they are taxed just like dividends received from stocks (at a 15% rate for most taxpayers, or a zero rate for individuals with very low income levels, although dividends from some foreign companies in international mutual funds may be taxed as ordinary income).

Capital Gain Distributions A mutual fund that realizes capital gains as a result of selling shares of stocks or bonds must distribute those capital gains to its investors in the same year. As with dividend distributions, mutual funds normally allow investors to choose whether to receive capital gains in the form of cash payments or as additional shares (which means the amount of the capital gains is reinvested to buy more shares of the fund). Distributions of long-term capital gains are taxed at the long-term capital gains rate, whereas short-term capital gains are taxed at the higher ordinary income tax rate.

Given the differences in tax rates for short-term and long-term gains, investors in high tax brackets will normally achieve higher performance by selecting mutual funds that generate long-term capital gains rather than short-term capital gains.

EXAMPLE

You invest in an index fund that has very little turnover and thus produces a small capital gains distribution and a significant amount of tax-favored dividend income for the year. You also invest in a technology mutual fund that attempts to take advantage of short-term price swings in its holdings while producing mostly short-term capital gains, which it distributes to its shareholders. The index fund distributed $200 of long-term capital gains and $800 of dividends, and the tech fund produced $100 of long-term gains and $900 of short-term capital gains. Your marginal tax rate on ordinary income is 28%, and your long-term capital gains tax rate is 15%.

Given this information, the taxes on the distributions are as calculated in Exhibit 17.2. Even though the two funds distributed the same amount to you, your taxes on the index fund distributions are $117 lower. Thus, your after-tax income from that fund is $117 higher than your income from the tech fund, as shown in the exhibit.

As the preceding example illustrates, individuals in higher tax brackets can reduce their tax liability by investing in mutual funds with low short-term capital gain distributions.

Capital Gain from Redeeming Shares You earn a capital gain if you redeem shares of a mutual fund when the share price exceeds the price at which you purchased the shares. For example, if you purchase 200 shares of a stock mutual fund at a price of $25 per share and sell the shares for $30, your capital gain will be:

$$\text{Capital Gain} = (\text{Selling Price per Share} - \text{Purchase Price per Share}) \times \text{Number of Shares}$$
$$= (\$30 - \$25) \times 200$$
$$= \$1,000$$

EXHIBIT 17.2   Potential Tax Implications from Investing in Mutual Funds

	Index Mutual Fund	Technology Mutual Fund
Dividends	$800	$0
ST capital gain	0	900
LT capital gain	200	100
Total income	$1,000	$1,000
Tax on dividends (15%)	$120	$0
Tax on ST capital gains (28%)	0	252
Tax on LT capital gains (15%)	30	15
Total taxes	$150	$267
After-tax income	$850	$733

If you held the shares for more than one year, you have a long-term capital gain. If you held them for one year or less, your gain is subject to your ordinary income tax rate.

Determining your capital gain is more difficult when you have reinvested distributions in the fund because each distribution results in the purchase of more shares at the prevailing price on that day. The capital gain on the shares purchased at the time of the distribution is dependent on the price you paid for them. Returns vary among stock mutual funds in any particular period. Although they are normally affected by general stock market conditions, stock mutual funds' returns can also vary with the specific sector or industry in which the stocks are concentrated. For example, technology stocks performed better than other types of stocks in the late 1990s, so mutual funds focusing on technology stocks performed well during that time. In the 2001–2003 period, stocks as a group did not perform well. Because of the significant rise in price that technology stocks had experienced in the 1990s (resulting more from speculation than from actual increases in earnings), the price declines were even greater than for nontechnology stocks. The same mutual funds whose performance was enhanced in the 1990s by focusing on technology stocks now suffered the greatest decline.

Because the returns are highly dependent on the performance of the sector in which the stock mutual fund is concentrated, be careful when comparing mutual funds. The difference between the performances of two stock mutual funds during a particular period may be attributed to the sector and not to the managers of the funds. Some investors tend to invest in whichever stock mutual fund performed well recently because they presume that the fund has the best portfolio managers. However, if the fund performed well just because its sector performed well, then it would be a mistake to judge the management based on past performance.

Risk from Investing in a Stock Mutual Fund

**ECONOMIC
IMPACT**

Although different types of stock mutual funds experience different performance levels in a given time period, they are all influenced by general stock market conditions. The performance of a stock mutual fund is dependent on the general movements in stock prices. When the stock market is weak, prices of stocks held by a stock fund decrease and the NAV of the fund declines as well. This susceptibility to the stock market is often referred to as **market risk**. Many stock mutual funds experienced losses of 40% or more during the financial crisis in 2008–2009.

market risk
The susceptibility of a
mutual fund's perfor-
mance to general stock
market conditions.

Trade-Off Between Expected Return and Risk of Stock Funds

Some investors are willing to tolerate risk from investing in a stock mutual fund when they expect that the mutual fund may offer a very high return. The trade-off between the expected return and risk of different stock mutual funds is shown in Exhibit 17.3. On the conservative side, a stock index fund that represents a very broad index of stocks will show similar performance to the market in general. Thus, its expected return is somewhat limited, but so is its risk. A growth stock fund offers potential for higher returns than a broad index fund, but it also has more risk (more potential for a large decline in value). A fund that invests only in growth stocks within one sector (such as a technology fund) has potential for a very high return, but it also exhibits high risk. A fund that invests in growth stocks of small firms in a small foreign country has even more potential return and risk.

Risk from Investing in a Bond Mutual Fund

Although different types of bond mutual funds will experience different performance levels in a given time period, they are all influenced by general bond market conditions. The performance of a bond mutual fund is dependent on the general movements in interest rates. When interest rates rise, prices of bonds held by a bond fund decrease, and the

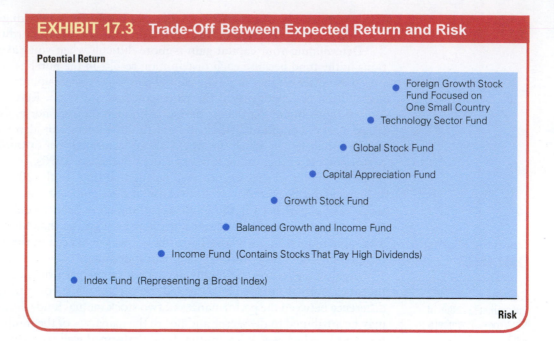

EXHIBIT 17.3   Trade-Off Between Expected Return and Risk

Potential Return

- Foreign Growth Stock Fund Focused on One Small Country
- Technology Sector Fund
- Global Stock Fund
- Capital Appreciation Fund
- Growth Stock Fund
- Balanced Growth and Income Fund
- Income Fund (Contains Stocks That Pay High Dividends)
- Index Fund (Representing a Broad Index)

Risk

interest rate risk
For a bond mutual fund, its susceptibility to interest rate movements.

NAV of the fund declines. This susceptibility to interest rate movements is often referred to as **interest rate risk**.

The prices of all bonds change in response to interest rate movements, but the prices of longer-term bonds are the most sensitive, as discussed in Chapter 16. Thus, investors who want to reduce exposure to interest rate movements can select a bond fund that focuses on bonds with short terms to maturity. Conversely, investors who want to capitalize on an expected decline in interest rate movements can select a bond fund that focuses on long-term bonds.

The performance of many bond mutual funds is also dependent on the default risk of the individual bond holdings. Bond funds that invest most of their money in bonds with a high degree of default risk tend to offer a higher potential return to investors, but they also exhibit a high degree of risk. Under favorable economic conditions, the issuers of those bonds may be able to cover their payments, and these bond funds will consequently perform very well. If economic conditions are weak, however, some of the bond issuers

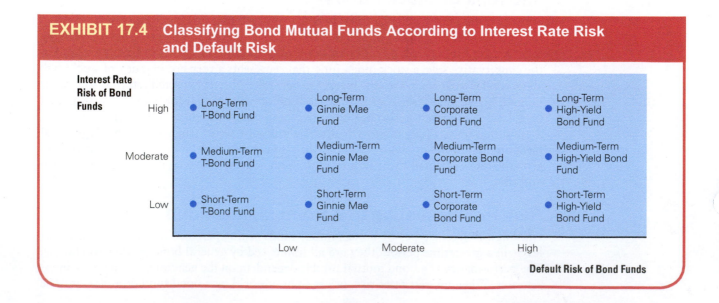

EXHIBIT 17.4   Classifying Bond Mutual Funds According to Interest Rate Risk and Default Risk

Interest Rate Risk of Bond Funds

High	Long-Term T-Bond Fund	Long-Term Ginnie Mae Fund	Long-Term Corporate Bond Fund	Long-Term High-Yield Bond Fund
Moderate	Medium-Term T-Bond Fund	Medium-Term Ginnie Mae Fund	Medium-Term Corporate Bond Fund	Medium-Term High-Yield Bond Fund
Low	Short-Term T-Bond Fund	Short-Term Ginnie Mae Fund	Short-Term Corporate Bond Fund	Short-Term High-Yield Bond Fund

Low   Moderate   High

Default Risk of Bond Funds

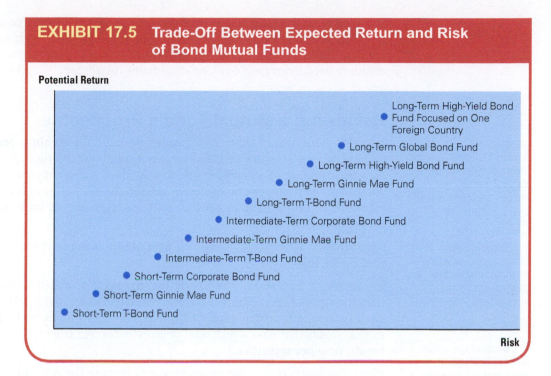

EXHIBIT 17.5   Trade-Off Between Expected Return and Risk of Bond Mutual Funds

may default on their payments, and these bond funds will provide relatively low or even negative returns to their shareholders.

The exposure of a bond fund to default risk is independent of its exposure to interest rate risk, as illustrated in Exhibit 17.4. Some bond funds, such as long-term Treasury bond funds, have no (or a low) default risk and a high level of interest rate risk. Other bond funds, such as short-term high-yield bond funds, have a low level of interest rate risk and a high level of default risk. Some bond funds, such as long-term high-yield bond funds, are highly exposed to both default risk and interest rate risk.

Trade-Off Between Expected Return and Risk of Bond Funds

The trade-off between the expected return and risk of different bond mutual funds is shown in Exhibit 17.5. On the conservative side, a Treasury bond fund that holds Treasury bonds with a short term remaining until maturity has no exposure to default risk and limited exposure to interest rate risk. Thus, the prices of the bonds it holds are not very sensitive to external forces, so the NAV of the fund will not be very sensitive to these forces. The expected return on this fund is relatively low, however. A high-yield bond fund that invests only in junk bonds with long terms to maturity has the potential for a very high return. Its value is subject to default risk, however, because the junk bonds could default. It is also subject to a high level of interest rate risk because of the long-term maturities. A bond fund that invests in bonds issued by risky firms in a small foreign country has even more potential return and risk.

Selecting Among Mutual Funds

Your decision to purchase shares of a specific mutual fund should be made once you determine your investment objectives, evaluate your risk tolerance, and decide which fund characteristics you desire.

Determine whether you are interested in a stock mutual fund or a bond mutual fund. If you want your investment to have high potential for increasing in value over time, you should consider capital appreciation funds. If you want periodic income, you should consider bond funds. If you want some income but also some potential for an increase in value, you might consider a hybrid fund. Some types of funds are segmented according to whether they focus their investment in stocks of large firms (large capitalization), medium-sized firms (mid-cap), or small firms (small-cap).

Reviewing a Mutual Fund's Prospectus

prospectus
A document that provides financial information about a mutual fund, including expenses and past performance.

For any mutual fund that you consider, you should obtain a **prospectus**, which is a document that provides financial information about the fund, including expenses and past performance. You may be able to download the prospectus from the mutual fund company's Web site, or you can order it from the mutual fund company over the phone, by e-mail or online. The prospectus contains considerable information, as described in the following paragraphs.

investment objective
In a prospectus, a brief statement about the general goal of the mutual fund.

Investment Objective The **investment objective** is a brief statement about the general goal of the fund.

investment strategy
In a prospectus, a summary of the types of securities that are purchased by the mutual fund to achieve its objective.

Investment Strategy The **investment strategy** (also called investment policy) summarizes the types of securities that are purchased by the mutual fund to achieve its objective. For example, a fund's investment strategy may be to focus on large stocks, technology stocks, stocks that have a high level of growth, foreign stocks, Treasury bonds, corporate bonds, or other securities.

Past Performance The prospectus will include the return on the fund over recent periods (such as the last year, the last three years, and the last five years). The performance is normally compared to a corresponding stock index (such as the S&P 500) or bond index, which is important because performance should be based on a comparison to general market movements. Although the past performance offers some insight into the ability of the fund's managers to select stocks, it will not necessarily persist in the future.

Fees and Expenses The prospectus will provide a breakdown of the following fees and expenses:

- The maximum load imposed on purchases of the fund's shares.
- The redemption fee or *back-end load* (if any) imposed when investors redeem their shares.
- Expenses incurred by the fund, including management fees resulting from monitoring the fund's portfolio, distribution fees resulting from the fund's advertising costs, and marketing costs that are paid to brokers who recommend the fund to investors. A fund can be classified as a no-load fund and yet still have substantial advertising and marketing fees.

The most important expense statistic mentioned in the prospectus is the expense ratio. Because it adjusts for the size of the fund, you can compare the efficiency of various mutual funds. The expense ratio may also be converted into the actual expenses that you would be charged if you had invested a specified amount in the fund (such as $1,000). The expense ratio may be as low as 0.1% for some funds and more than 4% for others. Expense ratios can change over time, so you should monitor them periodically when investing in a mutual fund.

Risk The prospectus of a stock fund typically states that the fund is subject to market risk or the possibility of a general decline in the stock market, which can cause a decline in the value of the mutual fund. In addition, the prices of individual stocks within the fund may experience substantial declines in response to firm-specific problems. Bond funds normally mention their exposure to interest rate risk and default risk. These risks are stated so that investors understand that there is some uncertainty surrounding the future performance of the mutual fund and that the value of the mutual fund can decline over time.

Financial Planning ONLINE

Go to:
http://www.fidelity.com

To get:
Detailed information about many individual mutual funds that you specify, including past performance and expense ratio. You can also review Web sites of other investment companies that sell mutual funds.

Distribution of Dividends and Capital Gains The prospectus explains how frequently the mutual fund makes distributions to investors. Most funds distribute their dividends to their shareholders quarterly and distribute their capital gains once a year (usually in December). The prospectus also describes the means by which dividends and capital gains are distributed.

Minimum Investment and Minimum Balance The prospectus states the minimum investment that can be made in the fund. In addition, it may require that you maintain a minimum balance, as it is costly for a fund to maintain an account that has a very small balance.

How to Buy or Redeem Shares The prospectus explains how you can invest in the fund. If the mutual fund is part of a family of funds operated by a single investment company, the prospectus explains how you can call the investment company to transfer money from one fund to another within the family. The prospectus also explains how you can sell your shares back to the mutual fund.

FREE APPS
for Personal Finance

Managing Your Investments

Application:

The Personal Capital Money and Investing app (by Personal Capital Corporation) allows you to easily monitor all your mutual fund accounts.

To Find It:

Search for the "Personal Capital Money and Investing" app on your mobile device.

Making the Decision

Once you have narrowed your list to a small number of possible mutual funds, you can create a table to compare the important characteristics. This process will help you select the mutual fund that will best satisfy your preferences.

EXAMPLE

Stephanie Spratt wants to invest $1,000 in a mutual fund that focuses on technology stocks. She also wants to avoid a load fee and to ensure that expenses charged by the mutual fund she selects are low. She creates a list of possible mutual funds that focus on technology stocks and require a minimum investment of $1,000. Using a prospectus for each fund that she downloaded online, she assesses the load fee, expense ratio, and past performance, as shown here:

Mutual Fund	Load Status	Expense Ratio	Recent Annual Performance
#1	No-load	1.5%	8%
#2	No-load	0.8%	7%
#3	No-load	2.0%	8%
#4	3% load	1.7%	7%

Stephanie immediately eliminates #4 because of its load and high expense ratio. She then removes #1 and #3 from consideration because of their high expense ratios. She selects #2 because it is a no-load fund and has a relatively low expense ratio. She does not place much weight on past performance in her assessment.

Stephanie also wants to invest $1,000 in a bond mutual fund. She is considering bond funds that contain AA-rated bonds. She is concerned about interest rate risk because she thinks that interest rates may rise. She creates a list of possible bond funds that allow a very small minimum investment and evaluates information from the prospectuses:

Bond Fund	Load Status	Expense Ratio	Typical Terms to Maturity
#1	4% load	1.0%	6–8 years
#2	No-load	0.9%	15–20 years
#3	No-load	0.8%	5–7 years
#4	No-load	1.2%	5–7 years

Stephanie eliminates #1 because it has a load. She eliminates #2 because it focuses on bonds with long terms to maturity, and that type of bond mutual fund would perform poorly if interest rates rise. She removes #4 from consideration because it has a relatively high expense ratio in comparison with #3. She decides to invest in #3 because it is a no-load fund, it has a low expense ratio, and its bonds have a relatively short term to maturity, which reduces the amount of interest rate risk. She also prefers bond fund #3 because it is in the same family of mutual funds as the stock mutual fund that she just selected. Thus, she will be able to easily transfer money between these two mutual funds.

Quotations of Mutual Funds

Financial newspapers such as *The Wall Street Journal* publish price quotations of open-end mutual funds, as shown in Exhibit 17.6. When an investment company offers several different mutual funds, its name is printed in bold, and the funds are listed below. For example, Blazer Funds (shown in Exhibit 17.6) is the name of an investment company that manages a growth fund and an equity income fund. Each fund's NAV is shown in the second column, the net change in the NAV is shown in the third column, and the return over the year to date (YTD) is shown in the fourth column. For example, Blazer's growth fund has a net asset value of $32.23 per share. The net change in the net asset value during the previous day was $0.15. The fund has generated a return of 8.26% since the new calendar year, and a 22.51% return over the last three years.

Price quotations of closed-end funds are also provided by financial newspapers such as *The Wall Street Journal*. An example is shown in Exhibit 17.7. Quotations of closed-end funds are listed on the exchanges where they are traded. The special listing in some financial newspapers may disclose the dividend of the fund, last-reported price, and the change in the price per share. The premium or discount of the closed-end fund (relative to the price) is not reported. Consider the closed-end fund Zumex Fund, which invests in various stocks. It paid an annual dividend of $2.24 per share. Its last price (at the time its shares were last traded) on the previous day was $29.41 per share. This reflects a gain of $.17 per share over the day. Financial Web sites also provide quotations for mutual funds and closed-end funds.

Financial Planning
ONLINE

Go to:
http://www.vanguard.com

To get:
Research on mutual funds and stocks, and online tools to help investors.

EXHIBIT 17.6   Example of Mutual Fund Price Quotations

	NAV	Net Change	YTD Annual Return	3-Year Return
Blazer Funds				
Growth Fund	32.23	+0.15	8.26%	22.51%
Equity Income Fund	45.10	+0.22	9.78%	26.34%

EXHIBIT 17.7   Example of Closed-End Fund Price Quotations

	DIV	LAST	NET CHG
Zumex Fund ZUX	2.24	29.41	+0.17

In any particular period, some types of mutual funds perform better than others. For example, in some years large stocks perform well, and small stocks perform poorly. In other years, smaller stocks perform better than large stocks. When investors want to assess the performance of a mutual fund, they compare the return on that mutual fund to the average return for that same type of mutual fund. In this way, investors can determine whether their mutual fund was managed effectively. Financial newspapers and financial Web sites commonly provide information about the performance of mutual funds over a recent period, such as the last quarter. The average return can vary substantially among types of mutual funds. In some periods, mutual funds that specialize in a particular type of stock (such as technology stocks or small stocks) perform much better than other mutual funds, primarily because the types of stocks in which they invest performed well. For this reason, many investors commonly switch from one type of mutual fund to another over time, hoping to properly guess the type of stocks that will perform relatively well in any particular period. However, the types of stocks that performed well in the most recent quarter will not necessarily perform well in the next quarter.

There are various information sources that indicate the mean performance level among mutual funds. For example, Lipper indexes indicate the mean return for various types of mutual funds. These indexes are periodically reported in *The Wall Street Journal* and are available on Lipper's Web site. Investors review the Lipper indexes to compare the performance of different types of mutual funds over time.

FREE APPS
for Personal
Finance

Performance of Mutual Funds

Application:

The Morningstar app (by Morningstar, Inc.) provides a performance review of mutual funds, exchange-traded funds, and index funds.

To Find It:

Search for the "Morningstar" app on your mobile device.

Diversification Among Mutual Funds

Financial Planning
ONLINE

Go to:
http://www.mfea.com

To get:
General information about investing in mutual funds.

If you plan to invest in more than one mutual fund, you may want to consider diversifying across several types of mutual funds to achieve a lower level of risk. When a stock mutual fund that contains large stocks is performing poorly, another stock mutual fund that contains small stocks may be performing well. Diversification benefits can be limited, though, because when the stock market declines, the values of most stock mutual funds decline as well. Therefore, diversifying among stock mutual funds that invest in U.S. stocks has only limited effectiveness in reducing risk.

Diversification across bond mutual funds may result in less risk than investing in a bond fund that focuses only on long-term bonds. Virtually all bond funds are adversely affected by an increase in interest rates, however, so diversification among bond funds is not an effective means of reducing exposure to interest rate risk.

A more effective diversification strategy is to diversify across stock and bond mutual funds, as Stephanie Spratt chose to do earlier in the chapter. The returns of stock mutual funds and bond mutual funds are not highly correlated, so diversifying among stock and bond funds can be effective. When U.S. stock market conditions are poor, stock funds focused on U.S. stocks will perform poorly, but the bond funds may still perform well. If U.S. interest rates rise, the bond funds may perform poorly, but the stock funds may still perform well. Another possibility might be to invest in a hybrid fund that combines stocks and bonds in its portfolio.

Impact of the Financial Crisis on Diversification Benefits

ECONOMIC IMPACT

During the financial crisis in 2008–2009, diversification among different types of mutual funds had limited effectiveness. Financial stocks and housing stocks performed very poorly, so diversification into mutual funds that contained other stocks beyond financial and housing stocks reduced the adverse effects of the crisis. However, as the crisis intensified, the entire economy was affected. Most stock mutual funds performed poorly because virtually all types of stocks performed poorly.

Mutual funds that contained Treasury bonds continued to perform well during the financial crisis because Treasury bonds are not subject to default risk. However, bond mutual funds containing bonds that could default performed poorly. The values of these bonds plummeted as investors recognized that these bonds might default due to such weak economic conditions.

International Diversification of Mutual Funds

You may be able to reduce your overall risk further by diversifying among mutual funds that represent different countries. International stock funds tend to be susceptible to the market conditions of the countries (or regions) where the stocks are based and to the exchange rate movements of the currencies denominating those stocks against the dollar. Thus, the returns of international stock funds are less susceptible to U.S. stock market conditions. International bonds are primarily influenced by the interest rates of their respective countries, so they are also less susceptible to U.S. interest rate movements.

Consider a strategy of investing in the portfolio of mutual funds listed in the first column of Exhibit 17.8. The primary factor that affects each mutual fund's return is shown in the second column. Notice that each fund is primarily affected by a different factor, so one adverse condition (such as a weak U.S. market) will have only a limited adverse effect

EXHIBIT 17.8   Variation in the Primary Factor that Affects the Return on Mutual Funds

Your Return from Investing in:	Is Primarily Affected by:
U.S. growth stock fund	U.S. stock market
U.S. corporate bond fund	U.S. interest rates
European stock fund	European stock markets and the value of the euro
Latin American stock fund	Latin American stock markets and the values of Latin American currencies
Australian bond fund	Australian interest rates and the value of the Australian dollar
Canadian bond fund	Canadian interest rates and the value of the Canadian dollar

on your overall portfolio of mutual funds. Any adverse conditions in a single country should affect only a mutual fund focused on that country.

Diversification Through Mutual Fund Supermarkets

mutual fund supermarket
An arrangement offered by some brokerage firms that enables investors to diversify among various mutual funds (from different mutual fund families) and to receive a summary statement for these funds on a consolidated basis.

A **mutual fund supermarket** enables investors to diversify among various mutual funds (from different mutual fund families) and receive summary statement information for these funds on a consolidated basis. Charles Schwab created the first mutual fund supermarket.

You can also achieve consolidated summary statements of all of your mutual funds by selecting all of your funds from a single family. To the extent that you select funds from a fund family that has low expenses and wide offerings (such as Vanguard), you can probably invest in all the types of mutual funds you desire and reduce the expenses that you are indirectly charged.

Other Types of Funds

hedge funds
Limited partnerships that manage portfolios of funds for wealthy individuals and financial institutions.

In addition to mutual funds and closed-end funds, there are other types of funds that pool money of investors and invest it for them. **Hedge funds** sell shares to wealthy individuals and financial institutions and use the proceeds to invest in securities. They require a much larger initial investment (such as $1 million) than mutual funds. Although many hedge funds have performed well, they typically charge high management fees and also are exposed to much risk. They have been subject to minimal regulation, which has allowed some hedge funds to engage in fraudulent activity.

Madoff Fund Scandal Bernard Madoff managed a hedge fund that invested money for many institutions, charities, and wealthy individuals. This fund consistently reported very favorable returns for its investors for many years. However, in 2008, Madoff admitted that his financial reporting was a big lie, and it turned out that the actual return on his fund was much worse than he had reported. Consequently, many investors (including charities) who invested money in his fund lost most of the money that they invested. As a result of this scandal, hedge funds have been subjected to more regulatory oversight by the Securities and Exchange Commission.

PSYCHOLOGY
of Personal Finance

In retrospect, some of the investors who had invested in Madoff's fund should have been suspicious that this fund was continually achieving superior performance, even when many other types of investment funds were struggling. The high performance was simply achieved by fraudulent reporting. Perhaps investors were easily convinced that the reporting was accurate because they were receiving the news that they wanted to receive. That is, investors wanted to believe that the reports were true because they were benefitting from the news.

How Mutual Funds Fit Within Your Financial Plan

The following are the key decisions about mutual funds that should be included within your financial plan:

- Should you consider investing in mutual funds?
- What types of mutual funds should you invest in?

Stephanie Spratt's first concern should be maintaining adequate liquidity and being able to make her existing loan payments. As she accumulates money, however, she plans to invest in mutual funds. Exhibit 17.9 provides an example of how mutual fund decisions apply to Stephanie's financial plan.

EXHIBIT 17.9   How Mutual Funds Fit Within Stephanie Spratt's Financial Plan

GOALS FOR INVESTING IN MUTUAL FUNDS

1. *Determine if and how I could benefit from investing in mutual funds.*
2. *If I decide to invest in mutual funds, determine what types of mutual funds to invest in.*

ANALYSIS

Characteristics of Mutual Funds	Opinion
■ I can invest small amounts over time.	*Necessary for me*
■ Each fund focuses on a specific type of investment (growth stocks versus dividend-paying stocks, etc.).	*Desirable*
■ Mutual fund managers decide how the money should be invested.	*Desirable*
■ Investment is well diversified.	*Desirable*
■ I can withdraw money if I need to.	*Necessary for me*

Type of Stock Mutual Fund	Opinion
Growth	*Some potential for an increase in value.*
Capital appreciation	*Much potential for an increase in value, but may have high risk.*
Equity income	*Provides dividend income, but my objective is appreciation in value.*
Balanced growth and income	*Not as much potential for an increase in value as some other types of funds.*
Sector	*May consider in some periods if I believe one sector will perform well.*
Technology	*Much potential for an increase in value, but may have high risk.*
Index	*U.S. index funds should have less risk than many other types of funds.*
International	*Too risky for me at this time.*

Type of Bond Mutual Fund	Opinion
Treasury	*Low risk, low return.*
Ginnie Mae	*Low risk, low return.*
Corporate bond (AA-rated bonds)	*Moderate risk, moderate return.*
High-yield bond	*Higher risk, higher potential return.*
Municipal bond	*Offers tax advantages, but my tax rate is still relatively low.*
Index bond	*Low risk, low return.*
International bond	*Higher risk, higher potential return.*

DECISIONS

Decision on Whether to Invest in Mutual Funds:

Mutual funds would allow me to invest small amounts of money at a time, and I could rely on the fund managers to make the investment decisions. I will likely invest most of my excess money in mutual funds.

Decision on Which Mutual Funds to Consider:

At this time, I would prefer stock mutual funds that offer greater potential for capital appreciation. In particular, I believe that technology stocks should perform well because the prices of many technology stocks have declined lately and may be bargains. However, I am not confident about selecting any particular technology stocks myself and prefer to rely on a stock mutual fund manager who specializes in these stocks.

I prefer the AA-rated bond funds to the other bond mutual funds at this time because they offer adequate returns, and I think the risk is minimal right now. My financial situation and my preferences may change, so I may switch to other types of mutual funds. I will always select a specific mutual fund that not only achieves my investment objective, but also is a no-load fund and has a relatively low expense ratio.

DISCUSSION QUESTIONS

1. How would Stephanie's mutual fund investing decisions be different if she were a single mother of two children?

2. How would Stephanie's mutual fund investing decisions be affected if she were 35 years old? If she were 50 years old?

SUMMARY

Background on Mutual Funds. Mutual funds can be broadly distinguished according to the securities (stocks or bonds) in which they invest. They allow you to invest in a broadly diversified portfolio with a small initial investment, and investors can rely on managers to manage the fund.

Types of Mutual Funds. The common types of stock mutual funds include growth funds, capital appreciation funds, income funds, sector funds, and index funds. The income funds typically have a lower expected return than the other funds and a lower level of risk. The capital appreciation funds tend to have a higher potential return than the other funds and a higher level of risk.

The common types of bond mutual funds are Treasury bond funds, Ginnie Mae funds, corporate bond funds, high-yield bond funds, municipal bond funds, index bond funds, and international bond funds. Treasury bond funds with short maturities have low potential return and low risk. High-yield bond funds have higher potential return and high risk (because some of their bonds may default). Any bond funds that invest in long-term bonds are subject to a high level of interest rate risk.

Return-Risk Trade-Off in Mutual Funds. Mutual funds provide returns to investors in the form of dividend distributions and capital gain distributions. Some mutual funds have the potential to achieve a high return because they invest in stocks with greater growth potential. However, these funds also could experience large losses because the stocks in which they invest commonly experience losses when economic conditions are weak. Other mutual funds that invest in safer stocks tend to have less potential for very high returns, but also less potential for large losses.

Choosing Among Mutual Funds. When choosing among stock mutual funds, you should select a fund with a required initial investment that you can afford, an investment objective that satisfies your needs, and a relatively low expense ratio. The prospectus of each fund provides information on these characteristics. When choosing among bond mutual funds, you should select a fund with a required initial investment that you can afford, an investment objective that satisfies your needs, and a relatively low expense ratio.

Mutual Fund Quotations. Mutual fund quotations are provided in *The Wall Street Journal* and other business periodicals and are also provided by many financial Web sites. These quotations can be used to review the prevailing prices, net asset values (NAVs), expense ratios, and other characteristics. The quotations can also be used to assess recent performance.

Diversification Among Mutual Funds. When diversifying among mutual funds, recognize that most stock funds are affected by general stock market conditions, whereas most bond funds are affected by bond market (interest rate) conditions. You can achieve more effective diversification by investing across stock and bond mutual funds. You may also consider including international stock and bond funds to achieve a greater degree of diversification.

How Investing in Mutual Funds Fits Within Your Financial Plan. Mutual funds allow you to diversify your investments, even if you have a small amount of money to invest. Thus, they enable you to make investments that offer the potential for high return, while also allowing for diversification to limit your risk. To the extent that mutual funds can help you accumulate wealth to satisfy future spending or retirement goals, they can help you achieve your financial plan.

REVIEW QUESTIONS

All Review Questions are available in MyFinanceLab *at* http://www.myfinancelab.com.

1. **Categories of Mutual Funds.** What are mutual funds? What two broad categories of mutual funds exist, and how are they different? Do investors select the securities the mutual fund invests in?

2. **Investing in Mutual Funds.** List three reasons for investing in mutual funds.

3. **NAV.** What is a mutual fund's net asset value (NAV)? How is the NAV calculated and reported?

4. **Open-End Funds.** What is an open-end mutual fund? What types of companies usually manage open-end funds? Describe how these funds work on a day-to-day basis.

5. **Closed-End Funds.** What is a closed-end fund? Describe how closed-end funds function.

6. **Load Funds.** What is the difference between no-load and load mutual funds? How do loads affect a fund's return? Why do some investors purchase load funds? How does an investor purchase a no-load fund?

7. **Mutual Fund Expenses.** What kinds of expenses do mutual funds incur? How are expense ratios calculated? Why should investors pay attention to expense ratios?

8. **Expense Ratios.** Describe the three components of the expense ratio. How can a no-load fund compensate brokers?

9. **Types of Stock Mutual Funds.** List and briefly describe the different types of stock mutual funds.

10. **Index Funds.** Why do investors invest in index funds? Discuss the popularity of index fund investment as it relates to expenses. What tax advantage do index funds offer relative to other types of mutual funds?

11. **Types of Bond Mutual Funds.** List and briefly describe the types of bond mutual funds.

12. **Bond Fund Expenses.** Why are some U.S. investors attracted to international and global bond funds? What risk is associated with these funds that investors are not subject to when investing strictly in U.S. bond funds? Discuss the expenses associated with international and global bond funds relative to domestic bond funds.

13. **How Mutual Funds Generate Returns.** Describe the three ways a mutual fund can generate returns for investors.

14. **Stock Mutual Fund Performance.** Is a stock mutual fund's past performance necessarily an indicator of future performance? What type of risk affects all stock mutual funds? Describe the trade-off between the expected return and risk of stock funds.

15. **Bond Mutual Fund Risk.** Discuss return and risk as they relate to bond mutual funds. What type of risk are all bond funds subject to? What other risk is associated with some bond funds? Describe the trade-off between risk and the expected return of bond mutual funds.

16. **Investing in Mutual Funds.** What should investors consider when deciding whether to purchase shares of a mutual fund? What characteristics of a mutual fund should be considered? Briefly discuss each characteristic.

17. **Mutual Fund Prospectus.** What is a prospectus? How does an investor obtain one? What information does a prospectus provide?

18. **Closed-End Fund Quotations.** Where can an investor find price quotations for closed-end and open-end funds? What information will be provided in a quotation for open-end funds? What information will be provided in a quotation for closed-end funds?

19. **Lipper Indexes.** Explain how Lipper indexes are used.

20. **Diversification.** Discuss diversification among mutual funds. Describe some strategies that make diversification more effective. What is a mutual fund supermarket?

21. **Exchange-Traded Funds.** What are exchange-traded funds (ETFs)?

22. **Fund Family.** What is a fund family? What are the benefits of using a fund family?

23. **Socially Responsible Stock Funds.** What are socially responsible stock funds? What types of stocks would this type of fund typically avoid owning?

24. **Hybrid Fund.** What is a hybrid fund? What are some of the advantages of hybrid funds?

25. **Life-Cycle Fund.** What is a life-cycle fund? What are the advantages of this type of mutual fund?

26. **Junk Bond Fund.** What is a junk bond fund? What type of investor might be attracted to junk bond funds?

27. **International Bond Funds.** What are international bond funds? What specific type of risk do these funds have that domestic bond funds do not have?

28. **Mutual Funds and Your Financial Plan.** What factors do you need to consider when deciding whether to add mutual fund investing to your financial plan?

FINANCIAL PLANNING PROBLEMS

All Financial Planning Problems are available in MyFinanceLab at http://www.myfinancelab.com.

1. **Amount of Shares Purchased.** Hope invested $9,000 in a mutual fund when the price per share was $30. The fund has a load fee of $300. How many shares did she purchase?

2. **Amount of Shares Purchased.** If Hope (from problem 1) had invested the same amount of money in a no-load fund with the same price per share, how many shares could she have purchased?

3. **Expense Ratio.** Mark owns a mutual fund with a NAV of $45.00 per share and expenses of $1.45 per share. What is the expense ratio for Mark's mutual fund?

4. **Estimating Returns.** Hope (from problem 1) later sells her shares in the mutual fund for $37 per share. What would her return be in problems 1 and 2?

5. **Estimating Returns.** Hunter invested $7,000 in shares of a load mutual fund. The load of the fund is 7%. When Hunter purchased the shares, the NAV per share was $70. A year later, Hunter sold the shares at a NAV of $68 per share. What is Hunter's return from selling his shares in the mutual fund?

6. **Tax Consequences.** Rena purchased 200 shares of a no-load stock mutual fund. During the year she received $3 per share in dividend distributions, $200 in long-term capital gain distributions, and capital gains of $1,100 when she sold the stock after owning it eight months. What are the tax consequences of Rena's ownership of this stock fund? Rena is in a 35% marginal tax bracket.

7. **Tax Consequences.** Ronnie owns 600 shares of a stock mutual fund. This year he received dividend distributions of 60 stock mutual fund shares ($40 per share) and long-term capital gain distributions of 45 stock mutual fund shares (also $40 per share). What are the tax consequences of Ronnie's stock mutual fund ownership if he is in a 25% marginal tax bracket?

8. **Ethical Dilemma.** In the past, some mutual funds often engaged in a practice called "after-hours trading" that allowed some of their larger shareholders to reap profits or avoid losses in a manner not available to all investors. To understand how this practice works, one must remember that mutual fund prices (NAVs) are based on the underlying prices of the securities in which they are invested. Mutual fund prices are established each day at 4 P.M. Eastern Time, when the market closes. For this reason, mutual fund orders to buy or sell must be placed by investors prior to 4 P.M. The after-hours trading practice allowed certain large investors the opportunity to place and execute mutual fund trades after 4 P.M. Thus, if a news release occurred at 5 P.M. that would have a detrimental effect on the stock of a company held by a mutual fund, a large investor could sell the mutual fund shares based on a price prior to the announcement and therefore avoid a potential loss.

   a. Discuss the ethics of this practice.

   b. If you knew about this practice, would it have stopped you from investing in mutual funds? Discuss.

FINANCIAL PLANNING ONLINE EXERCISES

1. Go to the mutual funds section of http://www.fidelity.com.

   a. Select one of the mutual funds offered by Fidelity in which you have an interest and summarize the description provided by Fidelity. Do you think this type of mutual fund has potential for a high return? Why? Do you think this mutual fund is risky? Why?

   b. What is the expense ratio of this mutual fund?

2. Go to the mutual funds section of http://www.bloomberg.com. Briefly describe the type of information that is provided.

3. Go to the mutual funds section of http://www.vanguard.com, under the personal investors section. Describe the type of information provided about mutual funds.

PSYCHOLOGY OF PERSONAL FINANCE: Investing in Mutual Funds

1. Investors are naturally attracted to mutual funds and hedge funds that perform well. However, they should be suspicious when a fund reports that it is continually achieving superior performance, even when many other types of investment funds are struggling. The high performance may be due to fraudulent reporting. Investors want to believe that the reports are true even when they should be suspicious. Describe your behavior when investing. Are you suspicious when a fund suggests that its performance is always better than that of other funds?

2. Read one practical article about how psychology affects decisions when investing in mutual funds. You can easily retrieve possible articles by doing an online search using the terms "psychology" and "investing in mutual funds." Summarize the main points of the article.

WEB SEARCH EXERCISE

You can develop your personal finance skills by conducting an Internet search for related articles. Find a recent online article about personal finance that reinforces one or more concepts covered in this chapter. If your class has an online component, your professor may ask you to post your summary of the article there and provide a link to the article so that other students can access it. If your class is live, your professor may ask you to summarize your application of the article in class. Your professor may assign specific students to complete this assignment or may allow any student to do the assignment on a volunteer basis.

For recent online articles related to this chapter, consider using the following search terms (be sure to include the current year as a search term to ensure that the online articles are recent):

- Open-end mutual funds
- Closed-end mutual funds
- Load mutual funds
- Selecting a stock mutual fund
- Selecting a bond mutual fund
- Risk of mutual fund

VIDEO EXERCISE: Investing in Mutual Funds

Go to one of the Web sites that contain video clips (such as http://www.youtube.com), and review some video clips about investing in mutual funds. You can use search phrases such as "tips on investing in mutual funds." Select one video clip on this topic that you would recommend for the other students in your class.

1. Provide the Web link for the video clip.

2. What do you think is the main point of this video clip?

3. How might you change your process of investing in mutual funds as a result of watching this video clip?

BUILDING YOUR OWN FINANCIAL PLAN

Mutual funds provide a relatively inexpensive investment medium for meeting many financial goals. With a relatively small investment, you can obtain diversification and receive professional management of your portfolio.

There are thousands of individual mutual funds that invest in a wide variety of portfolios ranging from very conservative bond portfolios to very aggressive funds. Fortunately, various Web sites provide information to help you select mutual funds that will best meet your individual financial goals.

In this case, you will explore one of these Web sites and begin the process of selecting some mutual funds that will help you reach the goals you established in Chapter 1.

Go to the worksheets at the end of this chapter to continue building your financial plan.

THE SAMPSONS—A Continuing Case

Over the last month, the Sampsons have been struggling with how to invest their savings to support their children's college education. They previously considered stocks and bonds and are now seriously considering investing their money in mutual funds. They find the prospect of relying on an investment professional's advice without having to pay for one-on-one service from a brokerage firm appealing. They are looking to you for advice on which type of funds would be appropriate and whether they should invest their savings in one mutual fund or in several.

Go to the worksheets at the end of this chapter to continue this case.

CHAPTER 17: BUILDING YOUR OWN FINANCIAL PLAN

YOUR GOALS FOR CHAPTER 17

1. Determine if and how you could benefit from investing in mutual funds.

2. If you decide to invest in mutual funds, choose the best types of funds for your needs.

ANALYSIS

1. Assume that you have $10,000 to invest in stock mutual funds today. Given your financial situation, select one of the following types of mutual funds that would be the most suitable to satisfy your financial goals. Enter your findings in the following table.

Type of Stock Mutual Fund	Suitable Investment Option?	Reasoning
Growth		
Capital Appreciation		
Equity Income		
Balance Growth and Income		
Sector		
Technology		
Index		
International		

2. Assume that you also have $10,000 to invest in bond mutual funds today. Given your financial situation, select one of the following types of bond mutual funds that would be the most suitable to satisfy your financial goals. Enter your findings in the following table.

Type of Bond Mutual Fund	Suitable Investment Option?	Reasoning
Treasury		
Ginnie Mae		
Corporate Bond		
High-Yield Bond		
Municipal Bond		
Index Bond		
International Bond		

DECISIONS

1. What is your decision regarding the ideal type of stock mutual fund to invest in? Explain why you selected that type of stock mutual fund.

_____

_____

_____

_____

_____

_____

_____

_____

_____

_____

_____

_____

2. What is your decision regarding the ideal type of bond mutual fund to invest in? Explain why you selected that type of bond mutual fund.

_____

_____

_____

_____

_____

_____

_____

_____

_____

_____

_____

CHAPTER 17: THE SAMPSONS—A Continuing Case

CASE QUESTIONS

1. Why might mutual funds be more appropriate investments for the Sampsons than individual stocks or bonds?

_____

_____

_____

_____

_____

_____

_____

_____

2. Should the Sampsons invest their savings in mutual funds? Why or why not?

_____

_____

_____

_____

_____

_____

_____

_____

3. What types of mutual funds should the Sampsons consider, given their investment objective?

_____

_____

_____

_____

_____

_____

_____

_____

Asset Allocation

There is an old saying that is good advice for investors: "Do not put all of your eggs in one basket." Consider the case of Nicki and Jack Saizon. The Saizons worked for the same company in the telecommunications field. From that vantage point, they had seen the tremendous rise in telecom stocks in past years. They invested all their savings, which up to that time had been invested conservatively in a

AUKARAWATCYBER/Shutterstock

certificate of deposit, into a telecommunications mutual fund. Hoping that this would be the way to quick wealth, they ignored the advice that they had read regarding diversification of an investment portfolio. The Saizons reasoned that diversification would limit their potential gain. Also, they expected some diversification benefits within the mutual fund they selected.

Within two years, their fund was worth half of their original investment. Nicki and Jack began to appreciate that the benefit of diversification—lower portfolio risk—far outweighed the potential gain they might have made by concentrating their investment in one sector.

Asset allocation is an important strategy for investors. In prior chapters you learned about building your wealth by investing in stocks, bonds, and mutual funds. Now that you are familiar with each of these types of investments, you can determine how to distribute your money among the various types of financial assets. The primary goal of asset allocation is reducing your risk while still achieving an acceptable return on your investment.

MyFinanceLab helps you master the topics in this chapter and study more efficiently. Visit http://www.myfinancelab.com for more details.

The objectives of this chapter are to:

- Explain how diversification among assets can reduce risk
- Describe strategies that can be used to diversify among stocks
- Explain asset allocation strategies
- Identify factors that affect your asset allocation decisions
- Explain how asset allocation fits within your financial plan

How Diversification Reduces Risk

If you knew which investment would provide the highest return for a specific investment period, investment decisions would be easy. You would invest all your money in that particular investment. In the real world, there is a trade-off between risk and return when investing. Although the return on some investments (such as a Treasury security or a bank CD) is known for a specific investment period, these investments offer a relatively low rate of return. Many investments, such as stocks, some types of bonds, and real estate, offer the prospect of high rates of return, but their future return is uncertain. They could offer a return of 20% or more this year, but they could also experience a loss of 20% or even worse.

Benefits of Portfolio Diversification

asset allocation
The process of allocating money across financial assets (such as stocks, bonds, and mutual funds) with the objective of achieving a desired return while maintaining risk at a tolerable level.

Because the returns from many types of investments are uncertain, it is wise to allocate your money across various types of investments so that you are not completely dependent on any one type. **Asset allocation** is the process of allocating money across financial assets (such as stocks, bonds, and mutual funds). The objective of asset allocation is to achieve your desired return on investments while maintaining your risk at a tolerable level.

Building a Portfolio You can reduce your risk by investing in a **portfolio**, which is a set of multiple investments in different assets. For example, your portfolio may consist of various stocks, bonds, and real estate investments. By constructing a portfolio, you diversify across several investments rather than focus on a single investment. Investors who have all their funds invested in stock or bonds of a firm that goes bankrupt typically lose their entire investment. Given the difficulty in anticipating when a particular investment might experience a major decline in its value, you can at least reduce your exposure to any one stock or bond by spreading your investments across several firms' stocks and bonds. A portfolio can reduce risk when its investments do not move in perfect tandem. Even if one investment experiences very poor performance, the other investments may perform well and can offset the adverse effects.

portfolio
A set of multiple investments in different assets.

Determining Portfolio Benefits

To determine a portfolio's diversification benefits, you compare the return on its investments to the overall portfolio.

EXAMPLE

You are considering investing in a portfolio consisting of investments A and B. Exhibit 18.1 illustrates the portfolio diversification effect of using these two stocks. The exhibit shows the return per year for investments A and B, as well as for a portfolio with 50% of the investment allocated to A and 50% to B. The portfolio return in each year is simply the average return of A and B. Notice how the portfolio's range of returns is less than the range of returns of either stock. Also, notice that the portfolio's returns are less volatile over time than the returns of the individual stocks. Because the portfolio return is an average of A and B, it has a smoother trend than either individual investment. The smoother trend demonstrates that investing in the portfolio is less risky than investing in either individual investment. You decide to create a diversified portfolio of both investments to reduce your risk.

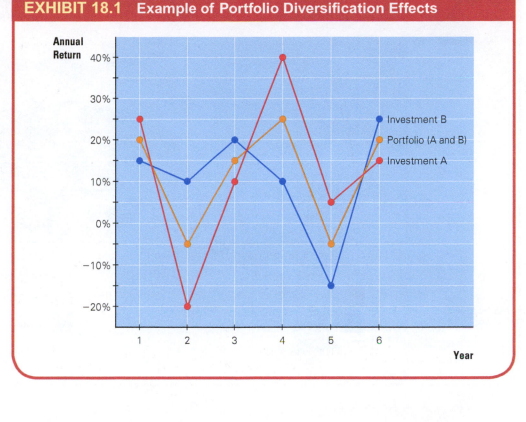

EXHIBIT 18.1   Example of Portfolio Diversification Effects

As the previous example illustrates, the main benefit of diversification is that it reduces the exposure of your investments to the adverse effects of any individual investment. In Exhibit 18.1, notice that when investment A experienced a return of −20% in year 2, the portfolio return was −5%. The adverse effects on the portfolio were limited because B's return was 10% during that year. Investment A's poor performance still affected the portfolio's performance, but less than if it had been the only investment. When B experienced a weak return (such as −15% in year 5), its poor performance was partially offset because A's performance was 5% in that year.

Factors That Influence Diversification Benefits

A portfolio's risk is often measured by its degree of volatility because the more volatile the returns, the more uncertain the future return on the portfolio. Some portfolios are more effective at reducing risk than others. By recognizing the factors that reduce a portfolio's risk, you can ensure that your portfolio exhibits these characteristics. The volatility of a portfolio's returns is influenced by the volatility of returns on each individual investment within the portfolio and by how similar the returns are among investments.

Volatility of Each Individual Investment As Exhibit 18.2 illustrates, the more volatile the returns of individual investments in a portfolio, the more volatile the portfolio's returns are over time (holding other factors constant). The left graph shows the returns of investment A (as in Exhibit 18.1), C, and an equal-weighted portfolio of A and C. The right graph shows the individual returns of investments A and D along with the return of an equal-weighted portfolio of A and D. Comparing the returns of C on the left with the returns of D on the right, it is clear that C is much more volatile. For this reason, the portfolio of A and C (on the left) is more volatile than the portfolio of A and D (on the right).

Impact of Correlations Among Investments The more similar the returns of individual investments in a portfolio, the more volatile the portfolio's returns are over time. This point is illustrated in Exhibit 18.3. The left graph shows the returns of A, E,

EXHIBIT 18.2 **Impact of an Investment's Volatility on Portfolio Diversification Effects**

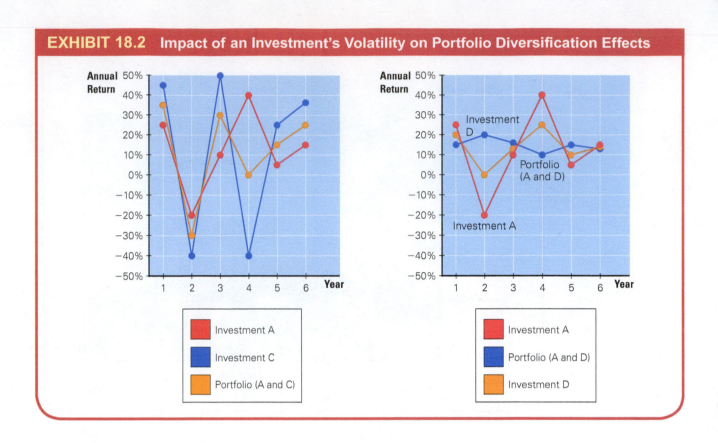

and an equal-weighted portfolio of the two investments. Notice that the investments have very similar return patterns. When investment A performs well, so does E; when A performs poorly, so does E. Consequently, the equal-weighted portfolio of A and E has a return pattern that is almost identical to that of either A or E. Thus, this portfolio exhibits limited diversification benefits.

The middle graph in Exhibit 18.3 shows the returns of A, F, and an equal-weighted portfolio of the two investments. Notice that the return patterns of the investments are opposite to one another. When A performs well, F performs relatively poorly. When A performs poorly, F performs well. The returns of A and F are therefore negatively correlated. As a result, the equal-weighted portfolio of A and F has a very stable return pattern because the returns of the stocks moved in opposite directions. Due to the negative correlation of returns, this portfolio offers substantial diversification benefits.

The right graph in Exhibit 18.3 shows the returns of A, G, and an equal-weighted portfolio of the two investments. Notice that the return patterns of the two stocks are independent of each other. That is, A's performance is not related to G's performance. The return pattern of the equal-weighted portfolio of A and G is more volatile than the returns of the portfolio of A and F (middle graph), but less volatile than the returns of the portfolio of A and E (left graph). Thus, the portfolio of investments A and G exhibits more diversification benefits than a portfolio of two investments that are positively related, but fewer diversification benefits than a portfolio of negatively correlated investments.

This discussion suggests that when you compile a portfolio, you should avoid including investments that exhibit a high positive correlation. Although finding investments that are as negatively correlated as A and F may be difficult, you should at least consider investments whose values are not influenced by the same conditions. In reality, many investments are similarly influenced by economic conditions. If economic conditions deteriorate, most investments perform poorly. Nevertheless, some are influenced to a higher degree than others.

Financial Planning
ONLINE

Go to:
The finance section of Yahoo.com and insert a stock symbol.

To get:
A trend of the stock price. Notice that you can customize the trend to focus on the period in which you are interested.

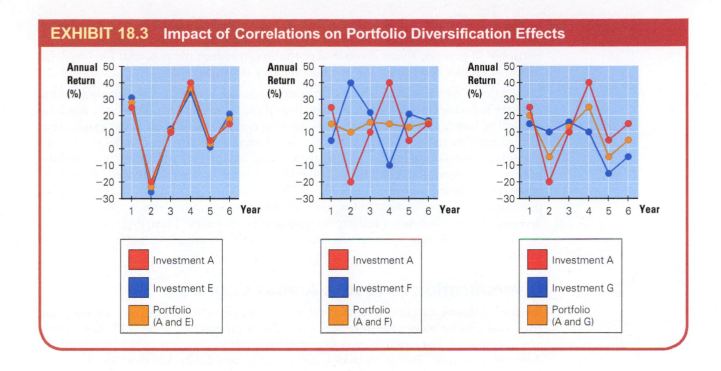

EXHIBIT 18.3   Impact of Correlations on Portfolio Diversification Effects

Monitoring Your Asset Allocation

Application:

The Betterment—Smarter Investing app (by Betterment) allows you to monitor your investment accounts and assess the performance of your investments.

To Find It:

Search for the "Betterment" app on your mobile device.

Strategies for Diversifying

There are many different strategies for diversifying among investments. Some of the more popular strategies related to stocks are described here.

Diversification of Stocks Across Industries

When you diversify your investments among stocks in different industries, you reduce your exposure to one particular industry. For example, you may invest in the stock of a firm in the automobile industry, the stock of a firm in the retail food industry, the stock of a firm in the health care industry, and so on. When economic conditions decline, people may avoid buying new cars, so your automobile stock may perform poorly; however, people still need food and health care, so your food and health care stocks may perform relatively better. Thus, a portfolio of stocks diversified across industries is less risky than a portfolio of stocks that are all based in the same industry.

When adding more stocks to the portfolio, the diversification benefits are even greater because the proportional investment in any stock is smaller. Thus, the portfolio is less exposed to poor performance of any single stock. To illustrate how diversification benefits would be even stronger for a more diversified portfolio, consider the returns from investing in 500 large U.S. stocks (the S&P 500 index), which is shown on many financial Web sites. This trend would be more stable than the trend of returns in a small stock portfolio. In general, a very diversified portfolio can reduce the potential for very large losses, but it can also reduce the potential for very large gains.

Limitations of Industry Diversification   Although diversification among stocks in different industries is more effective than diversification within an industry, the portfolio can still be highly susceptible to general economic conditions. Stocks exhibit market risk, or susceptibility to poor performance because of weak stock market conditions. A stock portfolio composed of stocks of U.S. firms based in different industries may perform poorly when economic conditions in the United States are weak. Indeed, during the weak economic conditions in the 2008–2009 period, there were some months in which the returns of stocks in most industries experienced significant losses, so investors who diversified across industries still experienced significant losses. Thus, diversification will not necessarily prevent losses when economic conditions are poor, but it can limit the losses.

Diversification of Stocks Across Countries

Because economic conditions (and therefore stock market conditions) vary among countries, you may be more able to reduce your risk by diversifying your stock investments across countries. For example, you may wish to invest in a variety of U.S. stocks across different industries, European stocks, Asian stocks, and Latin American stocks. Many investment advisers recommend that you invest about 80% of your money in U.S. stocks and allocate 20% to foreign countries.

Diversifying among stocks based in some countries outside the United States makes you less vulnerable to conditions in the United States. Economic conditions in countries can be interrelated, however. In some periods, all countries may simultaneously experience weak economic conditions, causing stocks in all countries to perform poorly at the same time. When investing in stocks outside the United States, recognize that they are typically even more volatile than U.S.-based stocks, as they are subject to more volatile economic conditions. Therefore, you should diversify among stocks within each foreign country rather than rely on a single stock in any foreign country. It is also important to keep in mind that the returns in stock markets of small developing countries may be very volatile, so an international portfolio may be less risky if it is focused on developed countries that have well-established stock markets with very active trading.

Economic Impact on Global Diversification Benefits

ECONOMIC IMPACT   Economic conditions are somewhat integrated across countries. Therefore, international diversification does not completely insulate investors from a weak local economy. For example, during the financial crisis in 2008–2009, the U.S. stock market experienced very weak performance. However, non-U.S. stock markets also performed poorly because the weak conditions in the United States affected conditions in other countries. Some countries were more adversely affected than others. Those U.S. investors who maintained internationally diversified portfolios of stocks during the credit crisis may have had smaller losses than if their portfolios had consisted entirely of U.S. stocks. However, they still likely experienced losses because most stock markets around the world performed poorly during this period.

Asset Allocation Strategies

When investors make asset allocation decisions, they should not restrict their choices to stocks. All stocks can be affected by general stock market conditions, so diversification benefits are limited. Greater diversification benefits can be achieved by including other financial assets, such as bonds, real estate investment trusts (REITs), and stock options. The size of your portfolio and knowledge level will help determine the financial assets you will include in your portfolio.

Including Bonds in Your Portfolio

The returns from investing in stocks and from investing in bonds are not highly correlated. Stock prices are influenced by each firm's expected future performance and general stock market conditions. Bond prices are inversely related to interest rates and are not directly influenced by stock market conditions. Therefore, by including bonds in your portfolio, you can reduce your susceptibility to stock market conditions. The expected return on bonds is usually less than the return on stocks, however.

As you allocate more of your investment portfolio to bonds, you reduce your exposure to market risk, but increase your exposure to interest rate risk. Your portfolio is more susceptible to a decline in value when interest rates rise because the market values of your bonds will decline. Recall from Chapter 16 that you can limit your exposure to interest rate risk by investing in bonds with relatively short maturities because the prices of those bonds are less affected by interest rate movements than the prices of long-term bonds.

In general, the larger the proportion of your portfolio that is allocated to bonds, the lower your portfolio's overall risk (as measured by the volatility of returns). The portfolio's value will be more stable over time, and it is less likely to generate a loss in any given period. Investors who are close to retirement commonly allocate much of their portfolio to bonds because they are relying on it to provide them with periodic income. Conversely, investors who are 30 to 50 years old tend to focus their allocation on stocks because they can afford to take risks to strive for a high return on their portfolio.

Including Real Estate Investments in Your Portfolio

Many individuals include real estate investments in their portfolio. One method of investing in real estate is to purchase a home and rent it out. Doing this requires a substantial investment of time and money, however. You must conduct credit checks on prospective renters and maintain the property in good condition. An alternative is to invest in **real estate investment trusts (REITs)**, which pool investments from individuals and use the proceeds to invest in real estate. REITs commonly invest in commercial real estate such as office buildings and shopping centers.

real estate investment trusts (REITs)
Trusts that pool investments from individuals and use the proceeds to invest in real estate.

REITs are similar to closed-end funds in that their shares are traded on stock exchanges; the value of the shares is based on the supply of shares for sale (by investors) and investor demand for the shares. REITs are popular among individual investors because the shares can be purchased with a small amount of money. For example, an investor could purchase 100 shares of a REIT priced at $30 per share for a total of $3,000 ($30 × 100 shares). Another desirable characteristic of REITs is that they are managed by skilled real estate professionals who decide what properties to purchase and manage the maintenance of the properties.

equity REITs
REITs that invest money directly in properties.

mortgage REITs
REITs that invest in mortgage loans that help to finance the development of properties.

Types of REITs REITs are classified according to how they invest their money. **Equity REITs** invest money directly in properties, whereas **mortgage REITs** invest in mortgage loans that help to finance the development of properties. The performance of an equity REIT is based on changes in the value of its property over time, so returns are influenced by general real estate conditions. The performance of a mortgage REIT is based on the interest payments it receives from the loans it provided.

Role of REITs in Asset Allocation The values of most REITs tend to be highly influenced by real estate conditions. Although this can be favorable in some periods, it exposes investors to high risk. For example, during the 2008–2009 financial crisis, the real estate market suffered, and most REITs performed poorly. Therefore, individual investors who invest in REITs may want to further diversify their investment portfolios.

When stock market and/or bond market conditions are poor, real estate conditions may still be favorable. Thus, REITs can perform well in a period when stocks or bonds are performing poorly. Consequently, a portfolio that contains stocks, bonds, and REITs may be less susceptible to major declines because it is unlikely that all three types of investments will simultaneously perform poorly.

stock option
An option to purchase or sell stocks under specified conditions.

call option
Provides the right to purchase 100 shares of a specified stock at a specified price by a specified expiration date.

exercise (strike) price
The price at which a stock option is exercised.

premium
The price that you pay when purchasing a stock option.

Including Stock Options in Your Portfolio

When making your asset allocation decisions, you may want to consider **stock options**, which are options to purchase or sell stocks under specified conditions. Like stocks, stock options are traded on exchanges. Some employers include stock options in compensation packages, so you should be aware of them.

Call Options A **call option** on a stock provides the right to purchase 100 shares of a specified stock at a specified price (called the **exercise price** or **strike price**) by a specified expiration date. The advantage of a call option is that it locks in the price you have to pay to purchase the stock and also gives you the flexibility to let the option expire if you wish. The price that you pay when purchasing a call option is referred to as a **premium**. The premium of a call option is influenced by the number of investors who wish to buy call options on that particular stock. Investors can purchase call options through their brokerage firm, which charges a commission for executing the transaction.

EXAMPLE

On September 10, you pay a premium of $2 per share, or $200, to purchase a call option on Gamma stock. The stock price is currently $28. The call option gives you the right to buy 100 shares of Gamma stock at the exercise price of $30 at any time up until the end of November. Thus, no matter how much Gamma's stock price rises before the end of November, you can still buy the stock at $30 per share.

For every buyer of a call option, there must be a seller who is willing to sell the call option. The seller of a call option is obligated to sell the shares of the specified stock to the buyer for the exercise price if and when the buyer exercises the option.

EXAMPLE

Joan Montana sold you the call option on Gamma stock. Joan receives the $200 premium that you paid to buy the call option. She is obligated to sell 100 shares of stock to you for $30 per share if and when you exercise the call option.

Your net gain or loss from buying a call option can be determined by considering the amount received when you sell the stock, the amount you paid for the stock when exercising the option, and the amount you paid for the premium.

EXAMPLE

Recall that you paid a premium of $2 per share, or $200, to purchase the call option on Gamma stock. The price of Gamma stock increases from $28 to $35 per share by the end of November. You can exercise the option and then sell the stock in the market at its prevailing price of $35. Your gain is

Amount Received from Selling the Stock ($35 × 100 shares)	$3,500
Amount Paid for Gamma Stock ($30 × 100 shares)	−$3,000
Amount Paid for the Premium ($2 × 100 shares)	−$200
Net Gain	=$300

Because you paid $200 for the call option and your net gain was $300, your return can be derived as your net gain divided by the amount of your investment:

Return = Net Gain/Amount of Investment

= $300/$200

= 1.50, or 150%

Joan does not own shares of Gamma stock, so she has to buy it in the market at $35 per share before selling it to you at $30 per share. Thus, her net gain is

Amount Received from Selling the Stock ($30 × 100 shares)	$3,000
Amount Paid for Gamma Stock ($35 × 100 shares)	−$3,500
Amount Received from the Premium ($2 × 100 shares)	+$200
Net Gain	= −$300

Because her net gain is negative, it reflects a loss. Notice that the dollar amount of your gain is equal to the dollar amount of Joan's loss.

When investing in a call option on a stock rather than the stock itself, you can magnify your return. If you had purchased Gamma stock on September 10 at a price of $28 per share, your gain would have been $7 per share. The return from investing in the call option (150%) is much higher. However, the risk from investing in the call option is higher than the risk from investing in the stock itself.

put option
Provides the right to sell 100 shares of a specified stock at a specified price by a specified expiration date.

Put Options A **put option** on a stock provides the right to sell 100 shares of a specified stock at a specified exercise price by a specified expiration date. You place an order for a put option in the same way that you place an order for a call option. The put option locks in the price at which you can sell the stock and also gives you the flexibility to let the option expire if you wish. You buy a put option when you expect the stock's price to decline.

EXAMPLE

On January 18, you pay a $300 premium to purchase a put option on Winger stock, which has an exercise price of $50 and expires at the end of March. The stock price is currently $51 per share. The put option gives you the right to sell 100 shares of Winger stock at the exercise price of $50 at any time up until the end of March. Thus, no matter how much Winger's stock price decreases before the end of March, you can still sell the stock at $50 per share.

For every buyer of a put option, there must be a seller who is willing to sell the put option. The seller of a put option is obligated to buy the shares of the specified stock from the buyer of the put option for the exercise price if and when the buyer exercises the option.

The Role of Stock Options in Asset Allocation Although stock options have become a popular investment for individual investors who want to achieve very high returns, options are still very risky and should therefore play only a minimal role (if any) in asset allocation. Because asset allocation is normally intended to limit exposure to any one type of investment, any allocation to stock options should be made with caution. Many stock options are never exercised, which means that the investment generates a return of −100%.

Nevertheless, there are some ways of using stock options to reduce the risk of your portfolio. Two of the more common methods are discussed next.

First, you can limit the risk of stocks you hold by purchasing put options on them.

> **EXAMPLE**
>
> You invested in 100 shares of Dragon.com stock a year ago. Although the stock has performed well, you think it may perform poorly in the near future. The present price of the stock is $40 per share. You decide to pay a premium of $3 per share, or $300, for a put option on Dragon.com stock with an exercise price of $38. If the stock price stays above $38 per share, you will not exercise the put option. Conversely, if the stock price falls below $38 per share, you can exercise the put option by selling the shares you are holding for $38 per share.

In this example, your purchase of a put option locked in a minimum price at which you could sell a stock you were holding, no matter how much that stock's price declines. Thus, you were able to reduce your portfolio's risk by limiting your potential loss on this stock.

covered call strategy
Selling call options on stock that you own.

You can also reduce your risk by selling call options on stocks you hold. Doing so is referred to as a **covered call strategy** because the call option you sell is covered by stock that you already own.

> **EXAMPLE**
>
> Assume once again that you are concerned that the price of Dragon.com stock may decline in the near future. There is a call option available with an exercise price of $42 and a premium of $2. You decide to sell a call option on Dragon.com stock and receive a premium of $200 ($2 × 100 shares). If the price of Dragon.com stock rises above $42 per share, the call option will be exercised, and you will have to sell the stock to fulfill your obligation. However, you will at least sell the stock for a gain. Conversely, if the stock price remains below $42, the call option will not be exercised. In this case, the $200 that you earned from selling the call option can help offset the stock's poor performance, thereby reducing your potential losses from holding it.

How Asset Allocation Affects Risk

Some asset allocation strategies reduce risk to a greater degree than others. To maintain a very low level of risk, an asset allocation may emphasize money market funds, U.S. government bonds, and the stocks of large established U.S. firms. These types of investments tend to have low risk, but also offer a relatively low rate of return. To strive for a higher return, the asset allocation could include more real estate and stocks from developing countries. Exhibit 18.4 compares different asset allocation strategies in terms of risk and potential return.

Stocks, real estate, and low-rated corporate bonds all experienced losses in 2008. Therefore, an asset allocation strategy that diversified among these types of assets would have resulted in a large loss. Thus, even the most conservative asset allocation strategy can result in a loss over a given period.

An Affordable Way to Conduct Asset Allocation

When allocating money across a set of financial assets, you are subject to transaction fees on each investment that you make. Thus, it can be costly to invest in a wide variety of investments. You can reduce your diversification costs by investing in mutual funds. Because a typical stock mutual fund contains more than 50 stocks, you can broadly diversify by investing in just a few funds.

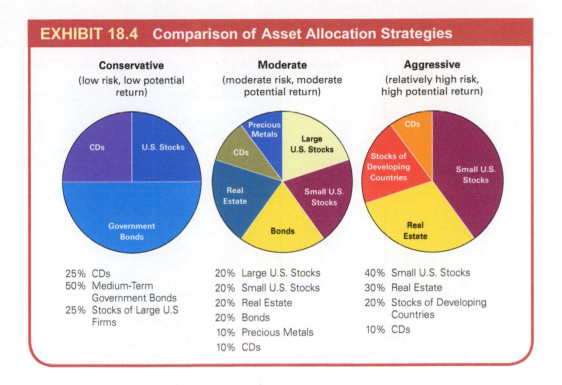

EXHIBIT 18.4   Comparison of Asset Allocation Strategies

Conservative
(low risk, low potential return)

25% CDs
50% Medium-Term Government Bonds
25% Stocks of Large U.S Firms

Moderate
(moderate risk, moderate potential return)

20% Large U.S. Stocks
20% Small U.S. Stocks
20% Real Estate
20% Bonds
10% Precious Metals
10% CDs

Aggressive
(relatively high risk, high potential return)

40% Small U.S. Stocks
30% Real Estate
20% Stocks of Developing Countries
10% CDs

For example, you could invest in a mutual fund focusing on stocks of large U.S. firms, another stock mutual fund that focuses on stocks of small U.S. firms, and a third stock mutual fund that focuses on a foreign country. You could also invest in a bond mutual fund that contains the types of bonds and maturities that you desire. You may also consider investing in a REIT to diversify your portfolio even further. With this type of portfolio, you can limit your exposure to adverse conditions such as a weak performance by a single firm, a single industry, or a single country, or events such as an increase in interest rates.

Your Asset Allocation Decision

Your ideal asset allocation will likely not be appropriate for someone else because of differences in your personal characteristics and investment goals. The asset allocation decision hinges on several factors, including your stage in life and your risk tolerance.

Your Stage in Life

Investors early in their career paths will need easy access to funds, so they should invest in relatively safe and liquid securities, such as money market investments. If you do not expect to need the invested funds in the near future, you may want to consider investing in a diversified portfolio of individual stocks, individual bonds, stock mutual funds, and bond mutual funds. Investors who expect to be working for many more years may invest in stocks of smaller firms and growth stock mutual funds, which have high growth potential. Conversely, investors nearing retirement age may allocate a larger proportion of money toward investments that will generate a fixed income, such as individual bonds, stock mutual funds containing high-dividend stocks, bond mutual funds, and some types of REITs.

Although no single asset allocation formula is suitable for everyone, the common trends in asset allocation over a lifetime are shown in Exhibit 18.5. Notice the heavy emphasis on stocks at an early stage of life, as individuals take some risk in the hope that they can increase their wealth. Over time, they gradually shift toward bonds or to stocks of stable firms that pay high dividends. The portfolio becomes less risky as it shifts to a higher proportion of bonds and stocks of stable firms. This portfolio is less likely to

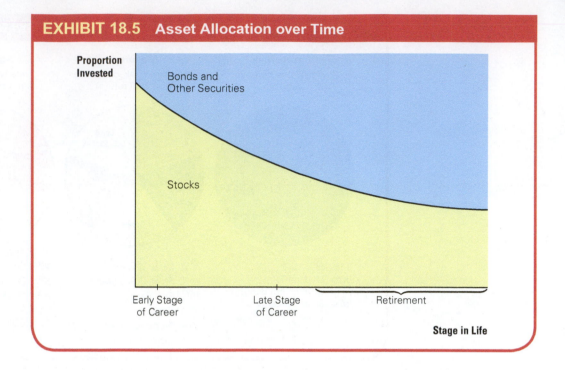

EXHIBIT 18.5   Asset Allocation over Time

generate large returns, but it will provide periodic income on retirement. In fact, your portfolio will likely be your main source of income after you retire. (Chapter 19 discusses the role of savings in retirement planning in detail.)

Exhibit 18.6 provides a more detailed example of how your asset allocation might change over time. In the early career stage, the allocation may be focused on stocks with much potential for growth and a relatively high level of risk. Although stocks can lose value, they typically perform well over long-term periods. You may be more willing to accept risk at an early stage in your career because even if stocks perform poorly over a short period of time, there is time for them to improve before you may want to sell the assets to use the cash. However, even at an early stage, you should maintain some very liquid assets (such as money market securities) that can be sold if you need cash to pay bills, make a down payment on a home, or for other reasons.

In the middle stage of your career, you may reduce your risky assets and hold a higher proportion of safer assets such as Treasury bonds. By the time you reach retirement, you may want to reduce your proportion of stocks even further and allocate more funds toward Treasury bonds. Ideally, the securities that you hold by the time you retire can generate sufficient income to support you for the rest of your life. If you have a large amount of stocks at that time, there is a risk that your stocks could lose much of their value, and your assets may no longer be able to provide adequate financial support.

Your Degree of Risk Tolerance

Investors also vary in their degree of risk tolerance. If you are unwilling to take much risk, you should focus on safe investments. For example, you might invest in Treasury bonds with relatively short maturities. If you are willing to accept a moderate level of risk, you may consider a stock mutual fund that represents the S&P 500 stock index and large-cap stock mutual funds that invest in stocks of very large and stable firms. These investments offer more potential return than an investment in Treasury bonds, but they may also result in losses in some periods.

If you are willing to tolerate a higher degree of risk to strive for higher returns, you may consider individual stocks. Smaller stocks that are focused on technology tend to have potential for high returns, but they are also very risky. Even if you can tolerate a

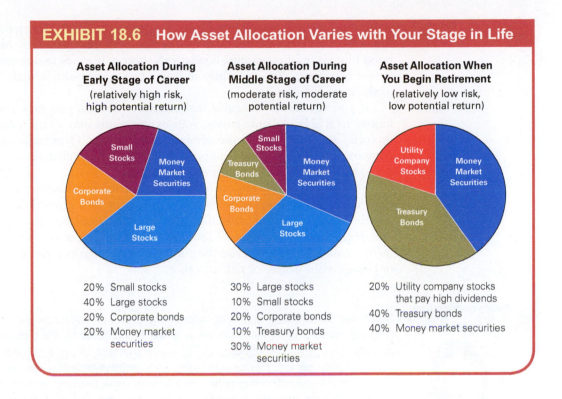

EXHIBIT 18.6   How Asset Allocation Varies with Your Stage in Life

Asset Allocation During Early Stage of Career
(relatively high risk, high potential return)

- 20% Small stocks
- 40% Large stocks
- 20% Corporate bonds
- 20% Money market securities

Asset Allocation During Middle Stage of Career
(moderate risk, moderate potential return)

- 30% Large stocks
- 10% Small stocks
- 20% Corporate bonds
- 10% Treasury bonds
- 30% Money market securities

Asset Allocation When You Begin Retirement
(relatively low risk, low potential return)

- 20% Utility company stocks that pay high dividends
- 40% Treasury bonds
- 40% Money market securities

high level of risk, you should still diversify your investments. You might consider various mutual funds that have the potential of achieving a high return, but contain a diversified set of stocks, so you are not overly exposed to a single stock. Recall from Chapter 17 that you can choose among various growth funds, capital appreciation funds, and even funds focused on various sectors such as health care or financial firms. You may also consider bond mutual funds that invest in corporate bonds. You can increase your potential return (and therefore your risk) by focusing on high-yield (junk) bond mutual funds with long terms to maturity.

Some investors use an unrealistic perception of the investment environment to justify their investment behavior. They are unwilling to recognize how much risk they are taking. They make investments that tend to generate a very strong return when economic conditions are favorable but a very weak return when economic conditions are unfavorable. When economic conditions are favorable, these investors are very pleased and believe that they have very good investment skills. However, when economic conditions are unfavorable, these types of investments perform poorly.

Some investors simply are unwilling to accept that unfavorable economic conditions might occur. They always have a very optimistic outlook on the economy, but they should be realistic rather than overly optimistic. That is, as they make risky investments, they should recognize that they could easily incur large losses if the economy weakens. If they are not in a position in which they can afford to incur large losses, they should seriously consider safer types of investments. Safer investments, however, are not as exciting because they do not offer the potential for high returns. Thus, some investors end up gambling their money in risky investments and therefore possibly risk major losses that they cannot afford.

Your Expectations About Economic Conditions

Your expectations about economic conditions also influence your asset allocation. If you expect strong stock market conditions, you may shift a larger proportion of your money into your stock mutual funds. Conversely, if you expect a temporary weakness in the stock market, you may shift a larger proportion of your money to your bond mutual funds. If you expect interest rates to decrease, you may consider shifting money from a bond mutual fund containing bonds with short maturities to one containing bonds with longer maturities. You can easily shift money among mutual funds if the funds are part of the same family.

If you anticipate favorable real estate conditions, you may allocate some of your money to REITs. As time passes, your expectations may change, causing some types of financial assets to become more desirable than others. Over time, you should change the composition of your investment portfolio in response to changes in your market expectations, investment goals, and life circumstances.

Because it is nearly impossible to predict economic conditions, it is difficult to determine which types of investments will perform best in a given period. Consequently, you may be better off basing your asset allocation decisions completely on your stage in life and degree of risk tolerance. Then, once you establish a diversified portfolio of investments, you will need to revise the portfolio only when you enter a different stage in life or change your degree of risk tolerance.

EXAMPLE

Stephanie Spratt wants to develop a long-term financial plan for allocating money to various financial assets. Specifically, she wants to set rough goals for the proportion of money that she will invest in stocks, bonds, and REITs over the next 10 years. Because she just recently started her career and may be working for another 30 years, she does not feel it is necessary to allocate a large proportion of her money to bonds at this time. She recognizes that bonds are typically safer than stocks, but plans to consider bond and stock mutual funds in the future. She recognizes that stocks are risky, but is comfortable taking some risk at this stage in her life. She plans to consider some equity income mutual funds, growth stock mutual funds, and international mutual funds.

As Stephanie accumulates more funds for investing over the next five years, she plans to invest in various stocks or stock mutual funds. She will invest in REITs only if her view of the real estate market throughout the United States becomes more favorable.

At the point when she is close to retirement, she will take a more conservative investment approach that reduces risk (and offers a lower potential return).

FREE APPS
for Personal
Finance

Valuing Your Investments

Application:

The SigFig Investing app (by SigFig) keeps track of the value of your asset portfolio by updating the values of each of your investments.

To Find It:

Search for the "SigFig Investing" app on your mobile device.

How Asset Allocation Fits Within Your Financial Plan

The following are the key asset allocation decisions that should be included within your financial plan:

- Is your present asset allocation of investments appropriate?
- How will you apply asset allocation in the future?

Exhibit 18.7 provides an example of how asset allocation decisions apply to Stephanie Spratt's financial plan. Stephanie's first concern is maintaining adequate liquidity and being able to make her existing loan payments. As she accumulates more money beyond what she needs for these purposes, she will allocate money to various investments.

EXHIBIT 18.7 **How Asset Allocation Fits Within Stephanie Spratt's Financial Plan**

GOALS FOR ASSET ALLOCATION

1. *Ensure that my present asset allocation is appropriate.*
2. *Determine a plan for asset allocation in the future as I accumulate more money.*

ANALYSIS

Investment	Market Value of Investment	Proportion of Invested Funds Allocated to This Investment
Common stock	$3,000	$3,000/$5,000 = 60%
Stock mutual fund	1,000	$1,000/$5,000 = 20%
Bond mutual fund	1,000	$1,000/$5,000 = 20%
Total	$5,000	

DECISIONS

Decision on Whether My Present Asset Allocation Is Appropriate:

My present asset allocation is too heavily concentrated on one stock. With just $5,000 in investments, I should probably have all of my money invested in mutual funds so that my investments are more diversified. I should consider selling the stock and investing the proceeds in a stock mutual fund. I already own shares of a mutual fund focused on technology firms. I will invest the proceeds from selling my stock in a different type of stock mutual fund so that I can achieve more diversification.

Decision on Asset Allocation in the Future:

Once I revise my asset allocation as described above, I will have $4,000 invested in stock mutual funds and $1,000 in bond mutual funds. This revision will result in a balance of 80% invested in stock funds and 20% invested in bond funds. The stock funds have a higher potential return than the bond funds. During the next few years, I will invest any extra money I have in stock or bond mutual funds, maintaining the same 80/20 ratio.

DISCUSSION QUESTIONS

1. How would Stephanie's asset allocation decisions be different if she were a single mother of two children?

2. How would Stephanie's asset allocation decisions be affected if she were 35 years old? If she were 50 years old?

SUMMARY

Diversification Effect on Risk. Asset allocation uses diversification to reduce your risk from investing. In general, a portfolio achieves more benefits when it is diversified among assets whose returns are less volatile and are not highly correlated with each other over time.

Stock Diversification Strategies. Common stock diversification strategies include diversifying among stocks across industries and across countries. You should consider using these two types of diversification so that you limit the exposure of your stock investments to any external forces that could affect their value.

Asset Allocation Strategies. Your asset allocation decision should not be restricted to stocks. Because bond returns are primarily influenced by interest rate movements rather than stock market conditions, they are not highly positively correlated with stock returns over time. Therefore, bonds can reduce the risk in an investment portfolio. Real estate investment trusts (REITs) are primarily influenced by real estate conditions and can also be useful for diversifying an investment portfolio. Stock options can also be used for diversification, but they can be very risky.

Factors That Influence Asset Allocation. Your asset allocation decision should take into account your stage in life, your degree of risk tolerance, and your expectations of economic conditions. If you are young, you may be more willing to invest in riskier securities to build wealth. If you are near retirement, you should consider investing more of your money in investments that can provide you with a stable income (dividends and interest payments) over time. If you are more willing to tolerate risk, you would invest in riskier stocks and bonds. Your asset allocation is also influenced by your expectations about future economic conditions. These conditions will affect the expected performance of stocks, bonds, and REITs and therefore should shape your decision of how to allocate your money across these financial assets.

How Asset Allocation Fits Within Your Financial Plan. Asset allocation determines how to diversify your investments. You may rely on your investments to build your wealth over time, and you may ultimately rely on that wealth to cover your future spending behavior. Therefore, your asset allocation decisions can help you achieve your financial plan.

REVIEW QUESTIONS

All Review Questions are available in *MyFinanceLab* at *http://www.myfinancelab.com*.

1. **Diversification.** Why is it important to diversify your financial holdings across financial assets? How does asset allocation enable you to accomplish diversification?

2. **Investment Portfolio.** What is a portfolio? How does a diverse portfolio help reduce risk?

3. **Portfolio Risk.** What factors influence a portfolio's risk? Explain.

4. **Diversification Strategies.** Describe two strategies for diversifying a stock portfolio.

5. **Portfolio Risk.** How can allocating some of your assets to bonds reduce the level of risk in your portfolio?

6. **REITs.** What are real estate investment trusts (REITs)? How are they classified? What are some attractive characteristics of REITs? How can REITs help diversify a portfolio?

7. **Stock Option.** What is a stock option? Why is it important for an investor to understand how stock options function?

8. **Asset Allocation Costs.** Why can asset allocation be expensive? How can you reduce the costs?

9. **Risk Tolerance Over Time.** Explain how your tolerance for risk when investing may have changed by the time you retire, and why.

10. **Call Option.** What is a call option? How does it work?

11. **Gain on Call Options.** How is a gain or loss calculated from the trading of call options?

12. **Put Option.** What is a put option? How does it work?

13. **Options in Asset Allocation.** "There is a right way and a wrong way to use stock options in asset allocation." Evaluate this statement.

14. **Asset Allocation Decision.** Discuss the role that your stage in life plays in the asset allocation decision.

15. **Risk Tolerance.** How does your risk tolerance affect the asset allocation decision?

16. **Economic Conditions.** How might your expectations of economic conditions influence your asset allocation? What is the problem with this strategy?

17. **Impact of Global Recession on Diversification Strategy.** Why would a global recession possibly limit the potential benefits from international diversification?

18. **U.S. Economic Impact on Other Countries.** Explain how economic conditions in the United States influence economies of other countries.

19. **Investment Correlation.** What is meant by correlations among investments? How does correlation impact portfolio risk?

20. **Puts and Risk Reduction.** Assume that 11 months ago you purchased stock in XYZ Company for $50 a share. The stock price is now $72 a share but you would like to wait another month before selling the stock in order to pay a lower capital gains tax rate. Explain how you can use a put to protect yourself from this stock falling in value before your expected sale date.

21. **Covered Call Strategy.** What is a covered call strategy?

22. **Mutual Funds and Asset Allocation.** Explain how mutual funds can help you conduct affordable asset allocation.

23. **Correlation Coefficients in Practice.** Juana wants to add another asset to her portfolio. She is trying to decide between two assets that have correlations with her portfolio of +.65 and −.12 respectively. Which asset will provide the greatest benefit, and why?

FINANCIAL PLANNING PROBLEMS

All Financial Planning Problems are available in MyFinanceLab at http://www.myfinancelab.com.

1. **Return on Stock Options.** Maryanne paid $300 for a call option on a stock. The option gives her the right to buy the stock for $27 per share until March 1. On February 15, the stock price rises to $32 per share, and Maryanne exercises her option. What is Maryanne's return from this transaction?

2. **Return on Stock Options.** Chris purchased a call option on a stock for $200. The option gives him the right to purchase the stock at $30 per share until May 1. On May 1, the price of the stock is $28 per share. What is Chris's return on the stock option?

3. **Return on Stock Options.** Teresa purchased a call option on a stock for $250. The option allows her to purchase the stock for $40 per share if she exercises the option by December 31. On December 15, the stock rises to $60 per share, and Teresa exercises the option. What is Teresa's return?

4. **Covered Call Strategy.** Carlos purchased 100 shares of stock in Company Alpha for $21 a share. He recently sold a call on the stock for $1.50 a share with a strike price of $40. The stock has since increased in price to $42 per share. How much will Carlos make on this stock if the option is exercised?

5. **Ethical Dilemma.** Mike has decided that it is time he put his money to work for him. He has accumulated a substantial nest egg in a savings account at a local bank, but he realizes that with less than 3% interest he will never reach his goals. After doing some research he withdraws the money, opens an account at a local brokerage firm, and buys 500 shares of a large blue-chip manufacturing company and 600 shares of a well-known retailing firm. From the beginning, Mike's broker insists that his portfolio is not sufficiently diversified with just two stocks. Over time, the broker convinces Mike to sell the shares of the two stocks and purchase stock in other companies.

Two years later, Mike owns stock in 14 different companies and views his portfolio as well diversified. His cousin, Ed, who has recently graduated from business school, looks at Mike's portfolio and comments, "You are not very well diversified, as 10 of the stocks you own are technology stocks." Mike tells Ed that he followed his broker's recommendations and sold his original stocks to purchase the new stocks so he would have a diversified portfolio. Ed comments that the brokerage firm where Mike does business specializes in technology companies. Mike is disappointed because he thought he was getting good advice toward building a well-diversified portfolio. After all, Mike followed his broker's advice to the letter, and why would his broker give a client bad advice?

a. Comment on Mike's broker's ethics in recommending the sale of the original stocks to purchase a portfolio weighted so heavily toward technology stocks. Include in your discussion reasons why the broker may have followed this course of action.

b. To achieve diversification, what other course of action could Mike have taken that would not involve buying individual stocks in a variety of companies?

FINANCIAL PLANNING ONLINE EXERCISES

1. Go to the personal investor section of http://www.vanguard.com.

   a. This Web site helps you determine an asset allocation strategy based on your specific situation. Describe the allocation that is recommended.

   b. Now adjust your tolerance for risk. How does the recommended asset allocation change? Explain why the asset allocation changes the way it does.

PSYCHOLOGY OF PERSONAL FINANCE: Investing in Mutual Funds

1. Investors are naturally attracted to mutual funds and hedge funds that perform well. However, they should be suspicious when a fund reports that it is continually achieving superior performance, even when many other types of investment funds are struggling. The high performance may be due to fraudulent reporting, but some investors want to believe that the reports are true even when they should be suspicious. Describe your behavior when investing. Are you suspicious when a fund suggests that its performance is always better than that of other funds?

2. Read one practical article about how psychology affects decisions when selecting asset allocation. You can easily retrieve possible articles by doing an online search using the terms "psychology" and "asset allocation." Summarize the main points of the article.

WEB SEARCH EXERCISE

You can develop your personal finance skills by conducting an Internet search for related articles. Find a recent online article about personal finance that reinforces one or more concepts covered in this chapter. If your class has an online component, your professor may ask you to post your summary of the article there and provide a link to the article so that other students can access it. If your class is live, your professor may ask you to summarize your application of the article in class. Your professor may assign specific students to complete this assignment or may allow any student to do the assignment on a volunteer basis.

For recent online articles related to this chapter, consider using the following search terms (be sure to include the current year as a search term to ensure that the online articles are recent):

- Benefits of portfolio diversification
- Determining your asset allocation
- Risk tolerance of your portfolio

VIDEO EXERCISE: Asset Allocation

Go to one of the Web sites that contain video clips (such as http://www.youtube.com), and review some video clips about selecting asset allocation. You can use search phrases such as "tips on asset allocation." Select one video clip on this topic that you would recommend for the other students in your class.

1. Provide the Web link for the video clip.

2. What do you think is the main point of this video clip?

3. How might you change your process of asset allocation as a result of watching this video clip?

BUILDING YOUR OWN FINANCIAL PLAN

Achieving the proper asset allocation balance in a portfolio is a significant part of any financial plan. By reviewing the selections you have made to meet your goals in investing, this case will help you determine the percentage of your funds that is allocated to each investment. Is your asset allocation conservative, moderate, or aggressive?

Asset allocation is an area of your personal financial plan that will change significantly as you get older and many of your goals have a shortened time horizon. Therefore, an annual review of your asset allocation is imperative.

Go to the worksheets at the end of this chapter to continue building your financial plan.

THE SAMPSONS—A Continuing Case

The Sampsons have been evaluating methods for investing money that will ultimately be used to support their children's college education. They have concluded that a mutual fund is better suited to their needs than investing in individual stocks or individual bonds. They are now seriously considering a biotechnology fund, which is composed of numerous biotechnology stocks. They have heard that biotechnology stocks can experience very high returns in some periods. They are not concerned about some biotechnology stocks performing poorly in any period because the biotechnology mutual fund that they are considering contains multiple biotechnology stocks and is therefore diversified.

Go to the worksheets at the end of this chapter to continue this case.

PART 5: BRAD BROOKS—A Continuing Case

As a result of watching a financial news network on cable, reading articles in some business magazines, and listening to a coworker tell how her portfolio doubled in value in six months, Brad is now convinced that his financial future lies in the stock market. His coworker's windfall was in technology stocks, so Brad has focused his portfolio on three highly speculative technology stocks. He believes that the three stocks will give him adequate diversification with maximum growth potential.

Although he has heard that it might be a good idea to buy bonds for diversification purposes, he finds bonds boring and their returns too low. Brad read an article on how day trading (buying stocks and holding them for only a day or even less) with a margin account can increase his return, and he's interested in your opinion. Brad admits that he has virtually no knowledge of investing or time to do research, but a broker gives him lots of "hot tips." He believes that is all he really needs.

Brad has heard about misleading financial statements issued by some firms, but believes that even if companies misstate their financial condition, this will not affect their stock prices. Brad would like to hear what you think of his plan.

Go to the worksheets at the end of this chapter to continue this case.

CHAPTER 18: BUILDING YOUR OWN FINANCIAL PLAN

YOUR GOALS FOR CHAPTER 18

1. Ensure that your current asset allocation is appropriate.

2. Determine a plan for future allocation.

ANALYSIS

1. Enter information about your current investments in the following chart. (If you input this information in the Excel template, the software will create a pie chart showing the market value of each investment.)

Type of Investment	Market Value of Investment	Goal(s) Met by Investment and Duration of Goal	Percentage of Funds Allocated to This Investment*
Checking Account			
Savings Account			
CDs			
Money Market			
Mutual Fund—Large Cap			
Mutual Fund—Small Cap			
Mutual Fund—International			
Mutual Fund—Corporate Bonds			
Mutual Fund—Government Bonds			
REITs			
Large-Cap Stock			
Small-Cap Stock			
International Stock			
Equity in Home			
Other Real Estate Holdings			
Investment in Collectibles (e.g., Antiques, Art)			
Other Investment			
Other Investment			
Other Investment			
Other Investment			
Total Investments			

*To compute the percentage manually, take the dollar amount in the "Market Value of Investment" column for each type of investment and divide it by the dollar amount for "Total Investments."

2. How would you rate your portfolio (i.e., conservative, moderate, or aggressive)?

_____

_____

_____

_____

_____

3. Does the risk level of your portfolio correspond to your personal risk tolerance? If it does not correspond, what actions will you need to take to align the risk level of your portfolio and your own personal risk tolerance?

_____

_____

_____

_____

_____

DECISIONS

1. Is your current asset allocation appropriate? If not, what changes will you make to better diversify your investments?

_____

_____

_____

_____

_____

2. As you make additional investments in the future, how do you plan to allocate your assets?

_____

_____

_____

_____

_____

CHAPTER 18: THE SAMPSONS—A Continuing Case

CASE QUESTIONS

1. Advise the Sampsons regarding the soundness of their tentative decision to invest all their children's college education money in a biotechnology mutual fund.

_____

_____

_____

_____

_____

_____

_____

2. The Sampsons are aware that diversification is important. Therefore, they have decided that they will initially invest in one biotechnology mutual fund and then invest in three other biotechnology mutual funds as they accumulate more money. In this way, even if one mutual fund performs poorly, they expect that the other biotechnology mutual funds will perform well. How can the Sampsons diversify their investments more effectively?

_____

_____

_____

_____

_____

_____

3. A good friend of Dave's informed him that the company he works for will announce a new product that will revolutionize the industry the friend works in. Dave is very excited about the prospective jump in the stock price. He is ready to buy some stock in the friend's company. Advise Dave on this course of action.

_____

_____

_____

_____

_____

PART 5: BRAD BROOKS—A Continuing Case

CASE QUESTIONS

1. Comment on each of the following elements of Brad's plan:

   a. Level of diversification with three technology stocks

   _____

   _____

   _____

   b. His view on bonds and not including them in his portfolio

   _____

   _____

   _____

   c. Day trading

   _____

   _____

   _____

   d. Margin trading

   _____

   _____

   _____

   e. Source of information ("hot tips")

   _____

   _____

   _____

2. Given Brad's lack of knowledge of investing and his limited time to learn or do research, what might be the best option for Brad to pursue and still get the benefit of the potential growth in the technology sector?

   _____

   _____

   _____

   _____

   _____

3. What factors will influence Brad's asset allocation? Based on these factors, what might be a suitable sample portfolio for Brad?

_____

_____

_____

_____

_____

4. How would your answer to the sample portfolio part of question 3 be affected if Brad were

   a. 45 years old?

   _____

   _____

   _____

   b. 60 years old?

   _____

   _____

   _____

5. Explain to Brad why misleading financial statements may be more common than he believes and why misleading financial statements can negatively affect a stock's price.

_____

_____

_____

_____

_____

6. Prepare a written or oral report on your findings and recommendations to Brad.

_____

_____

_____

_____

_____

_____

_____

_____

_____

Retirement and Estate Planning

The chapters in this part explain how you can protect the wealth that you accumulate over time through effective financial planning. Chapter 19 explains how to plan effectively for your retirement so that you can maintain your wealth and live comfortably. Chapter 20 explains how you can pass on as much of your estate as possible to your heirs.

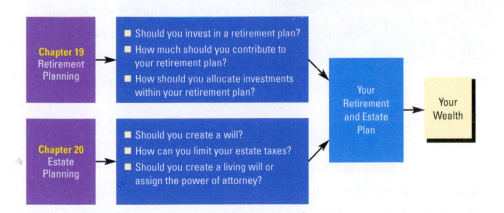

Chapter 19
Retirement Planning

- Should you invest in a retirement plan?
- How much should you contribute to your retirement plan?
- How should you allocate investments within your retirement plan?

Chapter 20
Estate Planning

- Should you create a will?
- How can you limit your estate taxes?
- Should you create a living will or assign the power of attorney?

Your Retirement and Estate Plan

Your Wealth

Retirement Planning

Vlacheslav Nikolaenko/Shutterstock

Patrick O'Toole, a divorcé, really wanted to retire at age 57. But, at 57, he was five years away from drawing Social Security, his mortgage still had 25 years of payments remaining, and after his divorce, he had only $225,000 accumulated in his retirement account. Even though he was unhappy in his present job, he needed to remain there as long as possible to build his retirement savings.

Three years later, Patrick had refinanced his mortgage and had only 15 years of payments remaining. In addition, his retirement assets had accumulated to $315,000. Patrick still had two years to go until he could draw early Social Security. At that time, he would be able to take a partial early retirement, although still not at the level of benefits he could have if he worked until age 66.

If you begin early in your working years to contribute to retirement plans, you can avoid the situation that Patrick was in. The quality and timing of your retirement will depend largely on your own decisions, even if your employer has a retirement plan available. It will take sound planning and diligent preparation to be financially prepared for retirement. This chapter describes the process and details some of the tools available to you.

MyFinanceLab helps you master the topics in this chapter and study more efficiently. Visit http://www.myfinancelab.com for more details.

The objectives of this chapter are to:

- Describe the role of Social Security

- Explain the difference between defined-benefit and defined-contribution retirement plans

- Present the key decisions you must make regarding retirement plans

- Identify the retirement plans offered by employers

- Explain the retirement plans available for self-employed individuals

- Describe types of individual retirement accounts

- Explain how annuities are used to prepare for retirement

- Illustrate how to estimate your future retirement account savings

- Explain how retirement planning fits within your financial plan

Social Security

Recall from Chapter 4 that Social Security is a federal program that taxes you during your working years and uses the funds to make payments to you on retirement (subject to age and other requirements). It is intended to ensure that you receive some income once you retire and therefore is an important part of retirement planning. However, Social Security does not provide sufficient income to support the lifestyle of most individuals. Therefore, additional retirement planning is necessary to ensure that you can live comfortably when you retire. Before discussing other means of retirement planning, we will describe how Social Security functions.

Qualifying for Social Security

To qualify for Social Security benefits, you need to build up a total of 40 credits from contributing to Social Security over time through payroll taxes. You can earn four credits per year if your income is at least $1,220 per quarter. In addition to receiving income at retirement, you will also receive Social Security benefits if you become disabled, as discussed in Chapter 12, or if you are the survivor when the breadwinner of the household dies. If the person who qualified for Social Security dies (the household's main income earner), the following benefits are provided to the survivors:

- A one-time income payment to the spouse

- Monthly income payments if the spouse is older than age 60 or has a child under the age of 16

- Monthly income payments to children under the age of 18 or up to age 19 if still attending secondary school full-time

Retirement Benefits

The amount of income that you receive from Social Security when you retire is dependent on the number of years you earned income and your average level of income. Social Security replaces about 40% of a worker's average annual income from his or her working years. Due to adjustments, however, this proportion is higher for individuals who had low-income levels and lower for those who had high-income levels.

You can receive retirement benefits starting at age 62, but the benefits will be lower than if you wait until you reach full retirement age. As a general rule, though, early retirement will give you about the same total Social Security benefits over your lifetime as full retirement benefits. Full retirement benefits begin at age 65 (for those born before 1938) to 67 (for those born in 1960 and later), depending on what year you were born (the age for qualification gradually increases over time). If you can wait until you are 70 to receive benefits, you will receive an even larger amount.

You can earn other income while receiving Social Security benefits. If you have not reached full retirement age, however, and your income from your job exceeds a specified limit ($15,720 in 2015), your Social Security benefits will be reduced. After you reach full retirement age, you can work as much as you want and still receive full benefits. In addition, depending on how much you earn and what other retirement income you have, a portion of your Social Security benefits may be taxed. You can obtain an estimate of your retirement benefits at http://www.ssa.gov.

**Financial Planning
ONLINE**

Go to:
http://www.ssa.gov

To get:
Estimates of how much earnings you have accumulated over time, how much taxes you have paid, estimates of retirement benefits, and additional information about Medicare and Social Security.

Concern About Retirement Benefits in the Future

There is some concern about whether the Social Security program will be available for retirees in the future. Today's retirees are living longer, which means that the program must provide income over a longer period to individuals on average. In addition, there will be more retirees in the future and fewer workers to support them. Therefore, given the program's uncertain future, many individuals are relying less on Social Security income in their retirement planning.

Even if the Social Security program continues, you may want more income after retirement than it provides. Many individuals accumulate their own retirement assets either through an employer-sponsored retirement plan or by establishing an individual retirement account.

Defined-Benefit Versus Defined-Contribution Plans

defined-benefit plan
An employer-sponsored retirement plan that guarantees a specific amount of income when you retire based on your salary and years of employment.

vested
Having a claim to a portion of the money in an employer-sponsored retirement account that has been reserved for you on your retirement even if you leave the company.

Employer-sponsored retirement plans are designed to help you save for retirement. Each pay period, you and/or your employer contribute money to a retirement account. The money in most of these accounts can be invested in a manner that you specify (within the range of options offered by your specific plan). The money you contribute to the retirement plan is not taxed until you withdraw it from the account. If you withdraw money from the account before you reach age $59\frac{1}{2}$, you will be subject to a 10% early withdrawal penalty tax. Any money you withdraw from the retirement account after you retire is taxed as ordinary income.

Employer-sponsored retirement plans are classified as defined-benefit or defined-contribution plans.

Defined-Benefit Plans

Defined-benefit plans guarantee a specific amount of income when you retire, based on factors such as your salary and years of employment. Your employer makes all the contributions to the plan. The specific formula varies among employers. Guidelines also determine when employees are **vested**, which means that they have a claim to a portion of the retirement money that has been reserved for them on retirement. For example, a firm may allow you to be 20% vested after two years, which means that 20% of the amount reserved for you through employer contributions will be maintained in your retirement account even if you leave the company. The percentage increases with the number of years with the employer, so you may be fully vested (able to retain 100% of your retirement account) after six years based on the guidelines of some retirement plans. Once you are fully vested, all money that is reserved for you each year will be maintained in your retirement account. These vesting rules encourage employees to stay at one firm for several years. One major advantage of a defined-benefit plan is that the benefits accumulate without the initiation of the employees. This helps employees who would not save money for retirement if they were given the money in the form of salary. Therefore, it ensures that people save for their retirement.

Defined-Contribution Plans

defined-contribution plan
An employer-sponsored retirement plan that specifies guidelines under which you and/or your employer can contribute to your retirement account and that allows you to invest the funds as you wish.

Defined-contribution plans specify guidelines under which you and/or your employer can contribute to your retirement account. The benefits that you ultimately receive are determined by the performance of the money invested in your account. You can decide how you want the money to be invested. You can also change your investments over time.

As a result of their flexibility, defined-contribution plans have become very popular. In the last 20 years, many employers have shifted from defined-benefit to defined-contribution plans. This places more responsibility on the employees to contribute money and to decide how the contributions should be invested until their retirement. Therefore, you need to understand the potential benefits of a defined-contribution plan and how to estimate the potential retirement savings that can be accumulated under this plan.

PSYCHOLOGY
of Personal
Finance

The Decision to Contribute Some people who have defined-contribution plans make the mistake of waiting too long before they save for retirement. They do not worry about saving for retirement when they are younger because they believe that they can save later. With this rationale, they may spend all the money that they earn. Then, as they get older, they may be forced to catch up on investing for retirement, but doing that severely cuts their funds available for spending. As a result, they might not save enough to have a comfortable retirement. The flexibility to postpone saving for retirement is one disadvantage of a defined-contribution plan for those people who lack the discipline to save on their own.

Benefits of a Defined-Contribution Plan A defined-contribution plan provides you with many benefits. Any money contributed by your employer is like extra income paid to you beyond your salary. In addition, having a retirement account can encourage you to save money each pay period by directing a portion of your income to be automatically added to the account before you receive your paycheck.

Investing in a defined-contribution plan also offers tax benefits. The retirement account allows you to defer taxes on income paid by your employer because your contribution to your account is deducted from your pay before taxes are taken out. If you invest $5,000 per year in your retirement account, you can reduce your taxable income by $5,000 each year, which reduces your taxes. If your marginal tax bracket is 25%, you could reduce your income tax by $1,250 (computed as 25% × $5,000) each year.

Also note that the income generated by your investments in a retirement account is not taxed until you withdraw the money after you retire. This tax benefit is very valuable because it provides you with more money that can be invested and accumulate in value. In addition, by the time you are taxed on the investments (when you withdraw funds from your retirement account), you will likely be in a lower tax bracket because you will have less taxable income.

Investing Funds in Your Retirement Account Most defined-contribution plans sponsored by employers allow some flexibility in how your retirement funds can be invested. You can typically select from a variety of stock mutual funds, bond mutual funds, or even money market funds. The amount of funds you accumulate will depend on how your investment in the retirement account performs.

Your Retirement Planning Decisions

Your key retirement planning decisions involve choosing a retirement plan, determining how much to contribute, and allocating your contributions. Several Web sites provide useful calculators to help you make these decisions, such as MSN.com's Retirement Planning Calculator and the Retirement Planner at http://www.marketwatch.com. Using the calculators can help you understand the trade-offs involved so that you can make retirement planning decisions that fit your specific needs. Each of your retirement planning decisions is discussed next.

Financial Planning
ONLINE

Go to:
The retirement section of http://www.vanguard.com

To get:
Guidance on your retirement decisions.

Which Retirement Plan Should You Pursue?

The retirement benefits from an employer-sponsored retirement plan vary among employers. Some employer-sponsored plans allow you to invest more money than others. If your employer offers a retirement plan, that should be the first plan you consider because your employer will likely contribute to it.

How Much to Contribute?

One of the most important retirement planning decisions is how much to contribute each pay period, as this decision will influence the amount of funds you have to spend during your retirement. However, many individuals do not invest in their retirement accounts in their early years, and therefore they do not take full advantage of the tax savings provided by retirement accounts. One reason for not saving for retirement is that the payoff comes so far in the future. When you're 25 years old, retirement is a long time away, and you may prefer to spend your money today in a way that will provide immediate satisfaction. The problem with that approach is that if you don't start saving for retirement early, you will have to save more in the years leading up to your retirement.

Given the difficulty of estimating how much income you will need at retirement, a safe approach is to recognize that Social Security will not provide sufficient funds and to invest as much as is allowed on a consistent basis in your retirement plan, especially when your contribution is matched by your employer. Alternatively, you can assess how much you need to cover your typical expenses and liquidity needs and invest the remainder in retirement accounts.

The size of your contribution should increase as your salary increases. If you tend to spend whatever excess funds you have after covering all your obligations, consider retirement contributions to be an obligation. As you notice your retirement account accumulating funds, the saving process will become easier because you will see how your retirement account balance grows over time.

How to Invest Your Contributions?

When considering changing investment alternatives within a defined-contribution retirement plan, you do not have to worry about tax effects. All the money you withdraw from your retirement account at the time you retire will be taxed at your ordinary income tax rate, regardless of how it was earned. Most financial advisers suggest a diversified set of investments, such as investing most of the money in one or more stock mutual funds and investing the remainder in one or more bond mutual funds.

Your retirement plan investment decision should take into account the number of years until your retirement, as shown in Exhibit 19.1. If you are far from retirement, you might consider mutual funds that invest in stocks with high potential for growth (such

EXHIBIT 19.1 Typical Composition of a Retirement Account Portfolio

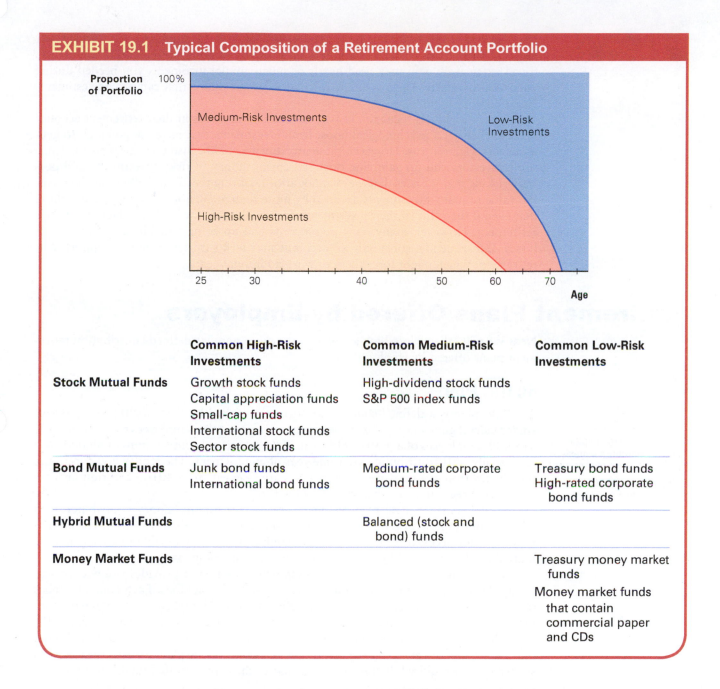

	Common High-Risk Investments	Common Medium-Risk Investments	Common Low-Risk Investments
Stock Mutual Funds	Growth stock funds Capital appreciation funds Small-cap funds International stock funds Sector stock funds	High-dividend stock funds S&P 500 index funds	
Bond Mutual Funds	Junk bond funds International bond funds	Medium-rated corporate bond funds	Treasury bond funds High-rated corporate bond funds
Hybrid Mutual Funds		Balanced (stock and bond) funds	
Money Market Funds			Treasury money market funds Money market funds that contain commercial paper and CDs

as a capital appreciation fund, a technology fund, and maybe an international stock or bond fund). If you are close to retirement, you might consider Treasury bond funds and a stock mutual fund that focuses on stocks of very large firms that pay high dividends. Some investments (such as a money market fund focused on Treasury bills or on bank certificates of deposit) are less risky, but also offer less potential return. Most retirement plans allow a wide variety of investment alternatives to suit various risk tolerances.

If you are young and far from retirement, you are in a position to take more risk with your investments. As you approach retirement, however, your investments should become more conservative.

The amount that you try to save by the time you retire is partially dependent on the retirement income that you will need to live comfortably. There are various methods of determining the amount that you should save for your retirement. Among the important variables to consider are the levels of your existing assets and liabilities, whether you will be supporting anyone besides yourself at retirement, your personal needs, the expected price level of products at the time of your retirement, and the number of years you expect to live while retired. Also think about what you plan to do in retirement. If you plan to travel extensively, you may need nearly as much annual income as you needed during your working years. Various online calculators are available that can provide estimates based on your input.

Some individuals focus too heavily on risky investments in their retirement account because they get a psychological boost from investments that have the potential to generate very high returns. However, these investments could cause very large losses. Thus, some investors end up gambling their retirement money in risky investments and possibly risking major losses that they cannot afford. During the 2008–2009 financial crisis, the value of many investments declined by more than 50%. Some investors may believe that even if the value of their investments decline, the value will rise by the time of their retirement. However, many risky investments end up being worthless, causing major losses. Consequently, some retirees' accounts may lack sufficient funds to support their retirement, which might force them to work additional years.

Retirement Plans Offered by Employers

Next we will take a close look at some of the more popular defined-contribution retirement plans offered by employers.

401(k) Plan

401(k) plan
A defined-contribution plan that allows employees to contribute a maximum of $18,000 ($24,000 if they are age 50 or older) per year on a pretax basis.

A **401(k) plan** is a defined-contribution plan established by firms for their employees. Under federal guidelines, in 2015 the maximum amount that employees can contribute is $18,000. Employees of age 50 or older can make additional contributions of $6,000. You can usually start contributing after one year of employment. The money you contribute is deducted from your paycheck before taxes are assessed. Your 401(k) contributions are fully vested regardless of when you leave the firm.

Employers offer a set of investment alternatives for the money contributed to a 401(k). For example, you may be able to invest in one or more mutual funds. The mutual funds are not necessarily part of a single family, so you may be able to choose among mutual funds sponsored by many different investment companies.

Some firms allow a managed account in which an adviser provides you with investment advice and account allocation based on your risk tolerance. Each company relies on a different program, so the prescribed allocation could depend on the company that manages your 401(k) plan. There are advisory fees, which normally range from 0.2% to 0.8% or higher per year. The company is required to disclose the amount of all fees, the historical performance of the investments available in the plan, its objectives, and its strategies. The required disclosures are similar to those that mutual funds must make.

Matching Contributions by Employers Some 401(k) plans require the entire contribution to come from the employee with no matching contribution from the employer. Other employers match the employee's contribution. In a dollar-for-dollar match, the employer matches the entire employee contribution up to the company's limit. So, for example, if an employee contributes $400 per month, the employer will provide an additional $400 per month to the employee's retirement account. Or the firm may match a percentage of the employee's contribution. For example, if the employee contributes $400, the employer may contribute 50% of that amount, or an additional $200. The amount of matching (if any) provided by the employer has a large impact on the savings that the employee will accumulate by retirement. More than 80% of all employers offering 401(k) plans match a portion or all of an employee's contributions.

Tax on Money Withdrawn from the Account If you withdraw money from your 401(k) account before age $59\frac{1}{2}$ you will be subject to a penalty equal to 10% of the amount withdrawn. Your withdrawal will also be taxed as regular income at your marginal income tax rate. However, if you are retired and over age $59\frac{1}{2}$ when you withdraw the money, you may not have much other taxable income and therefore will be in a very low marginal income tax bracket. Thus, the 401(k) plan allows you to defer paying taxes on the income you contributed for several years and may also allow you to pay a lower tax rate on the money once you withdraw it.

Roth 401(k) Plan

In 2006, the Roth 401(k) account was allowed as an alternative to the traditional 401(k) retirement account. The **Roth 401(k)** is available to people who are employed by firms that offer participation in the plan. Income contributed to a Roth 401(k) is taxed at the contributor's marginal tax rate at the time of the contribution. The advantage to the Roth 401(k) is that funds are not taxed when withdrawn from the account, as they are when withdrawn from a traditional 401(k) account. In essence, the Roth 401(k) plan allows contributors to avoid paying taxes on the interest or capital gains generated by the account. There are no restrictions on income level to contribute to a Roth 401(k) account.

The decision to invest in a Roth 401(k) or traditional account may depend on your marginal tax rate today versus your expected tax rate when you withdraw funds after retirement. If you are currently in a very low marginal tax bracket, you may benefit from using the Roth 401(k) because the taxes on your contribution will be small, and you will not be taxed on the funds at withdrawal. However, some people may prefer the traditional 401(k) because the tax benefit occurs now, which gives them more immediate disposable income. They may be less concerned about the tax benefit of the Roth 401(k) plan at their retirement, even if that benefit outweighs the immediate tax benefit from the traditional 401(k) plan.

403(b) Plan

Nonprofit organizations such as educational institutions and charitable organizations offer **403(b) plans**, which are very similar to 401(k) plans in that they allow you to invest a portion of your income on a tax-deferred basis. The maximum amount that you can contribute is dependent on your compensation and years of service, up to a limit of $18,000.

A 403(b) plan allows you to choose investment alternatives. You will be penalized for withdrawals before age $59\frac{1}{2}$, and when you withdraw the money at retirement, you will be taxed at ordinary income tax rates.

Simplified Employee Pension (SEP) Plan

A **Simplified Employee Pension (SEP) plan** is commonly set up by business owners for themselves and their employees. The employee is not allowed to make contributions. The employer can contribute up to 25% of the employee's annual income, up to a maximum annual contribution of $53,000 in 2015. SEPs give an employer a lot of flexibility in determining how much money to contribute. The employer may establish your SEP account at an investment company, depository institution, or brokerage firm of your choice. If it is established at an investment company, you will be able to invest the money in a set of mutual funds that the company offers. If the account is established at a depository institution, you will be able to invest the money in CDs issued by the institution. If it is established at a brokerage firm, you may be able to invest in some individual stocks or mutual funds that you choose. Withdrawals should occur only after age $59\frac{1}{2}$ to avoid a penalty, and the withdrawals are taxed at ordinary income tax rates at that time.

SIMPLE Plan

The **SIMPLE (Savings Incentive Match Plan for Employees) plan** is intended for firms with 100 or fewer employees. A SIMPLE plan can be established at investment companies, depository institutions, or brokerage firms. In 2015 the employee can contribute up to

$12,500 (additional contributions of $3,000 are allowed for employees who are age 50 or older). As with the other retirement plans mentioned so far, this contribution is not taxed until the money is withdrawn from the account. Thus, a SIMPLE account is an effective means of deferring tax on income. In addition, the employer can match a portion of the employee's contribution.

Profit Sharing

profit sharing
A defined-contribution plan in which the employer makes contributions to employee retirement accounts based on a specified profit formula.

Some firms provide **profit sharing**, in which the employer makes contributions to employee retirement accounts based on a specified profit formula. The employer can contribute up to 25% of an employee's salary each year, up to a maximum annual amount of $53,000 in 2015.

Employee Stock Ownership Plan (ESOP)

employee stock ownership plan (ESOP)
A retirement plan in which the employer contributes some of its own stock to the employee's retirement account.

With an **employee stock ownership plan** (**ESOP**), the employer contributes some of its own stock to the employee's retirement account. A disadvantage of this plan is that it is focused on one stock; if this stock performs poorly, your retirement account will not be able to support your retirement. Recall from Chapter 18 that a diversified mutual fund is less susceptible to wide swings in value because it contains various stocks that are not likely to experience large downturns simultaneously. An ESOP is generally riskier than retirement plans invested in diversified mutual funds.

Managing Your Retirement Account After Leaving Your Employer

When you leave an employer, you may be able to retain your retirement account there if you have at least $5,000 in it. Another option is to transfer your assets tax-free into your new employer's retirement account, assuming that your new employer allows such transfers (most employers do). However, some employers charge high annual fees to manage transferred retirement plans.

rollover IRA
An individual retirement account (IRA) into which you can transfer your assets from your company retirement plan tax-free while avoiding early withdrawal penalties.

You can also create a **rollover IRA** by transferring your assets tax-free from your company retirement plan to an individual retirement account (IRA). You can initiate a rollover IRA by completing an application provided by various investment companies that sponsor mutual funds or by various brokerage firms. By transferring your retirement account into a rollover IRA, you can avoid cashing in your retirement account and therefore can continue to defer taxes and avoid the early withdrawal penalty.

Retirement Plans for the Self-Employed

Self-employed individuals can use versions of many of the plans available to employed individuals. Two popular retirement plans for self-employed individuals are Simplified Employee Pension (SEP) plans and one-participant 401(k) plans.

Keogh Plan

Keogh plan
A retirement plan that enables high-income self-employed individuals to contribute part of their pretax income to a retirement account.

The first retirement plans for self-employed individuals were known as **Keogh plans,** named after the congressman who sponsored the bill creating them. Keogh plans are rarely used today because their rules are complicated and the plans are difficult to set up. Nevertheless, they still are used for certain high-income self-employed individuals. As with other retirement accounts, contributions are not taxed until they are withdrawn at the time of retirement.

Simplified Employee Pension (SEP) Plan

The **Simplified Employee Pension (SEP) plan** is available for self-employed individuals. If you are self-employed, you can contribute up to 25% of your annual net income, up to a maximum annual contribution of $53,000 in 2015. You can establish your SEP account at an investment company, depository institution, or brokerage firm of your choice. Another possibility is to establish a **one-participant 401(k) plan**, also known as a solo 401(k) or an individual 401(k). One-participant 401(k) plans are subject to the same rules and contribution limits as 401(k) plans for employees.

Individual Retirement Accounts

You should also consider opening an individual retirement account (IRA). There are two main types of IRAs: the traditional IRA and the Roth IRA.

Traditional IRA

The **traditional individual retirement account (IRA)** enables you to save for your retirement, separate from any retirement plan provided by your employer. In 2015, you can invest $5,500 per year ($11,000 per year for a married couple) in an IRA. The maximum level per year is adjusted periodically for inflation over time. Individuals who are age 50 or older can make additional contributions of $1,000 per year. Individuals who earn less than $61,000 per year and married couples who earn less than $98,000 per year receive a tax deduction on the entire amount of their contribution to a traditional IRA. However, if you are covered by an employer-sponsored plan and your gross income is above these limits, the tax deduction that you receive on your traditional IRA contribution is reduced. Individuals in low income brackets may also receive tax credits for contributing to the traditional IRA, meaning that the amount contributed to their IRA can offset a portion of their taxes owed. However, the credit is limited to a maximum of $1,000 for those who qualify. You are allowed to contribute to the IRA up to the tax deadline (usually April 15) in the following year to take advantage of the tax deduction in the previous year.

When you contribute to an IRA, your investment choices will depend on the retirement plan sponsor. For example, if you set up your IRA with the Vanguard mutual fund family, you can select among more than 60 mutual funds for your account. You can withdraw funds from an IRA without penalty at age $59\frac{1}{2}$ or later. You are taxed on the income earned by your investments at your ordinary income tax rate at the time you withdraw funds. If you withdraw the funds before age $59\frac{1}{2}$ you are not only taxed at your ordinary income tax rate, but also are typically charged a penalty equal to 10% of the withdrawn funds.

Roth IRA

The **Roth IRA** allows individuals who are under specific income limits to invest $5,500 per year ($11,000 per year for married couples). Individuals who are age 50 or older can make additional catch-up contributions with the same limits as the traditional IRA. You can withdraw funds from the Roth IRA at age $59\frac{1}{2}$ or later. You are taxed on money invested in the Roth IRA at the time of the contribution. However, you are not taxed when you withdraw the money, as long as you withdraw the money after age $59\frac{1}{2}$ and the Roth IRA has been in existence for at least five years. These tax characteristics differ from the traditional IRA, in which you are not taxed when contributing (if you are under specific income limits), but are taxed when you withdraw the money after retirement. You can invest in both a Roth IRA and a traditional IRA, but you are limited to a total IRA contribution. For example, if you are single and invest the maximum amount in a Roth IRA this year, you cannot invest in a traditional IRA. If you invest $1,000 less than the maximum amount in a Roth IRA this year, you can also invest $1,000 in a traditional IRA. You need not maintain a specific allocation between the two types of IRAs each year, but you are subject to the maximum total contribution.

Individuals whose income exceeds specified limits are not eligible for the Roth IRA. As of 2015, for married taxpayers filing jointly, eligibility for the Roth IRA phases out at annual adjusted gross income levels from $183,000 to $193,000, and they are not eligible if their annual adjusted gross income exceeds $193,000. For single taxpayers, the Roth IRA phases out at annual adjusted gross income levels from $116,000 to $131,000, with no contributions allowed if their annual adjusted gross income exceeds $131,000.

Comparison of the Roth IRA and Traditional IRA

To illustrate the difference between the Roth IRA and the traditional IRA, we will consider the effects of investing $4,000 in each type of IRA.

Advantage of the Traditional IRA over the Roth IRA
The income that you contribute to a traditional IRA is sheltered from taxes until you withdraw money from your account. Conversely, you pay taxes on your income contributed to a Roth IRA. For example, if you contribute $4,000 and are in a 25% tax bracket, you would incur a tax of $1,000 now (computed as $4,000 \times 25\%$) on the income contributed to a Roth IRA. Had you invested that income in a traditional IRA instead of a Roth IRA, you would not incur taxes on that income at this time.

Advantage of the Roth IRA over the Traditional IRA
IRA contributions should grow over time, assuming that you invest each year and that you earn a reasonable return. Assume that you are retired and withdraw $10,000 after several years of investing in your IRA. If you withdraw $10,000 from your Roth IRA, you will not pay any taxes on the amount withdrawn. Conversely, if you withdraw $10,000 from your traditional IRA, you will pay taxes on the amount withdrawn, based on your marginal income tax bracket. If your marginal tax bracket at that time is 25%, you will incur a tax of $2,500 ($10,000 \times 25\%$). Thus, you would incur a tax of $2,500 more than if you had withdrawn the money from a Roth IRA. Investment income accumulates on a tax-free basis in a Roth IRA, whereas money withdrawn from a traditional IRA is taxable.

Factors That Affect Your Choice
So which IRA is better? The answer depends on many factors, including your marginal income tax rate at the time you contribute money to your IRA and at the time that you withdraw money. If you are in a high tax bracket now and expect to be in a very low tax bracket when you withdraw money from the IRA, you may be better off with the traditional IRA. Because you are not taxed on the initial contribution, you will receive your tax benefit when you are working and subject to a high tax rate. If you withdraw money from the IRA after you retire, and you do not have much other income, the money withdrawn from the IRA will be taxed at a low tax rate.

A counterargument is that if you save a substantial amount of money in your employer-sponsored account and your IRA, you will be withdrawing a large amount of money from your accounts every year after you retire, so you will likely be in a high tax bracket. In this case, you may be better off paying taxes on the income now with a Roth IRA (as you contribute to your retirement account) rather than later.

Annuities

annuity
A financial contract that provides annual payments over a specified period.

When conducting your retirement planning, you should also consider investing in annuities. An **annuity** is a financial contract that provides annual payments until a specified year or for one's lifetime. The minimum investment in an annuity is usually $5,000. The investment in an annuity is not sheltered from income taxes. Thus, if you invest $5,000 in an annuity, you cannot reduce your taxable income by $5,000. The return on the investment in an annuity is tax-deferred, however, so any gains generated by the annuity are not taxed until the funds are paid to the investor. Although there are benefits from being able to defer the tax on your investment, they are smaller than the benefits from sheltering income by using a retirement account. Therefore, annuities are not suitable substitutes for retirement plans.

Fixed versus Variable Annuities

fixed annuity
An annuity that provides a specified return on your investment, so you know exactly how much money you will receive at a future point in time (such as retirement).

variable annuity
An annuity in which the return is based on the performance of the selected investment vehicles.

Annuities are classified as fixed or variable. **Fixed annuities** provide a specified return on your investment, so you know exactly how much money you will receive at a future point in time. **Variable annuities** allow you to allocate your investment among various subaccounts (specific stock and bond portfolios), so the return is dependent on the performance of those investments. However, the variable annuities do not guarantee a specific return to you over time. The amount of money that you receive depends on the performance of the types of investment you selected. You may periodically change your allocation. You can withdraw your investment as a lump sum or as a series of payments over time.

Variable annuities commonly provide a death benefit, so that when you die, your heirs receive the account balance or the amount that you initially invested in the annuity, whichever is greater. In most cases, the value of your investments should increase over time, so the guarantee that your heirs will receive the amount that you initially invested is not extremely beneficial. Furthermore, the company who sells you the annuity charges you for this death benefit, and the amount that it charges is typically much more than the expected benefit.

Annuity Fees

surrender charge
A fee that may be imposed on any money withdrawn from an annuity.

The main disadvantage of annuities is the high fees charged by the financial institutions (primarily insurance companies) that sell and manage annuities. These fees include management fees that are charged every year (similar to those for a mutual fund) and a **surrender charge** that may be imposed on any money withdrawn in the first eight years or so. The surrender charge is intended to discourage withdrawals. Some annuities allow you to swap one type of annuity for another, but when you do, you are typically charged surrender fees. The surrender charges are especially high if you withdraw money shortly after you purchase the annuity, and they decline over time. In addition, there may be "insurance fees" that are essentially commissions to salespeople for selling the annuities to you. These commissions commonly range from 5.75% to 8.25% of your investment. Some insurance companies have been criticized because their brokers aggressively sold annuities to customers without concern for the needs of their customers. Because brokers earn commissions on how much they sell, they may be tempted to make a sale without fully disclosing the disadvantages of annuities.

Some financial institutions now offer no-load annuities that do not charge commissions and also charge relatively low management fees. For example, Vanguard's variable annuity plan has total expenses between 0.58% and 0.86% of the investment per year, which are lower than what many mutual funds charge.

Estimating Your Future Retirement Savings

When you consider how much to contribute to retirement and how to invest your retirement funds, you will naturally want to know how your decision will affect your future retirement savings.

Recall from Chapter 3 that the future value of an investment today can be computed by using the future value interest factor (*FVIF*) table (Table C.1) in Appendix C. You need the following information:

- The amount of the investment
- The annual return that you expect on the investment
- The time when the investment will end

Copyright © Pears_____ucation, Inc. All rights reserved.

EXAMPLE

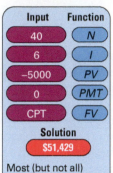

Input	Function
40	N
6	I
−5000	PV
0	PMT
CPT	FV

Solution

$51,429

Most (but not all) financial calculators, such as the Texas Instruments BAII PLUS, require a negative present value (*PV*) input. You should consult your manual to determine the requirements of your financial calculator.

You consider investing $5,000 this year, and this investment will remain in your account until 40 years from now when you retire. You believe that you can earn a return of 6% per year on your investment. Based on this information, you expect the value of your investment in 40 years to be:

$$\text{Value in 40 Years} = \text{Investment} \times FVIF\ (i = 6\%, n = 40)$$
$$= \$5,000 \times 10.285$$
$$= \$51,425$$

Your answer derived from this process may differ slightly from the answer when using a calculator due to rounding. Notice that a $5,000 investment can grow into more than $50,000 by the time you retire.

Estimating the Future Value of a Set of Annual Investments

If you plan to save a specified amount of money every year for retirement, you can easily determine the value of your savings by the time you retire. Recall that a set of annual payments is called an annuity. The future value of an annuity can be computed by using the future value interest factor of an annuity (*FVIFA*) table (Table C.3) in Appendix C. You need the following information:

- The amount of the annual payment (investment)
- The annual return that you expect on the investments
- The time when the investments will end

Relationship Between Size of Annuity and Retirement Savings Consider how the amount of your savings at retirement is affected by the amount that you save each year. As Exhibit 19.2 shows, for every extra $1,000 that you can save at the end

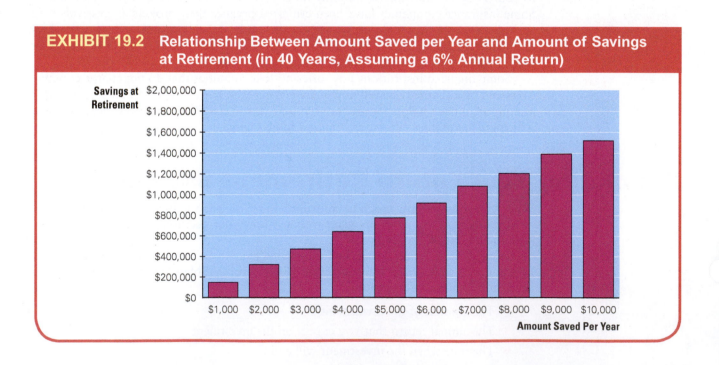

EXHIBIT 19.2   Relationship Between Amount Saved per Year and Amount of Savings at Retirement (in 40 Years, Assuming a 6% Annual Return)

of each year, you will accumulate an additional $154,760 at retirement, assuming a 6% annual return and 40 years of contributions.

EXAMPLE

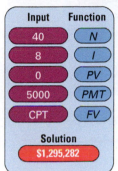

Input	Function
40	N
8	I
0	PV
5000	PMT
CPT	FV

Solution

$1,295,282

Stephanie Spratt is considering whether she should start saving toward her retirement. Although her retirement is 40 years away, she wants to ensure that she can live comfortably on her retirement income. She decides to contribute $3,600 per year ($300 per month) to her retirement through her employer's defined-contribution plan. Her employer will provide a partial matching contribution of $1,400 per year. Therefore, the total contribution to her retirement account will be $5,000 per year. As a result, Stephanie will have less spending money and will not have access to these savings until she retires in about 40 years. However, her annual contribution helps reduce her taxes now because the money she contributes is not subject to income taxes until she withdraws it at retirement.

Stephanie wants to determine how much money she will have in 40 years based on the total contribution of $5,000 per year. She expects to earn a return of 8% on her investment. She can use the future value of annuity tables (in Appendix C) to estimate the value of this annuity in 40 years. Her estimate of her savings at the time of retirement is

$$\text{Savings in Retirement Account} = \text{Annual Contribution} \times \textit{FVIFA} \ (i = 8\%, n = 40)$$

$$= \$5,000 \times 259.06$$

$$= \$1,295,300$$

The answer derived from this process may differ slightly from the answer when using a calculator due to rounding.

Stephanie realizes that she may be overestimating her return, so she reestimates her savings based on a 5% return:

$$\text{Savings in Retirement Account} = \text{Annual Contribution} \times \textit{FVIFA} \ (i = 5\%, n = 40)$$

$$= \$5,000 \times 120.797$$

$$= \$603,985$$

Even with this more conservative estimate, Stephanie will be able to accumulate more than $600,000 by the time she retires.

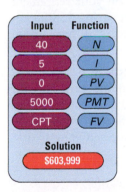

Input	Function
40	N
5	I
0	PV
5000	PMT
CPT	FV

Solution

$603,999

FREE APPS
for Personal Finance

Estimating Your Savings on Retirement

Application:

The Prudential Retirement Income Calculator app (by The Prudential Insurance Company of America) allows you to determine how the amount you would save by the time of your retirement would change based on various scenarios.

To Find It:

Search for the "Prudential Retirement Income" app on your mobile device.

Relationship Between Years of Saving and Retirement Savings The amount you will accumulate by the time you retire also depends on the number of years your investment remains in your retirement account. As Exhibit 19.3 shows, the longer your annual savings are invested, the more they will be worth at retirement. If you plan to retire at age 65, notice that if you start saving $5,000 per year at age 35 (and therefore

EXHIBIT 19.3 Relationship Between the Number of Years You Invest Annual Savings and Your Savings at Retirement (Assuming a $5,000 Annual Investment and a 6% Annual Return)

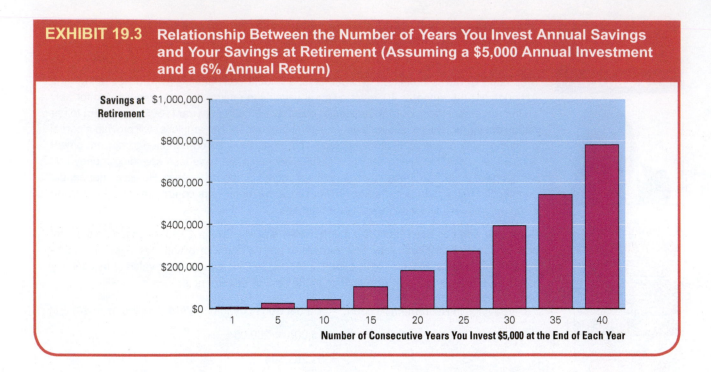

Number of Consecutive Years You Invest $5,000 at the End of Each Year

save for 30 years until retirement), you will have about $395,000 on your retirement (assuming a 6% annual return on investment). However, if you start saving $5,000 per year at age 25 (and therefore save for 40 years until retirement), you will have about $774,000 on your retirement.

Relationship Between Your Annual Return and Your Savings at Retirement

The amount you will have at retirement also depends on the return you earn on your annual savings, as shown in Exhibit 19.4. An annual return of 10% produces about $1.4 million more in accumulated retirement savings than an annual return of 6%. However, recognize that striving for higher returns on your investments can result in more risk.

EXHIBIT 19.4 Relationship Between the Annual Return on Your Annual Savings and Your Savings at Retirement (in 40 years, Assuming a $5,000 Annual Investment)

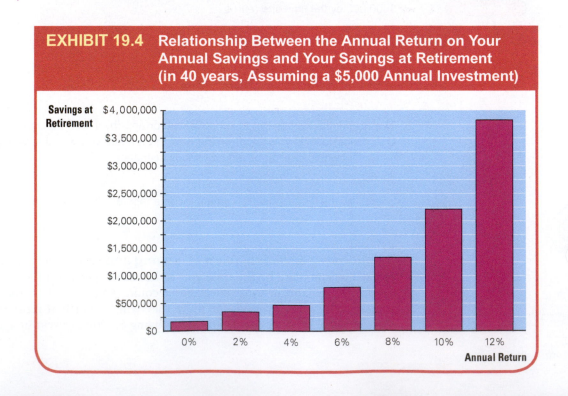

Annual Return

How Retirement Planning Fits Within Your Financial Plan

The following are the key retirement planning decisions that should be included within your financial plan:

- Should you invest in a retirement plan?
- How much should you invest in a retirement plan?
- How should you allocate investments within your retirement plan?

Exhibit 19.5 provides an example of how the retirement planning decisions apply to Stephanie Spratt's financial plan.

EXHIBIT 19.5   How Retirement Planning Fits Within Stephanie Spratt's Financial Plan

GOALS FOR RETIREMENT PLANNING

1. *Ensure an adequate financial position at the time I retire.*
2. *Reduce the tax liability on my present income.*

ANALYSIS

Type of Retirement Plan	Benefits
Employer's retirement plan	*I plan to contribute $3,600 of my income (tax-deferred) per year to my retirement plan. In addition, my employer provides a partial matching contribution of $1,400.*

Type of Retirement Plan	Benefits
Traditional IRA or Roth IRA	*I can contribute income each year (tax-deferred) to a traditional IRA. Alternatively, I could contribute to a Roth IRA; in that case, the contribution occurs after taxes, but the withdrawal after retire-ment will not be taxed.*
Annuities	*I can contribute money to annuities to supplement any other retirement plan. The only tax advantage is that any income earned on the money invested is not taxed until I withdraw the money after retirement.*

DECISIONS

Decision on Whether I Should Engage in Retirement Planning:

Even if Social Security benefits are available when I retire, they will not be sufficient to provide the amount of financial support that I desire. Given the substantial tax benefits of a retirement plan, I should engage in retirement planning. I plan to take full advantage of my employer's retirement plan. I will contribute $3,600 per year and my employer will match with $1,400. The benefits of traditional and Roth IRAs are also substantial. However, the trade-off is that I will not have access to any income that I invest in my retirement account for many years. Although I have not contributed to these retirement accounts in the past, I plan to do so as soon as possible. Annuities are not attractive to me at this point.

Decision on How Much to Contribute to Retirement:

I should attempt to contribute the maximum allowed to my employer's retirement plan and to a traditional or Roth IRA. These contributions will reduce the amount of money that I can dedicate toward savings and investments, but the trade-off favors retirement contributions because of the tax advantages. I will make sure that I maintain enough income to cover my monthly expenses and sufficient liquidity. Beyond that, I will attempt to maximize the amount of funds that I can contribute to retirement accounts.

Decision on Asset Allocation Within the Retirement Account:

I plan to invest the money slated for retirement in stock and bond mutual funds. I will invest about 70% or 80% of the money in a few diversified stock mutual funds and the remainder in a diversified corporate bond mutual fund.

DISCUSSION QUESTIONS

1. How would Stephanie's retirement planning decisions be different if she were a single mother of two children?

2. How would Stephanie's retirement planning decisions be affected if she were 35 years old? If she were 50 years old?

SUMMARY

Role of Social Security. Social Security provides income to qualified individuals to support them during their retirement. However, the income provided normally is not sufficient for most individuals to live comfortably. Therefore, individuals engage in retirement planning so that they will have additional sources of income when they retire.

Defined Benefit versus Contribution Plans. Retirement plans sponsored by employers are normally classified as defined-benefit plans or defined-contribution plans. Defined-benefit plans guarantee a specific amount of income to employees on retirement, based on factors such as their salary and number of years of service. Defined-contribution plans provide guidelines on the maximum amount that can be contributed to a retirement account. Individuals have the freedom to make decisions about how much to invest and how to invest for their retirement.

Retirement Planning Decisions. Two key retirement planning decisions are how much to contribute to your retirement plan and how to invest your contributions. When an employer is willing to match your retirement contribution, you should always contribute enough to take full advantage of the match. In addition, you should also try to contribute the maximum amount allowed, even if doing so means you will have less money to invest in other ways. Most financial advisers suggest investing most of your contribution in one or more diversified stock mutual funds and putting the remainder in a diversified bond mutual fund. The specific allocation depends on your willingness to tolerate risk.

Retirement Plans Offered by Employers. Retirement plans offered by employers include the 401(k) plan, 403(b) plan, Simplified Employee Pension (SEP) plan, SIMPLE, profit sharing, and ESOP. These plans offer similar types of benefits in that they encourage you to save for retirement and can defer your income from taxes. The specific

eligibility requirements and other characteristics vary among retirement plans.

In addition to these retirement plans, some firms began to offer Roth 401(k) plans in 2006. The advantage of the Roth 401(k) is that the funds withdrawn at the time of retirement are not taxed. However, the income contributed to the plan is taxed. Individuals who have the choice of a traditional 401(k) versus the Roth 401(k) must compare the benefits of deferring taxes with the traditional 401(k) plan versus avoiding taxes on withdrawal of retirement funds with the Roth 401(k) plan.

Self-Employed Retirement Plans. Self-employed individuals can use a SEP plan, which allows them to contribute up to 25% of their net income, up to a maximum of $53,000 in 2015. Alternatively, they can use a one-participant 401(k) plan, which is subject to the same rules and limits as 401(k) plans for employees. High-income self-employed individuals may choose to use a Keogh plan.

Individual Retirement Accounts. In addition to retirement accounts offered by employers, individuals can also establish an individual retirement account (IRA), such as a traditional IRA or a Roth IRA.

Annuities. An annuity is a financial contract that provides annual payments until a specified year or for one's lifetime. The return on the investment in an annuity is tax-deferred, however, so any gains generated by the annuity are not taxed until the funds are paid to the investor. However, this tax benefit is smaller than the benefit from sheltering income by using a retirement account.

Savings from Retirement Accounts. Your future savings from investing in a retirement account can easily be estimated based on information regarding the amount you plan to invest each year, the annual return you expect, and the number of years until retirement. The future savings reflect the future value of an annuity.

How Retirement Planning Fits Within Your Financial Plan. While you are working, you should be setting aside funds for your retirement. This will allow you to spend more money once you have retired and have more time for leisure activities. Retirement planning at an early age can have a major impact on your wealth by the time you retire.

REVIEW QUESTIONS

All Review Questions are available in MyFinanceLab *at http://www.myfinancelab.com.*

1. **Social Security.** How does Social Security fit into retirement planning? How does an individual qualify for Social Security benefits? When do you receive benefits?

2. **Retirement Benefits.** How are the retirement benefits under Social Security calculated? Describe some factors that affect the amount of your benefits.

3. **Concerns About Social Security.** Discuss some of the concerns about the future of Social Security.

4. **Employer-Sponsored Retirement Plans.** Describe how employer-sponsored retirement plans work in general.

5. **Defined-Benefit Plan.** What is a defined-benefit plan? What is vesting? What does it mean to be fully vested?

6. **Defined-Contribution Plan.** What is a defined-contribution plan? Why are many employers switching to this type of plan? List some of the benefits a defined-contribution plan offers to employees.

7. **Retirement Planning Decisions.** Briefly discuss the key retirement planning decisions an individual must make.

8. **401(k) versus 403(b) Plans.** Discuss the general characteristics of a 401(k) plan. What is a 403(b) plan?

9. **SEP versus SIMPLE Plans.** Compare and contrast a Simplified Employee Pension (SEP) plan and a Savings Incentive Match Plan for Employees (SIMPLE).

10. **ESOPs.** Discuss profit-sharing and employee stock ownership plans (ESOPs).

11. **Retirement Account.** Discuss the choices an employee has to manage a retirement account on leaving an employer.

12. **Self-Employment Retirement Plans.** Briefly describe two popular retirement plans for self-employed individuals.

13. **IRAs.** Compare and contrast a traditional IRA with a Roth IRA. Discuss the advantages of each. What factors will affect your choice of IRAs?

14. **Annuities.** What is an annuity? What is the difference between a fixed annuity and a variable annuity? What is the main disadvantage of annuities?

15. **Retirement Accounts.** Why are retirement accounts more beneficial than other investments that could be used for retirement? Describe an effective strategy for retirement planning.

16. **Projecting Retirement Funding.** When estimating the future value of a retirement investment, what factors will affect the amount of funds available to you at retirement? Explain.

17. **Projecting Retirement Funding.** When estimating the future value of a set of annual investments, what factors will affect the amount of funds available to you at retirement?

18. **Tax Benefits of a Retirement Account.** Explain the tax benefits of investing within a retirement account versus investing outside a retirement account.

19. **Retirement Planning.** What is the main advantage of retirement planning?

20. **Retirement Planning and Age.** Why is it important to begin retirement planning while you are young?

21. **Social Security and Retirement Age.** How does your retirement age impact the amount of Social Security benefits you will receive?

22. **Employer Matching.** What is an employer match? Why is it important to take advantage of an employer match?

23. **Investing Contributions.** What factors should you consider when deciding how to invest in your defined-contribution retirement fund?

24. **Profit Sharing.** What is a profit sharing plan? What are the contribution limits for profit sharing plans?

FINANCIAL PLANNING PROBLEMS

All Financial Planning Problems are available in MyFinanceLab *at http://www.myfinancelab.com.*

1. **Retirement Funding.** Barry has just become eligible for his employer-sponsored retirement plan. Barry is 35 and plans to retire at 65. Barry calculates that he can contribute $3,600 per year to his plan. Barry's employer will match this amount. If Barry can earn an 8% return on his investment, how much will he have at retirement?

2. **Retirement Funding.** How much would Barry (from problem 1) have at retirement if he had started this plan at age 25?

3. **Retirement Funding.** How much would Barry have if he could earn a 10% return on his investment beginning at age 35?

4. **Retirement Funding.** Assuming an 8% return, how much would Barry have if he could invest an additional $1,000 per year that his employer would match beginning at age 35?

5. **Retirement Funding.** How much will Marie have in her retirement account in 10 years if her contribution is $7,000 per year and the annual return on the account is 6%? How much of this amount represents interest?

6. **Retirement Plan Decision.** Thomas earns $45,000 per year. What retirement plan should Thomas consider under the following circumstances?

   a. He works for a large private firm.

   b. He works at a university.

   c. He owns a small firm with employees.

7. **Retirement Planning.** Tilly would like to invest $2,500 in before-tax income each year in a retirement account or in stock investments outside the retirement account. Tilly likes the stock investments outside the retirement account because they provide her with more flexibility and a potentially higher return. Tilly would like to retire in 30 years. If she invests money in the retirement account, she can earn 7% annually. If she invests in stock outside the account, she can earn 9% annually. Tilly is in the 25% marginal tax bracket.

   a. If Tilly invests all her money in the retirement account and withdraws all her income when she retires, what is her income after taxes?

   b. If Tilly invests all her money in stocks outside the account, what are her savings at retirement? (*Hint:* Remember that the income is taxed prior to investment.)

   c. Assuming a capital gains tax rate of 15%, what is the after-tax value of the stock investments?

   d. Should Tilly invest her money in the retirement account or in stocks outside the account?

8. **Retirement Account Withdrawal.** In need of extra cash, Troy and Lilly decide to withdraw $8,000 from their traditional IRA. They are both 40 years old. They are in a 25% marginal tax bracket. What will be the tax consequences of this withdrawal?

9. **IRAs.** Lisa and Mark married at age 22. Each year until their 30th birthdays, they put $4,000 into their traditional IRAs. By age 30, they had bought a home and started a family. Although they continued to make contributions to their employer-sponsored retirement plans, they made no more contributions to their IRAs. If they receive an average annual return of 8%, how much will they have in their IRAs by age 60? What was their total investment?

10. **IRAs.** Ricky and Sharon married at age 22, started a family, and bought a house. At age 30, they began making a contribution of $4,000 to a traditional IRA. They continued making these contributions annually until age 60. If the average return on their investment was 8%, how much was in their IRA at age 60? What was their total investment?

11. **Tax Savings.** Lloyd and his wife, Jean, have no retirement plan at work, but they contribute $4,000 each year to a traditional IRA. They are in a 25% marginal tax bracket. What tax savings will they realize for these contributions annually?

12. **Employer Matching.** Ezra works for a firm that offers a 100% match up to 4% of his salary on retirement contributions. How much will Ezra accumulate in 20 years if he contributes 4% of his salary of $100,000 per year assuming his account earns an 8% annual return?

13. **Profit Sharing.** Cedrick works for an employer that has a profit sharing retirement system. Assuming Cedrick made $133,000 last year, what is the maximum amount his employer can contribute to his retirement account?

14. **Ethical Dilemma.** Nancy and Al have been planning their retirement since they married in their early 20s. In their mid-40s and with two children in college, they are finding it harder to save and fear they will fall short of the savings needed to reach their retirement goals. Nancy's rich Uncle Charlie

assures her she has nothing to worry about. "You are my favorite niece and because you are so good to me, I am leaving my entire estate to you," he said. Nancy and Al begin devoting considerable time and energy to making Uncle Charlie's golden years as enjoyable as possible.

Factoring in their anticipated inheritance, Nancy and Al look forward to a comfortable retirement. Ten years later, Uncle Charlie passes away. At the reading of his will, Nancy is surprised to learn that Uncle

Charlie made the same comment to her four cousins. As the will is read, all five of the cousins are horrified to find that Uncle Charlie left his entire estate, valued at over $2 million, to a home for stray cats.

a. Fully discuss your views on the ethics of Uncle Charlie's actions.

b. Looking at Nancy and Al's experience, what lessons about retirement planning can be learned?

FINANCIAL PLANNING ONLINE EXERCISES

1. Go to http://www.socialsecurity.gov and then go to the Calculators section to estimate your benefits at retirement. Determine your monthly Social Security benefits.

2. Go to http://www.marketwatch.com and insert the search term "Retirement." Summarize the information provided by this Web site that can help you with your retirement planning.

PSYCHOLOGY OF PERSONAL FINANCE: Your Retirement

1. Some people find that it is much easier to save for retirement when they request that their employer automatically direct a portion of their income to their retirement account. Describe your strategy to invest in your retirement. Are you currently investing in a retirement account? If so, do you use a defined-contribution plan for this purpose?

2. Read one practical article about how psychology affects decisions when investing for retirement. You can easily retrieve possible articles by doing an online search using the terms "psychology" and "investing in retirement." Summarize the main points of the article.

WEB SEARCH EXERCISE

You can develop your personal finance skills by conducting an Internet search for related articles. Find a recent online article about personal finance that reinforces one or more concepts covered in this chapter. If your class has an online component, your professor may ask you to post your summary of the article there and provide a link to the article so that other students can access it. If your class is live, your professor may ask you to summarize your application of the article in class. Your professor may assign specific students to complete this assignment or may allow any student to do the assignment on a volunteer basis.

For recent online articles related to this chapter, consider using the following search terms (be sure to include the current year as a search term to ensure that the online articles are recent):

- Social Security benefits
- Defined-benefit plan
- Defined-contribution plan
- Your retirement plan
- Roth IRA
- Annuity
- Saving for your retirement

VIDEO EXERCISE: Retirement Planning

Go to one of the Web sites that contain video clips (such as http://www.youtube.com), and view some video clips about retirement planning. You can use search phrases such as "tips on retirement planning." Select one video clip on this topic that you would recommend for the other students in your class.

1. Provide the Web link for the video clip.
2. What do you think is the main point of this video clip?
3. How might you change your process of retirement planning as a result of watching this video clip?

BUILDING YOUR OWN FINANCIAL PLAN

Difficult as it may be to visualize, retirement really is "right around the corner." The reality is that the earlier you begin dealing with the issues of retirement, the more successful and enjoyable retirement will be.

You will very likely change jobs, if not careers, numerous times in your working life. Most of your employers will offer a defined-contribution plan, such as a 401(k), rather than a defined-benefit plan. It is therefore to your benefit to begin planning and executing a plan for your retirement as early as possible. The tax benefits of retirement planning should serve as an additional motivator. The key decisions you need to make are how much to save each month, what type of plan(s) to contribute to, and how to allocate various retirement investments.

A retirement plan, like a portfolio, should be reviewed annually. You will probably not make major changes to your plan, but an annual review will help you to see whether you are on target to achieve your goals and retirement needs.

Go to the worksheets at the end of this chapter to continue building your financial plan.

THE SAMPSONS—A Continuing Case

Next on the Sampsons' financial planning checklist is saving for retirement. Dave's employer offers a 401(k) plan, but Dave has not participated in it up to this point. Now he wants to seriously consider contributing. His employer will allow him to invest about $7,000 of his salary per year and match his contribution up to $3,000, for a total contribution of $10,000 per year.

The retirement funds will be invested in one or more mutual funds. Dave's best guess is that the retirement fund investments will earn a return of 7% per year.

Go to the worksheets at the end of this chapter to continue this case.

CHAPTER 19: BUILDING YOUR OWN FINANCIAL PLAN

YOUR GOALS FOR CHAPTER 19

1. Ensure an adequate financial position at the time you retire.
2. Reduce the tax liability on your present income.

ANALYSIS

1. Determine how much money you must save per year, based on an assumed rate of return, and the savings period until retirement to meet your goal for retirement savings. Experiment with different inputs using the financial planning Excel software.

   Future Value of an Annuity

Payment per Period	
Number of Periods	
Interest Rate per Period	
Future Value	

2. Once you estimate the savings you will need, if you need to save more than you had planned, identify possible adjustments to your personal cash flow statement.

DECISIONS

1. How much savings do you need to support yourself during retirement?

   _____

   _____

   _____

   _____

2. How much will you contribute to your retirement? Into what type of plan(s) will you contribute?

   _____

   _____

   _____

   _____

   _____

   _____

   _____

CHAPTER 19: THE SAMPSONS—A Continuing Case

CASE QUESTIONS

1. If Dave and his employer contribute a total of $10,000 annually, how much will that amount accumulate over the next 30 years, at which time Dave and Sharon hope to retire?

Future Value of an Annuity

Contribution	$10,000
Years	30
Annual Rate of Return	
Future Value	

2. Assuming that Dave's marginal tax bracket is 25%, by how much should his federal taxes decline this year if he contributes $7,000 to his retirement account?

3. The Sampsons' tax bracket has not changed. Assuming that Dave contributes $7,000 to his retirement account and that his taxes are lower as a result, by how much are Dave's cash flows reduced over the coming year? (Refer to your answer in question 2 when solving this problem.)

4. If Dave contributes $7,000 to his retirement account, he will have lower cash inflows as a result. How can the Sampsons afford to make this contribution? Suggest some ways that they may be able to offset the reduction in cash inflows.

Estate Planning

Iurii Sokolov/Fotolia

Ever since Jason Veer was a child, he wanted to help support charities. When he graduated from college, his busy career limited the amount of time he could devote to philanthropy. However, he made a promise to himself that he would donate a large amount of money to his favorite charities someday. He was not married and did not have any children. Jason lived very conservatively and accumulated considerable wealth over time. He wanted to have his large estate distributed among several charities that focused on improving health care for poor people and others that focused on improving the lives of children with no parents.

Although Jason had many good plans about how his large estate should be distributed to charities, he did not have a will. A month ago, Jason died unexpectedly. His only surviving family member was a brother, but he and Jason were estranged and had not communicated with each other for years. Nevertheless, under the laws in Jason's state, his brother received the entire amount of Jason's estate. None of the wealth that Jason had accumulated over the years was distributed to his favorite charities.

Estate planning is important because it ensures that your estate is distributed in the manner that you desire. In addition, proper planning may allow your estate to be legally insulated from taxes, so that your entire estate can be distributed to your family members or other beneficiaries that you identify in your will.

MyFinanceLab helps you master the topics in this chapter and study more efficiently. Visit http://www.myfinancelab.com for more details.

The objectives of this chapter are to:

- Explain the use of a will
- Describe estate taxes
- Explain the use of trusts, gifts, and contributions
- Introduce other aspects of estate planning
- Explain how estate planning fits within your financial plan

Purpose of a Will

estate
The assets of a deceased person after all debts are paid.

estate planning
The act of planning for how your wealth will be allocated on or before your death.

will
A legal request for how your estate should be distributed on your death. It can also identify a preferred guardian for any surviving children.

beneficiaries (heirs)
The persons specified in a will to receive a part of an estate.

intestate
The condition of dying without a will.

An **estate** consists of a deceased person's assets after all debts are paid. At the time of a person's death, the estate is distributed according to that person's wishes. **Estate planning** is the act of planning how your wealth will be allocated on or before your death. One of the most important tasks in estate planning is the creation of a **will**, which is a legal request for how your estate should be distributed on your death. It can also identify a preferred guardian for any surviving children who are minors.

Reasons for Having a Will

A will is critical to ensure that your estate is distributed in the manner that you desire. Once you have a positive net worth to be distributed on your death, you should consider creating a will. In your will, you can specify the persons you want to receive your estate—referred to as your **beneficiaries** (or **heirs**). If you die **intestate** (without a will), the court will appoint a person (called an administrator) to distribute your estate according to the laws of your state. In that case, one family member may receive more than you intended, while others receive less. You may think that you have little of value so you have no need for a will. But you're likely to have some personal property such as a baseball card collection or jewelry that you would like to leave to specific friends or relatives. With a will, you can ensure that they will receive that property. In addition, a will can prevent arguments after your death if several of your relatives want the same assets. Having an administrator also results in additional costs being imposed on the estate.

Furthermore, if there is no surviving spouse, the administrator will also decide who will assume responsibility for any children, and that might not be the person you would have chosen. For example, you might want your best friend to be your children's guardian because you and your friend have similar ideas on child rearing, but the administrator may choose your sister, who has a very different approach to raising children.

Creating a Valid Will

To create a valid will, you must be at least the minimum age, usually 18 or 21, depending on the state where you live. You must also be mentally competent and should not be subject to undue influence (threats) from others. A will is more likely to be challenged by potential heirs if there is some question about your competence or whether you were forced to designate one or more beneficiaries in the will. Some states require that the will be typed, although handwritten wills are accepted in other states. To be valid, a will must be dated and signed. Two or three witnesses who do not inherit anything under the will must also witness the signing of the will.

There are many different laws that you should understand when creating a will, and the laws can vary by state and change over time. Thus, while you can learn some of the basic principles for creating a will in this chapter, you may still benefit from discussing your will with an attorney who has expertise in this specific field.

Common Types of Wills

A **simple will** specifies that the entire estate be distributed to a person's spouse. It may be sufficient for many married couples. If the estate is valued at several million dollars or more, a simple will may not be appropriate, especially if the spouse also has a large amount of assets, because an estate in excess of $5.43 million (in 2015) could be subject to a high tax rate. Thus, if a wife dies and leaves her entire estate of $4 million to her husband who has $3 million of his own, the husband's estate will be worth $7 million and be subject to a high tax rate. A more appropriate will for large estates is the **traditional marital share will**, which distributes half of the estate to the spouse and the other half to any children or to a trust (discussed later in the chapter). This type of will is useful for minimizing taxes on the estate.

traditional marital share will
A will suitable for larger estates that distributes half of the estate to the spouse and the other half to any children or to a trust.

Key Components of a Will

Financial Planning ONLINE

Go to:
Go to the CNN Money web site and insert the search term "estate planning."

To get:
Guidance on estate planning.

A sample of a will is provided in Exhibit 20.1. The key components of a will are described next.

Distribution of the Estate The will details how the estate should be distributed among the beneficiaries. Because you do not know what your estate will be worth, you may specify your desired distribution according to percentages of the estate. For example, you could specify that two people each receive 50% of the estate. Alternatively, you could specify that one person receive a specific dollar amount and that the other person receive the remainder of the estate.

Executor In your will, you name an **executor** (also called a **personal representative**) to carry out your instructions regarding how your assets will be distributed. An executor may be required to collect any money owed to the estate, pay off any debts owed by the estate, sell specific assets (such as a home) that are part of the estate, and then distribute the proceeds as specified in the will. The executor must notify everyone who has an interest or potential interest in the estate. Most people select a family member, a friend, a business associate, a bank trust company employee, or an attorney as an executor. You should select an executor who would serve your interests in distributing the assets as specified in your will, who is capable of handling the process, and who is sufficiently organized to complete the process in a timely manner.

executor (personal representative)
The person designated in a will to execute your instructions regarding the distribution of your assets.

The executor must be a U.S. citizen, may not be a minor or convicted felon, and, under some states' laws, must reside in the same state as the person creating the will. The executor is entitled to be paid by the estate for services provided, but some executors elect not to charge the estate.

Guardian If you are a parent, you should name a guardian, who will be assigned the responsibility of caring for the children and managing any estate left to the children. You should ensure that the person you select as guardian is willing to serve in this capacity. Your will may specify an amount of money to be distributed to the guardian to care for the children.

Signature Your signature is needed to validate the will and ensure that someone else does not create a fake will.

letter of last instruction
A supplement to a will that can describe your preferences regarding funeral arrangements and indicate where you have stored any key financial documents.

Letter of Last Instruction You may also wish to prepare a **letter of last instruction**. This describes your preferences regarding funeral arrangements and indicates where you have stored any key financial documents such as mortgage and insurance contracts.

Changing Your Will

You may need to change your will if you move to a different state because state laws regarding wills vary. If you get married or divorced after creating your will, you may also need to change it.

EXHIBIT 20.1   A Sample Will

WILL of James T. Smith

I, James T. Smith of the City of Denver, Colorado, declare this to be my will.

ARTICLE 1

My wife, Karen A. Smith, and I have one child, Cheryl D. Smith.

ARTICLE 2 Payment of Debt and Taxes

I direct my Executor to pay my funeral expenses, my medical expenses, the costs of administration, and my debts.

ARTICLE 3 Distribution of the Estate

I direct that my estate be distributed to my wife, Karen A. Smith. If my wife predeceases me, my estate shall be distributed to my Trustee, to be managed as explained in Article 4.

ARTICLE 4 Trust for Children

4A. Purpose. This trust provides for the support of my daughter, Cheryl D. Smith, and any other children born to me.

4B. Use of Funds. The Trustee shall use as much of the trust income and principal as necessary to care for my child (or children). When the youngest of my children reaches the age of 25, the assets of this trust shall be split equally among the children.

4C. No Survivors. If no child of mine survives until age 25, assets of the trust shall be liquidated and 100% of the proceeds shall be donated to the San Diego Humane Society.

4D. Nomination of Trustee. I appoint my brother, Edward J. Smith, to serve as Trustee. If he is unable or unwilling to serve, I appoint my sister, Marie S. Smith, to serve as Trustee.

ARTICLE 5 Executor

I appoint my wife, Karen A. Smith, to serve as Executor. If she is unable or unwilling to serve, I appoint my brother, Edward J. Smith, to serve as Executor.

ARTICLE 6 Guardian

If my spouse does not survive me, I appoint my brother, Edward J. Smith, to serve as Guardian of my children. If he is unable to serve as Guardian, I appoint my sister, Marie S. Smith, to serve as Guardian.

ARTICLE 7 Power of Executor

My Executor has the right to receive payments, reinvest payments received, pay debts owed, pay taxes owed, and liquidate assets.

ARTICLE 8 Power of Trustee

My Trustee has the right to receive income generated by the trust, reinvest income received by the trust, sell assets in the trust, and use the proceeds to invest in other assets.

IN WITNESS WHEREOF, I hereby sign and declare this document to be my Will.

_____   _____
James T. Smith   Date

The above-named person signed in our presence, and in our opinion is mentally competent.

Signatures of Witnesses   Addresses of Witnesses

_____

Kenneth Tagan   44241 Lemon Street
                                                                    Denver, Colorado 80208

_____

Barbara Russell   101 Courtney Street
                                                                    Denver, Colorado 80208

If you wish to make major changes to your will, you will probably need to create a new will. The new will must specify that you are revoking your previous will, so that you do not have multiple wills with conflicting instructions. When you wish to make only minor revisions to your will, you can add a **codicil**, which is a document that specifies changes to your existing will.

codicil
A document that specifies changes in an existing will.

probate
A legal process that declares a will valid and ensures the orderly distribution of assets.

Executing the Will During Probate

Probate is a legal process that ensures that when people die, their assets are distributed as they wish, and the guardianship of children is assigned as they wish. The purpose of the probate process is for the court to declare a will valid and ensure the orderly distribution of assets. To start the probate process, the executor files forms in a local probate court, provides a copy of the will, provides a list of the assets and debts of the deceased person, pays debts, and sells any assets that need to be liquidated. The executor typically opens a bank account for the estate that is used to pay the debts of the deceased and to deposit proceeds from liquidating the assets. If the executor does not have time or is otherwise unable to perform these tasks, an attorney can be hired to complete them. Most states have a simplified probate process for small estates, but the rules vary from state to state

Estate Taxes

An estate may be subject to taxes before it is distributed to the beneficiaries. When a person dies and has a surviving spouse who jointly owned all the assets, the spouse becomes sole owner of the estate. In this case, the estate is not subject to taxes. If there is not a surviving spouse and the estate is to be distributed to the children or other beneficiaries, the estate is subject to taxes. The estate taxes are assessed after the value of the estate is determined during the probate process. You should estimate the estate taxes based on your net worth, so that you can take steps to minimize the tax liability on your death.

Determining Estate Taxes

The estate's value is equal to the value of all the assets minus any existing liabilities (including a mortgage) and funeral and administrative expenses. Life insurance proceeds from policies owned by the deceased are included in the estate and therefore may be subject to estate taxes.

A specified portion of an estate is exempt from federal estate taxes. In 2015, the first $5.43 million of an estate can be distributed to children or others tax-free. Beyond this specific limit, a federal estate tax is imposed with a top rate of 40%. The limit and estate tax rates may be changed over time. There are several ways of reducing your exposure to high estate taxes, as explained later in the chapter.

Other Related Taxes

Several states impose inheritance taxes or state excise taxes on an estate, although these taxes are being phased out in some states. To avoid state taxes on an estate, residents of such states sometimes retire in other states that do not impose them.

Valuing Your Estate to Assess Potential Estate Taxes

Because the potential estate tax you could incur someday is dependent on the value of your estate, you should periodically calculate the value of your estate. Many people will need estate planning to ensure that they can pass as much of their wealth as possible on to their beneficiaries. Once your net worth exceeds the tax-free limit, you should carefully plan your estate to minimize any potential tax liability.

Trusts, Gifts, and Contributions

trust
A legal document in which one person (the grantor) transfers assets to another (the trustee) who manages them for designated beneficiaries.

grantor
The person who creates a trust.

trustee
The person or institution named in a trust to manage the trust assets for the beneficiaries.

living trust
A trust in which you assign the management of your assets to a trustee while you are living.

revocable living trust
A living trust that can be dissolved.

irrevocable living trust
A living trust that cannot be changed, although it can provide income to the grantor.

standard family trust (credit-shelter trust)
A trust established for children in a family.

testamentary trust
A trust created by a will.

Estate planning commonly involves trusts, gifts, and contributions for the purpose of avoiding estate taxes. You may consider hiring an attorney to complete the proper documents.

Trusts

A **trust** is a legal document in which one person (called a **grantor**) transfers assets to another person (called a **trustee**), who manages the assets for designated beneficiaries. The grantor must select a trustee who is capable of managing the assets being transferred. Various types of investment firms can be hired to serve as trustees.

Living Trusts A **living trust** is a trust in which you assign the management of your assets to a trustee while you are living. You identify a trustee who you want to manage the assets (which includes making decisions on how to invest cash until it is needed or how to spend cash).

Revocable Living Trust With a **revocable living trust,** you can dissolve or revoke the trust at any time because you are still the legal owner of the assets. For example, you may revoke a living trust if you decide that you want to manage the assets yourself. Alternatively, you may revoke a living trust so that you can replace the trustee. In this case, you would create a new living trust with a newly identified trustee.

By using a revocable living trust, you can avoid the probate process. You are still the legal owner of the assets, however, so you do not avoid estate taxes. The assets are still considered part of your estate.

Irrevocable Living Trust An **irrevocable living trust** is a living trust that cannot be changed. This type of trust is a separate entity. It can provide income for you, but the assets in the trust are no longer legally yours. The assets are not considered part of your estate and therefore are not subject to estate taxes on your death.

Standard Family Trust A **standard family trust** (also called a **credit-shelter trust**) is a trust established for children in a family. The standard family trust is just one of many types of **testamentary trusts,** or trusts created by wills. It is a popular type of trust because it can be used to avoid estate taxes in a manner somewhat similar to the irrevocable living trust, except that it is not structured as a living trust. Consider the following example.

EXAMPLE

Stephanie Spratt's parents have an estate that is valued above the maximum allowable limit that can be passed on to children tax-free. Thus, a portion of their estate could be subject to high estate taxes. To legally avoid estate taxes, they revise their financial plan as follows. First, they split up the ownership of their assets, so that they are each owners of specific assets. In this way, the total amount of assets owned by either Mr. Spratt or Mrs. Spratt is below the maximum allowable limit that can be passed on to their children. Second, Mr. Spratt specifies in his will that if he dies first, his assets are to be distributed to a standard family trust for the children.

The trust will be managed by a trustee and will provide Mrs. Spratt with income while she is alive and, ultimately, will provide income for her children. The assets in the trust will not be legally owned by Mrs. Spratt. These assets will be distributed to the children when they reach an age specified in the trust document. Therefore, Mrs. Spratt will legally own an amount of assets that is below the maximum allowable level before estate taxes are imposed. Upon her death, her estate can be passed on tax-free to her children. The will could also state that if Mrs. Spratt dies first, her assets are to be distributed to a standard family trust.

Gifts

gift
A tax-free distribution of up to $14,000 per year from one person to another.

From an estate planning perspective, a **gift** is a tax-free distribution of funds from one person to another. As of 2015, the law allows up to $14,000 to pass by gift per year. The maximum amount of the gift allowed will increase over time with inflation.

If your goal is to ultimately pass on your estate to your children, but you are concerned about estate taxes, you can reduce the size of your estate by giving $14,000 tax-free to each of your children each year. The recipient does not have to report the gift as income, and therefore it is not subject to taxes. If you are married, you and your spouse can give $28,000 ($14,000 from each of you) to each of your children. Thus, a married couple with three children may give a total of $84,000 (3 × $28,000) in gifts to their children every year. Over a five-year period, the couple could give $420,000 (5 × $84,000) to their three children without any tax consequences to the parents or the children. Such gifts are especially important for people whose estate value exceeds the tax-free limit. Frequent gifts may enable the parents to ensure that their estate falls under the tax-free limit by the time of their death.

Contributions to Charitable Organizations

Many individuals wish to leave a portion of their estate to charitable organizations. Any money donated from an estate to charitable organizations is not subject to estate taxes. Consider an estate worth $200,000 more than the prevailing tax-free limit. If this entire estate is passed on to family members or other individuals, $200,000 of the estate will be subject to estate taxes. If $200,000 is donated to charitable organizations, however, none of the estate will be subject to estate taxes. Many individuals plan to leave donations for charitable organizations regardless of the tax implications, but it is nonetheless important to recognize the tax benefits.

Other Aspects of Estate Planning

In addition to wills and trusts, estate planning also involves some other key decisions regarding a living will and power of attorney.

Living Will

living will
A legal document in which individuals specify their preferences if they become mentally or physically disabled.

A **living will** is a simple legal document in which individuals specify their preferences if they become mentally or physically disabled. For example, many individuals have a living will that expresses their desire not to be placed on life support if they become terminally ill. In this case, a living will also has financial implications because an estate could be charged with large medical bills resulting from life support. In this way, those who do not want to be kept alive by life support can ensure that their estate is used in the way that they prefer.

Power of Attorney

power of attorney
A legal document granting a person the power to make specific decisions for you in the event that you are incapable.

A **power of attorney** is a legal document granting a person the power to make specific decisions for you in the event that you are incapacitated. For example, you may name a family member or a close friend to make your investment and housing decisions if you become ill. You should name someone who you believe would act to serve your interests.

durable power of attorney for health care
A legal document granting a person the power to make specific health care decisions for you.

A **durable power of attorney for health care** is a legal document granting a person the power to make specific health care decisions for you. A durable power of attorney ensures that the person you identify has the power to make specific decisions regarding your health care in the event that you become incapacitated. Although a living will states many of your preferences, a situation may arise that is not covered by your living will. A durable power of attorney for health care means that the necessary decisions will be made by someone who knows your preferences, rather than by a health care facility.

Financial Planning
ONLINE

Go to:
http://www.nolo.com

To get:
Guidance on creating a
will and other functions
of estate planning.

Maintaining Estate Plan Documents

Key documents such as your will, living will, and power of attorney should be kept in a safe, accessible place. You should tell the person (or people) you named as executor(s) and granted power of attorney where you keep these documents so that they can be retrieved if and when they are needed.

Here is a checklist of the important documents that you should keep together:

- Estate planning information, such as a will, living will, and power of attorney
- Life insurance policies and other insurance policies
- Retirement account information
- Home ownership and mortgage information
- Ownership of other real estate
- Personal property, such as cars or jewelry owned
- Personal loans
- Credit card debt information
- Ownership of businesses
- Personal legal documents
- The most recent personal tax returns
- Bank account information
- Investment information

How Estate Planning Fits Within Your Financial Plan

The following are the key decisions about estate planning that should be included within your financial plan:

- Should you create a will?
- Do you need to establish a trust?
- Should you create a living will or designate an individual to have power of attorney?

Exhibit 20.2 provides an example of how estate planning decisions apply to Stephanie Spratt's financial plan.

EXHIBIT 20.2 How Estate Planning Fits Within Stephanie Spratt's Financial Plan

GOALS FOR ESTATE PLANNING

1. *Create a will.*
2. *Establish a plan for trusts or gifts if my estate is subject to high taxes.*
3. *Decide whether I need to create a living will or assign power of attorney.*

ANALYSIS

Estate Planning and Related Issues

Issue	Status
Possible heirs to my estate?	*My sister and parents.*
Tax implications for my estate?	*Small estate at this point; exempt from taxes.*
Power of attorney necessary?	*Yes; I want someone to make decisions for me if I am unable.*
Living will necessary?	*Yes; I do not want to be placed on life support.*

DECISIONS

Decision Regarding a Will:

I will create a will that stipulates a contribution of $5,000 to a charity. I plan to make my parents my heirs if they are alive; otherwise, I will name my sister as the heir. I will designate my sister to be executor.

Decision Regarding Trusts and Gifts:

My estate is easily under the limit at which taxes are imposed, so it would not be subject to taxes at this point. Therefore, I do not need to consider establishing trusts or gifts at this time.

Decision on a Power of Attorney and Durable Power of Attorney:

I will assign my mother the power of attorney and the durable power of attorney. I will hire an attorney who can complete these documents along with my will in one or two hours.

DISCUSSION QUESTIONS

1. How would Stephanie's estate planning decisions be different if she were a single mother of two children?
2. How would Stephanie's estate planning decisions be affected if she were 35 years old? If she were 50 years old?

SUMMARY

Purpose of a Will. A will is intended to make sure that your preferences are carried out after your death. It allows you to distribute your estate, select a guardian for your children, and select an executor to ensure that the will is executed properly.

Estate Taxes. Estate taxes are imposed on estates that exceed a tax-free limit. This limit has changed over time. In 2015 it is $5.43 million.

Estate Planning. Estate planning involves the use of trusts, gifts, and charitable contributions. Trusts can be structured so that a large estate can be passed on to the beneficiaries without being subjected to estate taxes. Gifts are tax-free payments that can be made on an annualized basis; they allow parents to pass on part of their wealth to their children every year. By making annual gifts, parents may reduce their wealth so that when they die, their estate will not be subject to estate taxes. An estate's contributions to charity are not subject to estate taxes.

Living Will and Power of Attorney. In the event that you someday might be incapable of making decisions relating to your health and financial situation, you should consider creating a living will and power of attorney now. A living will is a legal document that allows you to specify your health treatment preferences, such as the wish that you do not want to be placed on life support. The power of attorney is a legal document that allows you to assign a person the power to make specific decisions for you if and when you are no longer capable of making these decisions.

How Estate Planning Fits Within Your Financial Plan. Estate planning fits within your financial plan because it helps prepare for financial support of family members or loved ones. It is a means by which you can ensure that the wealth you accumulated is properly directed to the people who you intended to receive it.

REVIEW QUESTIONS

All Review Questions are available in MyFinanceLab *at* http://www.myfinancelab.com.

1. **Estate Planning.** What is an estate? What is estate planning? What is the main goal of estate planning?

2. **Wills.** What is a will? Why is a will important? What happens if a person dies without a will?

3. **Valid Will.** List the requirements for a valid will.

4. **Types of Wills.** Describe two common types of wills.

5. **Components of a Will.** List and briefly discuss the key components of a will.

6. **Changing a Will.** When would you change your will? How can your will be changed?

7. **Probate.** What is probate? Describe the probate process.

8. **Estate Taxes.** Discuss estate taxes. When is an estate subject to and not subject to estate taxes? What is the top federal estate tax rate? What other taxes may be levied against an estate?

9. **Value of Estate.** Why is it important to calculate the value of your estate periodically?

10. **Estate Planning.** Beyond the will, what does estate planning involve?

11. **Trust.** What is a trust? What is the difference between a living trust and a testamentary trust?

12. **Revocable Living Trust.** What is a revocable living trust? How can a revocable living trust be used to help your estate? How does a revocable living trust affect estate taxes?

13. **Irrevocable Living Trust.** What is an irrevocable living trust?

14. **Standard Family Trust.** What is a standard family trust? Give an illustration.

15. **Estate Planning.** How do gifts fit into estate planning?

16. **Contributions.** How can contributions to charitable organizations help in estate planning?

17. **Living Will.** What is a living will? What are its implications for estate planning?

18. **Power of Attorney.** What is a power of attorney?

19. **Durable Power of Attorney.** What is a durable power of attorney for health care? Why is it needed even if you have a living will?

20. **Estate Plan Documents.** How should estate plan documents be maintained?

21. **Beneficiary.** What is a beneficiary? Why is it important to be specific with regard to beneficiaries and assets in your will?

22. **Executor.** What is an executor? Why is it important to name an executor in your will?

23. **Estate Taxes.** Jill just inherited $7 million from her grandfather in 2015. How much of the inheritance is subject to estate tax?

24. **Gifts.** How can you use annual gifts to reduce the tax burden on your heirs?

25. **Estate Planning Needs.** Lisa has an estate worth $3.21 million and three children who will receive her assets on her death. Should she create a will given that her estate is worth less than the $5.43 million threshold that is exempt from estate taxes?

26. **Ethical Dilemma.** In the nineteenth century, people traveled the country selling tonics that were guaranteed to cure all the ailments of humankind. In the twenty-first century, the "snake oil salesmen"

have been replaced with individuals making professional presentations on estate planning. At the conclusion of these presentations, they offer, for many hundreds of dollars, kits that will show you how to conduct estate planning without the expense of an attorney or tax professional.

One such group extols the virtues of a device called a charitable remainder trust (CRT). They tell you how to establish it following a boilerplate template that they provide. The CRT allows you to make tax-deductible contributions during your lifetime and, upon your death, pass the CRT to a family foundation managed by your children. This will allow the assets to avoid estate taxes and probate. The presenter purports this to be a cost-effective way to pass on your assets to your children. All of what is said in the presentations concerning CRTs is true.

What the presenter does not say about CRTs is that distributions from the family foundation can only be made to recognized charities. In other words, your children will own the estate, but they will not have access to it. These devices work well for a small percentage of the population, but for the majority of people they will not serve the desired purpose.

a. Discuss the presenter's ethics by not telling the full story. Keep in mind that what the presenter says is true, but does not reveal the whole truth.

b. If these seminars are the modern-day version of the snake oil salesmen of the nineteenth century, who should you look to instead for estate planning advice?

FINANCIAL PLANNING ONLINE EXERCISES

1. Go to a search engine, and type in "Create your own will." Read though several of these Web sites, and list the pros and cons of creating your own will.

2. Go to http://www.estateplanning.com. Click "10 Things You Need to Know About Estate Planning."

   a. Describe some of the key tasks involved in estate planning.

   b. Click "Tools." Enter your ZIP code and see how many estate planners live within 50 miles of your home.

   c. Click on "Learn" and then on "Trustee Responsibilities." Briefly describe the three responsibilities of a trustee.

3. Go to http://www.nolo.com. Click "Wills, Trusts & Probates" and then "Estate, Gift and Inheritance Taxes." Review the information provided on estate, gift, and inheritance taxes. What do you think the future of these taxes will be? Why?

PSYCHOLOGY OF PERSONAL FINANCE: Your Will

1. Some people put off creating a will because they do not want to think about financial planning for their death. In addition, they might struggle with the decision of how to distribute their estates. They may believe that it is too early to deal with estate planning because their plans for distributing their estate will change over time. What is your view on estate planning? Do you think it is too early for you to engage in estate planning?

2. Read one practical article about how psychology affects estate planning decisions. You can easily retrieve possible articles by doing an online search using the terms "psychology" and "estate planning." Summarize the main points of the article.

WEB SEARCH EXERCISE

You can develop your personal finance skills by conducting an Internet search for related articles. Find a recent online article about personal finance that reinforces one or more concepts covered in this chapter. If your class has an online component, your professor may ask you to post your summary of the article there and provide a link to the article so that other students can access it. If your class is live, your professor may ask you to summarize your application of the article in class. Your professor may assign specific students to complete this assignment or may allow any student to do the assignment on a volunteer basis.

For recent online articles related to this chapter, consider using the following search terms (be sure to include the current year as a search term to ensure that the online articles are recent):

- You need a will
- Decisions when creating a will
- Estate taxes
- Trusts and gifts
- Living will

VIDEO EXERCISE: Estate Planning

Go to one of the Web sites that contain video clips (such as http://www.youtube.com), and view some video clips about estate planning. You can use search phrases such as "tips on estate planning." Select one video clip on this topic that you would recommend for the other students in your class.

1. Provide the Web link for the video clip.

2. What do you think is the main point of this video clip?

3. How might you change your process of estate planning as a result of watching this video clip?

BUILDING YOUR OWN FINANCIAL PLAN

Wills, like life insurance, are something that many people mistakenly believe are necessary only if one is "wealthy." For today's college graduate, the accumulation of a $1 million estate is possible with disciplined savings. A will is necessary for anyone with positive net worth, and as the chapter has indicated, it is also necessary if you care about how and to whom your assets are distributed and to whom the guardianship of your children is assigned. Your key goals for estate planning are to create a will, establish a plan for trusts or gifts if your estate is subject to high taxes, and decide whether you need to create a living will or assign power of attorney.

The key events that necessitate the review and/or change of your will are marriage, divorce, death of your spouse, parenthood, and grandparenthood. Significant changes in your assets (such as the receipt of a significant bequest from a friend or relative's will) may also necessitate a review and/or change of your will.

Go to the worksheets at the end of this chapter to continue building your financial plan.

THE SAMPSONS—A Continuing Case

Dave and Sharon want to make sure that their family is properly cared for in the event of their death. They recently purchased term life insurance and want to make sure that the funds are allocated to best serve their children in the long run. Specifically, they have set the following goals. First, they want to make sure that a portion of the insurance proceeds is set aside for the children's education. Second, they want to make sure that the insurance proceeds are distributed evenly over several years, so that the children do not spend the money too quickly.

Go to the worksheets at the end of this chapter to continue this case.

PART 6: BRAD BROOKS—A Continuing Case

Brad tells you that he has revised his retirement plans. He has set an even more ambitious goal of retiring in 20 years instead of the original goal of 30 years. His goal is to save $500,000 by that time. He is not taking advantage of his employer's retirement match; his employer will match retirement plan contributions up to $300 per month. Factoring in the employer match, Brad could have a possible total annual retirement contribution of $7,200.

Brad also unveils his plans to provide for his two nephews' college education in the event of his death. He does not have a will and wonders if one is necessary.

Go to the worksheets at the end of this chapter to complete this case.

CHAPTER 20: BUILDING YOUR OWN FINANCIAL PLAN

YOUR GOALS FOR CHAPTER 20

1. Create a will.
2. Establish a plan for trusts or gifts if your estate is subject to high taxes.
3. Decide whether to create a living will or assign power of attorney.

ANALYSIS

1. Determine the size of your estate by reviewing your personal balance sheet and filling out the table below.

Gross Estate	Amounts
Cash	
Stocks and Bonds	
Notes and Mortgages	
Annuities	
Retirement Benefits	
Personal Residence	
Other Real Estate	
Insurance	
Automobiles	
Artwork	
Jewelry	
Other (Furniture, Collectibles, etc.)	
Gross Estate	

2. Next, consider the following estate planning issues. Indicate your action plan in the second column.

Issue	Status
Possible heirs to and executor for my estate	
Tax implications for my estate	
Are trusts and gifts needed?	
Is power of attorney necessary?	
Is durable power of attorney necessary?	
Is a living will appropriate?	

DECISIONS

1. Will you create a will on your own or with an attorney's assistance? What special stipulations (for an heir, executor, or donations to charity) will you include?

_____

_____

_____

_____

_____

_____

_____

_____

2. Do you need to establish trusts or gifts to reduce your estate's tax liability?

_____

_____

_____

_____

_____

_____

_____

_____

3. Will you assign power of attorney and/or durable power of attorney?

_____

_____

_____

_____

_____

_____

CHAPTER 20: THE SAMPSONS—A Continuing Case

CASE QUESTIONS

1. Advise the Sampsons about how they can plan their estate to achieve their financial goals.

_____

_____

_____

_____

_____

_____

_____

_____

_____

2. What important considerations are the Sampsons overlooking in their estate planning goals?

_____

_____

_____

_____

_____

_____

_____

_____

_____

3. Dave recently met with an estate planner who offered to create an elaborate estate plan without asking Dave specific questions. What should Dave have done before meeting with the estate planner?

_____

_____

_____

_____

_____

_____

_____

_____

PART 6: BRAD BROOKS—A Continuing Case

CASE QUESTIONS

1. With regard to Brad's revised retirement plans:

   a. How much will he have in 30 years if he invests $300 per month at 8%? Do not consider the employer's matched contribution at this point.

   Future Value of an Annuity

Payment per Year	
Number of Years	30
Annual Interest Rate	8%
Future Value	

   b. How much will he have to save per month at 8% to reach his $500,000 goal in 20 years? In 30 years?

Amount to Accumulate	$500,000
Number of Years	20
Annual Interest Rate	8%
Annual Deposit	
Monthly Deposit	

Amount to Accumulate	$500,000
Number of Years	30
Annual Interest Rate	8%
Annual Deposit	
Monthly Deposit	

   c. What impact could retiring 10 years earlier have on Brad's current standard of living?

   _____

   _____

   _____

   d. If Brad takes advantage of his employer's match, what will be the impact on his retirement savings (assume an 8% return)?

   Future Value of an Annuity

Payment per Year	
Number of Years	20
Annual Interest Rate	8%
Future Value	

   Future Value of an Annuity

Payment per Year	
Number of Years	30
Annual Interest Rate	8%
Future Value	

e. What other options are available to Brad to save for his retirement? Give the pros and cons of each.

_____

_____

_____

_____

2. If Brad really wishes to provide for his nephews' college education, how can a will help him achieve that goal? What else might Brad consider to ensure his nephews' college education?

_____

_____

_____

_____

3. How would your advice in questions 1 and 2 change if Brad was 40 years old?

_____

_____

_____

_____

4. Prepare a written or oral report on your findings and recommendations to Brad.

_____

_____

_____

_____

_____

_____

_____

_____

_____

_____

_____

_____

_____

Synthesis of Financial Planning

This part summarizes the key components of a financial plan. It also illustrates the interrelationships among the segments of a financial plan by highlighting how decisions regarding each component affect the other components.

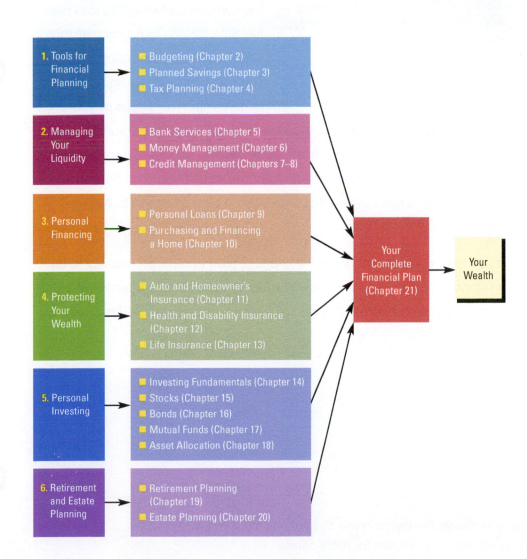

1. Tools for Financial Planning
- Budgeting (Chapter 2)
- Planned Savings (Chapter 3)
- Tax Planning (Chapter 4)

2. Managing Your Liquidity
- Bank Services (Chapter 5)
- Money Management (Chapter 6)
- Credit Management (Chapters 7–8)

3. Personal Financing
- Personal Loans (Chapter 9)
- Purchasing and Financing a Home (Chapter 10)

4. Protecting Your Wealth
- Auto and Homeowner's Insurance (Chapter 11)
- Health and Disability Insurance (Chapter 12)
- Life Insurance (Chapter 13)

5. Personal Investing
- Investing Fundamentals (Chapter 14)
- Stocks (Chapter 15)
- Bonds (Chapter 16)
- Mutual Funds (Chapter 17)
- Asset Allocation (Chapter 18)

6. Retirement and Estate Planning
- Retirement Planning (Chapter 19)
- Estate Planning (Chapter 20)

Your Complete Financial Plan (Chapter 21)

Your Wealth

Integrating the Components of a Financial Plan

Antonio Guillem/Shutterstock

Throughout the previous chapters, you have been asked to complete a number of assignments and online exercises regarding your own financial situation. Now that you have completed your journey through the components of a financial plan, it is time for you to compile all this information and the many decisions you have made. Your first step was to determine the status of your personal finances. To do this, you used financial planning tools to establish your personal balance sheet, prepare the cash flow statement, identify your financial goals, and address your concerns. After that you analyzed each part of the financial plan—liquidity, personal financing, insurance, investments, and retirement and estate planning—and established a plan of action to help you accomplish each of your goals.

As explained throughout this text, each component of a financial plan affects your ability to build wealth and achieve your financial goals. You have now learned many of the fundamentals relating to each component of a financial plan. This chapter will help you integrate that knowledge into a cohesive financial plan.

MyFinanceLab helps you master the topics in this chapter and study more efficiently. Visit http://www.myfinancelab.com for more details.

The objectives of this chapter are to:

- Review the components of a financial plan
- Illustrate how a financial plan's components are integrated
- Provide an example of a financial plan

Review of Components Within a Financial Plan

A key to financial planning is recognizing how the components of your financial plan are related. Each part of this text has focused on one of the six main components of your financial plan, which are illustrated once again in Exhibit 21.1. The decisions that you make regarding each component affect your cash flows and your wealth. The six components are summarized next, with information on how they are interrelated.

Budgeting

Recall that budgeting allows you to forecast how much money you will have at the end of each month so that you can determine how much you will be able to invest in assets. Most important, budgeting allows you to determine whether your cash outflows will exceed your cash inflows so that you can forecast any shortages in that month. Your spending decisions affect your budget, which affects every other component of your financial plan. Careful budgeting can prevent excessive spending and therefore help you achieve financial goals.

Budgeting Trade-Off The more you spend, the less money you will have available for liquidity purposes, investments, and retirement saving. Thus, your budgeting decisions involve a trade-off between spending today and allocating funds for the future. Your budget should attempt to ensure that you have net cash flows every month for savings or for retirement. The more funds you can allocate for the future, the more you will be able to benefit from compounded interest, and the more you will be able to spend in the future.

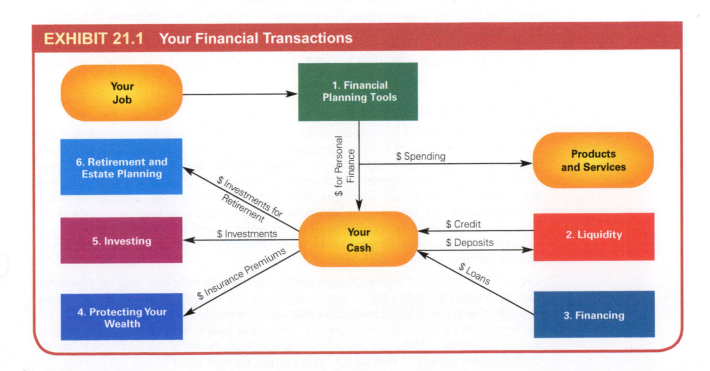

EXHIBIT 21.1 Your Financial Transactions

PSYCHOLOGY
of Personal
Finance

The most common problem that prevents effective financial planning is excessive spending. Although this problem has been discussed throughout the text, it deserves attention here because it affects all components of the financial plan. You learned that financial planning involves decisions regarding how much money to allocate for liquidity purposes (Part 2), insurance (Part 4), investments (Part 5), and retirement planning (Part 6). People have the choice of spending money versus allocating funds toward any of these purposes. Many people spend excessively and have no money left to allocate toward these other purposes. Some people would have been able to use 10% or more of their income for these other purposes if they simply spent money more wisely by planning ahead and attempting to purchase products when they are on sale.

The underlying psychology behind excessive spending is the complete focus on immediate satisfaction. One of the most common forms of excessive spending is the purchase of a car that is much more expensive than the person can afford. This results in large financing payments, which limit the amount of money they have for other purposes. Many people who have purchased a new car recently and have budget problems say that their $500 car loan payment every month uses up so much of their income that it is impossible for them to use money for liquidity, insurance, investments, or retirement planning. However, they are in denial. They would have had the ability to allocate money to other purposes if they had purchased a more affordable car. It was their spending decision on the new car that caused the very large car loan payment, which has prevented them from other forms of financial planning. If they had purchased a less expensive car, they could have allocated $200 per month or more to other financial planning purposes.

Many consumers use a decision-making process in which they decide on their spending first and then allocate funds to personal financing purposes only if they have any money left over. Using this process, they may never have anything left over because there are always lots of reasons to spend now to achieve immediate satisfaction, whereas using funds for financial planning purposes does not provide benefits until the future.

You can avoid this type of dilemma if you decide to set aside a specific amount of your income each month (such as $200 per month) for financial planning purposes, such as liquidity and retirement planning. If you comply with this budget rule, it will dictate how much you can spend each month for other purposes. With this approach, you may not be able to spend excessively. For example, if you are forced to set aside $200 per month, you may not be tempted to purchase a new car that would require car payments of $500 per month. Instead, you would be guided by your budget to buy a car that you can afford. Ultimately, this strategy will help you build your wealth so that you will have more money to spend in the future.

Managing Liquidity

You can prepare for anticipated cash shortages in a future month by ensuring that you have enough liquid assets to cover the deficiency. Some of the more liquid assets include a checking account, a savings account, a money market deposit account, and money market funds. The more funds you maintain in these types of assets, the more liquidity you will have to cover cash shortages. Even if you do not have sufficient liquid assets, you can cover a cash deficiency by obtaining short-term financing (such as using a credit card). If you maintain adequate liquidity, you will not need to borrow every time you need money. In this way, you can avoid major financial problems and therefore be more likely to achieve your financial goals.

Liquidity Trade-Off Because liquid assets generate relatively low returns, you forgo the opportunity to earn a higher return. Many checking accounts do not earn interest, and the other types of liquid assets have relatively low interest rates. If you choose to earn higher returns by investing all your money in stocks or bonds, however, you may not have sufficient liquidity. Thus, you should maintain enough money in liquid assets to satisfy your liquidity needs and then earn a higher return on your other assets.

Personal Financing

Personal financing allows you to make purchases now without having the full amount of cash on hand. Thus, financing can increase the amount of your assets. Financing is especially useful for large purchases such as a car or a home.

Personal Financing Trade-Off One advantage of personal financing with a mortgage or home equity loan is that the interest payments are tax-deductible.

A disadvantage is that financing can cause budgeting problems. When you borrow to pay for a car, to purchase a home, or even to pay off a credit card balance, you affect your future budget, because the monthly loan payment means that you will have less cash available at the end of each month. Although a loan allows you to make purchases now, it restricts your spending or saving in future months while you are paying off the loan. Therefore, an excessive amount of financing can prevent you from achieving your financial goals. In addition, excessive financing may prevent you from paying off your loans on time and therefore could damage your credit rating or even cause you to file for bankruptcy.

It is easier to cover the monthly loan payment if you select financing with a relatively long maturity. But the longer the maturity, the longer the loan will be outstanding, and the more interest you will pay.

You may want to consider paying off a loan before its maturity so that you can avoid incurring any more interest expenses, especially when the interest rate charged is relatively high. You should not use all your liquid funds to pay off a loan, however, because you will still need to maintain liquidity. Paying off loans rather than making additional investments is appropriate when the expected after-tax return on the investments you could make is lower than the interest rate you are paying on the loan.

Protecting Your Assets and Income

You can protect your assets or income (and therefore your wealth) by purchasing insurance. Recall from Chapters 11 and 12 that property and casualty insurance insures your assets (such as your car and home), health insurance covers health expenses, and disability insurance provides financial support if you become disabled. Life insurance (Chapter 13) provides your family members or other named beneficiaries with financial support in the event of your death. Thus, insurance protects against unexpected events that could reduce your income or your wealth.

Insurance Trade-Off Any money that is used to buy insurance cannot be used for other purposes such as investing in liquid assets, paying off loans, and making investments. However, your insurance needs should be given priority before investments. You are required to have insurance to cover your car and your home. You may also need life insurance to provide financial support to a family member.

Managing Investments

When making investments, recall that your main choices are stocks, bonds, and mutual funds. If you want your investments to provide periodic income, you may consider investing in stocks that pay dividends. The stocks of large, well-known firms tend to pay relatively high dividends, as these firms are not growing as quickly as smaller firms and can afford to pay out more of their earnings as dividends. Bonds also provide periodic income. If you do not need periodic income, you may consider investing in stocks of firms that do not pay dividends. These firms are often growing at a fast pace and therefore offer the potential for a large increase in the stock value over time.

Investment Trade-Off Investment decisions are exciting because they can potentially lead to large gains. However, whenever you use money for investments, you forgo the use of that money for some other purpose, such as investing in more liquid assets, paying off existing credit card debt, buying insurance, or investing in your retirement. You should make investments only after you have adequately covered the other personal finance functions.

If you try to earn high returns by investing all your money in stocks of smaller firms, you forgo some liquidity because the prices of these stocks are volatile, and you may want to avoid selling them when prices are relatively low. If you have sufficient liquid assets such as checking and savings accounts, however, you do not need additional liquidity from your investments in stocks.

By investing in the stocks of large, well-known firms, you may enhance your liquidity because you will receive dividend income and can easily sell the stocks if you need money. You can also enhance your liquidity by investing in Treasury bonds or highly rated corporate bonds because these bonds provide periodic income and can easily be sold if you need money.

By investing in stocks of smaller firms, you can potentially earn very high returns. However, such an investment is very risky because these stocks commonly experience larger losses than investments in stocks of large, well-known firms. You can invest in small stocks without being exposed to the specific risk of an individual stock by investing in a mutual fund that focuses on small stocks. When market conditions are weak, however, such funds can experience large losses, although not as much as a single stock of a small firm.

Retirement Planning

Retirement planning can ensure that you will have sufficient funds to maintain a comfortable standard of living at the time you retire. As discussed in Chapter 19, there are a variety of plans available and many tax advantages to retirement savings.

Retirement Account Trade-Off
The more money you contribute to your retirement account now, the more you will have when you reach retirement age. However, you should make sure you can afford whatever you decide to contribute. You need to have enough money to maintain sufficient liquidity so that you can afford any monthly loan payments before you contribute to your retirement.

When deciding whether to invest your money in current investments or in your retirement account, consider your goals. If you plan to use the investments for tuition or some other purpose in the near future, then you should not put this money into your retirement account. Funds invested in a retirement account are not liquid. Any money withdrawn early from a retirement account is subject to a penalty. One exception is the Roth IRA, which allows you to withdraw contributed dollars after five years without a penalty. If your goal is to save for retirement, you should allocate money to a retirement account. Although you will not have access to these funds, you are typically not taxed on contributions to your retirement account until the funds are withdrawn at the time of retirement. This deferral of taxes is very beneficial. In addition, some employers match part or all of your contribution to a retirement account.

Financial Planning ONLINE

Go to:
http://www.kiplinger.com

To get:
Useful information about a wide variety of financial planning topics that can help you complete and refine your financial plan.

Maintaining Your Financial Documents

To monitor your financial plan over time, you should store all finance-related documents in one place, such as a safe at home or a safety deposit box. The key documents are identified in Exhibit 21.2.

Integrating the Components

At this point, you have sufficient background to complete all the components of your financial plan. As time passes, however, your financial position will change, and your financial goals may change as well. You will need to revise your financial plan periodically to meet your financial goals. The following example for Stephanie Spratt illustrates how an individual's financial position can change over time, how a financial plan may need to be revised as a result, and how the components of the financial plan are integrated.

EXHIBIT 21.2   Documents Used for Financial Planning

Liquidity
- Certificates of deposit
- Bank account balances
- Any other money market securities owned

Financing
- Credit card account numbers
- Credit card balances
- Personal loan (such as car loan) agreements
- Mortgage loan agreement

Insurance
- Insurance policies
- Home inventory of items covered by homeowner's insurance

Investments
- Stock certificates
- Bonds
- Account balance showing the market value of stocks
- Account balance showing the market value of bonds
- Account balance showing the market value of mutual funds

Retirement and Estate Plans
- Retirement plan contracts
- Retirement account balances
- Will
- Trust agreements

EXAMPLE

Recall from Chapter 1 that Stephanie Spratt established the following goals:

- Purchase a new car
- Buy a home
- Make investments that will allow her wealth to grow over time
- Build a large amount of savings by the time of her retirement in 20 to 40 years

Stephanie purchased a new car and a home this year. She also made some small investments. She has clearly made progress toward her goal of building a large amount of savings by the time she retires.

Recall from Chapter 2 that Stephanie originally had a relatively simple personal balance sheet. Her assets amounted to $9,000, and she had credit card debt of $2,000 as her only liability. Thus, her net worth was $7,000 at that time. Since she created the balance sheet shown in Chapter 2, her assets, liabilities, and net worth have changed substantially.

Stephanie's current personal balance sheet is compared to her personal balance sheet from Chapter 2 in Exhibit 21.3. Notice how her personal balance sheet has changed:

1. Recall from Chapter 9 that Stephanie recently purchased a new car for $18,000. Even though the car is still new, the market value of a new car typically declines as soon as it is driven off the car dealer's lot. Stephanie estimates that her new car currently has a market value of $15,000.

EXHIBIT 21.3   Update on Stephanie Spratt's Personal Balance Sheet

	Initial Personal Balance Sheet (from Chapter 2)	As of Today
Assets		
Liquid Assets		
Cash	$500	$200
Checking account	3,500	200
Money market fund (MMF)	0	2,600
Total liquid assets	**$4,000**	**$3,000**
Household Assets		
Home	$0	$108,000
Car	1,000	15,000
Furniture	1,000	1,000
Total household assets	**$2,000**	**$124,000**
Investment Assets		
Stocks	$3,000	$3,200
Mutual funds	0	2,000
Investment in retirement account	0	800
Total investment assets	**$3,000**	**$6,000**
TOTAL ASSETS	**$9,000**	**$130,000**
Liabilities and Net Worth		
Current Liabilities		
Credit card balance	$2,000	$0
Total current liabilities	**$2,000**	**$0**
Long-Term Liabilities		
Car loan	$0	$17,000
Mortgage	0	100,000
Total long-term liabilities	**$0**	**$117,000**
TOTAL LIABILITIES	**$2,000**	**$117,000**
Net Worth	**$7,000**	**$13,000**

2. Recall from Chapter 10 that Stephanie recently purchased a home for $108,000 and estimates that her home still has a market value of $108,000.

3. Recall that Stephanie owned some stock (as explained in Chapter 2) and also invested in mutual funds (as explained in Chapter 18). Assume that her stock is presently worth $3,200, and her mutual funds are presently worth $2,000.

4. Recall that Stephanie recently started investing in her retirement account, as explained in Chapter 19. Assume that her retirement account now has a balance of $800.

Overall, Stephanie's assets have increased from $9,000 (in Chapter 2) to $130,000 today. Stephanie was able to increase her assets primarily by obtaining loans (financing). Thus, her substantial increase in assets resulted in a substantial increase in her long-term liabilities.

The main changes in Stephanie's liabilities are as follows:

1. Recall from Chapter 9 that Stephanie's recent purchase of a new car required her to obtain a car loan. She owes about $17,000 on the car.

2. Recall from Chapter 10 that Stephanie's recent purchase of a home required her to obtain a mortgage loan, which has a balance of about $100,000.

3. Recall that Stephanie had a credit card bill as explained in Chapter 2. Assume that she has paid off her credit card bill.

Exhibit 21.3 shows that Stephanie's liabilities are now $117,000. Thus, her net worth is

$$\text{Net Worth} = \text{Total Assets} - \text{Total Liabilities}$$
$$= \$130,000 - \$117,000$$
$$= \$13,000$$

The increase in her net worth since the beginning of the year is mainly a result of a bonus from her employer this year, which helped her cover the down payment on her house. Now that she has a car loan and a mortgage, she uses a large portion of her income to cover loan payments and will not be able to save much money.

Budgeting

Stephanie's recent cash flow statement is shown in Exhibit 21.4. The major change in her cash inflows from Chapter 2 is that her disposable income is now higher as a result of a promotion and salary increase at work. Her monthly cash inflows are now estimated to be $3,000.

The major changes in Stephanie's cash outflows are as follows:

1. As a result of purchasing a home, Stephanie no longer has a rent payment.

2. Assume that since buying her home, her electricity and water bill are now $80 per month, which is $20 more per month than when she rented an apartment.

3. Assume that as a result of buying a new car, Stephanie now saves about $100 per month on car maintenance because the car dealer will do all maintenance at no charge for the next two years.

4. Assume that since purchasing her home, Stephanie expects to spend more time at home and therefore will spend less money on recreation expenses. Overall, assume that her recreation expenses are now about $400 per month (a reduction of $200 per month from her initial estimate in Chapter 2).

5. Stephanie now has a car loan payment of $412 each month as a result of buying her new car (as explained in Chapter 9).

6. Stephanie now has a mortgage loan payment of $791 as a result of buying a home, as explained in Chapter 10. When also considering property tax and home insurance, her total home expenses will be about $966 per month.

7. Stephanie just started paying for disability insurance ($10 per month) as explained in Chapter 12 and life insurance ($10 per month) as explained in Chapter 13.

8. Stephanie recently started contributing $300 per month to her retirement account as explained in Chapter 19.

Budgeting Dilemma Although Stephanie's monthly cash inflows are now $500 higher than they were initially (from Chapter 2), her monthly cash outflows are now $800 higher than they were initially. Thus, her monthly net cash flows have declined from $400 to $0. This means that even though her salary (and therefore her cash inflows) increased, she should have just enough money to cover all of her monthly cash outflows.

EXHIBIT 21.4 Update on Stephanie Spratt's Monthly Cash Flow Statement

	Initial Cash Flow Statement	Most Recent Cash Flow Statement	Change in the Cash Flow Statement
Cash Inflows			
Disposable (after-tax) income	$2,500	$3,000	+$500
Interest on deposits	0	0	No change
Dividend payments	0	0	No change
Total cash inflows	**$2,500**	**$3,000**	**+$500**
Cash Outflows			
Rent	$600	$0	– $600
Internet	50	50	No change
Electricity and water	60	80	+20
Cellular	60	60	No change
Groceries	300	300	No change
Health and disability insurance and expenses	130	140	+10
Clothing	100	100	No change
Car insurance and maintenance	200	100	–100
Recreation	600	400	–200
Car loan payment	0	412	+412
Mortgage payment (includes property taxes and insurance)	0	966	+966
Life insurance payment	0	10	+10
Contribution to retirement plan	0	300	+300
Total cash outflows	**$2,100**	**$2,918**	**+$818**
Net cash flows	**$400**	**$82**	**–$318**

Budgeting Decision Stephanie reviews her personal cash flow statement to determine how she is spending her money. Some of her cash flows are currently being used to increase assets (her retirement account) or to reduce liabilities (such as loans). Even if she does not invest any of her net cash flows in stocks or mutual funds, her net worth will grow over time because she is paying down the debt on her home and on her car each month and is contributing to her retirement account.

Furthermore, she will now receive a tax refund from the IRS each year because she can itemize her mortgage expense. Overall, she decides that she is pleased with her cash flow situation. If she does not have sufficient cash to cover expenses in any month, she will use funds in her money market account or reduce her monthly retirement contribution to access more cash.

Long-Term Strategy for Budgeting Some of Stephanie's budget is determined by the bills that she incurs as a result of her car and home. Other parts of her budget are determined by the other components of her financial plan:

- The amount of cash (if any) allocated to liquid assets is dependent on her plan for managing liquidity.

- The amount of cash allocated to pay off existing loans is dependent on her plan for personal financing.
- The amount of cash allocated to insurance policies is dependent on her insurance planning.
- The amount of cash allocated to investments is dependent on her plan for investing.
- The amount of cash allocated to her retirement account is dependent on her retirement planning.

Managing Liquidity

Every two weeks, Stephanie's paycheck is direct-deposited to her checking account. She makes online payments from her checking account to pay all her bills and to cover the other cash outflows specified in Exhibit 21.4; she also pays her credit card bill each month. As shown in Exhibit 21.4, she expects to have about $82 at the end of each month after paying her bills and recreation expenses.

Stephanie wants to ensure that she has sufficient liquidity. Her most convenient source of funds to pay bills is her checking account; because her paycheck is deposited there, she knows she will have enough funds every month to pay her bills. If she had any other short-term debt (such as credit card debt), she would use her net cash flows to pay it off. She has a money market fund (MMF), which allows her to write a limited number of checks in the event that unanticipated expenses (such as home repair expenses) occur.

Liquidity Dilemma Stephanie must decide whether to change her liquidity position. She considers these options.

Stephanie's Options If She Changes Her Liquidity	Advantage	Disadvantage
Reduce liquidity position by transferring money from her MMF to a mutual fund	May earn a higher rate of return on her assets	Will have a smaller amount of liquid funds to cover unanticipated expenses
Increase liquidity position by transferring money from a mutual fund to her MMF	May earn a lower rate of return on her assets	Will have a larger amount of liquid funds to cover unanticipated expenses

Liquidity Decision Stephanie determines that she has access to sufficient funds to cover her liquidity needs. If she has any major unanticipated expenses beyond the funds in her MMF, she could sell shares of the stock or the mutual funds that she owns. She decides to leave her liquidity position as is.

Long-Term Strategy for Managing Liquidity Stephanie's plan for managing liquidity is to continue using her checking account to cover bills and to use funds from the MMF to cover any unanticipated expenses. She prefers not to invest any more funds in the MMF because the interest rate is low. Thus, she will use any net cash flows she has at the end of the month for some other purpose. If she ever needs to withdraw funds from her MMF, she will likely attempt to replenish that account once she has new net cash flows that can be invested in it.

Personal Financing

Stephanie has a car loan balance of $17,000 and a mortgage loan balance of $100,000. She should not need any additional loans. The interest expenses on the mortgage are tax-deductible, but the interest expenses on the car loan are not.

Financing Dilemma Stephanie wants to pay off the car loan as soon as she has saved a sufficient amount of money. She considers the following options for paying off her car loan early:

Stephanie's Options for Paying Off Her Car Loan Early	Advantage	Disadvantage
Withdraw funds from MMF	Would be able to reduce or eliminate monthly car loan payment	Will no longer have adequate liquidity
Withdraw funds from retirement account	Would be able to reduce or eliminate monthly car loan payment	Will be charged a penalty and will no longer have funds set aside for retirement
Sell stock	Would be able to reduce or eliminate monthly car loan payment	Would forgo the potential to earn high returns on stock
Sell mutual funds	Would be able to reduce or eliminate monthly car loan payment	Would forgo the potential to earn high returns on a mutual fund

Financing Decision Stephanie needs to maintain liquidity, so she eliminates the first option. She also eliminates the second option because she does not want to pay a penalty for early withdrawal of retirement funds and believes those funds should be reserved for retirement purposes.

The remaining options deserve more consideration. Stephanie's annual interest rate on the car loan is 7.60%. Once Stephanie has paid off most of the car loan and has a large enough investment in stocks and mutual funds to pay off the car loan (perhaps two or three years from now), she will decide whether to pay off the car loan early as follows:

- If she thinks that the investments will earn an annual after-tax return of less than 7.60%, she will sell them and use the money to pay off the car loan. In this way, she will essentially earn a return of 7.60% with that money because she will be paying off debt for which she was being charged 7.60%.

- If she thinks that the investments will earn an annual after-tax return greater than 7.60%, she will keep them. She will not pay off the car loan because her investments are providing her with a higher return than the cost of the car loan.

Long-Term Strategy for Financing Once Stephanie pays off her car loan, she will have an extra $412 per month (the amount of her car loan payment) that can be used to make more investments. Her only other loan is her mortgage, which has a 15-year life. If she stays in the same home over the next 15 years, she will have paid off her mortgage by that time. In this case, she will have no debt after 15 years. She may consider buying a more expensive home in the near future and would likely obtain another 15-year mortgage. She does not mind having a mortgage because she expects that the market value of her home will increase.

Protecting and Maintaining Wealth

Stephanie currently has auto, homeowner's, health, disability, and life insurance policies.

Insurance Dilemma Stephanie recognizes that she needs insurance to cover her car, home, and health expenses. In addition, she wants to protect her existing income in case she becomes disabled. She also wants to make sure that she can provide some financial support to her two nieces in the future.

Insurance Decision Stephanie recently decided to purchase disability insurance to protect her income in case she becomes disabled. She also decided to purchase life insurance to fund her nieces' college education if she dies. She is pleased with her current employer-provided health insurance policy.

Long-Term Strategy for Insurance Stephanie will maintain a high level of insurance to protect against liability resulting from owning her car or home. If she decides to have children in the future, she will purchase additional life insurance to ensure future financial support for her children. She will continue to review her policies to search for premium savings.

Managing Investments

Stephanie currently has an investment in one stock worth $3,200 and an investment in two mutual funds worth $2,000.

Investing Dilemma If the one stock that Stephanie owns performs poorly in the future, the value of her investments (and therefore her net worth) could decline substantially. She expects the stock market to do well but is uncomfortable leaving her investment in a single stock.

She considers the following options:

Stephanie's Options If She Changes Her Investments	Advantage	Disadvantage
Sell stock; invest the proceeds in bonds	Lower risk	Lower expected return than from her stock
Sell stock; invest the proceeds in her MMF	Lower risk and improved liquidity	Lower expected return than from her stock
Sell stock; invest the proceeds in a stock mutual fund	Lower risk	Lower expected return than from her stock

Investing Decision All three possibilities offer lower risk than the stock, but given that Stephanie expects the stock market to perform well, she prefers a stock mutual fund. She is not relying on the investment to provide periodic income at this time and wants an investment that could increase in value over time. She decides to sell her individual stock at the prevailing market value of $3,200 and to invest the proceeds in her stock mutual fund to achieve greater diversification.

Long-Term Strategy for Investing Once Stephanie's car loan is paid off, she will have an additional $412 in net cash flows per month that she can invest in the stock mutual fund or in other investments.

Retirement Planning

Stephanie recently started to contribute to a retirement account. This account is beneficial because her contributions will not be taxed until the funds are withdrawn during retirement. In addition, this account should grow in value if she consistently contributes to it each month and selects investments that appreciate in value over time.

Retirement Contribution Dilemma Recently, Stephanie started contributing $300 per month to her retirement account, which is partially matched by a contribution from her employer. She could also establish an individual retirement account (IRA), up to a limit of $5,500 per year. However, she cannot use any of the contributed funds until she retires.

She considers the following options:

Stephanie's Options Regarding Her Retirement Account	Advantage	Disadvantage
Do not contribute any funds to her retirement account	Can use all net cash flows for other purposes	Forgo tax benefits and contribution from employer; will have no money set aside for retirement
Continue to contribute $300 per month	Benefit from partial matching contribution, and achieve some tax benefits	Could use the $300 for other purposes
Contribute $300 per month and establish an IRA	Increased tax benefits	Could use the funds for other purposes

Retirement Contribution Decision Stephanie wants to know how much more she will have in 40 years (when she hopes to retire) if she saves an additional $100 per month ($1,200 per year). She expects to earn an annual return of 6% per year if she invests in an IRA. She can use the future value annuity table in Appendix C to determine the future value of her extra contribution. The *FVIFA* for a 6% interest rate and a period of 40 years is 154.758. In 40 years, her extra annual contribution of $1,200 per year would accumulate to:

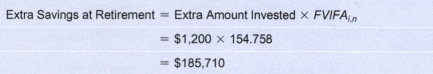

$$\text{Extra Savings at Retirement} = \text{Extra Amount Invested} \times FVIFA_{i,n}$$

$$= \$1,200 \times 154.758$$

$$= \$185,710$$

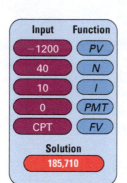

Input	Function
−1200	PV
40	N
10	I
0	PMT
CPT	FV

Solution

185,710

Stephanie would like to contribute $100 per month toward an individual retirement account (IRA) because she expects that it would result in $185,710 more at retirement. She also realizes that contributing the extra amount can provide tax benefits.

However, Stephanie could only afford to contribute $100 per month if she could reduce her monthly recreation expenses. Realistically, she believes that at this time it would be very difficult for her to reduce her monthly recreation expenses. She decides that once she pays off her car, she can reconsider contributing to an IRA.

Long-Term Strategy for Retirement Contributions Stephanie hopes to invest the maximum allowed in her retirement account in the near future so that she can take full advantage of the tax benefits. The maximum annual limit on her retirement contribution is dependent on her income. As her income increases over time, she will be able to increase her monthly contribution up to the maximum limit.

Financial Plan

Stephanie Spratt's financial plan is illustrated in Exhibit 21.5. It incorporates her most recent decisions (discussed earlier in this chapter). Her budget plan determines how she will use her cash inflows. Notice how she adjusts her budget plan in response to decisions regarding other components of her financial plan.

EXHIBIT 21.5   Stephanie Spratt's Financial Plan

BUDGET PLAN

My monthly salary of $3,000 after taxes is direct deposited to my checking account. I will use this account to cover all bills and other expenses. My total expenses (including recreation) should be about $2,918 per month. This leaves me with net cash flows of $82. I will also receive an annual tax refund of about $3,000. The taxes I pay during the year will exceed my tax liability, as the interest payments on my mortgage will reduce my taxable income.

I will use the net cash flows each month to cover any unanticipated expenses that occurred during the month. My second priority is to use the net cash flows to keep about $2,600 in my money market fund (MMF) to ensure liquidity. If this fund is already at that level, I will use the net cash flows each month to invest in a mutual fund.

PLAN FOR MANAGING LIQUIDITY

Since my salary is direct deposited to my checking account, I have a convenient means of covering my expenses. My backup source of liquidity is my MMF, which currently contains $2,600; I will maintain the account balance at about that level to ensure liquidity. If I ever need more money than is in this account, I could rely on my net cash flows. In addition, I could sell some shares of my mutual fund, or I could cover some expenses with a credit card, and would hope to use part of my next paycheck to pay off the credit card bill.

PLAN FOR FINANCING

I have two finance payments: a monthly car loan payment of $412, and a monthly mortgage payment of $966 (including property taxes and homeowner's insurance). I would like to pay off the car loan early if possible. The interest rate on that loan is 7.60%, and the interest is not tax-deductible. The principal remaining on the car loan will decrease over time as I pay down the debt with my monthly payments.

I may consider selling my shares of the mutual fund and using the proceeds to pay off part of the car loan. My decision will depend on whether I believe the mutual fund can provide a higher return to me than the cost of the car loan.

When I pay off the car loan, my cash outflows will be reduced by $412 per month. Thus, I should have more net cash flows that I can use to make investments and increase contributions to my retirement account.

INSURANCE PLAN

I have car insurance that covers the car and limits my liability. I have homeowner's insurance that covers the full market value of my home. I have health insurance through my employer. I have disability insurance that will provide financial support if I become disabled. I have life insurance, with my two nieces named as the beneficiaries. If I decide to have children in the future, I will purchase additional life insurance in which they would be named as the beneficiaries.

PLAN FOR INVESTING

I have an individual stock that I plan to sell, and I will use the proceeds to invest in a stock mutual fund. This creates more diversification and reduces my exposure to risk.

RETIREMENT AND ESTATE PLAN

I would like to allocate an additional $100 per month toward an individual retirement account (IRA) as I expect that it would increase my retirement fund by an estimated $185,710 at the time of my expected retirement. However, I am not likely to have an extra $100 each month that I could contribute to an IRA at this time. I will contribute even more income to my retirement (up to the maximum limit allowed) as my income increases over time.

I will also create a will to ensure that any wealth that I have accumulated is allocated in the manner that I desire.

A review of Stephanie's financial plan shows that she is building her net worth (wealth) over time by either reducing liabilities or increasing investment in assets:

- As she makes monthly payments on her car loan, she is reducing her car loan debt.
- As she makes monthly payments on her mortgage loan, she is reducing her mortgage loan debt.
- If she receives any extra cash inflows from earning a raise at work or for any other reason, she could increase her investment in a mutual fund.
- She is increasing her retirement account assets as she makes monthly contributions.

Stephanie's wealth may also increase for other reasons. The value of her home, mutual fund, and any investments she makes for her retirement account may increase over time. Overall, Stephanie's financial plan should provide her with sufficient wealth so that she can afford a very comfortable lifestyle in the future.

FREE APPS for Personal Finance

Your Personal Finance Decisions

Application:

The MSN Money app (by Microsoft) is useful for a wide variety of personal finance decisions, including spending, budgeting, saving, and financing.

To Find It:

Search for the "MSN Money" app on your mobile device.

SUMMARY

Financial Plan Components. A financial plan consists of a budget (Part 1), a plan for managing liquidity (Part 2), a financing plan (Part 3), an insurance plan (Part 4), an investment plan (Part 5), and a plan for retirement and estate planning (Part 6). The budget determines how you will spend or invest your money. Your plan for managing liquidity will ensure that you can cover any unanticipated expenses. Your financing plan is used to finance large purchases. Financing also involves decisions that affect the interest rate you are charged and the duration of any loans. Your plan for protecting your assets and income involves decisions about what types of insurance to purchase and how much insurance to buy. Your investment plan determines how much you allocate toward investments and how you allocate money across different types of investments. Your retirement and estate plan determines how much to periodically invest in your retirement account and how to distribute your estate to your heirs.

How Components Are Integrated. The components of a financial plan are integrated in that

they depend on each other. The budget plan is dependent on the other components of the financial plan. The amount of money available for any part of the plan is dependent on how much money is used for liquidity purposes, to make loan (financing) payments, to make investments, to buy insurance, or to contribute to retirement accounts. The more money you allocate toward any part of the financial plan, the less money you have for the other parts. Thus, a key aspect of financial planning is to decide which components of the financial plan deserve the highest priority because the decisions made about those components will influence the decisions for the others.

Financial Plan Example. The example featuring Stephanie Spratt's financial plan shows how the plan can be segmented into the six components. The example also illustrates how the components are integrated so that a decision about any one component can only be made after considering the others. As time passes and financial conditions change, you should reevaluate and update your financial plan.

REVIEW QUESTIONS

All Review Questions are available in MyFinanceLab *at* http://www.myfinancelab.com.

1. **Integrated Financial Plan.** Why is it important to integrate the components of your financial plan?

2. **Role of Budgeting.** How does budgeting fit into your financial plan? How is your financial plan affected by your spending? What is the budgeting trade-off?

3. **Role of Managing Liquidity.** Discuss how managing liquidity fits into your financial plan. What is the liquidity trade-off?

4. **Personal Financing.** Describe some advantages and disadvantages of using personal financing to achieve your financial goals. What is the personal financing trade-off?

5. **Managing Investments.** How does managing your investments fit into your financial plan? What is the investment trade-off?

6. **Maintaining and Protecting Wealth.** Discuss some methods for maintaining and protecting your wealth. What is the insurance trade-off?

7. **Impact of Timing on Your Plan.** How does time affect your financial plan?

8. **Change in Financial Position.** What do you think happens to your budget when your financial position changes?

9. **Financial Decision.** You have a $7,000 balance on your car loan at 11% interest. Your favorite aunt has just left you $10,000 in her will. You can put the money in a money market account at your bank and pay off your car loan, or you can invest the money in mutual funds. What factors must you consider in making your decision?

10. **Financial Decision.** In the previous question, you decide to pay off the car loan and invest the difference. Now you no longer have a $350 per month car payment. Suggest some ways you might use these additional funds.

11. **Investment Decision.** You have some extra cash in your budget that you wish to invest. You have narrowed your choices to a single stock, Treasury bonds, or stock mutual funds. What characteristics of each investment alternative should you consider in making your decision?

12. **Role of Insurance.** How does purchasing car insurance and homeowner's insurance help protect and maintain your wealth?

13. **Role of Insurance.** How does purchasing sufficient health insurance and disability insurance help protect and maintain your wealth?

14. **Life Insurance.** How does life insurance protect your wealth? Who needs life insurance?

15. **Impact of Spending on Financial Planning.** Explain how excessive spending can prevent effective financial planning.

16. **Goal Setting.** Explain why having very specific goals is important for financial planning.

17. **Tracking Expenditures and Budgeting.** Why is it important to track your expenditures for a few months? How does this practice impact your budget?

18. **Record Keeping.** Why is it important to keep financial records stored in a safe location? List some important documents that you should keep in a safe place.

FINANCIAL PLANNING PROBLEMS

All Financial Planning Problems are available in MyFinanceLab *at* http://www.myfinancelab.com.

1. **Interest Savings.** Judy has just received $12,500 as an inheritance from her uncle and is considering ways to use the money. Judy's car is one year old, and her monthly payment is $304. She owes 48 more payments. The amount to pay off the loan is $12,460. How much will Judy save in interest if she pays off her car loan now?

2. **Investment Decision.** Judy (from problem 1) is also considering investing the $12,500 in a certificate of deposit (CD). She is guaranteed a return of 4% on a four-year CD. How much would Judy earn from the CD? Which of the two alternatives offers the better return?

3. **Investment Value.** Judy pays off her car loan and now must decide how she wants to invest the extra $3,648 per year that she budgeted for car payments. She decides to invest this additional amount in her employer-sponsored retirement plan. Currently, the plan is averaging a 12% annual return. Judy has 15 years until retirement. How much more money will she have at retirement if she invests this additional amount?

4. **Investment Value.** Judy believes that another benefit of investing the extra $3,648 in her employer-sponsored retirement plan is the tax savings. Judy is in a 25% marginal tax bracket. How much will investing in this manner save her in taxes annually? Assuming she remains in a 25% marginal tax bracket until she retires, how much will it save her in total over the next 15 years, ignoring the time value of the tax savings?

5. **Retirement Savings.** Miguel, a recent 22-year-old college graduate, wants to retire a millionaire.

How much will he need to set aside annually to achieve his goal, assuming he plans to retire at age 67 and he can earn an 8% annual return on his investment?

6. **Retirement Considerations.** Referring to the previous question, what other factors should Miguel consider with regard to his retirement goal? What recommendation would you give Miguel regarding his goal?

FINANCIAL PLANNING ONLINE EXERCISES

1. Go to http://www.kiplinger.com, and click "Tools." Under the "College" heading, click "Should you go to grad school?" Fill in that information and report the results. How would this decision impact your financial plan?

2. Go to http://www.quicken.com and click on "Money Management Tips" at the bottom of the page.

   a. List five ways that you could save money.

   b. Watch one of the videos on money management and finances. What did you learn from this video?

   c. Go to your favorite search engine and find another Web site that provides helpful tips on saving money. What did you learn from this new Web site?

PSYCHOLOGY OF PERSONAL FINANCE: Your Financial Plan

1. Do you dedicate a sufficient amount of money toward financial planning purposes such as saving, insurance, investing, and your retirement? Explain how you could revise your spending now so that you would have more income that could be used for financial planning purposes.

2. Your financial plan should include plans for managing your liquidity, financing, insurance, investments, and retirement planning. Which of these plans causes you the greatest concern? Which of these plans will be most difficult for you to achieve? Explain.

WEB SEARCH EXERCISE

You can develop your personal finance skills by conducting an Internet search for related articles. Find a recent online article about personal finance that reinforces one or more concepts covered in this chapter. If your class has an online component, your professor may ask you to post your summary of the article there and provide a link to the article so that other students can access it. If your class is live, your professor may ask you to summarize your application of the article in class. Your professor may assign specific students to complete this assignment or may allow any student to do the assignment on a volunteer basis.

For recent online articles related to this chapter, consider using the following search terms (be sure to include the current year as a search term to ensure that the online articles are recent):

- Managing your liquidity
- Personal financing
- Managing your investments

- Retirement planning
- Integrating your financial plan
- Completing your financial plan
- Achieving your financial plan

VIDEO EXERCISE: Financial Plan

Go to one of the Web sites that contain video clips (such as http://www.youtube.com) and view some video clips about any aspect of financial planning. You can use search phrases such as "developing a financial plan." Select one video clip on this topic that you would recommend for the other students in your class.

1. Provide the Web link for the video clip.

2. What do you think is the main point of this video clip?

3. How might you change your process of developing a financial plan as a result of watching this video clip?

CERTIFIED FINANCIAL PLANNER EXERCISE

Stephanie Spratt comes to you for advice. Due to a very weak economy, she was just laid off from her job. She will receive $1,200 per month for the next six months. (Her cash budget and her personal balance sheet were provided earlier in this chapter.)

1. Offer advice to her on how she should revise her cash flow statement based on an income of $1,200 per month, assuming that she expects to be rehired within the next six months.

2. Assume that Stephanie might remain unemployed for an additional six months. Identify the possible ways that she could revise her personal cash budget and balance sheet to survive.

3. Explain the interaction between the personal balance sheet and the personal cash flow statement in a situation like this when income is not sufficient to cover monthly bills.

BUILDING YOUR OWN FINANCIAL PLAN

Congratulations! By completing the preceding 20 *Building Your Own Financial Plan* exercises, you have created a comprehensive financial plan. At this point, using the Excel-based software that accompanies your book, you should print out your completed plan and store it in a safe place.

As with any plan, periodic review and modification of your financial plan are essential. Many of the exercises have included prompts for when decisions should be reviewed or modified. The worksheets provided with this chapter will assist you in establishing your own timing for this review, tracking your progress toward meeting your goals, and keeping track of the location of important documents. Setting a specific time to do this review is helpful in preventing procrastination. Use the Excel spreadsheets that accompany this text to change your financial plan as needed. Remember that good financial planning is not the result of luck, but of informed decisions.

Go to the worksheets at the end of this chapter to complete building your financial plan.

THE SAMPSONS—A Continuing Case

With your help, Dave and Sharon Sampson have now established a financial plan. Among their key financial planning decisions were the following:

- **Budgeting.** They decided to revise their budget to make it possible to start saving. By reducing their spending on recreation, they freed up funds to be saved for a down payment on Sharon's new car and the children's college education.

- **Liquidity.** They maintain sufficient funds in their checking account in case of unexpected expenses.

- **Financing.** They paid off their credit card balance to avoid the high interest charges that they were accumulating. They also obtained a four-year car loan to finance Sharon's new car. In addition, they refinanced their mortgage to capitalize on lower interest rates, which allowed them to substantially reduce their monthly payments for their home.

- **Protecting Their Wealth.** They decided to increase their car insurance, reduce the deductible on their homeowner's insurance, and buy disability insurance. They also purchased a life insurance policy for Dave. They decided that Dave should invest at least $3,000 per year in his retirement account because his employer matches the contribution up to that amount. They made a will that designates a trustee who can allocate the estate to ensure that the children's college education is covered and that the children receive the benefits in small amounts (so they do not spend their inheritance too quickly).

- **Investments.** They decided not to buy individual stocks for now because of the risk involved. They decided that they will invest their savings for their children's education in mutual funds. They will not invest all the money in one mutual fund or one type of fund, but will diversify among several types of mutual funds.

Now that Dave and Sharon have completed their financial plan, they are relieved that they have a plan to deal with their budget, liquidity, financing, investing, insurance, and retirement.

Go to the worksheets at the end of this chapter to complete this case.

CHAPTER 21: BUILDING YOUR OWN FINANCIAL PLAN

YOUR GOALS FOR CHAPTER 21

1. Review your completed financial plan.
2. Record the location of your important documents.

ANALYSIS

1. Congratulations! You have completed your financial plan. Remember that financial planning is an ongoing task. Use the following table as a reminder to review key parts of your financial plan.

Item	When Reviewed	Date of Review
Short-Term Goals	As needed	
Intermediate-Term Goals	Annually	
Long-Term Goals	Annually	
Personal Cash Flow Statement	Annually	
Personal Balance Sheet	Annually	
Tax Situation	Annually, before year end	
Selection of Financial Institution	Biannually	
Credit Report	Annually	
Loans	As needed	
Risk Tolerance	Every 2–3 years	
Portfolio and Asset Allocation (Including Stocks, Bonds, and Money Market Instruments)	Annually	
Property and Casualty Insurance Needs	Annually	
Insurance Needs (Life, Health, Auto)	As dictated by critical events	
Retirement Plan	Annually	
Will and Estate Planning	As dictated by critical events	

2. Now that your plan is complete, store it for safekeeping. Along with your financial plan, keep a record of the location of your key assets and financial documents. Use the following worksheet as a guide.

Location of Important Documents

Estate Related	Location
Wills/Trusts	
Letter of Last Instruction	
Other	
Other	

Insurance	
Life	
Health	
Disability	
Auto	
Other	
Other	

Certificates and Deeds	
Automobile Titles	
Real Estate Deeds	
Birth Certificates	
Marriage Certificate	
Passports	
Other	
Other	

Investments and Savings	
Certificates of Deposit	
Stock Certificates	
Passbooks	
Mutual Fund Records	
Other	
Other	

Tax Records	**Location**
Last Year's Tax Return	
Last Seven Years of Tax Records	
Other	
Other	

Loans and Credit Cards	
Loan Notes (Still Outstanding)	
List of Credit Card Numbers	
Other	
Other	

3. Students who have completed the software worksheets throughout the semester can print out the final versions of the critical financial planning documents for safekeeping.

CHAPTER 21: THE SAMPSONS—A Continuing Case

CASE QUESTIONS

1. Explain how the Sampsons' budgeting affects all their other financial planning decisions.

   _____

   _____

   _____

   _____

2. How are the Sampsons' liquidity and investment decisions related?

   _____

   _____

   _____

   _____

3. In what ways are the Sampsons' financing and investing decisions related?

   _____

   _____

   _____

   _____

4. Explain how the Sampsons' retirement planning decisions are related to their investment decisions.

   _____

   _____

   _____

   _____

Financial Literacy POST-TEST

The following test will help you determine how much you learned about personal finance. It contains basic questions on material you learned from the text that can determine your ability to make proper financial planning decisions.

After taking the test, grade your performance based on the answers provided at the end of the test.

1. The _____ specifies the financial decisions that result from your personal financial planning.
   a. personal financial plan
   b. personal budget
   c. personal finance objective
   d. none of the above

2. When constructing a budget, it is helpful to use a personal cash flow statement, which measures a person's _____ and _____.
   a. cash inflows; cash outflows
   b. assets; expenses
   c. assets; liabilities
   d. none of the above

3. The time value of money implies that a dollar received today is worth _____ a dollar received tomorrow.
   a. more than
   b. the same as
   c. less than
   d. none of the above

4. Which of the following will not affect the amount of taxes you pay?
   a. Purchasing a home that will be financed with a mortgage
   b. Contributing a portion of your salary to your retirement account
   c. Taking a third job to enhance your wealth
   d. All of the above will affect the amount of taxes you pay.

5. _____ are not a type of depository institution.
   a. Credit unions
   b. Savings institutions
   c. Commercial banks
   d. Securities firms

6. Individuals with short-term funds would probably not invest them in _____.
   a. CDs
   b. NOW accounts
   c. corporate bonds
   d. checking accounts

7. Credit cards that allow consumers to borrow up to a specified maximum amount are examples of _____.
   a. installment credit
   b. collateral-based credit
   c. noninstallment credit
   d. revolving open-end credit

8. When applying for a credit card, you will probably not be asked for information regarding _____.
   a. your cash inflows and outflows
   b. your capital
   c. your credit history
   d. your criminal record

9. When applying for a loan, borrowers will probably need to provide information regarding their _____.
   a. personal balance sheet
   b. assets
   c. personal cash flow statement
   d. Borrowers probably need to provide information regarding all of the above.

10. The _____ the cost of a home, the _____ the insurance.
   a. higher; higher
   b. higher; lower
   c. lower; higher
   d. none of the above

601

11. _____ coverage is intended to cover any liability associated with property damage that you caused.
   a. Bodily injury liability
   b. Property damage liability
   c. Medical payments
   d. none of the above

12. _____ are not examples of private health care plans.
   a. Managed health care plans
   b. Indemnity plans
   c. Medicare plans
   d. Health maintenance organizations

13. Which of the following institutions are unlikely to offer life insurance policies?
   a. Financial institutions providing banking and brokerage services
   b. Subsidiaries of financial conglomerates
   c. Independent firms
   d. All of the above may offer life insurance policies.

14. A corporation issues stock to _____.
   a. distribute its ownership
   b. obtain funds to support operations
   c. incur fixed interest charges
   d. none of the above

15. In general, stocks perform _____ when interest rates are _____.
   a. better; high
   b. better; low
   c. poorer; low
   d. none of the above

16. Typical maturities for bonds are _____.
   a. 10 to 30 years
   b. 5 to 10 years
   c. 2 to 5 years
   d. 1 to 2 years

17. _____ mutual funds sell shares directly to investors and repurchase those shares whenever investors wish to sell them.
   a. Discount
   b. Premium
   c. Open-end
   d. Closed-end

18. A stock portfolio is subject to _____ risk, or the risk of poor performance due to weak stock market conditions.
   a. market
   b. interest rate
   c. business
   d. leverage

19. Individuals who defer their retirement are eligible to receive _____ level of annual income from the Social Security program.
   a. the same
   b. a lower
   c. a higher
   d. none of the above

20. A(n) _____ is a legal request for how one's estate should be distributed upon death.
   a. letter of last instruction
   b. asset distribution
   c. will
   d. none of the above

Answers

1. A	11. B
2. A	12. C
3. A	13. D
4. D	14. B
5. D	15. B
6. C	16. A
7. D	17. C
8. D	18. A
9. D	19. C
10. A	20. C

Appendix A
YOUR CAREER

Determining Your Career Path

What career path is optimal for you? Consider the factors described here when deciding your career path. Then, access the sources of information that are identified in the following sections to help make your selection.

Factors That May Affect Your Career Path

Perhaps the obvious first step in determining your career path is to consider your interests and then identify the careers that fit your interests. Most people identify several possible career interests, which makes the decision difficult. However, you may be able to screen your list based on the following factors.

Educational and Skill Requirements Some jobs may seem interesting, but they require more education and training than you are prepared to acquire. For example, the training required to be a doctor may be too extensive and time-consuming. In addition, the entrance requirements are very high. Review the education and skills that are needed for each career that appeals to you. From your list of possible career paths, focus on those in which you already have or would be willing to achieve the necessary background, education, and skills.

Job Availability People may find career paths that they would like to follow and feel they could do so successfully, but realize that these paths have a limited supply of open positions relative to applicants. For example, many people want to be fashion designers or chefs at expensive restaurants. Consider the number of job positions available compared to the number of applicants pursuing those jobs.

Compensation Most people consider compensation to be an important criterion when considering job positions. Some career tracks may be enjoyable but do not provide sufficient compensation. Information on compensation for various types of jobs is available on many Web sites. For example, at http://www.salary .com you can insert the type of job that you are curious about and obtain salary ranges for that position in a particular location in the United States.

Sources of Information That Can Help You Select Your Career Path

Consider the following sources of information as you attempt to establish a list of career options from which to select your optimal career path.

Books on Careers Many books identify careers and describe the necessary skills for each one. Some books provide a broad overview, while others are more detailed. A broad overview is usually ideal when you are first identifying the various types of possible careers. Then, once you narrow down the list, you can find a book that focuses on your chosen field, such as medicine, engineering, social work, and so on.

Courses Your college courses are a vital source of information about related careers. Courses in accounting can help you understand the nature of the work accountants do, nursing classes provide insight into the job descriptions of nurses, and courses in sociology may help you understand the jobs of social workers. Even courses that are broader in scope, for example, courses in management, may be applicable to many different types of jobs, including those of accountants, nurses, and social workers. If you enjoyed your basic management course, you may like a job in which you are involved in managing people, production processes, or services.

Job Experience Internships provide some exposure to a particular type of job and allow you to learn what tasks people in a field do as part of their daily work. Such experience is especially useful because many jobs are likely to differ from your perception.

Contacts For any specific job description that interests you, identify people who you know in that field. Set up an informational interview so that you can ask detailed questions about the job.

The Internet A lot of information on careers can be found on the Internet. To explore the types of careers that are available, and the skills needed for each, go to http://www.careers.org to learn about jobs in numerous fields, including finance, law, management, construction, health, agriculture, and broadcasting. Some Web sites such as http://www.careerbuilder.com list the most popular job categories so that you can determine the types of job positions that are frequently available. Be careful, however, to note the size of the pool of applicants for any type of job that interests you. It is much easier to land the job you want (assuming you have the requisite skills) when the number of openings is large compared to the number of qualified people interested in that position.

At some point, you have to narrow your choices so that you can spend more time focused on the careers that intrigue you the most. The Internet is very valuable in offering insight even after you narrow your choices. For example, http://www.monster.com offers targeted advice for many different fields.

Personality Tests You can get feedback on the type of career that fits you based on a personality test. Some of these tests are expensive, and views are mixed about whether they can more accurately pinpoint a job that fits your personality than if you simply use the criteria described earlier. Some tests are offered for free on Web sites, such as http://www.careerpath.com. Be aware that the free tests normally do not offer as detailed an analysis as the tests that you pay for.

Getting the Skills You Need

Once you decide on the type of position you want, your next step is to determine the training and education you will need to qualify for it.

Training

To gather general information, go to the Bureau of Labor Statistics site (http://www.bls.gov). There you will discover what training is needed for a specific job description and how to obtain it.

Be careful when reviewing information online about training courses that are available. Much information found on Web sites specifically devoted to training is provided by companies that want to sell you this training. For this reason, carefully evaluate whether the training offered will help get you the job that you want. As an extreme example, some companies provide training for modeling or acting. People are well aware of celebrities who became very rich by modeling or acting. However, taking a few courses is unlikely to lead to major success in those fields. Try to determine whether the market truly rewards people who pay for training by a particular company before you pay for it.

The training by some companies may be certified, which can distinguish it from others. However, a certificate does not always mean that the training is valuable or will lead to employment. In some cases, there may simply be fewer jobs than the number of people who are properly trained. In other cases, the training will not qualify you for a specific job position.

Education

Colleges and universities provide training in the form of education. Web sites such as http://www.collegeboard.com profile careers by college major to help you consider your career path and the education it requires. A degree in a career-oriented major, such as accounting or business, will prepare you for a job in that specific field. A liberal arts degree, on the other hand, will allow you to choose from a broad range of careers in areas such as marketing, journalism, teaching, and publishing.

The reputations of universities vary substantially, and some universities may be much more credible than others in preparing you for a specific job position. Some jobs require that your degree be acquired from an accredited university. Therefore, it may be important to learn whether the university you plan to attend is accredited. Because there are different accreditation agencies, determine the type of accreditation that would be important for the specific type of job you plan to pursue.

Learn as much as you can about the college or department of the university where you are considering taking courses. What percentage of recent graduates passes a standardized exam that must be taken after graduation (for fields like accounting and law)? Are recent graduates being hired in the field that you wish to enter? You may be able to get answers to these questions from the college department where you would be taking courses.

Internships

Internships offer a way to gain some experience in the type of job that you plan to pursue when you graduate. Many large well-known firms and small firms sponsor internships. You may be able to obtain an internship while you are still in college. Some companies may pay you for your work, although some internships are unpaid. Also, you may receive college credit for internships at some colleges.

Even if the internship does not offer pay or college credit, it can still be very worthwhile. An internship gives you some experience in your possible future career, which you can put on your résumé. If the firm sponsoring the internship has a job opening in the future, your internship experience there may give you an advantage over other applicants. An internship may also give you special insight into a particular career path, which could reinforce your desire to pursue this path when you graduate. Alternatively, it might make you realize that you do not want that career path, but even that outcome can be extremely valuable because it could help you find a more appropriate major.

You may be able to retrieve information about internships on corporate Web sites. In addition, your college may have internship programs.

Decisions About Your Education and Career

A common dilemma faced by most people at some point in their lives is whether to seek more education or a full-time job. The obvious disadvantage associated with pursuing more education is that you often must forgo income and incur additional education expenses. You might already be in debt and will have to borrow additional funds to support your education. Perhaps you were hoping that a full-time job would allow you to pay off existing debt and save money at this stage in your life.

This decision requires a comparison of the costs and benefits of pursuing a degree. The costs include your tuition, the forgone income you could have earned from working instead of going to school, and the forgone on-the-job experience that you could have gained by working instead of going to school. However, a degree may enable you to qualify for many additional types of jobs that require further education. Thus, the benefits of seeking a degree include better job opportunities, a better salary once you start working, greater potential for raises over time, and a more enjoyable career. In addition, you will achieve your education goals more quickly by going to college on a full-time basis.

How the Economy Can Affect Your Decision

There is a very close relationship between the number of jobs available and consumer demand for products and services. When consumer demand for products and services is strong, firms hire more employees so they can increase their production to satisfy the strong demand. They may also allow more workers to work overtime. These conditions tend to result in larger incomes for individuals, and this allows people to spend more money for products and services, which can create additional jobs.

Conversely, when the economy weakens, firms do not need as many employees to achieve their production goals or to serve consumers. Therefore, they eliminate some existing jobs, which results in layoffs. They are also less likely to create any new job positions, making it more difficult for people to find the type of job that they would like. In addition, the increased layoffs cause a reduction in income for some people, which limits the amount of funds that they have to spend. As their spending is reduced, the consumer demand for products and services is reduced further, which could cause additional layoffs.

Because of these effects during a weak economy, there will normally be more applicants for any job opening that occurs, which makes it more difficult to obtain the job you would like. Under these conditions, firms may even raise the required skills or education for the specific job opening, as they can be more selective when assessing job applicants.

The strategy of pursuing more education may be especially prudent when the economy is weak. Although jobs may be scarce during a weak economy, education is still available. For example, suppose that you just graduated from a community college, and your plan is to obtain a full-time job and go to a four-year college on a part-time basis. You may even have hoped that an employer would pay for your tuition while you take college courses. However, if jobs are scarce and you cannot obtain the job you would like, consider pursuing your education on a full-time basis instead of looking for a full-time job.

Comparative Analysis of Pursuing More Education versus a Job

Overall, the change in your career plan would have two major effects: (1) less (or perhaps zero) income during the period when you continue your education on a full-time basis, and (2) a quicker pace in achieving your college degree. You can conduct an analysis to compare the costs and the benefits of changing your career plan in this manner. First, forecast your annual cash inflows and outflows for the next several years for sticking with your original plan to pursue whatever full-time job you can obtain now (see Panel A in Exhibit A.1). Because this example assumes that you just finished your associate's degree at a community college, it would likely take you at least an additional six years to obtain your college degree on a part-time basis.

Now, forecast your annual cash inflows and outflows for the next several years for revising your original plan and pursuing your education full-time for the next two years. During the next two years, your cash inflows might be zero, and you should account for the full-time tuition within your cash outflows (see Panel B in Exhibit A.1). However, from Year 3 forward, your expected income will likely be higher than it would have been if you had pursued your original plan because you would have your college degree two years from now. Overall, your revised plan causes a large budget deficit in the first two years, but more favorable cash flows in all the years after that. Thus, the extra cash flows from Year 3 forward should more than offset the large budget deficit you created in the first two years. The exact number of years that it would take to offset your budget deficit depends on your specific situation.

Example of Analysis Exhibit A.1 illustrates how you could conduct an analysis. Panel A shows the expected cash flows based on the original plan of working full-time, with assumptions that you would go to school part-time and incur tuition expenses of $2,000 per year for the next six years. Panel B shows the expected cash flows based on the revised plan, in which you go to school full-time for two years instead of working, thus incurring all your tuition expenses over the next two years.

Once you have estimated the cash flows for the two alternative plans, you can compare them as shown in Exhibit A.2. Notice that the cumulative cash flows are shown here over an eight-year period, in which cash flows are accumulated on a yearly basis. In the first two years, the benefits of the original plan are obvious. However, by Year 8, the cumulative cash flows of the revised plan surpass those of the original plan. That is, the higher income earned starting in Year 3 due to finishing your degree allows you to

EXHIBIT A.1   Comparison of Original Career Plan to Revised Career Plan During a Weak Economy

Panel A: Original Career Plan: Pursue Full-Time Job Now and Finish Undergraduate Degree on a Part-Time Basis over the Next Six Years

Assumptions:

- You already have an associate's degree.
- You predict that your full-time job will provide a $1,000 raise every two years.
- You also predict that your salary will jump upon completion of your undergraduate degree starting in Year 7 and that your salary will increase by $1,000 every year after that.
- Tuition for part-time education will be $2,000 per year until the degree is completed.
- You expect to earn a salary of $35,000 when you obtain your college degree, with assumed raises of $1,000 per year.

Year	Annual Cash Inflows Due to Job	Annual Cash Outflows Due to Education	Annual Net Cash Inflows = Cash Inflows − Cash Outflows
1	$24,000	$2,000	$22,000
2	$24,000	$2,000	$22,000
3	$25,000	$2,000	$23,000
4	$25,000	$2,000	$23,000
5	$26,000	$2,000	$24,000
6	$26,000	$2,000	$24,000
7	$35,000	$0	$35,000
8	$36,000	$0	$36,000

Panel B: Revised Career Plan: Pursue Full-Time Education Now While the Economy Is Weak

Assumptions:

- You already have an associate's degree.
- You predict that you will receive your undergraduate degree in two years.
- Tuition for full-time education will be $6,000 per year until the degree is completed.
- You expect to earn a salary of $35,000 when you obtain your college degree, with assumed raises of $1,000 per year.

Year	Annual Cash Inflows Due to Job	Annual Cash Outflows Due to Education	Annual Net Cash Inflows = Cash Inflows − Cash Outflows
1	$0	$6,000	−$6,000
2	$0	$6,000	−$6,000
3	$35,000	$0	$35,000
4	$36,000	$0	$36,000
5	$37,000	$0	$37,000
6	$38,000	$0	$38,000
7	$39,000	$0	$39,000
8	$40,000	$0	$40,000

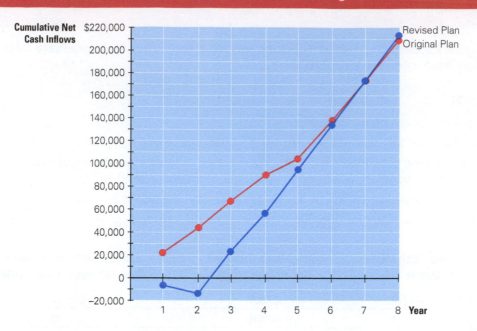

EXHIBIT A.2   Comparison of Net Cash Flows Between Original Plan and Revised Plan

Year	Original Plan: Annual Net Cash Inflows	Original Plan: Cumulative Net Cash Inflows	Revised Plan: Annual Net Cash Inflows	Revised Plan: Cumulative Net Cash Inflows
1	$22,000	$22,000	−$6,000	−$6,000
2	$22,000	$44,000	−$6,000	−$12,000
3	$23,000	$67,000	$35,000	$23,000
4	$23,000	$90,000	$36,000	$59,000
5	$24,000	$114,000	$37,000	$96,000
6	$24,000	$138,000	$38,000	$134,000
7	$35,000	$173,000	$39,000	$173,000
8	$36,000	$209,000	$40,000	$213,000

accumulate more cash flows over the following six years to offset the sacrifice you made in the first two years.

Refining the Analysis to Fit Your Situation Although an eight-year period is assessed here, you might need to consider the effects beyond that point. In this example, you were able to pursue a job requiring a college degree after two years with the revised plan, versus after six years with the original plan. Consequently, the revised career plan might lead to a faster career track over time, as you would have your undergraduate degree four years earlier. In general, the use of an eight-year period probably underestimates the potential benefits of the revised plan (in which you received your four-year degree more quickly) because you would probably be farther along in your career path by the end of eight years. Consequently, your cash flows may be higher in all years beyond the eight-year period assessed if you pursue the faster career track explained here.

The interest rate on the loan that you may have needed to cover your tuition was not considered in the analysis because this is unlikely to be much different for the two plans shown here. Some additional factors should be considered in this decision along with the analysis described earlier. The revised career plan may even offer additional benefits that do not show up in the analysis. The job that you obtain in Year 3 may provide not only more income but also more satisfaction. You can still decide to pursue additional education after obtaining this job in Year 3, but you would be in a position to take graduate courses instead of undergraduate courses.

In some situations, the analysis may lead you to conclude that pursuit of a full-time job now makes more sense than continuing your full-time education. For example, if you need a break from school and are not likely to perform well in school if you continue your education full-time, the revised career plan may not be appropriate for you. Also, if you already have all the qualifications required to obtain the type of job that you desire, additional education might not improve your marketability. In this special case, your cash flows over a long-term period would be more favorable if you stick with your original plan rather than continuing your education on a full-time basis.

This comparison of your original career plan to a revised career plan assumed that you had just completed your associate's degree. Although this example does not fit all profiles, you can easily adapt the analysis to fit your specific situation. For instance, if you have just received your college undergraduate degree, you may have various options to consider during a weak economy. You can pursue a full-time job, but even with your undergraduate degree, it may be difficult to obtain the type of job that you want during weak economic conditions. You could revise your career plan by pursuing a graduate degree on a full-time basis instead of looking for a full-time job while the economy is weak.

The trade-off is similar to that described in the previous example. Your revised career plan may result in no cash inflows (because of not having a job) and higher cash outflows (because of paying full-time tuition) for the next year or two. However, on graduation, your master's degree might allow you to pursue better jobs than those you could have pursued with an undergraduate degree. Thus, you may generate more income over time, which can recapture the loss of income while you were in a graduate program and the cost of tuition. The same type of analysis can be applied to help you make the proper decision. When conducting the analysis, it is important to use realistic data about income levels for various types of degrees. Some types of master's degrees may not necessarily lead to a higher income level than what you can expect to earn with your undergraduate degree.

Selecting Your School

Your choice of a college is a personal finance decision, as it can have a major impact on your future financial success. It could also affect your quality of life. If you are now at a community college, this section may help you consider the key factors for selecting a university once you earn your associate's degree. If you are already in an undergraduate program, you might apply this section to making a decision about a graduate school.

Factors to Consider When Choosing a College

You should consider many factors about colleges before you decide which one to attend. You can find a lot of information on the Internet about colleges and universities. Most colleges offer a great deal of information so that you can make an informed decision. In addition, some Web sites provide comparative statistics and opinions on universities, which can help you compare them. Some of the more important factors that you should consider when selecting a school are

- Admission requirements
- Tuition
- Major fields offered
- Reputation
- Convenience

Admission Requirements Universities commonly publicize their admission requirements. A review of admission requirements is a good first screen because this will let you spend most of your time focusing on the schools where you believe that you satisfy the admission requirements.

Tuition Tuition represents a major cost of education. The average tuition is about $31,000 per year for private universities, although there is much variation in tuition among them. The tuition at public universities is about $9,000 per year. Thus, going to a public university can save a student $22,000 per year on average. When students go to a public university that is outside their state of residence, they normally have to pay a large premium. The average premium charged by public universities is about $14,000 per year. Thus, the potential savings from going to a public university instead of a private one are reduced for students who go out-of-state. At two-year colleges, the average cost of tuition and fees is about $3,300.

Keep in mind that some colleges offer scholarships, so if you find a university that charges high tuition but seems to be perfect in every other way, you should investigate whether you could qualify for its scholarships. Some schools also offer grants for students who are less able to afford the tuition. There are also government programs that offer grants to students.

Major Fields Offered Each university offers its own set of major fields. Even if you are not sure of your exact major, you probably at least know your general interest, such as science or liberal arts or business. You can determine whether each school that you are considering offers majors in general areas that are aligned with your interests.

Reputation The reputation of a university can have a major impact on your marketability when you graduate. However, keep in mind that the impact of a university's reputation on your marketability is dependent on the major that you choose. A college that is known for having a great nursing program may enhance your marketability if you pursue a major in nursing, but that school's reputation might not have an impact on you if you pursue a major in an unrelated field.

Convenience Many students select a university based on convenience. For example, they may choose a local college because it allows them to live at home, or if they do go away, they select the university that is closest to their home so that they can come home on weekends. Some students put so much emphasis on convenience that they do not consider other relevant factors that could have enhanced their career. For example, they may select University A (located only 100 miles from home) instead of University B (located 200 miles from home) simply because it is closer to home and therefore more convenient. However, if University A does not offer a major that fits their interests, they may be forced to select a major that they do not like. They could have pursued their desired major at University B if they would have accepted a little less convenience.

FREE APPS
for Personal
Finance

Estimating the Cost of Your College Education

Application:

The 529 Calculator app (by TIAA-CREF) allows you to estimate the expenses of the college that you identify, and estimates how much you will need to invest or save to cover the expenses in the future.

To Find It:

Search for the "529 Calculator" app on your mobile device.

Commuting versus Going Away to College

If you plan to be working while you are pursuing your degree, your job may dictate the selection of your university due to convenience. However, if you are open to the possibility of going away to school, you may want to compare the advantages and disadvantages of each college before you finalize your decision.

Conduct Cash Flow Analysis Create a spreadsheet similar to that shown in Exhibit A.1 that displays what your expected cash inflows and outflows would be if you commute to college while working versus if you focus full-time on going to school. The obvious benefit to commuting is that you can earn income from your existing job, and your living arrangements may be less expensive than if you went away to school.

However, if you do not plan to work if you go away to college, you may be able to finish your degree more quickly, which would allow you to pursue your career sooner. Of course, if work is likely to slow your progress at school, you could also consider commuting without working. Either way, it is still possible that going away to college could make financial sense. Here are some situations in which going away to college may be worth considering.

- Even if both schools offer the major you desire, going away to college might result in lower expenses. For example, if you consider going away to a state university and the commuter university is private, you might be able to save a substantial amount of money by paying lower tuition at the state university.

- Going away to college may allow you to select your preferred major, which the commuter university might not offer. This could allow you to earn more income when you start your career. Your analysis should account for this difference when you estimate the income you would earn after graduating from either school. Even if it did not result in higher income, it might allow you to have a more enjoyable career.

- Even if both universities offer the major you desire, going away to college might allow you to be more marketable when you graduate if that school has a better reputation than the commuter university. This can be accounted for in your estimate of the higher income (cash inflow) that you might earn if you attend the university with the better reputation.

Even when you know that you will be going away to college, you can still conduct an analysis like this one when comparing two universities. Living expenses can vary substantially among schools. Also, the possible majors and minors vary among universities, and this could influence your future career. You can account for the differences in the majors when you estimate the income you will earn in the future for each possible major.

Consider Nonmonetary Factors In addition to your assessment of cash inflows and outflows, consider other factors that could also affect your decision. For example, is there a difference in the way courses (online versus classroom) are offered? Can you easily enroll in the courses you would want? Is the class size so large that it might reduce the quality of your education? Would your quality of life be better at one college? Would you have fewer distractions at another school and therefore be able to perform better there? To assess many of these characteristics, you can obtain information from college guides.

One of the most important nonmonetary factors students should consider is whether they have the discipline and maturity to go away to college. Some students may party less if they live at home and commute to a local college than if they go away to a university where there will be many temptations to enjoy an active social life. Other students, however, may thrive if they go away and live in a dorm where they can develop their social interaction skills and meet other students who have the same academic interests.

PSYCHOLOGY
of Personal
Finance

Consider visiting the campus of any college in which you still have an interest after conducting your analysis. You may find that your opinion of the campus and its town is quite different from those provided in college guides, and therefore it is important to assess the college campus yourself before making your final decision.

Selecting Your Major

The major that you select in college can have a very large impact on your future career, lifestyle, and income level. Therefore, this decision deserves much attention. You may be working in your career for 40 years or longer, so take the time to choose the proper major for your career.

For some people, selecting a major is easy because their career plans require a specific course of study. For example, if you want to be an accountant, you need to major in accounting. If you want to be a nurse, you need to major in nursing. However, many students have not decided on their future career, and therefore they struggle when selecting their major.

Some students select a major because their friends chose that major, because the courses are offered at a desirable time, because it is easy for them to obtain high grades in those classes, or because there is a study abroad semester for students in that major. That is, their decisions were driven by what is most convenient, or the least amount of work, or the most fun. Although these decisions might provide immediate satisfaction, they may backfire if they do not provide students with adequate knowledge or tools to pursue a job that they would like. Some majors that require very little work are not very marketable in the job market. Ideally, you can identify a major that would be of much interest to you and would also provide you with skills that can help you land a good job within your desired career path. It is worth your time to carefully assess possible majors so that you can make an informed decision.

Although there is no perfect formula for choosing the perfect major, there are some general guidelines that may be useful. As a starting point, broadly define the fields that you like or dislike. Examples of broad fields include the following:

- Science (such as chemistry or biology)
- Social science (such as sociology or anthropology)
- Business (such as marketing or management)
- Health (such as nursing or nutrition science)
- Arts (such as art or music)

By doing this, you can eliminate some fields that don't interest you. For the remaining broad fields, you can obtain information to learn more about the specific majors that are available. You may wish to consider the following criteria before selecting your major:

- Review the content of courses for majors
- Research different career paths
- Take tests that help identify your interests
- Conduct analyses to compare majors
- Consider whether you would be willing to work on an advanced degree

The following sections discuss how these approaches can help you make your decision.

Review Course Content

Review the content of the courses within any major that you might consider. You should be able to find these course descriptions in any college catalog. Note that these descriptions tend to be limited. However, if you do an online search of "syllabus" for the names of the courses, you can obtain additional information by looking at some syllabi that are posted online by professors for these types of courses. A syllabus might describe special projects and assignments that are required, which could help you determine whether the courses would fit your interests.

Research Possible Career Paths

You can find many Web sites that offer guidance on majoring in a specific field by searching for "majoring in" and the name of the field. You may even see blogs in which students majoring in a particular field share their insights. Some of the Web sites will indicate the types of careers and jobs for a particular major. You may be able to find these Web sites if you include "job," "career," or "salary" in your online search.

Be Cautious When Reviewing Information When you read about career paths, consider the source of the information. Some information can be misleading. For example, assume that you want to know the typical jobs and salary for a political science major in the first few years after graduation. Some Web sites may offer salary information for graduates with political science majors. However, many graduates with this degree pursue a law degree later. If the Web site shows the jobs and the average salary for political science majors who also obtained a law degree, this information would be misleading. Many of the jobs would only be possible because of the law degree and could not be attained with only the political science degree. The same argument applies to history majors, English majors, or any other undergraduate majors who later pursued a graduate or professional degree.

As another example, assume that you want to major in theater. You have read that many famous actors majored in theater. However, this does not really indicate the typical jobs and salaries for individuals who graduate with a theater major. You may also have read that many well-known writers majored in journalism. Again, this does not really indicate the typical jobs and salaries for individuals who graduate with a journalism degree. Keep in mind that many graduates with degrees in history, political science, and journalism do not pursue careers in their major field because the number of jobs available is less than the number of students who are graduating. You may still want to pursue such a major to pursue your dream career, but at least you should know about the odds of finding employment within that field before deciding on that major.

Recommendations Based on Self-Testing

Some Web sites such as http://www.luc.edu (insert the search term "what's my major") offer a quiz you can take that recommends an appropriate major based on your answers. You should also conduct your own evaluation of possible majors before making your decision.

Conduct Analysis to Compare Majors

Once you have narrowed your choices down to a few possible majors, you can conduct an analysis of the possible majors, similar to the analysis used for comparing colleges. If the possible majors are at the same college, your tuition or fees for all the majors may be similar. The example in Exhibit A.3 compares the cash flows based on majoring in X (the top table) versus Y (the bottom table). You can substitute your possible majors for X and Y, and you can also replace the numbers if you have estimates of starting salaries for the majors you are considering.

The example in Exhibit A.3 assumes that majoring in X leads to better job opportunities, which is why the starting salary (cash inflows) is higher after you graduate and why the expected salary over time increases by a higher percentage each year. Majoring in Y will lead to limited job opportunities, which is why the starting salary is lower. In addition, there may be limited chances for promotion, so the expected salary is increased by a relatively small amount each year.

PSYCHOLOGY of Personal Finance

EXHIBIT A.3   **Comparing Net Cash Flows Between Two Different Majors**

Assumptions:

- You already have an associate's degree.
- You predict that you will complete your undergraduate degree in two years if you major in X or in Y and you will start a full-time job after graduation.
- Tuition for full-time education is $8,000 per year until the degree is completed.

Expected Cash Flows over the Next Six Years Based on Majoring in X

Year	Annual Cash Inflows Due to Job	Annual Cash Outflows Due to Education	Annual Net Cash Inflows = Cash Inflows − Cash Outflows	Accumulated Net Cash Flows
1	$0	$8,000	−$8,000	−$8,000
2	$0	$8,000	−$8,000	−$16,000
3	$36,000	$0	$36,000	$20,000
4	$38,000	$0	$38,000	$58,000
5	$41,000	$0	$41,000	$99,000
6	$46,000	$0	$46,000	$145,000

Expected Cash Flows over the Next Six Years Based on Majoring in Y

Year	Annual Cash Inflows Due to Job	Annual Cash Outflows Due to Education	Annual Net Cash Inflows = Cash Inflows − Cash Outflows	Accumulated Net Cash Flows
1	$0	$8,000	−$8,000	−$8,000
2	$0	$8,000	−$8,000	−$16,000
3	$25,000	$0	$25,000	$9,000
4	$26,000	$0	$26,000	$35,000
5	$27,000	$0	$27,000	$62,000
6	$28,000	$0	$28,000	$90,000

Compare Results for Both Alternatives Once you have completed your spreadsheet, you can compare the results. The cash flows in this exhibit are estimated over the next six years (two final years of college plus four years of full-time work), but you can assess whatever period you desire. You can tally the results for the six years, as shown in the bottom right cell. Exhibit A.3 shows that majoring in X will result in substantially more net cash flows over time. After six years, your accumulated net cash flow is $145,000 if you major in X and only $90,000 if you major in Y. The financial benefits of majoring in X are obvious and would be even more pronounced if you extended the analysis over a longer period.

Account for Nonmonetary Factors This analysis does not include nonmonetary factors that should also be considered. Some people may find that the nonmonetary factors (such as their special interest in the Y major) are more important in their decision to major in Y, even though they know that doing so may not result in good job opportunities. Other people might decide that even though they have a greater interest in majoring in Y, they will not obtain the type of job that reflects their interest. Thus, they may decide to major in X because the jobs are more closely related to the major itself. Another group of people might have the same degree of interest in the X and Y majors and therefore select the X major because it provides better job opportunities. In addition, it results in larger net cash flows over time, which will allow them to spend more money without having to borrow funds.

Adjust Analysis If One Major Requires Longer Period When comparing the cash flows between two alternative majors, it is possible that a longer time period (such as an extra year) may be needed to complete the requirements for one of the majors. This is important because it means that you may not be pursuing a job until a year later with that major. This could be easily accounted for in the analysis shown in Exhibit A.3. Under these conditions, you would account for the tuition and fees in the third year, and because you would not be pursuing a job until you graduate at the end of the third year, you would not have any expected cash inflows until the fourth year.

Continuing Your Education

A master's degree or a Ph.D. provides you with additional knowledge and skills that may allow you to qualify for better jobs. However, there are costs associated with pursuing such degrees, and you must weigh them against the potential benefits.

Costs The cost of a graduate degree is substantial and should be estimated carefully before you make your decision to pursue one. Because the cost varies greatly among programs, you may find a program that is less expensive than others that still satisfies your needs. Consider tuition and fees, room and board, and the opportunity cost of pursuing the degree. If you enroll in a full-time program, your opportunity cost is the salary that you could have earned if you worked during that time. You may also find it necessary to give up some social activities as well.

Benefits Individuals often pursue a master's degree or doctorate to increase their marketability. There are many job positions that require a degree beyond a bachelor of arts or a bachelor of science. If your goal is to increase your marketability, determine what type of degree would make the biggest difference. For example, engineers commonly obtain a master's in business administration (MBA) rather than a master's in engineering because the MBA is intended to give them stronger management skills. In this way, the degree certifies their skills in managing projects and people.

If you decide to pursue a master's or doctorate, determine if the university you select would make a big difference in your marketability. Some programs have a national or international reputation, while others are known only within a local area.

In some cases, students realize only after they graduate that their undergraduate degree is not as marketable as they had hoped, and they attempt to correct the situation by pursuing a master's degree in the same field. This is especially true when they enjoyed their time while pursuing their undergraduate degree. They are comfortable in their existing environment and would like to continue doing what they have been doing. This type of decision provides immediate satisfaction because it allows them to continue the life they enjoyed as an undergraduate. However, this decision could have adverse long-term consequences if it does not help the students obtain a job in a field they might like after obtaining their graduate degree. In essence, getting this degree only allowed them to delay the serious decision about developing proper skills for obtaining a job that they might like.

If your undergraduate major does not help you find a job, conduct a careful evaluation before pursuing a master's degree in the same field. It is possible that there are very few jobs at the master's level or even at the doctoral level in that field. Furthermore, the competition might be fierce among job applicants with this degree because many other students also have graduate degrees in this field as they were unable to find jobs after completing their undergraduate studies. This has resulted in the situation that some people are overeducated in specific fields yet lack the specific skills that are desired for available jobs.

PSYCHOLOGY
of Personal
Finance

One alternative to pursuing a graduate degree in the same field as your undergraduate degree is to pursue another undergraduate degree in a more marketable field where there are job opportunities. There are some undergraduate degrees that are much more marketable than graduate degrees. You can apply the same type of cash flow analysis that was shown in Exhibit A.1 to determine which alternative would be more feasible. You can still consider nonmonetary factors as well to complement your analysis of cash flows.

Criteria Used to Assess Applicants

When you pursue a job, you will likely be competing against many other job seekers. By recognizing what the employer is seeking, you may be able to distinguish yourself from the other applicants. Understanding the criteria that employers use to assess applicants will help you determine whether you possess the right qualifications for the job.

Your Application

An application will likely request general information about your education background, such as the schools you attended and your major and/or minor in college. It will also request information about your previous work experience. Applications are used to determine whether the candidates have the knowledge and the experience to perform well in the job position.

Your Résumé

Your résumé should provide your educational background and work experience. Companies receive numerous résumés for job positions, so it helps to describe succinctly the skills that may help you stand out from other applicants. If you obtain the skills and training that you need to pursue the job that you desire, creating a résumé is relatively easy. Most career Web sites offer tips on how you can improve your résumé (the résumé section of http://www.monster.com, for example). You can also post your résumé on many Web sites such as http://www.monster.com and http://www.careers.com.

Although many Web sites offer guidance, keep in mind that no résumé format is perfect for all situations. When developing your résumé, you should attempt to use a format that clearly illustrates your strengths. For example, if you have had four jobs but only the most recent job is related to your existing and future occupation, you should devote much more attention to the most recent job. If your work experience is in one narrow occupation and you plan to remain in that field, you may consider describing your experience in depth. Thus, as you pursue other jobs within that same occupation, prospective employers can review how your skills might be different from others with a more general work experience.

Using Social Media

Social media facilitate interactions through Internet technologies. You may be able to use social media such as LinkedIn as a means to obtain a job or advance your career. Social media can help you in many ways.

Learning About Careers You can learn more about your specific field from the personal insights of others who explain their work experience. You may also learn about other careers that you wish to consider if you are not satisfied with your career.

Networking You can keep in contact with former coworkers, who may be a good source for learning more about other employers or other occupations.

Promoting Yourself You can describe your present occupation along with information about your work background, skills, expertise, and experience. You can also provide contact information so that prospective employers can get in touch with you.

Think Twice When Using Social Media When using social media, keep in mind that your comments or other content could be monitored by past, present, or prospective employers. Your posts on social media could be used against you by your present employer or a prospective employer if you:

- Divulge confidential information about your existing employer
- Make negative comments about your employer, supervisor, or coworkers
- Display content that suggests you might lack discipline in the workplace

Although you might consider some content harmless, prospective employers may screen out applicants based on an initial perception of their social media postings. Employers may not have the time to conduct a thorough evaluation of all applicants, so screening out questionable candidates based on their inappropriate social media content is a convenient method to reduce the applicant pool.

Your Interview

The interview process helps an employer obtain additional information, such as how you interact with people and respond to specific situations. Various personality traits can be assessed, such as:

- Your punctuality
- Your ability to work with others
- Your ability to communicate
- Your ability to grasp concepts
- Your listening skills
- Your ability to recognize your limitations
- Your ability to take orders
- Your ability to give orders
- Your potential as a leader

There are numerous books and Web sites that offer advice about various aspects of the interview, such as grooming, body language, etiquette, and even answering tough questions about deficiencies in your résumé. Another source of up-to-date information on interviewing is the career center at your college or university, which often offers seminars on effective interview techniques.

Comparing Job Offers

When you are applying for jobs, you will ultimately need to evaluate one or more job offers. Consider the following criteria during your evaluation.

Salary The salary is important, especially when you are supporting yourself. The salary can affect your level of spending that would be possible without borrowing funds. It can influence how quickly you can pay off existing debt and how much financing you can obtain for large purchases such as a car or home. But consider more than the starting salary. Some jobs have a low starting salary but give frequent raises so that, within a short time, the salary will be at a higher level. Other jobs may have a higher starting salary but provide few opportunities for raises and promotions.

Benefits Employers provide noncash benefits for their employees, such as health care benefits, contributions to your retirement fund, paid vacation time, special onsite day care and exercise facilities, and compensation for additional education.

Location The location of your employer determines the commuting time from your existing residence. Spending two hours per day commuting means that you will devote two additional hours per day to your job. If the job offer is based in a town that would require you to move, consider the costs of moving and the cost of living, the school system (if you have children), and the quality of life in the town of the employer. Also, consider the potential disadvantages if you will be moving away from family or friends, the potential complications if children must transfer to different schools, or if you need to sell a home before moving.

Changing Your Career

Many people do not realize which career would make them happy until they have pursued the wrong career. In some cases, they can use their existing experience in a new career, whereas in other cases, they must be retrained. The obvious barrier to switching careers is the amount of time that is already invested in a particular field. In addition, if training is necessary, the costs of changing careers may be high. Nevertheless, people should seriously consider switching if they truly believe a different career would be more satisfying, but first they should obtain detailed information about the new job prospects.

Be realistic in assessing any career change; look closely at your expectations. Would you really be more satisfied? How much training is involved? Would you have to stop working while you are retrained? How long will it take you to get a job once you are retrained? Is the compensation higher or lower in the new career versus your existing career? Are there more chances for advancement? Is there more job security?

Self-Employment

At some point in your life, you may decide that you want to leave your current job to be self-employed. Millions of people have started their own businesses and are much more satisfied than when they were employed by a firm or government agency. Self-employment, however, is not for everyone; some people are excellent workers but are not effective at creating business ideas or running a business.

First, to start your own business, you need a business plan that will be successful. Normally, this requires the creation of a product or service that is more desirable to customers than other products or services already offered in the market. Your advantage may be in creating a product that you can offer at a lower price than similar products in the market. Alternatively, your advantage may be higher quality. Keep in mind that competitors may be quick to adjust once you start your business, and it can be more difficult than you anticipated to gain market share. A business is accountable to its customers, and if it does not satisfy customers, it will not survive.

Conclusion

You have control over your career path. If you follow guidelines such as those described in this appendix, you can increase your chances of achieving the job and career path that you want. Keep in mind, however, that your career aspirations and opportunities may change over time. Therefore, your career planning does not end with your first job, but continues throughout your career and even plays a role in your decision when considering retirement.

Appendix B
PROJECTS

The following pages include projects for you to complete relating to specific aspects of personal finance.

- Assessing Your Credit
- Career Planning Project
- Leasing an Apartment
- Stock Market Project
- Comparison Shopping: Online versus Local Purchases

Assessing Your Credit

If you do not own a credit card, answer the following questions based on how you think you would use a credit card:

1. **Credit Spending.** How much do you spend per month on your credit card?

2. **Number of Credit Cards.** Do you have many credit cards? Are all of them necessary? Do you spend more money than you would normally as a result of having extra credit cards?

3. **Credit versus Cash.** Would you make the most of your purchases if you used cash instead of a credit card? Do you feel like purchases have no cost when you use a credit card instead of cash?

4. **Pay Off Part or All of Balance.** What is your normal strategy when you receive a credit card bill? Do you only pay the minimum amount required? Do you typically pay off your entire balance on a monthly basis? If you do not pay off the entire balance, is it because you cannot afford to pay it off, or because you would prefer to have extra cash on hand? If you have a positive balance, how do you plan to pay off that balance? Pay all of it off next month? Or pay only the minimum amount required next month?

5. **Credit Limit.** Consider the limit on the amount you can spend using your credit cards. Does the limit restrict your spending? Would you benefit if the limit were increased? Or reduced?

6. **Obtaining Your Credit Report.** Go to the Federal Trade Commission Web site, http://www.ftc.gov to obtain your free credit report. If you recently obtained your report, just review that report rather than obtaining a new one. Notice the types of companies that requested information on your credit. Is your credit report accurate? If not, you can write to the credit bureau to have the wrong information corrected, as explained in the text.

7. **Assessing Your Credit Report.** Are you satisfied with your existing credit rating? If not, what steps do you plan to take to improve your credit rating? For example, could you reduce some debt in the future? See Chapter 7 for more ideas on improving your credit rating.

Career Planning Project

Personal financial planning involves how you budget your money, manage your liquidity, finance purchases, protect your assets, invest your money, and plan your retirement and estate. All these activities are focused on your money. A related task is career planning, which determines the amount of money that you can earn over time. Furthermore, your career determines your quality of life. Most people think about their ideal career (such as rock star, professional athlete, movie star), but do not spend enough time planning a realistic career. This project allows you learn about possible career opportunities in which you might have an interest. Your instructor may offer you additional details regarding the deadline date and length of the project.

Information on Career Planning

Many Web sites can guide you toward careers that may fit your interests or skills. These sites tend to be general and do not focus on a particular industry. However, once you narrow your alternatives toward a specific career, you can do an Internet search for information about that career. For example, if you have an interest in health care, you can conduct a search using terms such as "health care careers." Within the field of health care careers, you can obtain more detailed information by using more specific search terms such as "nursing career" or "lab tech career."

The structure of this project allows you to consider a variety of alternative careers, to select one particular career, and to learn more in detail about that career.

1. **Career Goal.** What is your career goal? You can select a goal that requires more training, experience, or education than you presently have. However, it should be a goal that you believe is achievable. You should only select a goal requiring credentials that you are willing to obtain.

2. **Job Description.** What is the job description of the career you selected? What are the specific tasks involved in that career? What is the annual income you would expect to earn when starting this career? The Web site http://www.bls.gov may offer useful information that can help you answer this question.

3. **Skills Required.** What types of skills are critical to excel in the career that you wish to pursue? For example, do you need specific technical skills, computer skills, communication skills, or management skills for the career that you selected?

4. **Reasons for Your Career Goal.** Explain your career selection. Why would this career be ideal for you? What tasks are involved in this career that you would enjoy? Identify the specific tasks that you may be able to perform better than other people, once you have the proper training. Explain your answer.

5. **Concerns About Your Career Goal.** Any career might involve some tasks that are not desirable. Are there any tasks involved in this career that you may not like? Are there specific tasks that you may not be able to perform as well as other people, even with the proper training? Explain.

6. **Educational Background Required.** What is the typical educational background held by people with the career that you wish to pursue?

7. **Work Experience Needed.** What is the typical work experience required for people with the career that you wish to pursue? Do you have any work experience that is related to your career goal?

8. **Developing Your Résumé.** Consider your existing work experience. Create a résumé that summarizes your existing work experience in a manner that emphasizes its relationship to your career goals. For example, if your career goal is to be involved in management, make sure that your résumé emphasizes any experience you have managing employees, even if your title was not Manager.

9. **Steps to Achieve Your Goal.** Given your existing education and work experience, what additional education (if any) do you need to qualify for your desired career? Do you need to complete specific courses? Do you need a specific degree? Do you need specific work experience? If so, do you need any additional education to complete the work experience required? Explain.

10. **Conclusion About Your Ideal Career.** Now that you have researched your ideal career, do you still believe it is your ideal career? Or have you changed your mind? If you no longer think this career is ideal, what alternative career might be more suitable for you?

Leasing an Apartment

At some point in time, almost everyone will lease a place to live. Whether meeting a temporary or long-term housing need, leasing is a viable option for many individuals and families. In this project, you will explore the rights and responsibilities of leasing an apartment and compare it with other housing alternatives.

1. Look through the newspapers, the local apartment guide, or online sources to find a potential apartment to rent. Write down your reasons for selecting this particular place to live. When making your selection, you will want to consider its distance from work or school, its proximity to family or friends, the availability of public transportation or snow routes, and so on. You might also want to consider the desirability of the neighborhood, the amenities it offers, and other features that attracted you to this location.

2. You can obtain detailed information about apartments in a local newspaper, a local apartment guide, or on related Web sites.

   a. Determine the total monthly cost of living in the apartment.

   Monthly Rent _____

   Utilities (phone, gas, electric, Internet, etc.) _____

   Parking Fees _____

   Renter's Insurance _____

   Other Required Fees _____

   Other Optional Fees _____

   b. Determine the approximate cost of moving into the apartment.

   Application Fees _____

   Deposit on Apartment _____

   Deposits on Utilities _____

   Cleaning Fees _____

   Other Fees _____

   Moving Costs (rental truck, gasoline, etc.) _____

   c. Determine the move-out costs.

   Cleaning Fees _____

   Carpet Cleaning Fees _____

   Other Fees _____

3. Go online, and retrieve a standard apartment lease. Review your legal rights and responsibilities as outlined in the lease agreement. Review the landlord's rights and responsibilities as outlined in the lease agreement.

   Your lease agreement should address several important factors, such as:

   - What happens to your deposit when you decide to move out? Is it returned to you or held to cover other costs?
   - What happens if you break the lease?
   - What is the policy on subleasing the apartment?
   - What other restrictions (regarding pets, etc.) are imposed?

4. Research the tenant laws in your state. Some state laws tend to favor the land-lord over the tenant, whereas others tend to favor tenant rights. What conclu-sions do you have about the tenant laws in your state? What surprised you the most when researching the laws regarding property rental in your state?

5. Leasing an apartment is only one option available when renting a place to live. You may decide that leasing a house is a better alternative for you or your fam-ily. What factors would influence your decision on what type of residence to lease? How does leasing an apartment compare to leasing a house?

Most universities offer on-campus living options for their students. You can obtain information about university on-campus living options from various Web sites. Compare the terms of a university housing contract with a standard apartment lease. How is it similar? How is it different?

Stock Market Project

This project allows you to gain experience in making investment decisions, which are a key aspect of personal financial planning. Assume that you have $10,000 to invest. You will learn how to monitor your stock portfolio and measure your investment performance. You will also learn about the factors that affect a stock's performance over time.

Obtaining Stock Price and Dividend Information

Go to the Finance section of Yahoo!'s Web site (http://www.yahoo.com). Each stock has a ticker symbol. For example, the ticker symbol of Microsoft is MSFT. Insert the ticker symbol of the stock you select in the box that says "Get Quotes." You will see the stock price quoted, along with other financial information. Notice that the quarterly dividend is listed within the financial details, if the stock pays a dividend. The dividend quoted on the Yahoo! Finance site reflects the dividend provided per quarter.

Enter the Stock Information

1. Name of the stock in which you wish to invest _____

2. Ticker symbol of stock _____

3. Price per share of your stock at the time of purchase $ _____ per share

4. Number of shares that you purchased [$10,000 divided by the price per share of the stock] _____ shares

5. Dividend per share paid per quarter $ _____ per share

Your professor may ask you to submit this information at the beginning of the school term.

Determine Your Gain over the School Term

Near the end of the semester, you can determine your gain (or loss) from your investment in a stock.

6. Price per share of your stock on a date specified by your professor $ _____ per share

7. Total dollar value of your shares near the end of the school term. This is calculated as the number of shares purchased (from #4) multiplied by the price per share of your stock near the end of the school term (from #6). $ _____

8. Total dollar amount of dividends received. This is calculated as the dividend received per share (from #5) multiplied by the number of shares purchased (from #4). $ _____

9. Total dollars that you have at the end of the school term (#7 + #8) $ _____

10. Return on your investment = (total dollars based on #9 − $10,000)/$10,000   _____ %

Your professor may ask you to compare your results with other students in the class.

Comparing Your Stock to the General Market

Go to the Finance section of Yahoo!'s Web site (http://www.yahoo.com), and enter your stock in the "Get Quotes" box. A common benchmark used to measure general stock market conditions is the S&P 500 index. After you click 3m in the stock price chart to review a 3-month period, check the small S&P 500 box just above the chart. The Web site will provide a trend of the S&P 500 index on the same chart as your stock. This allows you to compare the performance of your stock to the stock market in general. Did your stock move in the same direction as the market for most of the school term? Did your stock perform better or worse than the market in general?

Team Project

If students were divided into teams, each team can determine its average return on investment and compare it against other teams.

Comparison Shopping: Online versus Local Purchases

Today's consumers have many options when deciding to make a purchase. Online commerce, or buying online, continues to grow and create more competition for local merchants. The Internet is an important source of product information for many consumers, even those who may not make online purchases. Online searches allow consumers to compare product features, prices, and availability, often saving time and energy when comparison shopping. This project will allow you to explore the advantages and disadvantages of buying online versus buying locally.

1. Select a product you would be interested in buying. Identify possible online sources and local sources where you can get reliable information about the product you want to buy. Remember, just because something is printed or posted on the Web does not mean the information is accurate.

2. Identify online sellers and local merchants where the product is available for sale. Generally, seller credibility is a bigger issue when shopping on the Web because the seller may be located anywhere and can be very difficult to track down if there are problems with the sale. For the most part, buyers have very limited knowledge about an online seller unless it is a well-branded company. Local merchants, however, can also pose a credibility risk, especially if they are small, single-location businesses that are new to the area.

3. Compare the cost of making the purchase online versus buying the product from a local merchant. List the costs associated with buying online, such as shipping and handling, potential postage for returning the product, restocking fees, Web

site membership fees, and so on. List the costs associated with buying a product locally, such as transportation (mileage/gasoline), time, restocking fees, membership fees, sales tax, and so on.

4. Compare the benefits of making online purchases versus buying the product locally. Some of these may include time, personal contact, ability to ask questions, and so on.

5. Online shopping is probably having an impact on local governments and local merchants. Prepare a presentation on the possible short-term and long-term costs and benefits of online shopping on your local area.

   Option 1. Talk with a local representative from the Chamber of Commerce or a local or state government official about the impact of online shopping on local tax revenues or local sales tax. How is online shopping affecting the number of jobs or the funds available to support local services such as schools, roads, and police?

   Option 2. Investigate a business that you follow (perhaps where you work or shop). Is it losing business to Web-based competitors, or is it using the Web to increase its appeal to consumers?

   Option 3. Conduct an Internet search to research your state's policy on Internet sales and possible loss of tax dollars. Is it attempting to recover some of the dollars lost to online sales?

Appendix C
FINANCIAL TABLES

Table C.1   Future Value Interest Factors for $1 Compounded at i Percent for n Periods:
$$FV = PV \times FVIF_{i,n}$$

Table C.2   Present Value Interest Factors for $1 Discounted at i Percent for n Periods:
$$PV = FV \times PVIF_{i,n}$$

Table C.3   Future Value Interest Factors for a $1 Annuity Compounded at i Percent for n Periods:
$$FVA = PMT \times FVIFA_{i,n}$$

Table C.4   Present Value Interest Factors for a $1 Annuity Discounted at i Percent for n Periods:
$$PVA = PMT \times PVIFA_{i,n}$$

TABLE C.1 Future Value Interest Factors for $1 Compounded at i Percent for n Periods: $FV = PV \times FVIF_{i,n}$

Period	1%	2%	3%	4%	5%	6%	7%	8%	9%	10%	11%	12%	13%	14%	15%	16%	17%	18%	19%	20%
1	1.010	1.020	1.030	1.040	1.050	1.060	1.070	1.080	1.090	1.100	1.110	1.120	1.130	1.140	1.150	1.160	1.170	1.180	1.190	1.200
2	1.020	1.040	1.061	1.082	1.102	1.124	1.145	1.166	1.188	1.210	1.232	1.254	1.277	1.300	1.322	1.346	1.369	1.392	1.416	1.440
3	1.030	1.061	1.093	1.125	1.158	1.191	1.225	1.260	1.295	1.331	1.368	1.405	1.443	1.482	1.521	1.561	1.602	1.643	1.685	1.728
4	1.041	1.082	1.126	1.170	1.216	1.262	1.311	1.360	1.412	1.464	1.518	1.574	1.630	1.689	1.749	1.811	1.874	1.939	2.005	2.074
5	1.051	1.104	1.159	1.217	1.276	1.338	1.403	1.469	1.539	1.611	1.685	1.762	1.842	1.925	2.011	2.100	2.192	2.288	2.386	2.488
6	1.062	1.126	1.194	1.265	1.340	1.419	1.501	1.587	1.677	1.772	1.870	1.974	2.082	2.195	2.313	2.436	2.565	2.700	2.840	2.986
7	1.072	1.149	1.230	1.316	1.407	1.504	1.606	1.714	1.828	1.949	2.076	2.211	2.353	2.502	2.660	2.826	3.001	3.185	3.379	3.583
8	1.083	1.172	1.267	1.369	1.477	1.594	1.718	1.851	1.993	2.144	2.305	2.476	2.658	2.853	3.059	3.278	3.511	3.759	4.021	4.300
9	1.094	1.195	1.305	1.423	1.551	1.689	1.838	1.999	2.172	2.358	2.558	2.773	3.004	3.252	3.518	3.803	4.108	4.435	4.785	5.160
10	1.105	1.219	1.344	1.480	1.629	1.791	1.967	2.159	2.367	2.594	2.839	3.106	3.395	3.707	4.046	4.411	4.807	5.234	5.695	6.192
11	1.116	1.243	1.384	1.539	1.710	1.898	2.105	2.332	2.580	2.853	3.152	3.479	3.836	4.226	4.652	5.117	5.624	6.176	6.777	7.430
12	1.127	1.268	1.426	1.601	1.796	2.012	2.252	2.518	2.813	3.138	3.498	3.896	4.334	4.818	5.350	5.936	6.580	7.288	8.064	8.916
13	1.138	1.294	1.469	1.665	1.886	2.133	2.410	2.720	3.066	3.452	3.883	4.363	4.898	5.492	6.153	6.886	7.699	8.599	9.596	10.699
14	1.149	1.319	1.513	1.732	1.980	2.261	2.579	2.937	3.342	3.797	4.310	4.887	5.535	6.261	7.076	7.987	9.007	10.147	11.420	12.839
15	1.161	1.346	1.558	1.801	2.079	2.397	2.759	3.172	3.642	4.177	4.785	5.474	6.254	7.138	8.137	9.265	10.539	11.974	13.589	15.407
16	1.173	1.373	1.605	1.873	2.183	2.540	2.952	3.426	3.970	4.595	5.311	6.130	7.067	8.137	9.358	10.748	12.330	14.129	16.171	18.488
17	1.184	1.400	1.653	1.948	2.292	2.693	3.159	3.700	4.328	5.054	5.895	6.866	7.986	9.276	10.761	12.468	14.426	16.672	19.244	22.186
18	1.196	1.428	1.702	2.026	2.407	2.854	3.380	3.996	4.717	5.560	6.543	7.690	9.024	10.575	12.375	14.462	16.879	19.673	22.900	26.623
19	1.208	1.457	1.753	2.107	2.527	3.026	3.616	4.316	5.142	6.116	7.263	8.613	10.197	12.055	14.232	16.776	19.748	23.214	27.251	31.948
20	1.220	1.486	1.806	2.191	2.653	3.207	3.870	4.661	5.604	6.727	8.062	9.646	11.523	13.743	16.366	19.461	23.105	27.393	32.429	38.337
21	1.232	1.516	1.860	2.279	2.786	3.399	4.140	5.034	6.109	7.400	8.949	10.804	13.021	15.667	18.821	22.574	27.033	32.323	38.591	46.005
22	1.245	1.546	1.916	2.370	2.925	3.603	4.430	5.436	6.658	8.140	9.933	12.100	14.713	17.861	21.644	26.186	31.629	38.141	45.923	55.205
23	1.257	1.577	1.974	2.465	3.071	3.820	4.740	5.871	7.258	8.954	11.026	13.552	16.626	20.361	24.891	30.376	37.005	45.007	54.648	66.247
24	1.270	1.608	2.033	2.563	3.225	4.049	5.072	6.341	7.911	9.850	12.239	15.178	18.788	23.212	28.625	35.236	43.296	53.108	65.031	79.496
25	1.282	1.641	2.094	2.666	3.386	4.292	5.427	6.848	8.623	10.834	13.585	17.000	21.230	26.461	32.918	40.874	50.656	62.667	77.387	95.395
30	1.348	1.811	2.427	3.243	4.322	5.743	7.612	10.062	13.267	17.449	22.892	29.960	39.115	50.949	66.210	85.849	111.061	143.367	184.672	237.373
35	1.417	2.000	2.814	3.946	5.516	7.686	10.676	14.785	20.413	28.102	38.574	52.799	72.066	98.097	133.172	180.311	243.495	327.988	440.691	590.657
40	1.489	2.208	3.262	4.801	7.040	10.285	14.974	21.724	31.408	45.258	64.999	93.049	132.776	188.876	267.856	378.715	533.846	750.353	1051.642	1469.740
45	1.565	2.438	3.781	5.841	8.985	13.764	21.002	31.920	48.325	72.888	109.527	163.985	244.629	363.662	538.752	795.429	1170.425	1716.619	2509.583	3657.176
50	1.645	2.691	4.384	7.106	11.467	18.419	29.456	46.900	74.354	117.386	184.559	288.996	450.711	700.197	1083.619	1670.669	2566.080	3927.189	5988.730	9100.191

TABLE C.1   (continued)

Period	21%	22%	23%	24%	25%	26%	27%	28%	29%	30%	31%	32%	33%	34%	35%	40%	45%	50%
1	1.210	1.220	1.230	1.240	1.250	1.260	1.270	1.280	1.290	1.300	1.310	1.320	1.330	1.340	1.350	1.400	1.450	1.500
2	1.464	1.488	1.513	1.538	1.562	1.588	1.613	1.638	1.664	1.690	1.716	1.742	1.769	1.796	1.822	1.960	2.102	2.250
3	1.772	1.816	1.861	1.907	1.953	2.000	2.048	2.097	2.147	2.197	2.248	2.300	2.353	2.406	2.460	2.744	3.049	3.375
4	2.144	2.215	2.289	2.364	2.441	2.520	2.601	2.684	2.769	2.856	2.945	3.036	3.129	3.224	3.321	3.842	4.421	5.063
5	2.594	2.703	2.815	2.932	3.052	3.176	3.304	3.436	3.572	3.713	3.858	4.007	4.162	4.320	4.484	5.378	6.410	7.594
6	3.138	3.297	3.463	3.635	3.815	4.001	4.196	4.398	4.608	4.827	5.054	5.290	5.535	5.789	6.053	7.530	9.294	11.391
7	3.797	4.023	4.259	4.508	4.768	5.042	5.329	5.629	5.945	6.275	6.621	6.983	7.361	7.758	8.172	10.541	13.476	17.086
8	4.595	4.908	5.239	5.589	5.960	6.353	6.767	7.206	7.669	8.157	8.673	9.217	9.791	10.395	11.032	14.758	19.541	25.629
9	5.560	5.987	6.444	6.931	7.451	8.004	8.595	9.223	9.893	10.604	11.362	12.166	13.022	13.930	14.894	20.661	28.334	38.443
10	6.727	7.305	7.926	8.594	9.313	10.086	10.915	11.806	12.761	13.786	14.884	16.060	17.319	18.666	20.106	28.925	41.085	57.665
11	8.140	8.912	9.749	10.657	11.642	12.708	13.862	15.112	16.462	17.921	19.498	21.199	23.034	25.012	27.144	40.495	59.573	86.498
12	9.850	10.872	11.991	13.215	14.552	16.012	17.605	19.343	21.236	23.298	25.542	27.982	30.635	33.516	36.644	56.694	86.380	129.746
13	11.918	13.264	14.749	16.386	18.190	20.175	22.359	24.759	27.395	30.287	33.460	36.937	40.745	44.912	49.469	79.371	125.251	194.620
14	14.421	16.182	18.141	20.319	22.737	25.420	28.395	31.691	35.339	39.373	43.832	48.756	54.190	60.181	66.784	111.119	181.614	291.929
15	17.449	19.742	22.314	25.195	28.422	32.030	36.062	40.565	45.587	51.185	57.420	64.358	72.073	80.643	90.158	155.567	263.341	437.894
16	21.113	24.085	27.446	31.242	35.527	40.357	45.799	51.923	58.808	66.541	75.220	84.953	95.857	108.061	121.713	217.793	381.844	656.841
17	25.547	29.384	33.758	38.740	44.409	50.850	58.165	66.461	75.862	86.503	98.539	112.138	127.490	144.802	164.312	304.911	553.674	985.261
18	30.912	35.848	41.523	48.038	55.511	64.071	73.869	85.070	97.862	112.454	129.086	148.022	169.561	194.035	221.822	426.875	802.826	1477.892
19	37.404	43.735	51.073	59.567	69.389	80.730	93.813	108.890	126.242	146.190	169.102	195.389	225.517	260.006	299.459	597.625	1164.098	2216.838
20	45.258	53.357	62.820	73.863	86.736	101.720	119.143	139.379	162.852	190.047	221.523	257.913	299.937	348.408	404.270	836.674	1687.942	3325.257
21	54.762	65.095	77.268	91.591	108.420	128.167	151.312	178.405	210.079	247.061	290.196	340.446	398.916	466.867	545.764	1171.343	2447.515	4987.883
22	66.262	79.416	95.040	113.572	135.525	161.490	192.165	228.358	271.002	321.178	380.156	449.388	530.558	625.601	736.781	1639.878	3548.896	7481.824
23	80.178	96.887	116.899	140.829	169.407	203.477	244.050	292.298	349.592	417.531	498.004	593.192	705.642	838.305	994.653	2295.829	5145.898	11222.738
24	97.015	118.203	143.786	174.628	211.758	256.381	309.943	374.141	450.974	542.791	652.385	783.013	938.504	1123.328	1342.781	3214.158	7461.547	16834.109
25	117.388	144.207	176.857	216.539	264.698	323.040	393.628	478.901	581.756	705.627	854.623	1033.577	1248.210	1505.258	1812.754	4499.816	10819.242	25251.164
30	304.471	389.748	497.904	634.810	807.793	1025.904	1300.477	1645.488	2078.208	2619.936	3297.081	4142.008	5194.516	6503.285	8128.426	24201.043	69348.375	191751.000
35	789.716	1053.370	1401.749	1861.020	2465.189	3258.053	4296.547	5653.840	7423.988	9727.598	12719.918	16598.906	21617.363	28096.695	36448.051	130158.687	*	*
40	2048.309	2846.941	3946.340	5455.797	7523.156	10346.879	14195.051	19426.418	26520.723	36117.754	49072.621	66519.313	88962.188	121388.437	163433.875	700022.688	*	*
45	5312.758	7694.418	11110.121	15994.316	22958.844	32859.457	46897.973	66748.500	94739.937	134102.187	*	*	*	*	*	*	*	*
50	13779.844	20795.680	31278.301	46889.207	70064.812	104354.562	154942.687	228345.875	339440.000	497910.125	*	*	*	*	*	*	*	*

*Not shown because of space limitations.

TABLE C.2 Present Value Interest Factors for $1 Discounted at *i* Percent for *n* Periods: $PV = FV \times PVIF_{i,n}$

Period	1%	2%	3%	4%	5%	6%	7%	8%	9%	10%	11%	12%	13%	14%	15%	16%	17%	18%	19%	20%
1	.990	.980	.971	.962	.952	.943	.935	.926	.917	.909	.901	.893	.885	.877	.870	.862	.855	.847	.840	.833
2	.980	.961	.943	.925	.907	.890	.873	.857	.842	.826	.812	.797	.783	.769	.756	.743	.731	.718	.706	.694
3	.971	.942	.915	.889	.864	.840	.816	.794	.772	.751	.731	.712	.693	.675	.658	.641	.624	.609	.593	.579
4	.961	.924	.888	.855	.823	.792	.763	.735	.708	.683	.659	.636	.613	.592	.572	.552	.534	.516	.499	.482
5	.951	.906	.863	.822	.784	.747	.713	.681	.650	.621	.593	.567	.543	.519	.497	.476	.456	.437	.419	.402
6	.942	.888	.837	.790	.746	.705	.666	.630	.596	.564	.535	.507	.480	.456	.432	.410	.390	.370	.352	.335
7	.933	.871	.813	.760	.711	.665	.623	.583	.547	.513	.482	.452	.425	.400	.376	.354	.333	.314	.296	.279
8	.923	.853	.789	.731	.677	.627	.582	.540	.502	.467	.434	.404	.376	.351	.327	.305	.285	.266	.249	.233
9	.914	.837	.766	.703	.645	.592	.544	.500	.460	.424	.391	.361	.333	.308	.284	.263	.243	.225	.209	.194
10	.905	.820	.744	.676	.614	.558	.508	.463	.422	.386	.352	.322	.295	.270	.247	.227	.208	.191	.176	.162
11	.896	.804	.722	.650	.585	.527	.475	.429	.388	.350	.317	.287	.261	.237	.215	.195	.178	.162	.148	.135
12	.887	.789	.701	.625	.557	.497	.444	.397	.356	.319	.286	.257	.231	.208	.187	.168	.152	.137	.124	.112
13	.879	.773	.681	.601	.530	.469	.415	.368	.326	.290	.258	.229	.204	.182	.163	.145	.130	.116	.104	.093
14	.870	.758	.661	.577	.505	.442	.388	.340	.299	.263	.232	.205	.181	.160	.141	.125	.111	.099	.088	.078
15	.861	.743	.642	.555	.481	.417	.362	.315	.275	.239	.209	.183	.160	.140	.123	.108	.095	.084	.074	.065
16	.853	.728	.623	.534	.458	.394	.339	.292	.252	.218	.188	.163	.141	.123	.107	.093	.081	.071	.062	.054
17	.844	.714	.605	.513	.436	.371	.317	.270	.231	.198	.170	.146	.125	.108	.093	.080	.069	.060	.052	.045
18	.836	.700	.587	.494	.416	.350	.296	.250	.212	.180	.153	.130	.111	.095	.081	.069	.059	.051	.044	.038
19	.828	.686	.570	.475	.396	.331	.277	.232	.194	.164	.138	.116	.098	.083	.070	.060	.051	.043	.037	.031
20	.820	.673	.554	.456	.377	.312	.258	.215	.178	.149	.124	.104	.087	.073	.061	.051	.043	.037	.031	.026
21	.811	.660	.538	.439	.359	.294	.242	.199	.164	.135	.112	.093	.077	.064	.053	.044	.037	.031	.026	.022
22	.803	.647	.522	.422	.342	.278	.226	.184	.150	.123	.101	.083	.068	.056	.046	.038	.032	.026	.022	.018
23	.795	.634	.507	.406	.326	.262	.211	.170	.138	.112	.091	.074	.060	.049	.040	.033	.027	.022	.018	.015
24	.788	.622	.492	.390	.310	.247	.197	.158	.126	.102	.082	.066	.053	.043	.035	.028	.023	.019	.015	.013
25	.780	.610	.478	.375	.295	.233	.184	.146	.116	.092	.074	.059	.047	.038	.030	.024	.020	.016	.013	.010
30	.742	.552	.412	.308	.231	.174	.131	.099	.075	.057	.044	.033	.026	.020	.015	.012	.009	.007	.005	.004
35	.706	.500	.355	.253	.181	.130	.094	.068	.049	.036	.026	.019	.014	.010	.008	.006	.004	.003	.002	.002
40	.672	.453	.307	.208	.142	.097	.067	.046	.032	.022	.015	.011	.008	.005	.004	.003	.002	.001	.001	.001
45	.639	.410	.264	.171	.111	.073	.048	.031	.021	.014	.009	.006	.004	.003	.002	.001	.001	.001	*	*
50	.608	.372	.228	.141	.087	.054	.034	.021	.013	.009	.005	.003	.002	.001	.001	.001	*	*	*	*

*PVIF is zero to three decimal places.

TABLE C.2 (continued)

Period	21%	22%	23%	24%	25%	26%	27%	28%	29%	30%	31%	32%	33%	34%	35%	40%	45%	50%
1	.826	.820	.813	.806	.800	.794	.787	.781	.775	.769	.763	.758	.752	.746	.741	.714	.690	.667
2	.683	.672	.661	.650	.640	.630	.620	.610	.601	.592	.583	.574	.565	.557	.549	.510	.476	.444
3	.564	.551	.537	.524	.512	.500	.488	.477	.466	.455	.445	.435	.425	.416	.406	.364	.328	.296
4	.467	.451	.437	.423	.410	.397	.384	.373	.361	.350	.340	.329	.320	.310	.301	.260	.226	.198
5	.386	.370	.355	.341	.328	.315	.303	.291	.280	.269	.259	.250	.240	.231	.223	.186	.156	.132
6	.319	.303	.289	.275	.262	.250	.238	.227	.217	.207	.198	.189	.181	.173	.165	.133	.108	.088
7	.263	.249	.235	.222	.210	.198	.188	.178	.168	.159	.151	.143	.136	.129	.122	.095	.074	.059
8	.218	.204	.191	.179	.168	.157	.148	.139	.130	.123	.115	.108	.102	.096	.091	.068	.051	.039
9	.180	.167	.155	.144	.134	.125	.116	.108	.101	.094	.088	.082	.077	.072	.067	.048	.035	.026
10	.149	.137	.126	.116	.107	.099	.092	.085	.078	.073	.067	.062	.058	.054	.050	.035	.024	.017
11	.123	.112	.103	.094	.086	.079	.072	.066	.061	.056	.051	.047	.043	.040	.037	.025	.017	.012
12	.102	.092	.083	.076	.069	.062	.057	.052	.047	.043	.039	.036	.033	.030	.027	.018	.012	.008
13	.084	.075	.068	.061	.055	.050	.045	.040	.037	.033	.030	.027	.025	.022	.020	.013	.008	.005
14	.069	.062	.055	.049	.044	.039	.035	.032	.028	.025	.023	.021	.018	.017	.015	.009	.006	.003
15	.057	.051	.045	.040	.035	.031	.028	.025	.022	.020	.017	.016	.014	.012	.011	.006	.004	.002
16	.047	.042	.036	.032	.028	.025	.022	.019	.017	.015	.013	.012	.010	.009	.008	.005	.003	.002
17	.039	.034	.030	.026	.023	.020	.017	.015	.013	.012	.010	.009	.008	.007	.006	.003	.002	.001
18	.032	.028	.024	.021	.018	.016	.014	.012	.010	.009	.008	.007	.006	.005	.005	.002	.001	.001
19	.027	.023	.020	.017	.014	.012	.011	.009	.008	.007	.006	.005	.004	.004	.003	.002	.001	*
20	.022	.019	.016	.014	.012	.010	.008	.007	.006	.005	.005	.004	.003	.003	.002	.001	.001	*
21	.018	.015	.013	.011	.009	.008	.007	.006	.005	.004	.003	.003	.003	.002	.002	.001	*	*
22	.015	.013	.011	.009	.007	.006	.005	.004	.004	.003	.003	.002	.002	.002	.001	.001	*	*
23	.012	.010	.009	.007	.006	.005	.004	.003	.003	.002	.002	.002	.001	.001	.001	*	*	*
24	.010	.008	.007	.006	.005	.004	.003	.003	.002	.002	.002	.001	.001	.001	.001	*	*	*
25	.009	.007	.006	.005	.004	.003	.003	.002	.002	.001	.001	.001	.001	.001	.001	*	*	*
30	.003	.003	.002	.002	.001	.001	.001	.001	*	*	*	*	*	*	*	*	*	*
35	.001	.001	.001	.001	*	*	*	*	*	*	*	*	*	*	*	*	*	*
40	*	*	*	*	*	*	*	*	*	*	*	*	*	*	*	*	*	*
45	*	*	*	*	*	*	*	*	*	*	*	*	*	*	*	*	*	*
50	*	*	*	*	*	*	*	*	*	*	*	*	*	*	*	*	*	*

*$PVIF$ is zero to three decimal places.

TABLE C.3 Future Value Interest Factors for a $1 Annuity Compounded at i Percent for n Periods: $FVA = PMT \times FVIFA_{i,n}$

Period	1%	2%	3%	4%	5%	6%	7%	8%	9%	10%	11%	12%	13%	14%	15%	16%	17%	18%	19%	20%
1	1.000	1.000	1.000	1.000	1.000	1.000	1.000	1.000	1.000	1.000	1.000	1.000	1.000	1.000	1.000	1.000	1.000	1.000	1.000	1.000
2	2.010	2.020	2.030	2.040	2.050	2.060	2.070	2.080	2.090	2.100	2.110	2.120	2.130	2.140	2.150	2.160	2.170	2.180	2.190	2.200
3	3.030	3.060	3.091	3.122	3.152	3.184	3.215	3.246	3.278	3.310	3.342	3.374	3.407	3.440	3.472	3.506	3.539	3.572	3.606	3.640
4	4.060	4.122	4.184	4.246	4.310	4.375	4.440	4.506	4.573	4.641	4.710	4.779	4.850	4.921	4.993	5.066	5.141	5.215	5.291	5.368
5	5.101	5.204	5.309	5.416	5.526	5.637	5.751	5.867	5.985	6.105	6.228	6.353	6.480	6.610	6.742	6.877	7.014	7.154	7.297	7.442
6	6.152	6.308	6.468	6.633	6.802	6.975	7.153	7.336	7.523	7.716	7.913	8.115	8.323	8.535	8.754	8.977	9.207	9.442	9.683	9.930
7	7.214	7.434	7.662	7.898	8.142	8.394	8.654	8.923	9.200	9.487	9.783	10.089	10.405	10.730	11.067	11.414	11.772	12.141	12.523	12.916
8	8.286	8.583	8.892	9.214	9.549	9.897	10.260	10.637	11.028	11.436	11.859	12.300	12.757	13.233	13.727	14.240	14.773	15.327	15.902	16.499
9	9.368	9.755	10.159	10.583	11.027	11.491	11.978	12.488	13.021	13.579	14.164	14.776	15.416	16.085	16.786	17.518	18.285	19.086	19.923	20.799
10	10.462	10.950	11.464	12.006	12.578	13.181	13.816	14.487	15.193	15.937	16.722	17.549	18.420	19.337	20.304	21.321	22.393	23.521	24.709	25.959
11	11.567	12.169	12.808	13.486	14.207	14.972	15.784	16.645	17.560	18.531	19.561	20.655	21.814	23.044	24.349	25.733	27.200	28.755	30.403	32.150
12	12.682	13.412	14.192	15.026	15.917	16.870	17.888	18.977	20.141	21.384	22.713	24.133	25.650	27.271	29.001	30.850	32.824	34.931	37.180	39.580
13	13.809	14.680	15.618	16.627	17.713	18.882	20.141	21.495	22.953	24.523	26.211	28.029	29.984	32.088	34.352	36.786	39.404	42.218	45.244	48.496
14	14.947	15.974	17.086	18.292	19.598	21.015	22.550	24.215	26.019	27.975	30.095	32.392	34.882	37.581	40.504	43.672	47.102	50.818	54.841	59.196
15	16.097	17.293	18.599	20.023	21.578	23.276	25.129	27.152	29.361	31.772	34.405	37.280	40.417	43.842	47.580	51.659	56.109	60.965	66.260	72.035
16	17.258	18.639	20.157	21.824	23.657	25.672	27.888	30.324	33.003	35.949	39.190	42.753	46.671	50.980	55.717	60.925	66.648	72.938	79.850	87.442
17	18.430	20.012	21.761	23.697	25.840	28.213	30.840	33.750	36.973	40.544	44.500	48.883	53.738	59.117	65.075	71.673	78.978	87.067	96.021	105.930
18	19.614	21.412	23.414	25.645	28.132	30.905	33.999	37.450	41.301	45.599	50.396	55.749	61.724	68.393	75.836	84.140	93.404	103.739	115.265	128.116
19	20.811	22.840	25.117	27.671	30.539	33.760	37.379	41.446	46.018	51.158	56.939	63.439	70.748	78.968	88.211	98.603	110.283	123.412	138.165	154.739
20	22.019	24.297	26.870	29.778	33.066	36.785	40.995	45.762	51.159	57.274	64.202	72.052	80.946	91.024	102.443	115.379	130.031	146.626	165.417	186.687
21	23.239	25.783	28.676	31.969	35.719	39.992	44.865	50.422	56.764	64.002	72.264	81.698	92.468	104.767	118.809	134.840	153.136	174.019	197.846	225.024
22	24.471	27.299	30.536	34.248	38.505	43.392	49.005	55.456	62.872	71.402	81.213	92.502	105.489	120.434	137.630	157.414	180.169	206.342	236.436	271.028
23	25.716	28.845	32.452	36.618	41.430	46.995	53.435	60.893	69.531	79.542	91.147	104.602	120.203	138.295	159.274	183.600	211.798	244.483	282.359	326.234
24	26.973	30.421	34.426	39.082	44.501	50.815	58.176	66.764	76.789	88.496	102.173	118.154	136.829	158.656	184.166	213.976	248.803	289.490	337.007	392.480
25	28.243	32.030	36.459	41.645	47.726	54.864	63.248	73.105	84.699	98.346	114.412	133.333	155.616	181.867	212.790	249.212	292.099	342.598	402.038	471.976
30	34.784	40.567	47.575	56.084	66.438	79.057	94.459	113.282	136.305	164.491	199.018	241.330	293.192	356.778	434.738	530.306	647.423	790.932	966.698	1181.865
35	41.659	49.994	60.461	73.651	90.318	111.432	138.234	172.314	215.705	271.018	341.583	431.658	546.663	693.552	881.152	1120.699	1426.448	1816.607	2314.173	2948.294
40	48.885	60.401	75.400	95.024	120.797	154.758	199.630	259.052	337.872	442.580	581.812	767.080	1013.667	1341.979	1779.048	2360.724	3134.412	4163.094	5529.711	7343.715
45	56.479	71.891	92.718	121.027	159.695	212.737	285.741	386.497	525.840	718.881	986.613	1358.208	1874.086	2590.464	3585.031	4965.191	6879.008	9531.258	13203.105	18280.914
50	64.461	84.577	112.794	152.664	209.341	290.325	406.516	573.756	815.051	1163.865	1668.723	2399.975	3459.344	4994.301	7217.488	10435.449	15088.805	21812.273	31514.492	45496.094

TABLE C.3 (continued)

Period	21%	22%	23%	24%	25%	26%	27%	28%	29%	30%	31%	32%	33%	34%	35%	40%	45%	50%
1	1.000	1.000	1.000	1.000	1.000	1.000	1.000	1.000	1.000	1.000	1.000	1.000	1.000	1.000	1.000	1.000	1.000	1.000
2	2.210	2.220	2.230	2.240	2.250	2.260	2.270	2.280	2.290	2.300	2.310	2.320	2.330	2.340	2.350	2.400	2.450	2.500
3	3.674	3.708	3.743	3.778	3.813	3.848	3.883	3.918	3.954	3.990	4.026	4.062	4.099	4.136	4.172	4.360	4.552	4.750
4	5.446	5.524	5.604	5.684	5.766	5.848	5.931	6.016	6.101	6.187	6.274	6.362	6.452	6.542	6.633	7.104	7.601	8.125
5	7.589	7.740	7.893	8.048	8.207	8.368	8.533	8.700	8.870	9.043	9.219	9.398	9.581	9.766	9.954	10.946	12.022	13.188
6	10.183	10.442	10.708	10.980	11.259	11.544	11.837	12.136	12.442	12.756	13.077	13.406	13.742	14.086	14.438	16.324	18.431	20.781
7	13.321	13.740	14.171	14.615	15.073	15.546	16.032	16.534	17.051	17.583	18.131	18.696	19.277	19.876	20.492	23.853	27.725	32.172
8	17.119	17.762	18.430	19.123	19.842	20.588	21.361	22.163	22.995	23.858	24.752	25.678	26.638	27.633	28.664	34.395	41.202	49.258
9	21.714	22.670	23.669	24.712	25.802	26.940	28.129	29.369	30.664	32.015	33.425	34.895	36.429	38.028	39.696	49.152	60.743	74.887
10	27.274	28.657	30.113	31.643	33.253	34.945	36.723	38.592	40.556	42.619	44.786	47.062	49.451	51.958	54.590	69.813	89.077	113.330
11	34.001	35.962	38.039	40.238	42.566	45.030	47.639	50.398	53.318	56.405	59.670	63.121	66.769	70.624	74.696	98.739	130.161	170.995
12	42.141	44.873	47.787	50.895	54.208	57.738	61.501	65.510	69.780	74.326	79.167	84.320	89.803	95.636	101.840	139.234	189.734	257.493
13	51.991	55.745	59.778	64.109	68.760	73.750	79.106	84.853	91.016	97.624	104.709	112.302	120.438	129.152	138.484	195.928	276.114	387.239
14	63.909	69.009	74.528	80.496	86.949	93.925	101.465	109.611	118.411	127.912	138.169	149.239	161.183	174.063	187.953	275.299	401.365	581.858
15	78.330	85.191	92.669	100.815	109.687	119.346	129.860	141.302	153.750	167.285	182.001	197.996	215.373	234.245	254.737	386.418	582.980	873.788
16	95.779	104.933	114.983	126.010	138.109	151.375	165.922	181.867	199.337	218.470	239.421	262.354	287.446	314.888	344.895	541.985	846.321	1311.681
17	116.892	129.019	142.428	157.252	173.636	191.733	211.721	233.790	258.145	285.011	314.642	347.307	383.303	422.949	466.608	759.778	1228.165	1968.522
18	142.439	158.403	176.187	195.993	218.045	242.583	269.885	300.250	334.006	371.514	413.180	459.445	510.792	567.751	630.920	1064.689	1781.833	2953.783
19	173.351	194.251	217.710	244.031	273.556	306.654	343.754	385.321	431.868	483.968	542.266	607.467	680.354	761.786	852.741	1491.563	2584.665	4431.672
20	210.755	237.986	268.783	303.598	342.945	387.384	437.568	494.210	558.110	630.157	711.368	802.856	905.870	1021.792	1152.200	2089.188	3748.763	6648.508
21	256.013	291.343	331.603	377.461	429.681	489.104	556.710	633.589	720.962	820.204	932.891	1060.769	1205.807	1370.201	1556.470	2925.862	5436.703	9973.762
22	310.775	356.438	408.871	469.052	538.101	617.270	708.022	811.993	931.040	1067.265	1223.087	1401.215	1604.724	1837.068	2102.234	4097.203	7884.215	14961.645
23	377.038	435.854	503.911	582.624	673.626	778.760	900.187	1040.351	1202.042	1388.443	1603.243	1850.603	2135.282	2462.669	2839.014	5737.078	11433.109	22443.469
24	457.215	532.741	620.810	723.453	843.032	982.237	1144.237	1332.649	1551.634	1805.975	2101.247	2443.795	2840.924	3300.974	3833.667	8032.906	16579.008	33666.207
25	554.230	650.944	764.596	898.082	1054.791	1238.617	1454.180	1706.790	2002.608	2348.765	2753.631	3226.808	3779.428	4424.301	5176.445	11247.062	24040.555	50500.316
30	1445.111	1767.044	2160.459	2640.881	3227.172	3941.953	4812.891	5873.172	7162.785	8729.805	10632.543	12940.672	15737.945	19124.434	23221.258	60500.207	154105.313	383500.000
35	3755.814	4783.520	6090.227	7750.094	9856.746	12527.160	15909.480	20188.742	25596.512	32422.090	41028.887	51868.563	65504.199	82634.625	104134.500	325394.688	*	*
40	9749.141	12936.141	17153.691	22728.367	30088.621	39791.957	52570.707	69376.562	91447.375	120389.375	*	*	*	*	*	*	*	*
45	25294.223	34970.230	48300.660	66638.937	91831.312	126378.937	173692.875	238384.312	326686.375	447005.062	*	*	*	*	*	*	*	*

*Not shown because of space limitations.

TABLE C.4 Present Value Interest Factors for a $1 Annuity Discounted at *i* Percent for *n* Periods: $PVA = PMT \times PVIFA_{i,n}$

Period	1%	2%	3%	4%	5%	6%	7%	8%	9%	10%	11%	12%	13%	14%	15%	16%	17%	18%	19%	20%
1	.990	.980	.971	.962	.952	.943	.935	.926	.917	.909	.901	.893	.885	.877	.870	.862	.855	.847	.840	.833
2	1.970	1.942	1.913	1.886	1.859	1.833	1.808	1.783	1.759	1.736	1.713	1.690	1.668	1.647	1.626	1.605	1.585	1.566	1.547	1.528
3	2.941	2.884	2.829	2.775	2.723	2.673	2.624	2.577	2.531	2.487	2.444	2.402	2.361	2.322	2.283	2.246	2.210	2.174	2.140	2.106
4	3.902	3.808	3.717	3.630	3.546	3.465	3.387	3.312	3.240	3.170	3.102	3.037	2.974	2.914	2.855	2.798	2.743	2.690	2.639	2.589
5	4.853	4.713	4.580	4.452	4.329	4.212	4.100	3.993	3.890	3.791	3.696	3.605	3.517	3.433	3.352	3.274	3.199	3.127	3.058	2.991
6	5.795	5.601	5.417	5.242	5.076	4.917	4.767	4.623	4.486	4.355	4.231	4.111	3.998	3.889	3.784	3.685	3.589	3.498	3.410	3.326
7	6.728	6.472	6.230	6.002	5.786	5.582	5.389	5.206	5.033	4.868	4.712	4.564	4.423	4.288	4.160	4.039	3.922	3.812	3.706	3.605
8	7.652	7.326	7.020	6.733	6.463	6.210	5.971	5.747	5.535	5.335	5.146	4.968	4.799	4.639	4.487	4.344	4.207	4.078	3.954	3.837
9	8.566	8.162	7.786	7.435	7.108	6.802	6.515	6.247	5.995	5.759	5.537	5.328	5.132	4.946	4.772	4.607	4.451	4.303	4.163	4.031
10	9.471	8.983	8.530	8.111	7.722	7.360	7.024	6.710	6.418	6.145	5.889	5.650	5.426	5.216	5.019	4.833	4.659	4.494	4.339	4.192
11	10.368	9.787	9.253	8.760	8.306	7.887	7.499	7.139	6.805	6.495	6.207	5.938	5.687	5.453	5.234	5.029	4.836	4.656	4.486	4.327
12	11.255	10.575	9.954	9.385	8.863	8.384	7.943	7.536	7.161	6.814	6.492	6.194	5.918	5.660	5.421	5.197	4.988	4.793	4.611	4.439
13	12.134	11.348	10.635	9.986	9.394	8.853	8.358	7.904	7.487	7.013	6.750	6.424	6.122	5.842	5.583	5.342	5.118	4.910	4.715	4.533
14	13.004	12.106	11.296	10.563	9.899	9.295	8.745	8.244	7.786	7.367	6.982	6.628	6.302	6.002	5.724	5.468	5.229	5.008	4.802	4.611
15	13.865	12.849	11.938	11.118	10.380	9.712	9.108	8.560	8.061	7.606	7.191	6.811	6.462	6.142	5.847	5.575	5.324	5.092	4.876	4.675
16	14.718	13.578	12.561	11.652	10.838	10.106	9.447	8.851	8.313	7.824	7.379	6.974	6.604	6.265	5.954	5.668	5.405	5.162	4.938	4.730
17	15.562	14.292	13.166	12.166	11.274	10.477	9.763	9.122	8.544	8.022	7.549	7.120	6.729	6.373	6.047	5.749	5.475	5.222	4.990	4.775
18	16.398	14.992	13.754	12.659	11.690	10.828	10.059	9.372	8.756	8.201	7.702	7.250	6.840	6.467	6.128	5.818	5.534	5.273	5.033	4.812
19	17.226	15.679	14.324	13.134	12.085	11.158	10.336	9.604	8.950	8.365	7.839	7.366	6.938	6.550	6.198	5.877	5.584	5.316	5.070	4.843
20	18.046	16.352	14.878	13.590	12.462	11.470	10.594	9.818	9.129	8.514	7.963	7.469	7.025	6.623	6.259	5.929	5.628	5.353	5.101	4.870
21	18.857	17.011	15.415	14.029	12.821	11.764	10.836	10.017	9.292	8.649	8.075	7.562	7.102	6.687	6.312	5.973	5.665	5.384	5.127	4.891
22	19.661	17.658	15.937	14.451	13.163	12.042	11.061	10.201	9.442	8.772	8.176	7.645	7.170	6.743	6.359	6.011	5.696	5.410	5.149	4.909
23	20.456	18.292	16.444	14.857	13.489	12.303	11.272	10.371	9.580	8.883	8.266	7.718	7.230	6.792	6.399	6.044	5.723	5.432	5.167	4.925
24	21.244	18.914	16.936	15.247	13.799	12.550	11.469	10.529	9.707	8.985	8.348	7.784	7.283	6.835	6.434	6.073	5.746	5.451	5.182	4.937
25	22.023	19.524	17.413	15.622	14.094	12.783	11.654	10.675	9.823	9.077	8.422	7.843	7.330	6.873	6.464	6.097	5.766	5.467	5.195	4.948
30	25.808	22.396	19.601	17.292	15.373	13.765	12.409	11.258	10.274	9.427	8.694	8.055	7.496	7.003	6.566	6.177	5.829	5.517	5.235	4.979
35	29.409	24.999	21.487	18.665	16.374	14.498	12.948	11.655	10.567	9.644	8.855	8.176	7.586	7.070	6.617	6.215	5.858	5.539	5.251	4.992
40	32.835	27.356	23.115	19.793	17.159	15.046	13.332	11.925	10.757	9.779	8.951	8.244	7.634	7.105	6.642	6.233	5.871	5.548	5.258	4.997
45	36.095	29.490	24.519	20.720	17.774	15.456	13.606	12.108	10.881	9.863	9.008	8.283	7.661	7.123	6.654	6.242	5.877	5.552	5.261	4.999
50	39.196	31.424	25.730	21.482	18.256	15.762	13.801	12.233	10.962	9.915	9.042	8.304	7.675	7.133	6.661	6.246	5.880	5.554	5.262	4.999

TABLE C.4 (continued)

Period	21%	22%	23%	24%	25%	26%	27%	28%	29%	30%	31%	32%	33%	34%	35%	40%	45%	50%
1	.826	.820	.813	.806	.800	.794	.787	.781	.775	.769	.763	.758	.752	.746	.741	.714	.690	.667
2	1.509	1.492	1.474	1.457	1.440	1.424	1.407	1.392	1.376	1.361	1.346	1.331	1.317	1.303	1.289	1.224	1.165	1.111
3	2.074	2.042	2.011	1.981	1.952	1.923	1.896	1.868	1.842	1.816	1.791	1.766	1.742	1.719	1.696	1.589	1.493	1.407
4	2.540	2.494	2.448	2.404	2.362	2.320	2.280	2.241	2.203	2.166	2.130	2.096	2.062	2.029	1.997	1.849	1.720	1.605
5	2.926	2.864	2.803	2.745	2.689	2.635	2.583	2.532	2.483	2.436	2.390	2.345	2.302	2.260	2.220	2.035	1.876	1.737
6	3.245	3.167	3.092	3.020	2.951	2.885	2.821	2.759	2.700	2.643	2.588	2.534	2.483	2.433	2.385	2.168	1.983	1.824
7	3.508	3.416	3.327	3.242	3.161	3.083	3.009	2.937	2.868	2.802	2.739	2.677	2.619	2.562	2.508	2.263	2.057	1.883
8	3.726	3.619	3.518	3.421	3.329	3.241	3.156	3.076	2.999	2.925	2.854	2.786	2.721	2.658	2.598	2.331	2.109	1.922
9	3.905	3.786	3.673	3.566	3.463	3.366	3.273	3.184	3.100	3.019	2.942	2.868	2.798	2.730	2.665	2.379	2.144	1.948
10	4.054	3.923	3.799	3.682	3.570	3.465	3.364	3.269	3.178	3.092	3.009	2.930	2.855	2.784	2.715	2.414	2.168	1.965
11	4.177	4.035	3.902	3.776	3.656	3.544	3.437	3.335	3.239	3.147	3.060	2.978	2.899	2.824	2.752	2.438	2.185	1.977
12	4.278	4.127	3.985	3.851	3.725	3.606	3.493	3.387	3.286	3.190	3.100	3.013	2.931	2.853	2.779	2.456	2.196	1.985
13	4.362	4.203	4.053	3.912	3.780	3.656	3.538	3.427	3.322	3.223	3.129	3.040	2.956	2.876	2.799	2.469	2.204	1.990
14	4.432	4.265	4.108	3.962	3.824	3.695	3.573	3.459	3.351	3.249	3.152	3.061	2.974	2.892	2.814	2.478	2.210	1.993
15	4.489	4.315	4.153	4.001	3.859	3.726	3.601	3.483	3.373	3.268	3.170	3.076	2.988	2.905	2.825	2.484	2.214	1.995
16	4.536	4.357	4.189	4.033	3.887	3.751	3.623	3.503	3.390	3.283	3.183	3.088	2.999	2.914	2.834	2.489	2.216	1.997
17	4.576	4.391	4.219	4.059	3.910	3.771	3.640	3.518	3.403	3.295	3.193	3.097	3.007	2.921	2.840	2.492	2.218	1.998
18	4.608	4.419	4.243	4.080	3.928	3.786	3.654	3.529	3.413	3.304	3.201	3.104	3.012	2.926	2.844	2.494	2.219	1.999
19	4.635	4.442	4.263	4.097	3.942	3.799	3.664	3.539	3.421	3.311	3.207	3.109	3.017	2.930	2.848	2.496	2.220	1.999
20	4.657	4.460	4.279	4.110	3.954	3.808	3.673	3.546	3.427	3.316	3.211	3.113	3.020	2.933	2.850	2.497	2.221	1.999
21	4.675	4.476	4.292	4.121	3.963	3.816	3.679	3.551	3.432	3.320	3.215	3.116	3.023	2.935	2.852	2.498	2.221	2.000
22	4.690	4.488	4.302	4.130	3.970	3.822	3.684	3.556	3.436	3.323	3.217	3.118	3.025	2.936	2.853	2.498	2.222	2.000
23	4.703	4.499	4.311	4.137	3.976	3.827	3.689	3.559	3.438	3.325	3.219	3.120	3.026	2.938	2.854	2.499	2.222	2.000
24	4.713	4.507	4.318	4.143	3.981	3.831	3.692	3.562	3.441	3.327	3.221	3.121	3.027	2.939	2.855	2.499	2.222	2.000
25	4.721	4.514	4.323	4.147	3.985	3.834	3.694	3.564	3.442	3.329	3.222	3.122	3.028	2.939	2.856	2.499	2.222	2.000
30	4.746	4.534	4.339	4.160	3.995	3.842	3.701	3.569	3.447	3.332	3.225	3.124	3.030	2.941	2.857	2.500	2.222	2.000
35	4.756	4.541	4.345	4.164	3.998	3.845	3.703	3.571	3.448	3.333	3.226	3.125	3.030	2.941	2.857	2.500	2.222	2.000
40	4.760	4.544	4.347	4.166	3.999	3.846	3.703	3.571	3.448	3.333	3.226	3.125	3.030	2.941	2.857	2.500	2.222	2.000
45	4.761	4.545	4.347	4.166	4.000	3.846	3.704	3.571	3.448	3.333	3.226	3.125	3.030	2.941	2.857	2.500	2.222	2.000
50	4.762	4.545	4.348	4.167	4.000	3.846	3.704	3.571	3.448	3.333	3.226	3.125	3.030	2.941	2.857	2.500	2.222	2.000

INDEX

FREE APPS
for Personal Finance

Free Apps for Personal Finance highlights useful apps students can download to their mobile devices for free that apply to some of the key concepts covered in the chapter.
To Find These: Search for the app name on your mobile device.

CHAPTER 1

Your Spending Decisions: The Spending Tracker app (MH Riley Ltd)

Help on Personal Finance: The Dollarbird–Smart Personal Finance app (Halcyon MD SRL)

CHAPTER 2

Managing Your Budget in Real Time: The Mint Money Manager, Budget, and Personal Finance app (Mint.com)

Establishing a 12-Month Budget Plan: The moneyStrands app (Strands, Inc.)

Updating Your Visual Budget: The Visual Budget app (Kiwi Objects)

CHAPTER 3

Estimating Growth in Savings: The Future Value of Your Money app (Garinet Media Network, LLC)

Calculating Your Savings: The Quick Compound Interest Calculator app (Goran Rauker)

CHAPTER 4

Qualifying for the Earned Income Tax Credit: The TurboTax Tax Preparation app (Intuit)

Estimating Your Tax: The TaxCaster app (Intuit)

CHAPTER 5

Your Banking Services: The Chase Mobile app (JPMorgan Chase & Co.)

Finding an ATM Nearby: The ATM Hunter app (Mastercard)

Paying Your Bills: The Mint Bills & Money app (Intuit Mint Bills, Inc.)

CHAPTER 7

Monitoring Your Credit Score: The Credit Karma app (Credit Karma, Inc.)

Identifying Permissions You Allowed in the Past: The MyPermissions app (Online Permissions Technologies Ltd.)

CHAPTER 9

Estimating the Time to Repay Your Debt: The Debts Break app (LINKSLINKS LTD)

Estimating Your Monthly Car Loan Payment: The RoadLoans app (RoadLoans.com)

Searching for Cars in Your Location: The AutoTrader app (Autotrader.com, Inc.)

Your Decision to Lease a Car: The Leasify app (Level Software LLC)

CHAPTER 10

Searching for a Home: The Real Estate by Zillow app (Zillow.com)

Generating an Amortization Schedule: The Zillow Mortgages app (Zillow.com)

Searching for an Apartment: The Zillow Rentals app (Zillow.com)

CHAPTER 11

Managing Your Insurance Policy: The GEICO Mobile app (GEICO)

Auto Insurance Information: The Go–Compare Car Insurance app (Go Inc.)

CHAPTER 12

Your Health Insurance: The Florida Blue app (Blue Cross and Blue Shield of Florida)

Finding a Health Insurance Plan: The onpatient PHR app (drchrono Inc.)

CHAPTER 13

Estimating the Amount of Life Insurance Needed: The Life Happens Needs Calculator app (Life and Health Insurance Foundation for Education)

Life Insurance Quotations: The i-Illustrate Lite app (John Hancock)

CHAPTER 14

Customized Financial News on Your Stocks: The Yahoo! Finance app (Yahoo! Inc.)

Financial Market Analysis: The Bloomberg Business app (Bloomberg Finance LP)

CHAPTER 15

Obtain Real-Time Stock Quotes: The Stock Tracker app (Wei Tang)

Manage Your Stocks: The Fidelity Investments app (Fidelity Investments)

Financial Data Analysis: The CNNMoney Business and Finance News app (CNNMoney.com)

Investing Game: The Stock Wars app (Continuous Integration Inc.)

CHAPTER 16

Analysis of Interest Rates: The Fed app (the Federal Reserve Bank of Chicago)

CHAPTER 17

Monitoring Exchange-Traded Funds: The Vanguard app (The Vanguard Group, Inc.)

Managing Your Investments: The Personal Capital Money and Investing app (Personal Capital Corporation)

Performance of Mutual Funds: The Morningstar app (Morningstar, Inc.)

CHAPTER 18

Monitoring Your Asset Allocation: The Betterment–Smarter Investing app (Betterment)

Valuing Your Investments: The MyBalanceSheet app (SigFig)

CHAPTER 19

Estimating Your Time Until Retirement: The Retirement Countdown app (MandellMobileApps)

Estimating Your Savings on Retirement: The Prudential Retirement Income Calculator app (The Prudential Insurance Company of America)

CHAPTER 21

Your Personal Finance Decisions: The MSN Money app (Microsoft)

APPENDIX A

Estimating the Cost of Your College Education: The 529 Calculator app (TIAA-CREF)